THE BOOK OF
1993
BASEBALL
CARDS

ISBN: 0-7853-0127-5

Contributing Writer: Tom Owens

Photo credits: Allsport USA: Otto Greule Jr., S. Halleran, Bill Hickey, Ken Levine, Lonnie Major.

Special thanks to: AU Sports Memorabilia, Skokie, Illinois; Steve Gold.

Tom Owens is a freelance writer and former editor of *Sports Collector's Digest*. He is the author of *Greatest Baseball Players of All Time* and *Collecting Sports Autographs*.

PUBLICATIONS INTERNATIONAL, LTD.

CONTENTS

Dave Winfield

CARD SHARKS

They're out there before the first pitch is thrown. They're around long before players begin arriving for spring training. Baseball card collectors keep their ever-trained eyes peeled for new cards, good deals, and that elusive card that is needed to fill in their collection.

The Book of 1993 Baseball Cards can help prepare you for the upcoming season. You might even become a regular card shark, able to circle the myriad of issues available, choosing the best investment material without letting your purchases devour all of your pocket money. This publication has become an innovative hobby tradition. Each season, collectors get an in-depth profile of more than 600 different players who could be key performers for their clubs. Every '93 card of each included player that was available at press time is displayed in this book in full color, giving fans an early preview of the best possible card investments.

Every fan can benefit from *The Book of 1993 Baseball Cards.* Casual followers of the game will want 1992 and career statistics to help predict the top teams and stars of 1993. Collectors will value the expert investment advice for each player's cards. Several factors are used to rate the cards, including: the technical quality, aesthetics and composition of the photo; integration of the photo into the card design; and the presentation of information on the back of the card. Hobbyists should take these factors into account when rating the 1993 cards.

This publication will focus on five sets from Donruss, Fleer, Score, Topps, and Upper Deck, all ranging in size from 720 to 900 cards. Due to Score's later issue date for their base set, we have included cards from the Score Select set. The availability of our selected sets guarantees participation by collectors of all ages and incomes. While fewer cards from Topps' newest 792-card set will hit the $1 level by the World Series, it's safe to say that you'll be able to find, afford, and collect those cards initially. Premium cards often go directly to hobby dealers. Suggested retail prices of $1.50 to $2 for premium-card packs seldom hold true. Even toy store managers read monthly price guides, and company-suggested prices are doubled or tripled when these high-end sets get hot.

What can you expect from these sets in 1993? For starters, expect a new level of competitiveness among manufacturers. In the late 1980s, companies wanted to be first with their "new" sets, offering cards for a new season by Christmas. Now, companies feel that being the best outranks being the first when new sets are offered. When cards were printed four months before the season began, trades and rookie call-ups weren't depicted. Collectors began to feel that companies were rushing out their sets just to create a necessity for an "update" set.

Donruss continued their successful two-series distributions in 1993. This allowed late transactions to be noted on cards, so players could be identified with their newest teams. Likewise, Upper Deck

Frank Thomas

will have a 100-card high-number series available to complete the 1993 set by midseason.

Topps and Fleer have relied on in-pack promotions and giveaways in the 1990s to stimulate individual sales. Their sets have tended to be smaller in quantity than the competition. Yet, when Marvel Comics acquired the Fleer Corporation, collectors marveled at the creative possibilities future cards might bring.

More early surprises were forecast for the major sets. In 1992, Fleer and Donruss became set stars early. Both companies offered redesigned looks with improved card stock, color photos on backs, and ultraviolet coatings. Additionally, both Fleer and Donruss have raised per-pack prices to suggested retails ranging from 89 to 99 cents apiece.

Upper Deck was expected to be the most expensive pack to begin 1993. In 1992, retail prices averaged $1 to $1.29 per pack. Most hobbyists argue that Upper Deck's unique beauty is worth a higher price. The California company, with its

heavy card stock, tamper-resistant foil packs, and counterfeit-proof holograms, can be credited or blamed for sparking the premium-card revolution.

The biggest mystery surrounding the unveiling of the 1993 sets involved the two expansion teams, the Florida Marlins and the Colorado Rockies. When players were chosen in the expansion draft, how were the changes going to be noted? Cards were going to be created before either team plays its first-ever games. In this situation in the past, companies have utilized everything from cap-less photos and airbrushed logo changes to shots of players at press conferences for cards.

Collectors should be aware of the potential for first-year team cards. Cards showing players on famed expansion teams such as the 1962 Mets or 1969 Seattle Pilots have been popular choices by history buffs. While many of the cards for the new teams will be overlooked and underpriced as commons, their long-term investment potential looks inviting.

The booming baseball card hobby can be fun and profitable for any educated collector. In the 1960s and early 1970s, collectors paid little attention to individual players; most merely wanted to accumulate complete sets. Star and rookie cards were unheard-of concepts. Now, the hobby has exploded. Baseball cards are marketed in specialty shops and at large conventions that often draw thousands of collectors each day. Baseball cards are a legitimate investment commodity, right beside stocks and bonds.

That's why the information in this publication is so important. Anyone can become a successful investor with a little effort. It's possible to build an impressive collection on a small budget.

Lately, the supply and demand rule of economics has been limited to demand only when it comes to cards. When certain cards are available to the public in smaller quantities, the prices for those cards will be higher.

However, card companies have kept quiet for years over production figures.

Whispers that printings will be limited for a certain set often begin with dealers who'll be offering huge quantities of those cards. Two things that may have a great deal of influence concerning the availability of certain cards are the timing and geographic proximity to a company. These supposed shortages usually come from distribution problems, not true scarcity. Past rumors have claimed that 1990 Score or 1991 Donruss would be hard to find.

Usually, when people purchase a pack of cards from a candy store, they have an equal chance of acquiring any card. Although all major card companies keep their production numbers a secret, it's assumed that equal numbers of all cards are printed.

The only investment-worthy card of the 1990s is one that's in "mint" condition. Today's picky retailers and collectors won't accept anything less. Just because the card is fresh out of a wax pack doesn't mean it's a mint one. The hobby's grading standards, which vary slightly with different collector publications, classify mint cards as ones with four square, sharp corners. Any other minor production flaws—such as packaging stains, ink streaks, or paper creases—will lower the grade and value of the card.

After you acquire individual cards, make sure to preserve them. A variety of durable plastic sheets and cases are sold through hobby publications or by card merchants. Never use rubber bands to hold stacks of cards because, over time, the bands will slice small grooves into the cards.

Collectors expect mint cards to have well-focused photographs, free of imperfections. The photo on a mint card is centered so that all four sides seem equal in width. An off-center photo is a flaw that occurs before the card is shipped out of the factory. This is considered an imperfection and collectors should beware of this problem when buying singles. Never invest in new cards that have any of the above-mentioned problems.

Kirby Puckett

When you buy a dealer-assembled assortment of cards, don't assume the cards are all mint. It's possible that the dealer accidentally or purposely inserted a few battered cards into the middle of the stack. Likewise, if you're going to buy just one star card that is housed in a plastic protector, it's best to see the card up close, out of its packaging. A red flag should go up if you're not being allowed access to the card in order to conceal flaws. Dealers unwilling to assist serious buyers don't deserve your business. Cards with even minor flaws can lose one-third of their value instantly.

Here's a word of advice: Don't assume that you have to buy cards immediately, thinking that they'll soon skyrocket in price. In some instances, the prices of cards will actually decrease. The patient hobbyist can glean true bargains. Around World Series time, grocery and department stores may discount packs and boxes of baseball cards. Non-hobby sellers fear the public won't buy baseball cards after the season ends.

Ken Griffey Jr.

The most patient shoppers will wait months into the baseball season, until companies release factory-collated complete sets. During the Christmas season, larger stores will slash prices on these products. Hobby dealers occasionally will strip factory sets of their bonus cards. The dealers sell these premium inserts, such as the Leaf and Studio preview cards, which have been inserted in complete sets of Donruss cards. Dealers, in turn, will offer bargains on the remaining set. You still get all the cards from the set you really wanted in the first place, but at a lower price.

But if you're like most collectors, the temptation to get 1993 cards weeks before the season starts is overwhelming. Normally, complete sets aren't available for several months, so in the meantime, you might choose to buy packages of

cards. The most common packages are the poly and foil packs. Older collectors and dealers still call these "wax," due to the former type of wrapper used.

These containers come with an ever-changing amount of cards contained within. Companies produce special subsets of cards to be included only in the different types of packs. Often, the promotional subset card may be shown in the see-through packaging.

Wise collectors attempt to crack company "codes" by studying the mechanically collated cello packs. It's possible to detect the sorting patterns after studying a couple of boxes worth of cellos. Keep each opened pack in its original order and jot down the numerical sequences. Then, by seeing the top and bottom cards of future packs, it'll be possible to predict the middle cards in those packages.

This system works best with rack packs, which are packages of three cellophane pockets of cards that are often displayed vertically on store racks. Rack packs may reveal six cards in the pack—three top and three bottom cards. Remember that different collating methods may be used for rack packs and cellos, but the code-cracking procedure works the same. Unlike wax or cello packs, it's highly unlikely that a rack pack can be tampered with and resealed.

If you want to buy an entire box of foil or poly packs, see a hobby dealer first. Companies now seal the boxes with specially marked cellophane, giving buyers extra assurance that cards remain untampered.

When you decide what sources you'll use to obtain individual cards, it's time to make a "want list." This preparation can be valuable. Make a simple list that details specific cards you want to speculate on, how many cards of each player you want to invest in, and how much you want to pay. Being focused on a goal helps you avoid making needless impulse buys, and your research will win you respect from dealers you meet. Giving the impression that you can't be fooled may win you a better deal with a dealer.

Think about how committed you'll be to your investments. If you find a promising player who has 1993 cards selling at five cents each, it would be easy to invest in a hundred cards. However, trying to buy 200 cards of Frank Thomas might be an expensive proposition. You'll find that a few dealers will market 1993 cards of individual players in lots of 25, 50, and 100 cards. Buying large quantities of certain players will get you better discounts.

When you check hobby price guides to appraise your new stash of cards, realize that most guides list selling (or retail) prices. If *Beckett Monthly* says that a 1993 Ken Griffey Jr. is worth 75 cents, that means that dealers will ask that much for the card. Dealers may be willing to pay no more than 25 to 50 cents for that same card, simply because dealers want to make a profit for themselves.

If you're serious about card collecting, you'll want to be on top of the game. You'll want to know which cards are ready to rise and which are about to take a nosedive. The best thing to do is to study the sports pages—just like a Wall Street tycoon would scan the stock market section of the newspaper. The fall is a good time to learn which players may have future hot cards. By the 1992 All-Star break, investors had labeled Kenny Lofton and Dave Fleming as likely American League Rookie of the Year candidates. Early investors landed the best bargains.

Don't be concerned if a player slumps or excels on the field for a few days. Instead, look at indicators like All-Star balloting, to see which players are getting the best reception from fans. When someone receives midseason honors such as "NL Pitcher of the Month," the recognition is longer-lasting and will boost card prices quicker.

Be aware that some cards take years, even decades, before their value starts to escalate. Players with average abilities may be great card investments if they get a lot of publicity. Pittsburgh knuckleballer

Jack McDowell

Tim Wakefield will stay in the limelight for years, regardless of his yearly successes. Due to reviving this special pitch, Wakefield will be a player whose cards could bring long-term surprises.

In other instances, off-the-field activities can make a difference to card investors. Pitcher Jack McDowell looked like a hands-down Cy Young winner in 1992. Yet, he could advance to a post-baseball career as a musician. Other players who seem inclined to a future in the broadcast booth offer additional encouragement to investors. Just look at how past cards of Joe Garagiola and Bob Uecker took off after they hit the airwaves.

More insight into individual players can be found in various baseball magazines. Publications such as this one take a deeper look into a player's career and rank him against his contemporaries and

Tom Glavine

other accomplished players from baseball's past. During the preseason, a flood of baseball magazines will be found on newsstands. These once-a-year periodicals will include team-by-team scouting reports and will try to forecast the future of many up-and-coming players.

Don't think that you should monitor only the major leagues. Each year, several unknown faces will debut with many clubs. To get the scoop on these rookie hopefuls, it's best to scour baseball publications like *USA TODAY Baseball Weekly* and *Baseball America*. The latter title also provides background information on rookies, featuring amateur players from high school on up.

Hobby-oriented magazines and newspapers can be helpful, too. Many collectors will guard their investment strategies, but clues to top investments can be gathered from various advertisements. What cards are dealers advertising to buy? What cards of players are NOT being sold? Are those unmentioned cards simply cold, or hasn't anyone figured out their appeal yet? Ask these questions while forming your own hobby game plan.

Looking at both the buying and selling advertisements help determine a standard market price for a player's cards. Some hobby papers provide regular price guides that supposedly monitor price increases in certain cards. These guides are of only limited use, however. They seldom account for regional interest in cards.

Regional interest can have a big impact on the value of cards. East Coast collectors would likely pay more for cards of players on the New York Yankees, Boston Red Sox, or New York Mets. Moreover, regional buyers will welcome cards that may garner little or no attention elsewhere. Cubs and White Sox cards will always sell well in the Midwest. Study hobby advertisements to sell your non-selling cards to interested geographical regions.

Selling in the fall, directly after a World Series, can be a profitable move. Everyone on a World Championship team gets added respect, which translates to higher card prices. Division-winning members of the A's, Blue Jays, Pirates, and Braves saw their cards selling fastest in the fall of 1992.

Many hobbyists mishandle investments in cards of award-winning players. When a player wins his first Cy Young or Most Valuable Player, his cards will grow in price by at least 10 percent. Cautious investors may hang on to the card, thinking the award is a signal of future greatness. However, when that Cy Young recipient falls a few victories short of a second consecutive award-winning year, card values unfairly plummet.

How do you handle the sale of a card of a future Hall of Famer? Very carefully! Some superstars will keep climbing in value forever. Unless you truly need the cash, reconsider your sale. George Brett is a sure bet for the Hall of Fame. Cards from his playing career will always be big sellers. Their values may never level off. You won't see big increases, but the gains will be consistent.

"Star" cards, cards of veteran players at a crossroads in their careers, are tougher calls to make. If a player over age 30 has his first great season in his career, you may want to move quickly for a short term profit. Try to project the long-term success of a sudden star. Was his success a one-time affair? Could he succeed with a lower-quality club? Will his lifetime stats remain memorable, or perhaps earn him a spot in the Hall of Fame? If a player's future seems shaky, sell while there is still marginal interest in his card. Oakland hurler Dave Stewart was a great card to sell, as long as he owned a streak of 20-win seasons.

A pitcher may prove the most baffling card investment. Many hurlers may have pitched up to four years in college and possibly a few more seasons in the minors before making a major league debut. Several pitchers each year are permanently sidelined by arm injuries, simply because they've been active for so long. Unlike hitters who can succeed on any team, a great pitcher is helpless without a competent offense behind him.

Another sometimes-puzzling area is that of rookie cards. When St. Louis sent three-year veteran slugger Todd Zeile back to Triple-A in late 1992, investors in his rookie cards began sweating. Once a $2 value, these cards were unstable properties. Even after the righthanded Redbird returned, collectors wondered if the move would blight Zeile's card values forever.

In 1992, Dodger Eric Karros was a great subject for card speculators. Tabbed as a likely NL Rookie of the Year, his cards tripled in value by season's end. When handling an investment assortment, sell enough to regain your initial costs. Then, be daring with the remainder. Generally, though, investors feel that tripling your

Eric Karros

investment is good enough. The final decision rests with your sense of adventure.

None of the information contained within this publication is a solicitation on the part of the publisher or any other party to buy or sell cards. Instead, the prices and guidelines provided are intended to make collecting 1993 baseball cards a challenging and worthwhile endeavor.

One final word about collecting baseball cards. Don't let investing in baseball cards take away from your enjoyment of the game and the hobby. Collectors find that baseball cards provide more than financial rewards. Each pocket-size treasure captures in words and pictures special moments you'll never see during a ballpark visit or televised event. Look at a pack of cards and you'll understand how baseball became America's Pastime.

JIM ABBOTT

Position: Pitcher
Team: New York Yankees
Born: September 19, 1967
Flint, MI
Height: 6'3" **Weight:** 210 lbs.
Bats: Left **Throws:** Left
Acquired: Signed as a free
agent, 12/92

KYLE ABBOTT

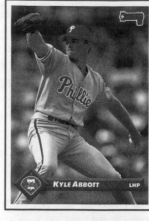

Position: Pitcher
Team: Philadelphia Phillies
Born: February 18, 1968
Newbury Port, MA
Height: 6'4" **Weight:** 195 lbs.
Bats: Left **Throws:** Left
Acquired: Traded from Angels
with Ruben Amaro Jr., for
Von Hayes, 12/91

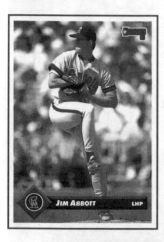
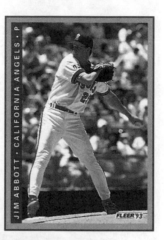

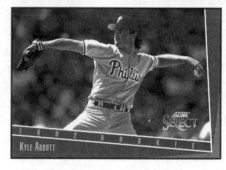

Jim Abbott proved that appearances can be deceiving. Abbott's sterling ERA (2.77 in '92) was eclipsed by inconsistent offensive support from his teammates, leading to a 7-15 record. In 1985, he turned down a 36th-round draft bid from Toronto, instead choosing college ball at Michigan. The 1988 U.S. Olympic baseball star was just the eighth overall selection in that year's first round of the free-agent draft. Active professionally since 1989, Abbott leapt to the majors without a single game of minor league seasoning. In 1991, Abbott was a career-best 18-11. That year, his ERA was slimmed down from his sophomore total of 4.51 to an impressive 2.89. He'll join the Yankees for '93.

Scoop up Abbott's 1993 cards if you see them at a nickel apiece. Even if he hung up his spikes forever, he'd still be one of baseball's most famed competitors of the 20th century. Get his 1989 draft pick card in his Michigan uniform. At a buck, it's a steal. Our pick for his best 1993 card is Score. We have chosen this card due to its unique photographic approach.

It is important to remember that in '92, Kyle Abbott—a solid pitcher while in the Angels' chain—was still only three years removed from being the ninth overall pick in the 1989 draft. When called upon to step into the starting role with Philly, he wasn't able to respond as hoped. In fact, he earned a trip back to Triple-A after going 0-7 with a 5.44 ERA in eight starts. That record is a bit misleading, though, because four of his eight outings were quality starts. His first start after his demotion to Scranton/Wilkes-Barre yielded a 3-0 shutout over Rochester. Abbott's hits and walks totals aren't too bad, but he must improve his work against lefthanded batters and do a better job of keeping the ball in the park. If he does that, you can expect him back in the majors to stay.

Buy Abbott's 1993s at a dime or less. Despite his losing record, he'll be a free-agent conversation piece. Our pick for his best 1993 card is Score. We have chosen this card because of its overall appeal and pleasing looks.

	W	L	ERA	G	CG	IP	H	ER	BB	SO
92 AL	7	15	2.77	29	7	211.0	208	65	68	130
Life	47	52	3.49	125	20	847.0	866	328	287	508

	W	L	ERA	G	CG	IP	H	ER	BB	SO
92 NL	1	14	5.13	31	0	133.1	147	76	45	88
Life	2	16	5.06	36	0	153.0	169	86	58	100

Series two cards from some companies were available at press time. If space allows, both cards are shown; if not, the most up-to-date cards are pictured.

RICK AGUILERA

Position: Pitcher
Team: Minnesota Twins
Born: December 31, 1961
San Gabriel, CA
Height: 6'5" **Weight:** 203 lbs.
Bats: Right **Throws:** Right
Acquired: Traded from Mets
with David West, Kevin
Tapani, Tim Drummond, and
Jack Savage for Frank Viola,
7/89

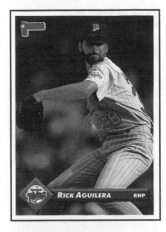

MANNY ALEXANDER

Position: Shortstop
Team: Baltimore Orioles
Born: March 20, 1971
San Padro de Macoris,
Dominican Republic
Height: 5'10" **Weight:** 150 lbs.
Bats: Right **Throws:** Right
Acquired: Signed as a free
agent, 2/88

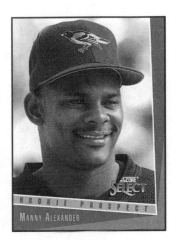

Give the Mets an error for packaging Rick Aguilera with four other pitchers in a 1989 swap for Frank Viola. While Viola gave the Mets only one-and-one-half solid seasons, Aguilera has become an airtight closer, ranking among the best in the league. He responded to a permanent switch to the bullpen at the onset of the 1990 campaign by converting 17 of his first 19 save opportunities. Aggie finished with 32 saves in '90. In 1991, he was even more effective, finishing with 42 regular-season saves, three more in the AL Championship Series, and two in the World Series win against Atlanta. That year saw him yield just one earned run between July 19 and September 25. He was rewarded with his first-ever spot on the All-Star team and earned a repeat appearance in '92. Aggie saved 41 games for the Twins in '92.

Relievers are shaky card gambles. Avoid Aguilera's 1993 nickel issues. Our pick for his best 1993 card is Upper Deck. We have chosen this card due to the outstanding photographic composition.

Manny Alexander gives the Orioles insurance against the day when Cal Ripken can't play every day. Alexander is a superb glove man who can hit and has the potential to steal 30 bases a year in the majors. Alexander played at Double-A Hagerstown in '92 and was voted the Eastern League's best defensive shortstop. He also started for the American League farmhands in the Double-A All-Star Game. It was the third time in four pro seasons that Alexander captured one honor or another. In '91, he made both the midseason and postseason All-Star teams, and was named by *Baseball America* as the top prospect in the Class-A Carolina League. Alexander broke into pro ball by making the Appalachian League All-Star team in '89. He was tabbed as the best shortstop in all five rookie leagues. Alexander won't hit with any power, but he'll put the ball in play.

Unless Alexander gets the opportunity to play full-time, pass on his '93s. Our pick for his best 1993 card is Upper Deck. We have chosen this card because it will increase in value.

	W	L	ERA	G	SV	IP	H	ER	BB	SO
92 AL	2	6	2.83	64	41	66.2	60	21	17	52
Life	51	46	3.29	308	122	749.2	705	274	220	582

	BA	G	AB	R	H	2B	3B	HR	RBI	SB
92 AA	.259	127	499	70	129	22	8	2	41	43
92 AAA	.292	6	24	3	7	1	0	0	3	2

LUIS ALICEA

Position: Second base
Team: St. Louis Cardinals
Born: July 29, 1965
Santurce, Puerto Rico
Height: 5′9″ **Weight:** 177 lbs.
Bats: Both **Throws:** Right
Acquired: First-round pick,
6/86 free-agent draft

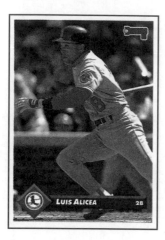

ROBERTO ALOMAR

Position: Second base
Team: Toronto Blue Jays
Born: February 5, 1968
Ponce, Puerto Rico
Height: 6′ **Weight:** 185 lbs.
Bats: Both **Throws:** Right
Acquired: Traded from Padres
with Joe Carter for Fred
McGriff and Tony Fernandez,
12/90

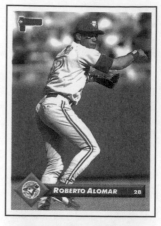

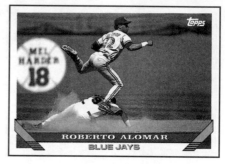

An injury to incumbent second baseman Jose Oquendo gave Luis Alicea his first starting chance in four years. Active in professional baseball since 1986, the switch-hitter debuted with the Cardinals in 1988. He inherited the second base position when Tom Herr was traded. A .212 showing in 93 games prompted a two-year exile to the minors. Following the 1989 season at Triple-A Louisville, Alicea discovered that he had fractured his wrist in May. After serving poorly as a pinch-hitter and utility infielder in 1991 (.191, 68 at-bats in 56 games), Alicea became a regular against lefties in 1992. His batting average at home remained near .300 throughout the season. Alicea may be locked in a three-way battle with Oquendo and infielder Geronimo Pena for starting second sacker duties in 1993.

Alicea's erratic hitting and lack of power make his cards perpetual commons. Ignore his 1993s. Our pick for his best 1993 card is Topps. We have chosen this card because of its overall appeal and pleasing looks.

Roberto Alomar is featured on the cover of the 1992 Blue Jays media guide. He got there after a dizzying AL debut season that included not only an All-Star start but a Gold Glove and team MVP honors as well. Starting all but four games at second, he finished the '91 season second in the league with 53 swipes and third with 11 triples. He teams with Devon White to make a productive batting order. When White doesn't reach, Alomar does, driving opposing pitchers crazy. His 82.8 percent success rate as a basestealer in '91 ranked second in the circuit. Alomar finished the '92 season with a .310 batting average, 76 RBI, and 49 stolen bases. He provided thrills both offensively and defensively with his performance in the '92 World Series.

The pride of Toronto, Alomar's cards are snappy choices at a dime or less. For an underrated card buy, grab the '89 Bowman of Alomar and his dad for a quarter. Our pick for his best 1993 card is Score. We have chosen this card because of its excellent combination of photography and design.

	BA	G	AB	R	H	2B	3B	HR	RBI	SB
92 NL	.245	85	265	26	65	9	11	2	32	2
Life	.224	234	630	51	141	22	15	3	56	3

	BA	G	AB	R	H	2B	3B	HR	RBI	SB
92 AL	.310	152	571	105	177	27	8	8	76	49
Life	.291	761	2962	439	862	146	31	39	302	192

SANDY ALOMAR

Position: Catcher
Team: Cleveland Indians
Born: June 18, 1968
    Salinas, Puerto Rico
Height: 6'5" **Weight:** 200
Bats: Right **Throws:** Right
Acquired: Traded from Padres
    with Carlos Baerga and Chris
    James for Joe Carter, 12/89

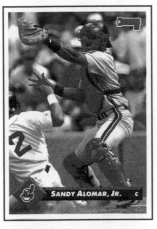

Cleveland receiver Sandy Alomar faced injuries for the second year in a row during 1992. A bruised throwing hand haunted him in May, while a partially torn knee ligament marred the second half of the season. Nevertheless, he received nearly one million votes to earn his third consecutive All-Star appearance. Alomar spent six seasons in the San Diego organization, overshadowed by incumbent backstop Benito Santiago. He escaped the minors in 1989, thanks to a Triple-A season of 13 home runs, 101 RBI, and a .306 average that won him a second Pacific Coast League Player of the Year title. Alomar became the toast of the AL in 1990, winning Rookie of the Year and Gold Glove honors.

If Alomar can't catch at least 100 games a season, he'll soon disappear from the minds of collectors. Give him one more chance, and adopt a few of his 1993 cards at a nickel apiece. For a buck, Alomar's 1989 Upper Deck sounds perfect. Our pick for his best 1993 card is Donruss. We have chosen this card for its technical merits.

	BA	G	AB	R	H	2B	3B	HR	RBI	SB
92 AL	.251	89	299	22	75	16	0	2	26	3
Life	.262	280	948	93	248	52	2	12	105	7

MOISES ALOU

Position: Outfield
Team: Montreal Expos
Born: July 3, 1966 Atlanta, GA
Height: 6'3" **Weight:** 190 lbs.
Bats: Right **Throws:** Right
Acquired: Traded from
    Pittsburgh with Scott Ruskin
    and Willie Greene for Zane
    Smith, 8/90

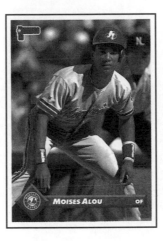

There's been much ballyhoo over Moises Alou. This talented young ballplayer is determined not to let injuries or lack of experience keep him down. Drafted by Pittsburgh in '86, Alou has taken longer to progress through the system because he never played organized ball until college. He then had to sit out the entire 1991 campaign due to shoulder surgery. By '92 he had mended, and when Ivan Calderon was injured, Alou got his chance. Moises had already played quite a few games in left field when his father, Felipe, replaced Tom Runnells as manager on May 22. Fans at Olympic Stadium soon began chanting the younger Alou's name, a real plus for a team having trouble at the gate. He has played all three outfield spots, indicating that his shoulder is sound. Alou has shown an ability to hit for average. He also tagged his first major league grand slam on September 23, 1992.

Be thrilled if you find Alou's 1993 cards for a dime each. Our pick for his best 1993 card is Score. We have chosen this card since the photograph captures the athletic ability of the player.

	BA	G	AB	R	H	2B	3B	HR	RBI	SB
92 NL	.282	115	341	53	96	28	2	9	56	16
Life	.277	131	361	57	100	28	3	9	56	16

WILSON ALVAREZ

Position: Pitcher
Team: Chicago White Sox
Born: March 24, 1970
Maracaibo, Venezuela
Height: 6'1" **Weight:** 175 lbs.
Bats: Left **Throws:** Left
Acquired: Traded from Rangers
with Scott Fletcher and
Sammy Sosa for Harold
Baines and Fred Manrique,
7/89

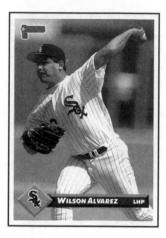 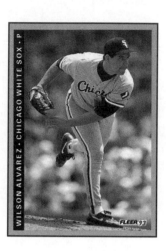

RUBEN AMARO JR.

Position: Outfield
Team: Philadelphia Phillies
Born: February 12, 1965
Philadelphia, PA
Height: 5'10" **Weight:** 170 lbs.
Bats: Both **Throws:** Right
Acquired: Traded from Angels
with Kyle Abbott for Von
Hayes, 12/91

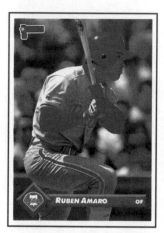 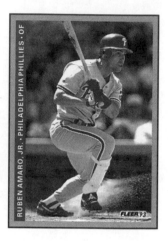

The Rangers inked Wilson Alvarez as an undrafted free agent in September 1986, following a noted amateur career in Venezuela that was highlighted by 12 no-hitters. His 165 Ks during a '91 Southern League campaign hinted at quality potential. However, no-hit wonder Alvarez looked remarkably human with the 1992 White Sox. After reeling off a 1991 no-no one day after being recalled from Double-A Birmingham, the young lefty was consistently inconsistent in his first full major league campaign. Constant struggles to keep his strikeout totals higher than his walks kept Alvarez banished to the ChiSox bullpen. In his five previous pro seasons, Alvarez had only seven career relief appearances. If he can get his control problems harnessed and lower his '92 ERA of 5.20, Alvarez could be a future strikeout king.

Don't count Alvarez out yet. His live arm and youth make him a possible card investment. Mull over his 1993 commons. Our pick for his best 1993 card is Fleer. We have chosen this card because of its overall appeal and pleasing looks.

Ruben Amaro Jr., is back in the city where he was born, where he was a batboy, and where his father played for years. Amaro got a chance to show his skills when center fielder Len Dykstra suffered an injury on Opening Day in '92. Amaro has the speed and arm to play all three outfield positions. His switch-hitting adds even more versatility. Amaro has the potential to be a very tough out. He hit above .325 at four different minor-league stops, never struck out more than 66 times in a season, and can draw a walk. He stole at least 27 bases a year in the California chain. His best season came with Edmonton in 1991, when he led the Pacific Coast League with 154 hits and a club-record 42 doubles. That year he also batted .326 and led the minors with 95 runs. His '92 batting average of .219 with 34 RBI were not his best numbers, but given more opportunity, he may shine.

Amaro's 1993 cards could be buried treasure at a nickel apiece. Our pick for his best 1993 card is Fleer. We have chosen this card because the design lends itself to the best use of the elements.

	W	L	ERA	G	SV	IP	H	ER	BB	SO
92 AL	5	3	5.20	34	1	100.1	103	58	65	66
Life	8	6	4.77	45	1	156.2	153	83	96	98

	BA	G	AB	R	H	2B	3B	HR	RBI	SB
92 NL	.219	126	374	43	82	15	6	7	34	11
Life	.219	136	397	43	87	16	6	7	36	11

BRADY ANDERSON

Position: Outfield
Team: Baltimore Orioles
Born: January 18, 1964
Silver Spring, MD
Height: 6'10 **Weight:** 185 lbs.
Bats: Left **Throws:** Left
Acquired: Traded from Red Sox
with Curt Schilling for Mike
Boddicker, 7/88

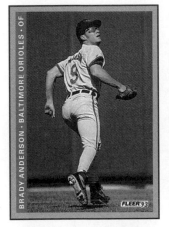

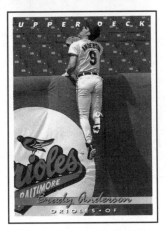

With left field vacant and the leadoff job open, Manager Johnny Oates gave Brady Anderson an extended trial during spring training in 1992 to work on his offense. The Maryland native quickly showed that his .272 average in the second half of 1991 was not just a fluke. In the '92 season, Anderson generated a .271 batting average, 80 RBI, 100 runs, and 21 homers over the course of 159 games. Anderson's sudden power surge was a pleasant surprise. He had produced a .219 average and 10 home runs in parts of four previous big league summers. Anderson reached 20 stolen bases in '92 faster than any Oriole since Luis Aparicio in '63. Baltimore fans are hoping that this feat is a sign of more good things to come.

Sideburns or not, his 1993 cards are good-looking investments at a nickel apiece. If you want an Anderson rookie card, his 1989 Bowman is affordable at 35 cents. Our pick for his best 1993 card is Score. We have chosen this card because it has a distinctive look.

	BA	G	AB	R	H	2B	3B	HR	RBI	SB
92 AL	.271	159	623	100	169	28	10	21	80	53
Life	.238	549	1704	239	406	70	21	31	168	106

ERIC ANTHONY

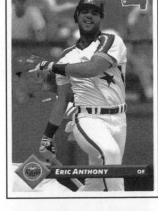

Position: Outfield
Team: Houston Astros
Born: November 8, 1967
San Diego, CA
Height: 6'2" **Weight:** 195 lbs.
Bats: Left **Throws:** Left
Acquired: 34th-round selection,
6/86 free-agent draft

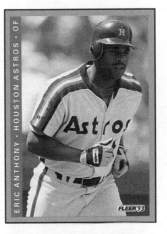

In what seemed like his last chance in the majors, Eric Anthony became one of Houston's leading sluggers in 1992. Aside from Jeff Bagwell, Anthony was the most consistent run producer for the uneven Astros, earning career highs in most categories. Despite being a low-round draft choice in 1986, Anthony paved the way for his 1989 major league debut with three consecutive home run titles. The highly touted outfielder blasted 10 home runs with Houston in '89, yet managed a meager .192 average (with 78 strikeouts in 84 games). After Anthony sank to .153 during a 39-game stint with Houston in 1991, his 1992 numbers—including a .239 batting average and 80 RBI—seem duly impressive. He did, however, strike out almost 100 times in 440 at-bats.

Strikeouts still dog the everlasting hopeful. Anthony's promise will dim eventually, as will the chances for his 1993 commons. Skip them. Our pick for his best 1993 card is Score. We have chosen this card since its design makes it a standout.

	BA	G	AB	R	H	2B	3B	HR	RBI	SB
92 NL	.239	137	440	45	105	15	1	19	80	5
Life	.210	285	858	89	180	31	1	34	123	11

Series two cards from some companies were available at press time. If space allows, both cards are shown; if not, the most up-to-date cards are pictured.

KEVIN APPIER

Position: Pitcher
Team: Kansas City Royals
Born: December 6, 1967
Lancaster, CA
Height: 6'2" **Weight:** 200 lbs.
Bats: Right **Throws:** Right
Acquired: First-round pick,
6/87 free-agent draft

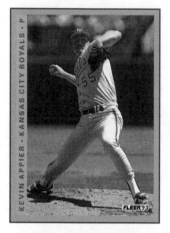

Kevin Appier has been a front-line starter for the Kansas City Royals for the last three seasons. He was AL Rookie Pitcher of the Year in 1990, when he went 12-8 with a 2.76 ERA, and finished third in the Rookie of the Year voting. In 1991, he went 13-10 with a 3.42 ERA after getting off to a 3-7 start. He led the staff in shutouts, starts, and innings while tying Bret Saberhagen for the team lead in victories. In August of '92, he pitched consecutive shutouts against the Red Sox and Yankees. Appier continued to go strong, even though the rest of the team struggled. On June 21, he pitched eight scoreless innings against Jimmy Key to beat the Toronto Blue Jays for the first time in his career. He finished 1992 a 15-game winner, boasting an impressive 2.46 ERA.

This young dean of Kansas City has some juicy cards. Get them in 1993 at a dime or less each. Our pick for his best 1993 card is Fleer. We have chosen this card for the interesting facts included on the reverse.

	W	L	ERA	G	CG	IP	H	ER	BB	SO
92 AL	15	8	2.46	30	3	208.1	167	57	68	150
Life	41	30	3.10	102	12	623.1	585	215	195	445

ALEX ARIAS

Position: Infield
Team: Florida Marlins
Born: November 20, 1967
New York, NY
Height: 6'3" **Weight:** 185 lbs.
Bats: Right **Throws:** Right
Acquired: Traded from Cubs
with Gary Scott for Greg
Hibbard, 11/92

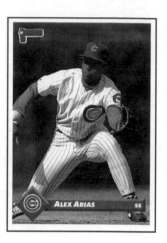

It just isn't time for the dawning of the age of Arias. But, by fully utilizing this opportunity with the Marlins, Alex Arias may just come into his own. In 1988, with Charleston of the South Atlantic League, Arias struck out once every 12.3 plate appearances, the league's fourth-best ratio. With Peoria of the Midwest League in 1989, Arias ranked third in the loop with 140 hits while leading his club with a .277 average. He made a career-high 42 errors with Charlotte of the Southern League in 1990, but led the league's shortstops in fielding percentage a year later and made the All-Star squad. Arias made it to the big leagues briefly in 1992, but faced big competition for a steady job with the Cubs. He will still have challenges in Florida, but he could make things happen. Arias is a singles hitter who will make contact and draw a walk, but delivers little power.

Wait to see what '93 brings before spending 15 cents for his new issues. Our pick for his best 1993 card is Donruss. We have chosen this card due to its unique photographic approach.

	BA	G	AB	R	H	2B	3B	HR	RBI	SB
92 AAA	.279	106	409	52	114	23	3	4	40	14
92 NL	.293	32	99	14	29	6	0	0	7	0

Series two cards from some companies were available at press time. If space allows, both cards are shown; if not, the most up-to-date cards are pictured.

RENE
AROCHA

Position: Pitcher
Team: St. Louis Cardinals
Born: February 24, 1966
    Havana, Cuba
Height: 6′ **Weight:** 180 lbs.
Bats: Right **Throws:** Right
Acquired: Signed as a free
    agent, 11/91

BILLY
ASHLEY

Position: Outfield
Team: Los Angeles Dodgers
Born: July 11, 1970 Taylor, MI
Height: 6′7″ **Weight:** 220 lbs.
Bats: Right **Throws:** Right
Acquired: Third-round pick,
    6/88 free-agent draft

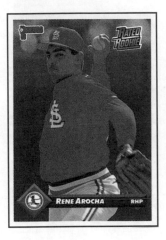  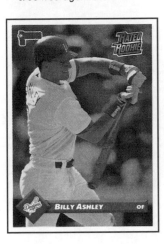 

Rene Arocha is one of the oldest prospects in baseball but there are unusual circumstances. He defected from Cuba in 1991, and the Cardinals won his rights in a lottery, beating out six other teams. His skills and maturity are at such an advanced level that even with no mainland experience, he was deemed ready for Triple-A ball. Arocha spent the '92 season with Louisville and was voted the best pitching prospect and owner of the best breaking pitch in the American Association. Opponents compiled only a .234 batting average against him in '92. He hurled two innings in the Triple-A All-Star Game, allowing three hits and one run. Arocha played with three title teams in Cuba in '85, '86, and '88, plus a World Cup winner in '87. In April 1991, he notched his 100th career victory. He also collected more than 1,000 strikeouts in Cuba.

Arocha could storm onto the big league scene. Pick up a few of his '93s. Our pick for his best 1993 card is Upper Deck. We have chosen this card because it will increase in value.

Billy Ashley blossomed as a big-time power hitter in 1992, and his emergence must have been a bit of a relief for the Dodgers. He had spent four years in pro ball, never reaching double figures in homers and never getting beyond Class-A. He also suffered through three trips to the DL in '91 with back and elbow injuries. Ashley responded to Double-A, however, showing enough to be named the best power prospect in the Texas League. He ranked among the leaders in the Dodgers' organization in both home runs and RBI and hit for a respectable average. He still doesn't walk as much as he should, especially for someone with his power. At least he seems to have outgrown his '90 season, when he struck out 135 times. With the Triple-A Pacific Coast League's tendency to pad power totals, you could be hearing quite a bit about him at Albuquerque in '93.

Unless the Dodgers can pull him up to the big league level, wait on his '93s. Our pick for his best 1993 card is Upper Deck. We have chosen this card because it will increase in value.

	W	L	ERA	G	CG	IP	H	ER	BB	SO
92 AAA	12	7	2.70	25	3	166.2	145	50	65	128
Life	12	7	2.70	25	3	166.2	145	50	65	128

	BA	G	AB	R	H	2B	3B	HR	RBI	SB
91 A	.252	61	206	18	52	11	2	7	42	9
92 AA	.279	101	380	60	106	23	1	24	66	13

PAUL ASSENMACHER

Position: Pitcher
Team: Chicago Cubs
Born: December 10, 1960
Detroit, MI
Height: 6'3" **Weight:** 200 lbs.
Bats: Left **Throws:** Left
Acquired: Traded from Braves
for Kelly Mann and Pat
Gomez, 9/89

 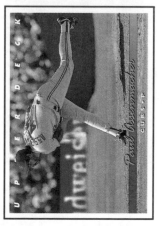

Paul Assenmacher bolstered the left side of the Cubs bullpen for the third consecutive year in 1992. Although his relief workload was lessened by fellow lefty Chuck McElroy, Assenmacher continued to excel in home games pitching against lefthanded hitters. For the last seven seasons, dating back to his 1987 debut with Atlanta, Assenmacher's totals exceed 50 appearances yearly. Through 1992, all but one of his 389 games in the majors has been in relief. Assenmacher's career peaked in 1991, when his 102.2 innings led National League relievers, and his 75 appearances and 117 strikeouts were second. An excellent fielder with remarkable control, Assenmacher remains one of the most underrated middle-men in baseball.

Not being a stopper has limited Assenmacher's chances for stardom. His 1993 commons have no investment chances. Our pick for his best 1993 card is Topps. We have chosen this card since the photograph captures the athletic ability of the player.

PEDRO ASTACIO

Position: Pitcher
Team: Los Angeles Dodgers
Born: November 28, 1969
Hato Mayor, Dominican
Republic
Height: 6'2" **Weight:** 174 lbs.
Bats: Right **Throws:** Right
Acquired: Signed as a free
agent, 11/87

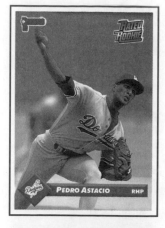

Pedro Astacio was a rare bright spot in the murky 1992 Dodgers collapse. Astacio, since his 1987 signing as an undrafted free agent, has been bred as a starter in the Dodgers farm system. He arrived from the Pacific Coast League on August 12, 1992. Ironically, at the time of his promotion, Astacio was a mere 6-6 with a 5.54 ERA in the minors. He suffered a temporary demotion back to Triple-A Albuquerque on August 24, simply to clear room for rehabilitated pitcher Tom Candiotti. Before leaving, Astacio's big league record included two shutouts, a 2-2 mark, and a 1.42 ERA. Only 10 days later, he returned when rosters expanded. Astacio posted a 1.98 ERA with five wins in 11 starts. He could be a rotation fixture in Los Angeles for years to come.

Expect Astacio's 1993 cards to begin at 10 to 15 cents each. He needs a full season in the bigs before investors can count on his issues. Our pick for his best 1993 card is Topps. We have chosen this card because of its great combination of photography and design.

	W	L	ERA	G	SV	IP	H	ER	BB	SO
92 NL	4	4	4.10	70	8	68.0	72	31	26	67
Life	37	29	3.44	459	47	552.2	512	211	203	524

	W	L	ERA	G	CG	IP	H	ER	BB	SO
91 AA	4	11	4.78	19	2	113.0	142	60	39	62
92 AAA	6	6	5.47	24	1	98.2	115	60	44	66

JIM AUSTIN

Position: Pitcher
Team: Milwaukee Brewers
Born: December 7, 1963
  Farmville, VA
Height: 6′2″ **Weight:** 200 lbs.
Bats: Right **Throws:** Right
Acquired: Traded from Padres
  with Todd Simmons for Dan
  Murphy, 2/89

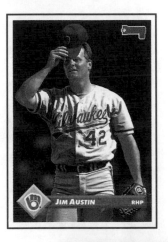

One of the reasons for Milwaukee's surprising pennant contention in 1992 was the addition of Jim Austin. Austin's career commenced in the sixth round of the 1986 free-agent draft. He was selected as a shortstop by San Diego but was revamped for pitching duties. In his first three seasons in the Padres organization, Austin never advanced beyond Double-A. Upon joining the Brewers farm system, he converted to relief and found a future calling in the majors. The righthander's success as a middle reliever was amazing, considering that he amassed an 8.31 ERA in a five-game debut with the Brewers in 1991. In 1992, he boasted a 1.85 ERA in 47 appearances.

Can you name the last rookie middle or short reliever whose cards acquired lasting value? It just doesn't happen often, and it's not likely to happen for Austin's 1993 cards, priced at 10 to 15 cents apiece. Our pick for his best 1993 card is Score. We have chosen this card due to the outstanding photographic composition.

	W	L	ERA	G	SV	IP	H	ER	BB	SO
92 AL	5	2	1.85	47	0	58.1	38	12	32	30
Life	5	2	2.69	52	0	67.0	46	20	43	33

STEVE AVERY

Position: Pitcher
Team: Atlanta Braves
Born: April 14, 1970
  Trenton, MI
Height: 6′4″ **Weight:** 190 lbs.
Bats: Left **Throws:** Left
Acquired: First-round selection,
  6/88 free-agent draft

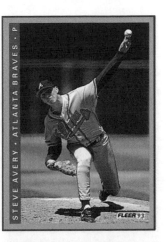

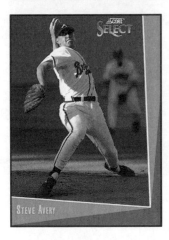

Steve Avery didn't share in the unmeasured success of many of his 1992 Atlanta teammates. The lefthander failed to recapture his 18-8 record from 1991, despite pitching more innings with a lower ERA. Likewise, Atlanta scored under an average of four runs per game when the lefty was pitching. Compare that to nearly 5 ½ runs per game in average leads for teammate Tom Glavine. Avery has struggled in the bigs before. During his 1990 rookie season, he was initiated with marks of 3-11 and a 5.64 ERA. The Michigan native was only 20 years old when he debuted with the Braves. He turned down a baseball scholarship from Stanford to begin his pro career.

Although Avery's job with the Braves is secure, his star billing isn't. With the emergence of starter Pete Smith and the addition of Greg Maddux, Avery could be an innocent bystander in '93. Don't assume his nickel-priced cards will retain their popularity. Our pick for his best 1993 card is Fleer. We have chosen this card for the superior presentation of information on its back.

	W	L	ERA	G	CG	IP	H	ER	BB	SO
92 NL	11	11	3.20	35	2	233.2	216	83	71	129
Life	32	30	3.71	91	6	543.0	526	224	181	341

Series two cards from some companies were available at press time. If space allows, both cards are shown; if not, the most up-to-date cards are pictured.

BOB AYRAULT

Position: Pitcher
Team: Philadelphia Phillies
Born: April 27, 1966
    Lake Tahoe, CA
Height: 6'4" **Weight:** 230 lbs.
Bats: Right **Throws:** Right
Acquired: Purchased from
    Reno, 7/89

CARLOS BAERGA

Position: Second base
Team: Cleveland Indians
Born: November 4, 1968
    San Juan, Puerto Rico
Height: 5'11" **Weight:** 165 lbs.
Bats: Both **Throws:** Right
Acquired: Traded from Padres
    with Chris James and Sandy
    Alomar for Joe Carter, 12/89

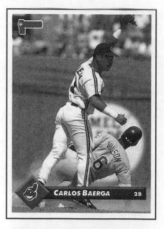

Bob Ayrault was a late but welcome addition to the 1992 Phillies bullpen. He began the year back in Triple-A, but earned a major league premier in June. At the time of his promotion, he was 5-1 with six saves. Big league righties hit a paltry .162 off Ayrault in '92. Altogether for his efforts in '92, he went 2-2 with a 3.12 ERA. In more than 43 innings of duty, the righthanded hurler never yielded a home run. The California native's pro career has seen some strange twists. He was drafted by San Diego in '86 and Pittsburgh in '87, but he declined to sign. Finally, he accepted a minor league contract with an unaffiliated team in '89. Bought by Philadelphia two months later, Ayrault's march to the majors began. His control makes him a valued addition to the Phillies staff.

Ayrault won't get lots of attention in middle relief. His cards won't either, so save your nickels. Our pick for his best 1993 card is Topps. We have chosen this card because of its great combination of photography and design.

The Padres' organization signed Carlos Baerga as an undrafted free agent on November 4, 1985, his 17th birthday. Traded to Cleveland late in '89, he has continued to improve each year, and proved a catalyst in the Tribe's 1992 revival. Hitting third in the order, Baerga raced Albert Belle throughout the year for the team lead in RBI. His pro career highs include 12 homers with Double-A Wichita in 1988 and 74 RBI with Triple-A Las Vegas in 1989. Despite finishing eighth in All-Star balloting for '92, he was named as an AL reserve. In the midseason classic, he produced an RBI double and scored a run. His rookie campaign featured seven homers, 47 RBI, and a .260 average. Those tallies grew to 11, 69, and .288 in 1991, and took an even greater leap in '92.

Baerga will be challenging for the title of top AL second baseman. Invest a nickel apiece in 1993 cards of the Cleveland keystoner. At fifty cents, Baerga's 1990 Score Traded card could take off. Our pick for his best 1993 card is Score. We have chosen this card for its artistic presentation.

	W	L	ERA	G	SV	IP	H	ER	BB	SO
92 NL	2	2	3.12	30	0	43.1	32	15	17	27
Life	2	2	3.12	30	0	43.1	32	15	17	27

	BA	G	AB	R	H	2B	3B	HR	RBI	SB
92 AL	.312	161	657	92	205	32	1	20	105	10
Life	.293	427	1562	218	457	77	5	38	221	13

JEFF BAGWELL

Position: First base
Team: Houston Astros
Born: May 27, 1968
    Boston, MA
Height: 6′ **Weight:** 195 lbs.
Bats: Right **Throws:** Right
Acquired: Traded from Red Sox
    for Larry Andersen, 8/90

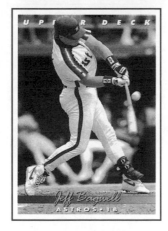

Jeff Bagwell greeted the 1992 Astros with sophomore power stats exceeding his award-winning premier production. Thanks to 1991 totals of 15 homers, 82 RBI, and a .294 batting average, Bagwell was voted the NL Rookie of the Year. While his batting average dipped a bit in '92 to .273, he managed to hit 18 dingers and 96 RBI. Ironically, during his two-year minor league career Bagwell owned a modest total of six career round-trippers. During his time with the Boston minor league organization, Bagwell never batted below .308. Throughout his career, the Massachusetts native has feasted on lefthanded pitching. Despite only five years of pro experience, Bagwell may procure more career highs in 1993.

Even at a dime apiece, Bagwell's cards are welcoming. His ability to go deep—even in the mammoth Astrodome—gives him staying power. If his '91s are overpriced, try the Upper Deck #702 for 75 cents, showing Bagwell, Luis Gonzalez, and Karl Rhodes. Our pick for his best 1993 card is Topps. We have chosen this card because of its overall appeal and pleasing looks.

	BA	G	AB	R	H	2B	3B	HR	RBI	SB
92 NL	.273	162	586	87	160	34	6	18	96	10
Life	.283	318	1140	166	323	60	10	33	178	17

HAROLD BAINES

Position: Designated hitter
Team: Baltimore Orioles
Born: March 15, 1959
    Easton, MD
Height: 6′2″ **Weight:** 195 lbs.
Bats: Left **Throws:** Left
Acquired: Signed as a free
    agent, 1/93

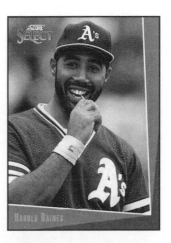

Harold Baines tallied his 1,000th career RBI with the 1992 A's. Despite his creaky knees, Baines left his traditional DH duties and subbed for injured Oakland outfielders in 17 regular season games. His hitting kept Oakland in pennant contention throughout the season, yet Baines endured one of the lowest averages of his career. The five-time All-Star is nearing 2,000 lifetime hits but hasn't survived fan hopes of eventual Hall of Fame status. Ever since the White Sox made him the first player in the nation drafted in June 1977, Baines has been considered star material. The label stuck after six consecutive seasons of 20-plus homers. Baines will return to his native Maryland, after signing with the Orioles for '93.

Despite impressive lifetime stats, Baines can't cut it in Cooperstown. Furthermore, his best offensive years are behind him. Any hope for his nickel-priced cards has been erased. Our pick for his best 1993 card is Topps. We have chosen this card because of its great combination of photography and design.

	BA	G	AB	R	H	2B	3B	HR	RBI	SB
92 AL	.253	140	478	58	121	18	0	16	76	1
Life	.286	1844	6744	865	1930	334	46	241	1066	30

SCOTT BANKHEAD

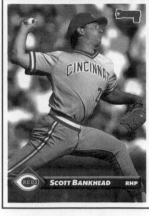

Position: Pitcher
Team: Boston Red Sox
Born: July 31, 1963
   Raleigh, NC
Height: 5'10" **Weight:** 185 lbs.
Bats: Right **Throws:** Right
Acquired: Signed as a free
   agent, 12/92

WILLIE BANKS

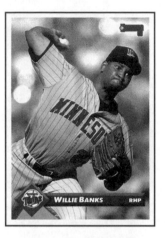

Position: Pitcher
Team: Minnesota Twins
Born: February 27, 1969
   Jersey City, NJ
Height: 6'1" **Weight:** 190 lbs.
Bats: Right **Throws:** Right
Acquired: First-round pick,
   6/87 free-agent draft

The Royals made pitcher Scott Bankhead a first-round draft choice in 1984, following his five victories for the U.S. Olympic baseball team. Seattle then obtained Bankhead in the 1986 Kansas City trade involving Danny Tartabull. While the Mariners gave up on his starting potential, they never considered how well the frequently disabled righty could fare in the bullpen. Going into 1992, Bankhead endured six stays on the DL. Because he appeared in only 21 total games in 1990-91, the M's ignored the hurler's free agency. Cincinnati gave Bankhead a shot as a middle reliever in 1992, and he became one of the best in the league. With a mended right shoulder, Bankhead heads to Boston for the '93 season.

But, how many middle relievers have investment-worthy cards? This reality hampers Bankhead's 1993 commons. Our pick for his best 1993 card is Upper Deck. We have chosen this card due to its unique photographic approach.

There's excitement about Willie Banks' fastball, and he's shown that he may have a complete repertoire. He was the first pitcher—and third overall—picked in 1987. His 1990 season was highlighted when the Southern League managers selected him as owner of the league's best fastball. Banks has been brought along slowly by the Twins, who had the luxury of not having to rush him. That's why even though Banks had a cup of coffee in the majors in 1991, he was sent back to Triple-A for seasoning. The extra work apparently helped. He won five of his first six decisions with Portland in the PCL in '92 and was among the chain's leaders in ERA and wins. His hits/inning ratio improved even as his strikeouts went down, a sign that Banks is learning how to pitch. His big league debut came on July 31, 1991, in Yankee Stadium. Banks earned his first major league win six days later against California.

A nickel each for Banks' 1993 cards sounds swell. Our pick for his best 1993 card is Score. We have chosen this card for the superior presentation of information on its back.

	W	L	ERA	G	SV	IP	H	ER	BB	SO
92 NL	10	4	2.93	54	1	70.2	57	23	29	53
Life	51	44	4.12	180	1	760.0	739	348	232	522

	W	L	ERA	G	CG	IP	H	ER	BB	SO
92 AL	4	4	5.70	16	0	71.0	80	45	37	37
Life	5	5	5.71	21	0	88.1	101	56	49	53

BRET BARBERIE

Position: Infield
Team: Florida Marlins
Born: August 16, 1967
    Long Beach, CA
Height: 5'11" **Weight:** 180 lbs.
Bats: Both **Throws:** Right
Acquired: First-round pick,
    11/92 expansion draft

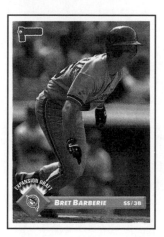
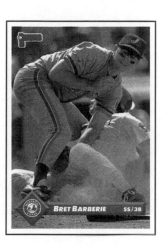

Bret Barberie's sophomore season with the Expos brought the dreaded second-year woes. Now with a brand-spanking new team, the former Olympian hopes to turn things around. After batting .353 in a 57-game trial with the 1991 Expos, he seemed set for a long life in the bigs. However, Barberie was terrorized by lefties in 1992, hitting only .164 against them. Throughout the season, his on-the-road batting average dipped as much or more than 100 points below his at-home marks, finishing with .183 and .288 averages respectively. When new skipper Felipe Alou arrived, he curtailed the transplanting of third baseman Tim Wallach to first. The result was far less playing time for Barberie, a fact that should change drastically in '93.

Without steady production at the plate, Barberie could be destined for life as a platoon player or utility infielder. Give him another season before considering his common-priced cards. Our pick for his best 1993 card is Donruss. We have chosen this card due to its unique photographic approach.

	BA	G	AB	R	H	2B	3B	HR	RBI	SB
92 NL	.232	111	285	26	66	11	0	1	24	9
Life	.271	168	421	42	114	23	2	3	42	9

BRIAN BARNES

Position: Pitcher
Team: Montreal Expos
Born: March 25, 1967
    Roanoke Rapids, NC
Height: 5'9" **Weight:** 170 lbs.
Bats: Left **Throws:** Left
Acquired: Fourth-round pick,
    6/89 free-agent draft

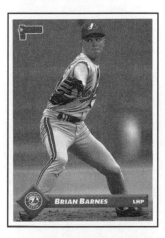
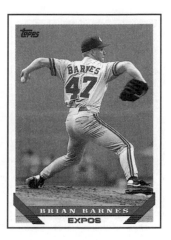
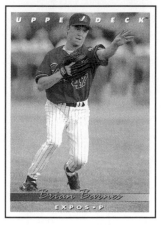

Brian Barnes played a small part in vaulting the Expos into surprise pennant contention in 1992. In 1990, Barnes made the jump from Double-A Jacksonville to the bigs. Barnes was the overall strikeout leader in professional baseball in 1990, considering his loop-best 213 Ks in the Southern League and 23 with the Expos. On June 19, 1992, he was again summoned, this time from the Triple-A American Association. He was a welcome lefty addition in the starting rotation. In seven of his first 14 games, Barnes lasted at least six innings and yielded three runs or less. At season's end in '92, he posted a 2.97 ERA over the course of 100 innings. Depending mainly on a fastball, curve, and changeup, the former Clemson University star should be in the majors permanently beginning in 1993.

Barnes needs to last a full season with Montreal before his common-priced cards can be taken seriously. Our pick for his best 1993 card is Donruss. We have chosen this card for its technical merits.

	W	L	ERA	G	CG	IP	H	ER	BB	SO
92 NL	6	6	2.97	21	0	100.0	77	33	46	65
Life	12	15	3.66	53	2	288.0	237	117	137	205

SKEETER BARNES

Position: Infield/outfield
Team: Detroit Tigers
Born: March 7, 1957
Cincinnati, OH
Height: 5'10" **Weight:** 180 lbs.
Bats: Right **Throws:** Right
Acquired: Signed as a free
agent, 1/91

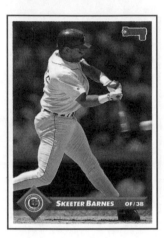

William Henry "Skeeter" Barnes III was a whirlwind of activity for the 1992 Tigers. The master utilityman appeared as a pinch-hitter, designated hitter, and in six different positions (all but pitcher, catcher, and shortstop) for the second season in a row. He finished '92 with a .273 batting average, 25 RBI, and three homers in 165 plate appearances. In January 1991, Barnes signed a minor league Triple-A contract with the Tigers. For that season, he hit .289 in 75 games, earning five homers and 16 RBI after 100 at-bats. In professional baseball since 1978, Barnes has played within the Cincinnati, Montreal, Philadelphia, St. Louis, Milwaukee, and Pittsburgh organizations. Although he first appeared in the majors via the 1983 Reds, Barnes owned a career total of just 75 games before joining Detroit.

Despite owning one of baseball's best nicknames, Barnes won't be making a buzz in hobby circles with part-time duties. Bypass his commons. Our pick for his best 1993 card is Topps. We have chosen this card because of its overall appeal and pleasing looks.

	BA	G	AB	R	H	2B	3B	HR	RBI	SB
92 AL	.273	95	165	27	45	8	1	3	25	3
Life	.249	245	433	67	108	22	3	11	52	15

SHAWN BARTON

Position: Pitcher
Team: Seattle Mariners
Born: May 14, 1963
Los Angeles, CA
Height: 6'3" **Weight:** 195 lbs.
Bats: Left **Throws:** Left
Acquired: Signed as a free
agent, 2/91

After waiting more than eight seasons, Shawn Barton finally enjoyed his first taste of the majors in 1992. Originally drafted by the Phillies in 1984, Barton served time in the Philadelphia and Mets farm systems, failing to exceed Triple-A. Before his big league premiere on August 6, 1992, against Milwaukee, Barton earned four saves in 30 appearances with Triple-A Calgary. The Mariners, in need of anything lefthanded, called upon the hurler for middle relief duties. The M's demoted veteran Juan Agosto to make room for the lefty. Although the entire team's bullpen ranked worst in the AL, Barton was earning one of the lowest ERAs on the squad, finishing '92 with a 2.92 average after facing 50 batters. Due to Seattle's 1992 mound misery Barton should receive an extended opportunity to stick with the 1993 M's.

Rookies nearing age 30 aren't wise selections for card investors. Even if Barton's 1993s approach 10 to 15 cents, save your money. Our pick for his best 1993 card is Donruss. We have chosen this card since the photograph captures the athletic ability of the player.

	W	L	ERA	G	SV	IP	H	ER	BB	SO
92 AL	0	1	2.92	14	0	12.1	10	4	7	4
Life	0	1	2.92	14	0	12.1	10	4	7	4

KEVIN BASS

Position: Outfield
Team: Houston Astros
Born: May 12, 1959
  Redwood City, CA
Height: 6′ **Weight:** 190 lbs.
Bats: Both **Throws:** Right
Acquired: Signed as a free
  agent, 1/93

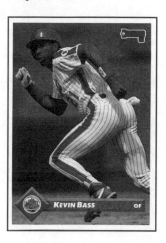

ROD BECK

Position: Pitcher
Team: San Francisco Giants
Born: August 3, 1968
  Burbank, CA
Height: 6′1″ **Weight:** 215 lbs.
Bats: Right **Throws:** Right
Acquired: Traded from
  Athletics for Charlie Corbell,
  3/88

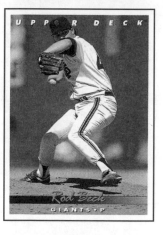

Late in '92, after almost 10 years of major league service, Kevin Bass ended a frustrating three-year stint with the Giants. The '92 season saw him produce a .269 average with nine homers and 39 RBI. In '93, he'll go back in time, at least regarding his team association. Bass signed with the Astros early in '93. His career began as a second-round pick of Milwaukee's in '77. Later, he was swapped to the Astros as a throw-in for the Don Sutton trade in '82. Bass enjoyed his best years in Houston from 1985-88. He sparked the 'Stros to a division title during his '86 All-Star season, batting .292 in NLCS competition. His career highs came during this period, including 20 homers (in '86) and 85 RBI (in '87). Bass signed a free-agency pact in '90. His Bay Area stay, however, was marked with slumps and knee injuries.

Common-priced cards of Bass aren't smart selections for 1993. A needed starting job and revitalization of his production would be a surprise. Our pick for his best 1993 card is Donruss. We have chosen this card for its technical merits.

Like many before him, Rod Beck was a starter in the minors who reached the majors only after moving to the bullpen. His 1992 campaign yielded a 3-3 record, a 1.76 ERA, and 17 saves in 42 appearances. Slightly better against lefties than righthanded batters, Beck struck out 87 of the 352 batters he faced in '92. The busiest reliever in the San Francisco bullpen last summer, he also had six blown saves and four holds. Although he broke into pro ball in '86, Beck did not become a full-time reliever until making the switch with Triple-A Phoenix of the Pacific Coast League in '91. That year, he was 4-3 with a 2.02 ERA, six saves, 35 strikeouts, and 13 walks in 71 innings pitched. A true California-boy, Beck was born and raised in Burbank, drafted by a California team, and then traded to another one.

Beck allows an awful lot of hits and middle relievers don't usually garner much attention. Ignore his '93s. Our pick for his best 1993 card is Fleer. We have chosen this card for the superior presentation of information on its back.

	BA	G	AB	R	H	2B	3B	HR	RBI	SB
92 NL	.269	135	402	40	108	23	5	9	39	14
Life	.269	1267	4112	509	1108	203	39	104	507	134

	W	L	ERA	G	SV	IP	H	ER	BB	SO
92 NL	3	3	1.76	65	17	92.0	62	18	15	87
Life	4	4	2.49	96	18	144.1	115	40	28	125

TIM BELCHER

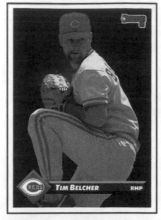

Position: Pitcher
Team: Cincinnati Reds
Born: October 19, 1961
   Sparta, OH
Height: 6′3″ **Weight:** 220 lbs.
Bats: Right **Throws:** Right
Acquired: Traded from Dodgers
   with John Wetteland for Kip
   Gross and Eric Davis, 11/91

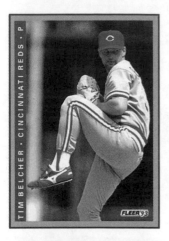

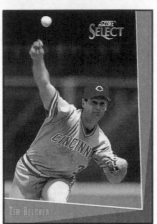

Although Tim Belcher posted one of the winningest seasons of his career in 1992, the Reds starter labored to reach a .500 record. As righthanded batters struggled to hit him (posting only a .179 average against the thirty-something righty), Belcher achieved double-digit (15) victories for the fourth time in five years. Belcher has ironman tendencies, evidenced by the league-leading eight shutouts and 10 complete games logged during his 15-12 campaign with the '89 Dodgers. During the Dodgers' 1988 World Championship season, Belcher was 3-0 in postseason play. He signed with the Yankees following the '84 draft. While he remains a safe bet for 10 wins and 30 starts annually, Belcher hasn't made any significant gains towards his quest for stardom.

Belcher's career stats have been enhanced by playing only for pennant contenders. His 1993 common-priced cards are shaky buys. Our pick for his best 1993 card is Upper Deck. We have chosen this card because the design lends itself to the best use of the elements.

	W	L	ERA	G	CG	IP	H	ER	BB	SO
92 NL	15	14	3.91	35	2	227.2	201	99	80	149
Life	65	52	3.20	173	23	1033.2	881	367	341	782

STAN BELINDA

Position: Pitcher
Team: Pittsburgh Pirates
Born: August 6, 1966
   Huntington, PA
Height: 6′3″ **Weight:** 187 lbs.
Bats: Right **Throws:** Right
Acquired: 10th-round pick,
   6/86 free-agent draft

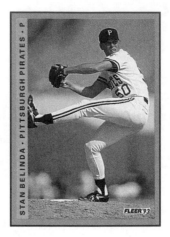

In 1992, Pittsburgh reliever Stan Belinda looked like a photocopy of his 1991 success as the Pirates tried to duplicate their pennant. After pitching two years of community college ball, Belinda was a low-round draft pick in 1986. Groomed exclusively in relief, he earned his major league debut in 1989. Since 1990, the sidearm specialist has tallied nearly one strikeout per inning while lowering his ERA. Before the start of the 1991 campaign, the Bucs dispatched high-priced stopper Bill Landrum, turning over the role to the younger Pennsylvania native. Belinda's save totals jumped from eight in 1990 to 16 in 1991 due to the job promotion. He bested his own figures for '92, posting a 6-4 record with 18 saves. During the 1992 season, Belinda was quite effective at home against lefties.

Few relievers ever have investment-quality commons. Belinda is talented, but won't gain the headlines needed to propel his card values. Our pick for his best 1993 card is Fleer. We have chosen this card because of its overall appeal and pleasing looks.

	W	L	ERA	G	SV	IP	H	ER	BB	SO
92 NL	6	4	3.15	59	18	71.1	58	25	29	57
Life	16	14	3.50	182	42	218.1	169	85	95	193

DEREK BELL

Position: Outfield
Team: Toronto Blue Jays
Born: December 11, 1968
  Tampa, FL
Height: 6'2" **Weight:** 200 lbs.
Bats: Right **Throws:** Right
Acquired: Second-round pick,
  6/87 free-agent draft

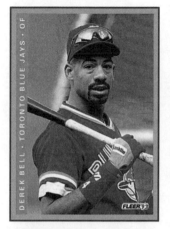

Coming off an award-winning year at Triple-A, Derek Bell suffered an early-season injury that delayed his impact on the big league club. In '92, Bell joined Philadelphia's Len Dykstra and St. Louis' Andres Galarraga on the disabled list during a spate of wrist injuries, went to Class-A Dunedin on rehab, and did not return to the majors until May. It was his fourth time on the DL in his career. Once back with the Jays, Bell slumped for a while, especially against righties. He also shows a marked improvement in batting on the road as opposed to at home, posting averages of .167 and .325, respectively. His record suggests a nice blend of pop and speed that should fit the SkyDome. Bell's best season came in 1991, when *Baseball America* named him the Minor League Player of the Year. He was also the MVP of the International League.

Bell's cards, at a dime each, would put some collectors in hobby heaven. Being part of a Championship team won't hurt, either. Our pick for his best 1993 card is Fleer. We have chosen this card due to the outstanding photographic composition.

	BA	G	AB	R	H	2B	3B	HR	RBI	SB
92 AL	.242	61	161	23	39	6	3	2	15	7
Life	.228	79	189	28	43	6	3	2	16	10

GEORGE BELL

Position: Designated hitter
Team: Chicago White Sox
Born: October 21, 1959
  San Pedro de Macoris,
  Dominican Republic
Height: 6'1" **Weight:** 202 lbs.
Bats: Right **Throws:** Right
Acquired: Traded from Cubs
  for Sammy Sosa and Ken
  Patterson, 4/92

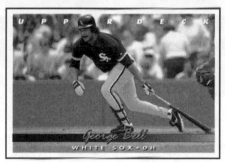

George Bell's return to the AL was triumphant, as he provided the '92 ChiSox with one of baseball's best DHers. Bell spent three years in the Phillies' organization before being drafted by Toronto in December 1980. In the '80s, he became infamous for his protests over DH duties, a role he seems to welcome with the Sox. A star slugger with Toronto from 1981-90, Bell's career highs of 47 round-trippers and league-best 134 RBI came with the '87 Blue Jays. Despite his '91 totals of .285 with 25 home runs and 86 RBI in the NL, the Cubs relieved themselves of Bell. His '92 ChiSox totals marked the ninth year in a row where he topped 80 RBI and the eighth time in nine campaigns he surpassed 20 homers.

Don't spend more than a nickel on Bell's 1993 cards. Prices could triple if he wins another postseason award or sparks the ChiSox to postseason play. If any Bell card gains value, it'll be his '82 Donruss rookie labeled "Jorge Bell." Prices over $5 are too risky. Our pick for his best 1993 card is Fleer. We have chosen this card for its artistic presentation.

	BA	G	AB	R	H	2B	3B	HR	RBI	SB
92 AL	.255	155	627	74	160	27	0	25	112	5
Life	.282	1485	5713	778	1613	291	32	252	938	66

JAY
BELL

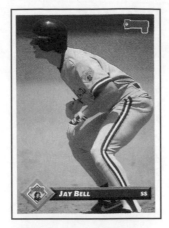

Position: Shortstop
Team: Pittsburgh Pirates
Born: December 11, 1965
   Eglin AFB, FL
Height: 6′ **Weight:** 185 lbs.
Bats: Right **Throws:** Right
Acquired: Traded from Indians
   for Felix Fermin, 3/89

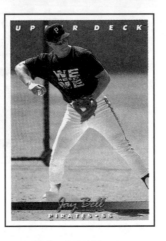

ALBERT
BELLE

Position: Outfield
Team: Cleveland Indians
Born: August 25, 1966
   Shreveport, LA
Height: 6′2″ **Weight:** 200 lbs.
Bats: Right **Throws:** Right
Acquired: Second-round pick,
   6/87 free-agent draft

Jay Bell suffered a minor power outage with the 1992 Pirates, following the biggest year of his career. With the 1991 Bucs, Bell batted .270 with 16 homers and 67 RBI, adding a 12-hit (.414) performance in the National League Championship Series. Part of his '92 decline was due to difficulties against left-handed pitchers. He remains one of baseball's most proficient sacrifice bunters, a stat ignored in many game accounts. In the field, Bell commits more errors than the average shortstop, yet he handles more chances than most infielders. Bell's career was launched as a first-round draft pick of the 1984 Twins. Acquired by Cleveland in a 1985 trade involving Bert Blyleven, Bell failed to win the Tribe's starting shortstop job in 1987 or '88.

Unfortunately, Bell's unselfish team play does little to improve his card values. In 1993, his common-priced cards can't compete. Our pick for his best 1993 card is Upper Deck. We have chosen this card because the design lends itself to the best use of the elements.

Although Cleveland shortened the dimensions of Municipal Stadium for '92, Albert Belle continued to do most of his long-ball blasting on the road. When he's on, Belle is one of the league's most feared sluggers. He accounted for 35.4 percent of his team's homers and 17.4 percent of its RBI during the '91 campaign. That was the year he had 28 homers and 95 RBI even though he missed 39 games because of suspensions and a brief punishment exile to the minors. The former LSU standout started the '92 season as Cleveland's DH but worked his way back into 52 games as a left fielder. He pounded out 34 home runs as well as 112 RBI during the '92 season. Perhaps even more noteworthy and admirable, he also seems to have conquered the alcohol-related problems and temper tantrums that hampered his progress.

Belle is a swell card investment at 15 cents each in 1993. For a reasonable gamble, buy the 1990 Bowman card of "Joey" Belle for 50 cents. Our pick for his best 1993 card is Score. We have chosen this card because of its overall appeal and pleasing looks.

	BA	G	AB	R	H	2B	3B	HR	RBI	SB
92 NL	.264	159	632	87	167	36	6	9	55	7
Life	.257	669	2444	349	627	125	26	39	239	38

	BA	G	AB	R	H	2B	3B	HR	RBI	SB
92 AL	.260	153	585	81	152	23	1	34	112	8
Life	.260	347	1287	164	335	62	7	70	247	13

RAFAEL BELLIARD

Position: Shortstop
Team: Atlanta Braves
Born: October 24, 1961
　　Pueblo Nuevo,
　　Dominican Republic
Height: 5′6″ **Weight:** 160 lbs.
Bats: Right **Throws:** Right
Acquired: Signed as a free
　　agent, 12/90

ESTEBAN BELTRE

Position: Infield
Team: Chicago White Sox
Born: December 26, 1967
　　Ingenio Quisfuella,
　　Dominican Republic
Height: 5′10″ **Weight:** 155 lbs.
Bats: Right **Throws:** Right
Acquired: Traded from Brewers
　　for John Cangelosi, 5/91

Shortstop Rafael Belliard wasn't taken for granted by the 1992 Braves. It's no secret that Belliard's biggest value to the Braves comes with his glove. Despite being outslugged by starting shortstop Jeff Blauser, Belliard has remained a late-inning defensive fixture for the last two seasons. Ironically, during the '91 World Series, Belliard was one of Atlanta's strongest hitters. His 6-for-16 efforts produced four RBI and a .375 average. He was all but silent in the '92 Series, however. Belliard's career commenced with the Pittsburgh organization in '80. By '82, he reached the majors. In '86, Belliard belted out a personal-best 31 RBI. The following year, he connected off Eric Show for his first home run. As Blauser's bat blossoms in '93, Belliard may become excess baggage for the Braves.

Defense alone cannot create a star or a star card. Skip Belliard's 1993 commons. Our pick for his best 1993 card is Upper Deck. We have chosen this card due to its unique photographic approach.

Due to a season-ending injury to Ozzie Guillen, Esteban Beltre got another chance for some major league playing time in 1992. His path thus far has not gone without some noteworthy accolades. He was rated the best infield arm in the PCL in 1991 by *Baseball America.* He led American Association shortstops with 580 total chances and 335 assists while with Indianapolis in 1990 and had also paced the Southern League in chances in '87. Originally signed as a non-drafted free agent by the Expos in '84, Beltre became a free agent on January 1, 1991, and landed in the Brewers' organization. Beltre made his big league debut in '91, getting his first hit off Seattle's Gene Harris. Beltre is a shortstop whose top assets are range and arm strength. He is also, however, a singles hitter with very little punch.

With the look of a utility infielder, Beltre's 1993 cards aren't worth a nickel apiece. Our pick for his best 1993 card is Topps. We have chosen this card for its technical merits.

	BA	G	AB	R	H	2B	3B	HR	RBI	SB
92 NL	.211	144	285	20	60	6	1	0	14	0
Life	.223	777	1689	171	377	31	12	1	113	38

	BA	G	AB	R	H	2B	3B	HR	RBI	SB
92 AAA	.267	40	161	17	43	5	2	0	16	4
92 AL	.191	49	110	21	21	2	0	1	10	1

FRED
BENAVIDES

Position: Infield
Team: Colorado Rockies
Born: April 7, 1966 Laredo, TX
Height: 6'2" **Weight:** 185 lbs.
Bats: Right **Throws:** Right
Acquired: Second-round pick,
  11/92 expansion draft

ANDY
BENES

Position: Pitcher
Team: San Diego Padres
Born: August 20, 1967
  Evansville, IN
Height: 6'6" **Weight:** 240 lbs.
Bats: Right **Throws:** Right
Acquired: First-round pick,
  6/88 free-agent draft

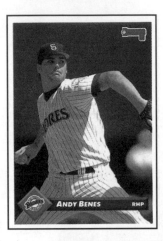

Fred Benavides is a slick fielder who has worked hard on his offense. After facing some pretty intense competition for the shortstop position held by All-Star Barry Larkin, Benavides will finally have a chance to come into his own as a member of the Rockies. He went 3-for-4 with the Reds against Los Angeles on May 25, acquiring his first big league hits. When Larkin went on the DL with a sprained knee in early '92, Benavides filled in at short and also saw some action at second. It was not a glamorous role, but he helped the Reds stay close until the regulars got back. Benavides sat down when Larkin returned, but on May 8, '92, his pinch-hit, two-run double helped in a 10-7 win over the Cubs. He went back to Triple-A Nashville in early June and took the honor of Sounds' Player of the Month.

Because of his punch, Benavides would be a decent 1993 card choice at a nickel. Our pick for his best 1993 card is Topps. We have chosen this card for the interesting facts included on the reverse.

Andy Benes was a much-heralded prospect in 1988, following his U.S. Olympic baseball team achievements. He was the first player in the nation chosen in the June '88 draft. His first-year efforts grabbed Rookie Pitcher of the Year honors from *The Sporting News*. Benes has really been learning on the job, receiving just 21 minor league starts before leaping to the majors in 1989. For 1992 Benes racked up his third consecutive year of double-digit victories for the Padres. Aside from Bruce Hurst, the 6' 6" hurler is San Diego's strongest starter. Yet, Benes did fall short of duplicating his 1991 stats of 15-11 with a 3.03 ERA. He is a durable moundsman and a yearly cinch for at least 30 starts and 200 innings pitched. At age 25, he could develop into a perpetual 20-game winner.

If you feel lucky, try a few cards of Benes for a nickel or less. He's young and strong with an unlimited future. Our pick for his best 1993 card is Donruss. We have chosen this card because of its overall appeal and pleasing looks.

	BA	G	AB	R	H	2B	3B	HR	RBI	SB
92 NL	.231	74	173	14	40	10	1	1	17	0
Life	.246	98	236	25	58	11	1	1	20	1

	W	L	ERA	G	CG	IP	H	ER	BB	SO
92 NL	13	14	3.35	34	2	231.1	230	86	61	169
Life	44	39	3.33	109	8	713.1	652	264	220	542

Series two cards from some companies were available at press time. If space allows, both cards are shown; if not, the most up-to-date cards are pictured.

MIKE BENJAMIN

Position: Shortstop
Team: San Francisco Giants
Born: November 22, 1965
   Euclid, OH
Height: 6'2" **Weight:** 175 lbs.
Bats: Right **Throws:** Right
Acquired: Third-round pick,
   6/87 free-agent draft

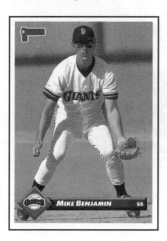 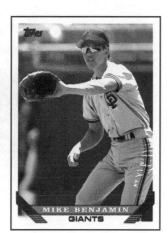

For the fourth consecutive season, Mike Benjamin teetered between Triple-A and a job with the Giants. Benjamin's hitting problems in the bigs were obvious: a .250 average against lefthanders, as compared to a .103 mark facing righties. His overall efforts in '92 for the Giants only added up to a .173 average with one homer and three RBI. Since '89, when he was slated as one of the team's future infield hopes, Benjamin has failed to capture a full-time role. The Arizona State product turned down an '85 draft offer from the Twins. Despite being a capable glove man, he's never hit better than .259 in a single professional season. Expect Benjamin, Royce Clayton, and incumbent Jose Uribe to tussle for San Francisco's starting duties again in 1993.

Benjamin's weak offense will stop him from becoming a household word in the majors. In fact, his hitting could threaten his big league future. Forget his 1993 commons. Our pick for his best 1993 card is Topps. We have chosen this card due to its unique photographic approach.

	BA	G	AB	R	H	2B	3B	HR	RBI	SB
92 NL	.173	40	75	4	13	2	1	1	3	1
Life	.160	130	243	29	39	8	2	5	14	5

DAMON BERRYHILL

Position: Catcher
Team: Atlanta Braves
Born: December 3, 1963
   South Laguna, CA
Height: 6' **Weight:** 205 lbs.
Bats: Both **Throws:** Right
Acquired: Traded from Cubs
   with Mike Bielecki for Turk
   Wendell and Yorkis Perez,
   9/91

Platoon catcher Damon Berryhill supplied Atlanta with part-time power in 1992. Despite sharing receiver duties with Greg Olson, Berryhill registered a career high in home runs. Originally a 13th-round Cub selection in the free-agent draft of January 1983, Berryhill's arrival in Chicago came in 1987. He won the starting job from Jody Davis in 1988, hitting .259 in 95 games. The brawny Californian was headed for offensive highs in 1989, but a rotator cuff injury stopped his season at 91 games. He returned to the majors for the final month of 1990, but couldn't regain his full-time position. Look for Berryhill and Olson to tussle for more playing time in 1993, with Berryhill's power providing an edge.

Yet, going into 1992, Berryhill had never caught 100 games in a single season. Without any substantial history as a starter, his common-priced cards are doomed to inexpensive obscurity. Our pick for his best 1993 card is Topps. We have chosen this card for the superior presentation of information on its back.

	BA	G	AB	R	H	2B	3B	HR	RBI	SB
92 NL	.228	101	307	21	70	16	1	10	43	0
Life	.236	379	1191	98	281	60	2	28	146	3

DANTE BICHETTE

Position: Outfield
Team: Colorado Rockies
Born: November 18, 1963
 West Palm Beach, FL
Height: 6'3" **Weight:** 225 lbs.
Bats: Right **Throws:** Right
Acquired: Traded from Brewers
 for Kevin Reimer, 11/92

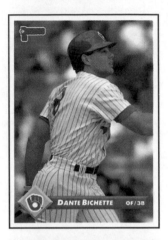 

MIKE BIELECKI

Position: Pitcher
Team: Cleveland Indians
Born: July 31, 1959
 Baltimore, MD
Height: 6'3" **Weight:** 195 lbs.
Bats: Right **Throws:** Right
Acquired: Signed as a minor-
 league free agent, 12/92

After being selected in the 17th round of the 1984 free-agent draft by California, Dante Bichette began his pro career as a third baseman. While he debuted with the Angels in 1988, he wasn't a regular until '90. The following season, he had the honor of being swapped for future Hall of Fame slugger Dave Parker. Although he earned the highest batting average of his major league career in '92, Bichette's power production dwindled. Following consecutive 15-homer, 50-plus RBI seasons in 1990 and '91, his long-ball lackings were considerable. To top it off, lefthanded hitting Darryl Hamilton decided to have a banner season in '92. Bichette got a vote of confidence from the expansion team in Colorado. His career may get a much needed boost with the Rockies in '93.

Bichette's increased batting average isn't enough for collectors. Look for more homers before getting excited over his nickel-priced cards. Our pick for his best 1993 card is Score. We have chosen this card because the design lends itself to the best use of the elements.

Hurler Mike Bielecki's good fortunes were short-circuited with the 1992 Braves. Among his 14 starts with Atlanta, seven went at least six innings in which he surrendered three or less runs. During the last week of July, however, Bielecki encountered problems when he strained a back muscle. Then, his season ended prematurely when a partially torn ligament was discovered in his pitching elbow. The Indians picked him up late in '92. He'll try to rehab with the Tribe, then duplicate his attempts from '89. That season, with the Cubs, he won a career-best 18 games. In '88, Bielecki earned the honor of starting the first-ever night game in Wrigley Field. Although his record was a respectable 13-11 in 1991 before leaving Chicago, Bielecki's ERA had inflated to 4.50.

Bielecki is considered a "one-year wonder" to many card collectors. Bielecki's cards can't escape their common-priced dungeon. Our pick for his best 1993 card is Topps. We have chosen this card because of its great combination of photography and design.

	BA	G	AB	R	H	2B	3B	HR	RBI	SB
92 AL	.287	112	387	37	111	27	2	5	41	18
Life	.254	424	1365	144	347	69	6	38	176	40

	W	L	ERA	G	CG	IP	H	ER	BB	SO
92 NL	2	4	2.57	19	1	80.2	77	23	27	62
Life	53	52	4.05	203	7	927.1	919	417	376	551

CRAIG BIGGIO

Position: Second base
Team: Houston Astros
Born: December 14, 1965
 Smithtown, NY
Height: 5'11" **Weight:** 180 lbs.
Bats: Right **Throws:** Right
Acquired: First-round pick,
 6/87 free-agent draft

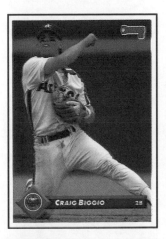

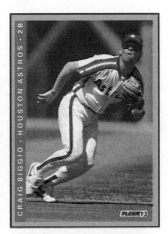

Before 1992, Craig Biggio was a rarity—a good-hitting catcher whose running speed was better than his throwing arm. So the Houston Astros did the logical thing, moving him to second base. Biggio quickly showed he could handle the new assignment with relative ease. Moreover, he didn't lose any of his offensive game while making the transition. Biggio led the Astros in hitting in both 1990 and '91. A first-time All-Star in '91, Biggio batted a career-best .295 and reached double figures in steals for the third season in a row. He had two four-hit games and tied Will Clark for sixth in the league with 48 multiple-hit games. Biggio, who hit .315 over the first half, also used his speed to keep out of double-plays. He once successfully stole 18 consecutive bases.

An All-Star nod means Biggio has card potential. Buy his 1993s, if you see them at a nickel or less. Investigate Biggio's '89 Fleer Update at the dollar level. Our pick for his best 1993 card is Upper Deck. We have chosen this card due to its unique photographic approach.

	BA	G	AB	R	H	2B	3B	HR	RBI	SB
92 NL	.277	162	613	96	170	32	3	6	39	38
Life	.274	645	2280	306	624	106	12	30	192	109

BUD BLACK

Position: Pitcher
Team: San Francisco Giants
Born: June 30, 1957
 San Mateo, CA
Height: 6'2" **Weight:** 185 lbs.
Bats: Left **Throws:** Left
Acquired: Signed as a free
 agent, 11/90

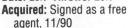

Harry Ralston "Bud" Black began his 12-year major league career with the 1981 Mariners. He was signed by Seattle as a 17th-round selection in the 1979 draft. Black's first full season in the major leagues came with the 1984 Royals. It was in '84 that he established a career-high 17-12 record. Between Kansas City and San Francisco, Black spent the 1989-90 seasons with Cleveland and Toronto. He had one of the fastest starts of his career in 1992. In his first 10 decisions, the veteran Giants hurler was 8-2 with a 2.90 ERA. However, Black remained prone to serving up gopher balls. In his first 25 starts, he was victimized for 20 home runs. At least he escaped a repeat of his 1991 fate, a National League-leading 16 losses.

Even while winning in double digits, Black is still a .500 pitcher at heart. For more return on your investment, pick up nickel-priced cards of a younger, more dominant pitcher. Our pick for his best 1993 card is Upper Deck. We have chosen this card since its design makes it a standout.

	W	L	ERA	G	CG	IP	H	ER	BB	SO
92 NL	10	12	3.97	28	2	177.0	178	78	59	82
Life	105	110	3.76	361	32	1858.0	1776	776	558	932

WILLIE BLAIR

Position: Pitcher
Team: Colorado Rockies
Born: December 18, 1965
Paintsville, KY
Height: 6'1" **Weight:** 185 lbs.
Bats: Right **Throws:** Right
Acquired: First-round pick,
11/92 expansion draft

Willie Blair brought mild relief to the Astros in 1992. Although he was an afterthought in the Cleveland deal involving Kenny Lofton, Blair made a modest addition to the staff after his June 12 recall from the Pacific Coast League. He filled in for demoted starter Daryl Kile, then shored up the right side of the Houston bullpen. In '93, he'll have the opportunity to make a contribution to the Rockies. It all began for Blair when he became Toronto's 11th-round draft choice in 1986. He premiered with the Blue Jays in 1990, but managed only a 3-5 mark with a 4.06 ERA in 27 games. In his short stint with the '91 Indians, Blair's fare was more of the same (2-3, 6.75 ERA in 11 appearances). Before Blair plans on improving his marks for 1993, he'll have to escape the Triple-A revolving door he's been spinning through for three years. He may do it in '93.

Blair needs to really overhaul his stats to revive his commons. Our pick for his best 1993 card is Donruss. We have chosen this card for its technical merits.

	W	L	ERA	G	CG	IP	H	ER	BB	SO
92 NL	5	7	4.00	29	0	78.2	74	35	25	48
Life	10	15	4.57	67	0	183.1	198	93	63	104

LANCE BLANKENSHIP

Position: Infield/outfield
Team: Oakland Athletics
Born: December 6, 1963
Portland, OR
Height: 6' **Weight:** 185 lbs.
Bats: Right **Throws:** Right
Acquired: 10th-round pick,
6/86 free-agent draft

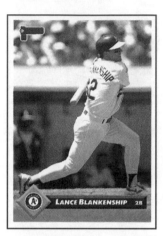 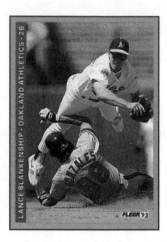

Lance Blankenship must have the path between Oakland and Triple-A Tacoma memorized. In '92, he continued to shuttle between the majors and Pacific Coast League for a sixth consecutive season. Even without a full-time job, Blankenship proved to be one of Oakland's most valuable assets in '92. Originally slated as the A's starting second baseman, he saw considerable outfield duty when numerous injuries occurred and with the emergence of second baseman Mike Bordick. Blankenship began his pro career in 1986 and joined the A's one year later. His top year in Tacoma came in 1988, thanks to nine homers, 52 RBI, and 40 stolen bases. A two-time All-American for the University of California baseball team, Blankenship has become a versatile fielder and constant threat on the base paths.

Although Blankenship seems like a valuable "tenth man," he needs a regular position before his common-price cards get solid recognition. Our pick for his best 1993 card is Fleer. We have chosen this card due to its unique photographic approach.

	BA	G	AB	R	H	2B	3B	HR	RBI	SB
92 AL	.241	123	349	59	84	24	1	3	34	21
Life	.232	367	798	133	185	40	2	7	69	41

JEFF BLAUSER

Position: Shortstop
Team: Atlanta Braves
Born: November 8, 1965
 Los Gatos, CA
Height: 6′ **Weight:** 170 lbs.
Bats: Right **Throws:** Right
Acquired: First-round selection
 in 6/84 free-agent draft

BERT BLYLEVEN

Position: Pitcher
Team: California Angels
Born: April 6, 1951
 Zeist, Holland
Height: 6′3″ **Weight:** 220 lbs.
Bats: Right **Throws:** Right
Acquired: Signed as a free
 agent, 1/92

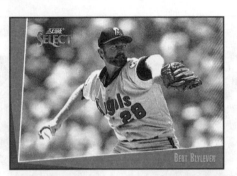

Jeff Blauser continued to show modest pop in 1992, reaching double figures in homers (14) for the third time in four years. He also hit .262 with 46 RBI. The Atlanta infielder's power is surprising, considering that he achieved just 35 homers in a five-year minor league career. In 1989, Blauser's first full major league season, he was Atlanta's starting third baseman. This was on the heels of Ron Gant's hot-corner problems. Blauser moved to the shortstop position in 1990, the spot he was groomed for while in the minors. Before signing with Atlanta in the free-agent draft of June 1984, Blauser turned down a first-round draft offer from the Cardinals in the January '84 draft. In 1993, Blauser should be appearing throughout the Atlanta infield.

If you want to invest in shortstop cards, pick Ozzie Smith or Barry Larkin. Blauser's commons are near misses. Our pick for his best 1993 card is Donruss. We have chosen this card because of its great combination of photography and design.

Future Hall of Fame pitcher Bert Blyleven received no special treatment from the Angels in 1992. After sitting out all of '91 with a rotator cuff tear and another subsequent surgery, California wouldn't guarantee a roster spot in '93. Following a seven-game rehab in Double- and Triple-A, Blyleven returned with a seven-inning shutout win against Cleveland. His last win had been July 20, 1990. During his comeback campaign, Blyleven passed Tom Seaver for third place on the all-time strikeout list. The ageless righty has been a major league fixture since the 1970 season with Minnesota. Blyleven's only season as a 20-game winner came with the 1973 Twins. Expect him to make a serious bid to enter the 300-win circle in '93.

Blyleven's 1993 cards, at a nickel apiece, will pay long-term dividends when he reaches Cooperstown. His '73 Topps card still goes for about $4, making it his earliest, most affordable card. Our pick for his best 1993 card is Topps. We have chosen this card for its technical merits.

	BA	G	AB	R	H	2B	3B	HR	RBI	SB
92 NL	.262	123	343	61	90	19	3	14	46	5
Life	.262	578	1769	237	464	90	15	49	207	25

	W	L	ERA	G	CG	IP	H	ER	BB	SO
92 AL	8	12	4.74	25	1	133.0	150	70	29	70
Life	287	250	3.31	692	242	4970.0	4632	1830	1322	3701

MIKE BODDICKER

Position: Pitcher
Team: Kansas City Royals
Born: August 23, 1957
  Cedar Rapids, IA
Height: 5'11" **Weight:** 186 lbs.
Bats: Right **Throws:** Right
Acquired: Signed as a free
  agent, 11/90

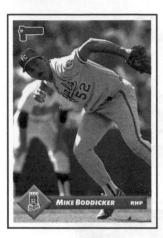 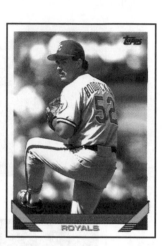

Mike Boddicker's tenure as a starting pitcher in the major leagues may have ended when Rickey Henderson rammed him with a line drive on September 25, 1991. When Boddicker returned to the Royals in '92, he was assigned to middle relief by manager Hal McRae. Boddicker did not shine. He gave up more than one hit per inning, and his strikeout-to-walk ratio was almost equal. These problems could be the result of a back problem that sent him to the disabled list in July. Relying on a good fastball and the ability to change speeds, Boddicker's best pitch is his "foshball," a blooping fastball that behaves like a screwball. Before the '92 season, he had posted wins in double figures for nine consecutive seasons. A third baseman in college, Boddicker won a Gold Glove in '90.

Despite his glory from years past, Boddicker's an unlikely candidate to leave the bullpen and return to his old form in the starting role. Our pick for his best 1993 card is Topps. We have chosen this card since the photograph captures the athletic ability of the player.

	W	L	ERA	G	SV	IP	H	ER	BB	SO
92 AL	1	4	4.98	29	3	86.2	92	48	37	47
Life	131	111	3.75	332	3	2069.2	2005	863	706	1306

JOE BOEVER

Position: Pitcher
Team: Houston Astros
Born: October 4, 1960
  St. Louis, MO
Height: 6'1" **Weight:** 200 lbs.
Bats: Right **Throws:** Right
Acquired: Signed as a free
  agent, 1/92

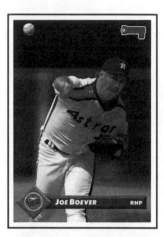 

Joe Boever was one of the most prosperous castoffs rescued by the Astros in 1992. The veteran righthander wasn't offered a new contract by the Phillies following the 1991 campaign and was netted for the bargain price of a Triple-A contract. The spring training invitee won an opening-day spot on Houston's roster, becoming a fixture in the 'Stros bullpen. Boever is a relief workhorse, appearing in 60-plus games annually for the last four seasons. Although working as a set-up man for closer Doug Jones in 1992, Boever has a noted past as a stopper. He gained a personal-best 21 saves with the 1989 Braves. Boever began in pro ball as an undrafted free agent in 1982, spending nearly six seasons in the Cardinals' organization. One of the best bargains of 1992, Boever will play a big part in Houston's 1993 revival.

Boever's bullpen duties do little to boost his card values. His 1993 cards are eternal commons. Our pick for his best 1993 card is Fleer. We have chosen this card because of its overall appeal and pleasing looks.

	W	L	ERA	G	SV	IP	H	ER	BB	SO
92 NL	3	6	2.51	81	2	111.1	103	31	45	67
Life	14	31	3.41	336	38	457.0	425	173	212	352

WADE BOGGS

Position: Third base
Team: New York Yankees
Born: June 15, 1958
   Omaha, NE
Height: 6′2″ **Weight:** 197 lbs.
Bats: Left **Throws:** right
Acquired: Signed as a free
   agent, 12/92

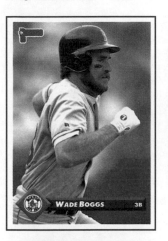 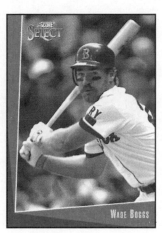

Wade Boggs broke into the majors with Boston in 1982 and hit a career-peak .368 three years later. Once a weak fielder, he worked hard to make himself one of the top defensive third basemen in the game. Boggs won five batting titles in his first 10 seasons and carried a .345 career average—baseball's best—into the 1992 campaign. He did stumble in '92, hitting only .259, but he still walked 74 times compared to 31 strikeouts. As a surprise to many, the BoSox didn't re-sign Boggs and the Yankees saw the opportunity to snap up the veteran. Blessed with a brilliant batting eye, his willingness to wait out a walk is reflected in his high on-base percentage. Boggs is a contact hitter who rarely strikes out.

   Get Boggs' 1993 cards at a dime each. Invest in his past and restored future. Early Boggs cards are overpriced, considering his 1992 showing. Save your money. Our pick for his best 1993 card is Score. We have chosen this card since its design makes it a standout.

	BA	G	AB	R	H	2B	3B	HR	RBI	SB
92 AL	.259	143	514	62	133	22	4	7	50	1
Life	.338	1625	6213	1067	2098	422	47	85	687	16

BRIAN BOHANON

Position: Pitcher
Team: Texas Rangers
Born: August 1, 1968
   Denton, TX
Height: 6′2″ **Weight:** 220 lbs.
Bats: Left **Throws:** Left
Acquired: First-round pick,
   6/87 free-agent draft

Pitcher Brian Bohanon didn't attract much attention with the Rangers in 1992. By contrast, he was a tidy 4-2 with a 2.73 ERA in nine starts with Triple-A Oklahoma City. The Texas native rocketed through three minor league levels before debuting with the Rangers in '91. His 4-3 mark and 4.84 ERA were a stern contrast to his '92 misfortunes, when he started the season on the disabled list. He rehabilitated in Double- and Triple-A, but was nicked for seven gopher balls upon his return to the bigs. A highly touted draft pick out of high school in '87, Bohanon endured three stays on the disabled list before '92. He uses a fastball, curve, slider, and changeup, but he needs good health to cement his comeback.

   Due to past elbow and shoulder worries, Bohanon isn't going to be a major force on the '93 Rangers staff. His common-priced cards have few financial possibilities. Our pick for his best 1993 card is Upper Deck. We have chosen this card due to the outstanding photographic composition.

	W	L	ERA	G	CG	IP	H	ER	BB	SO
92 AL	1	1	6.31	18	0	45.2	57	32	25	29
Life	5	7	5.74	40	1	141.0	163	90	66	78

BARRY BONDS

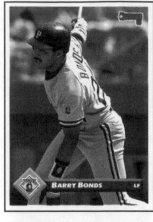

Position: Outfield
Team: San Francisco Giants
Born: July 24, 1964,
Riverside, CA
Height: 6'1" **Weight:** 185 lbs.
Bats: Left **Throws:** Left
Acquired: Signed as a free
agent, 12/92

For the last three seasons, Barry Bonds was the top all-around player in the NL. He was MVP in 1990, finished second a year later, and won top honors again in '92. In '93, he'll be a baseball giant in more ways than one. He signed a free-agent deal with San Francisco late in '92. A Gold Glove fielder with a golden bat, Bonds is also blessed with great speed. During the '90 campaign, he joined father Bobby as the only father-and-son tandem in the 30/30 Club. He and Eric Davis are the only players ever to steal 50 bases and hit 30 homers in the same season. In '91, Bonds became the first Buc since Willie Stargell to produce consecutive 100-RBI seasons. In '92, Bonds hit .311 with 34 home runs, knocked in 103 RBI, and swiped 39 bases. Bonds broke into pro ball in 1985 and advanced to Pittsburgh a year later.

His 1993 cards await big welcomes at a quarter apiece. The 1988 Fleer card of Bonds is an undiscovered early bargain at $1.50 or less. Our pick for his best 1993 card is Fleer. We have chosen this card because of its overall appeal and pleasing looks.

	BA	G	AB	R	H	2B	3B	HR	RBI	SB
92 NL	.311	140	473	109	147	36	5	34	103	39
Life	.275	1010	3584	672	984	220	36	176	556	251

RICKY BONES

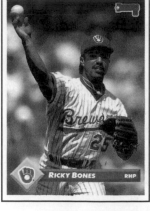

Position: Pitcher
Team: Milwaukee Brewers
Born: April 7, 1969
Salinas, Puerto Rico
Height: 6' **Weight:** 190 lbs.
Bats: Right **Throws:** Right
Acquired: Traded from Padres
with Jose Valentin and Matt
Mieske for Geoff Kellogg and
Gary Sheffield, 3/92

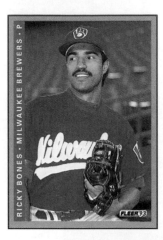

Ricky Bones had the unpleasant task of trying to replace a possible triple crown winner. As fans were reading reports about how Gary Sheffield was winning games for his new team, the pitcher obtained in the one-sided swap was faced with providing some kind of immediate return for Milwaukee. Bones began his pro career at age 17, signing as an undrafted free agent in 1986. In his first full major league season, Bones became a regular in the Brewers rotation. He exceeded his 4-6 record with the 1991 Padres, which was the culmination of six minor league seasons. His long career in the minors produced winning marks in five of his half-dozen years. While his 1992 stats with the Brew Crew aren't overwhelming, Bones remains a young, promising moundsman.

However, Bones isn't the overpowering type. With little hope of becoming a staff ace or strikeout champion, his 1993 commons are best forgotten. Our pick for his best 1993 card is Upper Deck. We have chosen this card because it has a distinctive look.

	W	L	ERA	G	CG	IP	H	ER	BB	SO
92 AL	9	10	4.57	31	0	163.1	169	83	48	65
Life	13	16	4.64	42	0	217.1	226	112	66	96

BOBBY BONILLA

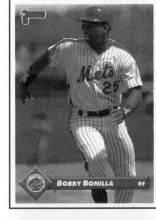

Position: Outfield
Team: New York Mets
Born: February 23, 1963,
New York, NY
Height: 6'3" **Weight:** 230 lbs.
Bats: Both **Throws:** Right
Acquired: Signed as a free
agent, 12/91

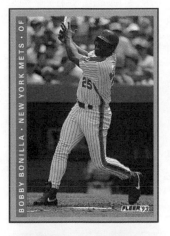

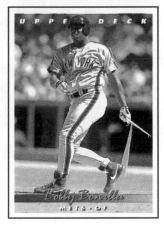

What happened? Bobby Bonilla finished second to teammate Barry Bonds in the 1990 MVP voting. In '91, he finished first in the league in doubles, fourth in hits, runs, and on-base percentage, fifth in walks, and sixth in batting and total bases. He also had a career-best 18-game hitting streak. In '92, however, Bonilla got off to a rocky start in his first year with the Mets. After signing a megabucks free agent contract that extended five seasons, Bonilla slammed two homers on Opening Day. The tide seemed to turn as he plunged into a prolonged slump. On June 1, however, Bonilla went 3-for-3 with three runs scored and six RBI as the Mets romped to a 14-1 win over San Francisco. He reached base on each of his five at-bats. On that night, he knocked in more runs than he had plated in 73 previous Shea Stadium at-bats.

Wait for a return to his former winning ways before buying his dime-priced 1993s. Check the 1987 Topps set for a $1.50 Bonilla rookie. Our pick for his best 1993 card is Topps. We have chosen this card due to its unique photographic approach.

	BA	G	AB	R	H	2B	3B	HR	RBI	SB
92 NL	.249	128	438	62	109	23	0	19	70	4
Life	.279	1046	3732	572	1040	224	37	135	596	32

BRET BOONE

Position: Second base
Team: Seattle Mariners
Born: April 6, 1969 El Cajon, CA
Height: 5'10" **Weight:** 180 lbs.
Bats: Right **Throws:** Right
Acquired: Fifth-round selection,
6/90 free-agent draft

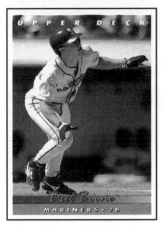

By the end of his third professional season, Bret Boone was a major league regular. The Mariners promoted Boone in August 1992, handing him the second base job that had been occupied by Harold Reynolds for years. Along with becoming an instant starter, Boone's performance suffered from the pressure of being a family record setter. He barely eked out a .194 batting average. As the son of Bob Boone, a star catcher for 19 seasons, and the grandson of Ray Boone, a big league infielder from 1948-60, Bret's Seattle call-up marked the first time a family had three generations represented in the majors. During his three-year collegiate career at the University of Southern California, Boone set four offensive records. The M's tried out Boone at shortstop before grooming him as a permanent second sacker.

Simply because of his noted relatives, Boone's cards are worth keeping. Invest heartily if you can find his 1993 cards at a dime or less. Our pick for his best 1993 card is Score. We have chosen this card for the interesting facts included on the reverse.

	BA	G	AB	R	H	2B	3B	HR	RBI	SB
92 AAA	.314	118	439	73	138	26	5	13	73	17
92 AL	.194	33	129	15	25	4	0	4	15	1

PAT BORDERS

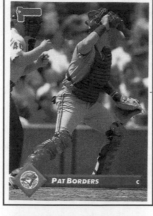

Position: Catcher
Team: Toronto Blue Jays
Born: May 14, 1963
    Columbus, OH
Height: 6'2" **Weight:** 195 lbs.
Bats: Right **Throws:** Right
Acquired: Sixth-round pick,
    6/82 free-agent draft

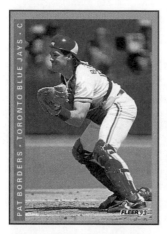

What a difference a year makes. With the arrival of catcher Greg Myers in 1991, Pat Borders sank to five home runs and 36 RBI in 105 games. He waited until his last 17 games of 1991 to hit four of those homers. However, Borders resembled his 1990 slugging self again in 1992. He reclaimed his starting job with the Blue Jays in 1992, posting one of the best offensive campaigns of his career. He decided to top off a fantastic comeback year by helping his team to take top honors in the World Series and being named Series MVP. First considered a third baseman upon his 1982 signing out of high school, Borders' first bow in the majors came in 1988. As a rookie, he played second, third, or catcher.

Borders does his job, but is usually overshadowed in a star-filled sky of Blue Jays. Don't expect too much from his 1993 common-priced cards. The World Series MVP is in the '88 Topps Traded set for 35 cents. Our pick for his best 1993 card is Upper Deck. We have chosen this card since the photograph captures the athletic ability of the player.

	BA	G	AB	R	H	2B	3B	HR	RBI	SB
92 AL	.242	138	480	47	116	26	2	13	53	1
Life	.258	518	1512	142	390	84	8	41	188	3

MIKE BORDICK

Position: Second base
Team: Oakland Athletics
Born: July 21, 1965
    Marquette, MI
Height: 5'11" **Weight:** 175 lbs.
Bats: Right **Throws:** Right
Acquired: Signed as a free
    agent, 7/86

Mike Bordick exceeded everyone's expectations with the 1992 A's. During the first two months of the season, he was a brief league batting leader, and he finished in the 10th spot in the AL for the year (.300). Yes, this was the same man who had never exceeded the .270s in the minors and the same A's utilityman who scraped out a .238 mark with no homers and 21 RBI in a 90-game '91. A shortstop by trade, Bordick adapted quickly to second base when Walt Weiss recovered to reclaim his starting job. Simply playing pro baseball is one of Bordick's biggest feats. Despite a three-year career at the University of Maine, he was not chosen in the 1986 draft. Instead, he was discovered while playing summer baseball. Now, he may be one of Oakland's steadiest players for 1993.

Bordick's 1992 overachievements could be temporary. Unless he actually does win a batting crown, his 1993 commons will stay common. Our pick for his best 1993 card is Upper Deck. We have chosen this card since the photograph captures the athletic ability of the player

	BA	G	AB	R	H	2B	3B	HR	RBI	SB
92 AL	.300	154	504	62	151	19	4	3	48	12
Life	.276	269	753	83	208	24	5	3	69	15

Series two cards from some companies were available at press time. If space allows, both cards are shown; if not, the most up-to-date cards are pictured.

CHRIS BOSIO

Position: Pitcher
Team: Seattle Mariners
Born: April 3, 1963
Carmichael, CA
Height: 6'3" **Weight:** 225 lbs.
Bats: Right **Throws:** Right
Acquired: Signed as a free
agent, 12/92

SHAWN BOSKIE

Position: Pitcher
Team: Chicago Cubs
Born: March 28, 1967
Hawthorne, NV
Height: 6'3" **Weight:** 205 lbs.
Bats: Right **Throws:** Right
Acquired: First-round selection,
1/86 free-agent draft

Pitcher Chris Bosio made surprise contenders out of the Brewers in 1992, submitting one of the finest seasons of his career. When he limited Boston to four hits and no runs over eight innings on September 14, the big righthander tied a team record with his eighth consecutive victory. Bosio seems to thrive on work. He's exceeded 30 games and 200 innings pitched in three of the last four seasons. Before becoming a Brewer in 1986, Bosio's 16 Pacific Coast League saves with Triple-A Vancouver led the league. In 1989, Bosio was named Milwaukee's Most Valuable Pitcher (15-10, 2.95 ERA, and 173 strikeouts). Bosio's career bottomed out in '90, when he was 4-9 in 20 starts. Two knee operations during 1990 hampered his progress. Bosio will be pitching in Seattle in '93, after signing a free-agent contract in late '92.

Don't forget that Bosio had a lifetime losing record going into 1992. His common-priced cards lack appeal. Our pick for his best 1993 card is Donruss. We have chosen this card for its technical merits.

Shawn Boskie, once touted as Chicago's future staff ace, was a mere afterthought for the Cubs in '92. In 1990 and '91, Boskie rode the organizational merry-go-round, spinning between Chicago and Triple-A Iowa. Despite a lackluster spring training, he made the Opening-Day roster in 1992. Neck and shoulder spasms sent him to the 15-day disabled list during the second half of the '92 campaign and could account for some of his ineffectiveness. Boskie was only the 10th overall selection in the first-round of the free-agent draft in January 1986. Before joining the Cubs rookie league team, Boskie was a third baseman. His major league debut, on May 20, 1990, was a complete-game win over the Mets. Since then, Boskie has been the victim of "can't-miss" expectations.

Boskie's future with the Cubs may be in the past. His 1993 commons are questionable purchases. Our pick for his best 1993 card is Donruss. We have chosen this card for its technical merits.

	W	L	ERA	G	CG	IP	H	ER	BB	SO
92 AL	16	6	3.62	33	4	231.1	223	93	44	120
Life	67	62	3.76	212	32	1190.0	1184	497	289	749

	W	L	ERA	G	CG	IP	H	ER	BB	SO
92 NL	5	11	5.01	23	0	91.2	96	51	36	39
Life	14	26	4.69	66	1	318.1	345	166	119	150

DARYL BOSTON

Position: Outfield
Team: Colorado Rockies
Born: January 4, 1963
  Cincinnati, OH
Height: 6'3" **Weight:** 195 lbs.
Bats: Left **Throws:** Left
Acquired: Signed as a free
  agent, 12/92

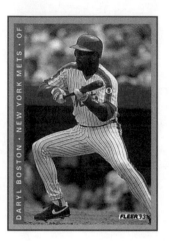

Daryl Boston was a solid but unspectacular presence with the 1992 Mets. The outfielder saw the most action in left field, but also filled in for injured center fielder Vince Coleman. Throughout the season, Boston's batting average against lefties soared almost 100 points over his marks against righties (.319 LHP; .236 RHP). Boston was an off-and-on starter with the White Sox from 1984-89, following his selection in the free-agent draft in '81. His ChiSox years peaked in '88, when he socked 15 homers and 31 RBI. He was abruptly released by Chicago after a mere five games in '90, but was signed by New York only five days later. That year, Boston repaid his adoptive Mets by hitting .273 with 12 home runs and a career-best 45 RBI. He'll be with the Colorado Rockies in '93.

Boston's future seems to be as a second-stringer or platoon player. Even with a new team, he won't get enough notice to revive his '93s. Our pick for his best 1993 card is Donruss. We have chosen this card because of its excellent combination of photography and design.

	BA	G	AB	R	H	2B	3B	HR	RBI	SB
92 NL	.249	130	289	37	72	14	2	11	35	12
Life	.250	882	2261	321	565	114	21	65	224	97

JEFF BRANSON

Position: Infield
Team: Cincinnati Reds
Born: January 26, 1967
  Waynesboro, MS
Height: 6' **Weight:** 180 lbs.
Bats: Left **Throws:** Right
Acquired: Second-round pick,
  6/88 free-agent draft

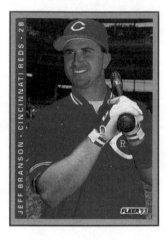

Jeff Branson is a versatile player who received his first look at the big leagues in 1992 when injuries hit the Reds. A member of the 1988 gold medal-winning U.S. Olympic team, Branson can play second and third as well as short. He broke into the pros by delivering 10 homers and 68 RBI en route to a berth on the Midwest League's 1989 postseason All-Star team. He slipped a bit in 1990, starting in Double-A Chattanooga but going back to Class-A Cedar Rapids. In 1991, though, Branson opened in Double-A and was boosted to Triple-A Nashville of the American Association in July. His batting average suffers greatly when on the road. In '91, Branson batted a very respectable .309 at home, but only managed .182 when away. Branson will steal the occasional base, but has reached double figures only once ('90).

As a possible successor to Bill Doran, Branson's 10 cent 1993 card could be a pleasant surprise. Our pick for his best 1993 card is Donruss. We have chosen this card due to the outstanding photographic composition.

	BA	G	AB	R	H	2B	3B	HR	RBI	SB
92 NL	.296	72	115	12	34	7	1	0	15	0
Life	.296	72	115	12	34	7	1	0	15	0

Series two cards from some companies were available at press time. If space allows, both cards are shown; if not, the most up-to-date cards are pictured.

CLIFF BRANTLEY

Position: Pitcher
Team: Philadelphia Phillies
Born: April 12, 1968
   Staten Island, NY
Height: 6'1" **Weight:** 190 lbs.
Bats: Right **Throws:** Right
Acquired: Phillies' second draft
   choice, 6/86

SID BREAM

Position: First base
Team: Atlanta Braves
Born: August 3, 1960
   Carlisle, PA
Height: 6'4" **Weight:** 220 lbs.
Bats: Left **Throws:** Left
Acquired: Signed as a free
   agent, 12/90

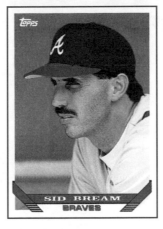

Cliff Brantley labored long in the minor leagues before getting to the majors. There is, however, more work to be done if he is to become an impact pitcher with the Phils. In a 13-game stretch with Philadelphia in 1992, Brantley issued 34 walks in 45 ⅓ innings. Also, the first nine men to attempt a steal were successful. On the bright side, Brantley allowed only one of his first inherited runners to score and did not permit a hit to the first batter he faced over that span. Brantley reached the majors in 1991, his sixth season as a pro. He began the year at Double-A Reading and went 4-3 with a 1.94 ERA. He was Eastern League Pitcher of the Week for two starts during which he assembled a 15-inning scoreless streak. Brantley moved to Triple-A Scranton, where he put together another skein, this one of 20 ⅓ innings. He got the call from the Phillies and debuted September 3 against the Reds.

   Brantley's 1993s will be so-so buys at 10 to 15 cents. Our pick for his best 1993 card is Donruss. We have chosen this card since the photograph captures the athletic ability of the player.

Sid Bream upped his offensive output for the Braves in 1992, giving quiet but steady hitting support. His leadership doesn't show up in statistics, but it is credited as a large part of Atlanta's turnaround. Bream started his pro career as a second-round draft choice of Los Angeles in 1981. In mid-1985, he was traded to Pittsburgh with R.J. Reynolds and Cecil Espy in exchange for Bill Madlock. In 1986, his first full season with the Bucs, he posted career highs of 16 home runs and 77 RBI. In 1989, he survived for a mere 19 games. Going into 1992, Bream had undergone four knee operations in two years. He's preserved his fine fielding reputation, despite numerous stays on the disabled list. With Bream's past health concerns, he seems ideal for a future designated hitter's role in the AL.

   With other healthier players waiting in the wings, Bream can't last forever as Atlanta's first baseman. His '93s get a polite thumbs-down. Our pick for his best 1993 card is Score. We have chosen this card because of its overall appeal and pleasing looks.

	W	L	ERA	G	SV	IP	H	ER	BB	SO
92 NL	7	7	2.95	56	7	91.2	67	30	45	86
Life	24	14	2.94	246	42	391.2	345	128	173	308

	BA	G	AB	R	H	2B	3B	HR	RBI	SB
92 NL	.261	125	372	30	97	25	1	10	61	6
Life	.262	925	2770	311	726	172	11	81	413	46

GEORGE BRETT

Position: Designated hitter
Team: Kansas City Royals
Born: May 15, 1953
Glen Dale, WV
Height: 6′ **Weight:** 205 lbs.
Bats: Left **Throws:** Right
Acquired: Second-round
selection, 6/71 free-agent
draft

George Brett provided great drama for Royals fans in 1992. Going into the last weeks of the season, Brett was less than two dozen hits away from the coveted 3,000 hit mark. He achieved the goal, reaching 3,005. Going into '92, Brett's career had been interrupted by 10 separate stays on the DL. Yet, he's the first player ever to win batting titles in three different decades (1976, 1980, and 1990). He made his major league debut in '73. A 10-time All-Star, Brett is a Cooperstown shoo-in the moment he rides off into the Royal sunset.

Even with Brett sticking around for a few more hits in 1993, be assured it will be his last year depicted in card sets. Get these finale cards for less than a dime apiece. Upon his Hall of Fame calling, prices will boom. Brett's '75 Topps rookie card easily tops $200. Invest in the '77 Topps "Big League Brothers" of George and Ken Brett for $3. Our pick for his best 1993 card is Fleer. We have chosen this card due to the outstanding photographic composition.

	BA	G	AB	R	H	2B	3B	HR	RBI	SB
92 AL	.285	152	592	55	169	35	5	7	61	8
Life	.307	2562	9789	1514	3005	634	134	298	1520	194

GREG BRILEY

Position: Outfield
Team: Seattle Mariners
Born: May 24, 1965 Bethel, NC
Height: 5′9″ **Weight:** 170 lbs.
Bats: Left **Throws:** Right
Acquired: First-round selection,
6/86 free-agent draft

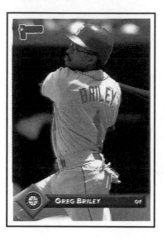 

Injuries and the lack of a full-time position haunted Greg Briley's 1992 season. In July, Briley landed on the 15-day disabled list with a sprained ligament in his throwing elbow. When he was healthy, the man known to Seattle fans as "Pee-Wee" saw duty at second base, third, designated hitter, and all three outfield spots. While the M's value his lefthanded bat, they usually keep him out of the lineup against lefties. Briley's lessened role with the Mariners comes because he hasn't recaptured his rookie-season glory from 1989, when he batted .266 with 13 homers and 52 RBI. In 1991, he stole a career-high 23 bases, compared to only nine thefts in '92. Before signing with the Mariners in 1986, the North Carolina native declined draft offers from the Dodgers and Indians in 1985.

Briley can't count on starting work from the Mariners in 1993. Therefore, his common-priced cards can't be counted on, either. Our pick for his best 1993 card is Topps. We have chosen this card because the design lends itself to the best use of the elements.

	BA	G	AB	R	H	2B	3B	HR	RBI	SB
92 AL	.275	86	200	18	55	10	0	5	12	9
Life	.260	478	1348	155	351	69	9	26	123	59

RICO BROGNA

Position: First base
Team: Detroit Tigers
Born: April 18, 1970
Turner Falls, MA
Height: 6'2" **Weight:** 202
Bats: Left **Throws:** Left
Acquired: First-round pick,
6/88 free-agent draft

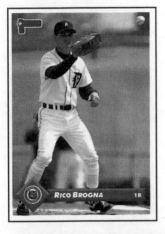

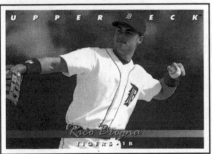

SCOTT BROSIUS

Position: Infield
Team: Oakland Athletics
Born: August 15, 1966
Hillsboro, OR
Height: 6'1" **Weight:** 185 lbs.
Bats: Right **Throws:** Right
Acquired: 20th-round selection,
6/87 free-agent draft

Rico Brogna is regarded as one of the Tigers' top prospects, but he'll have to do a lot more than he has if he wants to win a job. For one thing, he has Cecil Fielder ahead of him at the major league level, and there's probably no player in baseball who could unseat the home run and RBI machine. He did get a peek at the bigs in August '92. He didn't fare too well, hitting a weak .192 in his nine-game trial. Which brings up the second reason Brogna will have a tough go: He simply hasn't responded to Triple-A competition. After being a home run champion for London of the Double-A Eastern League in '90, he has failed to impress in more than one try at Triple-A Toledo. He is a below-average runner but not a bad performer with the glove. He was voted the Class-A top fielding first baseman in '89 by *Baseball America*.

Brogna has two chances of unseating Fielder—slim and none. Forgo his '93s. Our pick for his best 1993 card is Donruss. We have chosen this card because of its excellent combination of photography and design.

Scott Brosius joined the parade of injured players on the 1992 A's. Despite making the Opening-Day roster, Brosius was sidelined by a bruised hip in April and by a viral infection in July, missing more than a month of active duty. A trip back to Triple-A put more limits on his big league exposure. Yet, he made the most of his appearances, serving the A's in six different positions. Brosius got his first taste of the bigs in 1991, hitting .235 in 36 games with Oakland. He unveiled his full potential with Double-A Huntsville in 1990, smashing 23 homers and 88 RBI for a .296 average. If Brosius hangs around the Oakland organization, he could be the eventual successor at third base. However, this remote chance offers little hope for his 1993 prospects.

Put Brosius with another team, and he might be a semi-regular. With the A's, though, he could do lots of sitting. Until his employment picture clears, steer clear of his 1993 commons. Our pick for his best 1993 card is Donruss. We have chosen this card for its technical merits.

	BA	G	AB	R	H	2B	3B	HR	RBI	SB
91 AA	.273	77	293	40	80	13	1	13	51	0
92 AAA	.261	121	387	45	101	19	4	10	58	1

	BA	G	AB	R	H	2B	3B	HR	RBI	SB
92 AL	.218	38	87	13	19	2	0	4	13	3
Life	.226	74	155	22	35	7	0	6	17	6

KEVIN BROWN

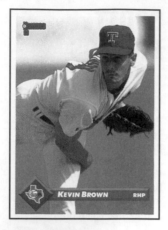

Position: Pitcher
Team: Texas Rangers
Born: March 14, 1965
McIntyre, GA
Height: 6'4" **Weight:** 195 lbs.
Bats: Right **Throws:** Right
Acquired: First-round pick,
6/86 free-agent draft

JERRY BROWNE

Position: Infield/outfield
Team: Oakland Athletics
Born: February 13, 1966
St. Croix, Virgin Islands
Height: 5'10" **Weight:** 170 lbs.
Bats: Both **Throws:** Right
Acquired: Signed as a free
agent, 4/92

Kevin Brown has been a solid starter for Texas for four seasons in a row. The former All-American from Georgia Tech broke into pro ball in '86. He even won a start for the Rangers that summer after working only six games in the minors. Periodic arm trouble hampered his progress, however, and he did not reach the Rangers to stay until '89. Not until '91 did Brown have his first injury-free campaign. Brown seized a piece of the public spotlight in '92 by becoming the third 10-game winner in the majors. He notched the 10th win in a 4-1 outing over Boston on June 21. This effort tied him with Rick Honeycutt ('83) as the earliest 10-game winner in Texas history. Brown achieved this in only his 15th start for '92.

Don't invest. Sudden stardom means his cards are overpriced at 15 cents or higher. If he loses any momentum in '93, they'll wilt. Brown shares a '89 Fleer rookie card with Kevin Reimer. At 50 cents, it's a steal. Our pick for his best 1993 card is Donruss. We have chosen this card because of its overall appeal and pleasing looks.

Jerry Browne could have been dubbed Oakland's master plumber in 1992, as he plugged leaks in the A's lineup throughout the season. Aside from catching, pitching, and playing first base, Browne was seen everywhere. He did play 58 of his 111 games at third base. His sole downfall was a .184 average against lefthanded pitching. In a cost-cutting move, Browne was cut during spring training from the '92 Cleveland roster. After signing a Triple-A contract with Oakland, he was promoted for good on April 20. Browne was swapped from Texas in 1988 with Pete O'Brien and Oddibe McDowell in exchange for future batting champion Julio Franco. After two years as an Indians starter at second base, Browne was a utilityman in 1991. The switch-hitter could be seeing lots more reserve action for the A's in 1993.

Browne can't crack Oakland's starting lineup. Staying on the bench spells disaster for his 1993 commons. Our pick for his best 1993 card is Upper Deck. We have chosen this card since its design makes it a standout.

	W	L	ERA	G	CG	IP	H	ER	BB	SO
92 AL	21	11	3.32	35	11	265.2	262	98	76	173
Life	56	43	3.67	127	25	875.2	876	357	304	477

	BA	G	AB	R	H	2B	3B	HR	RBI	SB
92 AL	.287	111	324	43	93	12	2	3	40	3
Life	.272	728	2417	341	657	101	21	17	222	65

Series two cards from some companies were available at press time. If space allows, both cards are shown; if not, the most up-to-date cards are pictured.

TOM BROWNING

Position: Pitcher
Team: Cincinnati Reds
Born: April 28, 1960
  Casper, WY
Height: 6′1″ **Weight:** 195 lbs.
Bats: Left **Throws:** Left
Acquired: Ninth-round
  selection, 6/82 free-agent
  draft

Four consecutive years of 200-plus innings pitched took their toll on Tom Browning in 1992. A ruptured ligament in his left knee ended Browning's season in early June. This marked the first time in eight seasons that Browning did not win in double figures. The hurler's career began with the 1984 Reds. He finished second in 1985 Rookie of the Year balloting (to Vince Coleman), due in part to a career-best 20-9 season. The Wyoming native contributed to the team's 1990 World Championship with a 15-9 record and two postseason victories. Despite his injury, he moved into 12th on the all-time team wins list in 1992. If the Reds expect to contend again in 1993, they need a healthy Browning at their disposal.

Browning is signed through 1994 with the Reds. He'll need another 20-win season or pennant-winning participation to inflate the values of his common-priced cards. Our pick for his best 1993 card is Upper Deck. We have chosen this card because of its overall appeal and pleasing looks.

	W	L	ERA	G	CG	IP	H	ER	BB	SO
92 NL	6	5	5.07	16	0	87.0	108	49	28	33
Life	113	80	3.86	272	29	1756.1	1725	753	473	922

J.T. BRUETT

Position: Outfield
Team: Minnesota Twins
Born: October 8, 1967,
  Milwaukee, WI
Height: 5′11″ **Weight:** 175 lbs.
Bats: Left **Throws:** Left
Acquired: 11th-round pick,
  6/88 free-agent draft

J.T. Bruett is a whiz both on the basepaths and in the classroom. A major in industrial psychology, he earned the Bierman Award for athletic academics in his sophomore year at Minnesota. He also stole 61 bases for Kenosha in 1989, leading the Class-A Midwest League and getting voted best baserunner. Bruett builds his game around his ability to get on base, as illustrated by his .439 on-base percentage in '90, which led the Class-A California League. He has never hit under .267 for a full season, and has walked more than he has struck out at virtually every stop in his pro career. Bruett is also a fine defensive outfielder; Cal League managers once voted him the Best Defensive Outfielder. He made only two errors in 223 total chances with Triple-A Portland in '91. Bruett came to the majors in '92 and was used mostly as a reserve. He played all three outfield positions with the Twins in '92.

The jury's still out on Bruett. Try his 1993s at a dime each. Our pick for his best 1993 card is Topps. We have chosen this card due to the outstanding photographic composition.

	BA	G	AB	R	H	2B	3B	HR	RBI	SB
92 AL	.250	56	76	7	19	4	0	0	2	6
Life	.250	56	76	7	19	4	0	0	2	6

TOM BRUNANSKY

Position: Outfield
Team: Boston Red Sox
Born: August 20, 1960
  Covina, CA
Height: 6'4" **Weight:** 220 lbs.
Bats: Right **Throws:** Right
Acquired: Traded from
  Cardinals for Lee Smith, 5/90

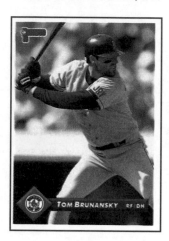 

STEVE BUECHELE

Position: Third base
Team: Chicago Cubs
Born: September 26, 1961
  Lancaster, CA
Height: 6'2" **Weight:** 200 lbs.
Bats: Right **Throws:** Right
Acquired: Traded from Pirates
  for Danny Jackson, 7/92

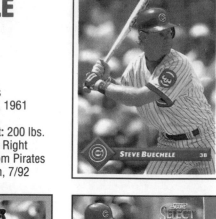

Tom Brunansky became a starter by default for the 1992 Red Sox. Boston's starting outfield of Mike Greenwell, Ellis Burks, and Phil Plantier fell to injuries and slumps, summoning reserves like Bruno. In his third Red Sox season, Brunansky's offensive totals looked strikingly similar to his past performance. His 1990 season of 16 homers and 73 RBI snapped an eight-year string of 20 or more homers annually. Although his average dropped to .229 in 1991, he managed 16 round-trippers and 70 RBI. A first-round draft pick of California's in 1978, Brunansky debuted with the Angels in 1981. A trade made him a Twins regular in '82. In Minnesota, he socked career highs of 32 homers in 1984 and '87. More than a slugger, Brunansky's outfield talents produced a game-ending diving catch as the BoSox clinched the pennant in '90.

Even in cozy Boston, Brunansky hasn't been able to preserve his power. His 1993 cards are forgettable commons. Our pick for his best 1993 card is Donruss. We have chosen this card for its technical merits.

Upon joining the Cubs in mid-1992, Steve Buechele marked time with his third team in two seasons. As usual, Buechele was a stronger hitter against lefthanded pitchers (.304 LHP; .233 RHP). He couldn't duplicate his 1991 combined totals of 22 home runs and 85 RBI, yet his everyday presence stabilized Chicago's eternal hot-corner problem. His affiliation with Texas began as a fifth-round draft pick in 1982, followed by a major league premiere in 1985. Buechele's employers started changing in August 1991. The Rangers feared that the upcoming free-agent would be unsignable and shuttled him to Pittsburgh for two minor leaguers. During the pennant drive, the former Stanford star contributed four homers and 19 RBI in 31 games. In the NLCS, Buechele batted .304.

Buechele has never been a popular card buy. His 1993 commons will be no different. Don't invest. Our pick for his best 1993 card is Score. We have chosen this card because it has a distinctive look.

	BA	G	AB	R	H	2B	3B	HR	RBI	SB
92 AL	.266	138	458	47	122	31	3	15	74	2
Life	.248	1656	5860	760	1454	287	29	255	856	66

	BA	G	AB	R	H	2B	3B	HR	RBI	SB
92 NL	.261	145	524	52	137	23	4	9	64	1
Life	.245	1056	3337	405	816	143	18	107	421	15

50   *Series two cards from some companies were available at press time. If space allows, both cards are shown; if not, the most up-to-date cards are pictured.*

JAY BUHNER

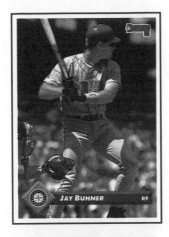

Position: Outfield
Team: Seattle Mariners
Born: August 13, 1964
   Louisville, KY
Height: 6'3" **Weight:** 205 lbs.
Bats: Right **Throws:** Right
Acquired: Traded from Yankees
   with Troy Evers and Rich
   Balabon for Ken Phelps, 7/88

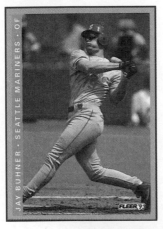

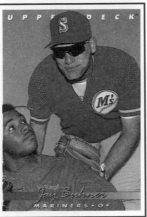

JIM BULLINGER

Position: Pitcher
Team: Chicago Cubs
Born: Aug. 21, 1965,
   New Orleans, LA
Height: 6'2" **Weight:** 185 lbs.
Bats: Right **Throws:** Right
Acquired: Ninth-round pick,
   6/86 free-agent draft

Amidst Seattle's dismal 1992 finish, outfielder Jay Buhner kept slugging. He exceeded 20 home runs (25) for the second season in a row. Most important to his '92 season was the fact that he stayed relatively healthy. Originally drafted by the Pirates in '84, he was swapped to the Yankees in a five-player deal at year's end. He debuted with the Yanks in '87. When the M's acquired Buhner in mid-1988, he quickly responded with 10 homers and 25 RBI in 60 games. His '89 season of nine homers and 33 RBI was extinguished after 58 games. A sprained wrist was the culprit. A broken wrist and a sprained ankle limited Buhner to 51 games in '90.

If you feel lucky, gamble a nickel or less on Buhner's 1993 commons. If he tops 30 homers and gets Seattle into pennant contention, your longshot could pay off. In the '88 Donruss "The Rookies," Buhner is available in the 25 cent range. Our pick for his best 1993 card is Upper Deck. We have chosen this card due to its unique photographic approach.

Jim Bullinger made news with his feat at the plate, but improved the Cubs' bullpen with his job on the hill. A converted shortstop who apparently never forgot how to hit a fastball, Bullinger became the 10th player in major league history to homer in his first at-bat. He also became the second pitcher in 1992 to do it, following San Diego's Dave Eiland. The homer came in the first game of a double-header in St. Louis, and helped the Cubs to a 5-2 win. In the nightcap, Bullinger went 1 1/3 innings for his first big league save. He quickly took over the closer role for the Cubs, helping them make a move out of the East Division basement. Bullinger spent four pro seasons at short, but his average never got above .256. His career took off once he went to the mound in '90. He was a starter for two years, climbing from Single- to Triple-A, then was used in the bullpen when he got to Chicago.

Reliever cards aren't stable investments. Skip Bullinger's 1993s. Our pick for his best 1993 card is Score. We have chosen this card because it has a distinctive look.

	BA	G	AB	R	H	2B	3B	HR	RBI	SB
92 AL	.243	152	543	69	132	16	3	25	79	0
Life	.246	490	1599	212	393	72	9	81	261	4

	W	L	ERA	G	SV	IP	H	ER	BB	SO
92 NL	2	8	4.66	39	7	85.0	72	44	54	36
Life	2	8	4.66	39	7	85.0	72	44	54	36

TIM BURKE

Position: Pitcher
Team: Cincinnati Reds
Born: February 15, 1959
    Omaha, NE
Height: 6′3″ **Weight:** 205 lbs.
Bats: Right **Throws:** Right
Acquired: Signed as a free
    agent, 12/92

Tim Burke made an unusual crosstown move during the 1992 season. After beginning the year with the New York Mets, he was dispatched to the Yankees in an even-up June transaction. While the Yanks valued Burke's ability to neutralize lefties, they let him become a free agent after the season. The Reds picked him up late in '92. Although he was an important middle relief man in New York's restructured bullpen, they didn't use Burke in many save opportunities. Burke was a second-round draft choice by Pittsburgh in '80. Although he was first acquired by the Yankee organization in 1982, he only served in the minors and was swapped to the Expos one year later. The righty was a dominant stopper in Montreal from 1987-90, racking up a personal-best 28 saves in 1989.

Burke has several good years left, but none of them will be as a stopper. When relegated to set-up work, his 1993 commons will be ignored. Our pick for his best 1993 card is Topps. We have chosen this card because of its excellent combination of photography and design.

	W	L	ERA	G	SV	IP	H	ER	BB	SO
92 AL	2	2	3.25	23	0	27.2	26	10	15	8
Life	49	33	2.72	498	102	699.1	624	211	219	444

JOHN BURKETT

Position: Pitcher
Team: San Francisco Giants
Born: November 28, 1964
    New Brighton, PA
Height: 6′3″ **Weight:** 205 lbs.
Bats: Right **Throws:** Right
Acquired: Sixth-round pick,
    6/83 free-agent draft

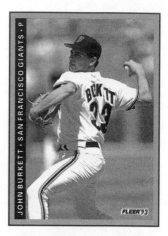

John Burkett was one of many disappointments for the 1992 San Francisco Giants. Before posting his first shutout with a 5-0 win over Atlanta on July 30, he had split 12 decisions and fashioned a somewhat inflated ERA. Burkett is often victimized by the home run ball. He doesn't beat himself with walks, however. He usually whiffs twice as many as he walks. He's most effective against righthanded batters and pitches better in his home ballpark. In '92, opponents compiled a .264 batting average, a .308 on-base average, and a .382 slugging percentage against him. He allowed lefty hitters to bat .295, while he allowed righthanded batters to hit only .210. Blessed with great hand-eye coordination, Burkett hopes to try pro bowling when he's through with baseball. He's never pitched a perfect game but he's turned the trick in bowling three times.

If bowling pins were batters, you could bet on Burkett. Skip his '93s. Our pick for his best 1993 card is Topps. We have chosen this card for its technical merits.

	W	L	ERA	G	SV	IP	H	ER	BB	SO
92 NL	13	9	3.84	32	3	189.2	194	81	45	107
Life	39	27	3.95	104	8	606.1	625	266	169	361

ELLIS BURKS

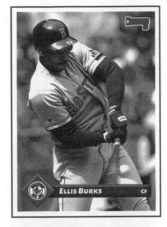

Position: Outfield
Team: Chicago White Sox
Born: September 11, 1964
    Vicksburg, MS
Height: 6'2" **Weight:** 205 lbs.
Bats: Right **Throws:** Right
Acquired: Signed as a free
    agent, 1/93

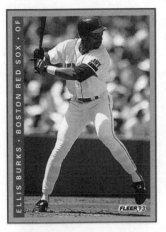 

Ellis Burks was a major factor in the 1992 Red Sox collapse. Actually, the loss of the potent outfielder accounted for Boston's sputtering offense. He appeared in only 66 games during the '92 season. Burks is now a Sox of a different color. He signed with the Chicago White Sox early in '93, hoping to fix some of their right field woes. A BoSox regular since '87, Burks has topped 20 homers twice. From 1987 through '89, the Mississippi native exceeded 20 stolen bases annually. He drove in a career-high 92 runs in '88, followed by 89 RBI in '90. In '91, assorted woes ranging from a bulging back disc to a pulled hamstring kept him out of 32 games. He was burdened for most of the '92 season with lower back ailments.

After repeated health problems, and a possible allergy to lefthanded pitching, Burks is an unpredictable choice for collectors. Still, his cards could be longshot surprises in 1993 for a nickel each. Our pick for his best 1993 card is Upper Deck. We have chosen this card because of its overall appeal and pleasing looks.

	BA	G	AB	R	H	2B	3B	HR	RBI	SB
92 AL	.255	66	235	35	60	8	3	8	30	5
Life	.281	722	2794	440	785	160	27	93	387	93

TODD BURNS

Position: Pitcher
Team: Texas Rangers
Born: July 6, 1963
    Maywood, CA
Height: 6'2" **Weight:** 190 lbs.
Bats: Right **Throws:** Right
Acquired: Signed as a free
    agent, 12/91

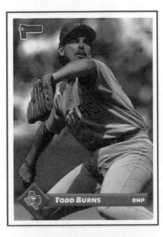 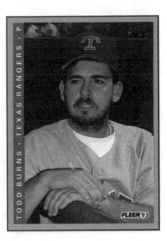

Todd Burns found a new home in 1992, pulling double duty for the pitching-strapped Rangers. Although he began the season at Triple-A Oklahoma City, Texas soon provided the veteran righthander with a second chance at major league employment in June. Burns found work both as a starter and middle reliever, responsibilities similar to his job in Oakland. Immediately, Burns submitted six innings of one-hit, scoreless baseball against the Mariners on June 9, but left with no decision. Burns began his pro career with the Athletics as a seventh-round draft pick in 1984. His initial season with the A's came in 1987, when he collected a career-best eight victories. He followed with eight saves and a 2.24 ERA in 1989. With a fastball, curve, slider, and change-up in his repertoire, Burns should spend a full season with Texas in 1993.

Pitching in relief won't raise card values for Burns. Veto his 1993 commons. Our pick for his best 1993 card is Topps. We have chosen this card because of its excellent combination of photography and design.

	W	L	ERA	G	SV	IP	H	ER	BB	SO
92 AL	3	5	3.84	35	1	103.0	97	44	32	55
Life	21	15	3.08	154	13	394.0	344	135	134	207

Series two cards from some companies were available at press time. If space allows, both cards are shown; if not, the most up-to-date cards are pictured.

MIKE BUTCHER

Position: Pitcher
Team: California Angels
Born: May 10, 1965
Davenport, IA
Height: 6'1" **Weight:** 200 lbs.
Bats: Right **Throws:** Right
Acquired: Signed as a free
agent, 7/88

Kansas City cast-off Mike Butcher offered surprising payoffs for the Angels in 1992. The righthanded reliever spent 2 ½ seasons in the Royals' organization, beginning with his second-round selection in the free-agent draft of June 1986. After his mid-1988 release, he signed with California. Converting from starting to relief in 1990 helped turn Butcher's career around. The Iowa native progressed from Triple-A Edmonton to the bigs after the All-Star break that year. A tidy ERA and a lean strikeout-to-walk ratio were hallmarks of Butcher's rookie-season success. His value as a short reliever and set-up man quickly became apparent. During his 1991 minor league season, 53 of Butcher's 70 strikeouts came in relief.

As a middle reliever, Butcher can't be expected to gain much acclaim. Don't overestimate his 1993 cards, which could be priced at 10 to 15 cents each. Our pick for his best 1993 card is Topps. We have chosen this card since the photograph captures the athletic ability of the player.

	W	L	ERA	G	SV	IP	H	ER	BB	SO
92 AL	2	2	3.25	19	0	27.2	29	10	13	24
Life	2	2	3.25	19	0	27.2	29	10	13	24

BRETT BUTLER

Position: Outfield
Team: Los Angeles Dodgers
Born: June 15, 1957
Los Angeles, CA
Height: 5'10" **Weight:** 160 lbs.
Bats: Left **Throws:** Left
Acquired: Signed as a free
agent, 12/90

Don't blame Brett Butler for the downfall of the 1992 Dodgers. His offensive marks were stellar once again. In his second year with LA, he exceeded 30 stolen bases for a 10th consecutive year. Since his 1981 debut in the majors, Butler has played with four different teams. He broke in with Atlanta, but was swapped to the Indians in 1984. Butler became a free-agent addition for San Francisco in 1988, before doing the same for the Dodgers in 1991. In his four-year stint with Cleveland, Butler earned two consecutive years of 50-plus RBI and a career-best 52 stolen bases. An adept lead-off man, skilled bunter, and a gifted center fielder, Butler is a born team leader. Whether on a last-place team or a pennant contender, Butler provides all-around support.

Any performance with a last-place team tends to go unappreciated. Butler's '92 exploits, therefore, will do little to spark his common-priced cards any higher. Our pick for his best 1993 card is Donruss. We have chosen this card because the design lends itself to the best use of the elements.

	BA	G	AB	R	H	2B	3B	HR	RBI	SB
92 NL	.309	157	553	86	171	14	11	3	39	41
Life	.288	1678	6169	1048	1777	216	99	44	439	437

Series two cards from some companies were available at press time. If space allows, both cards are shown; if not, the most up-to-date cards are pictured.

IVAN CALDERON

Position: Outfield
Team: Boston Red Sox
Born: March 19, 1962
　　Fajardo, Puerto Rico
Height: 6'1" **Weight:** 221 lbs.
Bats: Right **Throws:** Right
Acquired: Traded from Expos
　　for Mike Gardiner and Terry
　　Powers, 12/92

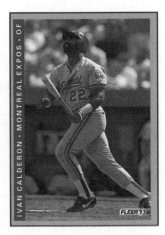

Ivan Calderon's honeymoon with Montreal ended in 1992. A laundry list of injuries—from a sore elbow to a strained rib cage to a pulled shoulder—documents some of Calderon's '92 torments before his midseason shoulder surgery. Yet, he rehabbed in the minors and rejoined the team for a pennant run during late September. Still, the Expos failed to earn a 1991 repeat from Calderon, who was named to his first-ever All-Star team. His NL debut campaign in '91 included 19 homers, 75 RBI, and a .300 average. The free-swinging slugger is famed for his enthusiasm at the plate, declining most opportunities for walks. He's been active in pro ball since 1979. Calderon's career bests, 28 homers and 83 RBI, came with the White Sox in 1987. He'll try to make a comeback with the BoSox in '93.

Calderon's ninth year in the majors is another above-average but unnoticed effort. His nickel-priced 1993s aren't exciting investments. Our pick for his best 1993 card is Score. We have chosen this card for the interesting facts included on the reverse.

	BA	G	AB	R	H	2B	3B	HR	RBI	SB
92 NL	.265	48	170	19	45	14	2	3	24	1
Life	.277	842	3073	444	851	190	23	103	422	93

KEN CAMINITI

Position: Third base
Team: Houston Astros
Born: April 21, 1963
　　Hanford, CA
Height: 6' **Weight:** 200 lbs.
Bats: Both **Throws:** Right
Acquired: Third-round pick,
　　6/84 free-agent draft

Ken Caminiti sampled life as a .300 hitter with the 1992 Astros. In the past three years as a starter, Caminiti looked destined for life in the .250s. But, during the last month of the season, his average in the Astrodome climbed into the .370s. With the unveiling of 1992 first-round draft selection Phil Nevin as the third baseman of the future, Caminiti knows his future is now. He tried to build on career highs of 13 home runs and 80 RBI achieved in 1991 (13 HR and 62 RBI in '92). Once, Caminiti was the Houston wonderboy, leaping from Double-A to a big league starting job in 1987. He's since developed a reputation as one of the National League's finest fielders. Some fans feel Caminiti's power totals could double if he could escape the clutches of the cavernous Astrodome.

Caminiti remains offensively lukewarm, unable to hit his 1993 cards past their modest values of three to five cents apiece. Our pick for his best 1993 card is Upper Deck. We have chosen this card due to its unique photographic approach.

	BA	G	AB	R	H	2B	3B	HR	RBI	SB
92 NL	.294	135	506	68	149	31	2	13	62	10
Life	.256	694	2492	271	639	121	11	44	295	27

Series two cards from some companies were available at press time. If space allows, both cards are shown; if not, the most up-to-date cards are pictured.

KEVIN CAMPBELL

Position: Pitcher
Team: Oakland Athletics
Born: December 6, 1964
Marianna, AK
Height: 6'2" **Weight:** 225 lbs.
Bats: Right **Throws:** Right
Acquired: Traded from Dodgers
for David Veres, 1/91

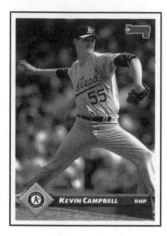 

CASEY CANDAELE

Position: Infield/outfield
Team: Houston Astros
Born: January 12, 1961
Lompoc, CA
Height: 5'9" **Weight:** 165 lbs.
Bats: Both **Throws:** Right
Acquired: Traded from Expos
for Mark Bailey, 7/88

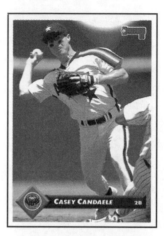 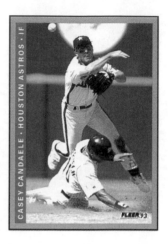

Kevin Campbell returned to the Oakland bullpen again in 1992, but couldn't recapture his rookie-season glory. The righthanded reliever grappled with occasional control problems, as his walks exceeded his strikeouts (45 BB; 38 Ks). A 5.12 ERA was another handicap. Campbell earned his 1991 debut in the majors, submitting a 9-2 record and 1.80 ERA at Triple-A Tacoma as proof. With the Athletics, his rookie campaign began on July 15, including a 1-0 mark and 2.74 ERA in 14 games of relief. The Arkansas native found his future in 1989, the first year he was transferred to bullpen duty. Following his fifth-round draft selection by the Dodgers in 1986, the former University of Arkansas star spent three years as a starter.

How can any Oakland reliever have worthwhile cards while working in the shadow of Dennis Eckersley? Campbell's challenge should freeze values on his 1993 common-priced cards. Our pick for his best 1993 card is Topps. We have chosen this card because of its excellent combination of photography and design.

After Casey Candaele achieved dream-like success with the 1991 Astros, he apparently woke up in 1992. Candaele played for the University of Arizona but was untouched in the 1982 free-agent draft. Signed by the Expos that July, he premiered with Montreal in 1986. He finished fourth in Rookie of the Year balloting in 1987, after hitting .272 with one homer and 23 RBI. He established numerous career bests in 1991, batting .262 with four homers and 50 RBI in 151 games. The reserve specialist appeared at six different positions with the '92 'Stros while fighting to keep his batting average above .200. Righthanded pitchers continued to plague Candaele, the same player whose personal-best batting average was a .286 average with Houston in 1990.

Candaele is the heart of Houston's bench strength. His versatile glove makes him an unlikely starter, and an unlikely card investment at three to five cents apiece. Our pick for his best 1993 card is Upper Deck. We have chosen this card since the photograph captures the athletic ability of the player.

	W	L	ERA	G	SV	IP	H	ER	BB	SO
92 AL	2	3	5.12	32	1	65.0	66	37	45	38
Life	3	3	4.50	46	1	88.0	79	44	59	54

	BA	G	AB	R	H	2B	3B	HR	RBI	SB
92 NL	.213	135	320	19	68	12	1	1	18	7
Life	.250	641	1743	175	435	75	20	9	124	34

TOM CANDIOTTI

Position: Pitcher
Team: Los Angeles Dodgers
Born: August 31, 1957
  Walnut Creek, CA
Height: 6'2" **Weight:** 200 lbs.
Bats: Right **Throws:** Right
Acquired: Signed as a free
  agent, 12/91

JOSE CANSECO

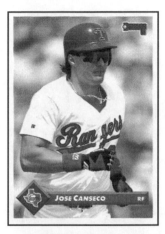

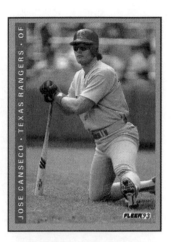

Position: Outfield
Team: Texas Rangers
Born: July 2, 1964,
  Havana, Cuba
Height: 6'4" **Weight:** 240 lbs.
Bats: right **Throws:** right
Acquired: Traded from
  Athletics for Ruben Sierra,
  Bobby Witt, and Jeff Russell,
  8/92

Tom Candiotti won in double digits for the sixth time in seven seasons with the lowly 1992 Dodgers. Although his stats were a near photocopy of his 1991 results, his production was tarnished due to life with a last-place team. Candiotti is only one of three knuckleballers active in the majors. His trick pitch, learned from Phil Niekro, has netted him more than 100 strikeouts in each of the last seven years. After playing with an unaffiliated minor league team in 1979, Candiotti was signed by the Royals. Drafted by Milwaukee in '80, his big league premiere came with the Brewers in 1983. Only a year earlier, he missed the entire season with a career-threatening elbow injury. Candiotti was one of 1991's hottest free agents, following his September heroics that year helping Toronto to a pennant.

  After his team's dreadful finish, collectors may find Candiotti guilty by association. Forget his 1993 common-priced cards. Our pick for his best 1993 card is Fleer. We have chosen this card for the superior presentation of information on its back.

In an act that caught many by surprise, the A's traded away their once-favorite son, Jose Canseco. In all five of his uninterrupted seasons before '92, Canseco reached triple figures in RBI. He was a unanimous MVP selection in '88, when he became the first player to hit 40 homers and steal 40 bases in the same season. He reached a personal peak in home runs (44) in '91. Canseco holds numerous Oakland slugging records, including most RBI in a season (124 in '88) and most 100-RBI campaigns (five). For the '92 season, Canseco was a bit more than disappointing, hitting his lowest batting average (.244) since hitting .240 in '86. He did manage 26 home runs and knocked in 87 RBI for '92, numbers well below his last three seasons of production.

  Canseco's 1993 cards may be a quarter apiece or more. Say no, because his health may limit his hitting. For a safe investment, snare the '88 Fleer combo card of Canseco and McGwire (#624) for 75 cents. Our pick for his best 1993 card is Fleer. We have chosen this card due to its unique photographic approach.

	W	L	ERA	G	CG	IP	H	ER	BB	SO
92 NL	11	15	3.00	32	6	203.2	177	68	63	152
Life	95	93	3.45	245	56	1608.1	1526	616	524	1030

	BA	G	AB	R	H	2B	3B	HR	RBI	SB
92 AL	.244	119	439	74	107	15	0	26	87	6
Life	.266	972	3655	614	974	171	8	235	734	128

JOE CARTER

Position: Outfield
Team: Toronto Blue Jays
Born: March 7, 1960,
Oklahoma City, OK
Height: 6'3" **Weight:** 215 lbs.
Bats: Right **Throws:** Right
Acquired: Traded from Padres
with Roberto Alomar for Fred
McGriff and Tony Fernandez,
12/90

BRAULIO CASTILLO

Position: Outfield
Team: Colorado Rockies
Born: May 13, 1968
Elias Pina, Dominican
Republic
Height: 6' **Weight:** 160 lbs.
Bats: Right **Throws:** Right
Acquired: Third-round pick,
11/92 expansion draft

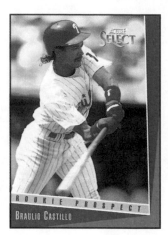

Joe Carter has finally found a home. He broke into pro ball in '81 and reached the Chicago Cubs two years later. It was his strong season at Triple-A Iowa, however, that convinced Cleveland to trade for him in '84. Convinced they would lose him to free agency, the Tribe sent him to San Diego after the '89 season. The first player to produce 100-RBI seasons for three different teams in consecutive years, Carter carved his niche in Toronto during '91. He hammered 33 homers and had his highest batting average since '86. He also stole 20 bases, extended his consecutive-game playing streak to 505 games, and made the All-Star team for the first time. To top off this stellar performance, he was a major factor for the Blue Jays in their first-ever World Championship. Going into '93, Carter has produced six 100-RBI seasons.

Sock away a few 1993 Carters at a dime apiece. Mr. RBI is worth it. At $6 to $8, Carter's '85 Donruss looks like a juicy investment. Our pick for his best 1993 card is Topps. We have chosen this card because of its overall appeal and pleasing looks.

Outfielder Braulio Castillo's second chance with the Phillies became his last in 1992. Returning from Triple-A to Philadelphia for a second consecutive season, Castillo hit .197 with two home runs and seven RBI in 28 games. He earned the call-up due to his International League totals of 13 homers, 47 RBI, and a .246 average. Upon his '91 arrival in the Phillies organization, Castillo had batted .300 with 15 RBI in 16 Triple-A games. His trial in the bigs in '91 netted only a .173 average in 28 games. Obtained from Los Angeles in exchange for reliever Roger McDowell, Castillo never caught on with the Dodgers. They signed the Dominican in '85, although he never progressed past Double-A. Castillo became a member of the Rockies for the '93 season.

Although he's struck out with two organizations, the third time could be a charm for Castillo. Longshot lovers might want to keep a few of his common-priced cards. Our pick for his best 1993 card is Donruss. We have chosen this card for its technical merits.

	BA	G	AB	R	H	2B	3B	HR	RBI	SB
92 AL	.264	158	622	97	164	30	7	34	119	12
Life	.263	1344	5201	727	1370	264	34	242	873	181

	BA	G	AB	R	H	2B	3B	HR	RBI	SB
92 NL	.197	28	76	12	15	3	1	2	7	1
Life	.188	56	128	15	24	6	1	2	9	2

Series two cards from some companies were available at press time. If space allows, both cards are shown; if not, the most up-to-date cards are pictured.

FRANK CASTILLO

Position: Pitcher
Team: Chicago Cubs
Born: April 1, 1969 El Paso, TX
Height: 6'1" **Weight:** 180 lbs.
Bats: Right **Throws:** Right
Acquired: Sixth-round pick,
6/87 free-agent draft

ANDUJAR CEDENO

Position: Shortstop
Team: Houston Astros
Born: August 21, 1969
La Romana, Dominican
Republic
Height: 6'1" **Weight:** 168 lbs.
Bats: Right **Throws:** Right
Acquired: Signed as a free
agent, 10/86

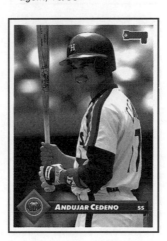

Frank Castillo bolstered the 1992 Cubs starting rotation, providing depth not apparent in his statistics. He finished the '92 season with a 10-11 record, fanning 135 batters and walking only 63. In 1991, Castillo was sidelined with a broken thumb and a strained arm, missing more than two months of the season. Despite three extended stays on the disabled list, Castillo's career has skyrocketed since his high school graduation in 1987. During his 1991 rookie year, Castillo's 6-7 record included four complete games in 18 starts. One year later, he was without a complete game for the entire season. Yet, he did pitch 205 ⅓ innings spread out over 33 games for an average of six innings per game. His work ethic, control, and youth are three reasons why Castillo will be active throughout the 1990s.

Castillo is young and strong. He could be worth at least a dozen wins yearly. Give him time before investing in his 1993 commons. Our pick for his best 1993 card is Upper Deck. We have chosen this card because the design lends itself to the best use of the elements.

Andujar Cedeno became a classic definition of the sophomore jinx in 1992. The Astros gave the young shortstop another chance at full-time work, but his offensive skills deteriorated quickly. Cedeno looked like a different player in 1991, when he represented Houston in 67 games. His stats included nine homers, 36 RBI, and a .243 average. Although Cedeno was a member of the 'Stros' 1992 Opening-Day roster, he was returned to Triple-A when he stopped producing against righthanders. The strikeout-prone infielder was a hapless hitter on the road in '92 (.152), yet was a sterling slugger back in the Pacific Coast League. Since his pro career began in 1988, Cedeno has zoomed through the Houston farm system. At age 23, he'll have to play his way out of a starting job.

Cedeno's offensive crash should make collectors beware. His common-priced cards will remain untouched if Cedeno can't resume hitting. Our pick for his best 1993 card is Donruss. We have chosen this card for its technical merits.

	W	L	ERA	G	CG	IP	H	ER	BB	SO
92 NL	10	11	3.46	33	0	205.1	179	79	63	135
Life	16	18	3.78	51	4	317.0	286	133	96	208

	BA	G	AB	R	H	2B	3B	HR	RBI	SB
92 NL	.173	71	220	15	38	13	2	2	13	2
Life	.207	145	479	42	99	26	4	11	49	6

WES CHAMBERLAIN

Position: Outfield
Team: Philadelphia Phillies
Born: April 13, 1966
   Chicago, IL
Height: 6'2" **Weight:** 210 lbs.
Bats: Right **Throws:** Right
Acquired: Traded from Pirates
   with Julio Peguero and Tony
   Longmire for Carmelo
   Martinez, 8/90

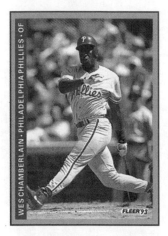

NORM CHARLTON

Position: Pitcher
Team: Cincinnati Reds
Born: January 6, 1963
   Fort Polk, LA
Height: 6'3" **Weight:** 205 lbs.
Bats: Both **Throws:** Left
Acquired: Traded from Reds
   for Kevin Mitchell, 11/92

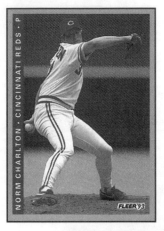

Philadelphia's Wes Chamberlain saw his 1992 campaign collapse at midseason over a sprained ankle. He landed on the 60-day DL on August 19, joining wounded outfield teammates Dale Murphy and Len Dykstra. The injury halted his attempts to repeat his 1991 totals of 13 home runs and 50 RBI. Chamberlain wowed the Phillies in his 1990 debut, hitting .283 with two homers and four RBI in 18 games. He was raised in the Pittsburgh organization, beginning with his fourth-round selection in the 1987 draft. The Pirates accidentally lost Chamberlain on waivers in 1990, and were forced to surrender him and two other prospects in a trade. Chamberlain is a vital ingredient in the 1993 Philadelphia lineup.

However, even while in the minors, Chamberlain never hit more than 21 homers in a season. With his modest power and mediocre defense, he's unlikely to reap stardom. Chamberlain's 1993 nickel-priced cards are unstable investments. Our pick for his best 1993 card is Donruss. We have chosen this card since the photograph captures the athletic ability of the player.

Norm Charlton inherited Cincinnati's closer role in 1992 and responded with one of his finest seasons ever. Rob Dibble became a mass of ineffectiveness, and the stopper's baton was passed to the former Expos farmhand. The baton will go back to Dibble, however, because Charlton was dealt to Seattle for slugger Kevin Mitchell. Charlton displayed his versatility in 1990, posting marks of 12-9 and a 2.79 ERA as a starter and reliever. He posted a win in the pennant-clinching game six during NLCS play in '90. Never shy about throwing at other batters to protect his team, Charlton's 1991 infamy included two stays on the suspended list, one for confessing he intentionally beaned Mike Scioscia. Additionally, he spent more than a month on the disabled list with shoulder problems.

Good or not, relievers like Charlton seldom achieve star power. His 1993 commons are iffy investments. Our pick for his best 1993 card is Fleer. We have chosen this card for its technical merits.

	BA	G	AB	R	H	2B	3B	HR	RBI	SB
92 NL	.258	76	275	26	71	18	0	9	41	4
Life	.250	195	704	86	176	37	3	24	95	17

	W	L	ERA	G	SV	IP	H	ER	BB	SO
92 NL	4	2	2.99	64	26	81.1	79	27	26	90
Life	31	24	3.00	238	29	500.2	429	167	190	421

Series two cards from some companies were available at press time. If space allows, both cards are shown; if not, the most up-to-date cards are pictured.

SCOTT CHIAMPARINO

Position: Pitcher
Team: Florida Marlins
Born: August 22, 1966
San Mateo, CA
Height: 6′2″ **Weight:** 205 lbs.
Bats: Left **Throws:** Right
Acquired: Third-round pick,
11/92 expansion draft

Pitcher Scott Chiamparino made slow but steady steps in regaining his once-glowing potential. Major reconstructive elbow surgery in 1991 halted his rising career. In his limited '92 appearances, however, two of his four losses included shutouts against his Texas teammates. Before his return, the righthander's minor league rehabilitation featured a 1.93 ERA in three Double-A starts and a 1-1 mark in Triple-A. Chiamparino was one of the young players sent from Oakland in the trade obtaining slugger Harold Baines in '90. Oakland nabbed the California native as a fourth-round draft selection in '87. His '90 premier with the Rangers included a 1-2 record and 2.63 ERA in six starts. Previously, he won a career-high 13 games with Triple-A Tacoma. In '93, Chiamparino will join the Florida Marlins.

Chiamparino's health is a factor in his future. See if he can endure a full season before laying claim to his common-priced cards. Our pick for his best 1993 card is Topps. We have chosen this card due to the outstanding photographic composition.

	W	L	ERA	G	CG	IP	H	ER	BB	SO
92 AL	0	4	3.55	4	0	25.1	25	10	5	13
Life	2	6	3.27	15	0	85.1	87	31	29	40

ARCHI CIANFROCCO

Position: Infield
Team: Montreal Expos
Born: October 6, 1966
Rome, NY
Height: 6′5″ **Weight:** 200 lbs.
Bats: Right **Throws:** Right
Acquired: Seventh-round pick,
6/87 free-agent draft

 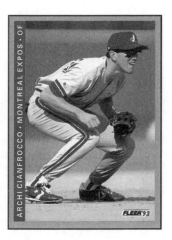

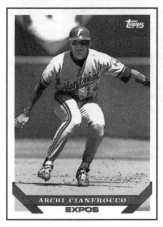

Archi Cianfrocco made the major league club as a non-roster player just when it seemed his career could stall at the Double-A level. But his third year in Double-A was better than the other two, and now the Expos have found a handy player who has some pop in his bat. Cianfrocco was signed as a second baseman and shortstop, but nowadays he plays first, third, and a little left field. To enjoy a long career he'll have to improve on his contact. He struck out in 27 percent of his first 125 official big league at-bats, while walking just five times over that span. Cianfrocco's best pro season came with Double-A Harrisburg of the Eastern League in 1991. His .316 mark was second behind teammate Matt Stairs, and his .465 slugging percentage placed him fifth. The need for a better eye at the plate was evidenced in his nine homers as opposed to 112 strikeouts, an unacceptable ratio.

Mull over Cianfrocco's 1993s at a dime apiece. Our pick for his best 1993 card is Topps. We have chosen this card for its technical merits.

	BA	G	AB	R	H	2B	3B	HR	RBI	SB
92 NL	.241	86	232	25	56	5	2	6	30	3
Life	.241	86	232	25	56	5	2	6	30	3

JACK CLARK

Position: Designated hitter
Team: Boston Red Sox
Born: November 10, 1955
New Brighton, PA
Height: 6'3" **Weight:** 210 lbs.
Bats: Right **Throws:** Right
Acquired: Signed as a free
agent, 12/90

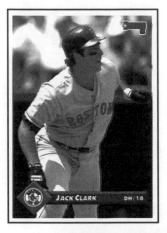

JERALD CLARK

Position: Outfield
Team: Colorado Rockies
Born: August 10, 1963
Crockett, TX
Height: 6'4" **Weight:** 205 lbs.
Bats: Right **Throws:** Right
Acquired: First-round pick,
11/92 expansion draft

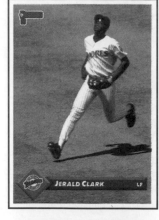

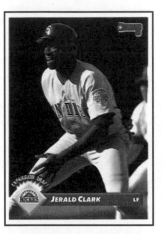

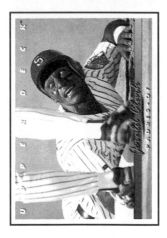

Jack Clark's tallies from 1992 were his worst in years. He saw his streak of 25 or more homers per season snapped. In fact, with his ailing shoulders and a sore hip, he yielded only five homers in '92. Although Clark's been active in the majors since '76, his collapse is sudden. His career bests, 35 homers and 106 RBI, came with the 1987 Cards. From 1987-90, Clark's walks exceeded his strikeouts, as his 100-plus annual free passes led the league three times in four years. In '91, he whacked 28 homers and 87 RBI. Clark, unfortunately, got more publicity in '92 off the field by declaring bankruptcy, a stress which was a definite factor in his decline. Throughout the '92 season, Clark struggled and lost in his attempts to hit on the road (.170) and against righthanders (.160).

The much-maligned slugger no longer commands respect in hobby circles. His cards, once interesting possibilities are now yawners. Our pick for his best 1993 card is Donruss. We have chosen this card for its technical merits.

Jerald Clark pounded career highs in 1992, his first legitimate season as a San Diego starter. Now he'll start all over again with the expansion team in Colorado. Clark received a 1984 draft offer from the Dodgers, but chose to continue his education at Lamar University. The Texas-born slugger earned his way to the majors by producing six consecutive seasons of .300 or better in the minors. His minor league career peaked with 22 homers, 83 RBI, and a .313 mark with Triple-A Las Vegas in 1989. He bounced between the Pacific Coast League and the majors for three years in a row before spending a full season with the Padres in '91. In '92, the new resident left fielder surpassed his '91 totals of 10 homers and 47 RBI, while providing the Padres with solid defense. He enhanced his value by serving as backup at first.

Clark made a fine start toward establishing a career in 1992. See what he does with a new club before investing. Our pick for his best 1993 card is Upper Deck. We have chosen this card due to its unique photographic approach.

	BA	G	AB	R	H	2B	3B	HR	RBI	SB
92 AL	.210	81	257	32	54	11	0	5	33	1
Life	.267	1994	6847	1118	1826	332	39	340	1180	77

	BA	G	AB	R	H	2B	3B	HR	RBI	SB
92 NL	.242	146	496	45	120	22	6	12	58	3
Life	.237	340	1022	88	242	45	7	28	126	5

MARK CLARK

Position: Pitcher
Team: St. Louis Cardinals
Born: May 12, 1968 Bath, IL
Height: 6'5" **Weight:** 225 lbs.
Bats: Right **Throws:** Right
Acquired: Ninth-round pick,
    6/88 free-agent draft

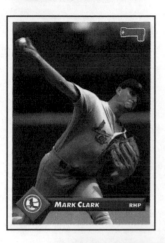

Mark Clark has posted impressive innings-to-walk and innings-to-hit ratios through his career, but now must work on translating them into wins. One indicator of a good pitcher is keeping hits below or near the amount of innings pitched, and Clark has done that. He has also shown good control, walking roughly three men per nine innings. For all that effort, however, Clark only once reached double figures in victories ('89), tying for the Class-A South Atlantic League with 14 victories. His problem in putting his game together was evident in 1991, when he made 29 starts covering Double-A, Triple-A, and major league ball, yet came away with just nine wins. In 1992, Clark received a chance to join the Cardinal rotation and showed the same kind of inconsistency. In New York on June 21, he carried a low-hit game into the late innings, but the Cardinals wound up losing.

His live arm gives investors hope at a dime each for 1993 cards. Our pick for his best 1993 card is Topps. We have chosen this card for the superior presentation of information on its back.

	W	L	ERA	G	CG	IP	H	ER	BB	SO
92 NL	3	10	4.45	20	1	113.1	117	4.45	36	44
Life	4	11	4.38	27	1	135.2	134	4.38	47	57

PHIL CLARK

Position: Outfield
Team: Detroit Tigers
Born: May 6, 1968
    Crockett, TX
Height: 6' **Weight:** 180 lbs.
Bats: Right **Throws:** Right
Acquired: First-round pick,
    6/86 free-agent draft

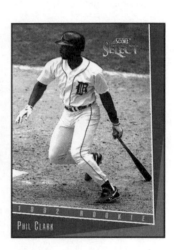

A continuation of hitting and a switch to a new position were just the ticket that gained Phil Clark admission to the 1992 Tigers roster. The former catcher escaped from behind the plate after the 1990 minor league season. An injury and subsequent knee operation caused the career change to the outfield. He was recalled from Toledo on September 7, at the conclusion of the Triple-A season in 1992. The promotion came after seven seasons in the Tigers organization, dating back to his first-round selection out of high school. In five of those seven years, he hit .290 or better. Baseball runs in the Clark family. Brother Jerald is a new member of the Colorado Rockies, while brother Isaiah spent time in the Milwaukee farm system.

Phil may be the next member of the Clark clan to become a full-time major leaguer. He could last the upcoming season as a Detroit part-timer, but that won't do enough to stimulate his 1993 commons. Our pick for his best 1993 card is Score. We have chosen this card for the interesting facts included on the reverse.

	BA	G	AB	R	H	2B	3B	HR	RBI	SB
92 AL	.407	23	54	3	22	4	0	1	5	1
Life	.407	23	54	3	22	4	0	1	5	1

WILL CLARK

Position: First base
Team: San Francisco Giants
Born: March 13, 1964
New Orleans, LA
Height: 6'1" **Weight:** 190 lbs.
Bats: Left **Throws:** Left
Acquired: First-round pick,
6/85 free-agent draft

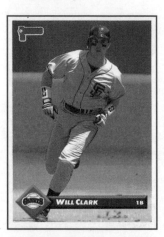

ROYCE CLAYTON

Position: Infield
Team: San Francisco Giants
Born: January 2, 1970
Burbank, CA
Height: 6' **Weight:** 175 lbs.
Bats: Right **Throws:** Right
Acquired: First-round pick,
6/88 free-agent draft

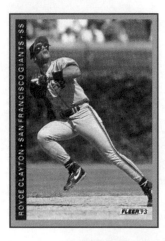

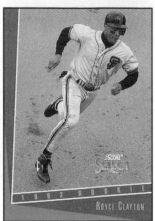

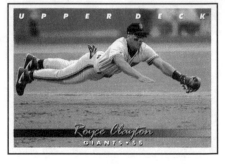

Usually the Giants can count on Will Clark to produce more than 20 homers, 100 RBI, and a .300 batting average every season. They know he's one of the best-fielding first baseman in the NL. He led the league in RBI in 1988 and finished second in the batting derby a year later. Clark was named MVP in the 1989 NLCS and won a Gold Glove in 1991. When Clark hit a career peak with 116 RBI in '91, it marked the fifth season in a row he had knocked in more than 90 runs. He also had career peaks with a .333 average in 1989 and 35 homers in '87. Clark's clouting started off as usual in '92, when he boasted a .321 average after the first 60 games. He stumbled a bit, however, and his end of the season totals dropped from their usual lofty shelf.

A slight Clark slip means his 1993s will be discounted. Invest if the price hits 15 cents apiece. Clark's first Topps card in '87 is an appealing $3 buy. Our pick for his best 1993 card is Score. We have chosen this card because of its overall appeal and pleasing looks.

Royce Clayton nearly made the difficult jump all the way from Double-A to the majors, but slumped a little and was optioned out in June 1992. There is little doubt he will be back—and in a big way. Clayton was named the top prospect in the entire minor leagues by *The Sporting News,* and made both the midseason and the Texas League All-Star teams. He then helped Double-A Shreveport take its second Texas League title in a row. Clayton made the big club out of spring training in '92, playing his way onto one of the best infields in the NL, beating out Jose Uribe. A very confident player, Clayton can make the spectacular play, but must bear down on the routine ones, especially on throws to first. He could eventually hit .250 with some power and speed. He'll go deep into the counts, getting both strikeouts and walks. His first big league home run came off a breaking ball, a good sign.

He has to be a starter someday. Find his 1993s at a dime or less. Our pick for his best 1993 card is Upper Deck. We have chosen this card since the photograph captures the athletic ability of the player.

	BA	G	AB	R	H	2B	3B	HR	RBI	SB
92 NL	.300	144	513	69	154	40	1	16	73	12
Life	.301	1028	3778	605	1139	222	35	162	636	50

	BA	G	AB	R	H	2B	3B	HR	RBI	SB
92 NL	.224	98	321	31	72	7	4	4	24	8
Life	.216	107	347	31	75	8	4	4	26	8

ROGER CLEMENS

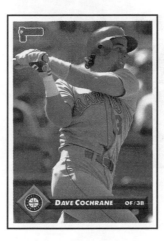

Position: Pitcher
Team: Boston Red Sox
Born: August 4, 1962,
   Dayton, OH
Height: 6'4" **Weight:** 220 lbs.
Bats: Right **Throws:** Right
Acquired: First-round pick,
   6/83 free-agent draft

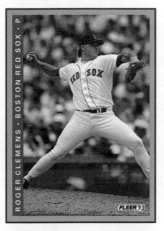

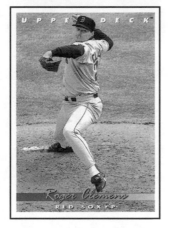

Even before the '92 season began, Roger Clemens had established himself as the best pitcher in baseball. In '92, he posted an 18-11 record with a 2.41 ERA with a team that finished in the cellar. He also struck out 208 while only walking 62. Previously, he won three Cy Young Awards—narrowly missing two others—and one MVP trophy. He led the league in shutouts four times, ERA three times, and victories and strikeouts twice each. Clemens, who followed Nolan Ryan's career with the Astros, enjoyed his best season in '86. That was the year he became the only man to win MVP honors in both the All-Star Game and the regular season as well as the Cy Young Award. He started '86 by winning 14 in a row, settling for a 24-4 record overall.

Even 15 cents apiece seems reasonable to spend on a few 1993 cards of Clemens. Early Clemens cards are overpriced for investing. Try the '87 Fleer Gooden/Clemens combo for 75 cents. Our pick for his best 1993 card is Fleer. We have chosen this card for the superior presentation of information on its back.

	W	L	ERA	G	CG	IP	H	ER	BB	SO
92 AL	18	11	2.41	32	11	246.2	203	66	62	208
Life	152	72	2.80	273	89	2031	1703	631	552	1873

DAVE COCHRANE

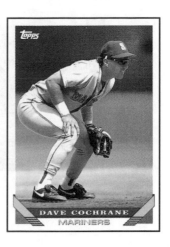

Position: Infield; outfield
Team: Seattle Mariners
Born: January 31, 1963
   Riverside, CA
Height: 6'2" **Weight:** 180 lbs.
Bats: Both **Throws:** Right
Acquired: Traded from Royals
   for Ken Spratke, 2/88

Dave Cochrane's 1992 season ended on August 1 when he underwent surgery to remove a bone from his right foot. Valued for his versatility, Cochrane hit a career-high .250 and hit a pair of homers in limited action for Seattle. He had a .309 on-base average and a .322 slugging percentage in '92. He's never appeared in more than 65 games a year, but has proven himself capable whenever he gets the nod. He's caught, played all four infield positions plus the outfield, and served as a designated hitter who bats from both sides. Cochrane even pitched in eight games for Triple-A Hawaii of the Pacific Coast League in 1987. Because he lacks speed but has a strong arm, his best position is catcher. Given a chance to play, he might recapture the batting stroke that helped him top 15 homers in six minor league seasons.

Wait and see if he retains his mobility when healthy. Unless he can find one position and stick with it, pass on his '93s. Our pick for his best 1993 card is Topps. We have chosen this card due to the outstanding photographic composition.

	BA	G	AB	R	H	2B	3B	HR	RBI	SB
92 AL	.250	65	152	10	38	5	0	2	12	1
Life	.235	218	514	43	121	24	1	8	43	1

CRAIG COLBERT

Position: Catcher
Team: San Francisco Giants
Born: February 13, 1965
Iowa City, IA
Height: 6′ **Weight:** 190 lbs.
Bats: Right **Throws:** Right
Acquired: 20th-round pick,
6/86 free-agent draft

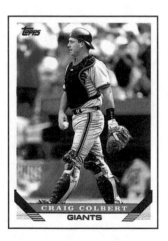

Craig Colbert quietly became San Francisco's next catcher of the future in 1992. While one-time "can't-miss" receiver Steve Decker was missing his chance in Triple-A, Colbert was challenging for the starting backstop role. The Giants demonstrated their respect for the Iowa native by placing him on the 40-man roster after the '91 season ended. Although he was an invitee to spring training, Colbert didn't make the Opening-Day '92 Giants roster. Instead, he headed back to Triple-A Phoenix for the third year in a row. Colbert began his pro career as a third baseman. He's only caught professionally since 1990. Since then, he's played every position except pitcher. Colbert's abilities as a utilityman should keep him in the majors throughout 1993.

Remember, collectors over-invested in Decker's cards. Yet, Colbert could be different, creating some hopeful financial chances for his 1993 cards at 10 to 15 cents each. Our pick for his best 1993 card is Score. We have chosen this card since the photograph captures the athletic ability of the player.

	BA	G	AB	R	H	2B	3B	HR	RBI	SB
92 NL	.230	49	126	10	29	5	2	1	16	1
Life	.230	49	126	10	29	5	2	1	16	1

GREG COLBRUNN

Position: First base/catcher
Team: Montreal Expos
Born: July 26, 1969
Fontana, CA
Height: 6′ **Weight:** 190 lbs.
Bats: Right **Throws:** Right
Acquired: Sixth-round pick,
6/87 free-agent draft

Greg Colbrunn was part of the committee elected to succeed departed first baseman Andres Galarraga. The California native, a converted catcher, was a moderate success. In his 44 starts, Colbrunn batted .302 against righthanders and .222 against lefties in 1992. Surprisingly, he walked just six times in 168 at-bats. In '91, Colbrunn began the year as a non-roster invitee to spring training, but was lost for the season following April elbow surgery. In '90, he was a star in Double-A ball, hitting .301 with 13 homers and 76 RBI for Jacksonville. Colbrunn turned down a Stanford baseball scholarship to sign with Montreal in '87. Following Gary Carter's departure, Colbrunn could wind up behind the plate if his throwing is sound.

Colbrunn will become invisible in the bigs among his contemporaries unless he finds a home run stroke quickly. Until then, postpone purchases of his common-priced cards. Our pick for his best 1993 card is Upper Deck. We have chosen this card because the design lends itself to the best use of the elements.

	BA	G	AB	R	H	2B	3B	HR	RBI	SB
92 NL	.268	52	168	12	45	8	0	2	18	3
Life	.268	52	168	12	45	8	0	2	18	3

Series two cards from some companies were available at press time. If space allows, both cards are shown; if not, the most up-to-date cards are pictured.

ALEX
COLE

Position: Outfield
Team: Colorado Rockies
Born: August 17, 1965
Fayetteville, NC
Height: 6'2" **Weight:** 170 lbs.
Bats: Left **Throws:** Left
Acquired: First-round pick,
11/92 expansion draft

Alex Cole joined his fifth organization in four years when he signed with the Colorado Rockies. Part of Cole's inability to stay in one place was a sub-.200 average against righties. He fell quickly from a .295 batting average, 27 stolen-base season in 1991. He had posted a .300, 40 steals campaign in 1990. He began the 1990 season with San Diego's Triple-A affiliate, but was swapped to Cleveland in midseason. He began the '92 season in the Indians lineup. However, the emergence of rookie outfield sensation Kenny Lofton made Cole excess baggage with the Tribe. He was picked up by the Pirates in July. Cole had been given a look by the Bucs in '84, when they drafted him in the 11th round but he turned them down in favor of college. Cole accepted a draft offer from St. Louis in 1985, but never progressed beyond Triple-A.

Cole could get things jump started with the new team in 1993. Gamblers might have some fun speculating on his common-priced cards. Our pick for his best 1993 card is Donruss. We have chosen this card for its artistic presentation.

	BA	G	AB	R	H	2B	3B	HR	RBI	SB
92 NL	.278	64	205	33	57	3	7	0	10	7
Life	.283	290	916	145	259	26	14	0	49	83

VICTOR
COLE

Position: Pitcher
Team: Pittsburgh Pirates
Born: January 23, 1968
Leningrad, Russia
Height: 5'10" **Weight:** 160 lbs.
Bats: Both **Throws:** Right
Acquired: Traded from Royals
for Carmelo Martinez, 5/91

Victor Cole made his major league debut in June 1992. He made a bit of history as well, becoming the first Russian-born player to appear in the bigs in almost three quarters of a century. He broke into pro ball in 1988 with the Royals with a combined 6-0 mark between Class-A Eugene and Double-A Baseball City. In '89, he again pitched both in Class-A and Double-A and was used exclusively as a starter for the only time as a pro. Cole spent the '90 season at Double-A Memphis, making just six starts in 46 appearances and notching 102 strikeouts in 107 ⅔ innings. He began the '91 campaign at Triple-A Omaha but, after being traded to Pittsburgh, spent time in their Class-A and Double-A systems. In '92, he notched four starts in eight big league appearances, going only 23 innings and accruing a whopping 5.48 ERA. While there's little doubt about his stuff, he needs to work on control.

His 1993 cards are toss-ups at a dime apiece. Our pick for his best 1993 card is Donruss. We have chosen this card due to the outstanding photographic composition.

	W	L	ERA	G	CG	IP	H	ER	BB	SO
92 NL	0	2	5.48	8	0	23	23	14	14	12
Life	0	2	5.48	8	0	23	23	14	14	12

VINCE
COLEMAN

Position: Outfield
Team: New York Mets
Born: September 22, 1961
  Jacksonville, FL
Height: 6′ **Weight:** 170 lbs.
Bats: Both **Throws:** Right
Acquired: Signed as a free
  agent, 12/90

CRIS
COLON

Position: Shortstop
Team: Texas Rangers
Born: January 3, 1969
  Laguaira, Venezuela
Height: 6′2″ **Weight:** 180 lbs.
Bats: Both **Throws:** Right
Acquired: Signed as a free-
  agent, 10/86

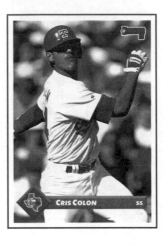 

In just eight big league seasons, Vince Coleman has established himself as one of the games' greatest base-stealers. He swiped 110 bases—a record for a rookie—with St. Louis in '85 and topped 100 in each of the next two seasons. Before hamstring problems disabled him for extended stretches of 1991, Coleman had led the NL in steals for six seasons in a row. He once successfully stole a record 50 consecutive bases. The switch-hitting left fielder was also bothered by hamstring problems in the spring of '92. By June 10, however, he was well enough to tie his own club record with three stolen bases in a game. Ten days later, he hit a rare home run to tie a game the Mets eventually won. Because of his speed, Coleman should be a .300 hitter but doesn't make enough contact at the plate. A .265 career hitter heading into '93, he's never hit higher than .292 in a season.

  Coleman should be healthy before his 1993 cards are considered. Our pick for his best 1993 card is Score. We have chosen this card because it has a distinctive look.

Cris Colon was one of four shortstop candidates for the 1992 Rangers. While with Double-A Tulsa in '92, Colon batted a respectable .263 with one homer and 44 RBI. However, he suffered through 33 errors in 119 games. With Texas, Colon batted a thin .143 against righthanders, compared to .200 against lefties. In contrast, he hit a combined .336 in '91 at two minor league stops. The nephew of Chico Carrasquel, a big league shortstop from 1950-59, Colon's defense has improved yearly. Colon suffered through a combined 75 errors in '88, his first full minor league season. Before signing as an undrafted free agent in '86, Colon enjoyed success at baseball and soccer at his Venezuela high school.

  Colon may belong to the "good-glove, no-bat" school of infielders. If so, his '93 cards will be the commonest of commons. Expect Colon to spend most of the '93 campaign ripening in Triple-A. Our pick for his best 1993 card is Upper Deck. We have chosen this card because it will increase in value.

	BA	G	AB	R	H	2B	3B	HR	RBI	SB
92 NL	.275	71	229	37	63	11	1	2	21	24
Life	.265	1021	4042	648	1071	124	62	18	255	610

	BA	G	AB	R	H	2B	3B	HR	RBI	SB
92 AL	.167	14	36	5	6	0	0	0	1	0
Life	.167	14	36	5	6	0	0	0	1	0

DAVID CONE

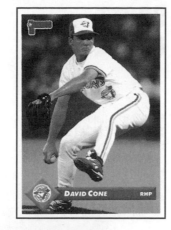

Position: Pitcher
Team: Kansas City Royals
Born: January 2, 1963
Kansas City, MO
Height: 6'1" **Weight:** 190 lbs.
Bats: Left **Throws:** Right
Acquired: Signed as a free
agent, 12/92

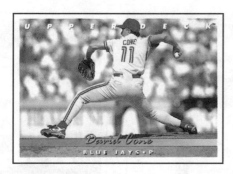

David Cone had the unique distinction in 1992 of not only being the No. 1 pitcher for the Mets, but also the ace in the hole for the World Champion Toronto Blue Jays. He thrived on the Mets while the rest of the team struggled during the first half of the '92 campaign. He struck out more than twice as many batters (214) as he walked (82). Cone pitched himself to a 13-7 record and a 2.88 ERA over 27 starts with New York in '92. The Blue Jays, setting their course for postseason play, picked him up in August '92 for Jeff Kent and Ryan Thompson. Cone did not disappoint the Jays and pitched eight scoreless innings in the second ALCS game against Oakland. After being signed as a free agent at the end of '92, he'll weave his magic for the Royals in '93. In '92 Cone missed his third strikeout crown in a row to John Smoltz by one K.

Cone cards sound tasty at a dime apiece. Investors might snag a '87 Donruss Cone rookie card for $2. Our pick for his best 1993 card is Upper Deck. We have chosen this card because of its overall appeal and pleasing looks.

	W	L	ERA	G	CG	IP	H	ER	BB	SO
92 AL	4	3	2.55	8	0	53.0	39	15	29	47
Life	84	51	3.10	201	34	1267.0	1059	437	460	1227

JEFF CONINE

Position: Infield
Team: Florida Marlins
Born: June 27, 1966
Tacoma, WA
Height: 6'1" **Weight:** 220 lbs.
Bats: Right **Throws:** Right
Acquired: First-round pick,
11/92 expansion draft

Jeff Conine was one of the most promising hitters in the Royals' chain until suffering wrist problems in '91. He underwent two operations and in between hit .257 with three homers in 51 games. Conine was back better than ever in 1992 at Triple-A Omaha of the American Association. The Florida Marlins are excited about his recovery. The new team demonstrated their confidence by slating him to handle first base for them in '93. Conine has already assembled an impressive career. He can hit for power and average and, until the wrist injury, stole at least 20 bases a season. He likes to hit the ball in the alleys, and doesn't strike out too often for someone who hits the ball with such authority. He was the Southern League MVP in 1990 while with Double-A Memphis, and was the Royals' Minor League Player of the Year. He was voted the league's top prospect behind Frank Thomas.

This possible slugger seems like a tidy buy at a dime per card. Our pick for his best 1993 card is Score. We have chosen this card because of its great combination of photography and design.

	BA	G	AB	R	H	2B	3B	HR	RBI	SB
92 AAA	.302	110	397	69	120	24	5	20	72	4
92 AL	.253	28	91	10	23	5	2	0	9	0

DENNIS COOK

Position: Pitcher
Team: Cleveland Indians
Born: October 4, 1962
   Lamarque, TX
Height: 6'3" **Weight:** 185 lbs.
Bats: Left **Throws:** Left
Acquired: Traded by Dodgers
   with Mike Christopher for
   Rudy Seanez, 12/91

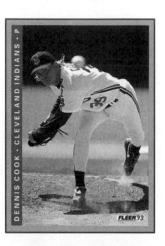

Dennis Cook didn't join in Cleveland's season-ending successes in 1992. Despite being the forth-busiest Tribe starter, his ERA swelled to 3.82, marring his first full year with a single big league team. In January '83, Cook declined a sixth-round draft bid from San Diego. Instead, following college, he took an 18th round offer from the Giants in June '85. Since his '88 debut in the majors, Cook has gotten cooked as each year progresses. Following fast starts, his ERA and losses seem to multiply as the season goes on. In '89, Cook divided his time between San Francisco and Philly. His best campaign was '90, piling up a 9-4 record between stays with the Phillies and Dodgers. The AL can't use Cook's talent at the bat, which garnered a home run off Fernando Valenzuela in '90.

A professional since 1985, Cook doesn't look like he'll ever win more than a dozen games per year. His common-priced cards aren't worthwhile. Our pick for his best 1993 card is Topps. We have chosen this card for its artistic presentation.

	W	L	ERA	G	CG	IP	H	ER	BB	SO
92 AL	5	7	3.82	32	1	158.0	156	67	50	96
Life	24	20	3.66	126	6	474.2	442	193	162	248

SCOTT COOPER

Position: Infield
Team: Boston Red Sox
Born: October 13, 1967
   St. Louis, MO
Height: 6'3" **Weight:** 205 lbs.
Bats: Left **Throws:** Right
Acquired: Third-round pick,
   6/86 free-agent draft

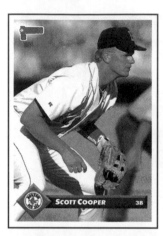
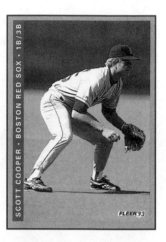

Scott Cooper is finally getting his share of major league at-bats after years of waiting behind Wade Boggs in the Red Sox chain. However, most of his playing time has come at first base, not at third, where Boggs still reigned. This took away some of Cooper's game because he was named the Triple-A International League's top defensive third baseman two years in a row by *Baseball America*. Another complication for last year's Triple-A Pawtucket MVP was the deep right field fence in Fenway. Still, Cooper led his club in base hits for four seasons in a row (1988-91), and he doesn't strike out much. Cooper compiled a .457 average during a 14-game stint with the Red Sox late in '91, getting his first hit September 12. Don't expect a blur on the bases; he's never stolen more than three in a year.

Is this a Wade Boggs replacement? Spend only a dime each on his 1993s, until the verdict is passed. Our pick for his best 1993 card is Fleer. We have chosen this card for its technical merits.

	BA	G	AB	R	H	2B	3B	HR	RBI	SB
92 AL	.276	123	337	34	93	21	0	5	33	1
Life	.292	139	373	40	109	25	2	5	40	1

WIL CORDERO

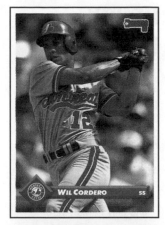

Position: Infield
Team: Montreal Expos
Born: October 3, 1971
Mayaguez, Puerto Rico
Height: 6'2" **Weight:** 185 lbs.
Bats: Right **Throws:** Right
Acquired: Signed as a free
agent, 5/88

RHEAL CORMIER

Position: Pitcher
Team: St. Louis Cardinals
Born: April 23, 1967
Moncton, New Brunswick,
Canada
Height: 5'10" **Weight:** 185 lbs.
Bats: Left **Throws:** Left
Acquired: Sixth-round pick,
6/88 free-agent draft

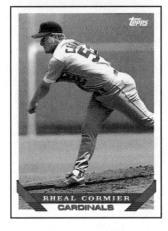

Wil Cordero missed a chance to take over the regular shortstop job in spring training of '92, and wound up going back to Triple-A Indianapolis for another year of seasoning. Despite a stint on the DL for the second season in a row, he still managed a productive year, hitting for average and chipping in with an occasional homer and steal. Cordero made the All-Star team in Double-A in '90. In '91, *Baseball America* tabbed him the third-best prospect in the American Association and the best in the Expos' organization. That same season, Cordero suffered a fractured hand when hit by a Mark Kiefer pitch. The injury may have cost him a trip to the bigs. He did join the Expos in September of that year for rehab, though he was not placed on the active roster. Cordero shows good range with a strong arm and good bat speed.

A healthy Cordero will challenge for playing time. Gamble a nickel apiece on his '93s. Our pick for his best 1993 card is Fleer. We have chosen this card because of its overall appeal and pleasing looks.

A minor league detour salvaged Rheal Cormier's 1992 season. He began the year in the St. Louis starting rotation, but was shipped back to Triple-A on May 31 with an 0-5 mark and 6.56 ERA. Following a week-long stay in the American Association, the lefthanded prospect looked like a new pitcher upon his big league return. Cormier's premiere with the 1991 Cardinals included a 4-5 record (and two consecutive complete games) in 10 starts. While he struck out 38 in 67 innings in '91, he walked just eight. The New Brunswick native played for the '88 Canadian Olympic baseball team before beginning his pro career in '89. His first win in '91 marked the first National League victory by a French-Canadian in 20 years.

Cormier is a keeper for 1993. With only four years of professional experience, he should blossom soon. At a dime or less per card, his '93 issues are promising purchases. Our pick for his best 1993 card is Donruss. We have chosen this card due to the outstanding photographic composition.

	BA	G	AB	R	H	2B	3B	HR	RBI	SB
92 AAA	.314	52	204	32	64	11	1	6	27	6
92 NL	.302	45	126	17	38	4	1	2	8	0

	W	L	ERA	G	CG	IP	H	ER	BB	SO
92 NL	10	10	3.68	31	3	186.0	194	76	33	117
Life	14	15	3.80	42	5	253.2	268	107	41	155

TIM COSTO

Position: First base
Team: Cincinnati Reds
Born: February 16, 1969
Melrose Park, IL
Height: 6'5" **Weight:** 220 lbs.
Bats: Right **Throws:** Right
Acquired: Traded from Indians
for Reggie Jefferson, 6/91

HENRY COTTO

Position: Outfield
Team: Seattle Mariners
Born: January 5, 1961
New York, NY
Height: 6'2" **Weight:** 180 lbs.
Bats: Right **Throws:** Right
Acquired: Traded from Yankees
with Steve Trout for Lee
Guetterman, Wade Taylor,
and Clay Parker, 12/87

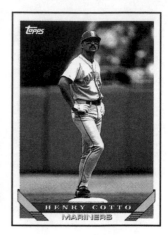

Tim Costo played first base for Double-A Chattanooga in '92 and battled Willie Greene for the home run title among Reds' farmhands. As is often the case with longball hitters, when Costo came to the plate, it seemed he either hit a homer or struck out. His RBI totals failed to keep pace with the home run output, and at one point he had 20 homers and just 11 doubles and triples combined. Costo came to the Reds when a front office mistake exposed top prospect Reggie Jefferson to a trade, but Costo looks like more than just a consolation prize. He will have to cut down his strikeouts, which have been in triple figures. None of this should obscure the fact Costo had a breakthrough season, more than doubling his home run totals of his first two pro campaigns.

Costo's a pack of dynamite when he connects. Pick up a few of his '93s and see what he does in the bigs. Our pick for his best 1993 card is Upper Deck. We have chosen this card because it will increase in value.

Henry Cotto remained Seattle's fourth outfielder in 1992, providing the team with his usual speed and defense. He soared past .300 against lefthanded pitchers (.321), yet struggled against righties, hitting a minute .175. However, he exceeded 20 stolen bases (23) for just the third time in his career. His pro career can be traced back to '80, when he was signed by the Cubs as an undrafted free agent. His '84 rookie season in Chicago consisted of defensive duties and pinch-hitting, as evidenced by his 146 at-bats in 105 games. Cotto's busiest season came in '88, batting nearly 400 times for the Mariners. In his first Seattle season, he was the team's starting center fielder before Ken Griffey Jr. In '89, he collected nine homers and 33 RBI in 100 games.

Cotto's part-time status shouldn't change in 1993. Spend your time and money investing in common-priced cards of starters. Our pick for his best 1993 card is Topps. We have chosen this card because of its great combination of photography and design.

	BA	G	AB	R	H	2B	3B	HR	RBI	SB
92 AA	.241	121	424	63	102	18	2	28	71	4
92 NL	.222	12	36	3	8	2	0	0	2	0

	BA	G	AB	R	H	2B	3B	HR	RBI	SB
92 AL	.259	108	294	42	76	11	1	5	27	23
Life	.263	776	1938	271	509	79	9	39	189	114

Series two cards from some companies were available at press time. If space allows, both cards are shown; if not, the most up-to-date cards are pictured.

CHAD
CURTIS

Position: Outfield
Team: California Angels
Born: November 6, 1968
Benson, AZ
Height: 5'10" **Weight:** 175 lbs.
Bats: Right **Throws:** Right
Acquired: 45th-round pick,
6/89 free-agent draft

Chad Curtis has arrived at just the right time; few baseball execs appreciate speed more than Angels GM Whitey Herzog does. In addition to stealing 43 bases in '92, he managed a nifty .259 batting average with 46 RBI and 51 walks. Curtis has come quickly through the system, proving his talent at every level. He has a good enough arm to play right or center field. Curtis finished third in the Triple-A Pacific Coast League in '91 with 46 steals but—surprise—found out it's a little tougher in the majors. Curtis was caught stealing in seven of his first 14 major league attempts. He hit 23 homers spanning the Double- and Triple-A levels. He has played a lot of second base as a pro. In fact, he made the Class-A Midwest League All-Star team in that position in '90.

Spending 50 to 75 cents each on 1993 Curtis cards might seem wild. But, another strong year could push those cards past the $1 range. Our pick for his best 1993 card is Upper Deck. We have chosen this card because the design lends itself to the best use of the elements.

	BA	G	AB	R	H	2B	3B	HR	RBI	SB
92 AL	.259	139	441	59	114	16	2	10	46	43
Life	.259	139	441	59	114	16	2	10	46	43

MILT
CUYLER

Position: Outfield
Team: Detroit Tigers
Born: October 7, 1968
Macon, GA
Height: 5'10" **Weight:** 185 lbs.
Bats: Both **Throws:** Right
Acquired: Second-round pick,
6/86 free-agent draft

A weak right knee put the brakes on Milt Cuyler's 1992 season with the Tigers. Even when he was in the lineup, Cuyler's running game was curtailed. Playing in only 89 games in '92, he hit .241, knocked in 28 RBI, and swiped a mere 10 bases. In 1991, his 41 stolen bases were the most by a Detroit rookie since 1909. His other rookie totals were .258 with three homers and 33 RBI. Most of all, he gave the Tigers a speedy glove man to roam center field for the first time in years. The aging club welcomed a youngster with 177 career stolen bases from five minor league seasons. He began his pro career right out of high school in 1986. For two consecutive seasons, Cuyler's batting average has remained higher on the road than at Tiger Stadium.

Look close. Cuyler's 1993 editions may be found for as little as a nickel each. Speed, defense, and youth are three reasons why Cuyler's cards could turn some quick profits. Our pick for his best 1993 card is Fleer. We have chosen this card because it has a distinctive look.

	BA	G	AB	R	H	2B	3B	HR	RBI	SB
92 AL	.241	89	291	39	70	11	1	3	28	8
Life	.251	262	817	124	205	29	9	6	69	50

KAL
DANIELS

Position: Outfield
Team: Chicago Cubs
Born: August 20, 1963
Vienna, GA
Height: 5'11" **Weight:** 205 lbs.
Bats: Left **Throws:** Right
Acquired: Traded from Dodgers
for Mike Sodders, 6/92

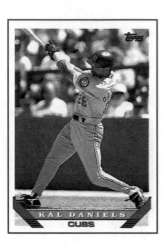

RON
DARLING

Position: Pitcher
Team: Oakland Athletics
Born: August 19, 1960
Honolulu, Hawaii
Height: 6'3" **Weight:** 195 lbs.
Bats: Right **Throws:** Right
Acquired: Traded from Expos
for Russ Comier and Matt
Grott, 7/91

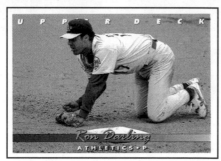

Even in homer-friendly Wrigley Field, Kal Daniels couldn't regain his power stroke. Daniels broke in with the 1986 Reds, hitting .320 with six homers and 23 RBI in 74 games. In 1987, he added 26 homers, 64 RBI, and a .334 average. His career climaxed in 1990, when he smashed career highs of 27 homers and 94 RBI. Although Daniels started the '92 season with Los Angeles, his days were numbered following the acquisition of Eric Davis. In 35 games with the Dodgers, he managed just two homers and eight RBI. Of course, his troublesome knees helped Daniels miss more than a month of the LA season. He didn't fare much better in the Windy City, hitting six homers with 25 RBI in 86 games. The controversial slugger will have a limited future, unless he's given the relatively safe job of designated hitter.

While Daniels still has above-average power, he remains a perennial candidate for the DL. Pass on his 1993 commons. Our pick for his best 1993 card is Topps. We have chosen this card for the superior presentation of information on its back.

Pitcher Ron Darling ended a two-year losing streak while becoming one of Oakland's steadiest starters in 1992. Three of his first 13 victories were shutouts. Of course, getting supported with at least five runs per game made a difference in Darling's '92 totals. His 15-10 record with a 3.66 ERA was a nice change from '91. The only real news Darling made that year was pitching with three different teams in one season. Swapped on July 15 from the Mets to the Expos, Darling made only three starts with Montreal. After an 0-2 record in two weeks, he was traded to the A's. Long before Darling began his whirlwind tour of teams, he had appeared with New York in '83, and followed with a career-best 17-9 effort in '88. Six consecutive years of double-digit wins ended in 1990, as Darling slipped to 7-9 and ended the year as a reliever.

Darling's career totals have been inflated by pitching only with contenders. His cards are overrated, too. Steer clear of his 1993 commons. Our pick for his best 1993 card is Upper Deck. We have chosen this card for its artistic presentation.

	BA	G	AB	R	H	2B	3B	HR	RBI	SB
92 NL	.241	83	212	21	51	11	0	6	25	0
Life	.285	727	2338	391	666	125	8	104	360	87

	W	L	ERA	G	CG	IP	H	ER	BB	SO
92 AL	15	10	3.66	33	4	206.1	198	84	72	99
Life	117	89	3.57	305	29	1918.1	1760	762	729	1318

Series two cards from some companies were available at press time. If space allows, both cards are shown; if not, the most up-to-date cards are pictured.

DANNY
DARWIN

Position: Pitcher
Team: Boston Red Sox
Born: October 25, 1955
   Bonham, TX
Height: 6'3" **Weight:** 195 lbs.
Bats: Right **Throws:** Right
Acquired: Signed as a free
   agent, 12/90

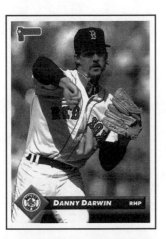

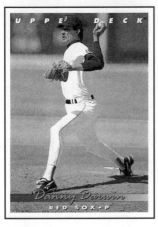

Danny Darwin rebounded from an injury-plagued 1991 to become one of Boston's most versatile pitchers in 1992. Working as a starter and reliever, the veteran moundsman exceeded 100 strikeouts for the eighth time in his long career. He finished the '92 season with a 9-9 record and three saves. The native Texan burst onto the big league scene in 1980, his first full season with the Rangers. In 53 games, Darwin developed a 13-4 record with 8 saves. In 1985, his first season with Milwaukee, the righty suffered through a career-worst 18 losses. Along with consecutive 11-4 seasons with the Astros in 1989-90, Darwin captured the '90 NL ERA title with a 2.21 mark. In 1991, his season ended on July 7, due to a sore shoulder later requiring surgery.

   Darwin's 1993 cards, at a nickel or less, are unimportant purchases. Even his unlikely chance of discovering a 20-win season would bring only small, temporary hikes to his card values. Our pick for his best 1993 card is Upper Deck. We have chosen this card because of its great combination of photography and design.

	W	L	ERA	G	SV	IP	H	ER	BB	SO
92 AL	9	9	3.96	51	3	161.1	159	71	53	124
Life	123	124	3.50	551	32	2142.0	2006	832	649	1431

DOUG
DASCENZO

Position: Outfield
Team: Texas Rangers
Born: June 30, 1964
   Cleveland, OH
Height: 5'8" **Weight:** 160 lbs.
Bats: Both **Throws:** Left
Acquired: Signed as a free
   agent, 12/92

Although Doug Dascenzo continued to shore up the Cubs reserves in 1992, he may find full-time work with the Texas Rangers in '93. A capable defensive outfielder and pinch-hitter, Dascenzo benefitted the Cubs in various roles since he joined the team in '88. In fact, Dascenzo has even filled in as emergency relief pitcher, throwing five innings of scoreless relief for Chicago. Despite switch-hitting abilities, Dascenzo continues to fare the best hitting righthanded. Never nearing the 30-plus steals he accumulated over five minor league seasons, Dascenzo registered a personal best 15 stolen bases in 1990. With several of the Cub outfielders suffering from recurring health problems, the able-bodied Dascenzo seemed like an outfield regular by default in 1992. With Texas in '93, Dascenzo hopes to find a permanent spot.

   Dascenzo's career destiny as an outfield fill-in bores collectors. Without a full-time job, his 1993s are everlasting deadwood. Our pick for his best 1993 card is Donruss. We have chosen this card due to the outstanding photographic composition.

	BA	G	AB	R	H	2B	3B	HR	RBI	SB
92 NL	.255	139	376	37	96	13	4	0	20	6
Life	.240	443	1070	133	257	37	9	3	80	47

DARREN
DAULTON

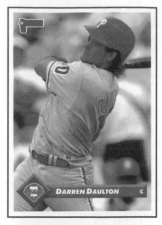

Position: Catcher
Team: Philadelphia Phillies
Born: January 3, 1962
    Arkansas City, KS
Height: 6'2" **Weight:** 195 lbs.
Bats: Left **Throws:** Right
Acquired: 25th-round pick,
    6/80 free-agent draft

CHILI
DAVIS

DARRY
DAULTON

Position: Designated hitter
Team: California Angels
Born: January 17, 1960
    Kingston, Jamaica
Height: 6'3" **Weight:** 219 lbs.
Bats: Both **Throws:** Right
Acquired: Signed as a free
    agent, 12/92

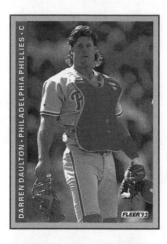

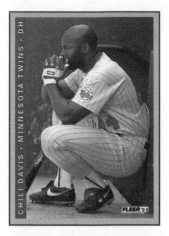

Darren Daulton redeemed himself in 1992, carving out career highs in numerous offensive categories. He outdid himself everywhere, even breaking double figures in steals (11). He hit well against both lefties (.257) and righties (.279), pounding out 27 homers. His RBI (109) were the most since Mike Schmidt drove in 113 in 1987. Daulton's success comes after some tough career breaks. In 1991, he was a passenger during Len Dykstra's infamous car accident, missing a total of 63 games due to the injuries he suffered. In '88, Daulton's month on the DL came after punching a wall and breaking his hand.

Despite his miracle rejuvenation, two facts remain. First, the catcher had six stays on the DL before 1992. Secondly, '92 was the first year he had ever topped 20 homers during his 13 pro seasons. His cards can't sustain values of more than a nickel apiece. Expect Daulton's '86 Fleer rookie at an affordable 75 cents. Our pick for his best 1993 card is Fleer. We have chosen this card for its artistic presentation.

Chili Davis did not pack his usual punch for the 1992 Twins, a team depending on him as a power source. The 1991 World Champions adopted Davis in January '91. He responded with personal bests of 29 home runs and 93 RBI that season, marking the fifth time he exceeded 20 round-trippers in a year. As those stats dwindled in '92, so did Minnesota. Davis will try to cook up some power production with the Angels in '93. Part of his offensive resurrection came with a full-time move to DH. His defensive skills declined over the years and seemed to distract him at bat. The two-time All-Star has surpassed .300 only once in his career, a .315 effort in 1984. Yet, he's topped 100 strikeouts in six seasons. Davis was San Francisco's 11th selection in the 1977 draft.

Since Davis suffered a 1992 letdown, 1993 cards of Chili should be cheaper than usual. However, don't expect his common-priced cards to regain any steam. Our pick for his best 1993 card is Upper Deck. We have chosen this card due to its unique photographic approach.

	BA	G	AB	R	H	2B	3B	HR	RBI	SB
92 NL	.270	145	485	80	131	32	5	27	109	11
Life	.233	706	2114	263	492	105	9	75	309	32

	BA	G	AB	R	H	2B	3B	HR	RBI	SB
92 AL	.288	138	444	63	128	27	2	12	66	4
Life	.270	1590	5698	799	1538	275	28	197	818	117

ERIC DAVIS

Position: Outfield
Team: Los Angeles Dodgers
Born: May 29, 1962
  Los Angeles, CA
Height: 6'3" **Weight:** 200 lbs.
Bats: Right **Throws:** Right
Acquired: Traded from Reds
  with Kip Gross for John
  Wetteland and Tim Belcher,
  11/91

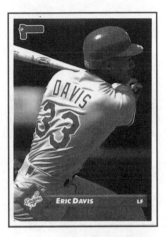

GLENN DAVIS

Position: First base
Team: Baltimore Orioles
Born: March 28, 1961
  Jacksonville, FL
Height: 6'3" **Weight:** 211 lbs.
Bats: Right **Throws:** Right
Acquired: Traded from Astros
  for Steve Finley, Curt
  Schilling, and Pete Harnisch,
  1/91

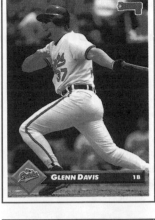

The much-awaited pairing of Eric Davis and childhood pal Darryl Strawberry in the 1992 Dodgers outfield produced few results. Instead, Davis and Strawberry had more injuries than statistics to compare. Davis was first sidelined by a strained shoulder in May. Finally, a sore wrist ended his season prematurely. The frustration replayed Davis' 1991 woes, when he played in only 89 games for the Reds, hitting .235 with 11 homers and 33 RBI. Although Davis was selected in the eighth round of the 1980 draft, he didn't become a Cincinnati regular until 1986. In that first full season, he smacked 27 homers and swiped 80 bases, joining Rickey Henderson as one of the rare few to crack the 20/80 barrier. His 30/30 season of 1987 included 37 dingers, 100 RBI, and 50 steals.

After a two-year decline, little movement can be expected on his new nickel-priced cards. Our pick for his best 1993 card is Score. We have chosen this card for the interesting facts included on the reverse.

Credit Glenn Davis for sparking the 1992 Orioles into surprise pennant contention. The injury-prone slugger was relegated to full-time DH duty. The first half of his season was spent on the DL, due to a rib cage injury, yet Davis exceeded double digits in home runs for the eighth season in a row. In '90, Davis injured his neck and was limited to 49 games. Despite his limited appearances that year, he produced 10 homers and 28 RBI. Before the trade from Houston, Baltimore had attempted to grab Davis in the '79 free-agent draft. Instead, after college, Davis was a first-round pick of the Astros in 1981. From 1985-90, he produced a minimum of 20 homers and 64 RBI a year.

Give Davis a full season to reestablish himself as one of baseball's resident sluggers. Only the most optimistic investors should toy with his 1993 nickel-priced cards. Surprisingly, a buck gets you an '86 Donruss Davis, his first company appearance. Our pick for his best 1993 card is Donruss. We have chosen this card because of its great combination of photography and design.

	BA	G	AB	R	H	2B	3B	HR	RBI	SB
92 NL	.228	76	267	21	61	8	1	5	32	19
Life	.265	932	3124	575	828	127	19	182	564	266

	BA	G	AB	R	H	2B	3B	HR	RBI	SB
92 AL	.276	106	398	46	110	15	2	13	48	1
Life	.262	985	3606	502	945	174	13	189	594	28

ANDRE DAWSON

Position: Outfield
Team: Boston Red Sox
Born: July 10, 1954 Miami, FL
Height: 6'3" **Weight:** 195 lbs.
Bats: Right **Throws:** Right
Acquired: Signed as a free agent, 12/92

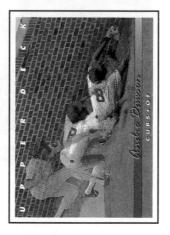

The knee problems that have plagued Andre Dawson resurfaced in '92. He began wearing a brace to avoid in-season surgery. Patella pains aside, the slugger still managed to put up impressive numbers. Dawson was first among the Cubs in all three Triple Crown categories. While no longer capable of repeating his 49-homer season of '87, Dawson remains one of the most respected clutch hitters. For this very reason, Boston snapped him up the very day after it was decided he could not come to terms with the Cubs. In '91, he and Ryne Sandberg became the first Cubs to produce consecutive 100-RBI campaigns since Ron Santo in 1969-70. Dawson and Willie Mays are the only players in baseball history with 2,000 hits, 300 homers, and 300 stolen bases.

The Hawk may soon fly to Cooperstown. Pay 15 cents each or less for his 1993 cards. Early Dawson cards are out of reach. Get one of his first Cubs cards, an '87 Topps Traded, for 35 cents. Our pick for his best 1993 card is Upper Deck. We have chosen this card due to its unique photographic approach.

	BA	G	AB	R	H	2B	3B	HR	RBI	SB
92 NL	.277	143	542	60	150	27	2	22	90	6
Life	.282	2310	8890	1259	2504	444	94	399	1425	310

ROB DEER

Position: Outfield
Team: Detroit Tigers
Born: September 29, 1960 Orange, CA
Height: 6'3" **Weight:** 225 lbs.
Bats: Right **Throws:** Right
Acquired: Signed as a free agent, 11/90

Rob Deer continued his all-or-nothing offensive production with the Tigers in 1992. For the seventh consecutive season, Deer broke the 20-homer milestone (32). However, Deer's batting average continued its annual flip-flop (.247 in '92, up from .179 in '91). As the outfield slugger tried to keep his batting average above his weight, Deer again exceeded 100 strikeouts (131). From 1986 through '91, Deer's strikeouts have ranged from 147 to 186 whiffs per season. A sprained ankle and bruised wrist and hand kept Deer out of some '92 action, but possibly stopped him from another year of record-setting strikeouts. Deer began seven years of minor league toil in 1978 in the San Francisco organization. His first full season came with the 1986 Brewers, producing a career-high 33 homers and 86 RBI.

The only records Deer will set might be for lifetime strikeouts. Don't depend on his 1993 common-priced cards. Our pick for his best 1993 card is Donruss. We have chosen this card because of its great combination of photography and design.

	BA	G	AB	R	H	2B	3B	HR	RBI	SB
92 AL	.247	110	393	66	97	20	1	32	64	4
Life	.222	1002	3365	503	746	128	12	205	536	38

RICH
DeLUCIA

Position: Pitcher
Team: Seattle Mariners
Born: October 7, 1964
Reading, PA
Height: 6' **Weight:** 180 lbs.
Bats: Right **Throws:** Right
Acquired: Sixth-round pick,
6/86 free-agent draft

DELINO
DeSHIELDS

Position: Second base
Team: Montreal Expos
Born: January 15, 1969
Seaford, DL
Height: 6'1" **Weight:** 170 lbs.
Bats: Left **Throws:** Right
Acquired: First-round pick,
6/87 free-agent draft

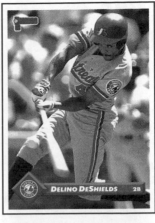

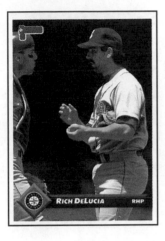
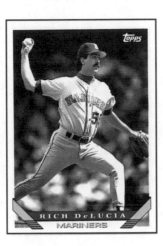

Rich DeLucia saw the bottom fall out of his high hopes for a successful 1992. After a 12-13 rookie season in '91, DeLucia was hoping that the on-the-job training he received would help him. His struggles just continued in '92, however, and he found himself assigned to the bullpen after making 11 starts. He lacks both the velocity and control to post a winning record—even if he was pitching with a team that would give him strong support. DeLucia yields more than a hit per inning and strikes out less than two batters for each walk he issues. In '92, opponents compiled a .293 batting average, a .361 on-base percentage, and a .490 slugging percentage against him. He's also prone to throwing the gopher ball. He gave up 13 homers in '92. The former University of Tennessee standout started his pro career in '86 and reached Seattle four years later.

Leave DeLucia's '93 issues alone. Our pick for his best 1993 card is Topps. We have chosen this card for its technical merits.

A September slump and a rib-cage injury hampered Delino DeShields in his quest for a career-best season in 1992. DeShields finished second in NL All-Star balloting for second sackers (although he didn't get named to the 1992 squad). He battled back from a 1991 slump, which included a league-leading 151 strikeouts and a .238 average. Amidst his hitting woes, DeShields upped his homer total to 10. DeShields' sophomore downfall was a contrast from his 1990 debut. Thanks to 42 stolen bases and a .289 average, he was runner-up to NL Rookie of the Year David Justice. During his brief minor league career, DeShields was a shortstop.

Young, fast, and unlimited in overall potential, DeShields and his cards have great futures. Once he cuts down on his strikeouts, nothing can stop DeShields from annual .300 performances. Spend up to a dime apiece for his 1993 editions. The '90 Upper Deck DeShields rookie looks right at 75 cents. Our pick for his best 1993 card is Score. We have chosen this card due to the outstanding photographic composition.

	W	L	ERA	G	SV	IP	H	ER	BB	SO
92 AL	3	6	5.49	30	1	83.2	100	51	35	66
Life	16	21	4.83	67	1	301.2	306	162	122	184

	BA	G	AB	R	H	2B	3B	HR	RBI	SB
92 NL	.292	135	530	82	155	19	8	7	56	46
Life	.272	415	1592	234	433	62	18	21	152	144

MIKE DEVEREAUX

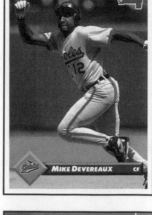

Position: Outfield
Team: Baltimore Orioles
Born: April 10, 1963
Casper, WY
Height: 6′ **Weight:** 195 lbs.
Bats: Right **Throws:** Right
Acquired: Traded from Dodgers
for Mike Morgan, 3/89

ROB DIBBLE

Position: Pitcher
Team: Cincinnati Reds
Born: January 24, 1964
Bridgeport, CT
Height: 6′4″ **Weight:** 230 lbs.
Bats: Left **Throws:** Right
Acquired: First-round pick,
6/83 free-agent draft

Mike Devereaux became the unlikely offensive savior of the 1992 Orioles. His pro career began with the Dodgers in '85, yeilding a major league debut in 1987. Skeptics labeled "Devo" a fluke in '91, after responding with career highs of 10 triples, 19 home runs, and 59 RBI. His '90 totals (12 homers, 49 RBI) may have matched those '91 stats, but Devereaux missed a month of the season due to a pulled hamstring. In '92, he broke the 100-RBI barrier for the first time, and set numerous other career highs.

Devereaux could compile another year or three's worth of eye-popping statistics. Yet, his late offensive accomplishments hint that his cards will never attain long-lasting value. Buy his 1993s at a nickel each. Be prepared to sell for a quick, short-term gain when Devereaux bats the Orioles into a pennant or contends for an individual title. Score's first set in '88 has a Devereaux rookie deal at 35 cents. Our pick for his best 1993 card is Fleer. We have chosen this card for the interesting facts included on the reverse.

Despite a late start and a fatter ERA (3.07), Rob Dibble maintained his fiery brand of relief with the 1992 Reds. His year started with a thud, suffering through an 8.10 ERA in six spring training games. Tendinitis in his pitching shoulder required Dibble to start the season on the DL, giving Norm Charlton the team's stopper role. As a result, Dibble couldn't duplicate his 31 saves from 1991 (25 in '92). Both in 1991 and '90, Dibble made All-Star game appearances, partly due to his astounding number of strikeouts per nine innings. He fanned 141 in 1989, 136 in 1990 and 124 in 1991. The righthanded flamethrower wasn't an overnight sensation for the Reds. He needed nearly six minor league seasons before his debut in the bigs on June 29, 1988, against San Diego.

Dibble's nickel-priced 1993 cards are a tough call. Look for Dibble's stats to grow with the departure of Charlton. His explosive "Nasty Boys" reputation can keep him and his card values popular. Our pick for his best 1993 card is Donruss. We have chosen this card because of its overall appeal and pleasing looks.

	BA	G	AB	R	H	2B	3B	HR	RBI	SB
92 AL	.276	156	653	76	180	29	11	24	107	10
Life	.259	584	2116	272	547	92	25	63	267	64

	W	L	ERA	G	SV	IP	H	ER	BB	SO
92 NL	3	5	3.07	63	25	70.1	48	24	31	110
Life	25	19	2.35	309	69	409.0	282	107	150	570

GARY DiSARCINA

GARY DiSARCINA SS

Position: Infield
Team: California Angels
Born: November 19, 1967
　Malden, MA
Height: 6′1″ **Weight:** 178 lbs.
Bats: Right **Throws:** Right
Acquired: Sixth-round pick,
　6/88 free-agent draft

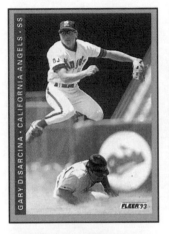

It was Gary DiSarcina's presence in the organization that enabled the Angels to trade shortstop Dick Schofield to the Mets for pitcher Julio Valera, and so a successful DiSarcina would have double the benefit toward the team's rebuilding. DiSarcina looks like he might be a better hitter than Schofield was, though no one should expect him to be a power man. The most homers he ever hit in his climb to the majors—even in the generous Pacific Coast League parks— was four. But offense won't matter much if DiSarcina doesn't cut down on his errors. He made 11 of them in his first 58 games of the 1992 season; 25 for the year. Some of that may be the adjustment to an everyday job in the majors; he led the PCL shortstops in 1991 with a .967 fielding percentage. That year he also assembled a 29-game errorless streak, hit .310, and was named Edmonton's "Trapper of the Year."

　Give him another year starting before buying his nickel-priced cards. Our pick for his best 1993 card is Fleer. We have chosen this card since the photograph captures the athletic ability of the player.

	BA	G	AB	R	H	2B	3B	HR	RBI	SB
92 AL	.247	157	518	48	128	19	0	3	42	9
Life	.234	195	632	61	148	22	1	3	45	10

JOHN DOHERTY

Position: Pitcher
Team: Detroit Tigers
Born: June 11, 1967
　Bronx, NY
Height: 6′4″ **Weight:** 200 lbs.
Bats: Right **Throws:** Right
Acquired: 19th-round pick,
　6/89 free-agent draft

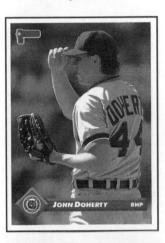

JOHN DOHERTY RHP

JOHN DOHERTY

John Doherty is one of the modern breed who comes to the majors as a relief specialist. In fact, in his first three years of pro ball, Doherty made only one start in 116 outings. All of that bullpen experience, however, did little to ease his nervousness on June 4, 1992, as he warmed up for his first appearance in Yankee Stadium, not far from where he grew up. "My first pitch in the bullpen, I almost threw it into the bleachers," he said. Doherty managed to hurl 1 ⅓ scoreless innings. He went on to be a workhorse for the Tigers in '92, going 7-4 with 3 saves and 10 holds over 47 games. Doherty owns adequate control and uses a sinking fastball. He received a four-game suspension for his role in a June 8 brawl against the Indians. He hit Glenallen Hill, then knocked down Sandy Alomar Jr., who charged the mound. Doherty then went on the disabled list with bruised ribs.

　As a reliever, Doherty's 1993 cards are doubtful dime purchases. Our pick for his best 1993 card is Score. We have chosen this card for the interesting facts included on the reverse.

	W	L	ERA	G	SV	IP	H	ER	BB	SO
92 AL	7	4	3.88	47	3	116.0	131	50	25	37
Life	7	4	3.88	47	3	116.0	131	50	25	37

CHRIS DONNELS

Position: Third base
Team: Houston Astros
Born: April 21, 1965
  Los Angeles, CA
Height: 6′ **Weight:** 185 lbs.
Bats: Left **Throws:** Right
Acquired: Claimed off waivers
  from Florida Marlins, 12/92

JOHN DOPSON

Position: Pitcher
Team: Boston Red Sox
Born: July 14, 1963
  Baltimore, MD
Height: 6′4″ **Weight:** 235 lbs.
Bats: Left **Throws:** Right
Acquired: Traded from Expos
  with Luis Rivera for Spike
  Owen and Dan Gakeler,
  12/88

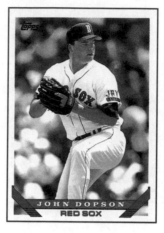 

The 1992 season is one Chris Donnels hopes he can leave far behind. He suffered through 45 games with the Mets, hitting only .174. The Florida Marlins expansion team picked him up in the expansion draft. His dreams of starting fresh in Florida were short-lived, however, thanks to a former teammate. When the Marlins signed free-agent Dave Magadan, their need for Donnels ceased. Now in Houston for '93, Donnels began as a first-round draft pick in '87. His potential skyrocketed in '89, when his Class-A stats of 17 homers, 78 RBI, and a .313 average won him Florida State MVP. Donnels was lackluster in his '91 debut with the Mets, hitting .225 with no homers and five RBI in 37 games.

Despite being free of New York's big-city pressure, Donnels has the distinction of being abandoned by two organizations in one year. Due to the presence of Houston cornermen Ken Caminiti and Jeff Bagwell, Donnels' '93 commons are risky ventures. Our pick for his best 1993 card is Topps. We have chosen this card because of its great combination of photography and design.

John Dopson beat the odds to become a steady Red Sox starter again in 1992. Dopson's pro career set sail in 1982 right after high school as Montreal's second-round draft selection. Following a 1985 audition in the bigs, his first and only full season as an Expo came in 1988. His 3-11 record obscured a 3.04 ERA. Dopson went through a shoulder operation in '87. Then, due to an injury to his pitching elbow that cropped up in the beginning of '89, the beleaguered righthander made only four starts in 1990. After 1990 surgery, Dopson pitched just seven games in 1991, six of which were in the minors. In '92, the Maryland native went 7-11. He was at his sharpest since going 12-8 in 28 starts in '89.

At age 29, Dopson's modest career stats, an ineffectiveness against righthanded hitters, and his numerous past health worries should discourage most collectors from considering these common-priced cards. Our pick for his best 1993 card is Topps. We have chosen this card due to the outstanding photographic composition.

	BA	G	AB	R	H	2B	3B	HR	RBI	SB
92 NL	.174	45	121	8	21	4	0	0	6	1
Life	.195	82	210	15	41	6	0	0	11	2

	W	L	ERA	G	CG	IP	H	ER	BB	SO
92 AL	7	11	4.08	25	0	141.1	159	64	38	55
Life	22	32	3.84	89	3	511.0	515	218	179	264

Series two cards from some companies were available at press time. If space allows, both cards are shown; if not, the most up-to-date cards are pictured.

BILL
DORAN

Position: Second base
Team: Cincinnati Reds
Born: May 28, 1958
  Cincinnati, OH
Height: 6′ **Weight:** 180 lbs.
Bats: Both **Throws:** Right
Acquired: Traded from Astros
  for Terry McGriff, Butch
  Henry, and Keith Kaiser, 9/90

D.J.
DOZIER

Position: Outfield
Team: San Diego Padres
Born: September 21, 1965
  Norfolk, VA
Height: 6′ **Weight:** 202 lbs.
Bats: Right **Throws:** Right
Acquired: Traded from Mets
  with Wally Whitehurst for
  Tony Fernandez, 10/92

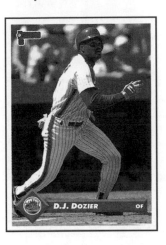

Bill Doran fought to remain a Cincinnati regular in 1992. Although his power totals were better than his 1989-90 efforts, Doran barely hit .200 against lefthanded pitching. He did manage .252 against righties (.235 overall), with 47 RBI, and 8 homers. The Cincinnati native joined his hometown in the last month of 1990, hitting .373 to help the Reds to a division title. Unfortunately, back surgery stopped Doran from participating in postseason play and the team's eventual World Championship. Doran was discovered out of Miami of Ohio, chosen in the sixth round of the 1979 draft. After only four years in the Houston farm system, Doran became an Astro regular. By 1985, his totals grew to .287 with 14 home runs and 59 RBI. Doran put up career-best numbers in 1987, belting 16 homers and 79 RBI.

  Doran's playing time could shrink in 1993. His 1993 cards aren't recommended, even at a nickel apiece. Our pick for his best 1993 card is Upper Deck. We have chosen this card for its artistic presentation.

D.J. Dozier belongs to the elite group of athletes talented enough to play football and baseball on the major league level. He broke in with the Vikings in 1987 and played in the NFL through 1991. Dozier's tools include size, speed, and strength. He won three letters in baseball in high school, but he was away from the sport for six years. Dozier was drafted by the Tigers in 1983, but attended Penn State, and was a four-year starter at halfback. Well into his grid career, Dozier reported to the Mets' extended spring training in 1989. He resumed baseball in 1990 with Class-A St. Lucie of the Florida State League, became an All-Star, and got a late season promotion to Double-A. Two years later, Dozier was in the majors. In '92, his last season with the Mets, he played in only 25 games. The Padres are counting on him to come alive with his new team in '93.

  Spend up to 15 cents each on cards of the next Bo Jackson. Our pick for his best 1993 card is Donruss. We have chosen this card for its technical merits.

	BA	G	AB	R	H	2B	3B	HR	RBI	SB
92 NL	.235	132	387	48	91	16	2	8	47	7
Life	.267	1425	5071	720	1353	216	39	84	491	208

	BA	G	AB	R	H	2B	3B	HR	RBI	SB
92 NL	.191	25	47	4	9	2	0	0	2	4
Life	.191	25	47	4	9	2	0	0	2	4

DOUG DRABEK

Position: Pitcher
Team: Houston Astros
Born: July 25, 1962
Victoria, TX
Height: 6'1" **Weight:** 185 lbs.
Bats: Right **Throws:** Right
Acquired: Signed as a free
agent, 12/92

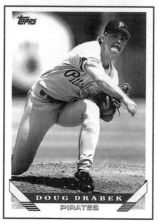

ROB DUCEY

Position: Outfield
Team: California Angels
Born: May 24, 1965 Toronto,
Ontario, Canada
Height: 6'2" **Weight:** 180 lbs.
Bats: Left **Throws:** Right
Acquired: Traded from Blue
Jays with Greg Myers for
Mark Eichhorn, 8/92

Traditionally a slow starter, Doug Drabek was among NL leaders in strikeouts, innings pitched, and opponents' batting average in the first half of '92. Even in '91, when he went only 15-14 in the wake of a Cy Young Award season, he finished fourth in the league in innings, seventh in complete games, and 10th in ERA. During the NLCS against Atlanta, he had a 0.60 ERA—pitching six shutout innings in the opener and taking a tough 1-0 loss on a ninth-inning run in Game 6. A hamstring injury prevented him from working more often. Houston, signing Drabek late in '92, is hoping he can coax them out of a .500 season. During his Cy Young season, Drabek hit career peaks with 22 wins and a 2.76 ERA. He wound up going 15-11 with a 2.77 ERA spread over 34 games in '92. He threw in four shutouts for good measure.

Spend a nickel apiece on Drabeck's 1993s. A hot card in a hot set, Drabek is an inviting $1.50 in the '86 Donruss "The Rookies." Our pick for his best 1993 card is Topps. We have chosen this card since the photograph captures the athletic ability of the player.

Rob Ducey's new lease on baseball life was short-lived with the 1992 Angels. At season's end, the team asked for special waivers, in order to demote the hard-luck outfielder back to the minors. He batted .188 in part-time duty with the Halos in '92, but earned only two RBI in 80 at-bats. A minor league return seemed inevitable for Ducey, who bounced between the bigs and Triple-A from 1987 through '92 with Toronto. In fact, Ducey's 80 plate appearances in '92 constituted a career high. Despite being a Toronto native, Ducey never could crack the talent-rich Blue Jays lineup. Known for his defense and above-average speed, Ducey has been a perennial prospect since his pro career began in '84. This brief Angel may be headed to baseball's beyond.

Ducey will be fortunate to stick in the majors throughout '93. His sporadic playing time and spotty offense make collectors shudder. Don't buy here. Our pick for his best 1993 card is Topps. We have chosen this card because of its great combination of photography and design.

	W	L	ERA	G	CG	IP	H	ER	BB	SO
92 NL	15	11	2.77	34	10	256.2	218	79	54	177
Life	99	70	3.11	226	36	1494.1	1353	517	387	896

	BA	G	AB	R	H	2B	3B	HR	RBI	SB
92 AL	.188	54	80	7	15	4	0	0	2	2
Life	.235	214	379	54	89	20	3	2	32	10

MARIANO DUNCAN

Position: Infield/outfield
Team: Philadelphia Phillies
Born: March 13, 1963
  San Pedro de Macoris,
  Dominican Republic
Height: 6′ **Weight:** 185 lbs.
Bats: Right **Throws:** Right
Acquired: Signed as a free
  agent, 12/91

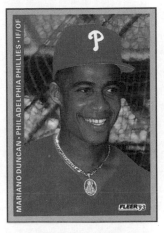

SHAWON DUNSTON

Position: Shortstop
Team: Chicago Cubs
Born: March 21, 1963
  Brooklyn, NY
Height: 6′1″ **Weight:** 175 lbs.
Bats: Right **Throws:** Right
Acquired: First-round pick,
  6/82 free-agent draft

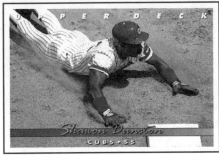

Before a September injury, Philadelphia's Mariano Duncan was polishing one of the finest offensive seasons of his unpredictable career. Near the end of the season, a then-healthy Duncan seemed prepared to erase his previous career highs set with the 1990 Reds (22 doubles, a league-leading 11 triples, 55 RBI, and a .306 average). He succeeded only in doubles (40). His home run high came in 1991, 12 dingers in just 100 games. Once a speedster, Duncan has slowed on the basepaths since notching a career-high 48 steals with the 1986 Dodgers. Annual trips to the disabled list have curtailed his thievery. Signed as an undrafted free agent out of the Dominican Republic in 1982, Duncan's childhood competitors included Tony Fernandez and Juan Samuel.

Despite having solid employment as Philadelphia's "10th man" in 1993, Duncan's health, and lack of one position to excel at, will stop his common-priced cards from gaining in value. Our pick for his best 1993 card is Score. We have chosen this card due to its unique photographic approach.

Due to surgery to mend a herniated disk in his back, Shawon Dunston's 1992 season was snuffed out early. Dunston is famed for being the first player in the nation selected in the 1982 free-agent draft. In '92, however, the veteran shortstop fell victim to the disabled list after only 18 games. Unfortunately, he was hitting a personal best .315 when injured. His disability erased a four-year streak of 50 or more RBI per season. Twice, in 1986 and 1990, Dunston reached a career high of 17 home runs. In 1989, Dunston batted .316 in the NL Championship Series against San Francisco. A two-time All-Star, Dunston's fame remains for his draft selection status, instead of his play.

Being a Cub with nation-wide cable TV exposure has helped Dunston's card popularity. His 1993 cards are dubious choices at a nickel each, though, due to his questionable health. Our pick for his best 1993 card is Upper Deck. We have chosen this card because the design lends itself to the best use of the elements.

	BA	G	AB	R	H	2B	3B	HR	RBI	SB
92 NL	.267	142	574	71	153	40	3	8	50	23
Life	.255	788	2830	368	722	123	27	53	253	147

	BA	G	AB	R	H	2B	3B	HR	RBI	SB
92 NL	.315	18	73	8	23	3	1	0	2	2
Life	.259	918	3333	407	863	157	38	73	342	133

LENNY DYKSTRA

Position: Outfield
Team: Philadelphia Phillies
Born: February 10, 1963
    Santa Ana, CA
Height: 5'10" **Weight:** 170 lbs.
Bats: Left **Throws:** Left
Acquired: Traded from Mets
    with Roger McDowell and
    Tom Edens for Juan Samuel,
    6/89

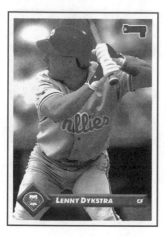 

DAMION EASLEY

Position: Third base
Team: California Angels
Born: November 11, 1969
    New York, NY
Height: 5'11" **Weight:** 155 lbs.
Bats: Right **Throws:** Right
Acquired: 30th-round selection,
    6/88 free-agent draft

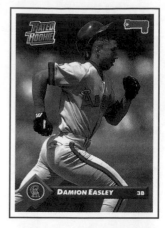

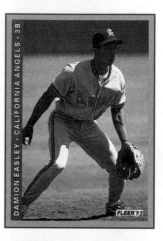 

Lenny Dykstra has worked hard to make himself into one of baseball's best leadoff men. In 1990, he led the NL in batting most of the year before finishing third with a .325 mark. That year, he led the majors with a .418 on-base percentage and tied for the league lead with 192 hits. He slipped to .297 in '91 only because his season was shortened by a May car crash that cost him a 60-day stint on the DL and a broken collarbone that ended his season in late August. Dykstra was back to his old tricks in 1992, however. He hit .301, took 40 walks, and swiped 30 bases. A hustler who's unhappy unless his uniform is dirty from head-first slides, Dykstra drops bunts, hits line drives, beats out infield hits, and rattles the opposition more than any other leadoff man in the NL East.

Dykstra's breakneck pace means he'll likely break something of his in 1993. Skip his nickel-priced issues. Our pick for his best 1993 card is Score. We have chosen this card for the interesting facts included on the reverse.

A position change was all it took for Damion Easley to earn his first trip to the majors in 1992. A full-time shortstop for each of his previous three pro seasons, Easley's hot defense and steady hitting helped him displace veteran third sacker Gary Gaetti in California. Easley was promoted from Triple-A Edmonton on August 12, 1992, when third baseman Rene Gonzalez went on the DL. Easley had a .969 fielding percentage for '92. His quick rise is surprising, considering that the low-round draft pick was chosen directly out of high school. He's expected to add considerable speed to the Halos' lineup, as evidenced by his 20-plus steals in three seasons in a row.

Easley may be a perennial .300 hitter. Although many fans might expect more home runs out of a third baseman, Easley could surprise the baseball world. At a dime apiece, his 1993 cards look like tempting diversions. Our pick for his best 1993 card is Upper Deck. We have chosen this card because of its great combination of photography and design.

	BA	G	AB	R	H	2B	3B	HR	RBI	SB
92 NL	.301	85	345	53	104	18	0	6	39	30
Life	.285	931	3219	533	916	190	28	52	283	220

	BA	G	AB	R	H	2B	3B	HR	RBI	SB
92 AAA	.289	108	429	61	124	18	3	3	44	26
92 AL	.258	47	151	14	39	5	0	1	12	9

Series two cards from some companies were available at press time. If space allows, both cards are shown; if not, the most up-to-date cards are pictured.

DENNIS ECKERSLEY

Position: Pitcher
Team: Oakland Athletics
Born: October 3, 1954
Oakland, CA
Height: 6'2" **Weight:** 195 lbs.
Bats: Right **Throws:** Right
Acquired: Traded from Cubs
with Don Rohn for Dave
Wilder, Brian Guinn, and
Mark Leonette, 4/87

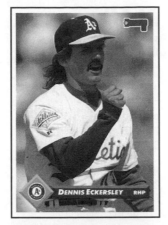

Age is no handicap to Dennis Eckersley. In '92, the 37-year-old closer converted 51 save opportunities for the A's. The '92 Cy Young winner became a full-time reliever in 1987—after the A's acquired his contract from the Cubs. He established solid credentials for Cooperstown only after switching to short relief. Over his five years as Oakland's closer, Eckersley saved at least 43 games four times. In one of those seasons, 1990, he reached a career peak with a 0.61 ERA—the lowest in major league history for anyone with a minimum of 25 innings pitched. That same season, he had more saves (48) than his combined total of hits (41) and walks (4) allowed. A six-time All-Star, Eckersley has compiled 11 saves in 21 postseason games. He was MVP of the 1988 ALCS, when he saved all four games against the Red Sox.

Grab Eckersley's 1993 cards at up to 15 cents apiece. Look for a '78 Topps Eck in the $4 range. Our pick for his best 1993 card is Fleer. We have chosen this card because of its overall appeal and pleasing looks.

	W	L	ERA	G	SV	IP	H	ER	BB	SO
92 AL	7	1	1.91	69	51	80.0	62	17	11	93
Life	181	145	3.43	740	239	2971.1	2747	1133	679	2118

JIM EISENREICH

Position: Outfield/
Designated hitter
Team: Kansas City Royals
Born: April 18, 1959
St. Cloud, MN
Height: 5'11" **Weight:** 195 lbs.
Bats: Left **Throws:** Left
Acquired: Claimed on waivers
by Royals, 10/86

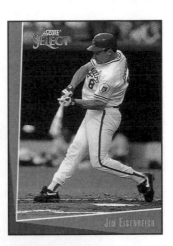

Jim Eisenreich found that a rib cage injury heightened his 1992 problems. Struggling for playing time, Eisenreich's August stint on the DL accentuated his declining value in manager Hal McRae's eyes. He hit .269 with two homers and 28 RBI in '92. Just one year earlier, Eisenreich's totals were two homers, 47 RBI, and a .301 average. In 1989, his first full season with the Royals, Eisenreich batted .293 with nine homers, 59 RBI, and 27 stolen bases. Originally, Eisenreich was a 16th-round selection by Minnesota in the 1980 draft. He debuted with the Twins in 1982, but was out of professional baseball entirely by 1985, due to a case of Tourette's Syndrome. After a two-year absence, Kansas City gave Eisenreich a second life in the majors. While he doesn't demonstrate patience at the plate, he rarely strikes out, usually putting the ball in play.

Eisenreich's career lack of power, and his 1992 fight to keep active casts doubts on his cards. Reject his common-priced 1993s. Our pick for his best 1993 card is Topps. We have chosen this card because the design lends itself to the best use of the elements.

	BA	G	AB	R	H	2B	3B	HR	RBI	SB
92 AL	.269	113	353	31	95	13	3	2	28	11
Life	.277	698	2144	251	594	121	23	25	237	67

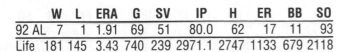

CAL ELDRED

Position: Pitcher
Team: Milwaukee Brewers
Born: November 24, 1967
Cedar Rapids, IA
Height: 6'4" **Weight:** 215 lbs.
Bats: Right **Throws:** Right
Acquired: First-round pick,
6/89 free-agent draft

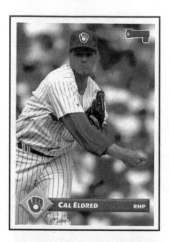

Opening his second season in Triple-A, Cal Eldred ranked among the organization's leaders in wins, strikeouts, and ERA. He went on to pitch 14 games for the big league team and went 11-2 with a 1.79 ERA. All this confirmed his status as one of Milwaukee's top prospects. He won the Ray Scarborough Award as the Brewers' minor league player of the year in 1991. He was named to the *Baseball America* Triple-A All-Star team and was rated the fourth-best prospect in the American Association by that publication. Eldred quickly rose through the ranks to get a taste of the majors. In 1990, he opened the season with Class-A Stockton and pitched a one-hitter. On May 18, 1990 he was promoted to Double-A El Paso, finishing fourth in the league with 7.59 strikeouts per nine innings. In 1991, Eldred led all of Triple-A with 168 strikeouts.

Eldred is hot stuff in the hobby. Spend as much as you can afford. His 1993s could open at 50 cents to $1. Our pick for his best 1993 card is Upper Deck. We have chosen this card because it will increase in value.

	W	L	ERA	G	CG	IP	H	ER	BB	SO
92 AL	11	2	1.79	14	2	100.1	76	20	23	62
Life	13	2	2.17	17	2	116.1	96	28	29	72

ALAN EMBREE

Position: Pitcher
Team: Cleveland Indians
Born: January 23, 1970
Vancouver, WA
Height: 6'2" **Weight:** 185 lbs.
Bats: Left **Throws:** Left
Acquired: Fifth-round pick,
6/89 free-agent draft

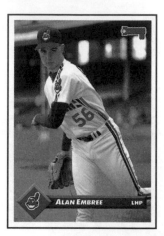

The Indians feel Alan Embree has one of the finest arms in all of the minor leagues. Embree has a scorching fastball, but still has a way to go in his command of the strike zone, in his knowledge of pitching, and in his approach. He did seem to sharpen his control a bit in '92. *Baseball America* called him the top pitching prospect in the Class-A Carolina League last summer. Embree jumped from Class-A to Double-A to Cleveland, and was among the top Cleveland farmhands in wins, ERA, and strikeouts. Embree broke into the pros in '90, and finished eighth in his Rookie-level league with a 2.64 ERA. He got a look at full-season Class-A in '91, and led Columbus with 10 wins, 155 1/3 innings, 137 strikeouts, and three complete games. In his last 12 starts, Embree struck out 80 in 81 innings.

While Embree may indeed join the bigs in '93, his lack of command at this stage should tell you to proceed with caution. Our pick for his best 1993 card is Upper Deck. We have chosen this card for the interesting facts included on the reverse.

	W	L	ERA	G	CG	IP	H	ER	BB	SO
92 AL	0	2	7.00	4	0	18	19	14	8	12
Life	0	2	7.00	4	0	18	19	14	8	12

SCOTT ERICKSON

Position: Pitcher
Team: Minnesota Twins
Born: February 2, 1968
Long Beach, CA
Height: 6'4" **Weight:** 225 lbs.
Bats: Right **Throws:** Right
Acquired: Fourth-round pick,
6/89 free-agent draft

Finishing second in the 1991 Cy Young award voting was a distant memory for Scott Erickson in '92. The righthander became one of the hard-luck Twins in his second full season with the club. Despite his 13-12 record and 3.40 ERA, Erickson lasted more than six innings in half his starts, yielding three runs or less. In 1991, Erickson was an untouchable 20-8, tying for most wins in the majors. His accomplishments came in spite of a two-week stay on the DL for a strained elbow. The righthander first joined Minnesota in mid-1990, after a total of only 27 minor league starts in Class-A and Double-A. His rookie-season total was 8-4 in 17 starts. Before signing with the Twins, Erickson vetoed draft bids from the Blue Jays ('88), Astros ('87), and Mets ('86).

As the Twins improve, so will Erickson. Here's the chance to buy his cards cheaper, while the team has a temporary downswing. Get his 1993s for less than a nickel for a solid investment. Our pick for his best 1993 card is Topps. We have chosen this card for its technical merits.

	W	L	ERA	G	CG	IP	H	ER	BB	SO
92 AL	13	12	3.40	32	5	212.0	197	80	83	101
Life	41	24	3.20	83	11	529.0	494	188	205	262

MONTY FARISS

Position: Infield/outfield
Team: Florida Marlins
Born: October 13, 1967
Cordell, OK
Height: 6'4" **Weight:** 205 lbs.
Bats: Right **Throws:** Right
Acquired: Third-round pick,
11/92 expansion draft

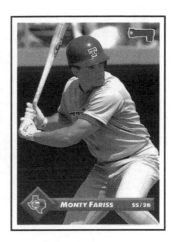

Monty Fariss will establish himself as a big leaguer if he does what he has done at every minor league level, namely, hit. In 67 games for the Texas Rangers in '92, he hit an anemic .217, knocking in 27 RBI. He also struck out 51 times, as compared to only 17 walks. In '93, he'll be attempting to make his mark with the Florida Marlins. Fariss began his pro career with Class-A Butte in '88 and batted .396 in 17 games to earn a promotion to Double-A. He was boosted to Triple-A two years later. There he ranked among American Association leaders in several offensive categories. He also started at second base for the American League squad in the Triple-A All-Star Game. He has played first, second, left field, and DH in the majors, but is not a defensive standout.

Could Fariss handle a full-time job? Until he answers that question, postpone his 1993 cards at a dime each. Our pick for his best 1993 card is Donruss. We have chosen this card due to the outstanding photographic composition.

	BA	G	AB	R	H	2B	3B	HR	RBI	SB
92 AAA	.299	187	28	56	13	3	9	38	31	42
92 AL	.217	67	166	13	36	7	1	3	21	0

Series two cards from some companies were available at press time. If space allows, both cards are shown; if not, the most up-to-date cards are pictured.

STEVE FARR

Position: Pitcher
Team: New York Yankees
Born: December 12, 1956
Cheverly, MD
Height: 5'11" **Weight:** 206 lbs.
Bats: Right **Throws:** Right
Acquired: Signed as a free
agent, 11/90

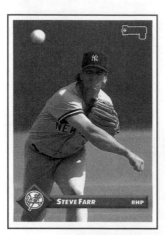

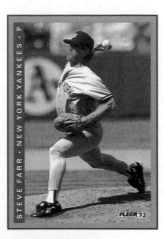

JEFF FASSERO

Position: Pitcher
Team: Montreal Expos
Born: January 5, 1963
Springfield, IL
Height: 6' **Weight:** 195 lbs.
Bats: Left **Throws:** Left
Acquired: Signed as minor
league free agent, 1/91

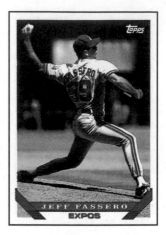

Reliever Steve Farr was better than ever in 1992, registering career highs in saves (30) and numerous other categories. The veteran righthander outdid his 1991 totals, which included 23 saves, a 5-5 record, and a 2.19 ERA. The Yankees have relied on Farr as a closer for two years. He was lured away from the Royals with big bucks. Kansas City replaced Farr as a stopper in 1991. His final season with the Royals consisted of a 1-7 record with one save, and a 1.98 ERA. The Pirates launched Farr's pro career in 1976, signing him as an undrafted free agent. After seven unfruitful seasons in the Pittsburgh minor league system, Farr was swapped to Cleveland. Ironically, the 1984 Indians released him after he went 3-11 with a 4.58 ERA in his rookie season.

Farr is an aging but underrated hurler. Time is against him in hopes of gaining widespread recognition. His 1993 commons are shaky buys. Our pick for his best 1993 card is Fleer. We have chosen this card for the superior presentation of information on its back.

Jeff Fassero stabilized the left side of the Montreal bullpen in 1992, providing the team with surprising relief depth. With a fastball, slider, and forkball as his chief weapons, the lefty exceeded 50 appearances (70) for a second consecutive season with the Expos. In 1991, Fassero was 2-5 with eight saves and a 2.44 ERA in his rookie campaign. During the course of the year, Fassero assembled an impressive streak of 9 1/3 hitless innings. The Illinois native's journey to the majors was a long one. His trip started when he was a 22nd-round draft pick of the Cardinals in 1984. He was drafted off the St. Louis minor league roster in 1989 by the White Sox. After one year, he received his release. Upon moving to Cleveland's Double-A affiliate, Fassero tried relief for the first time in his minor league career.

Without work as a closer, Fassero and his cards will turn invisible. Don't bother with his 1993 commons. Our pick for his best 1993 card is Topps. We have chosen this card due to the outstanding photographic composition.

	W	L	ERA	G	SV	IP	H	ER	BB	SO
92 AL	2	2	1.56	50	30	52.0	34	9	19	37
Life	44	42	3.10	430	103	749.0	666	258	288	609

	W	L	ERA	G	SV	IP	H	ER	BB	SO
92 NL	8	7	2.84	70	1	85.2	81	27	34	63
Life	10	12	2.68	121	9	141.0	120	42	51	105

MIKE FELDER

Position: Outfield
Team: Seattle Mariners
Born: November 18, 1962
  Richmond, CA
Height: 5′8″ **Weight:** 160 lbs.
Bats: Both **Throws:** Right
Acquired: Signed as a free
  agent, 11/92

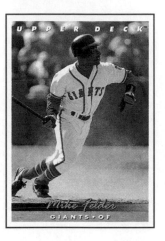

JUNIOR FELIX

Position: Outfield
Team: Florida Marlins
Born: October 3, 1967
  Laguna Sabada,
  Dominican Republic
Height: 5′11″ **Weight:** 165 lbs.
Bats: Both **Throws:** Right
Acquired: Third-round pick,
  11/92 expansion draft

Mike Felder anchored San Francisco's bench again in 1992. He split his time between left and center field. He hit .286 for the '92 season but swiped a lowly four bases. Felder's first—and last—year with the Giants was '91. He was signed by the Giants only one week after being released by the Brewers. In '93, he'll be a new addition to the Mariner team. In his NL debut season, Felder hit .264 with no homers, 18 RBI, and 21 stolen bases. Speed has been Felder's trademark through the years. He began his career as a third-round Milwaukee draft pick in 1981. In 1982, he led his Class-A league with 92 steals. By the time he rode the yo-yo between the majors and Triple-A from 1985-88, Felder had swiped more than 300 bases in the minors.

The man known as "Tiny" will make only a small impact in 1993. At age 30, Felder looks like a platoon player, which isn't enough to make his common-priced cards matter. Our pick for his best 1993 card is Upper Deck. We have chosen this card for its artistic presentation.

Junior Felix drove in the most runs of his four-year career with the 1992 Angels. The center fielder set career bests in games played (139), at bats (509), runs batted in (72), and strikeouts (128). In '93, he'll try to top those numbers again, except he'll be doing it for the Marlins in Florida. He missed six weeks of the '91 campaign due to a strained right calf muscle. So far, Felix hasn't duplicated his 1990 effort of 15 homers. The Blue Jays signed Felix as an 18-year-old free agent, discovered while participating in a track meet. Felix has been reprimanded at several levels for not displaying all-out effort. Prone to streaks of excellence, Felix could be an All-Star with the proper motivation.

Felix is an unpredictable but talented player. Still, his penchant for injuries and his questionable dedication should scare off many investors, even at a nickel per card. Our pick for his best 1993 card is Score. We have chosen this card because the design lends itself to the best use of the elements.

	BA	G	AB	R	H	2B	3B	HR	RBI	SB
92 NL	.286	145	322	44	92	13	3	4	23	14
Life	.257	732	1803	277	464	50	25	13	140	143

	BA	G	AB	R	H	2B	3B	HR	RBI	SB
92 AL	.246	139	509	63	125	22	5	9	72	8
Life	.259	442	1617	230	419	69	22	35	209	46

FELIX FERMIN

Position: Shortstop
Team: Cleveland Indians
Born: October 9, 1963
  Mao Valverde,
  Dominican Republic
Height: 5'11" **Weight:** 170 lbs.
Bats: Right **Throws:** Right
Acquired: Traded from Pirates
  with Denny Gonzales for Jay
  Bell, 3/89

ALEX FERNANDEZ

Position: Pitcher
Team: Chicago White Sox
Born: August 13, 1969
  Miami Beach, FL
Height: 6'1" **Weight:** 205 lbs.
Bats: Right **Throws:** Right
Acquired: First-round pick,
  6/90 free-agent draft

 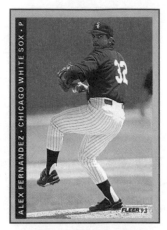

 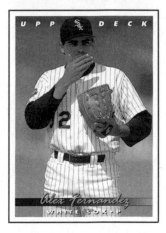

Felix Fermin suffered through a humbling 1992. Although he is a great glove man, he couldn't produce well enough with his bat to retain his starting job with the Cleveland Indians. The talented defensive shortstop lost his job to Mark Lewis. Fermin, however, remained a clubhouse leader who was ready to play when asked. Although he rarely hits homers or steals, Fermin is a contact hitter who is tough to fan. He doesn't walk much either. For his '92 efforts, he earned a .270 average in 215 at-bats. He does bunt and execute the hit-and-run play. He also produces surprisingly well in the clutch for a player who used to be an opposite-field hitter. In '92, he compiled a .326 on-base average and a .321 slugging percentage. On April 22, 1990, he hit a home run, his first in 2,915 professional at-bats. He had a .971 fielding percentage and 36 double plays at shortstop in '92.

Fermin is a solid fielding player. This alone does not a good card choice make. Our pick for his best 1993 card is Donruss. We have chosen this card for its technical merits.

A trip to the minors highlighted the 1992 frustrations of Alex Fernandez. The White Sox pitching prospect was shipped back to Triple-A Vancouver in June. By July 16, he was back in the bigs. He finished the '92 season at 8-11 with a 4.27 ERA. The refresher course seemed worthwhile for the righty, who earned just a month's minor league experience before joining the ChiSox in 1990. Fernandez logged a 9-13 record in his 1991 rookie season with the Pale Hose. The Brewers missed out on signing Fernandez in the first-round of the 1988 draft, when the righty opted for a college career. His choice was fruitful, earning the 1990 Golden Spikes award as the nation's top college player. In turn, Chicago made him the fourth overall selection in the first round of 1990.

Fernandez, even at age 23, is an older and wiser hurler. His nickel-priced cards will triple in value as soon as he nears 20 wins or the White Sox near a pennant. Our pick for his best 1993 card is Fleer. We have chosen this card for the superior presentation of information on its back.

	BA	G	AB	R	H	2B	3B	HR	RBI	SB
92 AL	.270	79	215	27	58	7	2	0	13	0
Life	.255	578	1692	169	431	42	9	1	111	17

	W	L	ERA	G	CG	IP	H	ER	BB	SO
92 AL	8	11	4.27	29	4	187.2	199	89	50	95
Life	22	29	4.28	76	9	467.0	474	222	172	301

Series two cards from some companies were available at press time. If space allows, both cards are shown; if not, the most up-to-date cards are pictured.

SID FERNANDEZ

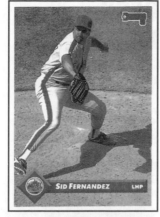

Position: Pitcher
Team: New York Mets
Born: October 12, 1962
    Honolulu, HI
Height: 6'1" **Weight:** 230 lbs.
Bats: Left **Throws:** Left
Acquired: Traded from Dodgers
    with Ross Jones for Bob
    Bailor and Carlos Diaz, 12/83

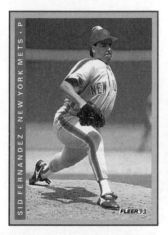

Sid Fernandez escaped a two-year slump, returning to the double-digit (14) winning circle for the fifth time in his career. He also fashioned five complete games and two shutouts. His team-leading win totals were an improvement from 1990, a season that consisted of a 1-3 mark in eight starts. Hit on the wrist in spring training that season, he needed three months to mend the break. Known as "El Sid," the husky lefty was chosen by Los Angeles in the third round of the 1981 draft. This was his first winning season since his 14-5 performance in 1989. In 1986, his 16-6 effort helped the Mets to a World Championship. He's exceeded 180 strikeouts in seven different New York campaigns.

Fernandez may win 10 to 15 games yearly for the next three to five seasons. However, even that output would keep him under 200 career victories, far from the marks needed to boost his common-priced cards. Our pick for his best 1993 card is Upper Deck. We have chosen this card because the design lends itself to the best use of the elements.

	W	L	ERA	G	CG	IP	H	ER	BB	SO
92 NL	14	11	2.73	32	5	214.2	162	65	67	193
Life	93	73	3.17	239	22	1471.0	1092	518	567	1377

TONY FERNANDEZ

Position: Shortstop
Team: New York Mets
Born: August 6, 1962
    San Pedro de Macoris,
    Dominican Republic
Height: 6'2" **Weight:** 175 lbs.
Bats: both **Throws:** right
Acquired: Traded from Padres
    for Wally Whitehurst and
    D.J. Dozier, 10/92

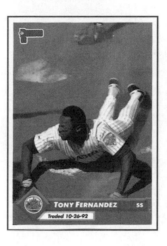

While playing for the Padres in 1992, Tony Fernandez hit .275 with 32 doubles. Although he walked 56 times, he also struck out 62 times. His base stealing efforts were 50-50, with 20 successful swipes in 40 attempts. In '93, he'll try to impress his new teammates in the Big Apple by bettering those stats all around. The switch-hitting shortstop has had at least 20 steals in six of the last seven seasons. He had career peaks with a .322 average and 32 steals for Toronto in 1987 and 17 triples for the Jays two years later. He also won four Gold Gloves in a row during his Toronto tenure. In 1991, his first year in the NL, he placed second at his position in putouts, assists, and total chances while tying for second in double plays.

Fernandez is consistent but unspectacular. Now that he is in New York, however, his cards could boom. His second-year '85 Donruss is great at 75 cents or less. Our pick for his best 1993 card is Score. We have chosen this card since its design makes it a standout.

	BA	G	AB	R	H	2B	3B	HR	RBI	SB
92 NL	.275	155	622	84	171	32	4	4	37	20
Life	.285	1328	5132	675	1465	251	70	48	479	181

MIKE FETTERS

Position: Pitcher
Team: Milwaukee Brewers
Born: December 19, 1964
　　Van Nuys, CA
Height: 6'4" **Weight:** 212 lbs.
Bats: Right **Throws:** Right
Acquired: Traded from Angels
　　with Glenn Carter for Chuck
　　Crim, 12/91

 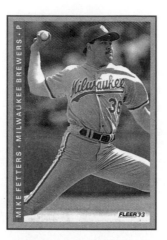

Switching teams gave Mike Fetters a new lease on his major league life. He joined the 1992 Brewers bullpen and revitalized his career. By the end of the '92 season, Fetters owned a 1.87 ERA, a dramatic reduction from his pre-1992 career average (4.51). He became a terror to righthanded batters—they hit a meager .164 against him—but all hitters struggled to top .200 when he was on the case. He relieved in 50 games for the Brew Crew in '92 as well. From 1989 through '91, Fetters had divided his time between Triple-A Edmonton and California. While he made only six starts in 46 career appearances with the Angels, Fetters worked as a starter in virtually all of his six minor league seasons. A high school basketball star, Fetters was chosen in the first round of the 1986 draft after playing college ball at Pepperdine.

Fetters can be applauded for his 1993 efforts. That acclaim is unlikely to translate into higher values for his common-priced cards, though. Our pick for his best 1993 card is Score. We have chosen this card due to the outstanding photographic composition.

	W	L	ERA	G	SV	IP	H	ER	BB	SO
92 AL	5	1	1.87	50	2	62.2	38	13	24	43
Life	8	7	3.58	96	3	178.1	173	71	73	106

CECIL FIELDER

Position: First base
Team: Detroit Tigers
Born: September 21, 1963
　　Los Angeles, CA
Height: 6'3" **Weight:** 230 lbs.
Bats: Right **Throws:** Right
Acquired: Signed as a free
　　agent, 1/90

Cecil Fielder does not look like a baseball star. But don't tell that to AL pitchers. In 1990, his first year as a big league regular, he had 51 homers and 132 RBI. In '91, he homered "only" 44 times but knocked in 133 runs. That placed Fielder in exclusive company. The only other players ever to lead the majors in homers and RBI two years in a row were Babe Ruth and Jimmie Foxx. Fielder's big league career actually began in '85, when he was a part-time player with the Blue Jays. In four Toronto seasons, however, he never appeared in more than 82 games. Given a chance to play regularly in Japan, the burly first baseman hit 38 homers for the Hanshin Tigers in 1989. Detroit decided to take a chance on him. Fielder responded by becoming the first player to crash the 50-homer barrier since George Foster in '77.

Even 25 cents each is reasonable for Cecil's '93 cards. While his 1990 cards could make small gains, his rookies are stalled in the $20-25 horizon. Our pick for his best 1993 card is Score. We have chosen this card for its artistic presentation.

	BA	G	AB	R	H	2B	3B	HR	RBI	SB
92 AL	.244	155	594	80	145	22	0	35	124	0
Life	.257	696	2297	353	590	91	3	161	473	0

CHUCK FINLEY

Position: Pitcher
Team: California Angels
Born: November 26, 1962
Monroe, LA
Height: 6′6″ **Weight:** 214 lbs.
Bats: Left **Throws:** Left
Acquired: 15th-round pick,
6/84 free-agent draft

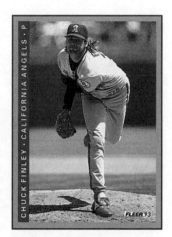

STEVE FINLEY

Position: Outfield
Team: Houston Astros
Born: March 12, 1965
Union City, TN
Height: 6′2″ **Weight:** 180 lbs.
Bats: Left **Throws:** Left
Acquired: Traded from Orioles
with Pete Harnisch and Curt
Schilling for Glenn Davis,
1/91

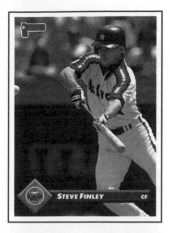

Pitcher Chuck Finley's season went from bad to worse in 1992. A toe injury delayed the start of his season. By the end of the '92 season, he had fallen to a 7-12 record and a 3.96 ERA. Lefthanded batters had a field day with Finley, hitting him at a .402 clip. Nonetheless, the lanky hurler exceeded 190 innings (204 ⅓) for the fifth consecutive season. Finley first found success with the Angels in 1989. That year, he won an All-Star berth with a remarkable turnaround. His 1988 totals of 9-15 with a 4.17 ERA turned into 16-9, a 2.57 ERA, and nine complete games. He improved to 18-9 in 1990, earning another All-Star spot. Although he repeated his 18-9 performance again in 1991, Finley's ERA climbed from 2.40 to 3.80.

Let Finley mend a season before considering his common-priced cards. He made a momentous rebound in 1989. Perhaps his best performances are sparked during odd-numbered years. Our pick for his best 1993 card is Upper Deck. We have chosen this card because it has a distinctive look.

In 1991, his first year with the Houston Astros, Steve Finley found that he liked the running game and artificial surfaces of the NL. Deployed as the center fielder and leadoff man, Finley finished third in the league with 10 triples, tied Jeff Bagwell for club leadership with 242 total bases, and collected 170 hits. He stole 17 bases in 81 games as a rookie but doubled his steal total when he reached career highs with a .285 average, eight homers, and 54 RBI for the '91 Astros. He continued to produce as Houston's No. 2 hitter in '92. He ranked second in the circuit with 13 triples and tied for third with 44 stolen bases. Finley, who once had trouble against lefties, began to pepper southpaws more regularly (.279 LHP, .299 RHP). A former standout at SIU, he began his pro career in '87 and reached Baltimore two years later.

Finley's above-average offense can't fuel his nickel card prices. Our pick for his best 1993 card is Topps. We have chosen this card because of its great combination of photography and design.

	W	L	ERA	G	SV	IP	H	ER	BB	SO
92 AL	7	12	3.96	31	4	204.1	212	90	98	124
Life	73	62	3.45	217	26	1198.2	1131	460	510	839

	BA	G	AB	R	H	2B	3B	HR	RBI	SB
92 NL	.292	162	607	84	177	29	13	5	55	44
Life	.276	544	1884	249	520	78	29	18	171	117

CARLTON FISK

Position: Catcher
Team: Chicago White Sox
Born: December 26, 1947
Bellows Falls, VT
Height: 6'2" **Weight:** 225 lbs.
Bats: Right **Throws:** Right
Acquired: Signed as a free
agent, 3/81

Carlton Fisk was saddled by injuries throughout '92, as he tried to add new pages to his record book. Going into '93, Fisk needs 25 games to break Bob Boone's all-time record of games caught (2,225). Already, Fisk holds records for most home runs by any catcher, and most homers hit by players over age 40. An 11-time All-Star, Fisk has played in four different decades. He played his first two games with the 1969 Red Sox. A Chicago institution since 1981, Fisk's personal bests of 37 homers and 107 RBI came with the 1985 White Sox. The Hall of Fame should welcome Fisk during his first year of eligibility.

Even at age 45, it's likely that Fisk will try for a last hurrah in 1993. This could produce the last-ever cards of Pudge as an active player, offering investors bargains at five to 10 cents apiece. For under $3, you can buy a pair of Fisks in the '82 Topps set. His regular in-action cards (#110-111) are wise buys. Our pick for his best 1993 card is Score. We have chosen this card since the photograph captures the athletic ability of the player.

	BA	G	AB	R	H	2B	3B	HR	RBI	SB
92 AL	.229	62	188	12	43	4	1	3	21	3
Life	.270	2474	8703	1274	2346	421	47	375	1326	128

JOHN FLAHERTY

Position: Catcher
Team: Boston Red Sox
Born: October 21, 1967
New York, NY
Height: 6'1" **Weight:** 195 lbs.
Bats: Right **Throws:** Right
Acquired: 25th-round pick,
6/88 free-agent draft

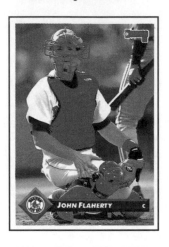

John Flaherty came a long way to keep a date with history. Taken in a low round, Flaherty climbed to the big leagues just in time to catch eight hitless innings by Matt Young in a game that does not qualify as a no-hitter. Flaherty now hopes to forge a career that will be more than a footnote. To do so, he will either have to show exceptional defensive skills or upgrade his offense. He hasn't shown much run production on his ascent through the minors; his career highs are six homers in '91 and 33 RBI in '90. He enjoyed one of his best seasons in '89, batting .260 for Class-A Winter Haven and making the league All-Star Team. He reached Triple-A in 1990. Flaherty opened the '92 season with the Red Sox and got valuable experience as a backup to Tony Pena. In his 35 games in '92, he accrued just 13 hits in 66 at-bats. His 195 ⅓ innings of work provided good exposure for the '93 season.

Unless he starts, Flaherty's cards can't top a nickel each. Our pick for his best 1993 card is Donruss. We have chosen this card for its artistic presentation.

	BA	G	AB	R	H	2B	3B	HR	RBI	SB
92 AAA	.250	104	11	26	3	0	9	25	17	53
92 NL	.197	35	66	3	13	2	0	0	2	1

DAVE FLEMING

Position: Pitcher
Team: Seattle Mariners
Born: November 7, 1969
  Queens, NY
Height: 6'3" **Weight:** 200 lbs.
Bats: Left **Throws:** Left
Acquired: Third-round pick,
  6/90 free-agent

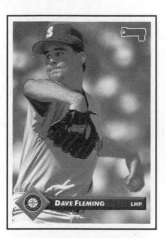 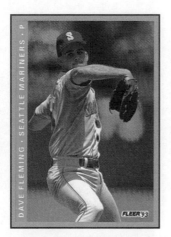

Dave Fleming was born not far from Shea Stadium less than a month after the Mets won their miracle world title. Some 22 years later, Fleming put together quite a year himself. When not much else was going right for the Mariners' pitchers, Fleming got off to one of the best starts in club history. Only Floyd Bannister won seven games as a Mariner more quickly than did Fleming. His walks (60) and strikeouts (112) don't blow you away, but he has a knack for victory (17-10). He keeps the ball in the park—not always easy in the Kingdome—and handles lefties. Fleming attended the University of Georgia, saving the title game of the 1990 College World Series. From there he went to pro ball, going 7-3 in 12 starts in Class-A. In '91, Fleming went from Double-A to the majors. He got the call while in an airport making a connection.

Spend all you can on Fleming cards. A quarter apiece would be a bargain investment. Our pick for his best 1993 card is Upper Deck. We have chosen this card due to the outstanding photographic composition.

	W	L	ERA	G	CG	IP	H	ER	BB	SO
92 AL	17	10	3.39	33	7	228.1	225	86	60	112
Life	18	10	3.62	42	7	246.0	244	99	63	123

SCOTT FLETCHER

Position: Second base
Team: Boston Red Sox
Born: July 30, 1958
  Fort Walton Beach, FL
Height: 5'11" **Weight:** 173 lbs.
Bats: Right **Throws:** Right
Acquired: Signed as a free
  agent, 12/92

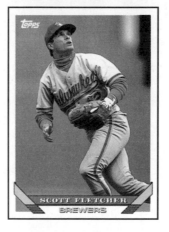

In 1992 Scott Fletcher became the latest veteran to head out of Milwaukee's revolving second-base door. After Willie Randolph abandoned the Brewers, they turned to Fletcher, an ignored free agent after being shunned by the White Sox. He hit .275 and knocked in 51 RBI in '92. In '93, he'll be working for the Red Sox. The ChiSox employed Fletcher from 1983-85. Swapped to Texas, he served as a Rangers regular in 1986-88. He batted a career-high .300 in 1986, then grew to personal bests of five homers and 63 RBI in 1987. The White Sox reacquired Fletcher in mid-89 but grew weary of his infrequent offense after a .206 disappointment in 1991. Fletcher turned down draft offers from the Dodgers, A's, and Astros before signing with the Cubs in '79.

Fletcher was one of 1992's top comeback players. Yet, this over-30 journeyman needs more than one improved season to redeem his unwanted common-priced cards. Our pick for his best 1993 card is Score. We have chosen this card since the photograph captures the athletic ability of the player.

	BA	G	AB	R	H	2B	3B	HR	RBI	SB
92 AL	.275	123	386	53	106	18	3	3	51	17
Life	.262	1361	4411	557	1155	193	31	25	437	74

TIM FORTUGNO

Position: Pitcher
Team: California Angels
Born: April 11, 1962
Clinton, MA
Height: 6'1" **Weight:** 195 lbs.
Bats: Left **Throws:** Left
Acquired: Drafted from
Brewers, 12/91

After six seasons of minor league travel, Tim Fortugno found a big league home in 1992. Drafted off the Milwaukee minor league roster following the '91 campaign, Fortugno began the '92 season in the Triple-A Pacific Coast League. Along with being a 30-year-old rookie, one of Fortugno's most dubious experiences of '92 was yielding George Brett's 3,000th career hit. Fortugno's career nearly died in '89. After turning down draft bids by the Athletics and Indians, he signed as a free-agent with the Mariners. Following a trade to the Philadelphia organization in '87, he received an unconditional preseason release from the Phillies in '89. Only by signing with an independent, unaffiliated Class-A team did Fortugno survive, benefitting by a sale to the Brewer organization after 18 games.

As one of baseball's oldest newcomers in 1993, Fortugno totes an extra burden. Varied bullpen chores won't boost his card values. Our pick for his best 1993 card is Topps. We have chosen this card because of its overall appeal and pleasing looks.

	W	L	ERA	G	SV	IP	H	ER	BB	SO
92 AL	1	1	5.18	14	1	41.2	37	24	19	31
Life	1	1	5.18	14	1	41.2	37	24	19	31

TONY FOSSAS

Position: Pitcher
Team: Boston Red Sox
Born: September 23, 1957
Havana, Cuba
Height: 6' **Weight:** 187 lbs.
Bats: Left **Throws:** Left
Acquired: Signed as a free
agent, 1/91

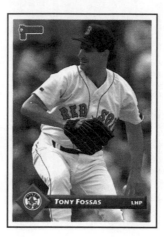
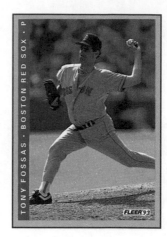

Reliever Tony Fossas was one of the few Red Sox with respectable stats in 1992. He served in 60 games for the '92 BoSox and earned a 2.43 ERA in the process. Boston acquired Fossas after he was released by the Brewers following the 1991 season. The Cuban-born hurler owned a career 4.12 ERA before the '92 season. While righthanders teed off on Fossas (.345), he kept his job by bedeviling lefties (.214). Sometimes, he'd be called upon to obtain even one difficult out against a lefty slugger. Before joining Boston in '91, Fossas had been released by three different organizations—the Rangers ('82), Cubs ('82, after less than a month), and Brewers ('90). He premiered with the '88 Rangers and appeared with Milwaukee for parts of '89 and '90.

Because of his low-profile relief work, Fossas can't accumulate the stats or recognition needed to fuel his common-priced cards. Our pick for his best 1993 card is Fleer. We have chosen this card because it has a distinctive look.

	W	L	ERA	G	SV	IP	H	ER	BB	SO
92 AL	1	2	2.43	60	2	29.2	31	8	14	19
Life	8	9	3.84	212	4	182.2	192	78	76	114

STEVE
FOSTER

Position: Pitcher
Team: Cincinnati Reds
Born: August 16, 1966
　Dallas, TX
Height: 6′ **Weight:** 180 lbs.
Bats: Right **Throws:** Right
Acquired: 12th-round pick,
　6/88 free-agent draft

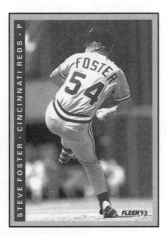

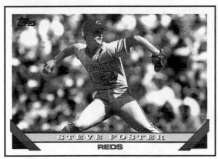

ERIC
FOX

Position: Outfield
Team: Oakland Athletics
Born: August 15, 1963
　LeMoore, CA
Height: 5′10″ **Weight:** 180 lbs.
Bats: Both **Throws:** Left
Acquired: Signed as minor
　league free agent, 3/89

Steve Foster had a stretch he would rather forget early in the 1992 season. Pitching in five games for the Reds, Foster did exactly what he had avoided for much of his climb through the minors—he allowed lots of baserunners and runs. After going 1-1 with a 2.88 ERA and 2 saves, he was optioned back to Nashville and resumed his usual sharpness. He even started for the first time in his pro career. Foster's future, however, still depends on his skill coming out of the bullpen. He collected three consecutive years of 20 or more saves but may shape up as more of a middle man for the Reds. He has always shown good control, beginning with his first major league stop in Billings in 1988. Entering the 1992 season, Foster owned 215 strikeouts in 232 ⅔ innings. Foster made his major league debut on August 22, 1991, with two scoreless innings against Atlanta.

　Foster's a marginal buy at a nickel each. Our pick for his best 1993 card is Fleer. We have chosen this card for the superior presentation of information on its back.

Eric Fox took an odd route to his 1992 major league debut with the A's. Called up July 7 when Rickey Henderson was injured, Fox was promoted from Double-A Huntsville. He had been sent down after beginning the year with a .192 mark at Triple-A Tacoma. Sent back to the Pacific Coast League on August 13, he was recalled two weeks later to be eligible for postseason play. He hit .238 in 51 games for the A's in '92. Originally a first-round draft choice of the Mariners in '86, Fox was released by the M's during '89 spring training. He signed an immediate contract with Double-A Huntsville, the beginning of his rebirth in the A's organization. His 1989 stats included 15 homers and 49 stolen bases.

　If the payroll-cutting A's bid several free agents goodbye, Fox could see an entire season's work with the 1993 Athletics. Wait to see his '93 status before speculating on his nickel- to dime-priced cards. Our pick for his best 1993 card is Score. We have chosen this card since the photograph captures the athletic ability of the player.

	W	L	ERA	G	SV	IP	H	ER	BB	SO
92 NL	1	1	2.88	42	2	50	52	16	13	34
92 AA	5	3	2.68	17	1	50.1	53	15	22	28

	BA	G	AB	R	H	2B	3B	HR	RBI	SB
92 AAA	.271	59	240	42	65	16	2	5	14	16
92 AL	.238	51	143	24	34	5	2	3	13	3

JOHN FRANCO

Position: Pitcher
Team: New York Mets
Born: September 17, 1960
Brooklyn, NY
Height: 5'10" **Weight:** 185 lbs.
Bats: Left **Throws:** Left
Acquired: Traded from Reds
with Don Brown for Kip
Gross and Randy Myers,
12/89

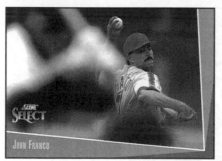

JULIO FRANCO

Position: Second base
Team: Texas Rangers
Born: August 23, 1961
San Pedro de Macoris,
Dominican Republic
Height: 6'1" **Weight:** 185 lbs.
Bats: Right **Throws:** Right
Acquired: Traded from Indians
for Jerry Browne, Pete
O'Brien, and Oddibe
McDowell, 12/88

John Franco is one of the most consistent relief pitchers in baseball. He had five 30-save seasons in a row from 1987-91 and showed he was still at the top of his game in 1992. Franco went 6-2 with a 1.64 ERA and 15 saves in '92. In his best season, Franco posted a 6-6 record, 39 saves, and a 1.57 ERA for the '88 Reds. The little lefty also led the NL in saves two years later, posting 33. Franco was a fifth-round draft choice of the Dodgers in 1981. He broke into pro ball that summer but was traded to the Cincinnati system two years later. Franco, who had been used as a starter in the minors, reached the Reds in 1984. He had been used exclusively as a reliever in all 500 of his big league appearances through 1991. At 32, Franco still has plenty of time to join the elite corps of closers with 300 career saves.

Wait and see what he does this next season before investing too heavily in Franco's '93s. Our pick for his best 1993 card is Score. We have chosen this card due to its unique photographic approach.

After winning the AL batting title with a career-best .341 average for the '91 Rangers, Julio Franco ran into a series of ailments that plagued him through much of the 1992 campaign. The toughest was a sore right knee that first sent him to the DL, then reduced him from regular second baseman to DH. It was an arrangement Franco didn't like. In 1991, he publicly complained when fans voting for the All-Star starting lineups chose him second to Toronto's Robby Alomar. Though selected to the AL squad for the third time that year, Franco did not appear in the game—perhaps because his carping had upset manager Tony LaRussa. Franco vented his frustration on AL pitchers, finishing with the best batting average in the history of the Rangers. He also became the first American Leaguer since Paul Molitor in '82 to finish with at least 100 runs scored, 200 hits, and 30 swipes.

Let Franco mend before viewing his '93s realistically. Our pick for his best 1993 card is Score. We have chosen this card because of its overall appeal and pleasing looks.

	W	L	ERA	G	SV	IP	H	ER	BB	SO
92 NL	6	2	1.64	31	15	33.0	24	6	11	20
Life	58	44	2.49	531	226	684.0	611	189	260	488

	BA	G	AB	R	H	2B	3B	HR	RBI	SB
92 AL	.234	35	107	19	25	7	0	2	8	1
Life	.301	1402	5416	807	1630	249	40	86	679	220

Series two cards from some companies were available at press time. If space allows, both cards are shown; if not, the most up-to-date cards are pictured.

TODD FROHWIRTH

Position: Pitcher
Team: Baltimore Orioles
Born: September 28, 1962
    Milwaukee, WI
Height: 6'4" **Weight:** 205 lbs.
Bats: Right **Throws:** Right
Acquired: Signed as a free
    agent, 12/90

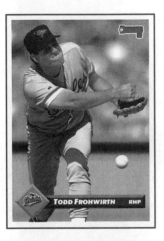 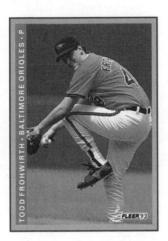

Todd Frohwirth proved to be more than a one-year wonder with the 1992 Orioles. The herky-jerky righty was Baltimore's biggest surprise in '91, going 7-3 with three saves, and a 1.87 ERA in 51 appearances. In '92, he remained effective despite an increased workload. He went 4-3 with a 2.46 ERA with four saves. For only the second time in nine years, he exceeded 60 games (65). Frohwirth dazzled the Phillies in his '87 big league premiere. In 10 appearances that season, he was 1-0 with 11 scoreless innings. Frohwirth has remained a fun pitcher to watch. His sidearm and submarine motions resemble the pitching style of relief great Dan Quisenberry. His three pitches of choice are a fastball, changeup, and a combined slider/curve dubbed a "slurve."

Frohwirth isn't getting substantial attention for his middle-relief successes. Unless he gains an all-star berth soon, his 1993 commons will be hopeless investments. Our pick for his best 1993 card is Upper Deck. We have chosen this card for its artistic presentation.

	W	L	ERA	G	SV	IP	H	ER	BB	SO
92 AL	4	3	2.46	65	4	106.0	97	29	41	58
Life	14	9	2.71	188	7	289.0	248	87	107	195

JEFF FRYE

Position: Second base
Team: Texas Rangers
Born: August 31, 1966
    Oakland, CA
Height: 5'9" **Weight:** 165 lbs.
Bats: Right **Throws:** Right
Acquired: 30th-round pick,
    6/88 free-agent draft

 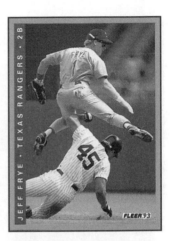

Rookie Jeff Frye was one of a platoon of fill-in second basemen for the 1992 Rangers. He shared the position with Al Newman and former teammate Monty Fariss. He started the season in Triple-A Oklahoma City, but was promoted on July 9. In his debut that day against Cleveland, he scored three runs, tripled, and drove in a run. In his 67 games for the Rangers in '92, he hit .256 and garnered 51 hits. Frye's first full season in pro ball came in 1989. His .313 average with Class-A Gastonia led the South Atlantic League. In two of his first four seasons in the minors, Frye won two league fielding titles.

Rumor has it that Texas could move Franco to the outfield, even if he's healthy in 1993. Therefore, the Rangers' second sacker job could remain open. Frye needs to do more at the plate before convincing the team he can be a full-timer. For now, pass on his cards, slated to start at 10 to 15 cents each. Our pick for his best 1993 card is Upper Deck. We have chosen this card due to its unique photographic approach.

	BA	G	AB	R	H	2B	3B	HR	RBI	SB
92 AAA	.300	87	337	64	101	26	2	2	28	11
92 AL	.256	67	199	24	51	9	1	1	12	1

TRAVIS FRYMAN

Position: Shortstop
Team: Detroit Tigers
Born: April 25, 1969
 Lexington, KY
Height: 6'1" **Weight:** 180 lbs.
Bats: Right **Throws:** Right
Acquired: First-round
 supplemental pick, 6/87 free-
 agent draft

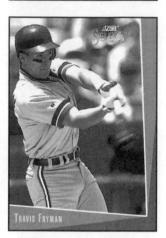

Travis Fryman staked his claim with another offensive sideshow in 1992. With incumbent shortstop Alan Trammell out with injuries, Fryman handled his natural position throughout the season. He hit .266 with 20 homers and knocked in 96 RBI in '92. In '91, despite no experience at third, Fryman roamed the hot corner to remain a full-time player. A foreign position didn't influence him offensively, as proven by his 21 home runs and 91 RBI. Fryman's slugging developed quickly. In four minor league seasons, his highest yearly totals were 10 homers and 56 RBI. Fryman was snatched up in '87, using a supplemental draft pick acquired in exchange for losing free-agent catcher Lance Parrish.

Consider it a bargain investment if you find Fryman's 1993 cards at a dime apiece. This power-hitting shortstop could be the next incarnation of Cal Ripken. For less than 50 cents, you may be able to sneak away with a Fryman rookie. Our pick for his best 1993 card is Donruss. We have chosen this card since the photograph captures the athletic ability of the player.

	BA	G	AB	R	H	2B	3B	HR	RBI	SB
92 AL	.266	161	659	87	175	31	4	20	96	8
Life	.268	376	1448	184	388	78	8	50	214	23

GARY GAETTI

Position: Third base
Team: California Angels
Born: August 19, 1958
 Centralia, IL
Height: 6' **Weight:** 200 lbs.
Bats: Right **Throws:** Right
Acquired: Signed as a free
 agent, 1/91

Gary Gaetti fell from grace with the Angels in 1992. He went into the last month of the season as a backup at third base, first base, and designated hitter. Although he was the first '92 Angel to break double digits in homers (12), Gaetti's dwindling batting average (.226) was a cause for concern. The Angels inked Gaetti to a four-year free-agent contract (estimated to be worth more than $11 million) before the 1991 season. During a nine-year reign with the Minnesota Twins, Gaetti was a third base standout, winning four Gold Gloves and two All-Star spots. He belted 201 homers there, including two consecutive years of 30-plus dingers. While the team feels the need to get their money's worth out of Gaetti for 1993, the Angels may be seeing fewer dividends on their investment.

Gaetti's career may have taken a permanent plunge in 1992. As a platoon player, his common-priced cards will spook investors. Our pick for his best 1993 card is Topps. We have chosen this card because it has a distinctive look.

	BA	G	AB	R	H	2B	3B	HR	RBI	SB
92 AL	.226	130	456	41	103	13	2	12	48	3
Life	.253	1643	6031	745	1523	287	28	231	872	82

Series two cards from some companies were available at press time. If space allows, both cards are shown; if not, the most up-to-date cards are pictured.

GREG GAGNE

Position: Shortstop
Team: Kansas City Royals
Born: November 12, 1961
   Fall River, MA
Height: 5'11" **Weight:** 172 lbs.
Bats: Right **Throws:** Right
Acquired: Signed as a free-
   agent, 12/92

 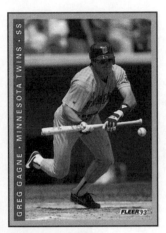

ANDRES GALARRAGA

Position: First base
Team: Colorado Rockies
Born: June 18, 1961
   Caracas, Venezuela
Height: 6'3" **Weight:** 235 lbs.
Bats: Right **Throws:** Right
Acquired: Signed as a free-
   agent, 11/92

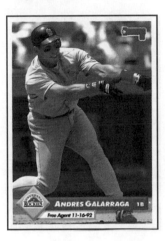 

Greg Gagne's eighth season as the Twins' shortstop wasn't that much different from the first seven—except that it was his last one in Minnesota. The KC free-agent signee hit .246 with 23 doubles and knocked in 35 runs for the Twins in '92. A Twins regular since '85, Gagne's career bests include 14 home runs (in '88) and 54 RBI (in '86). Nicknamed "Gags," he was one of the team's most consistent players. Hitting lower in the batting order, Gagne's slick defense makes up for his modest offense. Since a '85 back sprain held him out of the lineup nearly a month, Gagne has been worth at least 135 games per year. Although he was the Yankees' fourth choice in the '79 draft, Gagne never advanced beyond Class-A. His debut with the Twins came in '83.

   Gagne's respectable but unspectacular career is reflected in his common-priced cards. Now into his 30s, Gagne isn't a good choice for investors. Our pick for his best 1993 card is Fleer. We have chosen this card for its technical merits.

Andres "Big Cat" Galarraga was a small addition to the 1992 Cardinals. He hopes to have more of an impact with the Rockies in their inaugural year. The once-awesome slugger played in only 95 games for the Cards in '92. His .243 batting average, 10 homers, and 39 RBI, however, were an improvement on his '91 season, when he tallied nine homers, 33 RBI, and a .219 average in 107 games. From 1988 through '90, Galarraga was the cornerstone of Montreal's offense, surpassing 20 homers and 80 RBI yearly. Both in 1987 and '88, Galarraga's average topped .300. His career highs include 29 round-trippers and 92 RBI (in 1988). Yet, the first baseman has never been a flawless hitter. In 1988-90, he was the NL leader in strikeouts.

   Galarraga's future may very well depend on his performance for the Rockies in the '93 season. Now is the worst time to be considering his common-priced cards. Our pick for his best 1993 card is Topps. We have chosen this card because of its great combination of photography and design.

	BA	G	AB	R	H	2B	3B	HR	RBI	SB
92 AL	.246	146	439	53	108	23	0	7	39	6
Life	.249	1140	3386	452	844	183	35	69	335	79

	BA	G	AB	R	H	2B	3B	HR	RBI	SB
92 NL	.243	95	325	38	79	14	2	10	39	5
Life	.267	942	3407	432	909	182	16	116	472	59

MIKE GALLEGO

Position: Infield
Team: New York Yankees
Born: October 31, 1960
   Whittier, CA
Height: 5'8" **Weight:** 160 lbs.
Bats: Right **Throws:** Right
Acquired: Signed as a free
   agent, 1/92

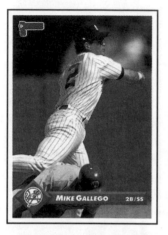

Mike Gallego became a free-agent fiasco with the 1992 Yankees. Although he hit a blistering .422 in spring training, Gallego's woes included a bruised heel in April and a broken wrist in June. Playing in only 53 games, he did manage a .254 batting average. The Yankees amazed the baseball world by signing Gallego to a hefty free-agent deal through '94. He won big bucks based on his 1991 stats with Oakland, including career highs of 12 homers, 49 RBI and a .247 average. Nevertheless, he began 1992 with a lifetime .232 average. The A's landed Gallego in the '81 draft, choosing him after a three-year career playing for UCLA. In college, his famous teammates included Don Slaught, Tim Leary, and Matt Young. Gallego may be paid like a famous starter for 1993, but that doesn't eliminate his utilityman's limitations.

Selling Gallego's cards might be harder than pronouncing his name in 1993. Even if you're a linguist, stay away from his commons. Our pick for his best 1993 card is Topps. We have chosen this card due to the outstanding photographic composition.

	BA	G	AB	R	H	2B	3B	HR	RBI	SB
92 AL	.254	53	173	24	44	7	1	3	14	0
Life	.234	782	1916	243	448	70	10	26	174	21

RON GANT

Position: Outfield
Team: Atlanta Braves
Born: March 2, 1965
   Victoria, TX
Height: 6' **Weight:** 172 lbs.
Bats: Right **Throws:** Right
Acquired: Fourth-round pick,
   6/83 free-agent draft

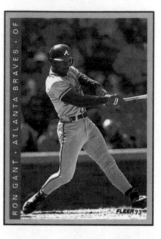

In 1992, Ron Gant fell short in his quest for a third consecutive 30/30 season. Before his second 30/30 notch in '91, only Willie Mays and Bobby Bonds had compiled consecutive marks in the majors. Unfortunately, Gant's homer total in '92 reached only 17, but he still hit .259 for the season. Gant, a good-hit, no-field second baseman as a 1988 rookie, proved more of a defensive disaster at third before finding his niche in the outfield. Stationed in center, he was 1990 Comeback Player of the Year. However, he still failed to make an All-Star squad before 1992. That changed when Gant's average began to rise. He started to go with the individual pitch instead of trying to pull every ball. As his average climbed, so did his recognition.

Pay attention to Gant's slump. Expect his 1993 cards at under a dime. If the '88 Donruss Gant rookie drops below $3, investors will go wild. Our pick for his best 1993 card is Donruss. We have chosen this card because it has a distinctive look.

	BA	G	AB	R	H	2B	3B	HR	RBI	SB
92 NL	.259	153	544	74	141	22	6	17	80	32
Life	.259	701	2586	402	670	131	23	111	363	131

Series two cards from some companies were available at press time. If space allows, both cards are shown; if not, the most up-to-date cards are pictured.

CARLOS GARCIA

Position: Infield
Team: Pittsburgh Pirates
Born: October 15, 1967
Tachira, Venezuela
Height: 6'1" **Weight:** 185 lbs.
Bats: Right **Throws:** Right
Acquired: Signed as a non-
drafted free agent, 1/87

Carlos Garcia owns a nice mixture of skills, including the punch that is part of the Pirate tradition and the speed for the artificial surface at Three Rivers Stadium. In '92, he got his third—and earliest—taste of the majors in as many years. Much of the campaign, however, was spent with Triple-A Buffalo, where he hit for average, stole bases, and added some extra-base pop. After laboring low in the minors for two years, his career began taking off in '89. He was named Player of the Month for both May and June at Class-A Salem, then received a promotion to Double-A Harrisburg. The next season was even better, as Garcia was picked to play in the Eastern League All-Star Game, was boosted to Buffalo, and finally got a call to the majors. Garcia spent most of '91 in Triple-A, then got his second shot at the bigs.

He was hot at Triple-A. Put away his '93s at a dime apiece, especially if he starts at second for the Bucs in '93. Our pick for his best 1993 card is Score. We have chosen this card due to the outstanding photographic composition.

	BA	G	AB	R	H	2B	3B	HR	RBI	SB
92 NL	.205	22	39	4	8	1	0	0	4	0
Life	.239	38	67	7	16	1	2	0	5	0

MIKE GARDINER

Position: Pitcher
Team: Montreal Expos
Born: October 19, 1965
Sarnia, Ontario, Canada
Height: 6' **Weight:** 200 lbs.
Bats: Both **Throws:** Right
Acquired: Traded from Red Sox
with Terry Powers for Ivan
Calderon, 12/92

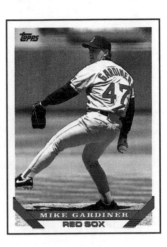

Mike Gardiner's losing record (4-10) with the '92 Red Sox was deceptive. Although he wasn't fooling many hitters, he received just over three runs per game in support from his teammates. He hopes to get more support with Montreal in '93. Gardiner kept his ERA (4.75) lower than in '91, when he was 9-10 with a 4.85 ERA. He debuted with the M's in '90, but was 0-2 in five games. The righty was drafted by Seattle in '87. The Canadian moundsman attended Indiana State University and, before starting his professional career, was a member of Canada's 1984 Olympic baseball team. Despite being one of baseball's few switch-hitting pitchers, Gardiner's possible offensive skills were limited by the designated hitter rule.

Gardiner has faced two straight losing seasons with Boston. For his career, assume that three flops and he's out. Don't bank on his 1993 common-priced cards. Our pick for his best 1993 card is Topps. We have chosen this card because of its great combination of photography and design.

	W	L	ERA	G	CG	IP	H	ER	BB	SO
92 AL	4	10	4.75	28	0	130.2	126	69	58	79
Life	13	22	5.07	55	0	273.1	288	154	110	176

MARK GARDNER

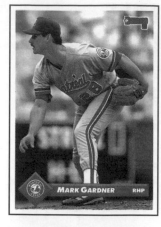

Position: Pitcher
Team: Kansas City Royals
Born: March 1, 1962
Clovis, CA
Height: 6'1" **Weight:** 200 lbs.
Bats: Right **Throws:** Right
Acquired: Traded from Expos
with Doug Piatt for Tim
Spehr and Jeff Shaw, 12/92

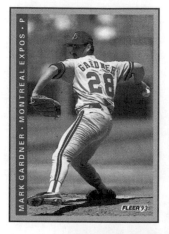

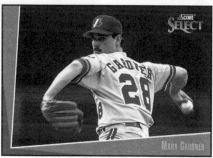

Mark Gardner was an off-and-on force with the 1992 Expos. He lasted until the sixth inning or longer in approximately half his '92 starts, and won in double digits (12-10) for the first time in his big league career. Yet Gardner's ERA remained above 4.00, a steady growth from the 3.42 level he reached in 1990. Gardner made the Expos for the first time in '89, following his 12-4 efforts in Triple-A. He's climbed to the majors on just three pitches: a fastball, curveball, and change-up. Gardner became the victim of great expectations following his near-perfect game in LA on July 26, 1991. Although he held the Dodgers hitless for nine innings, Gardner lost the game in the 10th. In '93, the righty will try to better his '92 stats while pitching for the Royals.

Who'll forget Gardner's near no-no in '91? Card collectors will, for starters. Gardner needs a bigger season in 1993 before his common-priced cards can take off. Our pick for his best 1993 card is Fleer. We have chosen this card for the superior presentation of information on its back.

	W	L	ERA	G	CG	IP	H	ER	BB	SO
92 NL	12	10	4.36	33	0	179.2	179	87	60	132
Life	28	33	3.96	94	3	527.0	473	232	207	395

BERNARD GILKEY

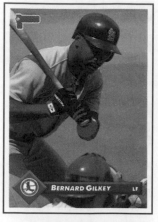

Position: Outfield
Team: St. Louis Cardinals
Born: September 24, 1966
St. Louis, MO
Height: 6' **Weight:** 190 lbs.
Bats: Right **Throws:** Right
Acquired: Signed as free agent,
8/84

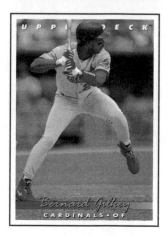

In 1992, Bernard Gilkey looked like the player the St. Louis Cardinals thought they had signed. Gilkey got his first peek at the bigs in '90. He looked impressive during the 18 game stint, hitting .297. In '91, however, after earning an Opening-Day start in left field, Gilkey struggled with injuries. His stats reflected those problems, as he only managed a .216 batting average and 14 swipes over the course of 81 games. Sent back to Triple-A Louisville for the end of '91, he came back with a vengeance. In '92, he hit .302 with 43 RBI in 131 games. His steals were still down, as he swiped only 18 for the '92 season. After stealing over 200 bases in his minor league career, the Cards expected Gilkey to burn up the basepaths.

The Cardinals are drowning in outfield talent. Unless Gilkey changes employers, he may get fewer chances to prove himself. His common-priced cards are tempting but unsafe choices. Our pick for his best 1993 card is Score. We have chosen this card for its artistic presentation.

	BA	G	AB	R	H	2B	3B	HR	RBI	SB
92 NL	.302	131	384	56	116	19	4	7	43	18
Life	.270	230	716	95	193	31	8	13	66	38

JOE GIRARDI

Position: Catcher
Team: Colorado Rockies
Born: October 14, 1964
  Peoria, IL
Height: 5′11″ **Weight:** 195 lbs.
Bats: Right **Throws:** Right
Acquired: First-round pick,
  11/92 expansion draft

DAN GLADDEN

Position: Outfield
Team: Detroit Tigers
Born: July 7, 1957
  San Jose, CA
Height: 5′11″ **Weight:** 181 lbs.
Bats: Right **Throws:** Right
Acquired: Signed as a free
  agent, 12/91

Joe Girardi rebounded from a frustrating, injury-filled season to become a solid part of the Cubs catching platoon in 1992. Throughout the season, Girardi's average remained near .300 when batting at home in Wrigley Field, or when hitting against lefthanders. While Girardi continued to suffer from home run amnesia, he did pump his average back up to match his '90 level of .270. The resurgence in his batting and a hope that he stays healthy could be why the Rockies chose him for '93 in the first round of the expansion draft. He has had some health problems. In '91, a strained back kept him out of action for all but 21 games. His premiere with the Cubs came during 1989, when he split his time between Chicago and Triple-A Iowa. Girardi played ball at Northwestern University before being drafted by Chicago in 1986.

Girardi's best has come and gone. Look elsewhere for a common-priced card investment. Our pick for his best 1993 card is Score. We have chosen this card because the design lends itself to the best use of the elements.

Dan Gladden was a free-agent fizzler with the 1992 Tigers. A fractured thumb sidelined him for more games than he'd lost since 1986. Oddly, Gladden had difficulties at Tiger Stadium, hitting .226 there. Overall, he hit .254 with seven homers and 42 RBI for the '92 season. A major leaguer since 1983, Gladden began his pro career in the San Francisco organization as an undrafted free agent in 1979. The gung-ho outfielder was a sparkplug for Minnesota in 1987-91. He made his presence known quickly with the eventual World Champions, earning 16 hits and 12 RBI in postseason play. His '88 career bests include 11 homers and 62 RBI. The Twins let Gladden escape via free-agency due to his modest power. One of the league's most aggressive left fielders, Gladden also swiped 20 or more bases from 1984-90.

Gladden's infrequent homers and inconsistent play make him an undependable card investment choice. His 1993 commons aren't safe bets. Our pick for his best 1993 card is Upper Deck. We have chosen this card for its technical merits.

	BA	G	AB	R	H	2B	3B	HR	RBI	SB
92 NL	.270	91	270	19	73	3	1	1	12	0
Life	.262	304	893	73	234	39	3	3	70	10

	BA	G	AB	R	H	2B	3B	HR	RBI	SB
92 AL	.254	113	417	57	106	20	1	7	42	4
Life	.270	1106	4145	611	1120	187	38	61	390	214

TOM
GLAVINE

Position: Pitcher
Team: Atlanta Braves
Born: March 25, 1966
  Concord, MA
Height: 6'1" **Weight:** 190 lbs.
Bats: Left **Throws:** Left
Acquired: Second-round pick,
  6/84 free-agent draft

LEO
GOMEZ

Position: Third base
Team: Baltimore Orioles
Born: March 2, 1967
  Carnovanas, Puerto Rico
Height: 6' **Weight:** 202 lbs.
Bats: Right **Throws:** Right
Acquired: Signed as a free
  agent, 12/85

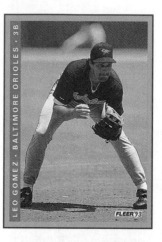

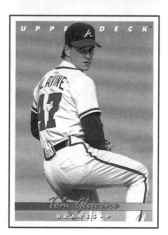

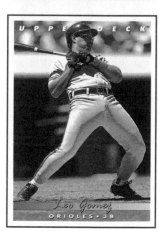

Tom Glavine had a dream season in 1991. He started the All-Star Game, pitched his team to a pennant, won a World Series game, and received the NL's Cy Young Award. He finished with a 20-11 record and 2.55 ERA. When skeptics suggested he had just completed a "career year," Glavine paid no attention. He merely set out to engineer a repeat performance in '92. He made another All-Star appearance in '92 and finished 20-8 with a 2.76 ERA. Glavine started 33 games, the fourth time in his pro career that he has tossed 33 or more. He almost snagged another Cy Young along the way to heading up another pennant-winning season with the Braves. The soft-spoken southpaw has long had the respect of his rivals for his abilities as a hitter and fielder. Glavine is an accomplished bunter and has good speed on the bases.

Test the water with his '93 cards at under a dime. Glavine's '88 Score rookie may break $2 quickly, a so-so investment level. Our pick for his best 1993 card is Fleer. We have chosen this card because of its overall appeal and pleasing looks.

Leo Gomez helped thump the Orioles into surprise pennant contenders in '92. He improved on his rookie season totals of 16 homers and 45 RBI from '91, and he lifted his batting average up from its .233 horizon. For '92, he hit .265 with 17 homers and 64 RBI. A 12-game stint with the 1990 Orioles provided Gomez with a major league audition. He owned 71 minor league home runs over the span of five seasons before jumping to the bigs. By 1991, he unseated Craig Worthington for the O's starting third sacker job. After he got his first '91 homer on June 9, he was on his way as a full-timer.

If Gomez levels off at 20 homers and 80 RBI yearly, that will be enough to guarantee his hot-corner job. However, competing against third-base contemporaries like Robin Ventura and Gregg Jefferies, Gomez won't have enough to keep his common-priced cards alive for collectors. Our pick for his best 1993 card is Donruss. We have chosen this card due to the outstanding photographic composition.

	W	L	ERA	G	CG	IP	H	ER	BB	SO
92 NL	20	8	2.76	33	7	225.0	197	69	70	129
Life	73	60	3.60	172	24	1117.2	1058	447	353	644

	BA	G	AB	R	H	2B	3B	HR	RBI	SB
92 AL	.265	137	468	62	124	24	0	17	64	2
Life	.249	267	898	105	224	41	2	33	110	3

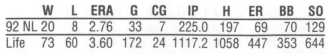
Series two cards from some companies were available at press time. If space allows, both cards are shown; if not, the most up-to-date cards are pictured.

RENE GONZALES

Position: Third base
Team: California Angels
Born: September 3, 1961
   Austin, TX
Height: 6'3" **Weight:** 201 lbs.
Bats: Right **Throws:** Right
Acquired: Signed as a free
   agent, 1/92

JUAN GONZALEZ

Position: Outfield
Team: Texas Rangers
Born: October 16, 1969
   Vega Baja, Puerto Rico
Height: 6'3" **Weight:** 200 lbs.
Bats: Right **Throws:** Right
Acquired: Signed as a free
   agent, 5/86

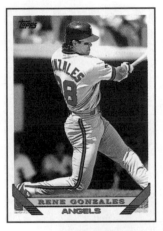

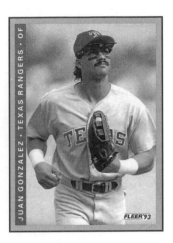

Rene Gonzales was thrust into the limelight with the 1992 Angels. Due to Gonzales' career-best hitting, the Angels shuttled third sacker Gary Gaetti to first, giving Gonzales a starting job for the first time in his career. With the increased opportunity, he carved out career highs in numerous offensive categories. By contrast, the Texas native previously owned a grand total of 15 career home runs from both his major and minor league days. Gonzales has bounced around baseball since signing as an undrafted free agent with Montreal in 1982, debuting in the bigs in 1984. He was brought to Baltimore in a 1986 trade which sent hurler Dennis Martinez to the Expos. With the 1988 Orioles, he played five different positions in 92 games. Swapped again, he subbed for the Blue Jays in 1991.

Gonzales may be a mere stop-gap for the Angels until Damion Easley is a regular. Therefore, his common-priced cards are liabilities. Our pick for his best 1993 card is Score. We have chosen this card for its artistic presentation.

When Juan Gonzalez drove in 102 runs for the 1991 Rangers, he became the 18th player to reach the 100-RBI plateau before age 22. He did it in his first full big league season—even while slowed by arthroscopic knee surgery at the start and lower back problems at the end. Gonzalez maintained his high standards in '92, slugging three homers in a single game against Minnesota on June 7. He also struck out a whopping 143 times. The '92 longball champ broke into pro ball at age 16 in '86 and has shown increased power every year. He proved ready for the majors after winning 1991 American Association MVP honors by leading the league with 29 homers, 101 RBI, and 252 total bases.

Gonzalez looks great as a card investment. Be grateful if the '93s come in for under a quarter each. His 1990 Fleer rookie at $1.50 won't be cheap forever. Our pick for his best 1993 card is Score. We have chosen this card because of its great combination of photography and design.

	BA	G	AB	R	H	2B	3B	HR	RBI	SB
92 AL	.277	104	329	47	91	17	1	7	38	7
Life	.233	482	1069	125	249	36	3	13	91	16

	BA	G	AB	R	H	2B	3B	HR	RBI	SB
92 AL	.260	155	584	77	152	24	2	43	109	0
Life	.259	346	1279	172	331	68	4	75	230	4

LUIS GONZALEZ

Position: Outfield
Team: Houston Astros
Born: September 3, 1967
　Tampa, FL
Height: 6'2" **Weight:** 180 lbs.
Bats: Left **Throws:** Right
Acquired: Fourth-round pick,
　6/88 free-agent draft

Luis Gonzalez suffered a second-half slump, marring his 1992 sophomore season with the Astros. While Gonzalez managed to hit .350 against lefties, he only hit .243 overall with 55 RBI over the course of 122 games. He saw his playing time decline due to the acquisition of veteran left fielder Pete Incaviglia. Gonzales played college ball for South Alabama before getting drafted in 1988. He skipped Triple-A, jumping right from Double-A Columbus to the bigs in 1990. He tied for the Double-A Southern League lead in homers (with 24) and swiped 27 bases. In '91, Gonzalez produced 13 homers, 69 RBI, and 10 stolen bases. His 50 extra-base hits that season set a Houston single-season record for rookies.

　Eric Anthony, not Gonzalez, seems to be the hottest card subject in the 1993 Astros outfield. Common-priced cards of Gonzalez are big gambles. Our pick for his best 1993 card is Fleer. We have chosen this card for the superior presentation of information on its back.

	BA	G	AB	R	H	2B	3B	HR	RBI	SB
92 NL	.243	122	387	40	94	19	3	10	55	7
Life	.247	271	881	92	218	49	12	23	124	17

DWIGHT GOODEN

Position: Pitcher
Team: New York Mets
Born: November 16, 1964
　Tampa, FL
Height: 6'3" **Weight:** 210 lbs.
Bats: Right **Throws:** Right
Acquired: First-round pick,
　6/82 free-agent draft

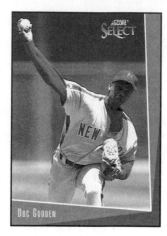

Dwight Gooden faced the first losing season of his career in 1992, as he went 10-13 with a 3.67 ERA. The letdown was surprising, considering that Gooden entered the season with a record-setting .714 career winning percentage. His problems may be traced to the season-ending shoulder surgery from September 1991. On July 18, 1992, the same shoulder flared up, placing Doc on the 15-day DL. Gooden was the fifth player chosen in the first round of the 1982 free-agent draft, following his high school graduation. His career soared after winning the 1984 Rookie of the Year award and the 1985 Cy Young.

　Due to his illustrious past and his association with a well-publicized team, Gooden's cards have remained 10 to 15 cent items. With his 1992 slump, optimistic investors can find bargain prices in hopes that Doctor K will be operating again soon. Don't overlook the 1984 Fleer Gooden at $2 or less. Our pick for his best 1993 card is Score. We have chosen this card for the interesting facts included on the reverse.

	W	L	ERA	G	CG	IP	H	ER	BB	SO
92 NL	10	13	3.67	31	3	206.0	197	84	70	145
Life	142	66	2.99	269	60	1919.2	1664	638	575	1686

TOM GORDON

Position: Pitcher
Team: Kansas City Royals
Born: Nov. 18, 1967
    Sebring, FL
Height: 5'9" **Weight:** 180 lbs.
Bats: Right **Throws:** Right
Acquired: Sixth-round selection
    in 6/86 free-agent draft

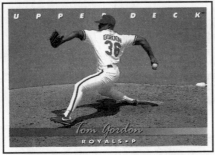

Pitcher Tom "Flash" Gordon was another talented hurler caught on Kansas City's sinking ship. Battered by left-handed hitters, Gordon had problems both as a starter and reliever in 1992. From 1989 through '91, Gordon exceeded 150 strikeouts per year, peaking with 175 Ks during his 1990 campaign. In 1989 Gordon finished second in AL Rookie of the Year balloting with a 17-9 record. He devoted himself to starting duty in 1990, and finished at 12-11 with six complete games. Prior to his 1989 premiere with the Royals, Gordon assembled a sleek 29-6 career record in three minor league seasons. Gordon earned high school letters in football, basketball and baseball before being drafted by Kansas City in 1986.

With a past ratio of nearly one strikeout per inning, Gordon might have a shot at stardom if he could focus on a full-time starting position. Don't count on him and his nickel-priced cards for 1993, as long as the Royals keep shuffling him between jobs. Our pick for his best 1993 card is Fleer. We have chosen this card because of its great combination of photography and design.

	W	L	ERA	G	SV	IP	H	ER	BB	SO
92 AL	6	10	4.59	40	0	117.2	116	60	55	98
Life	44	46	3.93	171	2	649.2	575	284	334	611

JIM GOTT

Position: Pitcher
Team: Los Angeles Dodgers
Born: August 3, 1959
    Hollywood, CA
Height: 6'4" **Weight:** 220 lbs.
Bats: Right **Throws:** Right
Acquired: Signed as a free
    agent, 12/89

Jim Gott achieved a new level of activity in 1992, appearing in a career-high 68 games. The former closer adapted well to his new duties of middle relief, providing a steadying influence on an unstable bullpen. While Roger McDowell's ERA grew and Jay Howell's injuries continued, Gott was the team's leading righthanded reliever (2.45 ERA). Gott's previous personal best of 67 appearances came with the '88 Pirates, when his 34 saves were second highest in the NL. His 1989 campaign was limited to one game in April, followed by season-ending elbow surgery. Gott, whose career began as a starter, was initially drafted by the Cardinals in 1977. He debuted with the 1982 Blue Jays, and spent 1985 through mid-'87 with the Giants.

Without a bucket of saves, relievers are ignored by card collectors. Despite his success, Gott's commons will be overlooked in 1993. Our pick for his best 1993 card is Donruss. We have chosen this card for its technical merits.

	W	L	ERA	G	SV	IP	H	ER	BB	SO
92 NL	3	3	2.45	68	6	88.0	72	24	41	75
Life	45	59	3.84	430	61	974.2	926	416	417	722

MARK GRACE

Position: First base
Team: Chicago Cubs
Born: June 28, 1964
   Winston-Salem, NC
Height: 6'2" **Weight:** 190 lbs.
Bats: Left **Throws:** Left
Acquired: 24th-round pick,
   6/85 free-agent draft

JOE GRAHE

Position: Pitcher
Team: California Angels
Born: June 14, 1967
   West Palm Beach, FL
Height: 6' **Weight:** 200 lbs.
Bats: Right **Throws:** Right
Acquired: Second-round pick,
   6/89 free-agent draft

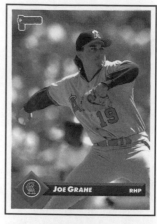

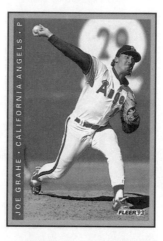

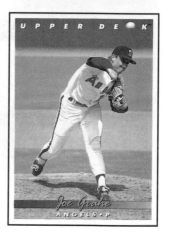

The Chicago Cubs can't complain about the play of Mark Grace over the past five seasons. A paragon of consistency, Grace took a .297 career average into the 1992 campaign. In the '92 season, he hit .307 with 37 doubles, knocking in 79 runs as well. He also supplied his usual strong defense in the field (.998 fielding percentage). In a 16-game stretch starting June 1, Grace hit .417. Sid Fernandez eventually stopped his hitting streak at 13. During that skein, he hit .429 and scored nine runs. When he missed the June 10 game because of a contusion on his right big toe, Grace ended a string of 230 consecutive games played. Although his average fell to a career-low .273 in '91, Grace led all big league first basemen in putouts, assists, and chances.

Grace is a great nickel-per-card choice. Consider his '93s. Grace is a jewel in the 1988 Topps Traded set for $2. Our pick for his best 1993 card is Fleer. We have chosen this card because it has a distinctive look.

When California relief ace Bryan Harvey was lost to the Angels early in 1992, the team's gray mood quickly turned to Grahe—Joe Grahe, that is. With Harvey's July trip to the DL an eventual season-ending elbow surgery, Grahe got the chance for which he had been waiting. In just his third pro season, his first as a reliever, Grahe paced the team in saves (21). For the '92 season, he pitched 94 ⅔ innings of relief spread over 39 games with a 3.52 ERA. As a starter, Grahe was a lackluster performer for California. He reached the majors for the first time on August 4, 1990, after a mere 23 starts. The result was a 3-4 mark in eight starts. He bounced between Anaheim and Triple-A Edmonton in 1991, winding up with a 3-7 record in the bigs.

Collectors who invested in Bryan Harvey's cards in 1992 wonder if Grahe could be the next fallen Angels' closer. Give Grahe another full and healthy season before respecting his common-priced issues for 1993. Our pick for his best 1993 card is Score. We have chosen this card for its artistic presentation.

	BA	G	AB	R	H	2B	3B	HR	RBI	SB
92 NL	.307	158	603	72	185	37	5	9	79	6
Life	.299	751	2807	370	840	148	18	46	355	41

	W	L	ERA	G	SV	IP	H	ER	BB	SO
92 AL	5	6	3.52	46	21	94.2	85	37	39	39
Life	11	17	4.27	72	21	211.0	220	100	95	104

CRAIG GREBECK

Position: Infield
Team: Chicago White Sox
Born: December 29, 1964
  Cerritos, CA
Height: 5′7″ **Weight:** 160 lbs.
Bats: Right **Throws:** Right
Acquired: Signed as an
  undrafted free agent, 8/86

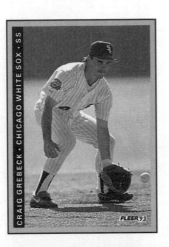

While unexpected knee surgery for Ozzie Guillen made Craig Grebeck a surprise starter for the 1992 White Sox, his season had the same unhappy ending as Guillen's did. Grebeck's duty ended abruptly when a broken foot on August 8 ended his season. In his 88 games in '92, Grebeck hit .268 with 35 RBI. His fielding was above average for shortstops in the AL as he wound up with a .980 percentage. In '91, Grebeck batted .281 with six home runs and 31 RBI, in only 107 games and 224 plate appearances. Grebeck's future in the majors was doubtful after his 1990 rookie season. In 59 games, he batted .168. Ironically, his first and only home run that year came off Nolan Ryan.

Still, overshadowed in a healthy infield of Guillen, Steve Sax, Frank Thomas, and Robin Ventura, Grebeck could be overlooked again in 1993. His cards are unappreciated commons. Our pick for his best 1993 card is Topps. We have chosen this card because of its great combination of photography and design.

	BA	G	AB	R	H	2B	3B	HR	RBI	SB
92 AL	.268	88	287	24	77	21	2	3	35	0
Life	.254	254	630	68	160	40	6	10	75	1

TOMMY GREENE

Position: Pitcher
Team: Philadelphia Phillies
Born: April 6, 1967
  Lumberton, NC
Height: 6′5″ **Weight:** 227 lbs.
Bats: Right **Throws:** Right
Acquired: Traded from Braves
  with Dale Murphy for Jim
  Vatcher, Victor Rosario, and
  Jeff Parrett, 8/90

Tommy Greene's 1992 season was abbreviated due to nagging shoulder problems. Tendinitis hampered his early starts, and slapped the hurler on the DL in May. He pitched in only 13 games (64 ⅓ innings pitched) in '92. Perhaps Greene's '91 workload, which exceeded 200 innings, contributed to his physical woes in 1992. Greene's '91 season began in the bullpen. In his second start of that season, he no-hit Montreal. He ended 1991 with a 13-7 record, a 3.38 ERA, and a career-high 154 strikeouts. Harvested out of his North Carolina high school by Atlanta in '85, Greene debuted in the majors in '89. Ironically, Greene appeared to be a meaningless "throw-in" from Atlanta in the '89 transaction that sent him to Philadelphia.

Risk-takers take note. Due to his injury, Greene's '93 cards will be available for nearly nothing. Short-term profits await if Greene can win in double figures again. Our pick for his best 1993 card is Topps. We have chosen this card due to the outstanding photographic composition.

	W	L	ERA	G	CG	IP	H	ER	BB	SO
92 NL	3	3	5.32	13	0	64.1	75	38	34	39
Life	20	15	4.04	68	4	349.2	324	157	132	231

Series two cards from some companies were available at press time. If space allows, both cards are shown; if not, the most up-to-date cards are pictured.

WILLIE GREENE

Position: Third base
Team: Cincinnati Reds
Born: September 23, 1971
Milledgeville, GA
Height: 5'11" **Weight:** 160 lbs.
Bats: Left **Throws:** Right
Acquired: Traded from Expos
with Dave Martinez and Scott
Ruskin for John Wetteland
and Bill Risley, 12/91

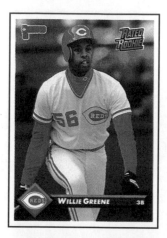 

Willie Greene is a bit of a puzzle. Although he doesn't look it, his 1992 figures stamped him as one of the top power hitters not only in the Reds' chain but in all of the minors. His bat produces a distinctive crack when it meets ball. Yet Greene's height and weight are those of an average-size infielder. He has been in three organizations and reached double figures in homers for each. Originally drafted by the Pirates as their No. 1 choice in '89, Greene was traded to Montreal as part of the deal that brought Zane Smith to Pittsburgh in '90. Then, late in '91, Greene came to Cincinnati in a transaction that sent John Wetteland to Montreal. Wetteland worked out very well for the Expos, but they may one day regret parting with Greene. Greene was drafted as a shortstop, but played third base in '92.

Greene is untested in the bigs. His power potential, however, suggests that you should sock a few of his '93s away. Our pick for his best 1993 card is Upper Deck. We have chosen this card because it will increase in value.

	BA	G	AB	R	H	2B	3B	HR	RBI	SB
92 AA	.278	96	349	47	97	19	2	15	66	8
92 NL	.269	29	93	10	25	5	2	2	13	0

MIKE GREENWELL

Position: Outfield
Team: Boston Red Sox
Born: July 18, 1963
Louisville, KY
Height: 6' **Weight:** 205 lbs.
Bats: Left **Throws:** Right
Acquired: Third-round pick,
6/82 free-agent draft

Mike Greenwell's 1992 season ended mercifully after only 49 games. The left fielder was being roasted at the plate, batting only .230 and being accused by fans of aiding Boston's downfall. An injured wrist, followed by surgeries on his elbow and knee, wiped out his year. Gone were the predictions that Greenwell could be the next great BoSox outfield slugger. Even in '91, when he was in top form, Greenwell couldn't maintain the career-best tradition he began in '88 when he belted 22 home runs and 119 RBI. In '87, Greenwell notched a personal-high .328 in 125 games. The Kentucky native debuted in Boston in 1985. Before 1992, he had never batted lower than .297.

Even if Greenwell is healthy enough to return to his pre-1992 level of performance, Boston would love to unload his salary. Collectors may consider both Greenwell and his nickel-priced cards unwanted, damaged goods. Our pick for his best 1993 card is Upper Deck. We have chosen this card due to the outstanding photographic composition.

	BA	G	AB	R	H	2B	3B	HR	RBI	SB
92 AL	.233	49	180	16	42	2	0	2	18	2
Life	.306	831	2980	418	912	167	26	84	489	60

Series two cards from some companies were available at press time. If space allows, both cards are shown; if not, the most up-to-date cards are pictured.

KEN GRIFFEY JR.

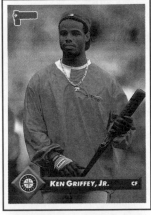

Position: Outfield
Team: Seattle Mariners
Born: November 21, 1969
Donora, PA
Height: 6'3" **Weight:** 195 lbs.
Bats: Left **Throws:** Left
Acquired: First-round pick,
6/87 free-agent draft

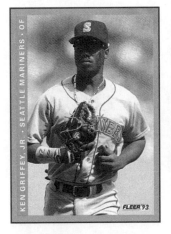

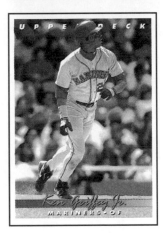

MARQUIS GRISSOM

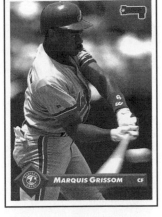

Position: Outfield
Team: Montreal Expos
Born: April 17, 1967
Atlanta, GA
Height: 5'11" **Weight:** 190 lbs.
Bats: Right **Throws:** Right
Acquired: Third-round pick,
6/88 free-agent draft

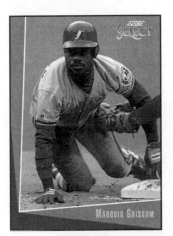

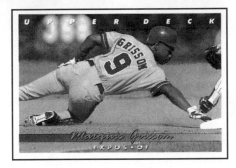

Ken Griffey Jr. seems to be improving as he gains experience. One of the game's youngest and most talented stars, he made his big league bow at 19 in 1989 and wasted little time making an impression. A Gold Glove center fielder, Griffey finished the '91 campaign with a .327 average, 22 homers, 100 RBI, and 18 stolen bases. He also became the first Seattle player selected by the fans to start in an All-Star Game. Griffey later became the 17th player to collect 100 RBI before the age of 22. He was slowed in '92 by a sprained right wrist that sent him to the DL for two weeks in June. He finished '92 hitting .308 with 27 homers and 103 RBI despite his injury.

In quantity, Griffey's '93s might be less than 50 cents each. Invest, because he's unlikely to get cheaper. Forget deals on early Griffeys. The '92 Upper Deck showing him with father and brother is the ultimate investment at 75 cents. Our pick for his best 1993 card is Fleer. We have chosen this card because of its overall appeal and pleasing looks.

Before the Montreal Expos had finished the first month of the 1992 season, Marquis Grissom had been in three different spots in the lineup. The fleet-footed center fielder, who prefers to hit sixth, had hit second and sixth most of the spring but moved into the leadoff slot on April 23. When Felipe Alou replaced Tom Runnells as manager in May, he left Grissom alone at the top of the order. That was a wise decision as Grissom's hitting has steadily improved since his rookie year of 1990. He also has more speed and confidence on the basepaths than most of his teammates. In '91, he led the majors with 76 stolen bases, the fourth highest total in club history. He topped that in '92, successfully swiping 78, being caught only 13 times.

Grab Grissom's '93 cards at a dime or less each. For a surprise, buy Upper Deck's 1990 #702 of Grissom, Delino DeShields, and Larry Walker together for 35 cents. Our pick for his best 1993 card is Donruss. We have chosen this card for its artistic presentation.

	BA	G	AB	R	H	2B	3B	HR	RBI	SB
92 AL	.308	142	565	83	174	39	4	27	103	10
Life	.301	578	2165	311	652	132	12	87	344	60

	BA	G	AB	R	H	2B	3B	HR	RBI	SB
92 NL	.276	159	653	99	180	39	6	14	66	78
Life	.268	431	1573	230	422	78	17	24	136	177

BUDDY GROOM

Position: Pitcher
Team: Detroit Tigers
Born: June 10, 1965 Dallas, TX
Height: 6'2" **Weight:** 200 lbs.
Bats: Left **Throws:** Left
Acquired: Drafted from White
  Sox organization, 12/90

Wedsel Gary "Buddy" Groom was a co-conspirator in saddling the 1992 Tigers with the league's worst pitching staff. His walks exceeded his strikeouts as lefthanders ripped him at a .355 clip. The winless lefty made seven starts for the Bengals. By comparison, he owned a strikeout/walk ratio exceeding 3-to-1 with Triple-A Toledo in '92. He sported a 7-7 mark with a 2.80 ERA. Originally a 12th-round draft pick of the White Sox in '87, Groom never progressed past Double-A ball in four seasons with Chicago's farm system. Yet, he owned consecutive 13-win seasons in 1988-89. Being a coveted lefthander, Groom will always get extra opportunities in pro ball. However, Groom could get the broom if the new Detroit owner demands a personnel overhaul.

Groom can't be expected to be a major factor in relief. His '93 commons will find no relief, either. Our pick for his best 1993 card is Topps. We have chosen this card because of its great combination of photography and design.

	W	L	ERA	G	SV	IP	H	ER	BB	SO
92 AL	0	5	5.82	12	1	38.2	48	25	22	15
Life	0	5	5.82	12	1	38.2	48	25	22	15

KEVIN GROSS

Position: Pitcher
Team: Los Angeles Dodgers
Born: June 8, 1961
  Downey, CA
Height: 6'5" **Weight:** 215 lbs.
Bats: Right **Throws:** Right
Acquired: Signed as a free
  agent, 12/90

Kevin Gross helped the Dodgers forget their last-place troubles for at least one game in 1992. On August 24, he earned his first career no-hitter with a 2-0 whitewashing of San Francisco. He still, however, posted his seventh consecutive losing season. He went 8-13 with a 3.17 ERA for the '92 season. His troubles began after a 15-13 showing with the '85 Phillies. In '85, ironically, Gross broke up a June 24 no-hitter by poking a sixth-inning double. He got his name in the history books years before his no-hitter. In '87, he was found with sandpaper in his glove and suspected of doctoring baseballs. As a result, he was slapped with a 10-day suspension by the National League. The California native has been active in the majors since 1983, with five seasons of double-digit wins.

Even with a no-no to his credit, Gross hasn't erased his lifetime losing record. Don't even think about his common-priced cards in 1993. Our pick for his best 1993 card is Upper Deck. We have chosen this card due to the outstanding photographic composition.

	W	L	ERA	G	CG	IP	H	ER	BB	SO
92 NL	8	13	3.17	34	4	204.2	182	72	77	158
Life	98	114	3.89	345	33	1789.2	1752	774	710	1249

Series two cards from some companies were available at press time. If space allows, both cards are shown; if not, the most up-to-date cards are pictured.

KELLY GRUBER

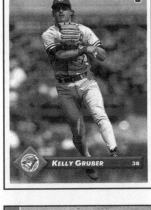

Position: Third base
Team: California Angels
Born: February 26, 1962
　Bellaire, TX
Height: 6′ **Weight:** 185 lbs.
Bats: Right **Throws:** Right
Acquired: Traded from Blue
　Jays for Luis Sojo, 12/92

MARK GUBICZA

Position: Pitcher
Team: Kansas City Royals
Born: August 14, 1962
　Philadelphia, PA
Height: 6′5″ **Weight:** 225 lbs.
Bats: Right **Throws:** Right
Acquired: Second-round pick,
　6/81 free-agent draft

Kelly Gruber didn't get many chances to recapture his past offensive brilliance for Toronto in 1992. A sprained knee and strained hamstring limited his second-half appearances. His fielding was below the '92 average for third basemen. His '91 accomplishments were limited to 20 homers and 65 RBI in 113 games, due to two separate hand injuries. The Blue Jays, perhaps disillusioned with his maladies, traded him late in '92 to the Angels. In '90, Gruber garnered career highs with 31 homers and 118 RBI (second-best in the American League). Although Gruber made his big league premiere with Toronto in 1984, he didn't become a starting third baseman until '88. He won a Gold Glove in 1990.

Gruber is an admirable overachiever, but his nickel-priced cards won't withstand the test of time. An overlooked plus in the '86 Donruss "The Rookies" is Gruber's card for $2. Our pick for his best 1993 card is Upper Deck. We have chosen this card because it has a distinctive look.

The 1990s continued to be a decade of doom for hurler Mark Gubicza in '92. Shoulder problems caused him to miss more than half the season. His 7-6 record for '92 marked another mediocre season. Gubzica's problems date back to June 29, 1990, when his season was ended by injury. Rotator cuff surgery followed that August, marking the end of his last, truly effective season. His career peaked in '88 with a personal-best 20-8 season. Gubzica earned his first of two All-Star game berths, carved out a career-best 183 strikeouts, and finished third in Cy Young balloting. Through '89, Gubicza was a double-digit winner annually. However, his '91 season concluded with seven losses in his last nine decisions, foreshadowing his '92 troubles.

After three years of frustration, Gubicza has given collectors legitimate doubts about his career and his cards. Stay away from his 1993 commons. Our pick for his best 1993 card is Upper Deck. We have chosen this card because the design lends itself to the best use of the elements.

	BA	G	AB	R	H	2B	3B	HR	RBI	SB
92 AL	.229	120	446	42	102	16	3	11	43	7
Life	.259	921	3094	421	800	145	24	114	434	80

	W	L	ERA	G	CG	IP	H	ER	BB	SO
92 AL	7	6	3.72	18	2	111.1	110	46	36	81
Life	104	92	3.75	259	37	1651.2	1586	689	618	1091

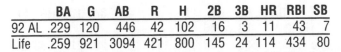

Series two cards from some companies were available at press time. If space allows, both cards are shown; if not, the most up-to-date cards are pictured.

JUAN GUERRERO

Position: Infield
Team: Houston Astros
Born: February 1, 1967
   Los Llanos, Dominican
   Republic
Height: 5'11" **Weight:** 160 lbs.
Bats: Right **Throws:** Right
Acquired: First-round pick,
   12/91 Rule 5 draft

PEDRO GUERRERO

Position: First base
Team: St. Louis Cardinals
Born: June 29, 1956
   San Pedro de Macoris,
   Dominican Republic
Height: 6' **Weight:** 195 lbs.
Bats: Right **Throws:** Right
Acquired: Traded from Dodgers
   for John Tudor, 8/88

Juan Guerrero came to the Astros in the Rule 5 draft and they liked him so much in spring training they decided to carry him. Guerrero entered the '92 season never having played above the Double-A level, but he filled in at third, second, short, and in the outfield. He understandably got off to a slow start at the plate, but he improved as the season progressed. He put one of his skills on display July 4, when he squeezed home a run to help the Astros beat the Mets in the nightcap of a double-header. His best season thus far was in '91, when Guerrero finished third in the Double-A Texas League with a .334 average. He was named to the All-Star team, and hit a two-run homer in the deciding game of the league's title series against El Paso. Guerrero was signed by the Giants as a non-drafted free agent in 1986.

Weak-hitting infielders make poor card investment subjects. Stay away from his '93 issues. Our pick for his best 1993 card is Donruss. We have chosen this card for its technical merits.

Pedro Guerrero's move to left field was a quickly curtailed experiment for the 1992 Cardinals. After only 10 games, he was sent back to first, replacing injured starter Andres Galarraga. A sore shoulder and pinched nerve in his neck, however, stopped Guerrero cold. He lasted for only 43 games in '92, hitting a woeful .219 with 16 RBI and striking out 25 times. Health woes are nothing new to Guerrero. Before '92, Pete had served eight stays on the disabled list. He followed his career-high 33 homers in 1985 by missing all but 31 games in 1986, due to a knee injury. In '89, his first full season with the Cardinals, Guerrero told another story. He hit .311 with 17 homers and 117 RBI, playing in all 162 games.

The injury-prone Guerrero could extend his career in the relatively safe job of DH with a patient AL employer. He has no future in the Cardinals' youth movement. Don't believe in his '93 commons. Our pick for his best 1993 card is Donruss. We have chosen this card for the interesting facts included on the reverse.

	BA	G	AB	R	H	2B	3B	HR	RBI	SB
92 NL	.200	79	125	8	25	4	2	1	14	1
Life	.200	79	125	8	25	4	2	1	14	1

	BA	G	AB	R	H	2B	3B	HR	RBI	SB
92 NL	.219	43	146	10	32	6	1	1	16	2
Life	.300	1536	5392	730	1618	267	29	215	898	97

Series two cards from some companies were available at press time. If space allows, both cards are shown; if not, the most up-to-date cards are pictured.

LEE GUETTERMAN

Position: Pitcher
Team: New York Mets
Born: November 22, 1958
  Chattanooga, TN
Height: 6'8" **Weight:** 230 lbs.
Bats: Left **Throws:** Left
Acquired: Traded from Yankees
  for Tim Burke, 6/92

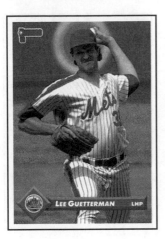 

OZZIE GUILLEN

Position: Shortstop
Team: Chicago White Sox
Born: January 20, 1964
  Ocumare del Tuy, Miranda,
  Venezuela
Height: 5'11" **Weight:** 150 lbs.
Bats: Left **Throws:** Right
Acquired: Traded from Padres
  in seven player deal, 12/84

In 1992, Lee Guetterman sampled National League life for the first time in his diverse career. In June, he was sent to the Mets for righthanded reliever Tim Burke. The swap marked the third team Guetterman has served during his six major league seasons. The '92 season wasn't pretty, as he toiled in 43 games (43 1/3 innings) with a 3-4 record and only two saves. He began in the pros as a fourth-round draft choice of the Mariners in 1981. The 6'8" reliever first appeared with Seattle in '84. In 1987, his only big league year as a starter, Guetterman gave the M's an 11-4 performance. From 1989-91, Guetterman made over 60 appearances per season. His 1989 totals included 13 saves, five wins, and a 2.45 ERA in 70 games. He matched his personal-best 11 victories in relief for the 1990 Yanks.

The towering reliever can't count his lofty 5.82 ERA as job security for '93. Guetterman's common-priced cards have even less of a guarantee. Our pick for his best 1993 card is Topps. We have chosen this card due to the outstanding photographic composition.

Shortstop Ozzie Guillen's 1992 season never got off the ground after he landed there. The speedy fielder was upended in a collision with left fielder Tim Raines while chasing a blooper. The injury resulting from the accident necessitated knee surgery. Guillen was lost for the year on April 21; his season screeching to a halt after just 12 games. The three-time All-Star had played in a minimum of 149 games in his previous seven major league seasons, averaging more than 25 stolen bases per year. He's driven in more than 50 runs three times. The slick fielder, winner of a 1990 Gold Glove, first rose to fame as the 1985 AL Rookie of the Year. Before joining the ChiSox, Guillen spent four seasons in the Padres' organization.

Guillen isn't enough of an offensive threat to gain enduring respect from the baseball world or from collectors. His 1993 common-priced cards don't look to be price gainers. Our pick for his best 1993 card is Upper Deck. We have chosen this card because it has a distinctive look.

	W	L	ERA	G	SV	IP	H	ER	BB	SO
92 NL	3	4	5.82	43	2	43.1	57	28	14	15
Life	35	31	4.37	345	23	584.1	644	284	185	251

	BA	G	AB	R	H	2B	3B	HR	RBI	SB
92 AL	.200	12	40	5	8	4	0	0	7	1
Life	.266	1095	3841	432	1021	143	42	10	338	136

BILL GULLICKSON

Position: Pitcher
Team: Detroit Tigers
Born: February 20, 1959
   Marshall, MN
Height: 6'3" **Weight:** 225 lbs.
Bats: Right **Throws:** Right
Acquired: Signed as a free
   agent, 12/90

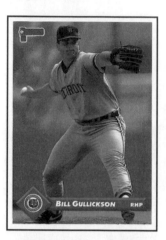 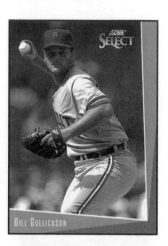

 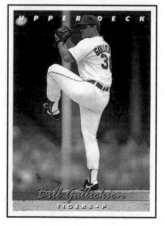

Bill Gullickson is not a strikeout pitcher. He allows opposing hitters to put balls into play, where his fielders record the outs. After losing his first two games of 1992, he won seven of his next eight decisions to retain his ranking as the No. 1 starter on the Detroit staff. He went 14-13 with a 4.34 ERA and logged 221 ⅔ innings of work during '92. In 1991, his first Detroit campaign, Gullickson went 20-9 to tie for the major league lead in victories. Detroit's first 20-game winner since Jack Morris in '86, Gullickson also led the team with 226 ⅓ innings pitched. He walked only 44, his lowest walk total since 1984 and beat every team except Texas, whom he did not face. In addition to the Expos and Astros, Gullickson has also pitched for the Reds and Yankees.

Workhorse Gullickson isn't getting younger. His '93 cards aren't wise buys, even at a nickel each. Our pick for his best 1993 card is Topps. We have chosen this card because of its great combination of photography and design.

	W	L	ERA	G	CG	IP	H	ER	BB	SO
92 AL	14	13	4.34	34	4	221.2	228	107	50	64
Life	145	122	3.73	349	51	2285.1	2317	947	553	1144

MARK GUTHRIE

Position: Pitcher
Team: Minnesota Twins
Born: September 22, 1965
   Buffalo, NY
Height: 6'4" **Weight:** 196 lbs.
Bats: Both **Throws:** Left
Acquired: Seventh-round pick,
   6/87 free-agent draft

 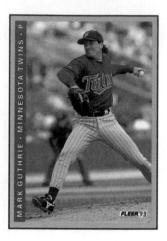

Mark Guthrie remained Minnesota's top lefty reliever in 1992. He appeared in more than 50 games (54) for the first time in his career and ranked among the league leaders in holds (19—tied with Boston's Greg Harris). Best of all, he shaved nearly a point-and-a-half off his previous year's ERA of 4.32 (2.88) and had over three times as many strikeouts (76) as walks (23). In 1991, Guthrie was utilized as a spot starter 16 times. He finished at 7-9 with two saves. He's become adept at holding baserunners, as indicated by his 13 pickoffs in 1990. The Twins drafted Guthrie out of LSU in 1987. His amateur career included work for Team USA in 1985. He concentrated on starting chores during his four minor league seasons. Now, however, he seems like a solid fixture in the Twins' bullpen of the future.

Guthrie's past undefined role with the Twins makes speculating on his 1993 commons difficult. His cards have little appeal. Our pick for his best 1993 card is Fleer. We have chosen this card because the design lends itself to the best use of the elements.

	W	L	ERA	G	SV	IP	H	ER	BB	SO
92 AL	2	3	2.88	54	5	75.0	59	24	23	76
Life	18	21	3.86	132	7	375.0	395	161	124	287

Series two cards from some companies were available at press time. If space allows, both cards are shown; if not, the most up-to-date cards are pictured.

JOSE GUZMAN

Position: Pitcher
Team: Chicago Cubs
Born: April 9, 1963
Santa Isabel, Puerto Rico
Height: 6'3" **Weight:** 195 lbs.
Bats: Right **Throws:** Right
Acquired: Signed as a free
agent, 12/92

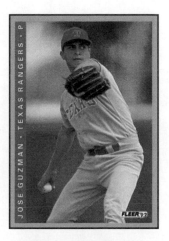

Jose Guzman enjoyed the winningest season of his major league career with the '92 Rangers. He was a team workhorse, surpassing 200 innings (224) and 30 starts (33) with ease. His hard work paid off, at least in the eyes of Cub fans who will be anxious to watch him weave his magic in Chicago in '93. He spent the entire '89 campaign on the DL, recuperating from rotator cuff surgery and shoulder problems. However, he returned in full form, posting a 13-7 record in 1991. He won AL Comeback Player of the Year honors from *The Sporting News* for his efforts. Before '91, Guzman hadn't enjoyed a winning season in the majors. His struggles began with a 9-15 mark in his '86 rookie campaign. His 14-14 performance in '87 fell to 11-13 in '88.

At a nickel each, Guzman's cards aren't promising. Pennant contention by the Cubs and a 20-win season from Guzman are two scenarios needed to jump-start his card values. Our pick for his best 1993 card is Fleer. We have chosen this card for its technical merits.

	W	L	ERA	G	CG	IP	H	ER	BB	SO
92 AL	16	11	3.66	33	5	224.0	229	91	73	179
Life	66	62	3.90	159	24	1013.2	983	439	395	715

JUAN GUZMAN

Position: Pitcher
Team: Toronto Blue Jays
Born: October 28, 1966
Santo Domingo,
Dominican Republic
Height: 5'11" **Weight:** 195 lbs.
Bats: Right **Throws:** Right
Acquired: Traded from Dodgers
for Mike Sharperson, 9/87

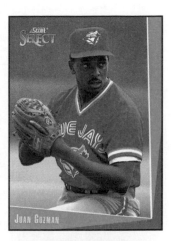

When the Toronto Blue Jays agreed to trade Mike Sharperson to the Los Angeles Dodgers in '87, the player they wanted in return was a minor league infielder named Jose Offerman. When the Dodgers refused, the Jays settled instead for Juan Guzman. A hard thrower deemed expendable by the Dodgers because of wildness, Guzman served primarily as a reliever until '90. Little did anyone know that he would become one of the premier pitchers for Toronto in their World Series quest in '92. For the regular season, he posted a 16-5 record with a 2.64 ERA. He mowed down opposing batters, striking out 165 in his 180 ⅔ innings of work. The '92 All-Star team member continued his brilliant performance in the postseason, turning in sparkling performances in ALCS and World Series play.

Guzman was great in '92. Try to find his '93s at 15 cents apiece. Any 1992 Guzman for 75 cents is a fair investment. Our pick for his best 1993 card is Score. We have chosen this card for the interesting facts included on the reverse.

	W	L	ERA	G	CG	IP	H	ER	BB	SO
92 AL	16	5	2.64	28	1	180.2	135	53	72	165
Life	26	8	2.79	51	2	319.1	233	99	138	288

TONY GWYNN

Position: Outfield
Team: San Diego Padres
Born: May 9, 1960
  Los Angeles, CA
Height: 5′11″ **Weight:** 205 lbs.
Bats: Left **Throws:** Left
Acquired: Third-round pick,
  6/81 free-agent draft

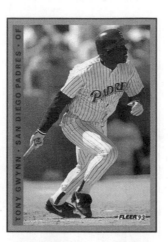

JOHN HABYAN

Position: Pitcher
Team: New York Yankees
Born: January 29, 1964
  Bayshore, NY
Height: 6′2″ **Weight:** 191 lbs.
Bats: Right **Throws:** Right
Acquired: Traded by Orioles for
  Stanley Jefferson, 7/89

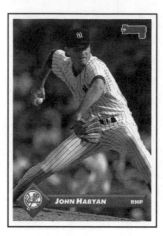

Now that the NL has added two expansion teams, will Tony Gwynn make a run at a .400 season? With pitching diluted throughout the league, the San Diego rightfielder might have the best chance of anyone in the game. He rarely strikes out and has the speed to beat out infield hits. In '87, he batted .370, the highest single-season mark of any active player. He just missed a fifth batting crown in '91 but did win his fifth Rawlings Gold Glove in six years. He has previously shown good speed, topping 30 steals four times, including a personal peak of 56 in 1987. In the '92 season, Gwynn hit .317, poked in 41 RBI, walked 46 times, and struck out a mere 16 times in 520 at-bats. The multi-talented lefty snagged a .982 fielding percentage, making only five errors in his 1,127 ⅔ innings of work.

Gwynn's 1993 cards look cool at 15 cents apiece. An early Gwynn sleeper is a 1985 Topps for $3 or less. Our pick for his best 1993 card is Donruss. We have chosen this card because it has a distinctive look.

In 1992, converted starter John Habyan found new success in the Yankees bullpen, tallying a career-high number of saves (seven). Oddly, opponents hit the righty more than 100 points better at Yankee Stadium (.355) than on the road (.223) during his 56 games in '92. Before '92, Habyan had only three saves in a six-year major league career. New York became addicted to Habyan in '91, using him a career-high 66 times. In his previous nine seasons, the righty's primary job had been as a starter. His best year in the rotation was a 6-7 showing with the '87 Orioles. Baltimore drafted Habyan in '82, following his high school graduation. He made his first appearance with the O's in '85. Habyan has developed one of the league's best pickoff throws.

Habyan's seesaw career hasn't produced big statistics so far. Although he'll keep contributing to New York's bullpen, his work won't augment future value of his common-priced cards. Our pick for his best 1993 card is Topps. We have chosen this card since the photograph captures the athletic ability of the player.

	BA	G	AB	R	H	2B	3B	HR	RBI	SB
92 NL	.317	128	520	77	165	27	3	6	41	3
Life	.327	1463	5701	842	1864	275	75	59	591	249

	W	L	ERA	G	SV	IP	H	ER	BB	SO
92 AL	5	6	3.84	56	7	72.2	84	31	21	44
Life	18	18	3.75	170	10	331.1	326	138	105	202

Series two cards from some companies were available at press time. If space allows, both cards are shown; if not, the most up-to-date cards are pictured.

DARRYL HAMILTON

Position: Outfield
Team: Milwaukee Brewers
Born: December 3, 1964
  Baton Rouge, LA
Height: 6'1" **Weight:** 180 lbs.
Bats: Left **Throws:** Right
Acquired: 11th-round pick,
  6/86 free-agent draft

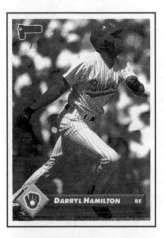 

Darryl Hamilton made right field his own with a banner year for the 1992 Brewers. He submitted career highs in home runs (five), RBI (62), and stolen bases (41). In addition, Hamilton filled in at center and left field when needed, preserving his status as one of the AL's most gifted flyhawkers. Expanding on his 57 RBI, .311 batting average, and 16 steals in 1991, Hamilton has the looks of a Milwaukee institution. His recent performances have been stark turnarounds from his '88 rookie debut with the Brew Crew. His 44-game audition yielded an unremarkable .184 with one homer and 11 RBI. He was promoted after only one full season in the minors. Following a year of seasoning with the '89 Pacific Coast League, Hamilton was back in the bigs for good.

Hamilton's an able starter, but won't be another Robin Yount. Until he finds a long-ball stroke, his common-priced cards will go unheeded. Our pick for his best 1993 card is Upper Deck. We have chosen this card for its artistic presentation.

	BA	G	AB	R	H	2B	3B	HR	RBI	SB
92 AL	.298	128	470	67	140	19	7	5	62	41
Life	.292	383	1134	172	331	43	13	8	148	74

CHRIS HAMMOND

Position: Pitcher
Team: Cincinnati Reds
Born: January 21, 1966
  Atlanta, GA
Height: 6'1" **Weight:** 190 lbs.
Bats: Left **Throws:** Left
Acquired: Sixth-round pick,
  6/86 free-agent draft

Chris Hammond's improved health didn't improve his 1992 season with Cincinnati. The hurler seemed mended from the elbow tendinitis he suffered in July 1991, along with his 1990 shoulder stiffness. Hammond's year end totals were 7-10 with a 4.21 ERA over 147 ⅓ innings of work. The '92 Reds' offense was weak, lending but four runs per game when Hammond was on the mound. He faced the same lack of offensive support in 1990. A five-game losing streak during six starts was caused in part by Cincinnati scoring just nine runs over that span. Hammond dominated the Triple-A American Association that year, leading the league with a 15-1 record, 149 strikeouts, and a 2.17 ERA. With Double-A Chattanooga in '88, he notched a loop-best 16 wins.

After an off-year by Hammond and many of the Reds, his 1993 commons look like unfavorable investments. Our pick for his best 1993 card is Fleer. We have chosen this card because of its overall appeal and pleasing looks.

	W	L	ERA	G	CG	IP	H	ER	BB	SO
92 NL	7	10	4.21	28	0	147.1	149	69	55	79
Life	14	19	4.25	51	0	258.1	254	122	115	133

ERIK
HANSON

Position: Pitcher
Team: Seattle Mariners
Born: May 18, 1965
  Kinnelon, NJ
Height: 6'6" **Weight:** 210 lbs.
Bats: Right **Throws:** Right
Acquired: Second-round pick,
  6/86 free-agent draft

 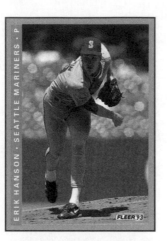

MIKE
HARKEY

Position: Pitcher
Team: Chicago Cubs
Born: October 25, 1966
  San Diego, CA
Height: 6'5" **Weight:** 220 lbs.
Bats: Right **Throws:** Right
Acquired: First-round pick,
  6/87 free-agent draft

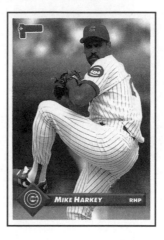 

Pitcher Erik Hanson nearly became baseball's only 20-game loser in 1992. The Mariners righthander was placed on the disabled list on August 23, due to a strained back. The media speculated that he was held out of action longer than necessary to avoid the humiliation of 20 losses. Once, Seattle fans thought Hanson could compile 20 wins in a season. After bursting onto the big league scene in 1988, the New Jersey native electrified the league with an 18-9, 211 strikeout performance in 1990. While his back was the worry of 1992, Hanson's elbow problems brought about an 8-8 decline in 1991. In 1989, tendinitis in his right shoulder was the culprit. Despite owning one of the American League's sharpest curveballs, Hanson faces a career crossroads in 1993.

Health problems have clouded Hanson's future. While his 1993 cards are affordable commons, they'll be useless clutter in your investment portfolio. Our pick for his best 1993 card is Topps. We have chosen this card because of its great combination of photography and design.

Pitcher Mike Harkey experienced baseball's oddest injury in 1992. In mid-September, during some pre-game horseplay, a failed backflip tore a tendon in his left knee. This injury sent Harkey to surgery and shortened his season. In the seven games he was able to participate in, he provided the Cubs with a 4-0 record and a 1.89 ERA, striking out 21 batters over 38 innings of work. Ironically, he began the season on the 60-day DL, recovering from the '91 shoulder surgery that cost him all but four starts that year. Injuries are nothing new to Harkey. Knee surgery and a shoulder ailment ruined his '89 progress at Triple-A Iowa. He missed two weeks of major league duty in '90 when his pitching shoulder flared up again. Harkey was named NL Rookie Pitcher of the Year in '90 when he was 12-6 with a 3.27 ERA in 27 starts.

Harkey's 1993 nickel-priced cards shouldn't be invested in until he stays healthy for two consecutive seasons. Our pick for his best 1993 card is Score. We have chosen this card due to the outstanding photographic composition.

	W	L	ERA	G	CG	IP	H	ER	BB	SO
92 AL	8	17	4.82	31	6	186.2	209	100	57	112
Life	45	42	3.76	114	14	752.1	734	314	225	577

	W	L	ERA	G	CG	IP	H	ER	BB	SO
92 NL	4	0	1.89	7	0	38.0	34	8	15	21
Life	16	11	3.12	43	2	265.0	241	92	95	148

Series two cards from some companies were available at press time. If space allows, both cards are shown; if not, the most up-to-date cards are pictured.

PETE HARNISCH

Position: Pitcher
Team: Houston Astros
Born: September 23, 1966
Commack, NY
Height: 6′ **Weight:** 207 lbs.
Bats: Right **Throws:** Right
Acquired: Traded from
Baltimore with Steve Finley
and Curt Schilling for Glenn
Davis, 1/91

BRIAN HARPER

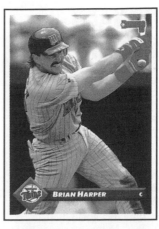

Position: Catcher
Team: Minnesota Twins
Born: October 16, 1959
Los Angeles, CA
Height: 6′2″ **Weight:** 208 lbs.
Bats: Right **Throws:** Right
Acquired: Signed as a free
agent, 1/88

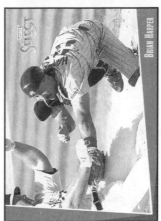

Houston starter Pete Harnisch, one of the team's brightest hopes for 1992, couldn't recapture his 1991 magic. He wound up with a 9-10 record and a 3.70 ERA, working 206 ⅔ innings. In '91, his first NL season, Harnisch was a career-best 12-9, earning his initial All-Star game appearance. One of his '91 season highlights came on September 6, when he struck out the Philadelphia side on nine pitches. He led the '91 'Stros in eight different categories. The Fordham University star was a first-round draft pick of Baltimore's in '87, debuting with the Orioles one year later. He began to show his full potential in '90, when he was 11-11 in 31 starts. Harnisch has given the Astros 30-plus starts in each of the last two years. After an off-season, Harnisch could try to attain his previous lofty ambitions again in 1993.

It would take a 20-win season for collectors to take notice of Harnisch's 1993 cards. Currently, his nickel issues are so-so choices. Our pick for his best 1993 card is Topps. We have chosen this card since its design makes it a standout.

Brian Harper continued to be the AL's top-hitting catcher in 1992. The Minnesota backstop was outmatched offensively only by Baltimore counterpart Mickey Tettleton, despite hitting more than 50 points higher (.307) than the O's receiver (.238). Harper managed career highs in hits (154) and RBI (73) in '92. The resident Twins catcher since '89, Harper was a bargain. After his '87 release by the A's, he was signed to a Triple-A contract. He had been dumped earlier that year by the Tigers and in '86 by the Cardinals. Due to his talented but underrated bat, the Twins have considered lengthening Harper's career by making him a designated hitter. Since debuting with the '79 Twins, Harper has seen action in three big league decades. If he continues to shine offensively, Harper's a cinch to play in a fourth.

Harper's 1993 commons just won't make it as investments. Unfortunately, they'll be just as overlooked as this talented catcher. Our pick for his best 1993 card is Upper Deck. We have chosen this card since the photograph captures the athletic ability of the player.

	W	L	ERA	G	CG	IP	H	ER	BB	SO
92 NL	9	10	3.70	34	0	206.2	182	85	64	164
Life	37	41	3.73	118	9	728.1	650	302	306	538

	BA	G	AB	R	H	2B	3B	HR	RBI	SB
92 AL	.307	140	502	58	154	25	0	9	73	0
Life	.295	788	2363	264	697	145	6	47	323	7

DONALD HARRIS

Position: Outfield
Team: Texas Rangers
Born: November 12, 1967
Waco TX
Height: 6'1" **Weight:** 185 lbs.
Bats: Right **Throws:** Right
Acquired: First-round pick,
6/89 free-agent draft

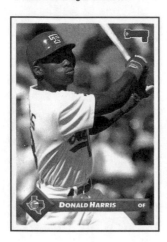 

LENNY HARRIS

Position: Infield
Team: Los Angeles Dodgers
Born: October 28, 1964
Miami, FL
Height: 5'10" **Weight:** 205 lbs.
Bats: Left **Throws:** Right
Acquired: Traded from Reds
with Kal Daniels for Mariano
Duncan and Tim Leary, 7/89

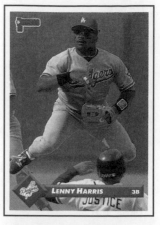

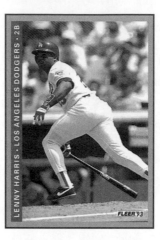 

 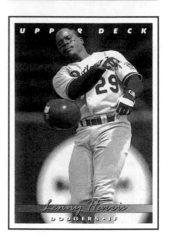

Outfielder Donald Harris failed to duplicate his 1991 debut with the Rangers in his second audition with the club. In '91, he hit .375 with one homer in an 18-game trial with Texas. The Texas native returned to Double-A in '92, collecting 11 homers, 39 RBI, and a .254 mark. However, his return to the bigs met with a deflated .182 average. He played in just 24 games for the Rangers in '92, only producing at the plate during road games. Discovered at Texas Tech University, where he made the team as a walk-on, Harris was the fifth player selected in the first round of the free-agent draft in June '89. Known for his gutsy defense and penchant for strikeouts, Harris remains a question mark in the '93 Texas outfield.

Following his 1992 slippage, Harris seems stuck behind the rising talent of David Hulse in center field. His nickel-priced cards will collect dust if he's trapped in Triple-A. Our pick for his best 1993 card is Donruss. We have chosen this card for its technical merits.

Lenny Harris played five different positions with LA in '92, often playing none of them particularly well. In fairness, the entire team suffered defensive setbacks. However, being a utilityman allowed Harris to commit errors (14) in various capacities. At the plate, Harris was another story. Although in '92 he only batted .139 against lefties, Harris broke his '90 career high of 15 stolen bases, swiping 19. He was solid against righties (.286), his usual nemeses. Before his mid-1989 trade to the Dodgers, Harris had served nearly seven years in the Cincinnati organization. Launched as a fifth-round selection in the '83 draft, Harris made a memorable Reds debut in '88. He batted .372 in 16 games. Although valued in the past for his versatility, Harris may lose his appeal with continued glove problems.

Harris doesn't have a full-time position. He doesn't have great lifetime stats. Investing in his commons doesn't make sense. Our pick for his best 1993 card is Upper Deck. We have chosen this card because it has a distinctive look.

	BA	G	AB	R	H	2B	3B	HR	RBI	SB
92 AL	.182	24	33	3	6	1	0	0	1	1
Life	.220	42	41	7	9	1	0	1	3	2

	BA	G	AB	R	H	2B	3B	HR	RBI	SB
92 NL	.271	135	347	28	94	11	0	0	30	19
Life	.279	548	1585	191	443	54	6	8	131	64

MIKE
HARTLEY

Position: Pitcher
Team: Minnesota Twins
Born: August 31, 1961
   Hawthorne, CA
Height: 6′1″ **Weight:** 197 lbs.
Bats: Right **Throws:** Right
Acquired: Traded from Phillies
   for David West, 12/92

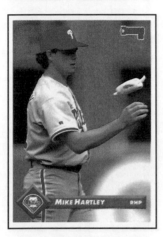 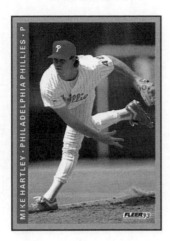

Mike Hartley started his second decade of pro ball with the Phillies in 1992. He served quietly in the Philadelphia bullpen, working anonymously in middle relief. Happily, he neared his past big league ratios of nearly a strikeout (53) per inning (55). The righthander notched his second consecutive season of 40-plus appearances (46) in '92. Hartley began the '91 season on the Dodgers' Opening-Day roster. He became a vital ingredient in the July trade which sent reliever Roger McDowell from the Phillies. His pro career, which began as an undrafted free-agent for St. Louis in '81, has been centered around relief work. He earned his first big league call-up with LA in '89, through the strength of seven wins and 18 saves in Triple-A. If he stays healthy, he should be a frequent worker in the '93 Twins' bullpen.

Being over 30 without a set role on the pitching staff mars Hartley. His 1993 commons aren't desirable. Our pick for his best 1993 card is Fleer. We have chosen this card because of its great combination of photography and design.

	W	L	ERA	G	SV	IP	H	ER	BB	SO
92 NL	7	6	3.44	46	0	55.0	54	21	23	53
Life	17	11	3.50	141	3	223.2	188	87	100	196

BRYAN
HARVEY

Position: Pitcher
Team: Florida Marlins
Born: June 2, 1963,
   Chattanooga, TN
Height: 6′2″ **Weight:** 219 lbs.
Bats: Right **Throws:** Right
Acquired: First-round pick,
   11/92 expansion draft

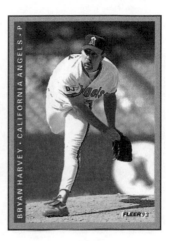 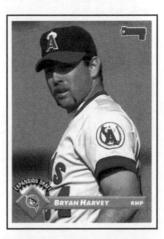

Throwing too many split-fingered fastballs may have caught up with Bryan Harvey in 1992. He was placed on the DL in June with elbow problems. He was only able to work in 28 ⅔ innings during his injury-shortened '92. When healthy, Harvey is one of the game's premier relief specialists. In 1991, he had a 2-4 record, 1.60 ERA, and 101 strikeouts in 78 ⅔ innings pitched. He converted 46 of 52 save opportunities, held opposing hitters to a .178 batting average, and made the AL All-Star team for the first time. He and starter Jim Abbott shared Angel MVP honors but the reliever was all alone at the top of the league's Rolaids Relief Man Award standings—the first time an Angel closer had done it. The hard-throwing righthander will continue mixing high heat and a 95 mph fastball with a splitter in '93, but he'll be doing it for the Florida Marlins.

Harvey's injury puts his cards on hold. Our pick for his best 1993 card is Fleer. We have chosen this card because the design lends itself to the best use of the elements.

	W	L	ERA	G	SV	IP	H	ER	BB	SO
92 AL	0	4	2.83	25	13	28.2	22	9	11	34
Life	16	20	2.49	250	126	307.2	219	85	126	365

BILLY HATCHER

Position: Outfield
Team: Boston Red Sox
Born: October 4, 1960
   Williams, AZ
Height: 5'10" **Weight:** 190 lbs.
Bats: Right **Throws:** Right
Acquired: Traded from Reds
   for Tom Bolton, 7/92

Billy Hatcher, star of the 1990 World Series, didn't shine in 1992. Cincinnati, who earned the '90 World Championship with Hatcher's record-setting nine hits being a key factor, virtually ignored the veteran outfielder for the first half of the '92 campaign. On July 9, after his playing time dwindled, Hatcher was unceremoniously shipped to Boston in exchange for a little-known pitcher. While he's sparkled in postseason play, many of Hatcher's regular-season exploits have been low-key. His greatest production came for the 1987 Astros, a season highlighted by 11 homers, 63 RBI, 53 stolen bases, and a .296 average. From 1986 through '90, Hatcher snatched at least 24 bases per year. The Arizona native began his pro career as a sixth-round draft choice of the Cubs in January '81.

   Batches of Hatchers will be untouched among common-priced 1993 cards. Keep it that way, if you're a smart investor. Our pick for his best 1993 card is Donruss. We have chosen this card for its technical merits.

	BA	G	AB	R	H	2B	3B	HR	RBI	SB
92 AL	.238	75	315	37	75	16	2	1	23	4
Life	.263	1004	3521	474	926	171	25	42	311	196

CHARLIE HAYES

Position: Third base
Team: Colorado Rockies
Born: May 29, 1965
   Hattiesburg, MS
Height: 6' **Weight:** 210 lbs.
Bats: Right **Throws:** Right
Acquired: First-round pick,
   11/92 expansion draft

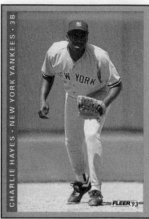

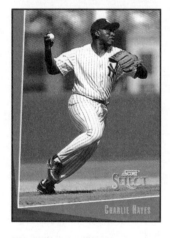

Third baseman Charlie Hayes escaped his stormy relationship with the Phillies and found a brief respite with the 1992 Yankees. After being criticized by Philly brass for defensive lapses, questionable motivation, and a potential weight problem, Hayes knew his days with the Phils were numbered. Practically given away to New York prior to spring training, Hayes returned the Yanks' hospitality with one of his best seasons ever. Never before in his previous nine pro seasons had Hayes hit more than a dozen homers in a year. His career-high RBI total was 57 with the 1990 Phillies. Not since Graig Nettles have the Yankees enjoyed such consistency at the hot corner. His performance did not go unnoticed by others, though, as he was snapped up as the second pick by the Colorado Rockies.

   Take a chance on a few 1993 commons of Hayes. His cards could boom if the third baseman helps put the Rockies on the map. Our pick for his best 1993 card is Donruss. We have chosen this card because it has a distinctive look.

	BA	G	AB	R	H	2B	3B	HR	RBI	SB
92 AL	.257	142	509	52	131	19	2	18	66	3
Life	.250	530	1845	168	461	77	4	48	219	13

Series two cards from some companies were available at press time. If space allows, both cards are shown; if not, the most up-to-date cards are pictured.

DAVE HENDERSON

Position: Outfield
Team: Oakland Athletics
Born: July 21, 1958
   Merced, CA
Height: 6'2" **Weight:** 220 lbs.
Bats: Right **Throws:** Right
Acquired: Signed as free agent
   12/87

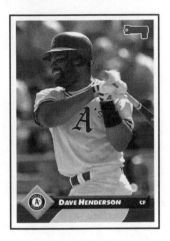

RICKEY HENDERSON

Position: Outfield
Team: Oakland Athletics
Born: December 25, 1958
   Chicago, IL
Height: 5'10" **Weight:** 190 lbs.
Bats: Right **Throws:** Left
Acquired: Traded from Yankees
   for Luis Polonia, Eric Plunk,
   and Greg Cadaret, 6/89

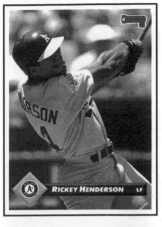

Dave Henderson, a fixture on past Oakland pennant winners, barely contributed to the team's 1992 division title. Not since his 59-game rookie season with the 1981 Mariners was Henderson so inactive. The cause was a hamstring pull, limiting Hendu to only 20 games. He was coming off a banner year in 1991, which produced his first All-Star game appearance. He smashed a personal-best 25 home runs, marking the ninth time he topped double digits in dingers. Oakland signed Henderson as a free agent before the 1988 campaign, and he responded with 24 homers, 94 RBI, and a career-high .304 average that first year.

   Henderson's success is his curse, too. Although he was a key to Oakland's 1988-90 league domination, teammates like McGwire and "another" Henderson got the credit. Especially after the injury, Henderson (and his common-priced cards) are overshadowed by other A's. Our pick for his best 1993 card is Donruss. We have chosen this card because of its overall appeal and pleasing looks.

Although hamstring problems sent Rickey Henderson to the DL early in the 1992 season, the speed merchant managed to compile impressive numbers anyhow. For the '92 season, he batted .283, smacked 15 homers, knocked in 46 RBI, swiped 48 bases, and walked 95 times. He struck out only 56 times in a total of 396 at-bats. At age 34, Henderson holds both single-season and career records for stolen bases. Though he no longer has world-class speed, he still ranks near the top of the league. Henderson's best season was 1990, when he was named AL MVP in a close vote over Detroit's Cecil Fielder. In '91, the swift left fielder surpassed Lou Brock as the leading base-stealer of all time.

   Henderson's 1993 cards won't pay short-term returns. However, he will up those 15 cent values with a race to Cooperstown. Any 1980s Henderson is a near-untouchable investment. An oddball possibility is the '92 Score "Dream Team" at a quarter or less. Our pick for his best 1993 card is Upper Deck. We have chosen this card since the photograph captures the athletic ability of the player.

	BA	G	AB	R	H	2B	3B	HR	RBI	SB
92 AL	.143	20	63	1	9	1	0	0	2	0
Life	.262	1375	4550	646	1191	253	16	172	624	48

	BA	G	AB	R	H	2B	3B	HR	RBI	SB
92 AL	.283	117	396	77	112	18	3	15	46	48
Life	.291	1859	6879	1472	2000	329	54	199	725	1042

TOM HENKE

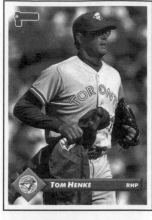

Position: Pitcher
Team: Texas Rangers
Born: December 21, 1957
  Kansas City, MO
Height: 6'5" **Weight:** 225 lbs.
Bats: Right **Throws:** Right
Acquired: Signed as a free
  agent, 12/92

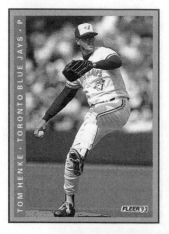

MIKE HENNEMAN

Position: Pitcher
Team: Detroit Tigers
Born: December 11, 1961
  St. Charles, MO
Height: 6'4" **Weight:** 195 lbs.
Bats: Right **Throws:** Right
Acquired: Fourth-round pick,
  6/84 free-agent draft

For the fourth time in his career, Tom Henke enjoyed a 30-save season. He'll try for a fifth as a Ranger in '93. After reaching 32 saves both in 1990 and '91, the lanky reliever seemed ready for a decline. Fellow reliever Duane Ward has adopted an increasing workload, giving Henke fewer save opportunities. Yet, Henke has maintained a sub-three ERA for the last six years. In '92, he ended up 3-2 with a 2.26 ERA and 34 saves in 57 games. A bargain acquisition in 1985, Henke was provided as compensation when Toronto lost free-agent catcher Cliff Johnson to Texas. Bred in the Texas farm system, Henke made his big league debut in 1982. Even at age 35, he continues as one of baseball's best closers.

Strangely, a handful of 30-save seasons isn't enough to convince collectors of Henke's card appeal. His 1993s will beg for buyers at a nickel apiece. Our pick for his best 1993 card is Topps. We have chosen this card due to the outstanding photographic composition.

Detroit reliever Mike Henneman compiled a career high in saves (24) with the 1992 Tigers, exceeding 20 saves for the fourth time in a six-year career. Most importantly, the Detroit bullpen institution surpassed 55 appearances (60) for the sixth consecutive season. He worked in 77 1/3 innings in '92, maintaining a 3.96 ERA. Before the '92 season, he averaged nearly 10 wins per year. A product of Oklahoma State University, the righthander needed less than four seasons of minor league exposure before becoming a relief regular for the 1987 Bengals. Henneman reeled off 13 consecutive saves in 1988, on the way to 22 saves, nine wins, and a 1.87 ERA. He was named to the 1989 All-Star team.

Henneman can't hold a candle to American League contemporaries like Dennis Eckersley or Tom Henke. His common-priced cards have never been hot. For 1993, they'll be icy cold. Our pick for his best 1993 card is Score. We have chosen this card for the superior presentation of information on its back.

	W	L	ERA	G	SV	IP	H	ER	BB	SO
92 AL	3	2	2.26	57	34	55.2	40	14	22	46
Life	32	30	2.64	487	220	623.0	477	183	198	695

	W	L	ERA	G	SV	IP	H	ER	BB	SO
92 AL	2	6	3.96	60	24	77.1	75	34	20	58
Life	51	27	3.05	369	104	534.0	488	181	192	371

Series two cards from some companies were available at press time. If space allows, both cards are shown; if not, the most up-to-date cards are pictured.

BUTCH HENRY

Position: Pitcher
Team: Colorado Rockies
Born: October 7, 1968
   El Paso, TX
Height: 6'1" **Weight:** 195 lbs.
Bats: Left **Throws:** Left
Acquired: Second-round pick,
   11/92 expansion draft

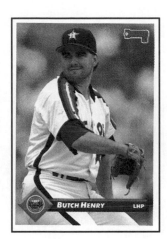

After five years of minor league frustration, hurler Floyd Bluford "Butch" Henry was welcomed to the Houston lineup. After posting a 4-0 record with a 1.57 ERA in spring training, Henry was a sure thing for the majors. Houston's awkward offense provided the rookie with just over three runs per game, accounting for his thin 1992 record. Yet, the Astros found that the young lefthander could carry a large workload. For the '92 season, he worked over 165 innings. The 'Stros acquired Henry in the 1990 Bill Doran deal. Henry had been a draft pick of the Reds in '87, but had never advanced above Double-A. He'll hook up with the Colorado Rockies for '93.

Although Henry seems recovered from 1989 elbow surgery, he can't be expected to top 10-12 wins per season, at best. Don't mess with his 1993 commons. Our pick for his best 1993 card is Donruss. We have chosen this card because of its great combination of photography and design.

	W	L	ERA	G	CG	IP	H	ER	BB	SO
92 NL	6	9	4.02	28	2	165.2	185	74	41	96
Life	6	9	4.02	28	2	165.2	185	74	41	96

DOUG HENRY

Position: Pitcher
Team: Milwaukee Brewers
Born: December 10, 1963
   Sacramento, CA
Height: 6'4" **Weight:** 185 lbs.
Bats: Right **Throws:** Right
Acquired: Eighth-round pick,
   6/85 free-agent draft

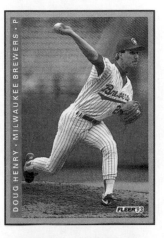

Despite a bulging 4.02 ERA, Doug Henry continued to anchor the Milwaukee bullpen in 1992. Although his ERA ballooned, his save total (29) rose accordingly. Ironically, the righthander may owe his current success to past elbow surgery. He spent the first four years of his minor league career as a starter. Once his elbow needed mending, the Milwaukee organization converted Henry to relief duties. The righthander blossomed into the Brewers Rookie of the Year in 1991, thanks to a record of 2-1 with 15 saves and a 1.00 ERA in 32 games. These exploits occurred after a July 14 promotion from Triple-A Denver. Despite an impressive collegiate career at Arizona State University, Henry remained overlooked through much of the 1985 free-agent draft.

Henry was an unnoticed influence in Milwaukee's 1992 pennant run. The hurler's age would be the only negative factor to observe when investing in his 1993 commons. Our pick for his best 1993 card is Fleer. We have chosen this card because of its overall appeal and pleasing looks.

	W	L	ERA	G	SV	IP	H	ER	BB	SO
92 AL	1	4	4.02	68	29	65.0	64	29	24	52
Life	3	5	2.94	100	44	101.0	80	33	38	80

DWAYNE HENRY

Position: Pitcher
Team: Cincinnati Reds
Born: February 16, 1962
   Elkton, MD
Height: 6'3" **Weight:** 205 lbs.
Bats: Right **Throws:** Right
Acquired: Claimed off waivers
   from Houston, 11/91

Besides being one of three pitchers named Henry throughout the majors, Dwayne Henry didn't have many significant accomplishments with the 1992 Reds. He was a worthy spot reliever, as evidenced by a .192 average by opposing righthanded hitters. Following his 1980 high school graduation, the pitcher's first 12 pro seasons were spent playing for teams throughout the south. Beginning as a Texas draft choice in '80, he debuted with the Rangers in '84. Henry ping-ponged between the minors and Texas from 1984-88. Swapped to Atlanta, he served parts of '89 and '90 with the Braves. After his '91 release from the Astros, Henry appeared in a career-high number of games with the Reds.

A low-profile reliever, Henry became obliterated by the statistics and personalities of Reds bullpen mates Rob Dibble and Norm Charlton. As he's lost among such names, Henry's 1993 commons will be lost forever. Our pick for his best 1993 card is Topps. We have chosen this card for the superior presentation of information on its back.

	W	L	ERA	G	SV	IP	H	ER	BB	SO
92 NL	3	3	3.33	60	0	83.2	59	31	44	72
Life	11	13	4.21	212	7	267.1	225	125	167	229

PAT HENTGEN

Position: Pitcher
Team: Toronto Blue Jays
Born: November 13, 1968
   Detroit, MI
Height: 6'2" **Weight:** 200 lbs.
Bats: Right **Throws:** Right
Acquired: Fifth-round pick,
   6/86 draft

Pat Hentgen, described by some as the Blue Jays' top starting pitching prospect, did lots of relieving in 1992. In fact, 26 of his 28 games were from the bullpen. He won five decisions and, in 229 batters faced, allowed 30 earned runs. That computes, over the course of the '92 season, to a 5.04 ERA. Hentgen had some trouble keeping the ball in the park, permitting four homers in his first 25 innings. Such stats reflect a pitcher who has trouble harnessing good stuff. In his first six professional seasons, Hentgen never allowed more hits than innings pitched, and only twice did he have an ERA over 4.00. Hentgen, however, only reached double figures in victories once, even though he had at least 28 starts five times. He'll have to work on getting more outs early in the count. His walk and strikeout totals are both high.

Let Hentgen get some more quality experience before mulling over his 1993s. Our pick for his best 1993 card is Score. We have chosen this card because of its great combination of photography and design.

	W	L	ERA	G	SV	IP	H	ER	BB	SO
92 AL	5	2	5.36	28	0	50.1	49	30	32	39
Life	5	2	4.99	31	0	57.2	54	32	35	42

CARLOS HERNANDEZ

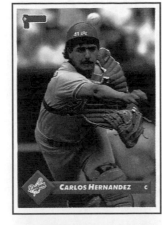

Position: Catcher
Team: Los Angeles Dodgers
Born: May 24, 1967
    Bolivar, Venezuela
Height: 5'11" **Weight:** 185 lbs.
Bats: Right **Throws:** Right
Acquired: Signed as free agent,
    10/84

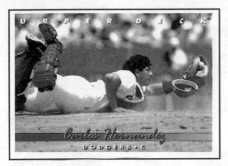

CESAR HERNANDEZ

Position: Outfield
Team: Cincinnati Reds
Born: September 28, 1966
    Yamasa, Dominican
    Republic
Height: 6' **Weight:** 160 lbs.
Bats: Right **Throws:** Right
Acquired: Claimed off waivers
    from Expos, 12/91

Carlos Hernandez became the heir apparent to the Dodgers catching throne in 1992. As veteran Mike Scioscia slumped amidst his drive to free agency, Hernandez became an increasingly active force in the LA lineup. His sole downfall was hitting righthanded pitching (.215). Other than that, for the '92 season the backstop hit .260 overall with three homers and 17 RBI in his 173 at-bats. In '91, Hernandez passed his final minor league test by hitting .345 in Triple-A. He was named to the Pacific Coast League All-Star team for his efforts. Hernandez batted a combined .206 in his two brief auditions, far less than his 1992 accomplishments. Ironically, the Dodgers signed Hernandez as an infielder in 1984, moving him behind the plate only in 1986.

Expect Hernandez to contend for the Dodgers' starting receiver's job in 1993. The homer-shy Hernandez and his common-priced cards will lose out in most investment battles. Our pick for his best 1993 card is Score. We have chosen this card because it has a distinctive look.

Cesar Hernandez sneaked onto an injury-filled Reds roster in 1992, enjoying his first taste of the majors in seven professional seasons. The sampling was bittersweet for the veteran Dominican. Incredibly, Hernandez hit .077 against major league righthanders, compared to a .342 mark against lefties. Before the '92 Cincinnati promotion, he was hitting .281 with three homers and 25 RBI at Double-A Chattanooga. Originally a first-round draft pick by Montreal in '85, Hernandez failed to reach the Triple-A level after six minor league seasons. His biggest numbers were 19 homers and 60 RBI in the Class-A Midwest League in '88.

With the loss of outfielders Glenn Braggs and Dave Martinez, Hernandez could land a reserve spot with Cincy. The thin promise of possible part-time play isn't enough to energize his common-priced cards, however. Our pick for his best 1993 card is Topps. We have chosen this card due to the outstanding photographic composition.

	BA	G	AB	R	H	2B	3B	HR	RBI	SB
92 NL	.260	69	173	11	45	4	0	3	17	0
Life	.251	94	207	14	52	6	0	3	19	1

	BA	G	AB	R	H	2B	3B	HR	RBI	SB
92 AA	.277	93	328	50	91	23	4	3	27	12
92 NL	.275	34	51	6	14	4	0	0	4	3

Series two cards from some companies were available at press time. If space allows, both cards are shown; if not, the most up-to-date cards are pictured.

JEREMY HERNANDEZ

Position: Pitcher
Team: San Diego Padres
Born: July 7, 1966
　　Burbank, CA
Height: 6'6"　**Weight:** 205 lbs.
Bats: Right　**Throws:** Right
Acquired: Traded from
　　Cardinals for Randall Byers,
　　4/89

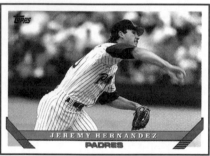

Jeremy Hernandez spent the first four years of his pro career as a starter. After spending 1990 at Double-A Wichita going 7-6 with a 4.53 ERA in a career-high 26 starts, the Padres switched him to the bullpen during '91. That route proved to be his ticket to the majors. Hernandez saved 13 games for Las Vegas of the Pacific Coast League, and got a call to the Padres on September 1. With San Diego, he appeared in nine games and went 14 ⅓ scoreless innings, picking up two saves. In '92, he spent more time in the minors, again pitching out of the bullpen. During his time with the Padres in the '92 season, he notched a 1-4 record with a 4.17 ERA and one save over the course of 36 ⅔ innings. The righty struck out 25 of the 157 batters he faced, allowing 17 earned runs.

A so-so relief campaign in 1992 means 1993 cards of Hernandez are stale choices at ten cents each. Our pick for his best 1993 card is Donruss. We have chosen this card for its technical merits.

	W	L	ERA	G	SV	IP	H	ER	BB	SO
92 NL	1	4	4.17	26	1	36.2	39	17	11	25
Life	1	4	3.00	35	3	51.0	47	17	16	34

ROBERTO HERNANDEZ

Position: Pitcher
Team: Chicago White Sox
Born: November 11, 1964
　　Santurce, Puerto Rico
Height: 6'4"　**Weight:** 220 lbs.
Bats: Right　**Throws:** Right
Acquired: Traded from Angels
　　for Mark Davis, 8/89

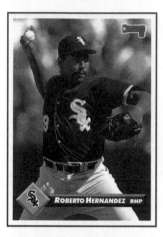

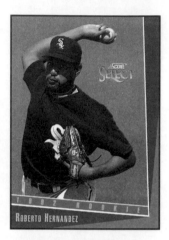

Roberto Hernandez was a little old for a rookie in 1992, but he was a big help in the White Sox bullpen. The batting average against Hernandez in his first eight appearances was .114, and he picked up two wins over that stretch. He was able to maintain his good showing during his other 18 outings during '92, winding up with a 7-3 record, a 1.65 ERA, 12 saves, and four holds over 71 innings of work. Hernandez struck out 68 of the 277 batters he faced during his campaign for '92, allowing only 13 earned runs and finishing 27 of the games he came in to relieve. His pitching was all the more impressive after surgery in '91 to treat numbness in his right hand. Hernandez was a first-round draft pick of California in 1986. After being dealt to Chicago, the White Sox converted him to a reliever.

Hernandez quietly made an impression in 1992. Get his 1993 cards for 15 cents or less. He's here to stay. Our pick for his best 1993 card is Upper Deck. We have chosen this card because it has a distinctive look.

	W	L	ERA	G	SV	IP	H	ER	BB	SO
92 AL	7	3	1.65	43	12	71.0	45	13	20	68
Life	8	3	2.72	52	12	86.0	63	26	27	74

XAVIER HERNANDEZ

Position: Pitcher
Team: Houston Astros
Born: August 16, 1965
   Port Arthur, TX
Height: 6'2" **Weight:** 185 lbs.
Bats: Left **Throws:** Right
Acquired: First-round pick,
   12/89 Rule 5 draft

 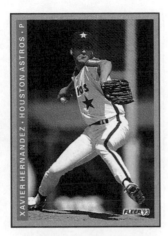

 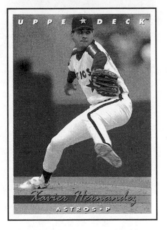

Xavier Hernandez made the Houston bullpen his own with a career-best season in 1992. Not only was he one of the Astros' most dependable and effective pitchers, Hernandez erased the blots on his record caused by consecutive disappointments in 1990 and '91. As proof, he carved more than two full points off his lifetime ERA. For the '92 season, Hernandez went 9-1 with a 2.11 ERA, seven saves, and three holds, striking out 96 of the batters he faced along the way. The righthander made his big league debut with the Blue Jays in 1989, going 1-0 in seven appearances. His National League arrival ended with an unspectacular 2-1 record and a 4.62 ERA in 34 games.

No matter how much Hernandez keeps improving, there are others who will be earning all the glory for the Astro bullpen in 1993. Middle relievers get no respect, and Hernandez cards will get yawns at three to five cents each. Our pick for his best 1993 card is Fleer. We have chosen this card due to the outstanding photographic composition.

	W	L	ERA	G	SV	IP	H	ER	BB	SO
92 NL	9	1	2.11	77	7	111.0	81	26	42	96
Life	14	9	3.58	150	10	259.0	232	103	106	182

OREL HERSHISER

Position: Pitcher
Team: Los Angeles Dodgers
Born: September 16, 1958
   Buffalo, NY
Height: 6'3" **Weight:** 190 lbs.
Bats: Right **Throws:** Right
Acquired: 17th-round pick,
   6/79 free-agent draft

Orel Hershiser's restored health didn't prevent the downfall of the 1992 Dodgers. However, the veteran pitcher reaped big dividends for staying off the DL. An incentive clause in his contract offered $250,000 for every start he made after his 30th. Los Angeles was concerned about Hershiser's medically reconstructed shoulder, which limited him to a combined total of four games over 1990 and '91. The righty went 10-15 with a 3.67 ERA in 33 starts for the '92 Dodgers. Hershiser's career peaked in 1988, when he pitched LA to a World Championship. His Cy Young-winning totals included a 23-8 record and a record-breaking 59 consecutive scoreless innings. Hershiser won't escape the 10 to 15 wins per year syndrome unless he gets steady run support.

If the Dodgers begin 1993 with more losses, cards of Hershiser and his teammates will become fireplace kindling. Avoid his nickel-priced issues. Our pick for his best 1993 card is Score. We have chosen this card since the photograph captures the athletic ability of the player.

	W	L	ERA	G	CG	IP	H	ER	BB	SO
92 NL	10	15	3.67	33	1	210.2	209	86	69	130
Life	116	82	2.87	289	59	1805.0	1587	576	539	1230

GREG HIBBARD

Position: Pitcher
Team: Chicago Cubs
Born: September 13, 1964
New Orleans, LA
Height: 6' **Weight:** 190 lbs.
Bats: Left **Throws:** Left
Acquired: Traded from Marlins
for Alex Arias and Gary
Scott, 11/92

Greg Hibbard topped double figures in wins (10) for the third season in a row. The White Sox lefty continued a streak started in 1990, when he was a career-best 14-9. Most impressively, Hibbard maintained his reputation as one of Chicago's most durable pitchers. He's exceeded 175 innings for three consecutive years. Although Hibbard's 11-11 record from 1991 seemed reasonable, the ChiSox shipped him back to Triple-A in July for a week. In '92, he was at his best while pitching at home in Comiskey Park (.247) or against lefthanded (.224) hitters. It remains to be seen if he can continue this pattern with the crosstown Cubs in '93. Surprisingly, Hibbard wasn't always a starter. After being picked by the Royals in the 16th round of the 1986 draft, he spent his first season as a reliever.

Hibbard's average past and his lackluster future aren't hopeful signs for card investors. Decline his 1993 common-priced issues. Our pick for his best 1993 card is Topps. We have chosen this card for its artistic presentation.

	W	L	ERA	G	CG	IP	H	ER	BB	SO
92 AL	10	7	4.40	31	0	176.0	187	86	57	69
Life	41	34	3.78	119	10	718.1	727	302	210	287

BRYAN HICKERSON

Position: Pitcher
Team: San Francisco Giants
Born: October 13, 1963
Bemidji, MN
Height: 6'2" **Weight:** 195 lbs.
Bats: Left **Throws:** Left
Acquired: Traded by Twins with
Jose Dominguez and Ray
Velasquez for David Blakely
and Dan Gladden, 3/87

Bryan Hickerson provided a stable foundation for the Giants bullpen in 1992, his first full year with the team. As the season progressed, he surpassed Dave Righetti as the team's top lefty reliever. In '91, Hickerson divided his time between San Francisco and Triple-A Phoenix. With the Giants, he was 2-2 in 17 appearances, earning 43 strikeouts in 50 innings. Hickerson turned down an '85 draft offer from the Cardinals in order to earn a degree in sports and exercise science from the University of Minnesota. He was chosen by the Twins in the seventh round of the '86 draft. During Class-A ball in 1987, Hickerson reeled off an 11-0 record in 17 games. The lefthander's major league progress is remarkable, considering that he missed the entire '88 campaign due to reconstructive elbow surgery.

His age and shifting mound responsibilities make Hickerson's cards undependable at a nickel each. Our pick for his best 1993 card is Donruss. We have chosen this card for its technical merits.

	W	L	ERA	G	SV	IP	H	ER	BB	SO
92 NL	5	3	3.09	61	0	87.1	74	30	21	68
Life	7	5	3.28	78	0	137.1	127	50	38	111

GLENALLEN HILL

Position: Outfield
Team: Cleveland Indians
Born: March 22, 1965
  Santa Cruz, CA
Height: 6'2" **Weight:** 210 lbs.
Bats: Right **Throws:** Right
Acquired: Traded from Blue
  Jays with Mark Whiten,
  Denis Boucher, and cash for
  Tom Candiotti and Turner
  Ward, 6/91

KEN HILL

Position: Pitcher
Team: Montreal Expos
Born: December 14, 1965
  Lynn, MA
Height: 6'2" **Weight:** 175 lbs.
Bats: Right **Throws:** Right
Acquired: Traded by Cardinals
  for Andres Galarraga, 11/91

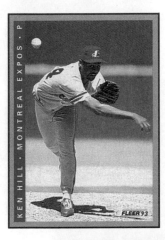

Glenallen Hill shared duties in left field with Thomas Howard for the 1992 Cleveland Indians. Hill began '92 by hitting .367 with one homer and eight RBI in spring training. However, he was sidelined by a pulled groin in April. Nevertheless, he achieved career highs in home runs (18), RBI (49), and stolen bases (9). By the end of the '92 season, the strong-armed but erratic flyhawk owned five assists and six errors. Hill's Toronto career commenced in '83, when he was a ninth-round draft selection out of high school. He labored through seven minor league seasons before getting his first shot with the Blue Jays in '89. He batted .288 in that 19-game audition. Returning for a full season in 1991, Hill hit 12 homers and 32 RBI in an injury-shortened 84-game slate.

Hill needs to play a healthy, complete season to display his full potential. For now, his 1993 commons remain tempting longshots. Our pick for his best 1993 card is Donruss. We have chosen this card for its technical merits.

Ken Hill became one of baseball's biggest surprises in 1992. The Expos looked foolish at first glance, trading a known slugger like Andres Galarraga for an unproven package like Ken Hill. Going into 1992, he owned a lifetime mark of 23-32 with a 4.03 ERA. For his '92 efforts, he garnered a 16-9 record with a 2.68 ERA over 218 innings. Montreal looked deeper and found talent in a young hurler who relies on a fastball, forkball, and changeup. Hill's 11-10 with the '91 Cardinals was the winningest season he ever experienced in his first seven years as a pro. His career began when he signed as an undrafted free agent by Detroit in '85. Contrast Hill's '92 achievements to his 7-15 record with the '89 Cards, when his 99 walks led National League pitchers.

Quietly scoop up Hill's 1993 commons. If the upcoming Expos team sneaks into a pennant on the strength of a 20-win season by Hill, those cards could hit the 15-cent mark fast. Our pick for his best 1993 card is Upper Deck. We have chosen this card because of its overall appeal and pleasing looks.

	BA	G	AB	R	H	2B	3B	HR	RBI	SB
92 AL	.241	102	369	38	89	16	1	18	49	9
Life	.245	277	902	118	221	35	6	39	113	25

	W	L	ERA	G	CG	IP	H	ER	BB	SO
92 NL	16	9	2.68	33	3	218.0	187	65	75	150
Life	39	41	3.61	117	6	688.2	615	276	280	447

MILT
HILL

Position: Pitcher
Team: Cincinnati Reds
Born: August 22, 1965
  Atlanta, GA
Height: 6′ **Weight:** 180 lbs.
Bats: Right **Throws:** Right
Acquired: 28th-round pick,
  6/87 free-agent draft

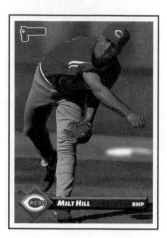
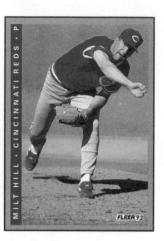

ERIC
HILLMAN

Position: Pitcher
Team: New York Mets
Born: April 27, 1966 Gary, IN
Height: 6′10″ **Weight:** 225 lbs.
Bats: Left **Throws:** Left
Acquired: 16th-round pick,
  6/87 draft

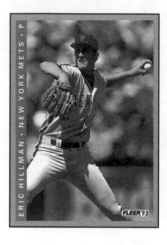

Milt Hill carved a niche in the Reds bullpen in 1992, becoming a terminator against lefthanded hitters. Lefties hit barely .040 off the Georgia native, compared to .304 earned by righthanders. Overall in '92, Hill went 0-0 with a 3.15 ERA. The righthander debuted with the Reds in '91, going 1-1 in 22 games. In 33 ⅓ relief innings, he surrendered only one home run. The Atlanta native recorded his first victory in the majors against the Braves. Throughout his six-year professional career, Hill has pitched exclusively in relief. He tallied consecutive 13-save seasons in 1988-89, before beginning a three-year stint at Triple-A Nashville. He paved the way for his '92 Cincinnati return by earning a career-best 16 saves in the American Association.

Despite the departure of reliever Norm Charlton, Hill will be overshadowed by Rob Dibble. Don't bet more than a nickel apiece on his '93 cards. Our pick for his best 1993 card is Fleer. We have chosen this card because of its great combination of photography and design.

Eric Hillman is the tallest player ever to come to camp for the Mets. Despite his size, however, Hillman has yet to step forward as another in a series of stars to grace Shea Stadium's mound. He got to the majors in the first half of the 1992 season, but things did not go well. In his 11 outings during the '92 campaign, Hillman went 2-2 with a 5.33 ERA. That debut, combined with his age, means Hillman must raise his game a notch, or he could be caught and passed by upcoming prospects. He did show some good signs for Tidewater in '92, going 2-1 with a 3.45 ERA in his first 19 games. All but one of those 19 appearances came out of the bullpen, representing a departure from the first five years of his career. Since Hillman's stuff does not seem to be enough for a closing role, his future would appear to be in long relief.

The Mets like Hillman. You might like him, too. Try his 1993 issues at 15 cents each. Our pick for his best 1993 card is Fleer. We have chosen this card for the superior presentation of information on its back.

	W	L	ERA	G	SV	IP	H	ER	BB	SO
92 NL	0	0	3.15	14	1	20.0	15	7	5	10
Life	1	1	3.54	36	1	53.1	51	21	13	30

	W	L	ERA	G	SV	IP	H	ER	BB	SO
92 NL	2	2	5.33	11	0	52.1	67	31	10	16
Life	2	2	5.33	11	0	52.1	67	31	10	16

STERLING HITCHCOCK

Position: Pitcher
Team: New York Yankees
Born: April 29, 1971
Fayetteville, NC
Height: 6'1" **Weight:** 200 lbs.
Bats: Left **Throws:** Left
Acquired: Ninth-round pick,
6/89 free-agent draft

CHRIS HOILES

Position: Catcher
Team: Baltimore Orioles
Born: March 20, 1965
Bowling Green, OH
Height: 6' **Weight:** 206 lbs.
Bats: Right **Throws:** Right
Acquired: Traded from Tigers
with Cesar Mejia and
Robinson Garces for Fred
Lynn, 9/88

 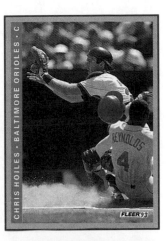

Sterling Hitchcock did his best to shine in the bigs in 1992. He received a call-up late in the summer of '92 and made the most of it, debuting on September 11 against the Royals. In that outing, he allowed just one run in six innings. He should get a long look in spring training in '93, along with fellow phenoms Sam Militello and Bob Wickman. The fact that Hitchcock is lefthanded is all the better. Yankee Stadium is not quite the haven for lefties that it used to be, but every club loves a southpaw who can throw the ball over the plate. Hitchcock signed out of Armwood High School in Florida and dominated in his first look at the pros. He was named the Gulf Coast League "Star of Stars," and was tabbed Topps Player of the Month for August. Hitchcock pitched a no-hitter while working in the Class-A Sally League in '90.

Hitchcock certainly seems to be the real thing. Grab up his '93s for a refreshing payoff when he makes his full-time splash in the bigs. Our pick for his best 1993 card is Upper Deck. We have chosen this card because it will increase in value.

Chris Hoiles made the most of his limited opportunities with the 1992 Orioles. He hit the 20-homer mark in just over 90 games, despite a broken bone in his right wrist after being beaned by a pitch. Hoiles bested his '91 efforts of 11 home runs, 31 RBI, and a .253 average in 107 games. He did not fare well in tryouts with Baltimore in '89 and '90, never clearing .200 in either trip to the bigs. Hoiles joined the O's organization in mid-1988, as one of three prospects received from Detroit. The Tigers snared Hoiles in the '86 draft, discovering him out of Eastern Michigan University. A strong-armed, competent receiver, expect a healthy Hoiles to terrorize AL pitchers even more in '93.

Hoiles could bring some unexpected payoffs to collectors who invest in his 1993 commons. If the young catcher turns up his offense a notch, he could homer the Orioles to a pennant. Search out Hoiles in the 1990 Score Traded set for 50 cents. Our pick for his best 1993 card is Fleer. We have chosen this card since its design makes it a standout.

	W	L	ERA	G	CG	IP	H	ER	BB	SO
92 AA	6	9	2.58	24	2	147.0	116	42	42	156
92 AL	0	2	8.31	3	0	13.0	23	12	6	6

	BA	G	AB	R	H	2B	3B	HR	RBI	SB
92 AL	.274	96	310	49	85	10	1	20	40	0
Life	.250	232	723	92	181	29	1	32	78	0

DAVE HOLLINS

Position: Third base
Team: Philadelphia Phillies
Born: May 25, 1966
Buffalo, NY
Height: 6'1" **Weight:** 207 lbs.
Bats: Both **Throws:** Right
Acquired: Drafted from Padres,
12/89, Rule 5 Draft

Dave Hollins became the classic "one who got away" story for San Diego in 1992. Drafted off the Padres roster in '89, Hollins became Philly's '92 team leader in homers (27) and RBI (93). His hitting continues to be a strength, as he managed a .270 average over the course of 156 games. Before the season, he owned a mere 11 homers and 36 RBI in 128 games spread over two seasons. Following the trade of third baseman Charlie Hayes, the Phillies cleared the hot corner and utilized Hollins on a full-time basis. In limited duty, his '91 totals were impressive: six homers, 21 RBI, and a .298 average. Hollins capped his '90 debut with the Phils by socking a record-tying three pinch-hit home runs. Before going to San Diego in the 1987 draft, Hollins played for the U.S. Olympic baseball team in 1986.

Expect to pay at least a dime apiece for Hollins' 1993 cards. Dealers claim he's the next coming of Mike Schmidt. Let the buyer beware. Our pick for his best 1993 card is Upper Deck. We have chosen this card for its technical merits.

	BA	G	AB	R	H	2B	3B	HR	RBI	SB
92 NL	.270	156	586	104	158	28	4	27	93	9
Life	.263	284	851	136	224	38	6	38	129	10

JESSE HOLLINS

Position: Pitcher
Team: Chicago Cubs
Born: January 27, 1970
Conroe, TX
Height: 6'3" **Weight:** 200 lbs.
Bats: Right **Throws:** Right
Acquired: 40th-round pick,
6/88 free-agent draft

Jesse Hollins is one of the better pitching prospects in the Cubs' organization, and he seemed to come into his own in 1992. After his first three pro years, during which he moved between the rotation and the bullpen, Hollins carved a niche for himself as a closer. Pitching at the highest level of his career, he became the runaway save leader in the Cubs' minor league system. Hollins reached the 20-save mark in late July by escaping a bases-loaded jam in the ninth. He has been compared to Lee Smith. However, he has not always thrown the ball over the plate. Hollins walked nearly one man per inning in '91. He won the Junior College World Series in '89. He had some success as a starter in '90 when he led the Class-A New York-Penn League with his 10 wins. He was Topps Player of the Month for August that year.

Although he will probably make the bigs in the near future, don't expect another Lee Smith. Save your pennies when it comes to Hollins' '93s. Our pick for his best 1993 card is Upper Deck. We have chosen this card because it will increase in value.

	W	L	ERA	G	SV	IP	H	ER	BB	SO
92 AA	3	4	3.20	63	25	70.1	60	25	32	73
92 NL	0	0	13.50	4	0	4.2	8	7	5	0

DARREN
HOLMES

Position: Pitcher
Team: Colorado Rockies
Born: April 25, 1966
   Asheville, NC
Height: 6' **Weight:** 199 lbs.
Bats: Right **Throws:** Right
Acquired: First-round pick,
   11/92 expansion draft

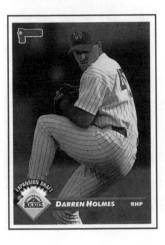 

SAM
HORN

Position: Designated hitter
Team: Baltimore Orioles
Born: November 2, 1963
   Dallas, TX
Height: 6'5" **Weight:** 247 lbs.
Bats: Left **Throws:** Left
Acquired: Signed as a free
   agent, 2/90

For the third consecutive year, Darren Holmes danced between the majors and Triple-A, hoping to win a permanent job in the bigs. The righthanded reliever presented his most convincing argument yet, submitting a 1992 ERA (2.55) more than two points lighter than his career mark, complemented by personal bests in wins (4) and saves (6). Holmes specialized in short relief, a marked change for this veteran starter. He worked in 41 games for the '92 campaign, generally not staying on the mound more than one inning per outing. Through '89, he mainly worked the starting rotation. A switch to the bullpen in '90 revitalized Holmes. He was 12-2 with 13 saves and a 3.11 ERA in Triple-A, earning his first promotion to LA. The Dodgers selected Holmes following his high school graduation.

It remains to be seen what Holmes will do in his bullpen capacity with the Rockies. Don't acquire his 1993 commons. Our pick for his best 1993 card is Donruss. We have chosen this card because of its great combination of photography and design.

Sam Horn offered only surges of power for the 1992 Orioles. Used as a designated hitter against righthanded pitching, Horn struck out 60 times in 162 plate appearances. Overall in the '92 season, Horn had a .235 average, five homers, and 19 RBI. He wasn't offered a new contract by the Orioles, in an effort to lower the streaky slugger's salary. Horn made a splendid comeback with the O's in '90 after being abandoned by the Red Sox. His first season with Baltimore included 14 homers, 45 RBI, and a .248 average. Although he slipped to .233 in '91, Horn was one of the league's top designated hitters with 23 home runs and 61 ribbies. Although a highly lauded first-round draft selection by Boston in '82, Horn never spent a full season with the BoSox.

Horn doesn't have the speed or defensive capabilities to be a full-time position player. Don't blow anything on Horn and his 1993 cards. Our pick for his best 1993 card is Topps. We have chosen this card due to the outstanding photographic composition.

	W	L	ERA	G	SV	IP	H	ER	BB	SO
92 AL	4	4	2.55	41	6	42.1	35	12	11	31
Life	5	9	4.10	95	9	136.0	140	62	49	109

	BA	G	AB	R	H	2B	3B	HR	RBI	SB
92 AL	.235	63	162	13	38	10	1	5	19	0
Life	.234	366	998	124	234	48	1	58	171	0

VINCE HORSMAN

Position: Pitcher
Team: Oakland Athletics
Born: March 9, 1967
Halifax, Nova Scotia
Height: 6'2" **Weight:** 180 lbs.
Bats: Right **Throws:** Left
Acquired: Acquired on waivers
from Blue Jays, 3/92

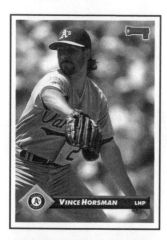 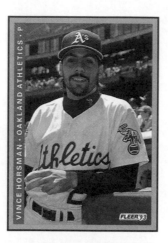

Vince Horsman is a native Canadian who has found in Oakland the home he never had in Toronto. Picked up on waivers in the spring of '92, Horsman became a valued member of the Athletics' bullpen. He got a chance when Joe Klink went down with an injury, and allowed only eight inherited runners to score in his first 29 appearances. He picked up one save and five holds over that span. Horsman doesn't knock you out with his strikeout capabilities or his control, but he does just what you want from a middle reliever—goes about an unglamorous job and gets it done. In '92, he trotted in totals of 2-1 with a 2.49 ERA. Horsman has been in the bullpen for most of his career, though he did make 28 starts in Double-A in '87. He wound up 7-7 with a 3.32 ERA, but obviously the Blue Jays thought his future was in relief. Toronto was right, but they may regret that it's not with them.

A bullpen trooper, Horsman's 1993 cards look smart at 10 to 15 cents each. Our pick for his best 1993 card is Fleer. We have chosen this card because of its overall appeal and pleasing looks.

	W	L	ERA	G	SV	IP	H	ER	BB	SO
92 AL	2	1	2.49	58	1	43.1	39	12	21	18
Life	2	1	2.28	62	1	47.1	41	12	24	20

STEVE HOSEY

Position: Outfield
Team: San Francisco Giants
Born: April 2, 1969
Oakland, CA
Height: 6'3" **Weight:** 215 lbs.
Bats: Right **Throws:** Right
Acquired: First-round pick,
6/89 free-agent draft

Steve Hosey could be the starting right fielder for the Giants in 1993 and well beyond that. He made his major league debut on August 29, 1992, and saw quite a bit of action during the final month. His numbers weren't spectacular, but he may just need a chance to get the feel of the big leagues. Once he does that, Hosey will likely be just the kind of player he was in the minors—good average, solid extra-base power, and more than a few stolen bases. He led the Class-A California League with 139 strikeouts in '90. He made an impact in his first pro season, being named to the Topps-National Association short season Class-A All-Star squad. In '91, he helped Double-A Shreveport win the Texas League title, getting four hits in game two of the finals.

Hosey should adjust and make an impact in the bigs with the Giants. The impact on his '93 cards, however, won't be as immense. Be frugal. Our pick for his best 1993 card is Upper Deck. We have chosen this card because it will increase in value.

	BA	G	AB	R	H	2B	3B	HR	RBI	SB
92 AAA	.286	126	462	64	132	28	7	10	65	15
92 NL	.250	21	56	6	14	1	0	1	6	1

CHARLIE HOUGH

Position: Pitcher
Team: Florida Marlins
Born: January 5, 1948
Honolulu, Hawaii
Height: 6'2" **Weight:** 190 lbs.
Bats: Right **Throws:** Right
Acquired: Signed as a free
agent, 12/92

THOMAS HOWARD

Position: Outfield
Team: Cleveland Indians
Born: December 11, 1964
Middletown, OH
Height: 6'2" **Weight:** 205 lbs.
Bats: Both **Throws:** Right
Acquired: Traded by San Diego
for Jason Hardtke and Chris
Maffett, 4/92

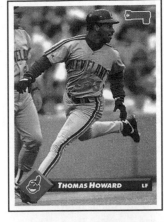

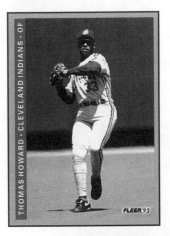

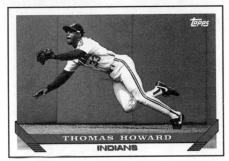

Charlie Hough notched his 200th victory with the '92 White Sox. He went 7-12 with a 3.93 ERA for the season. More importantly, however, Hough missed winning in double digits for only the second time in 11 years—all without the benefit of a single 20-win season. His highest total was 18 victories in '87. Combine Hough's 200 lifetime wins with his 61 career saves, and it's obvious what an impact he has made in baseball since his '70 debut. Hough, not Nolan Ryan, is the all-time victories leader for Texas. Hough hurled for the Rangers from 1980-90. When the Dodgers signed him in '66, he was inked as a third baseman. After hurting his arm in '69, he switched to pitching, learned the knuckler and began a new era of baseball history.

As a knuckleballer, Hough is among the last of a rare breed. His finale may come in '93. Hough's common-priced cards will only pay off if he gets lucky at Cooperstown. Our pick for his best 1993 card is Upper Deck. We have chosen this card for its technical merits.

While Thomas Howard couldn't match the power of left field mate Glenallen Hill in '92, Howard's .277 average was 36 points higher than Hill's. Howard also posted a better fielding percentage (.983) than Hill (.950). His offensive shortcomings were evidenced in his two lonely homers and 17 walks against 60 strikeouts in the '92 campaign. On April 14, the Padres had sent the little-used Howard to the Indians. Howard was San Diego's first choice in the '86 draft. He earned his first taste of the majors in '90, batting .273 in 20 games. Although he opened the season with the '91 Padres, Howard was demoted to Triple-A after four days. Upon his return, Howard ended the year with four homers, 22 RBI, and a .249 average in 106 big-league games.

Howard's limited long-ball punch will stop him from full-time work with the Tribe. Therefore, his 1993 commons may not produce many profits. Our pick for his best 1993 card is Donruss. We have chosen this card because the design lends itself to the best use of the elements.

	W	L	ERA	G	CG	IP	H	ER	BB	SO
92 AL	7	12	3.93	27	4	176.1	160	77	66	76
Life	202	191	3.67	803	106	3483.1	2963	1420	1542	2171

	BA	G	AB	R	H	2B	3B	HR	RBI	SB
92 AL	.277	117	358	36	99	15	2	2	32	15
Life	.265	248	686	71	182	29	5	6	54	25

JAY HOWELL

Position: Pitcher
Team: Los Angeles Dodgers
Born: November 22, 1955
  Miami, FL
Height: 6'3" **Weight:** 203 lbs.
Bats: Right **Throws:** Right
Acquired: Traded from
  Athletics with Jesse Orosco
  and Alfredo Griffin for Bob
  Welch, Jack Savage, and
  Matt Young, 12/87

PAT HOWELL

Position: Outfield
Team: Minnesota Twins
Born: August 31, 1968
  Mobile, AL
Height: 5'11" **Weight:** 165 lbs.
Bats: Both **Throws:** Right
Acquired: Traded from Mets for
  Darren Reed, 11/92

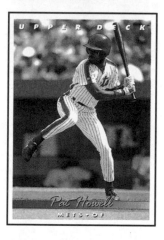

Relief ace Jay Howell continued two traditions in 1992—frequent injuries and frequent success on the mound. For the '92 season, he went 1-3 with a 1.54 ERA, four saves, and five holds. A sore shoulder was his early-season undoing. Going into '92, Howell had served seven stints on the DL dating back to '83. When healthy, Howell has been unstoppable. In '85, he earned a career-high 29 saves and nine victories in 63 games for the A's. Hurling for Los Angeles in '89, Howell harvested 28 saves, a 5-3 record, and a 1.58 ERA in 56 games. The Reds chose Howell in the '76 draft. He debuted with Cincinnati in '80. Stops with the Cubs and Yankees preceded his years with the A's and Dodgers.

Howell's career has been uneventful, excluding his frequent shoulder, elbow, and knee injuries. Even if he can stay healthy in 1993, he's not likely to pile up big numbers with the Dodgers. Pass up his commons. Our pick for his best 1993 card is Topps. We have chosen this card because of its great combination of photography and design.

Pat Howell stole his way into the majors in 1992, but the Mets' prospect found a holey bat waiting for him when he arrived at the big league plate. Righthanders especially troubled him, as evidenced by his .163 average. After a promotion from Triple-A Tidewater, Howell owned 243 stolen bases for his six-year career in the minor leagues. His career high was a loop-best 79 steals to pace the South Atlantic League in '90. Howell's return to the Twins is a rerun of sorts. Minnesota drafted Howell from the Mets organization in December '90, but returned him before the '91 season started. The Alabama native has shown a willingness to adapt, as evidenced by adopting switch-hitting after the '89 season.

With Kirby Puckett, Shane Mack, and Pedro Munoz set in the '93 Minnesota outfield, Howell could do a lot of sitting in the bigs. Such an inactive forecast should limit investments to a nickel per card. Our pick for his best 1993 card is Donruss. We have chosen this card for its technical merits.

	W	L	ERA	G	SV	IP	H	ER	BB	SO
92 NL	1	3	1.54	41	4	46.2	41	8	18	36
Life	51	49	3.29	474	153	743.1	690	272	259	607

	BA	G	AB	R	H	2B	3B	HR	RBI	SB
92 AAA	.244	104	405	46	99	8	3	1	22	21
92 NL	.187	31	75	9	14	1	0	0	1	4

Series two cards from some companies were available at press time. If space allows, both cards are shown; if not, the most up-to-date cards are pictured.

KENT HRBEK

Position: First base
Team: Minnesota Twins
Born: May 21, 1960
  Minneapolis, MN
Height: 6'4" **Weight:** 250 lbs.
Bats: Left **Throws:** Right
Acquired: 17th-round pick,
  6/78 free-agent draft

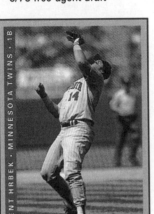

TIM HULETT

Position: Infield
Team: Baltimore Orioles
Born: January 12, 1960
  Springfield, IL
Height: 6' **Weight:** 199 lbs.
Bats: Right **Throws:** Right
Acquired: Signed as a free
  agent, 11/88

AL pitchers had a tough time with the middle of the Twins' lineup over the past few seasons: Kent Hrbek teamed with Kirby Puckett in one of the game's most productive left-right tandems. Hrbek went on the DL at the start of the '92 campaign. When healthy, Hrbek can break up a game with a single swing. Heading into '92, he had eight seasons in a row of at least 20 homers and five different years with at least 90 RBI. Working hard to lose 15 pounds, Hrbek had better mobility around first base, where he is already a fine fielder, and he gained better running speed on the basepaths in the process. He finished '92 with a .244 batting average, 15 homers, 58 RBI, and a .997 fielding percentage. A .289 career hitter through '91, Hrbek has personal peaks of a .312 average ('88), 34 homers ('87), and 107 RBI ('84).

Hrbek's health and stats have started slipping. Steer clear of his 1993 nickel-priced cards. Our pick for his best 1993 card is Fleer. We have chosen this card because the design lends itself to the best use of the elements.

Handy Tim Hulett continued to bolster Baltimore's bench in 1992, his fourth season with the club. Along with pinch-hitting, he filled in at second base, shortstop, third base, and designated hitter. His season was shortened by a leave of absence, due to a family tragedy in July. Overall in '92, he had a .289 batting average with 21 RBI. Hulett became a first-round draft selection of the White Sox in '80, making a big-league debut in '83. His finest season with the Pale Hose came in '86, including 17 home runs and 44 RBI during a career-high 150 games. Traded to Montreal in '88, he was released after a season at the Triple-A level. Before his professional career commenced, Hulett was coached at the University of South Florida by Hall of Famer Robin Roberts.

Hulett is a fine reserve, at most. His limited future and rocky past make his nickel-priced cards needless buys. Our pick for his best 1993 card is Topps. We have chosen this card due to the outstanding photographic composition.

	BA	G	AB	R	H	2B	3B	HR	RBI	SB
92 AL	.244	112	394	52	96	20	0	15	58	5
Life	.286	1543	5526	809	1580	290	17	258	950	33

	BA	G	AB	R	H	2B	3B	HR	RBI	SB
92 AL	.289	57	142	11	41	7	2	2	21	0
Life	.242	595	1765	194	428	73	12	44	182	13

TODD HUNDLEY

Position: Catcher
Team: New York Mets
Born: May 27, 1969
  Martinsville, VA
Height: 5'11" **Weight:** 185 lbs.
Bats: Both **Throws:** Right
Acquired: Second-round pick,
  6/87 draft

BRIAN HUNTER

Position: First base
Team: Atlanta Braves
Born: March 4, 1968
  El Toro, CA
Height: 6' **Weight:** 195 lbs.
Bats: Right **Throws:** Left
Acquired: Eighth-round pick,
  6/87 free-agent draft

Todd Hundley was handed the starting job in spring training, and he owned it for much of the year. The Mets did, however, have to rest him because of his problems at the plate. While the best he could manage for '92 was a .209 batting average, seven homers, and 32 RBI, there is very little dispute about his defensive ability. Hundley is agile, quick, and alert, and he shows a fine sense of command for someone so young. He handled 96 chances without an error in 21 games with New York in '91. He threw out 48 percent of runners trying to steal on him in '90, best among regular catchers in his Double-A league. At the plate, he needs some work, but there were signs of improvement in '92. For one thing, he has the power to hit 20 homers in a season. If Hundley can get his average to around .240 with power, he'll be a star.

As his hitting grows, so will his card values. Collect Hundley's 1993s at a nickel apiece. Our pick for his best 1993 card is Fleer. We have chosen this card because it has a distinctive look.

Brian Hunter slipped in his '92 efforts to gain Atlanta's starting first base position. The young slugger's year brought sweet and sour results. Hunter came closer to .300 facing lefthanded pitching and while batting at home. On the road or against righties, however, Hunter hustled to keep his marks near the .200 level. Future greatness was forecast for Hunter after the '91 season, when he hit .333 in the NL Championship Series. His regular-season tallies in '91 included a .251 batting average and 50 RBI in 97 games. His drop is evidenced in comparison to his '92 stats of a .239 average and 41 RBI over 102 games. It took Hunter nearly five seasons to crawl through the Braves minor league season. Now, he'll be holding his breath one more year, looking for a tiny opening in the '93 Atlanta lineup.

Can Hunter maintain his hitting while waiting for first base to become his alone? Don't risk it or Hunter's nickel-priced 1993 cards. Our pick for his best 1993 card is Score. We have chosen this card because it has a distinctive look.

	BA	G	AB	R	H	2B	3B	HR	RBI	SB
92 NL	.209	123	358	32	75	17	0	7	32	3
Life	.200	180	485	45	97	23	1	8	41	3

	BA	G	AB	R	H	2B	3B	HR	RBI	SB
92 NL	.239	102	238	34	57	13	2	14	41	1
Life	.246	199	509	66	125	29	3	26	91	1

BRUCE HURST

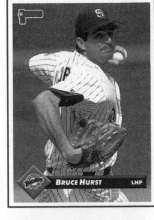

Position: Pitcher
Team: San Diego Padres
Born: March 24, 1958
   St. George, UT
Height: 6′3″ **Weight:** 220 lbs.
Bats: Left **Throws:** Left
Acquired: Signed as a free
   agent, 12/88

Bruce Hurst tried to duplicate his 1991 showing in '92. Unfortunately, as he was seeking a fourth season past the 15-win horizon, his ERA began to swell. However, he managed to register his 10th season in a row of double-digit victories (14) and bring his ballooning average down to 3.85. Since '82, his first full season in the majors, Hurst has been one of baseball's most durable starters. He was one of Boston's World Series heroes in '86, going 2-0 in three starts. In '88, Hurst unreeled a career-best 18-6 record with the Red Sox. After '92, Hurst owned 23 career shutouts and 83 complete games, picking off 79 baserunners in his career.

Hurst is a Don Sutton-type pitcher, someone who wins small but consistently. If the Padres decide to shed Hurst's big salary in the near future, he could end his career with a contender. His common-priced cards are far-fetched but tempting possibilities. Our pick for his best 1993 card is Score. We have chosen this card for the interesting facts included on the reverse.

	W	L	ERA	G	CG	IP	H	ER	BB	SO
92 NL	14	9	3.85	32	6	217.1	223	93	51	131
Life	143	110	3.85	366	83	2366.1	2395	1011	718	1656

JEFF HUSON

Position: Shortstop
Team: Texas Rangers
Born: August 15, 1964
   Scottsdale, AZ
Height: 6′3″ **Weight:** 180 lbs.
Bats: Left **Throws:** Right
Acquired: Traded from Expos
   for Drew Hall, 4/90

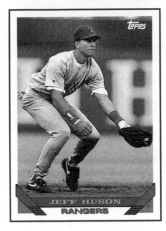
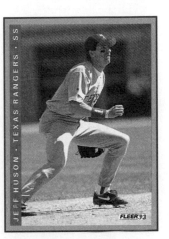

Whether at shortstop or second base, Jeff Huson was a plus for the 1992 Rangers. He played in more than 100 games for the third year in a row, providing Texas with solid defense up the middle. He managed a .261 batting average for '92, but could use some punch. Huson never clicked with the Expos, the team he was chosen by in '85. With Montreal in 1988-89, he filled in for a grand total of 55 games. He was named Rangers Rookie of the Year in '90, due in part to a .240 average and 28 RBI. After batting .213 with the '91 Rangers, some thought Huson couldn't hit in either league. However, a knee injury shelved him for a month, limiting his production. A rotator cuff injury is expected to keep him out of commission for most of '93.

Could Huson be a dependable, full-time infielder, set at one position? Texas may never let him know the answer. As a result, Huson's 1993 commons may never be worthwhile. Our pick for his best 1993 card is Upper Deck. We have chosen this card because it has a distinctive look.

	BA	G	AB	R	H	2B	3B	HR	RBI	SB
92 AL	.261	123	318	49	83	14	3	4	24	18
Life	.237	439	1098	150	260	41	8	6	83	43

Series two cards from some companies were available at press time. If space allows, both cards are shown; if not, the most up-to-date cards are pictured.

PETE
INCAVIGLIA

Position: Outfield
Team: Philadelphia Phillies
Born: April 2, 1964
   Pebble Beach, CA
Height: 6'1" **Weight:** 230 lbs.
Bats: Right **Throws:** Right
Acquired: Signed as a free
   agent, 12/92

JEFF
INNIS

Position: Pitcher
Team: New York Mets
Born: July 5, 1962 Decatur, IL
Height: 6'1" **Weight:** 180 lbs.
Bats: Right **Throws:** Right
Acquired: 13th-round pick,
   6/83 free-agent draft

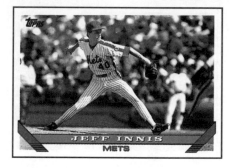

Pete Incaviglia got his first taste of NL pitching in 1992. Signed as a minor league free agent by Houston only weeks before spring training, Incaviglia served as a reserve outfielder for the second season in a row. In '93, he'll join his new Philadelphia teammates and try to get the team and his own career on the winning path again. The once-feared power hitter batted .214 with 11 home runs and 38 RBI for the '91 Tigers, playing only 97 games. He missed more than six weeks of the 1991 campaign, due to a chest injury and a sprained wrist. Despite a reputation for home runs, Incaviglia entered 1992 with more strikeouts (979) than games played (904). He was a Texas starter from 1985 through '90, beginning his big league career without a single game of minor league experience.

The slugger known as Inky may never be a full-timer again. Incaviglia's 1993 cards are risky nickel buys. Our pick for his best 1993 card is Topps. We have chosen this card because of its great combination of photography and design.

Jeff Innis gained the reputation as the busiest Mets reliever ever in 1992. Following a 69-game performance in '91, Innis became the first New York pitcher to exceed 70 games in a year since Roger McDowell hurled 75 contests in '86. For the '92 season, Innis spelled relief in 76 games, facing 373 batters over the course of 88 innings of work. His '92 ERA wound up at 2.86, underlining the fact that he only struck out 39. Before '91, the durable righty was volleyed between New York and Triple-A Tidewater for four seasons. He debuted with the Mets in '87, quickly finding his niche in middle relief. In the minors, however, he worked as a stopper. In 307 minor league appearances, the Illinois native earned 93 saves and 38 wins.

Look at stoppers, not middle-men like Innis, as card investment subjects. Innis cards will go untouched in 1993, even at three to five cents apiece. Our pick for his best 1993 card is Donruss. We have chosen this card for its technical merits.

	BA	G	AB	R	H	2B	3B	HR	RBI	SB
92 NL	.266	113	349	31	93	22	1	11	44	2
Life	.246	904	3135	402	772	154	15	146	470	29

	W	L	ERA	G	SV	IP	H	ER	BB	SO
92 NL	6	9	2.86	76	1	88.0	85	28	36	39
Life	8	17	2.76	221	2	283.1	256	87	83	156

Series two cards from some companies were available at press time. If space allows, both cards are shown; if not, the most up-to-date cards are pictured.

DANNY JACKSON

Position: Pitcher
Team: Philadelphia Phillies
Born: January 5, 1962
  San Antonio, TX
Height: 6′ **Weight:** 205 lbs.
Bats: Right **Throws:** Left
Acquired: Traded from Marlins
  for Joel Adamson and Matt
  Whiseant, 11/92

All of Danny Jackson's 1992 frustrations were erased on September 29, when he pitched Pittsburgh to another divisional title. His eighth victory of the season included seven innings of one-run baseball against the Mets, propelling the Pirates to their third consecutive NL East crown. The Bucs valued Jackson's postseason wisdom, acquired during his World Championship tours with the '85 Royals and the '90 Reds. Following his disastrous 1-5 woes with the Cubs in '91, Jackson's '92 wins sparkle by comparison. After spending nine previous stints on the DL before '92, it's amazing that he remains active. In '93, he'll try to help the Phillies out of the division cellar. In '88, Jackson's career blossomed into a 23-8 record with Cincinnati, his only All-Star season. After pitching 260 innings that year, three years of injuries followed.

Being with a division winner might have given Jackson temporary notoriety. But, don't be misled into buying his 1993 commons. Our pick for his best 1993 card is Score. We have chosen this card because of its overall appeal and pleasing looks.

	W	L	ERA	G	CG	IP	H	ER	BB	SO
92 NL	8	13	3.84	34	0	201.1	211	86	77	97
Life	81	92	3.83	247	36	1478.1	1462	629	598	865

DARRIN JACKSON

Position: Outfield
Team: San Diego Padres
Born: August 22, 1963
  Los Angeles, CA
Height: 6′ **Weight:** 185 lbs.
Bats: Right **Throws:** Right
Acquired: Traded from Cubs
  with Phil Stephenson and
  Calvin Schiraldi for Luis
  Salazar and Marvell Wynne,
  8/89

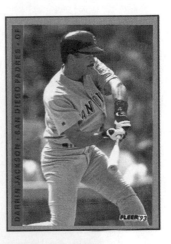

Darrin Jackson drove in a career-high 70 runs with the 1992 Padres. In his six major league seasons before '92, Jackson owned 98 career RBI. He's developed into a legitimate power hitter since '91, when he clubbed 21 homers. In '92, his sole offensive downfalls came hitting on the road (.208) or against lefties (.202). Jackson has been active in pro ball since '81, becoming a second-round draft pick of the Cubs. His first bow in the majors came with the Cubs in '85. By '88, he was a semi-regular in Chicago, working as a pinch-hitter and defensive substitute. Speaking of defense, the bazooka-armed Jackson made a strong bid for his first gold glove in '92, leading NL center fielders in assists (18).

Even after two notable offensive seasons, Jackson's hitting is still overshadowed by other outfield teammates. Overlook Jackson's 1993 commons. Our pick for his best 1993 card is Fleer. We have chosen this card because the design lends itself to the best use of the elements.

	BA	G	AB	R	H	2B	3B	HR	RBI	SB
92 NL	.249	155	587	72	146	23	5	17	70	14
Life	.252	517	1433	181	361	57	9	51	168	27

MIKE JACKSON

Position: Pitcher
Team: San Francisco Giants
Born: December 22, 1964
Houston, TX
Height: 6' **Weight:** 200 lbs.
Bats: Right **Throws:** Right
Acquired: Traded from Seattle
with Bill Swift and Dave
Burba for Kevin Mitchell and
Mike Remlinger, 12/91

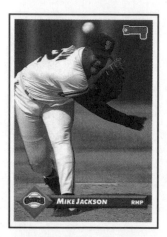

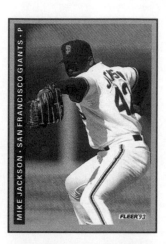

Mike Jackson's 1992 National League return was unmemorable. Swapped from Seattle as part of the Kevin Mitchell deal, Jackson was an unspectacular setup man out of the Giants bullpen. He did register nine holds and earn nearly one strikeout per inning, however. Before his arrival in San Francisco, Jackson mounted career highs with the '91 Mariners, including seven wins, 14 saves, and 72 appearances (second best in the American League). Active in pro ball since joining the Phillies organization in '84, Jackson has spent only one season in the minors as a starter. Since '87, his last season with Philadelphia, Jackson has appeared in 55 or more relief outings per year. The righthander was discovered by the Phils at a Texas junior college.

Unless he serves as a starter or closer, Jackson's talent and potential will be overlooked. His common-priced cards will remain ignored, too. Our pick for his best 1993 card is Fleer. We have chosen this card for its artistic presentation.

	W	L	ERA	G	SV	IP	H	ER	BB	SO
92 NL	6	6	3.73	67	2	82.0	76	34	33	80
Life	31	41	3.56	393	31	569.1	459	225	268	489

JOHN JAHA

Position: First base
Team: Milwaukee Brewers
Born: May 27, 1966
Portland, OR
Height: 6'1" **Weight:** 195 lbs.
Bats: Right **Throws:** Right
Acquired: 14th-round pick,
6/84 free-agent draft

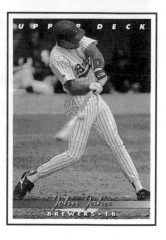

It took another year of minor league ball to prove himself, but John Jaha finally earned the Milwaukee starting first baseman's job in 1992. His adjustment to major league pitching wasn't immediate, as Jaha's batting average against lefthanders couldn't break the .200 barrier. But his fielding was first rate (1.000 average), and his overall performance displayed that the Brewers could pass the first base torch to this young Oregon native. Jaha's 1992 totals with Triple-A Denver included 18 homers, 69 RBI, and a .321 average.

With Paul Molitor's exit and fears that Robin Yount could escape the Brew Crew, younger sluggers like Jaha will be treasured commodities. So will his '93 cards. Jaha's cards seem like investment steals at 10 to 15 cents apiece. However, overzealous Milwaukee fans said the same about first baseman phenom Joey Meyer once. Joey who? Our pick for his best 1993 card is Donruss. We have chosen this card because of its overall appeal and pleasing looks.

	BA	G	AB	R	H	2B	3B	HR	RBI	SB
92 AL	.226	47	133	17	30	3	1	2	10	10
Life	.226	47	133	17	30	3	1	2	10	10

CHRIS JAMES

Position: Outfield
Team: Houston Astros
Born: October 4, 1962
Rusk, TX
Height: 6'1" **Weight:** 190 lbs.
Bats: Right **Throws:** Right
Acquired: Signed as a free
agent, 1/93

Chris James was more productive in spring training than during the regular season with the 1992 Giants. His preseason totals were .276 with two homers and a team-leading 17 RBI. During the year, he served infrequently as a pinch-hitter and spot starter. He fought to hit .200 against righthanders or anyone pitching at Candlestick Park. By contrast, he exceeded .300 against lefties and neared that rate on the road. Coming to Houston associates James with his fourth NL team. He was signed as an undrafted free agent by Philadelphia in '81, debuting with the Phils in '86. He batted .293 with 17 homers and 54 RBI in '87, his first full season. James bashed a career-high 19 homers with the '88 Phillies.

Due to his above-average power, James may stick around forever as a pinch-hitter and outfield substitute. That's not the same as starting, and not enough to generate additional values for his 1993 commons. Our pick for his best 1993 card is Topps. We have chosen this card because of its great combination of photography and design.

	BA	G	AB	R	H	2B	3B	HR	RBI	SB
92 NL	.242	111	248	25	60	10	4	5	32	2
Life	.260	779	2665	283	694	122	19	72	333	24

STAN JAVIER

Position: Outfield
Team: Philadelphia Phillies
Born: September 1, 1965
San Francisco de Macoris,
Dominican Republic
Height: 6' **Weight:** 185 lbs.
Bats: Both **Throws:** Right
Acquired: Traded from Dodgers
for Julio Peguero and Steve
Searcy, 7/92

Stan Javier's arrival with the 1992 Phillies marked the fourth team he's appeared with in an eight-year career. Known mainly for speed and outfield defense, he's never been able to keep a starting job in the majors. He stole successfully in 18 of 21 attempts in '92. His other stats are just about the same—okay, but not outstanding. He batted .249 with one homer and 29 RBI. Of his 130 appearances in '92, he only started 46 of them. Before joining up with Philly, Javier had enjoyed the best and worst of times with LA. He joined the Dodgers in '90, hitting .304 in 104 games. By '91, he was batting .205 in 121 contests. Although Javier debuted with the Yankees in '84, he spent the bulk of his career with Oakland.

Javier is a lock with the 1993 Phillies, but will settle for work as a fourth or fifth outfielder. Unless he stays in the starting lineup, his 1993 commons will be gathering dust. Our pick for his best 1993 card is Upper Deck. We have chosen this card because the design lends itself to the best use of the elements.

	BA	G	AB	R	H	2B	3B	HR	RBI	SB
92 NL	.249	130	334	42	83	17	1	1	29	29
Life	.246	758	1798	250	442	67	17	10	147	83

GREGG JEFFERIES

Position: Third base
Team: Kansas City Royals
Born: August 1, 1967
  Burlingame, CA
Height: 5'10" **Weight:** 185 lbs.
Bats: Both **Throws:** Right
Acquired: Traded from Mets
  with Keith Miller and Kevin
  McReynolds for Bret
  Saberhagen and Bill Pecota,
  12/91

REGGIE JEFFERSON

Position: Infield
Team: Cleveland Indians
Born: September 25, 1968
  Tallahassee, FL
Height: 6'4" **Weight:** 210 lbs.
Bats: Both **Throws:** Left
Acquired: Traded from Reds
  for Tim Costo, 6/91

Gregg Jefferies regained his star swing in 1992. Returning to third base helped ease the first-year burden of adjusting to a new league as well. The former Mets phenom flirted with .300 throughout the season, despite a prolonged September slump. He finished up the '92 season with a .285 batting average, 10 homers, 75 RBI, and 19 stolen bases. Jefferies was a first-round draft pick of New York's in '85. His Mets debut in '88 was a smashing success with a .321 average, six homers, and 17 RBI in 29 games. He became resident second baseman for the Mets in '89, with only occasional use at third. With a year's worth of AL experience, he can be expected to turn up the offensive heat in '93.

Jefferies is young, with untapped power potential. His 1993 cards present an inviting investment at a nickel apiece. The shortage and affordability of Jefferies' 1988 Donruss rookie at $1 is too good to be true. Our pick for his best 1993 card is Fleer. We have chosen this card due to the outstanding photographic composition.

Reggie Jefferson came to the Indians off a front-office mixup in Cincinnati, and the Indians are still waiting for him to become the coup that many people believed him to be. Unfortunately, Jefferson has been plagued by injuries, the latest one being a sprained ligament in his left elbow that made ashes of his 1992 season. He only made it into 24 games during '92, batting .337 and garnering 30 hits in his 89 at-bats. When healthy, Jefferson offers extra base power. He hit a career-high 18 homers with 90 RBI for Class-A Cedar Rapids in '88 and made the Midwest League All-Star team. In '89, Jefferson was promoted to Double-A, and finished second in the Reds' farm system with 17 homers and third with 80 RBI. Jefferson's health problems began in '90 with a season-ending stress fracture of his lower back, followed up with a bout of pneumonia in '91.

Jefferson isn't worth more than a dime per card in '93—not yet, at least. Our pick for his best 1993 card is Donruss. We have chosen this card because of its overall appeal and pleasing looks.

	BA	G	AB	R	H	2B	3B	HR	RBI	SB
92 AL	.285	152	604	66	172	36	3	10	75	19
Life	.278	617	2317	312	644	132	12	52	280	82

	BA	G	AB	R	H	2B	3B	HR	RBI	SB
92 AL	.337	24	89	8	30	6	2	1	6	0
Life	.259	55	197	19	51	9	2	4	19	0

Series two cards from some companies were available at press time. If space allows, both cards are shown; if not, the most up-to-date cards are pictured.

HOWARD JOHNSON

Position: Outfield
Team: New York Mets
Born: November 29, 1960
Clearwater, FL
Height: 5'10" **Weight:** 195 lbs.
Bats: Both **Throws:** Right
Acquired: Traded from Tigers
for Walt Terrell, 12/84

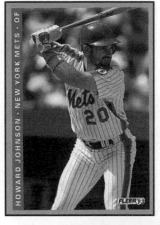

LANCE JOHNSON

Position: Outfield
Team: Chicago White Sox
Born: July 7, 1963
Lincoln Heights, OH
Height: 5'11" **Weight:** 160 lbs.
Bats: Left **Throws:** Left
Acquired: Traded from
Cardinals with Ricky Horton
and cash for Jose DeLeon,
2/88

Howard Johnson's 1992 switch to a new position produced few positive results for the Mets. HoJo tried to become a center fielder, but received lukewarm reviews for his defense. Worst of all, he saw the least action (100 games) since his 88-game season in '86. His '92 campaign ended early when he faced surgery on his left shoulder, both knees, and a fractured wrist. Along with games missed, the injuries explained his shrunken offense. Johnson's '91 feats, namely a league-leading 38 homers and 117 RBI, made him only the third Met in team history to lead the league in both categories in one season. From 1987-91, Johnson reached 90 or more RBI in four out of five seasons. His '92 woes broke a five-year string of 20 or more homers.

Johnson's 1993 cards aren't worth more than a nickel each. HoJo could stage an impressive one-year comeback, but his health hampers those odds. Our pick for his best 1993 card is Fleer. We have chosen this card because of its great combination of photography and design.

Speed and defense were only two of the assets Lance Johnson brought to the 1992 White Sox lineup. He broke his old career high of 36 stolen bases set in '90 by swiping 41 in '92, tying for ninth in the AL. In center field, he was one of the league's finest, topping 10 assists for the second year in a row, attaining a .987 fielding percentage overall. A White Sox regular since '90, Johnson led the league in triples in both '91 and '92. He began in the Cardinals organization in the '84 free-agent draft, appearing in St. Louis for 33 games in '87, including the NLCS and World Series. One of his teammates at Triton Junior College was Kirby Puckett, an opponent in that year's fall classic.

The low-homer guys in the ChiSox lineup like Johnson and Ozzie Guillen always get obscured by bashers like George Bell and Frank Thomas. Johnson's an above-average player, but his 1993 common-priced cards are hopeless. Our pick for his best 1993 card is Fleer. We have chosen this card because it has a distinctive look.

	BA	G	AB	R	H	2B	3B	HR	RBI	SB
92 NL	.223	100	350	48	78	19	0	7	43	22
Life	.253	1279	4309	672	1092	225	17	204	672	213

	BA	G	AB	R	H	2B	3B	HR	RBI	SB
92 AL	.279	157	567	67	158	15	12	3	47	41
Life	.273	583	2059	258	563	61	38	4	176	131

RANDY JOHNSON

Position: Pitcher
Team: Seattle Mariners
Born: September 10, 1963
Walnut Creek, CA
Height: 6'10" **Weight:** 225 lbs.
Bats: Right **Throws:** Left
Acquired: Traded from Expos
with Brian Holman and Gene
Harris for Mark Langston
and Mike Campbell, 5/89

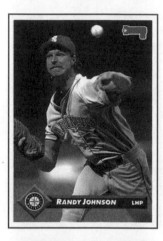

Randy Johnson's zany 1992 season was highlighted by his September 27 matchup against Texas. He fanned 18 Rangers in eight innings, one short of the AL record. Yet, he left the game with no decision. The towering lefty's year was filled with ups and downs. While he looked like a sure thing to capture the AL strikeout title, he was little help in getting Seattle out of last place. Control problems haunted Johnson throughout the first half of the season, until Nolan Ryan shared some pitching tips. Johnson's season-ending success wasn't enough to surpass his 14-11 record from '90. He was 13-10 in '91, with 228 strikeouts. Johnson also has a proclivity to walk a great number of batters.

His strikeout totals are exciting enough to merit investment in a few of his nickel-priced 1993 cards. If he licks his control difficulties, Johnson could be a 20-game winner. Johnson's rookie card, an '89 Fleer, can be nabbed for 35 cents or less. Our pick for his best 1993 card is Upper Deck. We have chosen this card for its artistic presentation.

	W	L	ERA	G	CG	IP	H	ER	BB	SO
92 AL	12	14	3.77	31	6	210.1	154	88	144	241
Life	49	48	3.95	130	16	818.0	649	359	519	818

CHIPPER JONES

Position: Shortstop
Team: Atlanta Braves
Born: April 24, 1972
Deland, GA
Height: 6'3" **Weight:** 185 lbs.
Bats: Both **Throws:** Right
Acquired: First-round pick,
6/90 free-agent draft

Chipper Jones made a smooth transition to Double-A in 1992. For the '92 season, he had a .353 on-base average and a .413 slugging average in Class-A and a .367 on-base average and a .594 slugging percentage in Double-A. Chipper Jones is among the highest-rated prospects in a Braves' organization that has already used its farm system to climb into baseball's top echelons. He was the first overall pick in the '90 draft, and he retains the look of a future major leaguer. Entering the '92 season, *Baseball America* named Jones the fourth-best prospect in baseball and first among position players. The publication also tabbed Jones the best defensive shortstop in the Class-A Carolina League after the '92 season, quite a tribute considering that he had suffered a bit of a problem in the field in '90, his first pro season.

Jones may make it into the bigs in '93. His cards, at a dime or less, are mild investments. Our pick for his best 1993 card is Upper Deck. We have chosen this card because it will increase in value.

	BA	G	AB	R	H	2B	3B	HR	RBI	SB
92 A	.277	70	264	43	73	22	1	4	31	10
92 AA	.346	67	266	43	92	17	11	9	42	14

DOUG JONES

Position: Pitcher
Team: Houston Astros
Born: June 24, 1957
Covina, CA
Height: 6'2" **Weight:** 195 lbs.
Bats: Right **Throws:** Right
Acquired: Signed as a free
agent, 1/92

JIMMY JONES

Position: Pitcher
Team: Houston Astros
Born: April 20, 1964 Dallas, TX
Height: 6'2" **Weight:** 190 lbs.
Bats: Right **Throws:** Right
Acquired: Signed as a free
agent, 3/91

Doug Jones set a new club record for the Astros in '92 by saving 36 games. With a 1.85 ERA and an 11-8 record in addition to his sparkling relief efforts, his success vindicated the decision of Astro management to take a chance on a veteran pitcher no one else wanted. The road that led him to Houston was not a short one. Jones launched his professional career in '78 and reached the majors in '82. He didn't stick, however, until '87. Jones, whose changeup is his best pitch, had saved 30-plus games three years in a row—and made the All-Star team each season—before hitting hard times in '91. He had a 1-7 record, 7.47 ERA, and five blown saves in 11 chances when Cleveland finally sent him to the minors. Jones did try his hand as a starter, but he was born to be a reliever.

Jones could last another one to three years. His nickel-priced cards have no long-term prospects. Our pick for his best 1993 card is Upper Deck. We have chosen this card because it has a distinctive look.

Jimmy Jones looked like an average pitcher with the 1992 Astros. Maintaining his average career, he once again struggled to win 10 games. For '92, Jones finished up with a 10-6 record, a 4.07 ERA, 39 walks, and 69 strikeouts over 139 1/3 innings. His ERA reflected his pre-1992 lifetime mark of 4.24. Incredibly, Jones was a highly touted high school prospect in '82. The Padres made him the third overall selection during the first round of that year's draft. He twirled a one-hit complete game for his first major league victory in '86. Unfortunately, Jones became human again too quickly. Before '92, his winningest season was a 9-7 production with the '87 Padres. He added another nine victories in '88, but hasn't come into his own since.

Jones will need to win 20 games in 1993 for his common-priced cards to develop any interest. Quite likely, the Astros will win the World Series before Jones hits it big. Don't hold your breath for either. Our pick for his best 1993 card is Donruss. We have chosen this card due to the outstanding photographic composition.

	W	L	ERA	G	SV	IP	H	ER	BB	SO
92 NL	11	8	1.85	80	36	111.2	96	23	17	93
Life	37	40	2.82	356	164	535.1	518	168	116	433

	W	L	ERA	G	CG	IP	H	ER	BB	SO
92 NL	10	6	4.07	25	0	139.1	135	63	39	69
Life	39	38	4.35	141	7	715.1	762	346	230	355

BRIAN JORDAN

Position: Outfield
Team: St. Louis Cardinals
Born: March 29, 1967
   Baltimore, MD
Height: 6'1" **Weight:** 205 lbs.
Bats: Right **Throws:** Right
Acquired: First-round pick,
   6/88 free-agent draft

RICKY JORDAN

Position: First base
Team: Philadelphia Phillies
Born: May 26, 1965
   Richmond, CA
Height: 6'3" **Weight:** 209 lbs.
Bats: Right **Throws:** Right
Acquired: First-round pick,
   6/83 free-agent draft

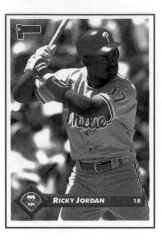 

Brian Jordan ended the suspense—and a lot of anxiety in St. Louis—in June 1992 when he agreed to give up his career with the Atlanta Falcons for a reported $2.26 million, three-year deal. Thus the Cardinals locked up a potential star, a speedster who could be a power hitter and major run-producer. Perhaps the pursuit of one career instead of two will leave Jordan a bit healthier. He was slowed by injury in '92, as he had been in '89 and '90. Playing in only 55 games in '92, he hit five homers and knocked in 22 RBI in 193 at-bats. Jordan played only 11 games in '89, his second pro season, due to an ankle injury. In '90, he went down with a wrist injury and only got 80 at-bats. Despite never having played a full season of minor league ball, Jordan has seemingly done a good job of fitting right in with the Cards.

He'll be back! At 15 cents each, Jordan's 1993s will be tempting. Our pick for his best 1993 card is Score. We have chosen this card for the interesting facts included on the reverse.

Ricky Jordan managed a passable offensive showing with the 1992 Phillies, but kept breaking the hearts of fans who remembered his past promise. Jordan was a part-time fill-in around Philly, appearing in only 94 games. A fractured jaw delayed the start of his season until May. His totals for '92 included batting .304 with 34 RBI, and four homers. By contrast, Jordan's '91 totals included nine homers, 49 RBI, and a .272 average. He burst upon the Philadelphia scene in '83, as a highly ranked first-round draft choice. By '88, he reached the majors, hitting .308 with 11 home runs and 43 RBI in just 69 games. Again in 1993 it appears there will be no room in the Philly lineup for this once-heralded hitter.

Jordan will be marking his first decade in the Philadelphia organization in 1993. Is time running out on this former rookie hopeful? It seems the clock has stopped on his common-priced cards. Our pick for his best 1993 card is Fleer. We have chosen this card because of its great combination of photography and design.

	BA	G	AB	R	H	2B	3B	HR	RBI	SB
92 NL	.207	55	193	17	40	9	4	5	22	7
Life	.207	55	193	17	40	9	4	5	22	7

	BA	G	AB	R	H	2B	3B	HR	RBI	SB
92 NL	.304	94	276	33	84	19	0	4	34	3
Life	.281	500	1697	207	477	98	7	41	245	10

TERRY JORGENSEN

Position: First base
Team: Minnesota Twins
Born: September 2, 1966
Kewaunee, WI
Height: 6'4" **Weight:** 213 lbs.
Bats: Right **Throws:** Right
Acquired: Second-round pick,
6/87 free-agent draft

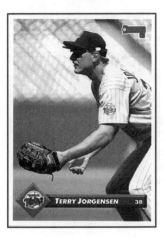 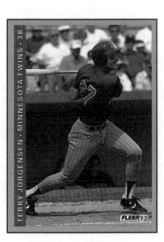

Terry Jorgensen's career hit a plateau in 1992. As a third baseman in Triple-A, his third consecutive season in the Pacific Coast League, he hit .292 with 14 home runs and 65 RBI. Minnesota offered Jorgensen a chance to spell injured Kent Hrbek at first base. The Wisconsin native responded with a .310 effort with 18 hits over 22 games. This avenged his 10-game debut with the '89 Twins, when he settled for a .174 average. Signed as an outfielder in '87, the Twins discovered Jorgensen when he helped his University of Wisconsin team to the NCAA World Series. An aggressive glove man and perennial defensive leader in the minors, Jorgensen could help the Twins at both infield corners in '93.

Even in the cozy Metrodome, Jorgensen would be blessed to manage 10 to 15 homers yearly. Those modest stats won't gain him stardom or increased values for his common-priced cards. Our pick for his best 1993 card is Fleer. We have chosen this card due to the outstanding photographic composition.

	BA	G	AB	R	H	2B	3B	HR	RBI	SB
92 AAA	.295	135	505	78	149	32	2	14	71	2
92 AL	.310	22	58	5	18	18	1	0	0	5

FELIX JOSE

Position: Outfield
Team: St. Louis Cardinals
Born: May 8, 1965
Santo Domingo,
Dominican Republic
Height: 6'1" **Weight:** 190 lbs.
Bats: Both **Throws:** Right
Acquired: Traded from
Athletics with Stan Royer
and Daryl Green for Willie
McGee, 8/90

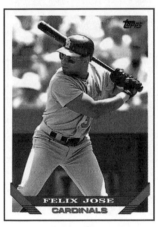 

Just ask the Oakland A's: They'll admit that they made a mistake in letting Felix Jose get away. In 1991, his first full season in the majors, the switch-hitting fielder hit .305 with eight homers, 77 RBI, and 20 stolen bases, tied Marquis Grissom for the league lead with 15 outfield assists, and made the All-Star team. He led his team in batting, hits, and extra-base hits, and finished second in the league in doubles and multi-hit games. To prove that showing was no fluke, Jose won NL Player of the Month honors in May '92. At the end of the season, his totals stood at a .295 batting average with 14 homers, 75 RBI, 40 walks, and 28 stolen bases. In his 1,117 ⅓ innings of play, he registered a .979 fielding percentage with 11 assists.

Jose's nickel-priced cards are subject to suspicion. Give him another year to make sure he solidifies. Jose's '89 Donruss Rookie is fair at 75 cents. Our pick for his best 1993 card is Upper Deck. We have chosen this card due to the outstanding photographic composition.

	BA	G	AB	R	H	2B	3B	HR	RBI	SB
92 NL	.295	131	509	62	150	22	3	14	75	28
Life	.287	439	1566	190	449	81	10	33	210	61

WALLY JOYNER

Position: First base
Team: Kansas City Royals
Born: June 16, 1962
    Atlanta, GA
Height: 6'2" **Weight:** 198 lbs.
Bats: Left **Throws:** Left
Acquired: Signed as a free
    agent, 12/91

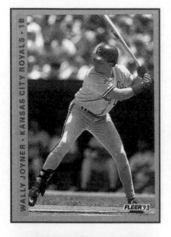

George Brett couldn't complain when the Royals told him he would be a full-time DH. The man taking his first-base job was Wally Joyner, one of the game's premier defensive players at the position. Signed even more for his offense than his defense, Joyner brought his sweet swing with him. Even while the Royals struggled, Joyner stood tough. In the '92 campaign, he hit .269 with 66 RBI, 36 doubles, and 55 walks. Defensively, he was part of 139 double plays, making only 10 errors in 1,262 ⅓ innings. Joyner, who had spent his entire career with the Angels before seeking greener pastures, brought career peaks of a .301 average ('91) and 34 homers and 117 RBI (both '87). He also had 100 RBI as a rookie in '86, but finished second to Jose Canseco in AL Rookie of the Year voting. He was the Angels' MVP a year later.

Dependable, but not very dynamic, Joyner's 1993 cards are marginal buys at a nickel apiece. Our pick for his best 1993 card is Upper Deck. We have chosen this card since the photograph captures the athletic ability of the player.

	BA	G	AB	R	H	2B	3B	HR	RBI	SB
92 AL	.269	149	572	66	154	36	2	9	66	11
Life	.285	995	3780	521	1079	206	13	123	584	39

DAVID JUSTICE

Position: Outfield
Team: Atlanta Braves
Born: April 14, 1966
    Cincinnati, OH
Height: 6'3" **Weight:** 200 lbs.
Bats: Left **Throws:** Left
Acquired: Fourth-round pick,
    6/85 free agent draft

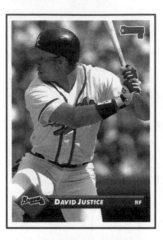

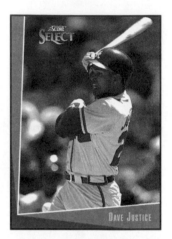

Still suffering from back problems first encountered in '91, David Justice didn't let the pain get in his way during the 1992 campaign. Although it took awhile for his swing to return, Justice finally jolted rival pitchers in June as the Braves raced toward the top of the NL West standings. After collecting only 13 RBI in his first 40 games, Justice showed his stuff. He wound up hitting .256, contributing 21 home runs, 72 RBI, and drawing 79 walks in his 509 at-bats. In his rookie season, he wasted no time in demonstrating his ability. The eventual 1990 NL Rookie of the Year hit 10 homers in a 12-game stretch from August 7-16 and 23 homers over the second half, tying Cecil Fielder for tops in the majors. Justice survived the sophomore jinx by collecting 21 homers and 87 RBI in 109 games in 1991.

Justice still leads the Braves. His 15-centers are decent card investments. A possibility is the 1990 Score Justice Rookie at $1.50. Our pick for his best 1993 card is Topps. We have chosen this card due to the outstanding photographic composition.

	BA	G	AB	R	H	2B	3B	HR	RBI	SB
92 NL	.256	144	484	78	124	19	5	21	72	2
Life	.269	396	1370	228	369	70	8	71	240	23

Series two cards from some companies were available at press time. If space allows, both cards are shown; if not, the most up-to-date cards are pictured.

SCOTT KAMIENIECKI

Position: Pitcher
Team: New York Yankees
Born: April 19, 1964
  Mt. Clemens, MI
Height: 6′ **Weight:** 197 lbs.
Bats: Right **Throws:** Right
Acquired: 14th-round pick,
  6/86 free-agent draft

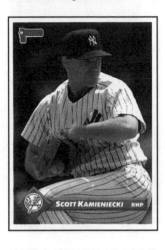

RON KARKOVICE

Position: Catcher
Team: Chicago White Sox
Born: August 8, 1963
  Union, NJ
Height: 6′1″ **Weight:** 215 lbs.
Bats: Right **Throws:** Right
Acquired: First-round pick,
  6/82 free-agent draft

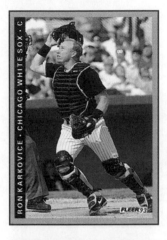

Scott Kamieniecki pitched his first full season with the Yankees in 1992, but didn't get the expected results. His less-than-spectacular season was marked by double-digit losses (14) and a hefty 4.36 ERA, reflecting his slow adjustment to the majors. Other '92 Kamieniecki totals include 28 games, six wins, 74 walks, and 88 strikeouts achieved while facing 804 batters. He looked like a different pitcher in 1991, when he was 4-4 in nine starts. His '91 campaign ended in August, due to a neck injury that led to surgery. Kamieniecki progressed through the New York farm system in less than five seasons. Although the Yankees snared him in the '86 free-agent draft, the righthander had declined previous offers from the Tigers ('82) and the Brewers ('85).

Kamieniecki has a name few collectors will forget. Unfortunately, many collectors have forgotten the hurler's rookie cards. His 1993s will be unloved commons. Our pick for his best 1993 card is Donruss. We have chosen this card for its technical merits.

Before the 1992 season, Ron Karkovice had never hit more than six homers a year. However, in '92, his slugging yielded that total in September alone. The reserve catcher was an unlikely hero against the first-place Athletics, banging out two homers in one game to keep Oakland from clinching the division in front of Comiskey Park fans. It's easy to argue that Karkovice was twice the hitter in 1992 that he was before. Just look at his stats. Previous career highs included six homers in '90, and 24 RBI in '89. He bettered those in '92 by hitting 13 homers and contributing 50 RBI. Before his '92 offensive explosion, he was known primarily as a strong-armed defensive substitute. Karkovice was a highly ranked amateur athlete, pitching and hitting his Florida high school to a state championship in '81.

Karkovice may have played with Carlton Fisk and backed him up, but Karkovice will never be another Fisk. Shy away from Karkovice commons. Our pick for his best 1993 card is Topps. We have chosen this card because it has a distinctive look.

	W	L	ERA	G	CG	IP	H	ER	BB	SO
92 AL	6	14	4.36	28	4	188.0	193	91	74	88
Life	10	18	4.25	37	4	243.1	247	115	96	122

	BA	G	AB	R	H	2B	3B	HR	RBI	SB
92 AL	.237	123	342	39	81	12	1	13	50	10
Life	.226	459	1171	145	265	55	3	36	145	20

ERIC KARROS

Position: First base
Team: Los Angeles Dodgers
Born: November 4, 1967
    Hackensack, NJ
Height: 6'4" **Weight:** 205 lbs.
Bats: Right **Throws:** Right
Acquired: Sixth-round pick,
    6/88 free-agent draft

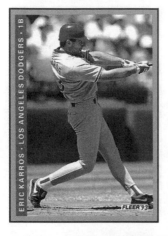

PAT KELLY

Position: Second base
Team: New York Yankees
Born: October 14, 1967
    Philadelphia, PA
Height: 6' **Weight:** 180 lbs.
Bats: Right **Throws:** Right
Acquired: Ninth-round pick,
    6/88 free-agent draft

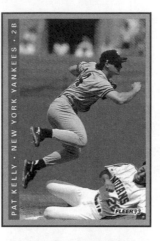

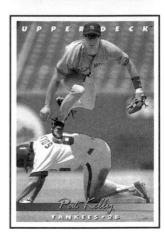

Eric Karros stepped in and provided pop when injuries stripped the Dodger lineup of Darryl Strawberry and Eric Davis. The first baseman's progress was all the more welcome because other Dodger prospects who had starred in the Triple-A Pacific Coast League flopped in the majors. For his '92 efforts, Karros produced a .257 batting average, 20 homers and 88 RBI. His efforts and accomplishments did not go unnoticed, as he was named the 1992 National League Rookie of the Year. Karros went to UCLA and made the team as a walk-on, becoming an All-American and leading the Bruins to the NCAA tournament. He made a spectacular entry into pro ball, hitting .366 with 12 homers and 55 RBI in just 66 games in rookie ball. Karros played for the Dodgers' Triple-A team in '91, where he hit at least .300 for the fourth year in a row.

    A half-buck for a 1993 card of Karros would be a sweet deal. In reality, prices may start at $1. Our pick for his best 1993 card is Upper Deck. We have chosen this card due to the outstanding photographic composition.

Pat Kelly's 1992 promotion with the Yankees lasted only weeks. When second baseman Steve Sax was traded, it was believed the swap was engineered to open the position for Kelly. Then, upon the signing of free-agent second baseman Mike Gallego and the promotion of rookie infielder Andy Stankiewicz, Kelly was in another battle for playing time. A thumb sprain in April hampered him for nearly a month. Kelly did log in 864 innings of playing time and 318 at-bats in '92. At least he wasn't jumping around between positions like he had to in '91. Kelly had never played third, but the Yankees used him at the hot corner for parts of that season. Before missing 21 games with a stiff back, he hit .242 with three homers and 23 RBI in 96 games. With Gallego's return projected for '93, Kelly isn't done sweating over a starting job yet.

    Kelly's cards and career hold promise, as long as he maintains a starting role. Grab a few of his 1993s at a nickel apiece. Our pick for his best 1993 card is Upper Deck. We have chosen this card because it has a distinctive look.

	BA	G	AB	R	H	2B	3B	HR	RBI	SB
92 NL	.257	149	545	63	140	30	1	20	88	2
Life	.252	163	559	63	141	31	1	20	89	2

	BA	G	AB	R	H	2B	3B	HR	RBI	SB
92 AL	.226	106	318	38	72	22	2	7	27	8
Life	.234	202	616	73	144	34	6	10	50	20

ROBERTO KELLY

Position: Outfield
Team: Cincinnati Reds
Born: October 1, 1964
    Panama City, Panama
Height: 6'4" **Weight:** 185 lbs.
Bats: Right **Throws:** Right
Acquired: Traded for Paul
    O'Neill, 11/92

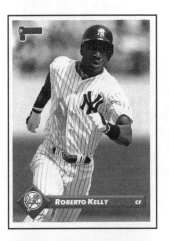

In 1992, his sixth major league season, Roberto Kelly won a reputation as the anchor of the New York Yankees. Firmly entrenched as the No. 3 hitter and center fielder, Kelly continued to give the club the combination of speed and power. In June '92, his two-run homer against Baltimore relief ace Gregg Olson tied a game in the ninth inning. The blast ended Olson's string of 7 ⅔ consecutive hitless innings. He hit .272 for the '93 season, with 31 doubles, 66 RBI, and 28 stolen bases. It was the first time in four years that he hadn't hit the 30-steal mark. A line-drive hitter with power to the opposite field, Kelly hit career highs with 20 homers and 69 RBI in '91—even though he was idled more than a month with a strained wrist. He joined Jose Canseco and Joe Carter as the only 20/20 players in the AL.

His 1993 cards are longshots at prices higher than a dime. Think about a 1988 Donruss Kelly for $1. Our pick for his best 1993 card is Topps. We have chosen this card because it has a distinctive look.

	BA	G	AB	R	H	2B	3B	HR	RBI	SB
92 AL	.272	152	580	81	158	31	2	10	66	28
Life	.280	638	2277	320	637	110	12	56	258	151

JASON KENDALL

Position: Catcher
Team: Pittsburgh Pirates
Born: June 26, 1974
    San Diego, CA
Height: 6' **Weight:** 180 lbs.
Bats: Right **Throws:** Right
Acquired: First-round pick,
    6/92 free-agent draft

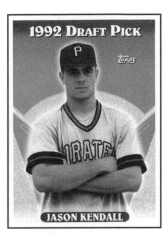

Jason Kendall is the son of former big league catcher Fred Kendall, whose 12-year career was spent mostly with the Padres. The younger Kendall has also chosen catching as a profession, and the Pirates obviously believe he has a future at the position. Kendall is a very good defensive catcher with an above-average throwing arm. He gets excellent grades for his leadership qualities, his makeup, and his overall athletic ability. He looked fine in his first pro season at bat, but the most important aspect of the game for a young catcher is defense, and he has many years to learn how to play behind the plate. The Pirates would love to see Kendall make it in the pros as their backstop. They need him to be a productive player.

Kendall should be a quality backstop for the Pirates when his time comes. It remains to be seen, however, whether he'll turn into a power hitter in the bigs. Proceed with caution. Our pick for his best 1993 card is Score. We have chosen this card because it has a distinctive look.

	BA	G	AB	R	H	2B	3B	HR	RBI	SB
92 R	.252	–	34	7	28	2	0	0	10	2
92 COL	.549	26	82	32	45	14	8	3	39	21

JEFF KENT

Position: Infield
Team: New York Mets
Born: March 7, 1968
   Bellflower, CA
Height: 6'1" **Weight:** 185 lbs.
Bats: Right **Throws:** Right
Acquired: Traded from Blue
   Jays with Ryan Thompson
   for David Cone, 8/92

Jeff Kent had never played above the Double-A level before the 1992 season. However, he found himself a job with the Blue Jays in '92. He filled in for Kelly Gruber at third, Roberto Alomar at second, and even played some first. He had a strange day on May 30, going from goat to hero. He came into the game as a pinch-runner, but was picked off by catcher Ron Karkovice. In the 11th, he doubled home the winning run. His 192 at-bats in '92 yielded 13 doubles, eight homers, and 35 RBI. He also struck out 35 times. Kent joined the pros as a third baseman and shortstop, but was converted to second in '90 while with Class-A Dunedin. He made the adjustment well enough to land on the midseason and postseason All-Star teams and was team MVP to boot. In '91, Kent ripped 12 homers, his third year in a row in double figures, and was team MVP with Double-A Knoxville. He'll start at second base for the Mets in '93.

The Mets now have Kent. You can, too, for only 15 cents for his 1993 cards. Our pick for his best 1993 card is Donruss. We have chosen this card due to the outstanding photographic composition.

	BA	G	AB	R	H	2B	3B	HR	RBI	SB
92 NL	.239	37	113	16	27	8	1	3	15	0
Life	.239	102	305	52	73	21	2	11	50	2

JIMMY KEY

Position: Pitcher
Team: New York Yankees
Born: April 22, 1961
   Huntsville, AL
Height: 6'1" **Weight:** 185 lbs.
Bats: Right **Throws:** Left
Acquired: Signed as a free
   agent, 11/92

 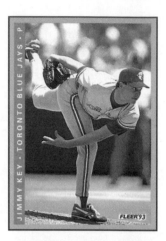

Jimmy Key wasn't Toronto's most successful 1992 starter, but he was one of the team's most durable hurlers. His performance that helped the Blue Jays win the '92 World Series was icing on the cake. He hurdled the double-digit winning plateau (13) for the eighth season in a row. Most impressively, he exceeded 30 starts (33) and 200 innings pitched (216 ⅔) for the sixth time in his career. The winner of the '91 All-Star game, Key has been a Blue Jays starter since '85. Key's only year as a reliever came in '84, his rookie season. In 63 appearances, he accumulated 10 saves. His career highs of 17 wins and a league-leading 2.76 ERA came in '87, when he was named AL Pitcher of the Year by *The Sporting News*.

Lefthanded batters still can't hit .200 off Key. The lefty hurler moves to Yankee Stadium, stepping out from the shadows cast by Jack Morris and Juan Guzman. Our pick for his best 1993 card is Upper Deck. We have chosen this card due to the outstanding photographic composition.

	W	L	ERA	G	CG	IP	H	ER	BB	SO
92 AL	13	13	3.53	33	4	216.2	205	85	59	117
Life	116	81	3.42	317	28	1695.2	1624	645	404	944

Series two cards from some companies were available at press time. If space allows, both cards are shown; if not, the most up-to-date cards are pictured.

JOHN KIELY

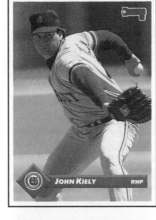

Position: Pitcher
Team: Detroit Tigers
Born: October 4, 1964
Boston, MA
Height: 6′3″ **Weight:** 210 lbs.
Bats: Right **Throws:** Right
Acquired: Signed as a free
agent, 9/87

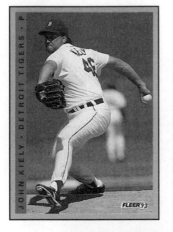

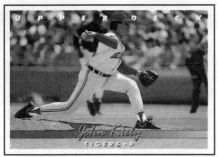

DARRYL KILE

Position: Pitcher
Team: Houston Astros
Born: December 2, 1968
Garden Grove, CA
Height: 6′5″ **Weight:** 185 lbs.
Bats: Right **Throws:** Right
Acquired: 30th-round pick,
6/87 free-agent draft

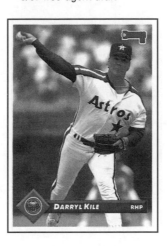

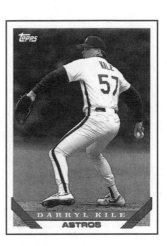

John Kiely became an important part of the Tigers bullpen in 1992. Throughout the season, Kiely struggled to keep his strikeout total higher than his walks. Yet, Kiely was a frequently called-upon member of the Detroit relief brigade. He was 2-0 in '92 spring training, but started the season in the Triple-A International League. The sidearm specialist was leading his Toledo club in saves when he was recalled by the Tigers in July. His '92 record of 4-2 with a 2.13 ERA was a contrast from his '91 big league debut of 0-1 with a 14.85 ERA in seven appearances. Kiely walked nine batters while striking out just one in his 6 ⅔ innings. Detroit discovered the Boston native as an undrafted free agent in '87.

Kiely's low ERA makes his 1993 cards tempting at a nickel each. Wait until he harnesses his control before making a commitment, just to be on the safe side. Our pick for his best 1993 card is Fleer. We have chosen this card because of its great combination of photography and design.

Darryl Kile's rising career was sidetracked by a minor league demotion in 1992. He went 0-2 with a 4.00 ERA in spring training, but made the '92 Opening-Day roster nonetheless. The Astros returned Kile to Triple-A at midseason. After nine starts and a 3-1 mark in Triple-A, he finished the season in Houston. In his first 20 starts, the Astros supported him with a tiny 2.94 runs per game. He finished the '92 season with a 5-10 record and a 3.95 ERA. After being almost overlooked in '87, he responded to Houston's faith in his ability, becoming a regular after just 64 games over three minor league seasons. Debuting with the 'Stros in '91, he compiled a 7-11 record and 3.69 ERA in 37 games.

If Kile becomes Houston's "swing man," bouncing between the bullpen and starting duty, his stats will vary wildly. In the process, the little interest remaining in his 1993 commons will die. Our pick for his best 1993 card is Topps. We have chosen this card because of its overall appeal and pleasing looks.

	W	L	ERA	G	SV	IP	H	ER	BB	SO
92 AL	4	2	2.13	39	0	55.0	44	13	28	18
Life	4	3	3.50	46	0	61.2	57	24	37	19

	W	L	ERA	G	CG	IP	H	ER	BB	SO
92 NL	5	10	3.95	22	2	125.1	124	55	63	90
Life	12	21	3.81	59	2	279.0	268	118	147	190

JEFF KING

Position: Third base
Team: Pittsburgh Pirates
Born: December 26, 1964
    Marion, IN
Height: 6'1" **Weight:** 185 lbs.
Bats: Right **Throws:** Right
Acquired: First-round pick,
    6/86 free-agent draft

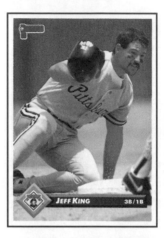 

Despite limited opportunities, Jeff King kept slugging for the 1992 Pirates. He began the year behind third baseman Steve Buechele, then wound up sharing playing time with third sacker John Wehner. While he hit 14 home runs and 65 RBI in '92, he also struck out more than twice for every walk he drew. In '91, he was the Opening-Day third baseman before he suffered a May back strain. His season ended after only 33 games, and climaxed with November back surgery. Stardom was forecast for King after he hit 14 homers and 53 RBI in '90. A starring third baseman at the University of Arkansas, King was named College Player of the Year by *The Sporting News* in '86. He was the first player to be chosen by any team in the '86 free-agent draft.

Want another shock? Kevin Young is a dazzling third base prospect waiting at Triple-A. The increased competition puts more heat on King and casts more doubts on his 1993 commons. Our pick for his best 1993 card is Donruss. We have chosen this card for its technical merits.

	BA	G	AB	R	H	2B	3B	HR	RBI	SB
92 NL	.231	130	480	56	111	21	2	14	65	4
Life	.230	365	1175	149	270	52	7	37	155	14

RYAN KLESKO

Position: First base
Team: Atlanta Braves
Born: June 12, 1971
    Westminster, CA
Height: 6'3" **Weight:** 220 lbs.
Bats: Left **Throws:** Left
Acquired: Sixth-round pick,
    6/89 free-agent draft

 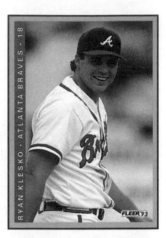

Ryan Klesko registered a disappointing season in his first look at Triple-A pitching. The Braves concede that he had some problems adjusting in 1992, but they believe he still is improving and can be an outstanding power hitter in the majors. Drafted as a pitcher, Klesko had arm trouble and was shifted to first. He has received a lot of attention. *Baseball America* listed him eighth on its list of baseball's top 100 prospects. So far, though, in five pro seasons, he has not put together an eye-popping home run total. Part of the reason in '92 was a hyperextension of the right elbow suffered in batting practice. Klesko did notch a .323 on-base average and a .435 slugging percentage last summer. He should get a legitimate shot to win a big league job in '93, but don't be surprised if he starts slowly.

Expect Klesko to get his chance soon. Until he can put together some solid numbers, proceed with caution on his '93s. Our pick for his best 1993 card is Fleer. We have chosen this card due to the outstanding photographic composition.

	BA	G	AB	R	H	2B	3B	HR	RBI	SB
92 AAA	.251	123	418	63	105	22	2	17	59	3
92 NL	.000	13	14	0	0	0	0	0	1	0

CHUCK KNOBLAUCH

Position: Second base
Team: Minnesota Twins
Born: July 7, 1968
   Houston, TX
Height: 5'9" **Weight:** 179 lbs.
Bats: Right **Throws:** Right
Acquired: First-round pick,
   6/89 free-agent draft

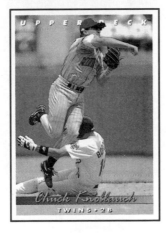

Chuck Knoblauch was no one-year wonder. After winning AL Rookie of the Year honors in 1991, he showed marked improvement in all areas as the Twins bid for a repeat title in '92. Knoblauch, hitting .297, came through again in '92. His 34 swipes showed impressive speed and, over his 1,339 ⅔ innings of work, he only erred six times. Knoblauch was able to fill a huge void when he jumped from Double-A to the majors during '91 spring training. The team's only other option at second base had been light-hitting Al Newman. A converted shortstop, Knoblauch finished '91 regular season play with a .281 average and 25 steals (tying a club record) but was more impressive in postseason play. That year, he hit .350 in the ALCS and .308 in the World Series.

With his sophomore improvement, Knoblauch could make year three really exciting. At a nickel apiece, investors should flock. The 1990 Score Knoblauch is sound at $1.50. Our pick for his best 1993 card is Upper Deck. We have chosen this card since the photograph captures the athletic ability of the player.

	BA	G	AB	R	H	2B	3B	HR	RBI	SB
92 AL	.297	155	600	104	178	19	6	2	56	34
Life	.289	306	1165	182	337	43	12	3	106	59

KURT KNUDSEN

Position: Pitcher
Team: Detroit Tigers
Born: February 20, 1967
   Arlington Heights, IL
Height: 6'3" **Weight:** 200 lbs.
Bats: Right **Throws:** Right
Acquired: Ninth-round pick,
   6/88 free-agent draft

Kurt Knudsen made an impression in spring training. It paid off within a couple of months, as he was brought to the big leagues and became one of the highlights in an otherwise discouraging year for Tiger pitchers. He began the '92 season at Triple-A Toledo and had a 3-1 record with a 2.08 ERA and one save when summoned to Detroit. Knudsen picked up his first major league win on May 20 against Milwaukee. Overall with the Tigers in '92, Knudsen went 2-3 with a 4.58 ERA. He walked more batters (28 in 55 innings of work) than you would like, and he must work on getting the first batter he faces out. With the 303 batters he faced for the Tigers in '92, he allowed 36 earned runs. His base hit and strikeout ratios have always been good. At Toledo in '91, for instance, Knudsen hurled 18 ⅓ innings, allowing just 13 hits while striking out 28.

Save your pennies. Knudsen could be swallowed up by the Tiger bullpen, making his '93 issues meaningless. Our pick for his best 1993 card is Fleer. We have chosen this card because of its great combination of photography and design.

	W	L	ERA	G	SV	IP	H	ER	BB	SO
92 AAA	3	1	2.08	12	1	21.2	11	5	6	19
92 AL	2	3	4.58	48	5	70.2	70	36	41	51

KEVIN KOSLOFSKI

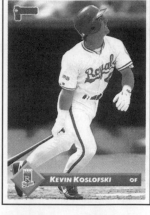

Position: Outfield
Team: Kansas City Royals
Born: September 24, 1966
   Decatur, IL
Height: 5'8" **Weight:** 165 lbs.
Bats: Left **Throws:** Right
Acquired: 20th-round pick,
   6/84 free-agent draft

Kevin Koslofski was one of Kansas City's biggest surprises in 1992. He made his first appearance with the Royals on June 28, after batting .314 with four homers and 29 RBI at Triple-A Omaha. In his debut game at Baltimore, he notched three singles, an RBI, and scored a run. At the end of the '92 campaign, his first major league season, Koslofski had demonstrated hot hitting, notching a .429 average against lefthanded pitching and .333 when away from Royals Stadium. By contrast, his home batting average was a chilly .195. No one could call Koslofski an overnight sensation. Almost an afterthought in the 1984 draft, the Illinois native began an 8½-year climb to the majors. Before 1992, his minor league averages never topped the .260s.

Koslofski will be represented in card sets for the first time in 1993. Those cards will average about a dime apiece and seem like hazardous hobby choices. Our pick for his best 1993 card is Fleer. We have chosen this card because of its overall appeal and pleasing looks.

	BA	G	AB	R	H	2B	3B	HR	RBI	SB
92 AL	.248	55	133	20	33	0	2	3	13	2
Life	.248	55	133	20	33	0	2	3	13	2

BILL KRUEGER

Position: Pitcher
Team: Detroit Tigers
Born: April 24, 1958
   Waukegan, IL
Height: 6'5" **Weight:** 205 lbs.
Bats: Right **Throws:** Right
Acquired: Signed as a free
   agent, 12/92

When 1991 World Series MVP Jack Morris jumped to the Toronto Blue Jays via free agency, the Minnesota Twins knew they had a big hole to fill. The signing of southpaw Bill Krueger, who had just led the Seattle Mariners in ERA, went a long way toward filling that void. His efforts just weren't all the Twins needed though, so by August '92, Krueger was traded to Montreal. By the end of '92, Krueger was with the Tigers. His '92 totals included a 10-6 record with a 4.30 ERA. A control pitcher, Krueger's best big league season was '91. After making eight relief appearances, he became a starter in May and took to the new job so well that he was AL Pitcher of the Month for July with a 4-0 record and 1.19 ERA. He finished with 11 wins, all but one as a starter. Krueger began his pro career in '80 and reached the majors with Oakland three years later. He has also pitched with the Dodgers and Brewers.

Krueger's 10 wins aren't enough to spark his common-priced cards. Our pick for his best 1993 card is Donruss. We have chosen this card for its technical merits.

	W	L	ERA	G	CG	IP	H	ER	BB	SO
92 AL	10	6	4.30	27	2	161.1	166	77	46	86
Life	57	57	4.25	233	8	1024.0	1097	484	431	516

JOHN KRUK

Position: First base
Team: Philadelphia Phillies
Born: February 9, 1961
   Charleston, WV
Height: 5'10" **Weight:** 200 lbs.
Bats: Left **Throws:** Left
Acquired: Traded from Padres
   with Randy Ready for Chris
   James, 6/89

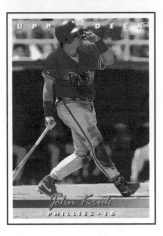

John Kruk took a six-year average of .291 into the 1992 campaign. He went on to finish third in the league for the '92 season with a .323 batting average—a new personal best. He also finished second among all National Leaguers with a .423 on-base percentage. He tallied over 1,330 innings of work during the '92 season, obtaining a .991 fielding percentage. Wielding an impressive bat, Kruk swatted 10 homers, 70 RBI, and drew 92 walks during '92. A good clutch hitter with some power, his career peaks include 21 homers, 92 RBI, and 84 runs scored ('91). In '91, Kruk made his first trip to the All-Star Game. He began that season by collecting 20 RBI in April, tying Mike Schmidt's club record. Kruk reached the majors with the '86 San Diego Padres and was traded to Philadelphia three years later.

Kruk's cards are iffy buys at rates higher than a dime each. The 1986 Topps Traded edition has Kruk at a classic price of a buck. Our pick for his best 1993 card is Fleer. We have chosen this card for the superior presentation of information on its back.

	BA	G	AB	R	H	2B	3B	HR	RBI	SB
92 NL	.323	144	507	86	164	30	4	10	70	3
Life	.297	930	2948	434	875	142	29	79	446	48

TIM LAKER

Position: Catcher
Team: Montreal Expos
Born: November 27, 1969
   Encino, CA
Height: 6'2" **Weight:** 175 lbs.
Bats: Right **Throws:** Right
Acquired: Sixth-round pick,
   6/88 free-agent draft

Tim Laker enjoyed the finest power season of his career in 1992, ranking among the top home run and RBI men in the Expos' minor league system. It was the latest step taken by a player who has made steady, though not spectacular, progress. Laker put himself on track for the majors with his 1990 season, when he made the Class-A Midwest League All-Star team and led loop catchers with 125 assists. He also paced his own club with 57 RBI and was second on the club with seven homers. Laker took another step in 1991, when he received his first promotion to Double-A and hit respectably there. But the highlight of Laker's '91 campaign came when he hit .310 over seven playoff games to help West Palm Beach capture the Class-A Florida State League title.

If Laker lives up to his billing—and keeps improving his hitting—he will play in Triple-A and maybe beyond in '93. Spend cautiously on his '93s. Our pick for his best 1993 card is Fleer. We have chosen this card for its artistic presentation.

	BA	G	AB	R	H	2B	3B	HR	RBI	SB
92 AA	.242	117	409	55	99	19	3	15	68	2
92 NL	.217	28	46	8	10	3	0	0	4	1

MARK LANGSTON

Position: Pitcher
Team: California Angels
Born: August 20, 1960
San Diego, CA
Height: 6'2" **Weight:** 183 lbs.
Bats: Left **Throws:** Left
Acquired: Signed as a free
agent, 12/89

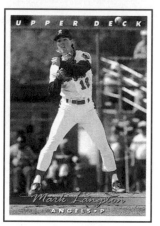

RAY LANKFORD

Position: Outfield
Team: St. Louis Cardinals
Born: June 5, 1967
Modesto, CA
Height: 5'11" **Weight:** 198 lbs.
Bats: Left **Throws:** Left
Acquired: Third-round pick,
6/87 free-agent draft

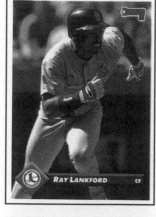

When Mark Langston threw his second shutout for the Angels in June 1992, he became the first Angel with back-to-back shutouts since Ken Forsch in '81. With Jim Abbott and Chuck Finley struggling during the first half of '92, Langston stepped forward as the Angels' ace. His complete game total for '92 (10) earned him sixth place in the league. A fine-fielding pitcher, Langston won his fourth Gold Glove Award in '92. The hard-throwing southpaw has always been a big winner. As an '84 rookie, he went 17-10 for the Mariners and fanned 204 enemy hitters, tops in the AL. Langston later won two more strikeout crowns. He has four 200-strikeout seasons, yet hasn't hit the 20-win plateau. He came closest in '91, posting 19 victories.

Spend no more than a nickel each on Langston's '93s, due to California's ever-shifting fortunes. Our pick for his best 1993 card is Score. We have chosen this card for the interesting facts included on the reverse.

Ray Lankford racked up numerous career highs with the 1992 Cardinals. The up-and-coming outfielder, playing in his second full season in the majors, bested most totals he had achieved during his '91 rookie campaign. In 1991, Lankford batted .251 with nine homers, 69 RBI and a league-leading 15 triples. For his efforts, Lankford finished third in NL Rookie of the Year balloting. He wasn't, however, content to stop there. In '92, he hit .293 with 20 homers and 86 RBI. He also demonstrated his fleet feet by swiping 42 bases. Although he drew 72 walks, Lankford did strike out a whopping 147 times. He was almost perfect in the field during '92, making only two errors in 1,369 innings.

Lankford's cards, incredibly, may still sell as commons in 1993. If the fast-rising star keeps the Cards in contention, his prices could triple soon. Any '91 Lankford card at less than a quarter is a deal. Our pick for his best 1993 card is Topps. We have chosen this card due to the outstanding photographic composition.

	W	L	ERA	G	CG	IP	H	ER	BB	SO
92 AL	13	14	3.66	32	9	229.0	206	93	74	174
Life	128	115	3.75	299	68	2072.2	1817	864	942	1805

	BA	G	AB	R	H	2B	3B	HR	RBI	SB
92 NL	.293	153	598	87	175	40	6	20	86	42
Life	.274	343	1290	182	353	73	22	32	167	94

Series two cards from some companies were available at press time. If space allows, both cards are shown; if not, the most up-to-date cards are pictured.

BARRY LARKIN

Position: Shortstop
Team: Cincinnati Reds
Born: April 28, 1964
  Cincinnati, OH
Height: 6′ **Weight:** 185 lbs.
Bats: Right **Throws:** Right
Acquired: First-round pick in
  6/85 free-agent draft

A sore left knee prevented Barry Larkin from contributing much early-season help to the Cincinnati Reds' comeback season in 1992. Larkin's recovery seemed to start slowly, but he finished the season posting impressive numbers that included a .304 average, 12 homers, 78 RBI, and 63 walks. He also swiped 15 bases in his over 1,200 innings of work in '92. The season also marked the fourth year in a row that he has hit at least .300. In '91, he hit .302 with 20 homers, 69 RBI, and 24 stolen bases while making the All-Star team for the fourth season. Larkin not only tied Leo Cardenas' '66 club record for homers by a shortstop but picked up five of them over a two-game stretch. A Cincinnati native who joined his hometown team in '86, Larkin led the Reds to victory in the '90 World Series with a .353 batting average against Oakland.

He's a card bargain at a dime apiece. A 1987 Topps rookie is a reasonable buy at $1. Our pick for his best 1993 card is Topps. We have chosen this card for its technical merits.

	BA	G	AB	R	H	2B	3B	HR	RBI	SB
92 NL	.304	140	533	76	162	32	6	12	78	15
Life	.296	835	3122	478	924	150	30	70	368	148

GENE LARKIN

Position: First base
Team: Minnesota Twins
Born: October 24, 1962
  Astoria, NY
Height: 6′3″ **Weight:** 199 lbs.
Bats: Both **Throws:** Right
Acquired: 20th-round pick,
  6/84 free-agent draft

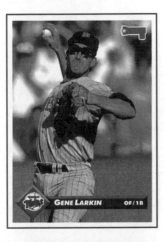
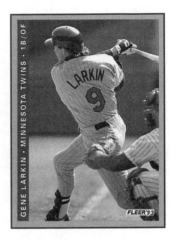

Gene Larkin rode to the rescue for the 1992 Twins, subbing for injured first baseman Kent Hrbek. While Larkin faced his usual problems hitting lefthanded pitchers, he was a defensive standout. He earned a .992 fielding percentage over 431 ⅔ innings of work. At bat, he couldn't match his career-high .286 average compiled in '91. He did, however, manage a .246 mark with 42 RBI in '92. In 1985-86, Larkin enjoyed two consecutive seasons of 100-plus RBI in the minors. He played in a career-high 149 games in '88, as reflected by his eight homers and 70 RBI. He is valued for his switch-hitting ability, and the Twins utilize Larkin at first, in the outfield, at DH, or as a pinch-hitter. At Columbia University, Larkin broke many offensive records previously held by Lou Gehrig.

Larkin's few homers and his infrequent playing time make his cards unattractive to collectors. Don't squander your nickels on his 1993s. Our pick for his best 1993 card is Topps. We have chosen this card because of its great combination of photography and design.

	BA	G	AB	R	H	2B	3B	HR	RBI	SB
92 AL	.246	115	337	38	83	18	1	6	42	7
Life	.266	702	2177	258	580	124	11	31	247	23

MIKE LaVALLIERE

Position: Catcher
Team: Pittsburgh Pirates
Born: August 18, 1960
 Charlotte, NC
Height: 5'10" **Weight:** 205 lbs.
Bats: Left **Throws:** Right
Acquired: Traded from
 Cardinals with Andy Van
 Slyke and Mike Dunne for
 Tony Pena, 4/87

For the third year in a row, Mike LaValliere was once again one of the best half-catchers in baseball. LaValliere continued to give Pittsburgh an excellent backstop platoon with Don Slaught in 1992. By combining the pair, the Pirates have a first-rate catcher. LaValliere was used primarily against righthanded pitchers. His average dropped approximately 100 points when facing lefties. He hit .267 against righties, but only .161 the other way. His other stats were very much the same as they have been in years past—a .256 batting average, two homers, 29 RBI. LaValliere began his pro career as an undrafted free agent with Philadelphia in '81. He debuted with the Phillies in '84 and played more than 100 games with the Cardinals in '86.

Even if you put the common-priced cards of catching mates LaValliere and Slaught together, hobbyists still don't have a worthy investment. Only invest your nickels in the cards of full-time players. Our pick for his best 1993 card is Donruss. We have chosen this card due to the outstanding photographic composition.

	BA	G	AB	R	H	2B	3B	HR	RBI	SB
92 NL	.256	95	293	22	75	13	1	2	29	0
Life	.269	736	2134	166	574	97	5	16	243	5

TERRY LEACH

Position: Pitcher
Team: Chicago White Sox
Born: March 13, 1954
 Selma, AL
Height: 6' **Weight:** 191 lbs.
Bats: Right **Throws:** Right
Acquired: Signed as a free-
 agent, 4/92

Terry Leach commemorated two events in 1992. First, he began the year, his 10th as a major leaguer, on the White Sox Opening-Day roster. His '92 spring training was with the Expos: Leach was one of the last cuts made from the Montreal roster, but was signed by Chicago early in April. After being released by the fifth organization of his career, he became a regular in the ChiSox bullpen. Secondly, for the sixth season in a row, he exceeded 40 appearances (51). Righthanders failed to hit .200 against the veteran sidearm specialist. At home he was equally effective, allowing batters only a .162 average. Before labelling Leach a baseball dinosaur, note that he didn't start his pro career until he was 25 years old. He was first drafted by the Red Sox in January '76, but didn't sign.

The only record Leach may near is total number of teams served in one career. His common-priced cards will be shrugged off in 1993. Our pick for his best 1993 card is Donruss. We have chosen this card due to the outstanding photographic composition.

	W	L	ERA	G	SV	IP	H	ER	BB	SO
92 AL	6	5	1.95	51	0	73.2	57	16	20	22
Life	38	27	3.16	362	9	684.0	673	240	195	328

TIM LEARY

Position: Pitcher
Team: Seattle Mariners
Born: December 23, 1958
   Santa Monica, CA
Height: 6′3″ **Weight:** 218 lbs.
Bats: Right **Throws:** Right
Acquired: Traded from Yankees
   with cash for Sean Twitty,
   8/92

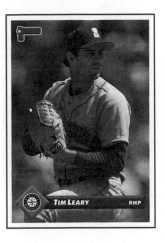

MANUEL LEE

Position: Shortstop
Team: Texas Rangers
Born: June 17, 1965
   San Pedro de Macoris,
   Dominican Republic
Height: 5′9″ **Weight:** 166 lbs.
Bats: Both **Throws:** Right
Acquired: Signed as a free
   agent, 12/92

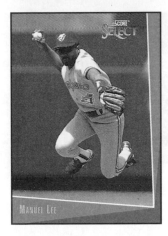

Tim Leary added a new facet to his career in 1992, slumping not with one, but two teams. In New York, Leary was a bust, despite getting a three-year free-agent contract worth nearly $6 million. His dismal '92 season found him with an 8-10 record with a hefty 5.36 ERA. Out of the 624 batters he faced, he walked 87 and struck out 46. In order to unload Leary to the Mariners, the Yanks accepted only one minor leaguer in return and paid a good share of his salary on the remaining contract. Once, Leary was a top-ranked starter. He rallied the Dodgers to a '88 World Championship with a 17-11 record. Only two seasons later, he led the AL with 19 losses. The Mets first discovered Leary out of UCLA, making him only the second player chosen in the first round of the '79 draft.

If Leary can't stand out on a pitching-poor last-place club like Seattle, his future cards will be useless to collectors. Don't buy his 1993 commons. Our pick for his best 1993 card is Donruss. We have chosen this card because it has a distinctive look.

Manuel Lee's eighth year with the Blue Jays—although typical in many ways for the veteran—was also his last. He signed with Texas for '93. Lee's 1992 adventures at the plate for the Jays were interesting. Batting in Toronto or against lefties, Lee scraped to top .200. The switch-hitter flirted with .300, however, when hitting on the road or against righties. Although he debuted with Toronto in '85, Lee started his career as an undrafted free agent in the Mets organization in '82. Until he signed with the Mets late in '92, Lee had been a fixture with the Blue Jays since '88. Toronto installed him as a starting shortstop in '90, after trading away Tony Fernandez. Through '92, his greatest production has been six homers and 41 RBI ('90), along with a .291 batting average ('88).

Lee's cards can't hold a candle to those of popular former double-play mate Roberto Alomar. Call him Manuel or call him Manny. Just don't call for his 1993 commons. Our pick for his best 1993 card is Score. We have chosen this card for its technical merits.

	W	L	ERA	G	CG	IP	H	ER	BB	SO
92	8	10	5.36	26	3	141	131	84	87	46
Life	66	95	4.21	253	25	1301	1342	609	466	811

	BA	G	AB	R	H	2B	3B	HR	RBI	SB
92 AL	.263	128	396	49	104	10	1	3	39	6
Life	.254	753	2152	231	547	67	17	16	199	26

CRAIG LEFFERTS

Position: Pitcher
Team: Baltimore Orioles
Born: September 29, 1957
Munich, West Germany
Height: 6'1" **Weight:** 210 lbs.
Bats: Left **Throws:** Left
Acquired: Traded from Padres
for Erik Schullstrom and
Ricky Gutierrez, 9/92

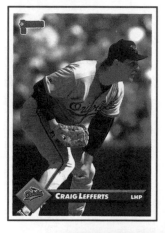

CHARLIE LEIBRANDT

Position: Pitcher
Team: Texas Rangers
Born: October 4, 1956
Chicago, IL
Height: 6'3" **Weight:** 200 lbs.
Bats: Right **Throws:** Left
Acquired: Traded from Braves
with Pat Gomez for Jose
Oliva, 12/92

 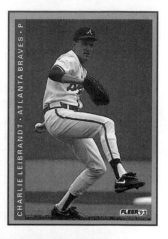

Switching from years of bullpen duty brought some big payoffs for Craig Lefferts in 1992. Before his trade to Baltimore, he was 13-9 with a 3.69 ERA as a starter for the Padres. Lefferts found the AL a little tougher to pitch in and in '92 he went 1-3 with a 4.09 ERA. While the Orioles got extra help in their pennant drive, the Padres got rid of a huge salary. Lefferts, owner of 100 career saves going into '92, performed like he'd been starting for years. Perhaps the biggest payoff the converted reliever will find is at the bank. Even before '92 ended, the possible free-agent seemed able to name his price for a '93 contract with numerous pitching-hungry teams.

Even though Lefferts will grab headlines as a free-agent possibility leading into the 1993 season, the publicity will offer few long-term benefits for his cards. Assume his common-priced cards will return to their low prices by the end of the year. Our pick for his best 1993 card is Score. We have chosen this card because of its overall appeal and pleasing looks.

For the eighth time in his career, Charlie Leibrandt won in double digits. In '92, the Braves' workhorse matched his 15 victories from '91, but not the career-best 17-9 mark assembled with the '85 Royals. He was traded late in '92 for third sacker Jose Oliva, underlining the fact that Atlanta is pitching-heavy. Leibrandt embarked on his lengthy career in '78, when he was picked by the Reds. The veteran lefty debuted with Cincinnati in '79, which gives him the distinction of pitching in three different decades. Along with his personal-high winning total obtained with Kansas City in '85, Leibrandt began a four-year streak of 30-plus starts and 230-plus innings pitched. This streak ended in '90, when his season started in June due to slight rotator cuff surgery.

Leibrandt—invisible when he was surrounded by young guns like Glavine, Smoltz, and Avery—will have a new home in '93. His three to five cent cards, however, shouldn't take up residence in yours. Our pick for his best 1993 card is Fleer. We have chosen this card because of its great combination of photography and design.

	W	L	ERA	G	CG	IP	H	ER	BB	SO
92 NL	13	9	3.69	27	0	163.1	180	67	35	81
Life	54	62	3.17	614	1	1027.2	956	362	282	634

	W	L	ERA	G	CG	IP	H	ER	BB	SO
92 NL	15	7	3.36	32	5	193.0	191	72	42	104
Life	131	109	3.65	368	51	2157.2	2221	876	611	1032

Series two cards from some companies were available at press time. If space allows, both cards are shown; if not, the most up-to-date cards are pictured.

MARK LEITER

Position: Pitcher
Team: Detroit Tigers
Born: April 13, 1963 Joliet, IL
Height: 6′3″ **Weight:** 210 lbs.
Bats: Right **Throws:** Right
Acquired: Traded from Yankees
  for Torey Lovullo, 4/91

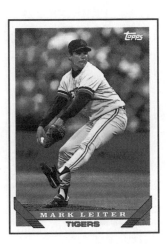

SCOTT LEIUS

Position: Third base
Team: Minnesota Twins
Born: September 24, 1965
  Yonkers, NY
Height: 6′3″ **Weight:** 180 lbs.
Bats: Right **Throws:** Right
Acquired: 13th-round pick,
  6/86 free-agent draft

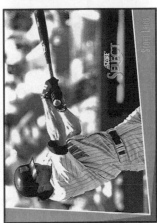

After winning six decisions in a row en route to a 9-7 rookie record with the 1991 Tigers, Mark Leiter had trouble finding the plate early in '92. At one point, he issued 16 walks in 12 ⅔ innings. Leiter eventually recovered and boosted his ratio of strikeouts-to-walks to 2-to-1. He yielded more hits than innings pitched, however, and threw his share of home-run balls. Opponents compiled a .277 batting average, a .342 on-base percentage, and a .415 slugging percentage against him in '92. He broke into pro ball in '83 but didn't reach the majors until '90, partly because he was sidelined by serious shoulder problems for three full years ('86 to '88). In '90 at Triple-A Columbus, he was 9-4 with a 3.60 ERA, nine walks, and 21 strikeouts in 26 ⅓ innings.

Leiter won't create much of a stir until he makes the unlikely change of gaining some much needed control. His past shoulder problems make his '93s poor card selections. Our pick for his best 1993 card is Upper Deck. We have chosen this card because it has a distinctive look.

Scott Leius saw his 1992 job description change instantly. Leius was scheduled to spend his sophomore season platooning at third base with Mike Pagliarulo. However, when eardrum surgery and a broken wrist eliminated Pagliarulo for most of the '92 campaign, Leius got his big chance. He started more than 100 games at the hot corner and also filled in at shortstop. For the '92 season, Leius posted a .249 batting average with 35 RBI and 34 walks against 61 strikeouts. His '92 fielding percentage of .955 placed him above the average for AL third basemen. In his rookie season, Leius rose to fame by hitting .357 in the '91 World Series. His 11-for-25 performance as a pinch-hitter set a Twins record. He was a four-sport star in high school, then played two years of amateur ball at Concordia College.

Leius will have to exceed .300 or start hitting homers by the handful. Otherwise, his 1993 commons will grow stale. Our pick for his best 1993 card is Fleer. We have chosen this card for its technical merits.

	W	L	ERA	G	SV	IP	H	ER	BB	SO
92 AL	8	5	4.18	35	0	112.0	116	52	43	75
Life	18	13	4.45	81	1	273.0	274	135	102	199

	BA	G	AB	R	H	2B	3B	HR	RBI	SB
92 AL	.249	129	409	50	102	18	2	2	35	6
Life	.261	252	633	89	165	26	4	8	59	11

MARK LEMKE

Position: Second base
Team: Atlanta Braves
Born: August 13, 1965
   Utica, NY
Height: 5′9″ **Weight:** 167 lbs.
Bats: Both **Throws:** Right
Acquired: 27th-round pick,
   6/83 free-agent draft

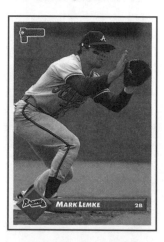

Mark Lemke flexed some home-run clout with the '92 Braves, but failed to show serious offensive potential. Atlanta nearly doubled Lemke's amount of plate appearances from '90 and '91, but Dirt did not deliver. His anemic stats for '92 included a .227 average, seven doubles, six homers, 26 RBI, and 50 walks. Lemke was the rage of the '91 World Series, despite being on the losing side. He paced the Braves with 10 hits (including a double and three triples), four RBI, and a .417 average. His first appearance with Atlanta came in '88. In 1990-91, he platooned at second base with Jeff Treadway.

   Lemke's cards would be worth a mint if he could make his regular season efforts near his postseason work. As it is, his 1993 nickel-priced cards will be popular only before the season starts, due to Atlanta's repeat postseason involvement in '92. Sell before the season starts and Lemke becomes human again. Our pick for his best 1993 card is Topps. We have chosen this card due to the outstanding photographic composition.

	BA	G	AB	R	H	2B	3B	HR	RBI	SB
92 NL	.227	155	427	38	97	7	4	6	26	0
Life	.226	423	1048	108	237	37	7	10	82	1

JESSE LEVIS

Position: Catcher
Team: Cleveland Indians
Born: April 14, 1968
   Philadelphia, PA
Height: 5′9″ **Weight:** 180 lbs.
Bats: Left **Throws:** Right
Acquired: Fourth-round pick,
   6/89 free-agent draft

Jesse Levis has a good future in the majors if he keeps building on what he has accomplished so far. He doesn't figure to dislodge Sandy Alomar Jr. at the big league level, but talent like his will emerge eventually. Levis got a trip to the majors early in 1992 when outfielder Glenallen Hill was sidelined. With the Indians in '92, Levis hit .279 and made only one error in 87 ⅔ innings. At the time of his promotion, Levis was hitting .472 with two homers and eight RBI in 12 games with Cleveland's Triple-A club in Colorado Springs. Levis has occasional power, but his chief offensive gift is an ability to put the ball in play. In '90, he was third in his Class-A league in on-base percentage with .398. In '91 in Double-A, he fanned once every 11.89 at-bats, third-best ratio in the league. He led all Double-A Eastern League catchers with 733 total chances, 644 putouts, and 77 assists.

   With limited playing prospects, 1993 cards of Levis are tossups at 15 cents each. Our pick for his best 1993 card is Donruss. We have chosen this card for its technical merits.

	BA	G	AB	R	H	2B	3B	HR	RBI	SB
92 AL	.279	28	43	12	2	4	0	1	3	0
Life	.279	28	43	12	2	4	0	1	3	0

DARREN LEWIS

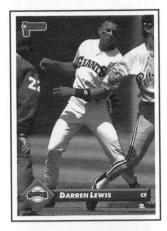

Position: Outfield
Team: San Francisco Giants
Born: August 28, 1967
    Berkeley, CA
Height: 6′ **Weight:** 175 lbs.
Bats: Right **Throws:** Right
Acquired: Traded from
    Athletics with Pedro Pena for
    Ernest Riles, 12/90

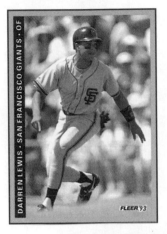

MARK LEWIS

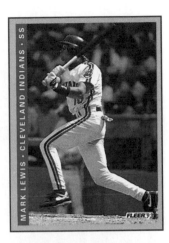

Position: Shortstop
Team: Cleveland Indians
Born: November 30, 1969
    Hamilton, OH
Height: 5′10″ **Weight:** 170 lbs.
Bats: Right **Throws:** Right
Acquired: First-round pick,
    6/88 free-agent draft

Speed alone should guarantee Darren Lewis a long tenure in the major leagues. Any way he gets on first, he is a threat to steal second to get a man in scoring position. He spent much of '92 sharing San Francisco's center field job with Mike Felder and Cory Snyder, before the Giants decided Lewis needed more seasoning. At Triple-A Phoenix in '92, he batted .228 with 22 runs scored, nine stolen bases, 11 walks, and 15 strikeouts in 158 at bats. His total of 28 big league stolen bases is impressive for someone who doesn't play every day or hit for a high average. He had a .295 on-base average and a .272 slugging percentage in 1992. Lewis should enjoy his first full big league season in '93.

While Lewis needs a full-time job before attracting major attention in the card hobby, his speed on the basepaths merits watching. Pick up a few of his '93s. Our pick for his best 1993 card is Upper Deck. We have chosen this card since the photograph captures the athletic ability of the player.

After four pro seasons, Mark Lewis became Cleveland's starting shortstop in 1992. Despite hitting .172 in spring training, Lewis made the Opening-Day roster. While his power and overall offensive efforts ranked a notch above '91 starter Felix Fermin, Lewis seemed set on leading AL shortstops in errors. In fact, Lewis made 25 errors in his 44 games during '92, a high-water mark that tied him with Gary DiSarcina for the dubious honor. The Indians drafted Lewis out of high school in '88, making him the second player chosen in the first round of that year's draft. Being a top draft pick piled great expectations on Lewis. After two mediocre seasons, his true offensive potential emerged in Double-A, where he hit .272 with 10 home runs and 60 RBI in '90.

After only one full season in the majors, Lewis doesn't electrify the imaginations of card collectors. His '93 commons are marginal investments. Our pick for his best 1993 card is Upper Deck. We have chosen this card due to its unique photographic approach.

	BA	G	AB	R	H	2B	3B	HR	RBI	SB
92 NL	.231	100	320	38	74	8	1	1	18	28
Life	.237	197	577	83	137	13	4	2	34	43

	BA	G	AB	R	H	2B	3B	HR	RBI	SB
92 AL	.264	122	413	44	109	21	0	5	30	4
Life	.264	206	727	73	192	36	1	5	60	6

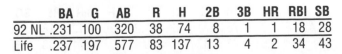

JIM LEYRITZ

Position: Designated hitter
Team: New York Yankees
Born: December 27, 1963
   Lakewood, OH
Height: 6'3" **Weight:** 190 lbs.
Bats: Right **Throws:** Right
Acquired: Signed as a free
   agent, 8/85

DEREK LILLIQUIST

Position: Pitcher
Team: Cleveland Indians
Born: February 20, 1966
   Winter Park, FL
Height: 6' **Weight:** 214 lbs.
Bats: Left **Throws:** Left
Acquired: Claimed on waivers,
   11/91

Jim Leyritz enjoyed his most productive offensive season with the Yankees in 1992. The multifaceted glove man exceeded his previous big league bests of five home runs and 25 RBI achieved in 92 games with the '90 Yanks, hitting seven and 26 respectively for the '92 season. He began '92 on New York's Opening-Day roster, projected as a third-string catcher. However, he saw most of his action as a DH, along with brief appearances at first base, second, third, and in right field. In '89, Leyritz paced the Double-A Eastern League in batting with a loop-best .315 average. In Triple-A in '91, he banged out a career-high 11 home runs. Leyritz attracted little attention in the '85 draft. The Yankees signed him later that year, beginning his six-year journey to the majors.

Leyritz might be one of the American League's most versatile players. That talent means nothing to card investors, who'll shun his 1993 commons. Our pick for his best 1993 card is Topps. We have chosen this card because the design lends itself to the best use of the elements.

Derek Lilliquist matched his previous career stats in one season as a Cleveland reliever. Before 1992, Lilliquist had appeared in 66 major league games, mostly as a starter. However, in the '92 Tribe bullpen, he passed that horizon in mid-September. Best of all, he assembled an ERA (1.75) that dipped more than three points lower than his pre-1992 mark. Only on the road did batters better a .200 average (.219) against him. He was toughest at home (.154) or when facing righthanders (.178). Lilliquist had been with the Padres organization, where he bombed in '91. In six games, he was a miserable 0-2 with an 8.79 ERA. As a starter, Lilliquist looked sharpest in '89, his first season with Atlanta. His rookie totals included an 8-10 mark and a 3.97 ERA.

While Lilliquist may find long-term employment as a middle reliever, he won't win any supporters for his common-priced cards. Leave his 1993 issues alone. Our pick for his best 1993 card is Topps. We have chosen this card because of its great combination of photography and design.

	BA	G	AB	R	H	2B	3B	HR	RBI	SB
92 AL	.257	63	144	17	37	6	0	7	26	0
Life	.246	187	524	53	129	22	1	12	55	2

	W	L	ERA	G	CG	IP	H	ER	BB	SO
92 AL	5	3	1.75	71	6	61.2	39	12	18	47
Life	18	26	4.23	137	6	363.2	402	171	98	196

JOSE LIND

Position: Second base
Team: Kansas City Royals
Born: May 1, 1964
  Toabaja, Puerto Rico
Height: 5'11" **Weight:** 175 lbs.
Bats: Right **Throws:** Right
Acquired: Traded from Pirates
  for Dennis Moeller and Joel
  Johnston, 11/92

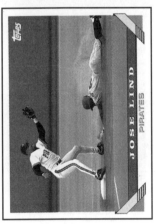

Jose Lind was one of the weakest links in the 1992 Pirates offense. His offense plunged from '91 totals of three home runs, 54 RBI, and a .265 average. Yet, his defensive leadership remained intact. In 1990 and '91, he led NL second sackers in putouts and won a Gold Glove for his efforts in '92. Lind's 311 putouts in '92 were second only in the league to Craig Biggio. Known as Chico to teammates, the scrappy second baseman has been a Pirates regular since '88. He debuted in Pittsburgh in '87, following five years in the minor leagues. His brother, pitcher Orlando Lind, was his teammate at Class-A and Double-A in '85 and '86. From '88 through '91, he appeared in at least 150 games yearly. He'll play with the Royals in '93.

Without a .300 average or a hatful of homers, Lind doesn't have the qualifications needed to sway card investors. His 1993s will have bleak futures at a nickel apiece. Our pick for his best 1993 card is Score. We have chosen this card because it has a distinctive look.

	BA	G	AB	R	H	2B	3B	HR	RBI	SB
92 NL	.235	135	468	38	110	14	1	0	39	3
Life	.255	779	2816	292	717	111	23	8	249	50

DOUG LINTON

Position: Pitcher
Team: Toronto Blue Jays
Born: September 2, 1965
  Santa Ana, CA
Height: 6'1" **Weight:** 185 lbs.
Bats: Right **Throws:** Right
Acquired: 43rd-round pick,
  6/86 free-agent draft

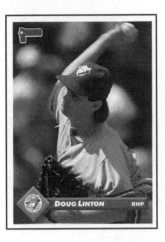

Despite debuting with a World Championship team, Doug Linton's bow with the 1992 Blue Jays was anything but sweet. Racked for five homers in 24 innings, the righthander relieved in five of his eight appearances. Overall, his '92 efforts with the Blue Jays posted a 1-3 record with a whopping 8.63 ERA, facing a total of 116 batters. Those batters, lefthanded or righthanded, all hit Linton hard during his peek at the bigs. He advanced to the majors following a healthy Triple-A season of 12-10 with seven complete games and a team-leading 126 strikeouts. Five seasons earlier, *Baseball America* had rated Linton as one of the top 10 prospects of the Class-A South Atlantic League. However, his Toronto turmoil casts a cloud over his prospect status.

Let Linton try to redeem himself from his 1992 nightmare before taking any stock in his 1993 cards. His rookie issues will sell for 10 to 20 cents, a dangerous price for speculators. Our pick for his best 1993 card is Topps. We have chosen this card for its technical merits.

	W	L	ERA	G	CG	IP	H	ER	BB	SO
92 AAA	12	10	3.69	25	7	170.2	83	70	70	126
92 AL	1	3	8.63	8	0	24	23	23	17	16

PAT LISTACH

Position: Shortstop
Team: Milwaukee Brewers
Born: September 12, 1967
Natchitoches, LA
Height: 5'9" **Weight:** 170 lbs.
Bats: Right **Throws:** Right
Acquired: Second-round pick,
6/88 free-agent draft

SCOTT LIVINGSTONE

Position: Third base
Team: Detroit Tigers
Born: July 15, 1965 Dallas, TX
Height: 6' **Weight:** 190 lbs.
Bats: Left **Throws:** Right
Acquired: Second-round pick,
6/88 free-agent draft

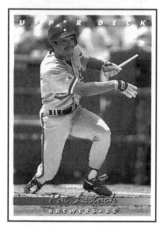

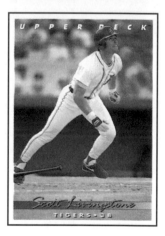

In his very first season at the major league level, Pat Listach established himself as a manager's dream—the kind of player whose name is automatically written into the lineup. He lacks power, but that's about the only thing missing from his bag of talents. He was so impressive and promising in '92 that he snagged AL Rookie of the Year honors. His totals included hitting a solid .345 against lefties and .324 on the road. Some of his acclaim can be accredited to the fact that he demonstrated excellent speed on the basepaths. Out of his 72 steal attempts in the '92 season, Listach was successful 54 times. He averaged 43 stolen bases a year over four minor league campaigns. A shortstop who can also play second, Listach made 24 errors in his 149 games in '92, but that may settle down with experience.

Listach and Kenny Lofton dominate the letter "L" and the card parade for '93. A half-buck for Listach's 1993 cards would seem reasonable. Our pick for his best 1993 card is Score. We have chosen this card for the interesting facts included on the reverse.

If anyone benefitted from Detroit injuries in 1992, it was Scott Livingstone. While Alan Trammell spent most of the year on the DL, '91's third baseman, Travis Fryman, got the chance to fill in at shortstop. In turn, Livingstone played more than 100 games at the hot corner. At the end of the '92 season, he was hitting .335 on the road, but only .229 at home. Livingstone remained a hot amateur property before and during his collegiate career at Texas A&M. He turned down a sixth-round offer from Toronto in '84, a 26th-round pick by the Yankees in '86, and a third-round selection by Oakland in '87. The Texas native was chosen as a college All-American by *The Sporting News* in '87 and '88.

Third basemen with little slugging ability are an endangered species in the majors. Livingstone's 1993 job may be up for grabs. Don't grab his '93 cards, even at a nickel apiece. Our pick for his best 1993 card is Fleer. We have chosen this card because of its overall appeal and pleasing looks.

	BA	G	AB	R	H	2B	3B	HR	RBI	SB
92 AL	.290	149	579	93	168	19	6	1	47	54
Life	.290	149	579	93	168	19	6	1	47	54

	BA	G	AB	R	H	2B	3B	HR	RBI	SB
92 AL	.282	117	354	43	100	21	0	4	46	1
Life	.285	161	481	62	137	26	0	6	57	3

KENNY LOFTON

Position: Outfield
Team: Cleveland Indians
Born: May 31, 1967
  East Chicago, IN
Height: 6′ **Weight:** 180 lbs.
Bats: Left **Throws:** Left
Acquired: Traded from Astros
  with Dave Rohde for Ed
  Taubensee and Willie Blair,
  12/91

Kenny Lofton has become Cleveland's leadoff man and could hold the job for many years. This season's AL base-stealing champion, Lofton made 24 successful attempts in '92 before California's Lance Parrish finally caught him. The down side of that is Lofton's tendency to get picked off; it happened three times June 13-14 alone. However, that still left him with 66 steals in 78 tries for the '92 season. As he gains more experience, he should become even better. Lofton's .285 batting average was impressive as well, adding a sprinkling of five homers and 42 RBI to compliment his speed, which gives him a chance for doubles and triples. Lofton was selected by the Astros in the 17th round of the '88 draft, and made the big club three years later. The Astros then traded him to Cleveland as part of a deal that netted them Willie Blair and Ed Taubensee.

The sky is the limit for these 1993 cards. Feel lucky to find one under a buck. Our pick for his best 1993 card is Upper Deck. We have chosen this card because it has a distinctive look.

	BA	G	AB	R	H	2B	3B	HR	RBI	SB
92 AL	.285	148	576	96	164	15	8	5	42	66
Life	.275	168	650	105	179	16	8	5	42	68

JAVY LOPEZ

Position: Catcher
Team: Atlanta Braves
Born: November 5, 1970
  Ponce, Puerto Rico
Height: 6′3″ **Weight:** 185 lbs.
Bats: Right **Throws:** Right
Acquired: Signed as a free
  agent, 11/87

Catcher Javy Lopez has a chance to really stand out. He has nice size, hits for average and power, and can even run a little. His work behind the plate has come along to the point where he was named the top defensive catcher in the Double-A Southern League by *Baseball America* in 1992. He was part of the reason Greenville dominated in '92. He was the starting catcher in the Double-A All-Star Game, going 2-for-2 with a run scored. As the regular season wound down, Lopez owned a lead of more than 10 percentage points over his closest pursuer for the batting title among Braves' minor leaguers, which is remarkable for a catcher. He also had a .362 on-base average and a .507 slugging percentage. He has shown an ability to homer in double figures. His RBI totals were a little low in '92, though.

Unless Lopez can unseat Greg Olson, you should exercise caution with his '93s. Our pick for his best 1993 card is Upper Deck. We have chosen this card due to the outstanding photographic composition.

	BA	G	AB	R	H	2B	3B	HR	RBI	SB
92 AA	.321	115	442	64	142	28	3	16	60	7
92 NL	.375	9	16	3	6	2	0	0	2	0

SEAN LOWE

Position: Pitcher
Team: St. Louis Cardinals
Born: March 29, 1971
  Dallas, TX
Height: 6'2" **Weight:** 200 lbs.
Bats: Right **Throws:** Right
Acquired: First-round pick,
  6/92 free-agent draft

KEVIN MAAS

Position: Designated hitter
Team: New York Yankees
Born: January 20, 1965
  Castro Valley, CA
Height: 6'3" **Weight:** 209 lbs.
Bats: Left **Throws:** Left
Acquired: 22nd-round pick,
  6/86 free-agent draft

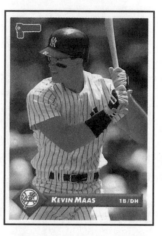

Sean Lowe was a surprise pick for the Cardinals in the 1992 free-agent draft. The righthanded pitcher was the 15th overall selection in the first round of the '92 draft and received an estimated signing bonus of $300,000. For his five starts in the short-season Class-A league, Lowe logged a 2-0 mark and 1.61 ERA. *Baseball America* ranked Lowe 54th out of 100 top prospects before the draft. Another Arizona State University discovery, Lowe transferred from a Texas community college team before the '92 amateur campaign. He entered the draft with single-season college stats of 8-4 with a 4.61 ERA. Most impressively, the Texan earned 106 strikeouts in 105 innings. Although he shows promise at this stage of his pro career, there is a long road in front of Lowe.

Despite Lowe's first-round hoopla, he may not be ready for the majors until '95. At that rate, his 15-cent rookie cards are iffy investments. Our pick for his best 1993 card is Score. We have chosen this card since the photograph captures the athletic ability of the player.

Kevin Maas made his major league mark in a hurry in 1990. Unfortunately, he couldn't make good on that promise for the '92 season. It all started for Maas in '90, when he hit his first homer off Bret Saberhagen on July 4. Maas promptly went on a home run tear, setting the major league record for fewest at-bats (77) needed to reach 10 home runs and fewest (133) needed for 15. That year, he out-homered all rookies except NL Rookie of the Year David Justice, finishing with 21 homers in 79 games (254 at-bats). Maas hit 23 more homers in '91 but watched his average fall as his strikeouts rose. He has the distinction of being the only Yankee since Tom Tresh in 1962-63 to reach 20 homers in each of his first two seasons in the majors. Maas finished '92 with a .248 batting average, 11 homers, and 35 RBI in his 286 at-bats.

Maas is in Yankee line-up limbo. For now, avoid his nickel-priced cards. Our pick for his best 1993 card is Score. We have chosen this card because the design lends itself to the best use of the elements.

	W	L	ERA	G	CG	IP	R	ER	BB	SO
91 COL	9	1	2.69	13	8	87	43	43	26	42
92 COL	8	5	4.49	22	3	114.1	68	57	85	111

	BA	G	AB	R	H	2B	3B	HR	RBI	SB
92 AL	.248	98	286	35	71	12	0	11	35	3
Life	.236	325	1040	146	245	35	1	55	139	9

MIKE MACFARLANE

Position: Catcher
Team: Kansas City Royals
Born: April 12, 1964
   Stockton, CA
Height: 6'1" **Weight:** 205 lbs.
Bats: Right **Throws:** Right
Acquired: Fourth-round pick,
   6/85 free-agent draft

Mike Macfarlane exceeded his modest 1991 power totals in '92, but it took the Royals catcher more than 40 extra games to do it. His '91 accomplishments of 13 home runs and 41 RBI came in 84 games, due to a season-shortening knee injury. In '92, he raced teammate Kevin McReynolds for the Kansas City lead in homers throughout the season and wound up winning by four. The California native was tormented at the plate by righthanded pitchers (hitting only .220) and when playing on the road (.229). Macfarlane's power potential first appeared in '90, when he drove in a career-best 58 runs. Oddly, in his four-year stint in the minors, Macfarlane's seasonal bests for homers were 12 ('86) and 13 ('87). Based on his sinking batting average (.234 in '92), 13 may be his unlucky number.

Macfarlane's limited overall skills and his streaky hitting don't inspire card collectors. His 1993 commons aren't inviting buys. Our pick for his best 1993 card is Fleer. We have chosen this card for its technical merits.

	BA	G	AB	R	H	2B	3B	HR	RBI	SB
92 AL	.234	129	402	51	94	28	3	17	48	1
Life	.251	484	1456	160	365	92	9	42	195	3

SHANE MACK

Position: Outfield
Team: Minnesota Twins
Born: December 7, 1963
   Los Angeles, CA
Height: 6' **Weight:** 185 lbs.
Bats: Right **Throws:** Right
Acquired: Rule 5 draft choice
   from Padres, 12/89

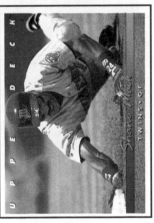

Shane Mack showed in 1992 that he could be one of baseball's best leadoff men. Handed the left field job after Dan Gladden's free-agency departure, Mack finished '92 with a .315 average, 101 runs scored, 75 RBI, and 26 stolen bases. Once an opposite-field hitter with little power, Mack spent five years in the San Diego system before the Padres tired of waiting for him to develop. Plucked out of the minors in the Rule 5 draft, the former UCLA All-American hit .326 in 1990 to win a regular outfield job. In '91, he finished at .310 with 18 homers and 74 RBI plus a .333 average in the Championship Series. Mack was an '84 Olympian and was San Diego's first-round draft choice that summer. A good defensive player, Mack is Minnesota's main man in left field.

Mack's late start on stardom scares off investors. Decline his nickel-priced '93s. Our pick for his best 1993 card is Topps. We have chosen this card due to the outstanding photographic composition.

	BA	G	AB	R	H	2B	3B	HR	RBI	SB
92 AL	.315	156	600	101	189	31	6	16	75	26
Life	.300	585	1712	271	514	82	21	46	230	61

GREG MADDUX

Position: Pitcher
Team: Atlanta Braves
Born: April 14, 1966
 San Angelo, TX
Height: 6′ **Weight:** 170 lbs.
Bats: Right **Throws:** Right
Acquired: Signed as a free
 agent, 12/92

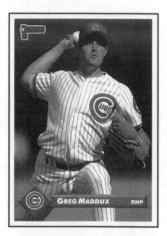 

Greg Maddux was the premier pitcher in the Chicago Cubs' rotation for the past five seasons. Although he won the Cy Young Award in '92 with personal bests of 20-11 and a 2.18 ERA, Maddux wanted more. Expressing his desire to pitch for a team that could assemble more than a "wait until next year " battle cry, Maddux took his show on the road and signed with the 1991-92 pennant-winning Atlanta Braves. With a plethora of mighty arms and big bats on the Braves' roster, he should be surrounded with enough talent to make his dream come true. No slouch defensively, Maddux snagged his third consecutive Gold Glove in '92. His 20 wins in '92 marked the fifth season in a row that he has won 15 or more.

His '92 accomplishments and hurling for a contender will help Maddux as a card investment. Buy his 1993 issues at a dime each. A 1987 Donruss Maddux is a moderate buy at $1.50. Our pick for his best 1993 card is Donruss. We have chosen this card for its technical merits.

	W	L	ERA	G	CG	IP	H	ER	BB	SO
92 NL	20	11	2.18	35	9	268.0	201	65	70	199
Life	95	75	3.35	212	42	1442.0	1352	536	455	937

MIKE MADDUX

Position: Pitcher
Team: New York Mets
Born: August 27, 1961
 Dayton, OH
Height: 6′2″ **Weight:** 190 lbs.
Bats: Right **Throws:** Right
Acquired: Traded from Padres
 for Roger Mason and Mike
 Freitas, 12/92

Mike Maddux kept the Padres bullpen afloat in 1992, his second— and last—year with the club. Maddux found relief to his liking, a role developed since joining San Diego days before the '91 season began. As a starter, Maddux never found his calling during stints with the Phillies (1986-89) and Dodgers ('90). In fact, the Phillies released Maddux at the end of the '89 season, ending an affiliation begun in '82. However, he blossomed into a top-notch middle reliever in '91, earning a 7-2 record with five saves and a 2.46 ERA in a career-high 64 appearances. His 50 appearances in '92 netted two wins and five saves, along with an ERA of 2.37. During his '86 rookie season with Philly, he started against his younger brother, Cy Young winner and former Cubs starter Greg Maddux. The young one won, 8-3.

Unlike his star brother, this Maddux isn't going to strike it rich in 1993. His common-priced cards will be just as unlucky. Our pick for his best 1993 card is Donruss. We have chosen this card due to the outstanding photographic composition.

	W	L	ERA	G	SV	IP	H	ER	BB	SO
92 NL	2	2	2.37	50	5	79.2	71	21	24	60
Life	19	18	3.74	189	11	426.1	421	177	142	272

Series two cards from some companies were available at press time. If space allows, both cards are shown; if not, the most up-to-date cards are pictured.

DAVE MAGADAN

Position: Third base
Team: Florida Marlins
Born: September 30, 1962
Tampa, FL
Height: 6'3" **Weight:** 195 lbs.
Bats: Left **Throws:** Right
Acquired: Signed as a free
agent, 12/92

One-time first baseman Dave Magadan played his shortest—and last—season for the Mets in five years. In 1992, he adapted defensively to full-time work at third base to make room for the acquisition of first baseman Eddie Murray. However, no one had planned for Magadan to fracture his wrist in August. A relay throw from Chicago shortstop Rey Sanchez hit Magadan as he was sliding to break up a double play. The mended Magadan will be with the Florida Marlins in '93. He batted a career-best .328 (third in the NL) with six homers and 72 RBI in '90. In '83, he won the Golden Spikes Award as the nation's top college player while at the University of Alabama.

Magadan's lack of power steamed many Mets fans. It doesn't do much good for his nickel-priced cards, either, and they'll be tough to sell in 1993. Our pick for his best 1993 card is Donruss. We have chosen this card for its technical merits.

	BA	G	AB	R	H	2B	3B	HR	RBI	SB
92 NL	.283	99	321	33	91	9	1	3	28	1
Life	.292	701	2088	275	610	110	11	21	254	5

MIKE MAGNANTE

Position: Pitcher
Team: Kansas City Royals
Born: June 17, 1965
Glendale, CA
Height: 6'1" **Weight:** 180 lbs.
Bats: Left **Throws:** Left
Acquired: 11th-round pick,
6/88 free-agent draft

Hurler Mike Magnante made Kansas City's Opening-Day roster in 1992, but didn't make the most of his opportunities. The lefty fooled few hitters, tallying more walks than strikeouts. He relieved in all but 12 of his 44 outings. Overall in '92, he went 4-9 with a 4.95 ERA, four holds, and no saves. Magnante was a solid middle reliever in his '91 rookie season with the Royals, earning a 2.45 ERA in 38 appearances. The lefty was used mostly as a starter throughout his minor league career, which began in '88. In '89, he registered a career-high 118 strikeouts with Double-A Memphis. His progress was sidetracked in '90, when his Triple-A season ended with June knee surgery. Before being drafted by the Royals, Magnante was a baseball standout at UCLA.

Most card investors run when middle relievers of any caliber are mentioned. Magnante's common-priced issues are just big disappointments waiting to happen. Our pick for his best 1993 card is Upper Deck. We have chosen this card because of its overall appeal and pleasing looks.

	W	L	ERA	G	SV	IP	H	ER	BB	SO
92 AL	4	9	4.94	44	0	89.1	115	49	35	31
Life	4	10	3.99	82	0	144.1	170	64	58	73

PAT MAHOMES

Position: Pitcher
Team: Minnesota Twins
Born: August 9, 1970
  Bryan, TX
Height: 6'1" **Weight:** 175 lbs.
Bats: Right **Throws:** Right
Acquired: Sixth-round pick,
  6/88 free-agent draft

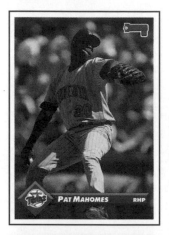
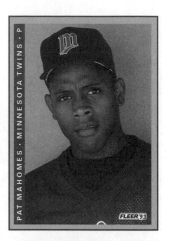

Pat Mahomes was the youngest starting pitcher in the American League for a brief period before being optioned to the minors early in 1992. He fell victim to control problems and had two bad starts before being sent out to make way for his friend, Willie Banks. Before demoting him, the Twins gave Mahomes a shot at the fifth starter's job, but only three of his first eight tries were quality starts. However, he didn't look out of place in the majors and actually won three of his first four decisions with an ERA just over 4.00. Mahomes was just 17 when he began his pro career with rookie-level Elizabethton of the Appalachian League. After two seasons in Class-A, Mahomes jumped to Double-A Orlando in '91, where he fanned 136 in 116 innings and was the winning pitcher in the All-Star Game. That earned him another jump, this time to Triple-A Portland, where he had a 3.44 ERA.

Minnesota needs Mahomes. You need to get his 1993 cards for a dime each. Our pick for his best 1993 card is Score. We have chosen this card because it has a distinctive look.

	W	L	ERA	G	CG	IP	H	ER	BB	SO
92 AL	3	4	5.04	14	0	69.2	73	39	37	44
Life	3	4	5.04	14	0	69.2	73	39	37	44

CANDY MALDONADO

Position: Outfield
Team: Chicago Cubs
Born: September 5, 1960
  Humacao, Puerto Rico
Height: 6' **Weight:** 195 lbs.
Bats: Right **Throws:** Right
Acquired: Signed as a free
  agent, 12/92

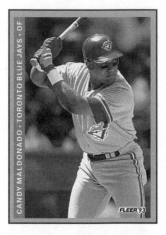

Candy Maldonado did more than hit homers for Toronto in '92. He was surprisingly adept in left field, throwing out more than a dozen baserunners. He broke double figures in home runs for the sixth time in his career. Maldonado also helped lead the Blue Jays to victory in the '92 World Series. Still, his career-finest numbers, 22 homers and 95 RBI with the '90 Indians, remain untouched. His play, however, did not go unnoticed, and the Cubs signed him on for '93. He accepted a non-roster invite to '91 spring training with the Brewers. Maldonado made their Opening-Day roster, but was shipped to the Blue Jays after 34 games. He graduated from high school in '79, one year after he began his pro career.

When surrounded by slugging teammates like Ryne Sandberg and Mark Grace, Maldonado's feats look tiny by comparison. Unfortunately, 1993 common-priced cards of Candy Man won't be sweet investments. Our pick for his best 1993 card is Score. We have chosen this card because the design lends itself to the best use of the elements.

	BA	G	AB	R	H	2B	3B	HR	RBI	SB
92 AL	.272	137	489	64	133	25	4	20	66	2
Life	.258	1196	3603	437	928	199	16	124	541	32

Series two cards from some companies were available at press time. If space allows, both cards are shown; if not, the most up-to-date cards are pictured.

KIRT MANWARING

Position: Catcher
Team: San Francisco Giants
Born: July 15, 1965 Elmira, NY
Height: 5'11" **Weight:** 190 lbs.
Bats: Right **Throws:** Right
Acquired: Second-round pick,
  6/86 free-agent draft

Kirt Manwaring was catcher by default in San Francisco again in 1992. While names like Steve Decker and Craig Colbert have been touted as backstops of the future, Manwaring has remained the Giants' catcher of the present. He enjoyed his first big league year of 100-plus games with career highs in more offensive categories. Although he hit barely .200 (.206) against righthanders, Manwaring manhandled lefties at a .300 clip (.305) in '92. In '91, a broken finger sent him back to the minors for a two-week medical rehabilitation. Previously, his only full season with San Francisco came in '89. Despite a broken foot interrupting his progress, Manwaring stayed on the DL for only two weeks.

Manwaring can't expect to survive in the majors without a healthier batting average. Even if he isn't displaced by the other young receivers, his 1993 cards won't retain their common values. Our pick for his best 1993 card is Upper Deck. We have chosen this card because of its overall appeal and pleasing looks.

	BA	G	AB	R	H	2B	3B	HR	RBI	SB
92 NL	.244	109	349	24	85	10	5	4	26	2
Life	.231	315	863	66	199	30	8	5	79	5

CARLOS MARTINEZ

Position: Infield
Team: Cleveland Indians
Born: August 11, 1965
  La Guira, Venezuela
Height: 6'5" **Weight:** 175 lbs.
Bats: Right **Throws:** Right
Acquired: Signed as a free
  agent, 3/91

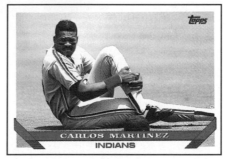

In 1992, Carlos Martinez posted similar numbers to his 1991 performance, but found fewer opportunities to play. His '92 marks included five homers, 35 RBI, and a .263 batting average, down a bit from his .284 mark in '91. The arrival of first baseman Paul Sorrento and return of third sacker Brook Jacoby hampered Martinez in finding a starting job in '92. Instead, Martinez filled in at third base and DH. Martinez is no stranger to the hot corner. When he debuted in the majors in '88, his first position with the White Sox was at third base. In '89, he appeared in a career-high 109 games, starting 91 times. Starting a trend, he notched five homers and 32 RBI, while hitting .300. He spent all of '90 with Chicago, but batted a disappointing .224 with four homers and 24 RBI in 92 games.

Don't expect the job competition to ease in 1993, which makes the forecast gloomy for common-priced Martinez cards. Our pick for his best 1993 card is Topps. We have chosen this card for its artistic presentation.

	BA	G	AB	R	H	2B	3B	HR	RBI	SB
92 AL	.263	69	228	23	60	9	1	5	35	1
Life	.265	359	1162	112	308	52	6	19	121	9

CHITO
MARTINEZ

Position: Outfield
Team: Baltimore Orioles
Born: December 19, 1965
Belize, Central America
Height: 5'10" **Weight:** 182 lbs.
Bats: Left **Throws:** Left
Acquired: Signed as minor
league free-agent, 11/90

DAVE
MARTINEZ

Position: Outfield
Team: San Francisco Giants
Born: September 26, 1964
New York, NY
Height: 5'10" **Weight:** 180 lbs.
Bats: Left **Throws:** Left
Acquired: Signed as a free
agent, 12/92

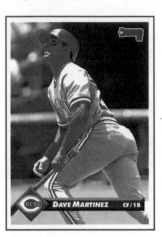 

Chito Martinez faced typical sophomore disappointments in 1992. He debuted with the '91 Orioles to the tune of 13 home runs and 33 RBI in 67 games. His second season was far less exciting, as he hit only five homers with 25 RBI in 83 games. In '92 spring training, Martinez made the biggest impact, busting three homers with nine RBI. During the '92 season, he took an instant liking to the new Orioles Park at Camden Yards, hitting approximately 100 points higher there (.310) than on the road (.224). Groomed in the Royals organization, Martinez was drafted in '84.

Martinez lost out in starting time to outfielder Joe Orsulak in '92. With fellow right fielder Luis Mercedes jockeying for position in '93, life will be tougher. Until Martinez plays a full season in Baltimore (or anywhere else), no one will be willing to speculate on his nickel-priced cards. Our pick for his best 1993 card is Donruss. We have chosen this card for its technical merits.

Dave Martinez maintained his part-time outfield job in 1992, only with a new employer. Obtained by the Reds to share center field duties with Reggie Sanders, Martinez even subbed at first base when needed. The Reds valued Martinez as a defensive substitute and pinch-hitter. Interestingly, he hit nearly 80 points better at Riverfront Stadium than in road games. In '93, Martinez will be hoping for more playing time with his new team, the Giants. Although he's been active in the majors since '86, Martinez has spent his entire career in the NL. In '87, his first full year in the majors, he hit .292 for the Cubs. Upon joining the Expos in mid-1988, he drove in a career-high 46 runs. By '90, he had clubbed a personal-high 11 homers with Montreal. For seven years in a row, Martinez has met or surpassed a dozen steals per year.

Martinez cards have never been big sellers. As he waits for full-time work, Martinez can watch his 1993 commons gather cobwebs. Our pick for his best 1993 card is Upper Deck. We have chosen this card because of its great combination of photography and design.

	BA	G	AB	R	H	2B	3B	HR	RBI	SB
92 AL	.268	83	198	26	53	10	1	5	25	0
Life	.268	150	414	58	111	22	2	18	58	1

	BA	G	AB	R	H	2B	3B	HR	RBI	SB
92 NL	.254	135	393	47	100	20	5	3	31	12
Life	.269	836	2555	329	688	99	37	39	228	107

Series two cards from some companies were available at press time. If space allows, both cards are shown; if not, the most up-to-date cards are pictured.

DENNIS MARTINEZ

Position: Pitcher
Team: Montreal Expos
Born: May 14, 1955
Granada, Nicaragua
Height: 6'1" **Weight:** 180 lbs.
Bats: Right **Throws:** Right
Acquired: Traded from Orioles
for Rene Gonzales, 6/86

EDGAR MARTINEZ

Position: Third base
Team: Seattle Mariners
Born: January 2, 1963
New York, NY
Height: 5'11" **Weight:** 175 lbs.
Bats: Right **Throws:** Right
Acquired: Signed as undrafted
free agent, 12/82

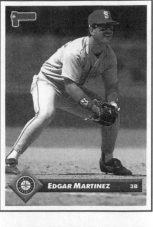

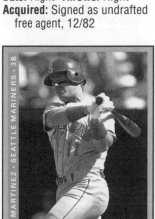

Despite his tremendous efforts, Dennis Martinez just couldn't pitch the Montreal Expos over the top in '92. It wasn't for lack of effort as his 16-11 record and 2.47 ERA will testify. Martinez was nothing short of brilliant as he worked to improve upon his '91 showing. Had he pitched for a contender in '91, Martinez would have received serious consideration for the NL's Cy Young Award. He finished with a 14-11 record but led the league with a 2.39 ERA, five shutouts, and nine complete games. He also pitched his first no-hitter, a perfect game, in the '91 season. Martinez has had seven strong seasons in a row for Montreal, the team that picked him off the minor league scrap heap in '86. He has won in double figures every season since and has won 16 games, a personal peak, four times.

The Expos have a real jewel in Martinez. His 1993 cards could shine at a nickel apiece. Our pick for his best 1993 card is Score. We have chosen this card for the interesting facts included on the reverse.

Although Edgar Martinez was the AL's surprise batting champ in '92, he paid a price. Shoulder ailments forced Martinez into DH duty. His chart-topping year ended on September 14, when he underwent surgery to remove a bone spur in his throwing shoulder. Yet, his .343 average led the league. At the same time, the Mariners tried and failed to stay out of the divisional cellar. Martinez improved on the career highs achieved during '91, which included 14 homers, 52 RBI, and a .307 average. Although Martinez premiered with Seattle in '87, he didn't win the team's starting hot corner job until '90, when he hit .302 with 11 homers and 49 RBI.

Just because Martinez has his first batting title, don't overpay for his 1993 cards. Paying more than a nickel each is dangerous, because The Edgar will likely slip and drive prices downward. A 1988 Fleer is tempting at $1.50. Our pick for his best 1993 card is Topps. We have chosen this card because of its great combination of photography and design.

	W	L	ERA	G	CG	IP	H	ER	BB	SO
92 NL	16	11	2.47	32	6	226.1	172	62	60	147
Life	193	156	3.62	523	108	3159.1	3050	1271	926	1693

	BA	G	AB	R	H	2B	3B	HR	RBI	SB
92 AL	.343	135	528	100	181	46	3	18	73	14
Life	.311	521	1805	295	561	122	8	45	204	17

RAMON
MARTINEZ

Position: Pitcher
Team: Los Angeles Dodgers
Born: March 22, 1968
   Santo Domingo,
   Dominican Republic
Height: 6'4" **Weight:** 173 lbs.
Bats: Right **Throws:** Right
Acquired: Signed as a free
   agent, 9/84

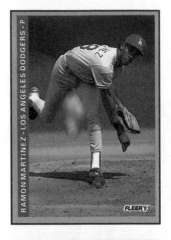

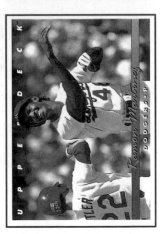

TINO
MARTINEZ

Position: First base
Team: Seattle Mariners
Born: December 7, 1967
   Tampa, FL
Height: 6'2" **Weight:** 205 lbs.
Bats: Left **Throws:** Right
Acquired: First-round pick,
   6/88 free-agent draft

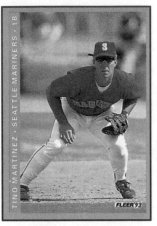

Although he entered the 1992 campaign as the No. 1 pitcher in the Dodgers' starting rotation, Ramon Martinez did not pitch with the consistency that made him an All-Star in '91. After sparking hope by throwing a 1-0 shutout against the Cubs on May 29, he finished the '92 season posting a disappointing 8-11 with a hefty 4.00 ERA. Martinez, who once fanned 18 Atlanta Braves in one game, appeared to have lost some velocity on his fastball. In his first 12 starts for '92, he pitched past the seventh inning only twice. The Dodgers are hoping the 25-year-old Martinez will regain some of his previous winning ways in '93. Martinez went 20-6 in '90 and 17-13 in '91—topping 220 innings pitched both years. The svelte Dominican righthander also threw four shutouts, one behind league-leader Dennis Martinez of Montreal, during the '91 campaign.

Put the brakes on buying any 1993s of Martinez, even at 15 cents or less. Our pick for his best 1993 card is Fleer. We have chosen this card because of its overall appeal and pleasing looks.

Constantino "Tino" Martinez made the most of what some wrongly considered his last chance with the Mariners. In 1992, Martinez shared first base with Pete O'Brien, but drove in more runs (66) than the veteran (52). In fact, Martinez bested O'Brien in virtually every category. He split his seasons in '90 and '91 between Triple-A Calgary and Seattle. Going into '92, Tino had failed two auditions in the majors. During his brief trial in '90, he batted .221 with no home runs and five RBI. He played in 36 games with the '91 M's, but fared even worse. After four homers, nine RBI and a .205 average, Martinez faced a crucial career test. Seattle grabbed Martinez in the first-round of the '88 draft, after he had been a member of the '88 U.S. Olympic baseball team.

Due to Seattle's horrendous 1992 finish, collectors may overlook 1993 cards of Martinez. If you're lucky, his issues might be harvested for three to five cents each. Invest while you can. Our pick for his best 1993 card is Fleer. We have chosen this card for its artistic presentation.

	W	L	ERA	G	CG	IP	H	ER	BB	SO
92 NL	8	11	4.00	25	1	150.2	141	67	69	101
Life	52	37	3.32	115	21	739.2	628	273	268	586

	BA	G	AB	R	H	2B	3B	HR	RBI	SB
92 AL	.257	136	460	53	118	19	2	16	66	2
Life	.244	196	640	68	156	25	2	20	80	2

ROGER MASON

Position: Pitcher
Team: San Diego Padres
Born: September 18, 1958
Bellaire, MI
Height: 6'6" **Weight:** 220 lbs.
Bats: Right **Throws:** Right
Acquired: Traded from Mets
with Mike Freitas for Mike
Maddux, 12/92

 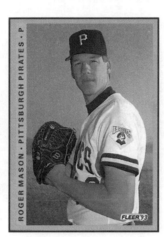

Roger Mason continued the second year of his second career in the majors with the 1992 Pirates. In '93, he'll have the opportunity to soldier on with the San Diego Padres, as he was traded late in '92. The long-time starter proved his '91 transition to the bullpen could stick. Even as a reliever, he reached career highs in wins (five) and saves (eight). Mason was released by the Astros near the end of '90 spring training. More than a month passed before Pittsburgh offered him a minor league job. Although he divided his time between starting and relieving at Triple-A Buffalo, the Bucs used him exclusively in relief upon his August '90 return to the majors. His '91 postseason highlights included one save and 4 ⅓ scoreless innings of work in NLCS play against the Braves.

Mason contributed to Pittsburgh's continued excellence in '92. Yet, his low-profile bullpen job, which will be even more so in San Diego, isn't conducive to future values for his '93 commons. Our pick for his best 1993 card is Donruss. We have chosen this card for its technical merits.

	W	L	ERA	G	SV	IP	H	ER	BB	SO
92 NL	5	7	4.09	65	8	88.0	80	40	33	56
Life	14	18	4.07	117	12	256.2	240	116	102	182

DON MATTINGLY

Position: First base
Team: New York Yankees
Born: April 20, 1961
Evansville, IN
Height: 6' **Weight:** 175 lbs.
Bats: Left **Throws:** Left
Acquired: 19th-round pick,
6/79 free-agent draft

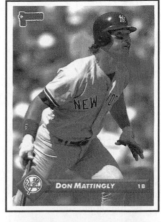

 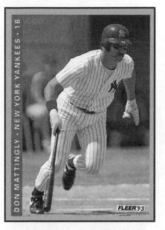

Although Don Mattingly didn't match his career power stats in 1992, he did post some solid numbers. The back problems that limited him to a career-low 102 games in '90 have taken a toll. The Yankee captain had only nine homers and 68 RBI in '91 while falling 12 points short of his seventh .300 season. In '92, he tied for third in the AL with 40 doubles, giving notice that his stroke and strength showed signs of returning. He also won his seventh Gold Glove. Mattingly's career peaks include a .352 average, 35 homers, and 145 RBI. He won the batting title in '84 and the MVP Award in '85. Mattingly, whose pro ball career began in '79, has knocked in 100 runs in five different big league seasons. In '87, he homered in eight consecutive games, tying Dale Long's record.

Mattingly means Hall of Fame in Yankee-speak. Buy his 1993 cards at 15 cents or less. All '84 Mattingly Rookies have nosedived recently. Try his '85 Donruss Diamond King for $2. Our pick for his best 1993 card is Topps. We have chosen this card because it has a distinctive look.

	BA	G	AB	R	H	2B	3B	HR	RBI	SB
92 AL	.287	157	640	89	184	40	0	14	86	3
Life	.311	1426	5643	808	1754	363	15	192	913	14

ROB MAURER

Position: First base
Team: Texas Rangers
Born: January 7, 1967
  Evansville, IN
Height: 6'3" **Weight:** 210 lbs.
Bats: Left **Throws:** Left
Acquired: Sixth-round pick,
  6/88 free-agent draft

Rob Maurer illustrates the depth of Texas' offensive power waiting in the wings behind Rafael Palmeiro. Although the lefty only played in parts of eight games for the Rangers in the '92 season, he demonstrated some real potential. In his brief excursion to the bigs in '92, he hit .333 at home. If he weren't locked in behind a .300 lifetime hitter, he might be able to get some more experience at the major league level. In the meantime, there are things to be worked on, such as lowering his strikeout totals. Maurer got a cup of coffee with Texas in September of '91, doubling off California's Scott Lewis for his first hit. Maurer was named the Rangers' Minor League Player of the Year and the American Association's Rookie of the Year in '91. He batted .301 for Oklahoma City and led the league with 41 doubles and 96 walks.

Can Maurer crash the '93 Texas lineup? If you're unsure, limit spending to a nickel each on '93 Maurers. Our pick for his best 1993 card is Donruss. We have chosen this card for its technical merits.

	BA	G	AB	R	H	2B	3B	HR	RBI	SB
92 AAA	.288	135	493	76	142	34	2	10	82	1
92 AL	.222	8	9	1	2	0	0	0	1	0

DERRICK MAY

Position: Outfield
Team: Chicago Cubs
Born: July 14, 1968
  Rochester, NY
Height: 6'4" **Weight:** 205 lbs.
Bats: Left **Throws:** Right
Acquired: First-round pick,
  6/86 free-agent draft

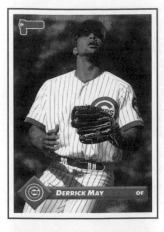

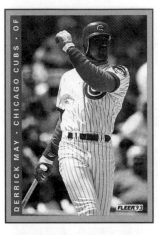

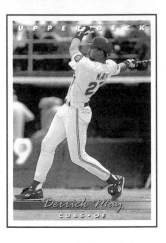

Derrick May capitalized on a 1992 stretch during which the Cubs were thin in outfielders. He homered twice against Philadelphia's Brad Brink on June 19, becoming the first Cub rookie in four years to have a two-homer game. Though he never reached double figures in homers as a minor leaguer, that aspect of his game could come around as he learns to use his size. May has fair speed, but his triple and stolen base totals have fallen off since the '89 season. He also has an arm good enough that he saw some action in right field. One factor to watch is May's right wrist, which was broken and reinjured in '91. May was the ninth player overall taken in '86, and he hit .320 in his first pro stop. He had two cups of coffee in the majors, the first in '90 and the second in '91. He hit one home run in each call-up.

With Kal Daniels gone, May owns left field for the Cubs. Spend 15 cents each to secure his 1993 commons. Our pick for his best 1993 card is Score. We have chosen this card because of its overall appeal and pleasing looks.

	BA	G	AB	R	H	2B	3B	HR	RBI	SB
92 NL	.274	124	351	33	96	11	0	8	45	5
Life	.267	156	434	45	116	16	0	10	59	6

BRENT MAYNE

Position: Catcher
Team: Kansas City Royals
Born: April 19, 1968
Loma Linda, CA
Height: 6'1" **Weight:** 190 lbs.
Bats: Left **Throws:** Right
Acquired: First-round pick,
6/89 free-agent draft

KIRK McCASKILL

Position: Pitcher
Team: Chicago White Sox
Born: April 9, 1961
Kapuskasing, Ontario,
Canada
Height: 6'1" **Weight:** 205 lbs.
Bats: Right **Throws:** Right
Acquired: Signed as a free
agent, 12/91

Brent Mayne faltered offensively in his sophomore season with the 1992 Royals. Mayne's main problem was lefthanders, as evidenced by a .136 mark against southpaws. His stats were a far cry from '91, when he debuted in Kansas City with three homers, 31 RBI, and a .251 average in 85 games. Ironically, two of his three rookie-season home runs were inside-the-park jobs. In a glimpse of his possible utilityman's future, Mayne also filled in at third base and designated hitter for the '92 Royals. A first-round draft pick in '89, Mayne began his collegiate career coached by his father at Orange Coast Junior College in California. He made the jump to the majors in '90, directly from Double-A ball.

Mayne can't outhit Kansas City catching rival Mike Macfarlane. Therefore, a distinct lack of playing time will deflate his common-priced card values. Our pick for his best 1993 card is Donruss. We have chosen this card for its artistic presentation.

Kirk McCaskill wasn't the instant ace the White Sox hoped for in 1992. He signed a fat three-year contract with Chicago, following his 10-19 record in '91. His '91 struggle was viewed optimistically. After all, California provided him with two runs or less in 14 of his 19 losses. For the '92 season, McCaskill went 12-13 and dragged along a 4.18 ERA. He did reach 200 innings (209) in '92, the first time since '89, when he was 15-10 for the Angels. His biggest success came with the Halos in '86, when he posted a career high of 17 victories and 10 complete games. McCaskill owns six seasons of double-digit triumphs in an eight-year career dating back to '82. One year before getting drafted by California, McCaskill was a fourth-round pick in the NHL draft.

McCaskill's a reasonable bet for at least 10 wins per season. He faces an undistinguishing career .500 record, which won't bring long-term appreciation for his common-priced cards. Our pick for his best 1993 card is Fleer. We have chosen this card because of its great combination of photography and design.

	BA	G	AB	R	H	2B	3B	HR	RBI	SB
92 AL	.225	82	213	16	48	10	0	0	18	0
Life	.239	172	457	40	109	18	0	3	50	2

	W	L	ERA	G	CG	IP	H	ER	BB	SO
92 AL	12	13	4.18	34	0	209.0	193	97	95	109
Life	90	87	3.91	226	30	1430.0	1384	621	543	823

LLOYD McCLENDON

Position: Outfield
Team: Pittsburgh Pirates
Born: January 11, 1959
  Gary, IN
Height: 5'11" **Weight:** 210 lbs.
Bats: Right **Throws:** Right
Acquired: Traded from Cubs
  for Mike Pomeranz, 9/90

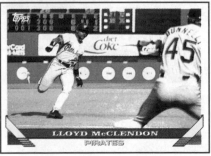

Lloyd McClendon continued to be one of the Pirates' most effective role players in 1992. McClendon shared right field duties with Cecil Espy and Alex Cole. As in past years, the utilityman (and third-string Pittsburgh catcher) hit lefthanders 50 points (.259) better than he hit righties (.208). His .253 overall batting average in '92 was a drop from his .288 in '91, his first full year with the Bucs. McClendon began his career in the Mets organization in '80. In '82 he became one of three prospects traded to Cincinnati. The Reds first summoned McClendon to the bigs in '87. His top big league output came with the '89 Cubs, and featured 12 home runs, 40 RBI, and a .286 average through 92 games.

  McClendon doesn't play enough to create any excitement for his common-priced cards. Particularly after Pittsburgh's three consecutive division titles, many of their starters will be better '93 card investments. Our pick for his best 1993 card is Topps. We have chosen this card due to its unique photographic approach.

	BA	G	AB	R	H	2B	3B	HR	RBI	SB
92 NL	.253	84	190	26	48	8	1	3	20	1
Life	.249	431	931	120	232	39	2	29	123	15

BOB McCLURE

Position: Pitcher
Team: Florida Marlins
Born: April 29, 1953
  Oakland, CA
Height: 5'11" **Weight:** 188 lbs.
Bats: Right **Throws:** Left
Acquired: Signed as a free
agent, 12/92

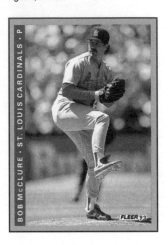

In 1992, Bob McClure celebrated his 20th season in pro ball. He appeared with the Cardinals, the sixth big league team he's served since his '75 debut with Kansas City. McClure's '92 performance netted him 71 relief appearances, marking the fifth time he has bested 50 games in the majors. His 1992 season added up to 54 innings, a 2-2 record, no saves, and 14 holds. McClure was a central figure in the Milwaukee bullpen for years, reaching a personal-best 10 saves in 1980. The Brew Crew converted McClure to starting duty in '82 through '84. His '82 achievements included a career-finest 12-7 record. Despite his age, McClure is a valued lefty, respected throughout the league for his top-notch pickoff move. He'll join the Marlin staff for '93.

  McClure will turn 40 during the '93 season as he continues as a spot reliever. His common-priced cards won't turn into good investments, so don't bother. Our pick for his best 1993 card is Fleer. We have chosen this card due to the outstanding photographic composition.

	W	L	ERA	G	CG	IP	H	ER	BB	SO
92 NL	2	2	3.17	71	0	54.0	52	19	25	24
Life	67	56	3.79	684	52	1152.1	1112	485	492	695

Series two cards from some companies were available at press time. If space allows, both cards are shown; if not, the most up-to-date cards are pictured.

BEN
McDONALD

Position: Pitcher
Team: Baltimore Orioles
Born: November 24, 1967
　　Baton Rouge, LA
Height: 6'7"　**Weight:** 214 lbs.
Bats: Right　**Throws:** Right
Acquired: First-round pick,
　　6/89 free-agent draft

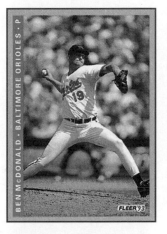

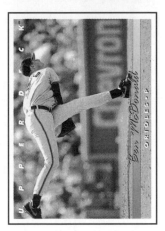

Big Ben McDonald enjoyed only fitful success with the 1992 Orioles. The Oriole hurler evened his record at 13-13. His last victory was in September, when he allowed just four hits and one run to defeat the Tigers. McDonald had not won in his previous eight starts. He gave up more than 30 homers to '92 opponents (32), rivaling only Detroit's Bill Gullickson in the gopher-ball derby. He did top 200 innings in '92 (227), a switch from two previous seasons of injuries. His most effective year was '90, when he fashioned an 8-5 record with a 2.43 ERA. McDonald was a star even before he played a game of pro ball. Winner of the '89 Golden Spikes award as the year's leading college player, McDonald was the first player chosen in that year's draft.

McDonald has struggled for two consecutive seasons. Investors hopeful for a 1993 comeback can easily find his cards at a nickel apiece. Our pick for his best 1993 card is Topps. We have chosen this card because of its great combination of photography and design.

	W	L	ERA	G	CG	IP	H	ER	BB	SO
92 AL	13	13	4.24	35	4	227.0	213	107	74	158
Life	28	26	4.02	83	8	479.1	435	214	156	311

JACK
McDOWELL

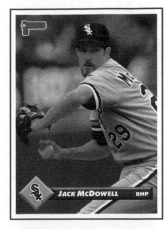

Position: Pitcher
Team: Chicago White Sox
Born: January 16, 1966
　　Van Nuys, CA
Height: 6'5"　**Weight:** 180 lbs.
Bats: Right　**Throws:** Right
Acquired: First-round pick,
　　6/87 free-agent draft

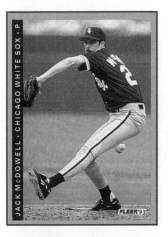

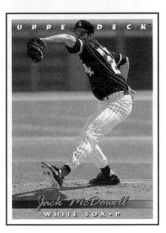

Even baseball's brightest stars know the law of averages will catch up with them eventually. Jack McDowell, the top starter of the Chicago White Sox, came to understand that in 1992. He won his first seven decisions, posting a 2.78 ERA along the way. Then he lost three in a row. The White Sox weren't worried about McDowell, however. He went on to top his '91 career best of 17-10 with a 20-10 record in '92. Black Jack worked over 260 innings and struck out 170 batters along the way. The former Stanford star led the majors with 15 complete games in '91. A former No. 1 draft choice, McDowell led Stanford to the College World Series title in '87, then broke into pro ball later that summer. Off the field, he moonlights as a progressive rock recording artist with a group called V.I.E.W.

Say yes, at 15 cents or less. He can even sing! Honest, McDowell's 1988 Donruss Rookie is still out there for $1. Our pick for his best 1993 card is Fleer. We have chosen this card since the photograph captures the athletic ability of the player.

	W	L	ERA	G	CG	IP	H	ER	BB	SO
92 AL	20	10	3.18	34	13	260.2	247	92	75	178
Life	59	39	3.49	132	33	906.0	811	351	308	633

ROGER McDOWELL

Position: Pitcher
Team: Los Angeles Dodgers
Born: December 21, 1960
    Cincinnati, OH
Height: 6'1" **Weight:** 182 lbs.
Bats: Right **Throws:** Right
Acquired: Traded from Phillies
    for Braulio Castillo and Mike
    Hartley, 7/91

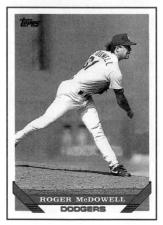 

Closer Roger McDowell had few leads to preserve with the 1992 Dodgers. Like most of his teammates, McDowell's stats reflected the team's last-place collapse. As his ERA ballooned to 4.09 and his losses mounted, McDowell still topped 60 appearances (65) for the seventh time in eight seasons. He struck out 50 of the 393 batters he faced over the course of his 83 ⅔ innings of work in '92. In better times, McDowell once helped the Mets to a World Championship ('86) with a 14-9 record and 22 saves. In '87, he saved a career-best 25 games to complement his 7-5 record. His career began as New York's third pick in the '82 free-agent draft. He progressed to the majors in '85, and finished sixth in NL Rookie of the Year balloting with 17 saves in 62 appearances.

Be careful about choosing cards of over-30 hurlers, even stoppers like McDowell. Due to his uneven amount of past saves, his 1993s aren't worth their nickel asking price. Our pick for his best 1993 card is Score. We have chosen this card because the design lends itself to the best use of the elements.

	W	L	ERA	G	SV	IP	H	ER	BB	SO
92 NL	6	10	4.09	65	14	83.2	103	38	42	50
Life	57	59	3.14	532	149	796.1	764	278	301	399

CHUCK McELROY

Position: Pitcher
Team: Chicago Cubs
Born: October 1, 1967
    Galveston, TX
Height: 6' **Weight:** 160 lbs.
Bats: Left **Throws:** Left
Acquired: Traded from Phillies
    with Bob Scanlan for Mitch
    Williams, 4/91

Chuck McElroy earned his keep with the 1992 Cubs, exceeding 70 appearances for the second season in a row. Unfortunately, he couldn't match the 1.95 ERA he sported in '91. In fact, his 3.55 ERA wasn't even close. His '91 and '92 strikeout and strikeouts per nine innings totals were very similar. However, his overall record—6-2 in '91 and 4-7 in '92—says more. He allowed the identical number of hits in '92 as he did in '91; he just did it in fewer innings. On the plus side, he did manage to double his save total from '91. McElroy was bred as a starter, but, upon becoming a reliever in '89, was a bullpen terror to lefthanded hitters. In '92, however, lefties hit .275 off McElroy whereas righties managed only .218.

The lefty reliever won't be hobby news until he drastically inflates his save total or joins the starting rotation. Don't bet on either possibility or on the chances for McElroy's 1993 commons to draw interest. Our pick for his best 1993 card is Fleer. We have chosen this card for its artistic presentation.

	W	L	ERA	G	SV	IP	H	ER	BB	SO
92 NL	4	7	3.55	72	6	83.2	73	33	51	83
Life	10	10	2.97	170	9	209.1	182	69	122	199

WILLIE McGEE

Position: Outfield
Team: San Francisco Giants
Born: November 2, 1958
San Francisco, CA
Height: 6'1" **Weight:** 195 lbs.
Bats: Both **Throws:** Right
Acquired: Signed as a free
agent, 12/90

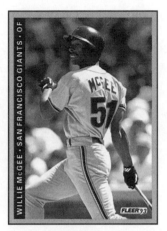

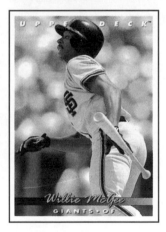

Willie McGee's 1992 season with San Francisco yielded more surprises than successes. The veteran tagged only one homer during the '92 campaign. Before '92, McGee owned 56 career homers, including a career-high 11 round-trippers in '87. For the first time in his career, McGee was forced to share playing time. He still managed a .297 batting average with 36 RBI and 13 stolen bases in '92. A four-time All-Star, McGee owns a lengthy resume of exploits. Three Gold Glove Awards, two batting titles, and the '85 NL MVP Award are some of McGee's feats. Although he's remembered for his nine-year reign in St. Louis, McGee's pro career began with the Yankees in '77.

McGee should retire as a career .300 hitter. However, if he can't regain a starting position in San Fran or elsewhere, his past accomplishments will be forgotten. Use caution in buying McGee's 1993 commons. Our pick for his best 1993 card is Fleer. We have chosen this card because the design lends itself to the best use of the elements.

	BA	G	AB	R	H	2B	3B	HR	RBI	SB
92 NL	.297	138	474	56	141	20	2	1	36	13
Life	.298	1462	5669	773	1689	257	83	57	639	307

FRED McGRIFF

Position: First base
Team: San Diego Padres
Born: October 31, 1963
Tampa, FL
Height: 6'3" **Weight:** 208 lbs.
Bats: Left **Throws:** Left
Acquired: Traded from Blue
Jays with Tony Fernandez for
Joe Carter and Roberto
Alomar, 12/90

Fred McGriff seems to like the pitching in the National League even better than the pitching in the American League. The mighty lefty swung his way through the '92 season, finishing up the campaign with a .286 batting average, pounding over 30 homers and 100 RBI. This was not the first time he had accomplished such a feat. In '91, his first NL season, he produced his fourth consecutive 30-homer season but his first 100-RBI campaign. He even became the fourth player in league history to hit grand-slams in consecutive games. Although McGriff has never hit over .300, it's not for lack of effort. In '92, he finished first in home runs (35), third in both slugging percentage (.556) and RBI (104), and fourth in on-base percentage (.394) in the National League.

Gobble up Crime Dog cards at a dime apiece. Also, consider McGriff's 1987 Topps Traded for $2. Our pick for his best 1993 card is Fleer. We have chosen this card because of its great combination of photography and design.

	BA	G	AB	R	H	2B	3B	HR	RBI	SB
92 NL	.286	152	531	79	152	30	4	35	104	8
Life	.279	883	3003	511	839	148	13	191	515	33

Series two cards from some companies were available at press time. If space allows, both cards are shown; if not, the most up-to-date cards are pictured.

MARK McGWIRE

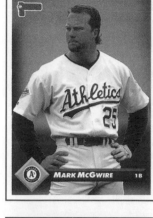

Position: First base
Team: Oakland Athletics
Born: October 1, 1963
  Pomona, CA
Height: 6'5" **Weight:** 225 lbs.
Bats: Right **Throws:** Right
Acquired: First-round pick,
  6/84 free-agent draft

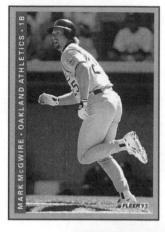

When Mark McGwire hit his 200th career home run on June 10, 1992, he became the fifth-fastest player to reach that plateau in big league history. The smooth-fielding Oakland first baseman joined the elite group in his 2,852nd at-bat. After taking a pay cut in the wake of his weak '91 performance, McGwire bolted from the starting gate in '92 with a pace that stamped him a potential threat to the single-season home run record of Roger Maris, who hit 61 in '61. Although he didn't reach that plateau, his 42 homers in '92 earned him the second highest mark in both leagues. High achievement is not unfamiliar territory to McGwire, who set an Oakland franchise record (and a record for rookies) when he connected 49 times in '87.

With Canseco gone, McGwire and his cards gain stardom. Buy many 1993s at 15 cents each. Don't think about a costly McGwire Rookie. Instead, choose an '88 Donruss Diamond King for 35 cents or less. Our pick for his best 1993 card is Topps. We have chosen this card due to the outstanding photographic composition.

	BA	G	AB	R	H	2B	3B	HR	RBI	SB
92 AL	.268	139	467	87	125	22	0	42	104	0
Life	.247	916	3123	504	772	128	5	220	608	6

TIM McINTOSH

Position: Catcher
Team: Milwaukee Brewers
Born: March 21, 1965
  Crystal, MN
Height: 5'11" **Weight:** 195 lbs.
Bats: Right **Throws:** Right
Acquired: Third-round pick,
  6/86 free-agent draft

Tim McIntosh saw little duty with the 1992 Brewers, a misfortune reflected in his offense. Although the traditional catcher served at first base, outfield, and DH when needed, he didn't reflect the promise in his 35 games in '92 that he's displayed in the past. A bruised finger on his throwing hand in August helped account for his limited appearances. McIntosh, following a three-year amateur career at the University of Minnesota, turned pro in '86. He made his big league debut in a five-game stint with the '90 Brew Crew, hitting .200. Back for a second consecutive season at Triple-A in '91, he smashed 18 homers and 91 RBI for a .292 average. In a September '91 call-up, he gave Milwaukee a .364 effort in his seven-game audition. Unproven in the majors but overqualified for Triple-A work, McIntosh could be facing a tough road ahead.

In three words, here's why McIntosh or his nickel-priced cards will never amount to much in Milwaukee: Surhoff and Nilsson. Our pick for his best 1993 card is Score. We have chosen this card due to its unique photographic approach.

	BA	G	AB	R	H	2B	3B	HR	RBI	SB
92 AL	.182	35	77	7	14	3	0	0	6	1
Life	.204	47	93	10	19	4	0	2	8	1

Series two cards from some companies were available at press time. If space allows, both cards are shown; if not, the most up-to-date cards are pictured.

MARK McLEMORE

Position: Second base
Team: Baltimore Orioles
Born: October 4, 1964
San Diego, CA
Height: 5'11" **Weight:** 195 lbs.
Bats: Both **Throws:** Right
Acquired: Signed as free agent,
2/92

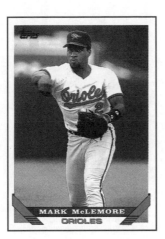

After spending three previous seasons in the minors, Mark McLemore worked himself back to the major league level last summer. He spent most of the year playing second fiddle to Baltimore second baseman Bill Ripken. Though McLemore offered superior speed and offense, he could not match Ripken's glovework. A better hitter against lefthanders, the switch-hitting McLemore is also solid on artificial turf, where speed helps. McLemore usually has a high success rate when he runs, but he was caught stealing five times in 16 attempts in '92. He had stolen 41 bases as the every-day second baseman for the '87 Angels. A contact hitter with little power, McLemore walks as often as he fans. He had a .308 on-base average and a .294 slugging percentage in 1992.

McLemore is okay on defense—range is his best asset—but he's no Ripken. Part-timers don't make big gains with hobbyists. Our pick for his best 1993 card is Topps. We have chosen this card because of its great combination of photography and design.

	BA	G	AB	R	H	2B	3B	HR	RBI	SB
92 AL	.246	101	228	40	56	7	2	0	27	11
Life	.229	402	1122	163	257	37	8	5	102	56

BRIAN McRAE

Position: Outfield
Team: Kansas City Royals
Born: August 27, 1967
Bradenton, FL
Height: 6' **Weight:** 185 lbs.
Bats: Both **Throws:** Right
Acquired: First-round pick,
6/85 free-agent draft

Brian McRae became one of Kansas City's biggest puzzles in 1992. Despite his low batting average, McRae was making steady gains at the plate. He drew nearly twice as many walks as he had in '91 and tried to curb his strikeouts (99 in '91). The center fielder knocked in over 50 runs for the second year in a row and remained one of his team's leading base stealers. During '91, his first full season as a Royal, McRae tallied eight home runs, 64 RBI, a .261 average, and 20 stolen bases. He was promoted from Double-A Memphis in '90 and responded with a .286 mark, including two homers and 23 RBI in 46 games. The fleet-footed son of current Royals manager Hal McRae was drafted out of high school in '85.

Due to his mild slump, McRae's 1993 cards will be a nickel or less. He's an inexpensive, promising investment, especially if the Royals return to pennant contention soon. Our pick for his best 1993 card is Upper Deck. We have chosen this card because it has a distinctive look.

	BA	G	AB	R	H	2B	3B	HR	RBI	SB
92 AL	.223	149	533	63	119	23	5	4	52	18
Life	.249	347	1330	170	331	59	17	14	139	42

KEVIN McREYNOLDS

Position: Outfield
Team: Kansas City Royals
Born: October 16, 1959
Little Rock, AR
Height: 6'1" **Weight:** 215 lbs.
Bats: Right **Throws:** Right
Acquired: Traded from Mets
with Keith Miller and Gregg
Jefferies for Bret Saberhagen
and Bill Pecota, 12/91

RUSTY MEACHAM

Position: Pitcher
Team: Kansas City Royals
Born: January 27, 1968
Stuart, FL
Height: 6'2" **Weight:** 165 lbs.
Bats: Right **Throws:** Right
Acquired: Acquired on waivers
from Detroit, 10/91

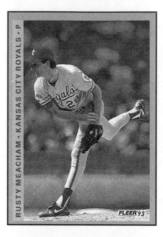

Kevin McReynolds made a quick adjustment to a new league in 1992, becoming one of Kansas City's top long-ball experts. McReynolds tagged 13 in '92, tossing in 49 RBI for good measure. The veteran outfielder choked against righthanders in '92, barely hitting .200. Lefties, meanwhile, were pounded in the mid-.300s. Since becoming a major league regular in '84, McReynolds has created some hefty offensive marks. Before his '92 arrival with the Royals, the Arkansas native's career minimums had been 15 homers and 74 RBI per season. Originally an '81 first-round draftee of San Diego's, his personal bests include 29 round-trippers (in '87) and 99 RBI (in '88).

McReynolds willingly appears in all sets now, unlike at the beginning of his career when he had open disputes with card companies. He'll need to turn up the offensive heat before anyone bites on his 1993 commons. Our pick for his best 1993 card is Score. We have chosen this card for the interesting facts included on the reverse.

Rusty Meacham became not only one of the top rookies but also one of the best relievers in baseball after the Tigers let him get away on a waiver claim. Meacham had finished above .500 at all but one of his pro stops, and he had usually shown superb control. But few people could have expected what Meacham delivered in '92. In his first 28 appearances, all out of the bullpen, he compiled an 0.42 ERA, while allowing just 29 of 160 batters to reach via a hit or walk. Over the '92 campaign, he posted a 10-4 record with a 2.74 ERA, two saves, and 14 holds, as he struck out 64 batters. He spelled real trouble for righties in '92, only allowing them to hit .188 off him. Detroit took Meacham in the '87 draft. One year later he led his Rookie level league with nine victories and was the MVP. He assembled two 15-win seasons in a row at the Class-A and Double-A levels, making the bigs in '91.

Spring for a few of Meacham's '93s, keeping the price to a dime each if possible. Our pick for his best 1993 card is Topps. We have chosen this card because of its overall appeal and pleasing looks.

	BA	G	AB	R	H	2B	3B	HR	RBI	SB
92 AL	.247	109	373	45	92	25	0	13	49	7
Life	.267	1341	4892	660	1307	251	29	196	744	89

	W	L	ERA	G	SV	IP	H	ER	BB	SO
92 AL	10	4	2.74	64	2	101.2	88	31	21	64
Life	12	5	3.27	74	2	129.1	123	47	32	78

Series two cards from some companies were available at press time. If space allows, both cards are shown; if not, the most up-to-date cards are pictured.

JOSE MELENDEZ

Position: Pitcher
Team: Boston Red Sox
Born: September 2, 1965
  Naguabo, Puerto Rico
Height: 6'2" **Weight:** 175 lbs.
Bats: Right **Throws:** Right
Acquired: Traded from Padres
  for Phil Plantier, 12/92

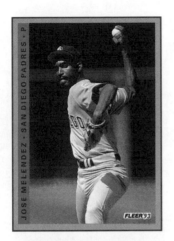

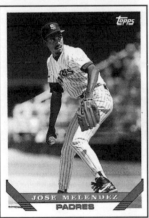

ORLANDO MERCED

Position: First base
Team: Pittsburgh Pirates
Born: November 2, 1966
  San Juan, Puerto Rico
Height: 5'11" **Weight:** 175 lbs.
Bats: Both **Throws:** Right
Acquired: Signed as a free
  agent, 2/85

Jose Melendez spent his first full season in the majors in 1992, bolstering the right side of the San Diego bullpen. His '92 success had odd parallels. While he held all road opponents and righthanded hitters to batting averages in the low .200s, Melendez wasn't as lucky in San Diego. At home or against lefthanders, foes batted .281 against him. In '91, Melendez was recalled from his Triple-A club on May 31, following his 7-0 start. While he was 5-3 as a Padres starter, Melendez was even better in 22 relief appearances. The bargain hurler made a three-game audition in '90. Melendez traces his pro career back to '83, when the Pirates signed him as an undrafted free agent. He'll join the BoSox in '93.

As a rule, relievers are less popular on cards than starters. Although common-priced cards of Melendez might seem unimportant now, the issues could bring unexpected bonuses if he moves to the starting rotation with success. Our pick for his best 1993 card is Upper Deck. We have chosen this card due to its unique photographic approach.

Orlando Merced lost his longball touch, but knocked in a career-high number of runs for the 1992 Pirates. His '92 problems of a lessened average and number of homers were balanced by his 60 RBI. In '91, Merced batted .275 with 10 home runs and 50 RBI, and finished second to Jeff Bagwell in '91 NL Rookie of the Year balloting. The common thread for Merced from 1991-92 is the struggle to hit .200 against lefthanded pitching. In '92, he didn't break that barrier, managing only a .190 average against southpaws. He did put together mid-.200 averages at home, on the road, or against righthanders. Merced's first promotion to the majors came with the '90 Bucs. He batted .208, going five-for-24 as a pinch-hitter.

Merced needs to pump up his power production before collectors can get pumped up over his common-priced cards. Invest elsewhere. Our pick for his best 1993 card is Upper Deck. We have chosen this card since the photograph captures the athletic ability of the player.

	W	L	ERA	G	CG	IP	H	ER	BB	SO
92 NL	6	7	2.92	56	0	89.1	82	29	20	82
Life	14	12	3.35	90	3	188.1	167	70	47	149

	BA	G	AB	R	H	2B	3B	HR	RBI	SB
92 NL	.247	134	405	50	100	28	5	6	60	5
Life	.260	279	840	136	218	46	7	16	110	13

KENT
MERCKER

Position: Pitcher
Team: Atlanta Braves
Born: February 1, 1968
Dublin, OH
Height: 6'2" **Weight:** 195 lbs.
Bats: Left **Throws:** Left
Acquired: First-round pick,
6/86 free-agent draft

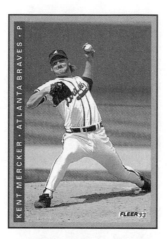

SAM
MILITELLO

Position: Pitcher
Team: New York Yankees
Born: November 26, 1969
Tampa, FL
Height: 6'3" **Weight:** 200 lbs.
Bats: Right **Throws:** Right
Acquired: Sixth-round pick,
6/90 free-agent draft

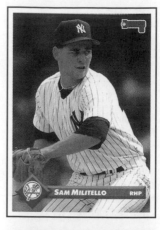
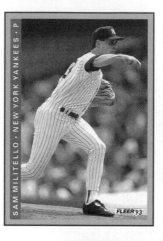

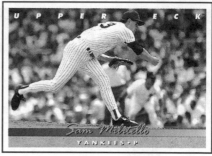

Kent Mercker's 1992 success was predictable. In 50 appearances, he earned six saves. Ironically, his '91 totals also included 50 games and six saves. The comparisons stop there, as Mercker's ERA rose from its '91 mark of 2.58. Atlanta used Mercker as a starter four times in '91, a practice since abandoned. The lefty began his career as a starter, following his first-round selection in the '86 draft. After a horrid two-game baptism with the '89 Braves, he returned the next year as a revamped reliever. Mercker was 4-7 with seven saves and a 3.17 ERA in 36 appearances. Surprisingly, lefthanders hit more than 50 points higher against Mercker than righthanders did in '92.

Look to the Braves starters, not their bullpen, for card investment possibilities. Mercker's 1993 cards have little promise, even at three to five cents apiece. If you want the cards of an Atlanta reliever, pick Wohlers or Stanton. Our pick for his best 1993 card is Topps. We have chosen this card for its artistic presentation.

Sam Militello was welcomed to the bigs for the first time in August 1992. He was summoned after dominating his Triple-A league with a 12-2 record, 2.29 ERA, and 152 strikeouts in 141 ⅓ innings. His Yankees debut—a seven-inning, one-hit victory against Boston—was August 9. For his efforts in the bigs in '92, he garnered a 3-3 record with a 3.45 ERA, striking out 42 batters over 60 innings. He split the '91 season between Double-A Albany and Class-A Prince William, going 14-4 with 168 strikeouts in 149 innings. His 1.57 ERA and .778 winning percentage were bests for all Yankee minor leaguers in '91. His minor league career ends with a 34-8 record and a 1.76 ERA.

Militello could be one of the hottest topics of conversation for rookie-card collectors. He's a reasonable investment at 10 to 15 cents each, and will be a likely double-digit winner for the 1993 Yanks. Our pick for his best 1993 card is Fleer. We have chosen this card due to the outstanding photographic composition.

	W	L	ERA	G	SV	IP	H	ER	BB	SO
92 NL	3	2	3.42	53	6	68.1	51	26	35	49
Life	12	12	3.24	141	19	194.1	158	70	100	154

	W	L	ERA	G	SV	IP	H	ER	BB	SO
92 AL	3	3	3.45	9	0	60.0	43	23	32	42
92 AAA	12	2	2.29	22	3	141.1	105	36	46	152

Series two cards from some companies were available at press time. If space allows, both cards are shown; if not, the most up-to-date cards are pictured.

KEITH MILLER

Position: Second base
Team: Kansas City Royals
Born: June 12, 1963
  Midland, MI
Height: 5'11" **Weight:** 185 lbs.
Bats: Right **Throws:** Right
Acquired: Traded from Mets
  with Gregg Jefferies and
  Kevin McReynolds for Bill
  Pecota and Bret Saberhagen,
  12/91

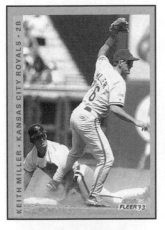

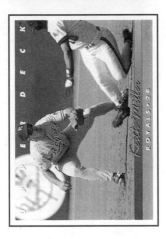

RANDY MILLIGAN

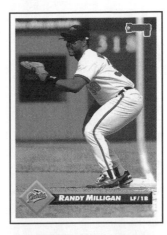

Position: First base
Team: Baltimore Orioles
Born: November 27, 1961
  San Diego, CA
Height: 6'1" **Weight:** 234 lbs.
Bats: Right **Throws:** Right
Acquired: Traded from Pirates
  for Pete Blohm, 12/88

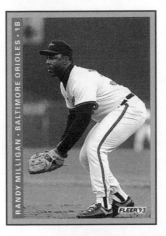

Keith Miller became Kansas City's free offensive bonus in 1992. Thrown in by the Mets to sweeten the preseason trade for Bret Saberhagen, Miller became one of the Royals' steadiest hitters. He batted .284 for the '92 season, consistently hitting right around .300 at home or against righties. When KC acquired Juan Samuel in the second half of the season, Miller's second base job was disrupted. Yet, Miller stole more than a dozen bases (16) for the third consecutive year while setting numerous career highs at the plate. A polished utilityman with New York from 1987 through '91, he played six different positions. Originally drafted by the Yankees in '84, his contract was canceled when a previous knee injury was discovered.

Miller will see frequent duty with Kansas City again in 1993. Don't expect him as a full-timer in one position, and don't expect his common-priced cards to bring any dividends. Our pick for his best 1993 card is Topps. We have chosen this card because it has a distinctive look.

Traditional slugger Randy Milligan began to expand his offense with the 1992 Orioles. He scored a career-high number of runs (71) while drawing more than 100 walks (106) for the first time in his 12-year pro career. Milligan's willingness to accept free passes balanced his lower batting average (.240) and decreased homer output (11). These are the lowest numbers the righty has posted in these two areas since before joining the Orioles late in '88. His hitting declined drastically during road games, as he could manage only a .193 batting average. The first baseman's career suffered a jolt on April 22, 1992, when he broadsided Billy Ripken while the pair sought the same grounder. Despite a concussion, Milligan missed only six games. Two of his career highs include pounding 20 homers in '90 and driving in 70 runs in '91.

Because he may not play full-time in 1993, avoid Milligan's commons. Our pick for his best 1993 card is Upper Deck. We have chosen this card because it has a distinctive look.

	BA	G	AB	R	H	2B	3B	HR	RBI	SB
92 AL	.284	106	416	57	118	24	4	4	38	16
Life	.271	414	1188	178	322	64	8	11	86	60

	BA	G	AB	R	H	2B	3B	HR	RBI	SB
92 AL	.240	137	462	71	111	21	1	11	53	0
Life	.256	554	1755	258	450	86	9	62	236	16

ALAN MILLS

Position: Pitcher
Team: Baltimore Orioles
Born: October 18, 1966
Lakeland, FL
Height: 6'1" **Weight:** 190 lbs.
Bats: Both **Throws:** Right
Acquired: Traded from Yankees
for Francisco de la Rosa,
2/92

 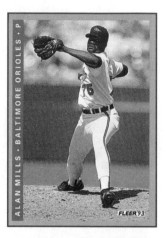

Alan Mills came from nowhere to the position of noted middle reliever in just one season. The Orioles adopted Mills with surprising results in 1992. He tamed righthanded hitters, allowing them only a .191 average against him, and handled 35 relief assignments with ease. He went 10-4 with a 2.61 ERA, but was shelved in mid-September due to a sore elbow. In six games with the '91 Yankees, Mills was 1-1 with a 6.41 ERA. Mills got his big league premiere with the '90 Yanks, but ended 1-5 in 36 relief outings. Originally, Mills was a first-round draft pick of the Angels in June '86. He spent his first four seasons in Class-A ball, mastering his control.

One good season does not a card investment make, especially when a middle reliever is the card in question. His 1993s are not advisable buys. If Baltimore gives Mills a chance in the starting rotation, think again about investing. Our pick for his best 1993 card is Score. We have chosen this card for its artistic presentation.

	W	L	ERA	G	SV	IP	H	ER	BB	SO
92 AL	10	4	2.61	35	2	103.1	78	30	54	60
Life	12	10	3.18	77	2	161.1	142	57	95	95

KEVIN MITCHELL

Position: Outfield
Team: Cincinnati Reds
Born: January 13, 1962
San Diego, CA
Height: 5'11" **Weight:** 210 lbs.
Bats: Right **Throws:** Right
Acquired: Traded from
Mariners for Norm Charlton,
11/92

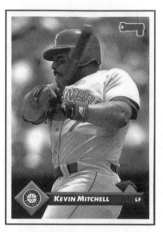 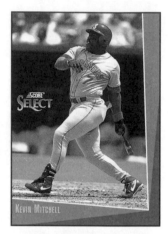

 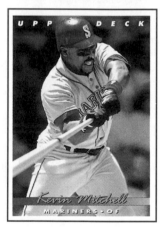

Kevin Mitchell's bubble of stardom burst with the 1992 Mariners. When the M's swapped half their bullpen for the controversial clubber, the media forecast that Mitchell might top 50 homers in the cozy Kingdome. Not quite. Instead, he failed to reach 10 four-baggers for the first time in his seven-year career. The only '92 statistic Mitchell led the league in may have been excuses. Each week, sportswriters relayed the newest reasons why Boogie Bear claimed he wasn't performing up to par. Despite a second-half comeback, a fractured foot wiped out his season on September 1 after 99 games. Mitchell's career peaks came in '89, his MVP-winning season with the Giants. He joins the Reds for '93.

Based on his past, Mitchell's nickel-priced 1993s are tempting. However, his physical condition and his questionable motivation are two negatives which should scare away most sane investors. If you're set on a Mitchell, buy him in the '87 Fleer Update set for $1. Our pick for his best 1993 card is Topps. We have chosen this card because it has a distinctive look.

	BA	G	AB	R	H	2B	3B	HR	RBI	SB
92 AL	.286	99	360	48	103	24	0	9	67	0
Life	.276	900	3109	469	859	162	20	171	548	26

Series two cards from some companies were available at press time. If space allows, both cards are shown; if not, the most up-to-date cards are pictured.

DAVE MLICKI

Position: Pitcher
Team: Cleveland Indians
Born: June 8, 1968
  Cleveland, OH
Height: 6'4" **Weight:** 185 lbs.
Bats: Right **Throws:** Right
Acquired: 17th-round pick,
  6/90 free-agent draft

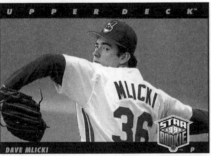

A hometown boy who made good would be the ideal description for David Mlicki. The young righthanded power pitcher, a Cleveland native, earned a big league premiere via four starts for the 1992 Tribe. In two of his four starts, Mlicki lasted six innings or longer while holding foes to three runs or less. Overall for the Tribe in '92, Mlicki went 0-2 with a 4.98 ERA. He managed to strike out one batter for each one he walked for the Indians in '92. He skipped Triple-A en route to the majors, thanks to an 11-9 record with 146 strikeouts in Double-A Canton-Akron. This followed 136 strikeouts in the Class-A South Atlantic League in '91, which ranked fourth overall in the entire Indians organization.

If the Indians harness Mlicki's pitching power, he could be the team's next Charles Nagy. Believers should grab a few of his 1993 cards at 10 cents apiece. Our pick for his best 1993 card is Upper Deck. We have chosen this card because it will increase in value.

PAUL MOLITOR

Position: Designated hitter/
  first base
Team: Toronto Blue Jays
Born: August 22, 1956
  St. Paul, MN
Height: 6' **Weight:** 185 lbs.
Bats: Right **Throws:** Right
Acquired: Signed as a free
  agent, 12/92

 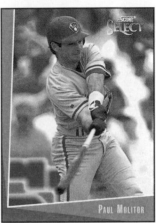

At age 36, Paul Molitor still swings a potent bat. A member of the Brewers from his 1978 major league debut through 1992, he shows no sign of slowing. He delivered a four-hit game against Seattle on June 14, 1992. His '92 batting average of .320 was fourth in the league. Proving he's still a threat on the basepaths, Molitor also swiped 31 bases. He's topped 40 steals four times in his career. The only player to produce a five-hit game in a World Series ('82), Molitor led both leagues with 216 hits and 133 runs scored in '91. That year, he finished with a .325 average, 17 homers, 75 RBI, and 19 stolen bases. Molitor now spends most of his time playing first or in the DH slot. The brittle star, who has been on the DL more than a dozen times, joins the Blue Jays.

If Molitor can hang tough and lead Toronto to another pennant, his dime-priced cards could take off. An early Molitor card of note is the '81 Fleer for $1 or less. Our pick for his best 1993 card is Fleer. We have chosen this card because the design lends itself to the best use of the elements.

	W	L	ERA	G	SV	IP	H	ER	BB	SO
92 AL	0	2	4.98	4	0	21.2	23	12	16	16
Life	0	2	4.98	4	0	21.2	23	12	16	16

	BA	G	AB	R	H	2B	3B	HR	RBI	SB
92 AL	.320	158	609	89	195	36	7	12	89	31
Life	.303	1856	7520	1275	2281	405	86	160	790	412

RICH MONTELEONE

Position: Pitcher
Team: New York Yankees
Born: March 22, 1963
  Tampa, FL
Height: 6'2" **Weight:** 236 lbs.
Bats: Right **Throws:** Right
Acquired: Traded from Angels
  with Claudell Washington for
  Luis Polonia, 4/90

JEFF MONTGOMERY

Position: Pitcher
Team: Kansas City Royals
Born: January 7, 1962
  Wellston, OH
Height: 5'11" **Weight:** 180 lbs.
Bats: Right **Throws:** Right
Acquired: Traded from Reds
  for Van Snider, 2/88

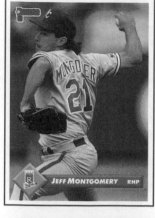

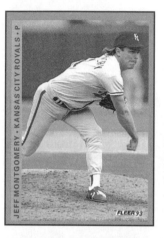

Rich Monteleone ended a five-year drought with a career turnaround in the 1992 Yankees bullpen. After entering the '92 campaign with a modest 5-4 record, the veteran righthander cleaned up in middle relief. His 92 ⅔ innings of work yielded a 7-3 record and a 3.30 ERA in '92. Although he seemed like an unimportant addition to the '90 trade for Luis Polonia, his '91 efforts at Triple-A Columbus paid off. He reeled off 17 saves and a 2.12 ERA in 32 games and was recalled by the Yankees that August. In '82, the Tigers made Monteleone their first-round draft pick. He joined the Seattle organization in '86, earning his big league debut as a Mariner in '87. Monteleone could be in the majors for years to come, but will be challenged for work by the abundance of young arms in the Yankees organization.

While Monteleone deserves credit for his 1992 success, his cards won't get any credit for investors. Punt his 1993 commons. Our pick for his best 1993 card is Donruss. We have chosen this card for its technical merits.

Jeff Montgomery is making Kansas City Royals fans forget Dan Quisenberry. By adding to his save totals each year, he stamps himself as a legitimate candidate to approach Quisenberry's club record of 45 saves in a season. Although the Royals got off to a ragged start in 1992, Montgomery notched his 14th save on June 10, lowering his ERA to 2.10 in the process. His final stats for the '92 season included an impressive 39 saves and a 2.18 ERA. Unlike Quisenberry, Montgomery averages nearly a strikeout per inning. Montgomery began his pro career in '83, reaching the majors four years later. He won seven games in a season twice and posted a career-best ERA of 1.37 in '89. In both '89 and '90, Montgomery had opened the year in a set-up role. With 33 saves in 39 opportunities in '91, he cemented his position as the club's top closer for the first time.

Closer cards seldom bring dividends. Avoid Montgomery's nickel issues. Our pick for his best 1993 card is Fleer. We have chosen this card due to the outstanding photographic composition.

	W	L	ERA	G	SV	IP	H	ER	BB	SO
92	7	3	3.30	47	0	92.2	82	34	27	62
Life	12	7	3.50	108	0	198	185	77	66	136

	W	L	ERA	G	SV	IP	H	ER	BB	SO
92 AL	1	6	2.18	65	39	82.2	61	20	27	69
Life	27	22	2.57	327	115	441.0	370	126	153	394

Series two cards from some companies were available at press time. If space allows, both cards are shown; if not, the most up-to-date cards are pictured.

MIKE MOORE

Position: Pitcher
Team: Detroit Tigers
Born: November 26, 1959
Eakly, Oklahoma
Height: 6′4″ **Weight:** 205 lbs.
Bats: Right **Throws:** Right
Acquired: Signed as a free
agent, 12/92

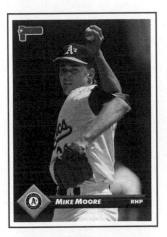 

Mike Moore's 1992 record may be deceiving. Granted, the righthander was a double-digit winner (17) with Oakland for a fourth consecutive season. Yet his wins came via an average of nearly five runs per game in support from A's teammates, obscuring Moore's four-plus ERA. Compare his stats to '91—a 17-8 effort with a 2.96 ERA. He may not receive all that offensive support from the Tigers in '93. Moore was the first overall pick of Seattle in the first round of the '81 draft. He debuted with the Mariners in '82, enduring four losing seasons in five years, aside from a 17-10 mark in '85. His career best of 19 victories came in '89, his first year with Oakland. For the last nine years, Moore has pitched 199 or more innings per season.

Before investing in Moore's 1993 commons, think. Will he enjoy the same success with Detroit? Unless he gets support, Moore's record may crumble faster than your investment in his cards. Our pick for his best 1993 card is Upper Deck. We have chosen this card because of its great combination of photography and design.

	W	L	ERA	G	CG	IP	H	ER	BB	SO
92 AL	17	12	4.12	36	2	223.0	229	102	103	117
Life	132	142	4.07	364	70	2331.0	2300	1053	910	1452

MICKEY MORANDINI

Position: Second base
Team: Philadelphia Phillies
Born: April 22, 1966
Kittanning, PA
Height: 5′11″ **Weight:** 167 lbs.
Bats: Left **Throws:** Right
Acquired: Fifth-round pick,
6/88 free-agent draft

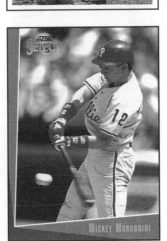

On September 20, Mickey Morandini became one of 1992's record setters. The Philadelphia second baseman made history by pulling an unassisted triple play against the Pirates, a feat last achieved in the National League 65 years earlier. Morandini's exploit didn't overshadow his steady progress at the plate throughout the year. While Morandini only hit .198 against lefthanded pitchers in '92, he hit almost .300 against righties. A member of the '88 U.S. Olympic baseball team, Morandini set numerous offensive highs in '92. He exceeded his 98-game totals with the '91 Phils, which included one homer, 20 RBI, and a .249 average. He began his pro career in '89, and rose to the majors in two quick seasons. He was unveiled in Philadelphia for 25 games in '90, causing incumbent second baseman Tom Herr to be swapped to the Mets.

Morandini is improving each year. His '93 common-priced cards are promising gambles. Our pick for his best 1993 card is Upper Deck. We have chosen this card due to its unique photographic approach.

	BA	G	AB	R	H	2B	3B	HR	RBI	SB
92 NL	.265	127	422	47	112	8	8	3	30	8
Life	.257	250	826	94	212	23	12	5	53	24

MIKE MORGAN

Position: Pitcher
Team: Chicago Cubs
Born: October 8, 1959
  Tulare, CA
Height: 6'2" **Weight:** 222 lbs.
Bats: Right **Throws:** Right
Acquired: Signed as a free
  agent, 12/91

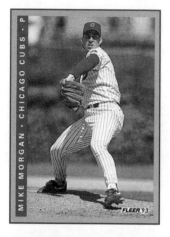

Although he didn't keep pace with 20-win teammate Greg Maddux, pitcher Mike Morgan enjoyed one of his finest seasons as a 1992 Cub. His 16 wins erased his previous career high (14), achieved in '91. He also kept his ERA below 3.00 for the second season in a row. In '92, Morgan struck out 123 batters, walking only 79. He owns five seasons of 11 or more wins, dating back to the '86 Mariners. Ironically, Morgan and Maddux attended the same Las Vegas high school, graduating six years apart. Morgan, after becoming a first-round draft choice of Oakland's in '78, debuted with the Athletics one week after graduation.

Morgan could collect one or two 20-win seasons before his career closes. This could bring a short-term price surge for his common-priced cards, especially if the Cubs near a pennant. However, Morgan's lifetime losing record will keep his cards from having lasting values. Our pick for his best 1993 card is Score. We have chosen this card due to the outstanding photographic composition.

	W	L	ERA	G	CG	IP	H	ER	BB	SO
92 NL	16	8	2.55	34	6	240.0	203	68	79	123
Life	83	112	3.87	298	41	1626.0	1651	699	546	783

HAL MORRIS

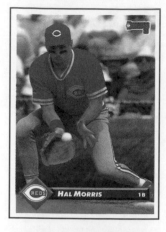

Position: First base
Team: Cincinnati Reds
Born: April 9, 1965
  Fort Rucker, AL
Height: 6'4" **Weight:** 215 lbs.
Bats: Left **Throws:** Left
Acquired: Traded from Yankees
  with Rodney Imes for Tim
  Leary and Van Snider, 12/89

After nearly winning the NL batting crown in 1991, Hal Morris encountered an early setback to his second bid in '92. On April 15, he suffered a broken right hand when hit by a Charlie Leibrandt pitch in the first inning. After he returned from the DL, Morris went 110 at-bats before hitting his first home run—against San Francisco lefthander Bryan Hickerson on June 16. That two-run shot in the sixth inning came on the reliever's first pitch and gave the Reds a 5-3 victory. As a rookie, Morris hit .340 with the '90 Reds, then followed with a .318 campaign. He came within a hit of the '91 batting title when he needed four hits on the last day to win and got three. He singled his first three times, then lined out to center in his last at-bat. The season ended with the frustrated Morris in the on-deck circle.

Past injuries have cast shadows on future cards. Limit spending to a nickel per '93 Morris. Our pick for his best 1993 card is Upper Deck. We have chosen this card since the photograph captures the athletic ability of the player.

	BA	G	AB	R	H	2B	3B	HR	RBI	SB
92 NL	.271	115	395	41	107	21	3	6	53	6
Life	.304	388	1220	166	371	76	7	27	152	25

JACK MORRIS

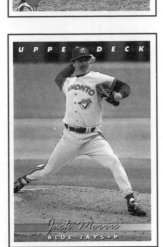

Position: Pitcher
Team: Toronto Blue Jays
Born: May 16, 1955
St. Paul, MN
Height: 6'3" **Weight:** 200 lbs.
Bats: Right **Throws:** Right
Acquired: Signed as a free
agent, 12/91

Jack Morris celebrated his '91 success with even more success and free-agent riches in '92. In an interesting bit of irony, Morris joined the Blue Jays, the team he had helped Minnesota beat in the '91 ALCS. In '92, the righty threw his first 21-win season since '86 and helped steer Toronto to their first-ever World Championship. While he did a stellar job of getting the Jays to the playoffs, he was shelled on arrival. The fact remains, however, that you can't win a Series until you outperform all others in the regular season. That is exactly what Morris did in '92. After 1990, he was written off as a has-been after two poor seasons with the Detroit Tigers. With the Twins in '91, Morris won 18 regular-season games and four more in postseason play, earning Series MVP honors.

These cards will sizzle at 15 cents apiece. His third card, in the '80 Topps set, is a decent buy at $4 or less. Our pick for his best 1993 card is Topps. We have chosen this card because of its great combination of photography and design.

TERRY MULHOLLAND

Position: Pitcher
Team: Philadelphia Phillies
Born: March 9, 1963
Uniontown, PA
Height: 6'3" **Weight:** 206 lbs.
Bats: Right **Throws:** Left
Acquired: Traded from Giants
with Charlie Hayes and
Dennis Cook for Steve
Bedrosian and Rick Parker,
6/89

Terry Mulholland's 13-11 record with the '92 Phillies placed him second on the team in wins to Curt Schilling. Lefties hit a pale .211 against Mulholland. In 17 of his 32 starts, Mulholland lasted six innings or longer while holding the opponents to three runs or less. However, his biggest feat was picking off 15 baserunners, tops in all of baseball. Mulholland won a team-leading 16 games for the '91 Phils. He became the first Philly pitcher this century to spin a nine-inning no-hitter, blanking San Francisco before a home crowd. Ironically, the Giants picked him in the first round of the '84 draft.

Mulholland could push his career winning record to .500 in '93, perhaps while approaching the 20-win circle. With a perennial contender like Oakland or Toronto, those marks would assure higher card values. In Philadelphia, though, his '93 commons won't be appreciated. Our pick for his best 1993 card is Donruss. We have chosen this card for its technical merits.

	W	L	ERA	G	CG	IP	H	ER	BB	SO
92 AL	21	6	4.04	34	6	240.2	222	108	80	132
Life	237	168	3.73	499	170	3530.0	3215	1464	1258	2275

	W	L	ERA	G	CG	IP	H	ER	BB	SO
92 NL	13	11	3.81	32	12	229.0	227	97	46	125
Life	45	49	3.87	148	30	857.2	868	369	215	453

MIKE MUNOZ

Position: Pitcher
Team: Detroit Tigers
Born: July 12, 1965
  Baldwin Park, CA
Height: 6'3" **Weight:** 195 lbs.
Bats: Left **Throws:** Left
Acquired: Traded from Dodgers
  for Mike Wilkins, 9/90

PEDRO MUNOZ

Position: Outfield
Team: Minnesota Twins
Born: September 19, 1968
  Ponce, Puerto Rico
Height: 5'10" **Weight:** 208 lbs.
Bats: Right **Throws:** Right
Acquired: Traded from Blue
  Jays with Nelson Liriano for
  John Candelaria, 7/90

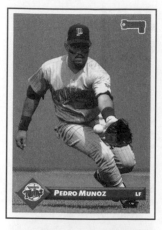

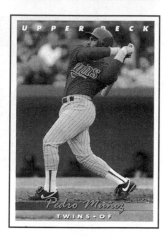

Being lefthanded gave Mike Munoz another shot at the majors in 1992. He impressed Detroit in spring training with a 1-0 record in seven preseason games, crafting a 1.59 ERA. The Tigers wound up keeping Munoz in reserve, sometimes to face only a single lefthanded hitter. Lefties hit under .200 off Munoz, defining his future role with the club. A third-round selection of the Dodgers in '86, Munoz devoted his first two years in the minors to starting duties. The lefty reliever celebrated his big league arrival with the '89 Dodgers. With Los Angeles in 1990, Munoz went 0-1 with a 3.18 ERA in eight relief assignments. After Munoz finished the '91 campaign with a 9.64 ERA in nine appearances, his return to Detroit looked doubtful.

Munoz may be a major leaguer in '93, but his limited scope in the Detroit bullpen will keep him out of the headlines. Cards of Munoz won't be popular, even at three to five cents each. Our pick for his best 1993 card is Topps. We have chosen this card because the design lends itself to the best use of the elements.

Despite a second-half collapse, new arrival Pedro Munoz was an offensive perk for the 1992 Twins. By mid-'92, he had clobbered 10 homers and 46 RBI. At the end of the '92 season, he had tallied up a .270 batting average, 12 homers, 71 RBI, and a .987 fielding percentage. Munoz was the reason the Twins never blinked when Dan Gladden left via free-agency for the Tigers. He easily exceeded Gladden's '91 totals of six homers and 52 RBI. Munoz was acquired by the Twins halfway through 1990; the next year, he slugged seven homers and 26 RBI, along with a .283 average, in 51 games. The strong-armed Munoz has become a defensive asset in right field, giving the Twins hope for an all-around star for '93.

Munoz needs to recapture his first-half hitting magic from '92. If he keeps his offense cranking throughout '93, his nickel-priced cards will be big price winners. Our pick for his best 1993 card is Fleer. We have chosen this card because of its overall appeal and pleasing looks.

	W	L	ERA	G	CG	IP	H	ER	BB	SO
92 AL	1	2	3.00	65	0	48.0	44	16	25	23
Life	1	3	4.52	82	0	65.2	69	33	35	31

	BA	G	AB	R	H	2B	3B	HR	RBI	SB
92 AL	.270	127	418	44	113	16	3	12	71	4
Life	.273	200	641	72	175	27	5	19	102	10

DALE MURPHY

Position: Outfield
Team: Philadelphia Phillies
Born: March 12, 1956
Portland, OR
Height: 6'4" **Weight:** 215 lbs.
Bats: Right **Throws:** Right
Acquired: Traded from Braves
with Tommy Greene for Jeff
Parrett, Jim Vatcher, and
Victor Rosario, 8/90

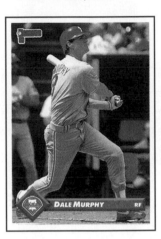 

EDDIE MURRAY

Position: First base
Team: New York Mets
Born: February 24, 1956
Los Angeles, CA
Height: 6'2" **Weight:** 222 lbs.
Bats: Both **Throws:** Right
Acquired: Signed as a free
agent, 11/91

 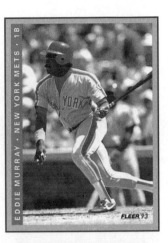

For Dale Murphy, the 1992 season was a total loss. Four months before spring training, he underwent arthroscopic knee surgery. The same knee had to be drained three times during the six-week training period. After playing 17 games in pain, Murphy went on the shelf again. His '92 totals added up to a .161 average with two homers and 17 RBI. He had arthroscopic surgery twice as doctors removed scar tissue and other debris. The future of the former superstar is clouded. Even with a clean bill of health, Murphy is only a shadow of the player who won Most Valuable Player awards in '82 and '83. Murphy still hits lefthanders and might finish out as a platoon player. He still has a fine arm in right field but had lost some speed even before his knee problems resurfaced.

It's highly unlikely that Murphy could ever regain his pre-injury form. His '93 cards should be avoided. Our pick for his best 1993 card is Score. We have chosen this card for the interesting facts included on the reverse.

Mickey Mantle is no longer the top run-producer among switch-hitters. That title went to Eddie Murray on June 6, 1992. When he singled against Pittsburgh's Dennis Lamp, Murray moved one ahead of Mantle's record of 1,509 RBI. The hit also placed him in 32nd place on the career RBI list. In addition to his 93 RBI in '92, Murray managed a .261 average, drew 66 walks, and swatted 16 homers. His RBI total for the '92 season was good for a three-way tie for seventh in the league. He also collected his 400th career homer, tops among active National Leaguers. Murray, who spent 12 years with the Orioles before coming to the Dodgers in '89, has always been one of the game's most accomplished clutch-hitters. In '91, 11 of his 19 homers put the Dodgers ahead or tied the game.

Murray is a future Hall of Famer. Get his 1993s at a dime each. How about Murray's 1981 Fleer card for $3? Our pick for his best 1993 card is Upper Deck. We have chosen this card for its artistic presentation.

	BA	G	AB	R	H	2B	3B	HR	RBI	SB
92 NL	.161	18	62	5	10	1	0	2	7	0
Life	.266	2154	7918	1196	2105	349	39	398	1259	161

	BA	G	AB	R	H	2B	3B	HR	RBI	SB
92 NL	.261	156	551	64	144	37	2	16	93	4
Life	.290	2444	9124	1343	2646	462	32	414	1562	90

Series two cards from some companies were available at press time. If space allows, both cards are shown; if not, the most up-to-date cards are pictured.

MIKE MUSSINA

Position: Pitcher
Team: Baltimore Orioles
Born: December 8, 1968
Williamsport, PA
Height: 6′ **Weight:** 182 lbs.
Bats: Right **Throws:** Right
Acquired: First-round pick,
6/90 free-agent draft

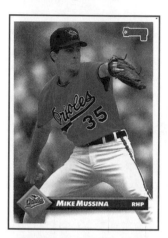
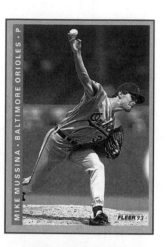

Mike Mussina took only three and one-half years to earn his economics degree from Stanford. He's still practicing what he learned, because he is the AL's most economical pitcher in doling out walks. Opponents in 1992 compiled a .239 batting average, a .278 on-base percentage, and a .348 slugging percentage against Mussina. Three of his first 12 wins last year were shutouts. He pitched only 28 games in the minors before reaching Baltimore in '91. At Triple-A Rochester in '91, he was 10-4 with a 2.87 ERA, 31 walks, and 107 strikeouts in 122 ⅓ innings. He was named the '91 International League Pitcher of the Year. One of baseball's smartest players, his locker overflows with books. Mussina strikes out three times more men than he walks, yields fewer hits than innings pitched, fields his position well, and keeps runners close.

Although he has a penchant for giving up the gopher ball, Mussina has star quality. His '93s are cardboard gold. Our pick for his best 1993 card is Upper Deck. We have chosen this card due to its unique photographic approach.

	W	L	ERA	G	CG	IP	H	ER	BB	SO
92 AL	18	5	2.54	32	8	241.0	212	68	48	130
Life	22	10	2.63	44	10	328.2	289	96	69	182

RANDY MYERS

Position: Pitcher
Team: Chicago Cubs
Born: September 19, 1962
Vancouver, WA
Height: 6′1″ **Weight:** 225 lbs.
Bats: Left **Throws:** Left
Acquired: Signed as a free
agent, 12/92

After a slow start, Randy Myers became the dean of the Padres bullpen in '92. His 66 appearances in '92 yielded a 3-6 record, 4.29 ERA, and 38 saves. The Chicago Cubs hope he can provide some much needed relief to save them from another mediocre season in '93. Myers' previous career high was 31 saves with the '91 Reds. New York made him a first-round draft choice in '82. After four minor league years as a starter, the Washington native debuted with the Mets in '85. He returned to Triple-A in '86 to master relief and became a Mets regular in '87. Going into '92, Myers had averaged 8.81 strikeouts per nine innings. He's worked in more than 50 games in each of the last six seasons.

The cost-conscious Padres dumped Myers and his big salary after '92. Playing with three teams in three years casts doubt on his common-priced cards. However, playing in Chicago might bring him some otherwise missed attention. Our pick for his best 1993 card is Upper Deck. We have chosen this card due to the outstanding photographic composition.

	W	L	ERA	G	SV	IP	H	ER	BB	SO
92 NL	3	6	4.29	66	38	79.2	84	38	34	66
Life	30	38	3.06	375	131	538.1	438	183	249	536

Series two cards from some companies were available at press time. If space allows, both cards are shown; if not, the most up-to-date cards are pictured.

CHRIS NABHOLZ

Position: Pitcher
Team: Montreal Expos
Born: January 5, 1967
  Harrisburg, PA
Height: 6'5" **Weight:** 212 lbs.
Bats: Left **Throws:** Left
Acquired: Second-round pick,
  6/88 free-agent draft

Lefthander Chris Nabholz set a new personal standard for wins with the 1992 Expos. Nabholz was one of four Montreal starters winning in double digits. His '92 campaign brought forth an 11-12 record with a 3.32 ERA. It also helped bring Montreal within nine games of first place for the season—quite a pleasant switch from their last place finish in '91. That season, his 8-7 record was influenced by more than six weeks on the DL with tendinitis in his left shoulder. He was named NL Pitcher of the Month in September '91, due to his 6-0 record. His first six-game winning streak came at the beginning of his rookie season in Montreal during 1990.

Even with 10 or more wins per season, Nabholz won't be an automatic card investment choice. Try Dennis Martinez or Ken Hill as the more dominant choices for nickel-priced 1993 purchases. Our pick for his best 1993 card is Donruss. We have chosen this card because of its great combination of photography and design.

	W	L	ERA	G	CG	IP	H	ER	BB	SO
92 NL	11	12	3.32	32	1	195.0	176	72	74	130
Life	25	21	3.35	67	3	418.2	353	156	163	282

TIM NAEHRING

Position: Shortstop
Team: Boston Red Sox
Born: February 1, 1967
  Cincinnati, OH
Height: 6'2" **Weight:** 190 lbs.
Bats: Right **Throws:** Right
Acquired: Eighth-round pick,
  6/88 free-agent draft

The bright promise Tim Naehring showed several springs ago is quickly fading into memory. Once regarded as a red-hot shortstop prospect because of his power, he was slowed by a sprained right wrist in 1992. He had a .308 on-base average and a .323 slugging percentage last season. He also spent time in the minor leagues, trying to recapture his home run stroke. His Triple-A Pawtucket efforts in '92 saw him bat .294 with two homers and five RBI in 34 attempts. He missed most of the '91 season with serious back problems, requiring surgery. In '90, Naehring hit 15 homers in 82 games for Triple-A Pawtucket, then added two more in a 24-game look with the Red Sox. He hit .275 with three homers and 31 RBI in 273 at-bats in Triple-A in '89. Naehring has played all three infield positions since turning pro in '88. He's best at short but will have to prove totally recovered from his back surgery.

He'll try for a comeback in '93. Wait for a healthy Naehring before investing. Our pick for his best 1993 card is Topps. We have chosen this card due to the outstanding photographic composition.

	BA	G	AB	R	H	2B	3B	HR	RBI	SB
92 AL	.231	72	186	12	43	8	0	3	14	0
Life	.221	116	326	23	72	15	0	5	29	0

CHARLES NAGY

Position: Pitcher
Team: Cleveland Indians
Born: May 5, 1967 Fairfield, CT
Height: 6'3" **Weight:** 200 lbs.
Bats: Left **Throws:** Right
Acquired: First-round pick,
    6/88 free-agent draft

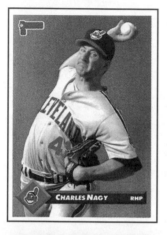

The Indians did not hesitate to trade veteran starting pitchers Tom Candiotti and Greg Swindell in '91. They knew Charles Nagy could step in as the ace of the staff. In '92, Nagy wasted no time proving them right. On June 17, he notched his fifth win in a row to bring his record to 9-3. The win extended his walkless string to 28 ⅔ consecutive scoreless innings. Even with the rest of the club struggling, Nagy posted a 17-win season. His 2.96 ERA for '92 was good for seventh-best in the AL. Nagy reached Cleveland in '90, earning a promotion from Double-A ball without Triple-A experience. He won 10 games in '91, his first full season in the majors. Nagy was a member of the '88 Olympic squad that won a gold medal in Seoul. During a 53-game schedule that summer, he led Team USA with a 1.05 earned run average.

Put out the welcome mat for Nagy cards at a dime each. If you can afford him, the '88 Topps Traded Nagy Olympian card should bloom at $2. Our pick for his best 1993 card is Upper Deck. We have chosen this card because it has a distinctive look.

	W	L	ERA	G	CG	IP	H	ER	BB	SO
92 AL	17	10	2.96	33	10	252.0	245	83	57	169
Life	29	29	3.71	75	16	509.0	531	210	144	304

JAIME NAVARRO

Position: Pitcher
Team: Milwaukee Brewers
Born: March 27, 1967
    Bayamon, Puerto Rico
Height: 6'4" **Weight:** 210 lbs.
Bats: Right **Throws:** Right
Acquired: Third-round pick,
    6/87 free-agent draft

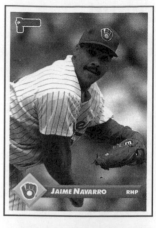

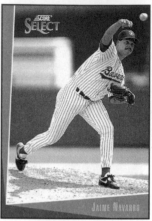

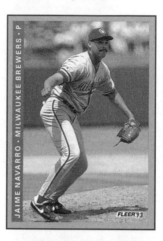

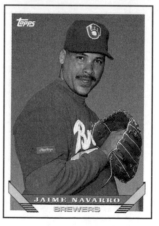

Credit Jaime Navarro with hoisting Milwaukee into 1992 surprise pennant contention. The righty achieved a career high of 17 victories and ranked among league leaders for starts (34) and innings pitched (246). Navarro paced himself throughout '92, as evidenced by his midseason record of 9-6. Remarkably, in 22 of his first 33 starts, he lasted into the sixth inning or better while surrendering three runs or less. Navarro first reached the Brewers in '89, going 7-8 with a 3.12 ERA. The next season, he improved to 8-7. Navarro capitalized on remaining with Milwaukee for a full season in 1991, when he finished with a 15-12 mark. His father, Julio Navarro, pitched in the majors from 1962-70.

Navarro's cards could be nickel-priced surprises in 1993. If the Brewers keep contending, and he nears 20 wins once more, his commons could double in value quickly. Our pick for his best 1993 card is Donruss. We have chosen this card because of its overall appeal and pleasing looks.

	W	L	ERA	G	CG	IP	H	ER	BB	SO
92 AL	17	11	3.33	34	5	246.0	224	91	64	100
Life	47	38	3.71	119	19	739.0	756	305	210	345

Series two cards from some companies were available at press time. If space allows, both cards are shown; if not, the most up-to-date cards are pictured.

DENNY NEAGLE

Position: Pitcher
Team: Pittsburgh Pirates
Born: September 13, 1968
  Prince Georges County, MD
Height: 6'4" **Weight:** 205 lbs.
Bats: Left **Throws:** Left
Acquired: Traded from Twins
  for John Smiley and Midre
  Cummings, 3/92

Denny Neagle enjoyed the rare pleasure of being traded from one contender to another. If he progresses as anticipated, he could help keep Pittsburgh in contention for some time. He came to the Pirates before the 1992 season as part of a package that sent lefty John Smiley to the Twins. Although Neagle didn't have the impact on the Pirates that Smiley once did, he was a useful pitcher who could start or relieve. His won-lost record (4-6 in '92) does not yet measure up to his hit-walk ratios, suggesting that he may be making bad pitches in key spots. Given time to mature in the majors, he should improve. Neagle, drafted by the Twins in the third round of the '89 draft, had a cup of coffee in the majors two seasons later. He put 20-3 and 9-5 years back-to-back in the minors and started the '91 Triple-A All-Star Game.

Who needs John Smiley? Neagle could blossom in '93. Try his cards at a dime each. Our pick for his best 1993 card is Score. We have chosen this card since its design makes it a standout.

	W	L	ERA	G	SV	IP	H	ER	BB	SO
92 NL	4	6	4.48	55	2	86.1	81	43	43	77
Life	4	7	4.40	62	2	106.1	109	52	50	91

JEFF NELSON

Position: Pitcher
Team: Seattle Mariners
Born: November 17, 1966
  Baltimore, MD
Height: 6'8" **Weight:** 225 lbs.
Bats: Right **Throws:** Right
Acquired: Drafted from
  Dodgers, 7/86 Rule 5 draft

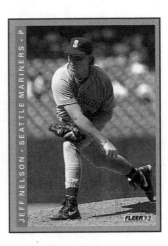

Jeff Nelson, who had never pitched in a big league game in his life, became a major league workhorse in 1992. The two scoreless innings he worked in his debut against Chicago represented a goal eight years in the making. Throwing for a total of 81 innings in '92, the righty managed to keep his ERA at 3.44 while saving six games. Nelson, first selected by the Dodgers as a low-round '84 draft choice, did not exactly have a cakewalk to the majors. After compiling a 0-12 mark in his first three minor league campaigns, he walked a horrific 84 in 71 1/3 innings for Class-A Bakersfield in '86. The M's must have seen some hope, picking him up in the Rule 5 draft. Three seasons later and a conversion from starter to closer saw Nelson soar. In '91, he saved 12 games at Double-A and seven more in Triple-A.

Not every Seattle pitcher reeked in 1992. Nelson's '93 cards are possibilities at 10 cents each. Our pick for his best 1993 card is Fleer. We have chosen this card due to the outstanding photographic composition.

	W	L	ERA	G	SV	IP	H	ER	BB	SO
92 AL	73	44	66	0	6	81.0	71	31	44	46
Life	73	44	66	0	6	81.0	71	31	44	46

ROD
NICHOLS

Position: Pitcher
Team: Cleveland Indians
Born: December 29, 1964
Burlington, IA
Height: 6'2" **Weight:** 190 lbs.
Bats: Right **Throws:** Right
Acquired: Fifth-round pick,
6/85 free-agent draft

DAVID
NIED

Position: Pitcher
Team: Colorado Rockies
Born: December 22, 1968
Dallas, TX
Height: 6'2" **Weight:** 175 lbs.
Bats: Right **Throws:** Right
Acquired: First-round pick,
11/92 expansion draft

Rod Nichols began 1992 in the Cleveland bullpen, then spent some time in the minors before returning to take Jack Armstrong's rotation spot. The velocity on Nichols's fastball had fallen to 84 mph at the time of his exile but was 7 mph faster when he returned. Opponents in '92 compiled a .273 batting average, a .323 on-base average, and a .429 slugging percentage against Nichols. The first batters he faced compiled a .389 average. Nichols yields more hits than innings pitched and has trouble keeping the ball in the park. At Triple-A Colorado Springs in '92, he was 3-3 with a 5.67 ERA, 16 walks, and 35 strikeouts in 54 innings pitched. Nichols has been used as both a starter and reliever over the last five seasons.

Nichols needs a specific role to find a niche. The keys are more control and fewer gopher balls. Until he harnesses his stuff, Nichols '93s aren't worth too many of your nickels. Our pick for his best 1993 card is Topps. We have chosen this card because of its great combination of photography and design.

David Nied pitched at Richmond of the Triple-A International League in 1992 and was a member of the All-Star team. He was among the victory, strikeout, and ERA leaders in the Atlanta system, including the major leaguers. He averaged about one strikeout per inning, very impressive for a starter, and walked only about two batters per start. The first player taken in the expansion draft, Nied is the kind of pitcher to anchor a starting staff. He has learned to pitch in the last couple of years, and that development has made him one of the top prospects in all of baseball. In fact, Nied will be ready to assume the role of the No. 1 starter on Colorado's staff in '93. Atlanta was loaded with pitching, but in two or three years they may kick themselves for not protecting Nied.

Nied will have a brand new team that will look for him to shine. If he gets run support, he could be a major force. Spend a dime on his '93s. Our pick for his best 1993 card is Upper Deck. We have chosen this card because it will increase in value.

	W	L	ERA	G	SV	IP	H	ER	BB	SO
92 AL	4	3	4.53	30	0	105.1	114	53	31	56
Life	11	30	4.39	91	1	399.2	437	195	114	208

	W	L	ERA	G	SV	IP	H	ER	BB	SO
92 NL	3	0	1.17	6	0	23.0	10	3	5	19
92 AAA	14	9	2.84	26	7	168.0	144	53	44	159

Series two cards from some companies were available at press time. If space allows, both cards are shown; if not, the most up-to-date cards are pictured.

MELVIN NIEVES

Position: Outfield
Team: Atlanta Braves
Born: December 28, 1971
San Juan, Puerto Rico
Height: 6'2" **Weight:** 186 lbs.
Bats: Both **Throws:** Right
Acquired: Signed as a free
agent, 5/88

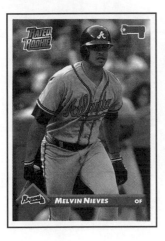

DAVE NILSSON

Position: Catcher
Team: Milwaukee Brewers
Born: December 14, 1969
Brisbane, Australia
Height: 6'3" **Weight:** 185 lbs.
Bats: Both **Throws:** Right
Acquired: Signed as free agent,
1/87

If Melvin Nieves is not the top power prospect in Atlanta's organization, he's got to be up there. Coming back from a leg injury that limited his 1991 season to 64 games, he rocked the Class-A Carolina League and the Double-A Southern League in '92. By the time he was finished, he was runaway leader for the RBI title among Atlanta farmhands and ranked with the leaders in batting average and RBI, too. In Class-A in '92, Nieves compiled a .395 on-base average and a .632 slugging percentage, and at Double-A he had a .381 on-base average and a .531 slugging percentage. His ability to switch-hit could make him a formidable obstacle late in games.

Nieves may be a year or two away from the bigs, especially if he doesn't immediately dominate Triple-A. A lot can happen in that time. Be cautious with his '93s. Our pick for his best 1993 card is Upper Deck. We have chosen this card because it will increase in value.

Dave Nilsson has become the third native-born Australian to play in the majors. He also has a chance to be the best of the three. Summoned when injuries cut into the Brewers' catching corps, Nilsson produced runs and did a nice job with the pitching staff. He also showed a good arm by gunning down 12 runners trying to steal. While Nilsson never hit more than seven homers in a season on his way to the big leagues, he cracked four in his 164 at-bats in '92. He also took one walk for almost every strikeout with the Brew Crew in '92. Nilsson was the minor leagues' top full-season hitter in '91 with a .366 average and was named to *USA Today's* All-Prospect Team. *Baseball America* put him on its Double-A All-Star team and tabbed him among the Texas League's best hopefuls.

Although he is coming along nicely, it is unlikely that he'll unseat B.J. Surhoff. Therefore, hold all card investments. Our pick for his best 1993 card is Donruss. We have chosen this card because the design lends itself to the best use of the elements.

	BA	G	AB	R	H	2B	3B	HR	RBI	SB
92 AA	.283	100	350	61	99	23	5	18	76	6
92 NL	.211	12	19	0	4	1	0	0	1	0

	BA	G	AB	R	H	2B	3B	HR	RBI	SB
92 AL	.232	51	164	15	38	8	0	4	25	2
Life	.232	51	164	15	38	8	0	4	25	2

OTIS NIXON

Position: Outfield
Team: Atlanta Braves
Born: January 9, 1959
  Evergreen, NC
Height: 6'2" **Weight:** 180 lbs.
Bats: Both **Throws:** Right
Acquired: Traded from Expos
  with Boi Rodriguez for Keith
  Morrison and Jimmy
  Kremers, 4/91

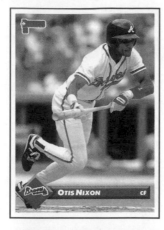

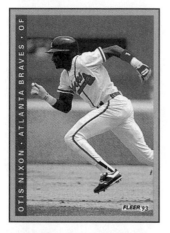

One reason Atlanta was able to duplicate its winning ways from 1991 was a strong repeat performance from Otis Nixon in '92. His .294 batting average and almost errorless fielding provided a solid force. When Nixon faced southpaws in '92, he was good for a tremendous .343 batting average. His only substantial decline came in stolen bases. He swiped a career-best 72 in '91, but his 41 in '92 were more than enough to earn career-steal number 600. It also tied for seventh best in the NL for the season. Nixon's '92 began belatedly in April, due to a suspension at the end of '91 for violating baseball's drug policy. The development soured a season filled with numerous personal records.

Nixon could be out of the picture in 1993 if a power-hitting outfielder steps forward. Aside from his past drug problems, he's never had the publicity needed to stimulate his common-priced cards. If you believe in Nixon, see his '86 Fleer Rookie for 50 cents. Our pick for his best 1993 card is Topps. We have chosen this card because of its overall appeal and pleasing looks.

	BA	G	AB	R	H	2B	3B	HR	RBI	SB
92 NL	.294	120	456	79	134	14	2	2	22	41
Life	.257	869	1996	381	513	53	10	6	123	305

MATT NOKES

Position: Catcher
Team: New York Yankees
Born: October 31, 1963
  San Diego, CA
Height: 6'1" **Weight:** 198 lbs.
Bats: Left **Throws:** Right
Acquired: Traded from Tigers
  for Clay Parker and Lance
  McCullers, 6/90

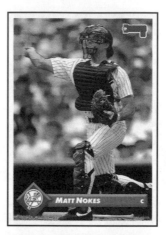

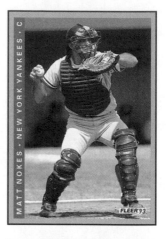

Matt Nokes was one of New York's most unpredictable players in 1992. After a very shaky first half, the backstop finished '92 with 22 homers, 59 RBI, and a weak .224 batting average. Even behind the plate, Nokes suffered. His caught-stealing percentage (23.4) was one of the lowest in the AL. A sore right shoulder limited his appearances and hindered his throwing. Originally a San Francisco farmhand, Nokes played in 19 games with the '85 Giants. He became a Detroit regular in '87, batting .289 with 32 homers and 87 RBI. Although Nokes hits well enough to stay employed in the majors, he may be better suited for a quiet spot in someone's outfield or a comfy designated hitter role.

Nokes has not developed into a solid backstop. His common-priced cards haven't been secure for years. Our pick for his best 1993 card is Score. We have chosen this card due to its unique photographic approach.

	BA	G	AB	R	H	2B	3B	HR	RBI	SB
92 AL	.224	121	384	42	86	9	1	22	59	0
Life	.256	762	2379	269	610	83	4	117	362	8

Series two cards from some companies were available at press time. If space allows, both cards are shown; if not, the most up-to-date cards are pictured.

CHARLIE O'BRIEN

Position: Catcher
Team: New York Mets
Born: May 1, 1961 Tulsa, OK
Height: 6'2" **Weight:** 190 lbs.
Bats: Right **Throws:** Right
Acquired: Traded from Brewers for Julio Machado and Kevin Brown, 8/90

Charlie O'Brien's production at the plate in 1992 was almost nonexistent; he batted .212 with two homers and 13 RBI. O'Brien has hit right around the .200 mark since '86 but has kept his spot in the major leagues because he's so valuable behind the plate. His throwing arm is like a howitzer. He nailed 15 of the first 25 runners who tried to steal last year, a 60 percent success rate that led both leagues. His season mark stood at 45.5 percent. Behind the plate, O'Brien gets high marks for handling pitchers, blocking the plate, and snaring wild pitches. At the plate, he doesn't strike out a lot. O'Brien hits routine grounders, pop-ups, and fly balls with alarming frequency, however. He actually hit six homers in 62 games for the '89 Brewers but then hit none the next year.

While he's a great backstop, O'Brien's inability to build a decent average doesn't excite investors. Our pick for his best 1993 card is Upper Deck. We have chosen this card because of its overall appeal and pleasing looks.

	BA	G	AB	R	H	2B	3B	HR	RBI	SB
92 NL	.212	68	156	15	33	12	0	2	13	0
Life	.205	339	889	87	182	48	3	12	92	0

PETE O'BRIEN

Position: First base/designated hitter
Team: Seattle Mariners
Born: February 9, 1958 Santa Monica, CA
Height: 6'2" **Weight:** 195 lbs.
Bats: Left **Throws:** Left
Acquired: Signed as a free agent, 12/89

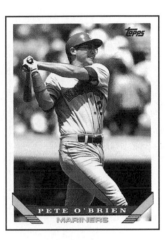

Pete O'Brien became Seattle's forgotten man in 1992. With the full-time promotion of first baseman Tino Martinez and the acquisition of left fielder Kevin Mitchell, O'Brien spent much of the season waiting and watching. O'Brien was supposed to be a one-man team when signed to a four-year free-agent deal by Seattle. However, he broke the hearts of Mariners fans by hitting .224 with five homers and 27 RBI in '90 in an injury-shortened debut. The limited exposure explained why his 14 homers and 52 RBI of 1992 dipped below his '91 feats of 17 homers and 88 RBI. Twice, in 1986-87, O'Brien reached career highs of 23 homers with Texas. During his Rangers tenure from 1982 through '88, he exceeded 80 RBI in four different campaigns.

O'Brien does not provide enough yearly homers or RBI to be respected by card investors. His 1993 issues are mistakes for collectors, even at three to five cents each. Our pick for his best 1993 card is Donruss. We have chosen this card because it has a distinctive look.

	BA	G	AB	R	H	2B	3B	HR	RBI	SB
92 AL	.222	134	396	40	88	15	1	14	52	2
Life	.262	1495	5227	624	1367	247	21	162	709	24

JOSE OFFERMAN

Position: Shortstop
Team: Los Angeles Dodgers
Born: November 4, 1968
   San Pedro de Macoris,
   Dominican Republic
Height: 6′ **Weight:** 160 lbs.
Bats: Both **Throws:** Right
Acquired: Signed as a free
   agent, 7/86

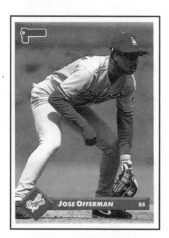 

 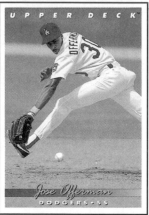

Jose Offerman suffered as the laughingstock of NL shortstops with the 1992 Dodgers. As he led the league in errors in his first season as an LA starter, he had to partially absorb blame for the team's last-place finish. However, he batted over .200 in the bigs for the first time in three years. In '91, Offerman struggled through 52 games, batting .195. Yet, LA had enough faith in the young infielder to release resident shortstop Alfredo Griffin before the '92 campaign began. Only in '90 was Offerman an offensive hero. He was named Triple-A Pacific Coast League Player of the Year for his league-leading 60 stolen bases, 11 triples, 56 RBI, and .326 average. Although Offerman was criticized by the media for his 40-plus errors, many forget the last Dodgers shortstop to reach the infamous mark: Maury Wills.

Maybe the same eventual stardom awaits Offerman. That's a big maybe, and may not be enough to keep interest in Offerman's 1993 commons. Our pick for his best 1993 card is Fleer. We have chosen this card because of its overall appeal and pleasing looks.

	BA	G	AB	R	H	2B	3B	HR	RBI	SB
92 NL	.260	149	534	67	139	20	8	1	30	23
Life	.241	230	705	84	170	22	8	2	40	27

BOB OJEDA

Position: Pitcher
Team: Cleveland Indians
Born: December 17, 1957
   Los Angeles, CA
Height: 6′1″ **Weight:** 195 lbs.
Bats: Left **Throws:** Left
Acquired: Signed as a free
   agent, 12/92

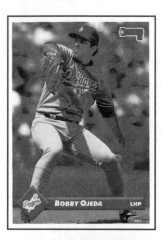 

Despite being the only lefthanded starter in Los Angeles at the close of 1992, Ojeda did little else to distinguish himself with the Dodgers. This was the main reason the Dodgers didn't mind letting him go to free agency after the '92 season. The Indians, in need of some pitching, sought out Ojeda for '93. In '92, the lefty failed to build on the 12-9 record and 3.18 ERA he created in '91, his first year with the Dodgers. The 12-year big league veteran started in 29 outings with Los Angeles last season and posted a 6-9 record with a 3.63 ERA, going the distance twice. His career-finest marks came with New York in '86, helping the team to a World Championship. Ojeda finished that season at 18-5 with seven complete games and a 2.57 ERA. After going 2-0 in postseason play, he finished fourth in Cy Young balloting.

Ojeda is nearing the twilight years of his rocky career. As he declines over the next couple years, so will his common-priced cards. Our pick for his best 1993 card is Topps. We have chosen this card for its technical merits.

	W	L	ERA	G	CG	IP	H	ER	BB	SO
92 NL	6	9	3.63	29	2	166.1	169	67	81	94
Life	113	97	3.60	340	41	1838.1	1774	735	649	1098

JOHN OLERUD

Position: First base
Team: Toronto Blue Jays
Born: August 5, 1968
  Bellevue, WA
Height: 6′5″ **Weight:** 218 lbs.
Bats: Left **Throws:** Left
Acquired: Third-round pick,
  6/89 free-agent draft

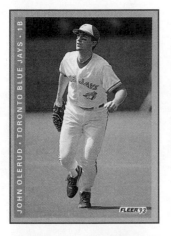

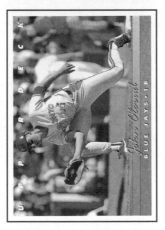

John Olerud provided the 1992 World Champion Blue Jays with a rerun of his '91 success. The young first baseman followed the script of his previous offense, which included 17 home runs, 68 RBI, and a .256 average. In '92, his average climbed to .291 when facing righties and .304 when on the road. He's handled first base on a regular basis since '91, when the team swapped incumbent first baseman Fred McGriff to open the spot for the younger slugger. Olerud, a star pitcher and hitter at Washington State University, graduated from college to the majors without a single game of minor league experience.

Remember, Olerud has never benefitted from minor league training. Therefore, he's been learning on the job. Expect his totals to grow with the 1993 Blue Jays, making his cards worthy nickel investments. Olerud's 1990 Donruss "The Rookies" is an easy choice at 50 cents. Our pick for his best 1993 card is Fleer. We have chosen this card for the superior presentation of information on its back.

	BA	G	AB	R	H	2B	3B	HR	RBI	SB
92 AL	.284	138	458	68	130	28	0	16	66	1
Life	.269	394	1278	177	344	73	2	47	182	1

STEVE OLIN

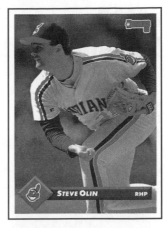

Position: Pitcher
Team: Cleveland Indians
Born: October 10, 1965
  Portland, OR
Height: 6′2″ **Weight:** 190 lbs.
Bats: Right **Throws:** Right
Acquired: 16th-round pick,
  6/87 free-agent draft

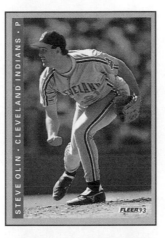

Steve Olin made up for the loss of Doug Jones by becoming the new dean of the Cleveland bullpen. Following his 1991 success, Olin once again paced the Indians in saves. In '91, he did it despite spending nearly two months in the minor leagues. Olin's '92 efforts marked many career highs. At season's end in '92, Olin had shaved more than a point off his '91 ERA of 3.36. Appearing in over 70 games for the Tribe again in '92, he set personal bests in ERA (2.34), saves (29), innings pitched (88 ⅓), and strikeouts (47). His previous high in saves was 24, achieved with Triple-A Colorado Springs in '89. If Olin can rack up numbers like this while Cleveland struggles to play .500 ball, wait until the Indians become a contender again.

Baseball pundits forecast a revival for the Indians by 1994. Olin could lead that drive, a thought which makes his common-priced cards tempting at three to five cents apiece. Our pick for his best 1993 card is Score. We have chosen this card since the photograph captures the athletic ability of the player.

	W	L	ERA	G	SV	IP	H	ER	BB	SO
92 AL	8	5	2.34	72	29	88.1	80	23	27	47
Life	16	19	3.10	195	48	273.0	272	94	90	173

OMAR OLIVARES

Position: Pitcher
Team: St. Louis Cardinals
Born: July 6, 1967
 Mayaguez, Puerto Rico
Height: 6'1" **Weight:** 193 lbs.
Bats: Right **Throws:** Right
Acquired: Traded from Padres
 for Alex Cole and Steve
 Peters, 2/90

JOE OLIVER

Position: Catcher
Team: Cincinnati Reds
Born: July 24, 1965
 Memphis, TN
Height: 6'3" **Weight:** 210 lbs.
Bats: Right **Throws:** Right
Acquired: Second-round pick,
 6/83 free-agent draft

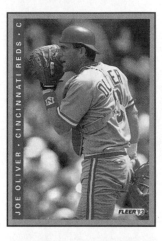

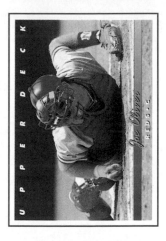

Omar Olivares was the most promising but inconsistent arm on the St. Louis staff in 1992. While he went 5-4 in the first half of '92, he suffered a second-half decline. Overall, he finished at 9-9 with a 3.84 ERA. He was strong against righthanded batters, but lefties ate him alive. His second-half decline was accented by complaints by St. Louis coaches that Olivares wasn't trying hard enough. Belonging to a team loaded with young pitchers, Olivares may be in trouble unless he can reclaim his winning ways from '91. Olivares gained fans in '91, his first full season with the Redbirds. His 11-7 mark came after a May recall from Triple-A Louisville. The Cards obtained the sinker-ball specialist before the '90 season. Olivares first started pro ball in the San Diego organization in '86.

Olivares isn't consistent or dominant enough to make collectors take notice of him or his common-priced cards. Our pick for his best 1993 card is Donruss. We have chosen this card for its technical merits.

Joe Oliver accidentally regained Cincinnati's starting catching job in 1992. When catcher Jeff Reed's season seemed lost due to April elbow surgery, the Reds let the other half of the backstop platoon assume full-time duty. Oliver reached a .270 batting average with 10 homers and 57 RBI for '92. He also struck out more than two times for every free pass he accepted. Behind the plate, he caught 87 potential basestealers, allowing 47 runners success in their theft endeavors. Although Oliver hadn't been this sound or performed this well in several years, don't make the mistake of thinking that he has escaped the part-time trap yet. Reed could be rehabilitated by '93. There is also prospect Dan Wilson in the wings, and he'll soon be ready to challenge for full-time receiving work.

Oliver is a streaky hitter. He seems at the top of his game, which isn't high enough to promote his 1993 commons. Our pick for his best 1993 card is Upper Deck. We have chosen this card because the design lends itself to the best use of the elements.

	W	L	ERA	G	CG	IP	H	ER	BB	SO
92 NL	9	9	3.84	32	1	197.0	189	84	63	124
Life	21	17	3.68	69	1	413.2	382	169	141	235

	BA	G	AB	R	H	2B	3B	HR	RBI	SB
92 NL	.270	143	485	42	131	25	1	10	57	2
Life	.247	407	1269	110	314	67	1	32	173	3

Series two cards from some companies were available at press time. If space allows, both cards are shown; if not, the most up-to-date cards are pictured.

GREG OLSON

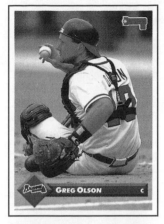

Position: Catcher
Team: Atlanta Braves
Born: September 6, 1960
Marshall, MN
Height: 6' **Weight:** 200 lbs.
Bats: Right **Throws:** Right
Acquired: Signed as a free
agent, 11/89

GREGG OLSON

Position: Pitcher
Team: Baltimore Orioles
Born: October 11, 1966
Omaha, NE
Height: 6'4" **Weight:** 210 lbs.
Bats: Right **Throws:** Right
Acquired: First-round pick,
6/88 free-agent draft

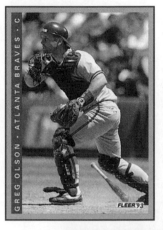

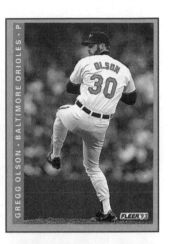

In 1992, his third year as the every-day catcher for the Braves, Greg Olson solidified his reputation as a strong defensive player and clubhouse leader who doesn't deliver much punch. Though he's had past problems with throwing, Olson improved his success rate against basestealers to nearly 40 percent in '92. At the same time, however, his batting average continued its three-year downward spiral. His power production—already minimal—also declined. He had a .316 on-base average and a .328 slugging percentage in 1992. He handles pitchers well and calls a good game. He saves wild pitches better than most of his colleagues, and he blocks the plate well. Olson is also more productive against lefthanded pitchers. At the end of the '92 season, he fractured his leg on a play at the plate, causing him to miss all of the postseason.

Olson needs to be healthy and gain some power before you invest in his '93s. Our pick for his best 1993 card is Fleer. We have chosen this card since its design makes it a standout.

Before yielding a game-tying, ninth-inning homer to Roberto Kelly last June 22, Gregg Olson had converted 19 consecutive save opportunities. His ERA dropped to 1.59 on July 1, 1992. Seven days later, however, he strained a muscle in his side and plunged into a slump. Unable to throw strikes with men on base, he blew his next six of 15 save chances. The youngest pitcher to post 100 saves, Olson averages nearly a strikeout an inning and fewer than eight hits per nine innings. Opponents compiled a .211 batting average, a .287 on-base average, and a .280 slugging percentage against him in '92. He has good control, keeps the ball in the park, and is especially effective at Camden Yards. Olson once worked 41 scoreless innings in a row, a relief record. The former All-American pitched only 16 games in the minors.

If Olson is healthy, he can save 30 or more games a season. If you believe, invest a few dimes in Olson's '93 issues. Our pick for his best 1993 card is Topps. We have chosen this card for the interesting facts included on the reverse.

	BA	G	AB	R	H	2B	3B	HR	RBI	SB
92 NL	.238	95	302	27	72	14	2	3	27	2
Life	.247	331	1013	109	250	51	3	16	107	4

	W	L	ERA	G	SV	IP	H	ER	BB	SO
92 AL	1	5	2.05	60	36	61.1	46	14	24	58
Life	17	19	2.36	270	131	305.1	244	80	140	303

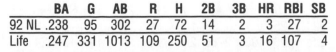

PAUL
O'NEILL

Position: Outfield
Team: New York Yankees
Born: February 25, 1963
    Columbus, OH
Height: 6'4" **Weight:** 215 lbs.
Bats: Left **Throws:** Left
Acquired: Traded from Reds
    with Joe DeBerry for Roberto
    Kelly, 11/92

When a righthander pitched against the Cincinnati Reds, Paul O'Neill usually hit fourth and played right field. In the first half of 1992, his power production sank as he was platooned with Glenn Braggs. O'Neill's overall '92 efforts netted a .246 batting average, 14 homers, and 66 RBI. He also took a pass 77 times while striking out on 85 different occasions. It took seven years of work for O'Neill, now with the Yankees, to become a big league regular. After several seasons of shuttling between Cincinnati and Triple-A, O'Neill hit 16 homers in 145 games for the '88 Reds. His power production stayed constant until '91, when batting tips from then-manager Lou Piniella helped O'Neill realize his potential. That season, he led the team with 28 homers, 91 RBI, 36 doubles, and 73 walks. That same year, O'Neill, who once pitched in a lopsided game, also led Reds outfielders with 13 assists in '91.

O'Neill cards are marginal choices at a dime apiece. Our pick for his best 1993 card is Fleer. We have chosen this card for its artistic presentation.

	BA	G	AB	R	H	2B	3B	HR	RBI	SB
92 NL	.246	148	496	59	122	19	1	14	66	6
Life	.259	799	2618	321	679	147	7	96	411	61

JOSE
OQUENDO

Position: Second base/
    shortstop
Team: St. Louis Cardinals
Born: July 4, 1963 Rio Piedras,
    Puerto Rico
Height: 5'10" **Weight:** 160 lbs.
Bats: Both **Throws:** Right
Acquired: Traded from Mets
    with Mark Davis for Argenis
    Salazar and John Young,
    4/85

Injuries ruined Jose Oquendo's season in 1992. First, he suffered a partial dislocation of the left shoulder that cost him seven weeks of playing time. After returning in June, he was sidelined with a heel spur that kept him out longer than expected. As a result, the Cardinals tried Geronimo Pena, Luis Alicea, and Rex Hudler at second base, Oquendo's best position. The versatile Oquendo, who once pitched four relief innings in an extra-inning game, also plays a fine game at shortstop. A patient contact hitter, he walks more often than he strikes out. For the 14 games he did play in '92, he hit .257 in 35 at-bats with a .350 on-base average and a .400 slugging percentage. Although he doesn't translate his speed into steals, Oquendo has fine range at both short and second, plus a strong arm. He makes very few errors (a record-low three at second base in '90).

Resist Oquendo's '93s. Unhealthy, he's a risk. Our pick for his best 1993 card is Donruss. We have chosen this card due to its unique photographic approach.

	BA	G	AB	R	H	2B	3B	HR	RBI	SB
92 NL	.257	14	35	3	9	3	1	0	3	0
Life	.261	1001	2780	288	726	94	19	12	224	33

Series two cards from some companies were available at press time. If space allows, both cards are shown; if not, the most up-to-date cards are pictured.

JOE ORSULAK

Position: Outfield
Team: New York Mets
Born: May 31, 1962
   Glen Ridge, NJ
Height: 6'1" **Weight:** 210 lbs.
Bats: Left **Throws:** Left
Acquired: Signed as a free
   agent, 12/92

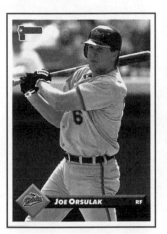 

 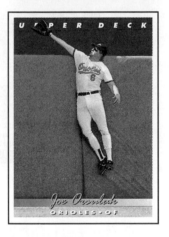

Joe Orsulak's 1992 efforts offered few improvements from his '91 marks. He shared right field with young slugger Chito Martinez and celebrated his fifth and last season with Baltimore. Signing with the New York Mets for '93, the New Jersey native may have escaped extinction for now. Last season, he accumulated a .289 batting average with only four homers and 39 RBI. Throughout the '92 season, Orsulak's batting average on the road or against righthanders hovered around .300. Although he's become best known for his outfield defense and throwing ability, Orsulak posted career bests of 11 homers and 57 RBI with the '90 Orioles.

Orsulak, due to his infrequent homers, won't find much better luck with the Mets. Even a new uniform may not spell full-time playing status for the lefty. It won't help the value of his common-priced cards, either. Our pick for his best 1993 card is Upper Deck. We have chosen this card because it has a distinctive look.

	BA	G	AB	R	H	2B	3B	HR	RBI	SB
92 AL	.289	117	391	45	113	18	3	4	39	5
Life	.278	930	2935	384	817	131	29	37	265	82

JUNIOR ORTIZ

Position: Catcher
Team: Cleveland Indians
Born: October 24, 1959
   Humacao, Puerto Rico
Height: 5'11" **Weight:** 176 lbs.
Bats: Right **Throws:** Right
Acquired: Signed as free agent,
   12/91

In 11 major league seasons, Ortiz has established several predictable patterns. He rarely homers, walks, or steals a base, but he makes contact often enough to produce a respectable career batting average. He also supplies solid defense whenever he's called upon in his role as backup catcher. Playing behind Sandy Alomar at Cleveland in '92, Ortiz hit 30 points below his lifetime average but did nail 33 percent of the runners who tried to steal against him. He handled the club's young pitchers well, saved wild pitches, and blocked the plate when necessary. A line-drive singles hitter who fares better against righthanders, Ortiz had a .296 on-base average and a .279 slugging percentage in '92. He once hit .335 for Minnesota in '90 and .336 for Pittsburgh in '86. He began his professional career in '77.

His time is running out. It's unlikely that he'll unseat Alomar. Unless Ortiz should win an everyday job, pass on his '93s. Our pick for his best 1993 card is Topps. We have chosen this card because of its overall appeal and pleasing looks.

	BA	G	AB	R	H	2B	3B	HR	RBI	SB
92 AL	.250	86	244	20	61	7	0	0	24	1
Life	.260	625	1569	120	408	56	4	5	157	7

JOHN ORTON

Position: Catcher
Team: California Angels
Born: December 8, 1965
　　Santa Cruz, CA
Height: 6'1" **Weight:** 192 lbs.
Bats: Right **Throws:** Right
Acquired: First-round pick,
　　6/87 free-agent draft

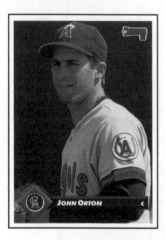

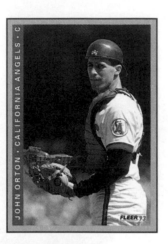

DONOVAN OSBORNE

Position: Pitcher
Team: St. Louis Cardinals
Born: June 21, 1969
　　Roseville, CA
Height: 6'2" **Weight:** 195 lbs.
Bats: Both **Throws:** Left
Acquired: First-round pick,
　　6/90 free-agent draft

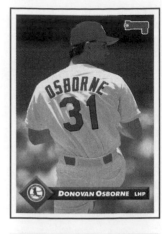

John Orton had a shot at California's backstop job in 1992, but couldn't hit well enough to win the post or stay in the majors. When veteran receiver Lance Parrish was released at midseason, Orton did not capitalize on the opening and wound up splitting another year between Anaheim and Triple-A Edmonton. His already meager '92 batting average of .219 dropped almost 100 points when a southpaw was on the mound. A notable strength, though, is the fact that he ranked among the top in the league (45%) in catching potential basestealers. Orton has bounced between the Pacific Coast League and the bigs since '89. Each time, however, he fails to survive offensively with the Halos. Although the starting catcher's job is within Orton's reach, late-season acquisition Greg Myers could contest for the spot.

Until he learns to hit left-handed pitching, Orton will only dream of full-time work. Don't risk your pennies on his 1993 commons. Our pick for his best 1993 card is Upper Deck. We have chosen this card for its technical merits.

The 13th overall pick in the country proved to be a lucky one for the Cardinals. Donovan Osborne flew through the Redbird farm system to become a member of the rotation within two years. Making 34 appearances in games for the Cards in '92, Osborne posted a very respectable 11-9 record with a 3.77 ERA. The southpaw struck out 104 of the batters he faced over his 179 innings of work. He has made an impression with his savvy, control, and changeup. He still needs to work on intimidating lefthanders and keeping the ball in the park. Still, he deserves credit for being a leader on the staff at his age. Osborne was part of a play that summed up an early-season injury blitz in '92. While fielding a bunt by Vince Coleman, Osborne injured an ankle. Coleman hurt his hamstring on the same play. *Baseball America* included Osborne in its top 10 Texas League prospects in '91.

Osborne's 1993 cards are upbeat buys at 10 to 15 cents apiece. Our pick for his best 1993 card is Score. We have chosen this card for the interesting facts included on the reverse.

	BA	G	AB	R	H	2B	3B	HR	RBI	SB
92 AL	.219	43	114	11	25	3	0	2	12	1
Life	.203	119	306	30	62	13	0	3	25	1

	W	L	ERA	G	CG	IP	H	ER	BB	SO
92 NL	11	9	3.77	34	0	179.0	193	75	38	104
Life	11	9	3.77	34	0	179.0	193	75	38	104

AL
OSUNA

Position: Pitcher
Team: Houston Astros
Born: August 10, 1965
  Inglewood, CA
Height: 6'3" **Weight:** 200 lbs.
Bats: Right **Throws:** Left
Acquired: 16th-round pick,
  6/87 free-agent draft

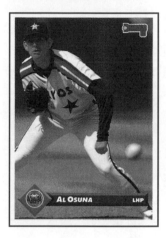

What a difference a year makes. Unfortunately for Al Osuna, the difference was not a pleasant one. Osuna fell from Houston's closer role to meaningless middle relief. At the end of the '92 campaign, Osuna owned a 6-3 record, 4.23 ERA, and no saves even though he had appeared in 66 games. His total innings of work for Houston added up to only 61 ⅔, less than one inning per appearance. Things were different in '91. That season his 12 saves were tops from the Astro bullpen, along with 71 appearances. However, that was before the arrival of super-stopper Doug Jones. Throughout the '92 season, Osuna failed to keep his strikeout total (37) higher than his walks (38). By contrast, the California native struck out 68 batters in 81 innings with the '91 'Stros.

Osuna won't be a major factor in Houston's 1993 bullpen plans. His '93 cards aren't going to grow from their current nickel values. Our pick for his best 1993 card is Topps. We have chosen this card for its technical merits.

	W	L	ERA	G	SV	IP	H	ER	BB	SO
92 NL	6	3	4.23	66	0	61.2	52	29	38	37
Life	15	9	3.84	149	12	154.2	121	66	90	111

SPIKE
OWEN

Position: Shortstop
Team: New York Yankees
Born: April 19, 1961
  Cleburne, TX
Height: 5'10" **Weight:** 170 lbs.
Bats: Both **Throws:** Right
Acquired: Signed as a free
  agent, 12/92

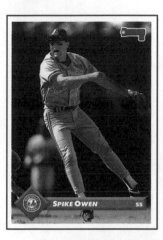

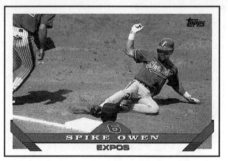

Even though he played in fewer games than he has in years past, Spike Owen upped his offensive production with the 1992 Expos. His season, interrupted by a groin pull and stiff neck, still culminated in the highest annual home run total in his 11-year pro career. He hit at a .291 clip when playing on the road and hit almost that well against lefties. Another striking stat from his '92 season is the fact that his nine errors were substantially below that of the NL average for shortstops. He also demonstrated a judicious batting eye in taking 50 walks and striking out only 30 times in his 386 at-bats in '92. The Yankees decided they could use a good glove like Owen in their lineup, so they signed him late in '92. In '91, Owen batted .255 with three home runs and 26 RBI in 139 games.

Unless Owen realizes a full-time job with the Yankees in '93, his card values will evaporate. His common-priced cards don't pass muster. Our pick for his best 1993 card is Topps. We have chosen this card because it has a distinctive look.

	BA	G	AB	R	H	2B	3B	HR	RBI	SB
92 NL	.269	122	386	52	104	16	3	7	40	9
Life	.243	1277	4110	499	1000	173	52	40	354	74

MIKE PAGLIARULO

Position: Third base
Team: Minnesota Twins
Born: March 15, 1960
Medford, MA
Height: 6'2" **Weight:** 195 lbs.
Bats: Left **Throws:** Right
Acquired: Signed as a free
agent, 1/91

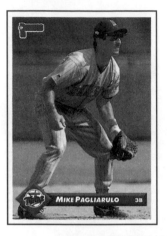

Mike Pagliarulo, part-time Twins third baseman, did not have an impressive 1992. Granted, he missed more than half the season due to two April injuries. Pagliarulo needed surgery during spring training to repair an eardrum. He was subsequently back on the disabled list in April '92, after breaking his right wrist. This time he was out for three months. By that time, replacement Scott Leius had made Pags but a memory at the hot corner. Instead of repeating his '91 work of batting a career-high .279, Pagliarulo rode the bench. Pagliarulo couldn't hit his weight against lefthanders, while Leius was hitting in the mid-.300s against lefties. For '92, Pagliarulo hit .200 with only 21 hits in 105 at-bats. He hit a career-high 32 blasts in '87.

These days, Pags lags as a card investment choice. His injuries and platoon work are statistics killers which sap the strength from his '93 commons. Our pick for his best 1993 card is Upper Deck. We have chosen this card since the photograph captures the athletic ability of the player.

	BA	G	AB	R	H	2B	3B	HR	RBI	SB
92 AL	.200	42	105	10	21	4	0	0	9	1
Life	.235	1044	3290	380	774	165	14	121	434	12

TOM PAGNOZZI

Position: Catcher
Team: St. Louis Cardinals
Born: July 30, 1962
Tucson, AZ
Height: 6'1" **Weight:** 190 lbs.
Bats: Right **Throws:** Right
Acquired: Eighth-round pick,
6/83 free-agent draft

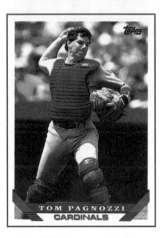

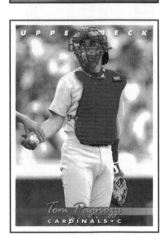

Tom Pagnozzi discovered a new power source in 1992, exceeding his four-year homer totals in a single season. Perhaps being a starter has put new zip in Pagnozzi's bat. Although he's been with the club since '87, Pags didn't see serious starting time until '91. After Card manager Joe Torre moved then-backstop Todd Zeile to third, Pagnozzi repaid the vote of confidence. In '91, Pagnozzi played in over 100 games for the first time in his career and snagged a Gold Glove in the process. He was able to keep that momentum going in '92, hitting .250 with new highs in doubles (26), and homers (7). He did not disappoint with his defensive abilities, either. Proving that he was in top form in '92, Pagnozzi made only one error for the entire season.

Pagnozzi may be a better all-around catcher than Zeile could have been. However, his modest power will keep him from becoming a hero among hobbyists. Decline his 1993 commons. Our pick for his best 1993 card is Donruss. We have chosen this card for its technical merits.

	BA	G	AB	R	H	2B	3B	HR	RBI	SB
92 NL	.249	139	485	33	121	26	3	7	44	2
Life	.255	508	1487	119	379	77	8	13	151	13

RAFAEL PALMEIRO

Position: First base
Team: Texas Rangers
Born: September 24, 1964
Havana, Cuba
Height: 6′ **Weight:** 180 lbs.
Bats: Left **Throws:** Left
Acquired: Traded from Cubs
with Drew Hall and Jamie
Moyer for Mitch Williams,
Paul Kilgus, Curt Wilkerson,
and Steve Wilson, 12/88

DEAN PALMER

Position: Third base
Team: Texas Rangers
Born: December 27, 1968
Tallahassee, FL
Height: 6′2″ **Weight:** 195 lbs.
Bats: Right **Throws:** Right
Acquired: Third-round pick,
6/86 free-agent draft

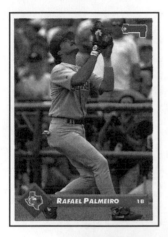

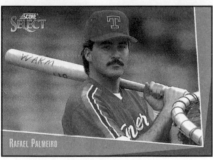

Rafael Palmeiro may never win a batting crown but he could figure to be a perennial challenger. He got off to a slow start in '92 but showed signs of regaining his former status with a four-hit game against Minnesota on June 4. Due to his stumble out of the gate, Palmeiro's figures dipped a bit in '92—most noticeably in his batting average and doubles—but he was still a formidable force for the Rangers. It would have been difficult to top his '91 production. That season, he hit career peaks with a .322 average, 26 homers, 88 runs batted in, and a best-in-baseball 49 doubles. Once criticized as an opposite-field singles hitter, the Cuban-born first baseman improved both his average and power production in each of his first three seasons with the Rangers.

Invest here, but only at a dime per card. In the 1988 Fleer set, Palmeiro is an asset at $1.25. Our pick for his best 1993 card is Score. We have chosen this card for the superior presentation of information on its back.

Dean Palmer needed only one full season in the bigs to prove his muscle. The Rangers drafted Palmer following his '86 Florida high school graduation. After a 5 ½-year journey through the minors, Palmer showed that he may handle the hot corner in Texas into the next century. In '92, he bested the career-high 25 home runs he belted with Double-A Tulsa in '89. He also knocked in 72 RBI during his 541 at-bats for the Rangers in '92. His success, however, wasn't universal. Palmer was the first American Leaguer to reach 150 strikeouts. In '91, Texas handed Palmer the third base job outright in the last month of the season, after swapping resident third sacker Steve Buechele to Pittsburgh. Palmer's '91 totals included 15 homers and 37 RBI in 81 games.

If Palmer's longball sideshows continue, he will receive the recognition he deserves in 1993. Buy his nickel-priced cards before it's too late for a bargain. Our pick for his best 1993 card is Donruss. We have chosen this card because of its overall appeal and pleasing looks.

	BA	G	AB	R	H	2B	3B	HR	RBI	SB
92 AL	.268	159	608	84	163	27	4	22	85	2
Life	.296	886	3270	463	968	194	23	95	421	28

	BA	G	AB	R	H	2B	3B	HR	RBI	SB
92 AL	.229	152	541	74	124	25	0	26	72	10
Life	.213	249	828	112	176	36	2	41	110	10

JEFF PARRETT

Position: Pitcher
Team: Oakland Athletics
Born: August 26, 1961
  Indianapolis, IN
Height: 6'3" **Weight:** 193 lbs.
Bats: Right **Throws:** Right
Acquired: Signed as a free
  agent, 2/92

LANCE PARRISH

Position: Catcher
Team: Los Angeles Dodgers
Born: June 15, 1956
  McKeesport, PA
Height: 6'3" **Weight:** 224 lbs.
Bats: Right **Throws:** Right
Acquired: Signed as a free
  agent, 1/93

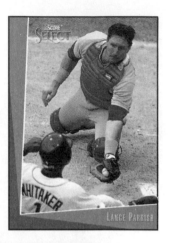

Jeff Parrett erased a two-year slump with a banner season out of the 1992 Athletics bullpen. Parrett, who had been with Atlanta since mid-1990, had been less than successful during his time with the Braves. In '92, Parrett won nine of his first 10 decisions with the A's. For the entire '92 season, Parrett posted a 3.02 ERA and 19 holds to highlight his 9-1 record. Over the course of his 66 appearances for the A's in '92, he finished 14 of those games and struck out 78 along the way. The journeyman hurler spent his first full season in the bigs with the Expos in '88. There he notched some career highlights, including six saves and 12 wins in 61 games. Traded to Philadelphia in '89, he captured another dozen victories in 72 appearances.

Middle relievers can never count on opportunities for wins or saves. Parrett will face an inevitable slip in his 1993 stats, causing his common-priced cards to fade fast. Our pick for his best 1993 card is Score. We have chosen this card for its technical merits.

Lance Parrish got the shock of his career in June 1992. After going on the disabled list with a bruised hand, he was released by the Angels. Less than a week later, he was signed by the Mariners. Parrish worked as a catcher, first baseman, and designated hitter for the M's. In '92, he logged 12 homers and 32 RBI though his batting average tumbled to .233. A 16-year major league veteran, Parrish strikes out almost three times as many times as he walks. His '92 campaign was no different, as he whiffed 70 times, accepting only 24 passes. Parrish, now with the Dodgers for '93, has hit 10 or more homers in 15 consecutive seasons. The three-time Gold Glove winner and eight time All-Star was signed out of high school by Detroit in '74.

Parrish is a far-fetched hope for the Hall of Fame. He's likely to serve as a reserve in '93. His common-priced cards are questionable investments. Our pick for his best 1993 card is Score. We have chosen this card because it has a distinctive look.

	W	L	ERA	G	SV	IP	H	ER	BB	SO
92 AL	9	1	3.02	66	0	98.1	81	33	42	78
Life	46	30	3.65	341	21	508.0	459	206	241	415

	BA	G	AB	R	H	2B	3B	HR	RBI	SB
92 AL	.233	93	275	26	64	13	1	12	32	1
Life	.253	1868	6743	829	1708	290	27	316	1030	26

DAN PASQUA

Position: Outfield
Team: Chicago White Sox
Born: October 17, 1961
Yonkers, NY
Height: 6′ **Weight:** 205 lbs.
Bats: Left **Throws:** Left
Acquired: Traded from Yankees
with Steve Rosenberg and
Mark Salas for Scott Nielsen
and Richard Dotson, 11/87

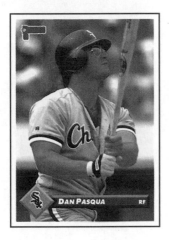
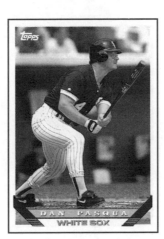

BOB PATTERSON

Position: Pitcher
Team: Texas Rangers
Born: May 16, 1959
Jacksonville, FL
Height: 6′2″ **Weight:** 192 lbs.
Bats: Right **Throws:** Left
Acquired: Signed as a free
agent, 12/92

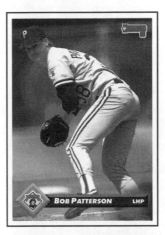
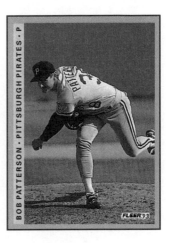

Dan Pasqua was a spotty contributor to the 1992 White Sox, showing only flashes of his past success. He batted .219 against righties as compared to .111 against southpaws. The huge difference explains his career as a platoon player. By season's end, Pasqua had seen his batting average tumble to .211, his lowest since '85. Pasqua's six home runs in '92 also marked the first time he had failed to reach double digits in homers in seven seasons. In '91, just one year earlier, Pasqua compiled 18 homers and a career-high 66 RBI. With the White Sox in '88, Pasqua's round-tripper total climbed as high as 20. With Chicago's increasingly crowded outfield picture, Pasqua will be on shaky ground in '93.

Due to his consistent failure against left-handed pitching, Pasqua won't be a starter with the White Sox or any other team in '93. Beware of his common-priced cards. Our pick for his best 1993 card is Topps. We have chosen this card because of its great combination of photography and design.

Bob Patterson reached a career high in saves while working out of the 1992 Pirates bullpen. The Texas Rangers, noting his success, decided to take advantage of Patterson's free agency and signed him at the end of '92. Last season, he bolstered the left side of the relief corps for the Bucs, taking pressure off rookie lefty relievers Steve Cooke and Denny Neagle. His efforts yielded a 6-3 record with a 2.92 ERA, nine saves, and ten holds. He scattered 64 ⅔ innings of work over 60 games. He struck out 43 of the 268 batters he faced and walked 23. Previously, Patterson's most productive season was '90, when he was 8-5 with five saves in 55 appearances. He had been a member of the Pirates organization since '86.

Patterson's age, limited opportunities to earn wins or saves, and tall shadow cast by talented teammates pose three strikes against his common-priced cards. Don't invest. Our pick for his best 1993 card is Donruss. We have chosen this card for its artistic presentation.

	BA	G	AB	R	H	2B	3B	HR	RBI	SB
92 AL	.211	93	265	26	56	16	1	6	33	0
Life	.247	816	2421	317	597	117	14	110	366	5

	W	L	ERA	G	SV	IP	H	ER	BB	SO
92 NL	6	3	2.92	60	9	64.2	59	21	23	43
Life	25	21	4.22	210	17	335.0	348	157	97	238

JOHN PATTERSON

Position: Infield
Team: San Francisco Giants
Born: February 11, 1967
  Key West, FL
Height: 5'9" **Weight:** 160 lbs.
Bats: Both **Throws:** Right
Acquired: 23rd-round pick,
  6/88 free agent draft

John Patterson began the 1992 season with the Giants, making the jump all the way from Double-A. His stay, however, lasted only a few weeks. During his time with the Giants in '92, he logged some innings at second base and filled in as a pinch hitter. In the 103 at-bats he took in the bigs in '92, he accrued 19 hits. He did markedly better against lefties, hitting .240 when there was a southpaw on the mound. Patterson will likely get more playing time in the majors. In '91, he batted .295 and led Double-A Shreveport to their league title. He went 1-for-2 in the Double-A All-Star Game in '91, too. He finished that season by ranking second in the league with 13 triples and 40 stolen bases and was selected by managers as the league's top defensive second baseman.

Robby Thompson, San Fran's incumbent second sacker, doesn't need to worry just yet. Patterson's hitting won't sell many of his 1993 cards, even at a nickel apiece. Our pick for his best 1993 card is Donruss. We have chosen this card because the design lends itself to the best use of the elements.

	BA	G	AB	R	H	2B	3B	HR	RBI	SB
92 NL	.184	32	103	10	19	1	1	0	4	5
Life	.184	32	103	10	19	1	1	0	4	5

ROGER PAVLIK

Position: Pitcher
Team: Texas Rangers
Born: October 4, 1967
  Houston, TX
Height: 6'3" **Weight:** 220 lbs.
Bats: Right **Throws:** Right
Acquired: Second-round pick,
  6/86 free-agent draft

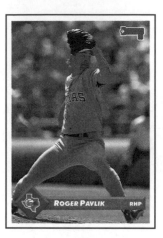

Roger Pavlik made his major league debut May 2, 1992, allowing one hit in six innings. However, he also walked six, demonstrating that there is still room for improvement. This hurt him in a long-awaited shot at the majors. For his '92 efforts with the Rangers, he earned a 4-4 record, hauling a hefty 4.21 ERA behind him. He did manage to strike out 45 of the 275 batters he faced and caught eight of the 11 runners who tried to steal on him. It took Pavlik six years in the minors to get the call in '92, but he was sent back down for more seasoning. Pavlik fought through arm trouble in '91. Playing for Triple-A Oklahoma City, he missed more than three months due to a sprained ligament in his elbow. He also had soreness in his right forearm but, after doing rehab over the winter, was ready for the '92 season.

Pavlik could stick in 1993. So could his cards, which look inexpensive at a dime apiece. Our pick for his best 1993 card is Donruss. We have chosen this card for its technical merits.

	W	L	ERA	G	SV	IP	H	ER	BB	SO
92 AAA	7	5	2.98	18	0	117.2	—	39	51	104
92 AL	4	4	4.21	13	1	62	66	29	34	45

Series two cards from some companies were available at press time. If space allows, both cards are shown; if not, the most up-to-date cards are pictured.

BILL PECOTA

Position: Third base
Team: Atlanta Braves
Born: February 12, 1960
   Redwood City, CA
Height: 6'2" **Weight:** 190 lbs.
Bats: Right **Throws:** Right
Acquired: Signed as a free
   agent, 1/93

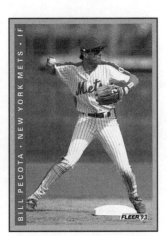

Bill Pecota returned from a year of full-time glory to become a Mets utilityman in 1992. Once thought of as the ultimate, pre-Kevin Seitzer replacement for George Brett at third base, Pecota never got extended opportunities with the Royals before '91. Then, when Seitzer broke his hand in early '91, Pecota became a regular third sacker. As a result, Pecota's six homers, 45 RBI, 16 stolen bases, and .286 batting average in '91 marked major league highs. His '92 efforts included more typical Pecota stats of a .227 average, two homers, 26 RBI, and nine swipes. For '93, he'll join the Atlanta Braves. Pecota debuted in Kansas City in '86. During his major league career, Pecota has appeared at all nine positions.

Pecota is an over-30 player without a full-time job. His part-time work, even with the Braves, won't make his common-priced cards friendly to investors. Our pick for his best 1993 card is Fleer. We have chosen this card due to the outstanding photographic composition.

	BA	G	AB	R	H	2B	3B	HR	RBI	SB
92 NL	.227	117	269	28	61	13	0	2	26	9
Life	.248	562	1353	195	336	65	10	20	127	50

ALEJANDRO PENA

Position: Pitcher
Team: Pittsburgh Pirates
Born: June 25, 1959
   Cambiaso, Dominican
   Republic
Height: 6'1" **Weight:** 203 lbs.
Bats: Right **Throws:** Right
Acquired: Signed as a free
   agent, 12/92

Alejandro Pena suffered a natural letdown following his season-ending 1991 heroics. Although he matched the combined 15 saves he earned with the Mets and Braves in '91, Pena wasn't well enough in '92 to improve on those marks. With a troublesome right elbow, he went on the DL August 21 and saw little action during the closing days of the pennant drive. When closer Jeff Reardon joined Atlanta during the last month of '92 to help the ailing stopper, Pena's future with the Braves became foggy. Pena joined Atlanta on August 29, 1991. He provided a 2-0 record, 11 saves, and 1.40 ERA, followed by three saves in NCLS play against Pittsburgh in '91. They must have remembered him, as the Bucs signed Pena to a free-agent deal late in '92. Pena debuted with Los Angeles in '81.

Pena's unclear responsibilities with the Pirates and his age are two reasons not to invest in his 1993 common-priced cards. Our pick for his best 1993 card is Topps. We have chosen this card due to the outstanding photographic composition.

	W	L	ERA	G	SV	IP	H	ER	BB	SO
92 NL	1	6	4.07	41	15	42.0	40	19	13	34
Life	50	48	2.95	433	67	969.2	878	318	301	743

GERONIMO PENA

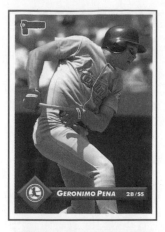

Position: Infield
Team: St. Louis Cardinals
Born: March 29, 1967
  Distrito Nacional,
  Dominican Republic
Height: 6'1" **Weight:** 195 LBS.
Bats: Both **Throws:** Right
Acquired: Signed as a free
  agent, 8/84

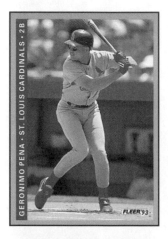

A broken collarbone and a sore shoulder couldn't stop Geronimo Pena from attaining some classy stats with the 1992 Cardinals. In 203 at-bats in '92, he collected 12 doubles, seven homers, 31 RBI, and 13 stolen bases, posting a .305 batting average. The only reason Pena returned to Triple-A Louisville was for medical rehab that ended in mid-August. Pena spent the bulk of his six minor league seasons playing second base. In a failed attempt to switch to third base in '90, he committed 20 of his 27 errors at the hot corner. He debuted with the Redbirds in '90. In '91, he batted .243 in 143 games, adding five homers, 17 RBI, and 15 steals in 20 attempts. Pena, a switchhitter, has hit home runs batting both lefthanded and righthanded.

Could Pena sustain his offensive might for an entire season? If he gets the chance to expand on his 1992 success, his cards will offer surprise bonuses. Take a shot on a few of his 1993 commons. Our pick for his best 1993 card is Topps. We have chosen this card for its technical merits.

	BA	G	AB	R	H	2B	3B	HR	RBI	SB
92 NL	.305	62	203	31	62	12	1	7	31	13
Life	.273	184	433	74	118	22	4	12	50	29

TONY PENA

Position: Catcher
Team: Boston Red Sox
Born: June 4, 1957
  Monte Cristi,
  Dominican Republic
Height: 6' **Weight:** 185 lbs.
Bats: Right **Throws:** Right
Acquired: Signed as a free
  agent, 11/89

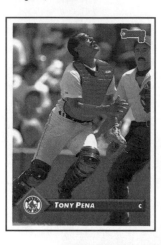

Tony Pena caught more than 100 games for the 11th consecutive season in 1992. However, the Red Sox receiver didn't accomplish much offensively, being another contributor to Boston's dismal finish. In '91, Pena batted .231 with five homers and 48 RBI. He won his fourth Gold Glove that year, too. His stats were virtually the same for '92, but the Gold Glove went to Ivan Rodriguez. Active in pro ball since '76, Pena became a Pittsburgh regular in '81. Between the Bucs and BoSox, Pena served the Cardinals from 1987-89. After batting .214 in '87, he adopted eyeglasses and hit .409 in the World Series. He's reached double figures in home runs six times in his career (capped by consecutive 15-homer seasons in 1983-84) and been on five All-Star teams.

Defensive stars seldom have popular cards. Pena's defense may hold, but his offense has been shrinking seasonally. Don't start with his 1993 common-priced cards. Our pick for his best 1993 card is Upper Deck. We have chosen this card because it has a distinctive look.

	BA	G	AB	R	H	2B	3B	HR	RBI	SB
92 AL	.241	133	410	39	99	21	1	1	38	3
Life	.267	1624	5550	584	1481	256	26	95	614	78

Series two cards from some companies were available at press time. If space allows, both cards are shown; if not, the most up-to-date cards are pictured.

TERRY PENDLETON

Position: Third base
Team: Atlanta Braves
Born: July 16, 1960
Los Angeles, CA
Height: 5′9″ **Weight:** 178 lbs.
Bats: Both **Throws:** Right
Acquired: Signed as a free
agent, 12/90

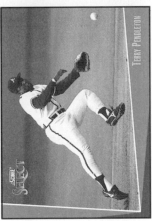

When experts suggested Terry Pendleton could never duplicate his 1991 career year that included a .319 average and 22 home runs, he wasted little time in proving them wrong. For the '92 campaign, Pendleton batted .311 with 21 homers, 105 RBI, and 39 doubles. Once again, his performance for the Braves helped them to the postseason. A durable performer who plays even when hurt, Pendleton was bothered during the '92 campaign by severe knee problems. He stayed in the lineup, however, and won a berth on the NL All-Star team for the first time in his nine-year career. In '90, the switch-hitting third baseman blossomed into a batting champion and MVP in his first year with Atlanta. His leadership, coupled with his sterling offense and defense, led the Braves out of last place in '90 all the way to first in '91.

Mr. MVP is a great card deal at 15 cents per card. Pendleton's 1985 Topps Rookie may be had for as low as $2. Our pick for his best 1993 card is Upper Deck. We have chosen this card due to its unique photographic approach.

	BA	G	AB	R	H	2B	3B	HR	RBI	SB
92 NL	.311	160	640	98	199	39	1	21	105	5
Life	.273	1240	4659	596	1274	228	33	87	633	114

MELIDO PEREZ

Position: Pitcher
Team: New York Yankees
Born: February 15, 1966
San Cristobal,
Dominican Republic
Height: 6′4″ **Weight:** 180 lbs.
Bats: Right **Throws:** Right
Acquired: Traded from White
Sox with Domingo Jean and
Bob Wickman for Steve Sax,
1/92

Even though the 1992 Yankees fell out of the pennant race early, Melido Perez chased another title down to the wire. His 218 strikeouts finished second only to Randy Johnson's 241 in the American League. In addition to his strikeout total, Perez earned other career highs in '92. For his 33 starts in '92, Perez went 13-16 with a 2.87 ERA over 247 ⅔ innings. Previously, he had never pitched more than 197 innings in a season. Perez started his pro career in the Kansas City organization in '84, debuting with the Royals in '87. The lanky righthander first joined Chicago in '88, going 12-10. In '90, when he ended the year at 13-14, Perez tossed a six-inning, rain-abbreviated no-hitter against the Yankees. His success in '92 was a contrast to his '91 efforts as a White Sox reliever.

If New York's offense improves in 1993, Perez will be that much better. His nickel-priced cards are investments worth pondering. Our pick for his best 1993 card is Topps. We have chosen this card because of its overall appeal and pleasing looks.

	W	L	ERA	G	SV	IP	H	ER	BB	SO
92 AL	13	16	2.87	33	10	247.2	212	79	93	218
Life	58	62	3.90	183	18	971.0	891	421	398	791

Series two cards from some companies were available at press time. If space allows, both cards are shown; if not, the most up-to-date cards are pictured.

233

MIKE
PEREZ

Position: Pitcher
Team: St. Louis Cardinals
Born: October 19, 1964
Yauco, Puerto Rico
Height: 6' **Weight:** 185 lbs.
Bats: Right **Throws:** Right
Acquired: 12th-round pick,
6/86 free-agent draft

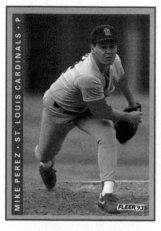

Mike Perez was yet another reason the Cardinals kept one of the National League's best bullpens in 1992. The righthander looked like a new pitcher, just one year after he was blown out of the National League. For his '92 efforts, he put together a 9-3 record with a 1.84 ERA. He made appearances in 77 games for the Redbirds in '92, throwing in a total of 93 innings. One year earlier, in '91, Perez made the Cardinals' Opening-Day roster. By May 13, however, he was back in the American Association, due to an 0-2 record and a 5.82 ERA. His '90 premier with the Redbirds had been promising. He posted a 1-0 record, one save, and 3.95 ERA in 13 games. During his career in the minors, Perez won league save titles at each level.

Working with Lee Smith would overshadow nearly any reliever, especially a young one like Perez. Be cautious about spending more than a nickel apiece on his 1993 cards. Our pick for his best 1993 card is Upper Deck. We have chosen this card because it has a distinctive look.

	W	L	ERA	G	SV	IP	H	ER	BB	SO
92 NL	9	3	1.84	77	0	93.0	70	19	32	46
Life	10	5	2.62	104	1	123.2	101	36	42	58

GENO
PETRALLI

Position: Catcher
Team: Texas Rangers
Born: September 25, 1959
Sacramento, CA
Height: 6'2" **Weight:** 180 lbs.
Bats: Left **Throws:** Right
Acquired: Signed as a free
agent, 5/85

Although Geno Petralli carried a 10-year average of .278 into the 1992 campaign, the advent of Ivan Rodriguez sharply curtailed his playing time. Rusting on the bench, he suffered through the worst season of his career. Never a robust hitter against southpaws, he didn't do much with righthanders either. Petralli has no power or speed. In '92, he had a .274 on-base average and a .276 slugging percentage. When he plays enough to stay sharp, Petralli makes fairly good contact. But he doesn't have the patience to wait for walks. In fact, the only thing keeping him in the major leagues is his versatility. In addition to being a lefty-hitting catcher, Petralli can play second and third base in a pinch. He is only average behind the plate. He's a good game-caller with a mediocre arm.

A utilityman with little punch and an average glove are signs that you should not pick up the veteran's '93s. Our pick for his best 1993 card is Donruss. We have chosen this card due to its unique photographic approach.

	BA	G	AB	R	H	2B	3B	HR	RBI	SB
92 AL	.198	94	192	11	38	12	0	1	18	0
Life	.269	750	1741	168	469	78	9	23	179	6

Series two cards from some companies were available at press time. If space allows, both cards are shown; if not, the most up-to-date cards are pictured.

TONY PHILLIPS

Position: Second base
Team: Detroit Tigers
Born: April 25, 1959
Atlanta, GA
Height: 5'10" **Weight:** 175 lbs.
Bats: Both **Throws:** Right
Acquired: Signed as a free
agent, 12/89

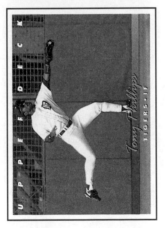

Detroit's Tony Phillips was one of the American League's most selective hitters in 1992. At season's end, his 114 free passes trailed only Baltimore's Mickey Tettleton and Chicago's Frank Thomas. Phillips reached his second consecutive season of double-digit homers, too. Defensively, he played everything but first base, catcher, and pitcher for the Tigers in '92. His first season in Detroit was '90, when he set career highs of 17 homers, 72 RBI, and a .284 average. From 1982 through '89, Phillips was with the Athletics and was regarded as Oakland's tenth man. His speed and versatile glove work kept him somewhere in the lineup regularly. Phillips has been in pro ball since '78, when he was the 10th player in the nation chosen that year.

Phillips can't be expected to have valued cards, as long as he bounces around the Bengal lineup. Even with his tidy offensive stats, don't assume his 1993 commons will bring profits. Our pick for his best 1993 card is Fleer. We have chosen this card due to the outstanding photographic composition.

	BA	G	AB	R	H	2B	3B	HR	RBI	SB
92 AL	.276	159	606	114	167	32	3	10	64	12
Life	.259	1292	4331	652	1120	190	37	68	450	97

MIKE PIAZZA

Position: Catcher
Team: Los Angeles Dodgers
Born: September 4, 1968
Norristown, PA
Height: 6'3" **Weight:** 200 lbs.
Bats: Right **Throws:** Right
Acquired: 62nd-round pick,
6/88 free-agent draft

Mike Piazza may have gone from godson to godsend. Tommy Lasorda is the young man's godfather. It was his talent, however, that got him to the majors. Piazza has become one of the top power prospects in the Los Angeles organization. He put up some big numbers in 1992, including a .441 on-base average and a .658 slugging average at Double-A San Antonio. For his '92 appearances in Triple-A, he had a .405 on-base average and a .564 slugging percentage. The fact that he's produced two years in a row is encouraging. Piazza has shown punch ever since he turned pro in '89. In '91, he topped all Class-A players with a .540 slugging percentage and with 58 extra-base hits. Piazza made the Class-A Northwest League All-Star team in '89, and helped Vero Beach win the Class-A Florida State League title in '90.

Piazza has a good shot at making the bigs in '93. If you have faith, check out his '93s for a dime. Our pick for his best 1993 card is Upper Deck. We have chosen this card because it will increase in value.

	BA	G	AB	R	H	2B	3B	HR	RBI	SB
92 NL	.232	21	69	5	16	3	0	1	7	0
Life	.232	21	69	5	16	3	0	1	7	0

HIPOLITO PICHARDO

Position: Pitcher
Team: Kansas City Royals
Born: August 22, 1969
   Esperanza,
   Dominican Republic
Height: 6′1″ **Weight:** 160 lbs.
Bats: Right **Throws:** Right
Acquired: Signed as a free
   agent, 12/87

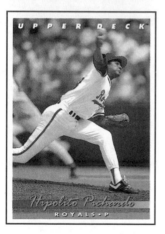

Hipolito Pichardo opened the season with Memphis of the Southern League, but was called to the majors in mid-April and worked his way into the starting rotation. Pichardo put up solid numbers in his first year in the bigs. For his '92 efforts, he earned a 9-6 record with a 3.95 ERA, striking out 59 of the 615 batters he faced and walking 49. He started 24 of the 31 games he appeared in for the '92 campaign, completing one. His arrival might have come sooner had it not been for arm and back troubles he suffered in '89 and '90. He went 5-4 with Class-A Appleton in '89, but missed the last month with a sore right forearm. He moved to the Class-A Florida State League in '90, going on the DL twice with a strained back. In '91, Pichardo reached Double-A, achieving varied success.

A winning record and unforgettable name help Pichardo look good for 1993. Spend a dime each on his cards. Our pick for his best 1993 card is Fleer. We have chosen this card due to its unique photographic approach.

	W	L	ERA	G	CG	IP	H	ER	BB	SO
92 AL	9	6	3.95	31	1	143.2	148	63	49	59
Life	9	6	3.95	31	1	143.2	148	63	49	59

PHIL PLANTIER

Position: Outfield
Team: San Diego Padres
Born: January 27, 1969
   Manchester, NH
Height: 5′11″ **Weight:** 195 lbs.
Bats: Right **Throws:** Right
Acquired: Traded from Red Sox
   for Jose Melendez, 12/92

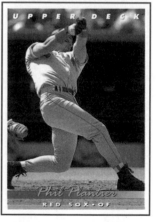

Phil Plantier opened 1992 as Boston's starting right fielder, but his season was filled with more disappointment than success. Despite postseason surgery in '91, Plantier's elbow still plagued him, as did a sore knee. For the '92 season with the BoSox, he managed a .246 batting average, seven homers, and 30 RBI. During a brief demotion in mid-'92 to the International League, Plantier hit .425 with five homers and 14 RBI in just 40 plate appearances. Those power totals were identical to the '92 spring training marks Plantier earned to get his return shot with the BoSox. Traded late in '92, he joins the San Diego Padres for '93. In '91, Plantier sparkled with a .331 average, 11 homers and 35 RBI in 53 games. He premiered with Boston in '90.

His move to San Diego may relieve a bit of the comeback pressure. Let him get used to his new teammates. Give him—and his nickel-priced '93s—another chance. Our pick for his best 1993 card is Upper Deck. We have chosen this card because of its great combination of photography and design.

	BA	G	AB	R	H	2B	3B	HR	RBI	SB
92 AL	.246	108	349	46	86	19	0	7	30	2
Life	.268	175	512	74	137	27	1	18	68	3

DAN
PLESAC

Position: Pitcher
Team: Chicago Cubs
Born: February 4, 1962
  Gary, IN
Height: 6'5" **Weight:** 215 lbs.
Bats: Left **Throws:** Left
Acquired: Signed as a free
  agent, 12/92

LUIS
POLONIA

Position: Outfield
Team: California Angels
Born: October 12, 1964
  Santiago City,
  Dominican Republic
Height: 5'8" **Weight:** 150 lbs.
Bats: Left **Throws:** Left
Acquired: Traded from Yankees
  for Claudell Washington and
  Rich Monteleone, 4/90

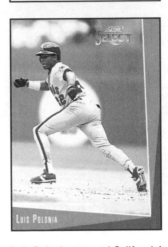

Although he made the All-Star team as a closer three times, Dan Plesac spent last summer as a middle reliever in the Milwaukee bullpen. Plesac regained some of his zip in '92, thanks in part to working out over the winter. He averaged nearly six and one-half strikeouts and gave up seven hits per nine innings. He had trouble locating the strike zone consistently, giving up four walks per nine innings. Opponents compiled a .229 batting average, a .317 on-base percentage, and a .343 slugging percentage against him in '92. Plesac had a 95 mph fastball and a slider that devoured lefthanded hitters before he ran into arm problems in 1990. After admitting to the ailment, he agreed to a cortisone shot and even tried starting in '91 after 331 consecutive relief outings.

Middle relievers are card-collecting poison. Unless Plesac stays healthy and snags a closing job with the Cubs in '93, hold onto your pennies. Our pick for his best 1993 card is Topps. We have chosen this card because of its great combination of photography and design.

Luis Polonia escaped California's 1992 decline, posting some of the finest offensive stats of his career. Even though he was bothered by a variety of injuries, Polonia is a good contact hitter. He also swiped more than 50 bases for the first time in his six-year major league career. The slight dip in his batting average, from its .296 level in '91, can be attributed to pesky lefthanders. Polonia battered righties near a .300 clip in '92, but fared more than 70 points worse against southpaws. Polonia has never been a big RBI man, but his lifetime average is very respectable. He began his pro career with Oakland in '84 and was a regular by '87. After joining the Yankees in June '89, Polonia spent parts of two seasons in New York.

Polonia needs to stop splitting seasons between the outfield and DH. His lack of homers and RBI may keep his nickel-priced 1993 cards from being taken seriously. Our pick for his best 1993 card is Fleer. We have chosen this card due to its unique photographic approach.

	W	L	ERA	G	SV	IP	H	ER	BB	SO
92 AL	5	4	2.96	44	1	79.0	64	26	35	54
Life	29	37	3.21	365	133	524.1	460	187	186	44

	BA	G	AB	R	H	2B	3B	HR	RBI	SB
92 AL	.286	149	577	83	165	17	4	0	35	51
Life	.299	753	2740	426	818	96	41	13	242	195

MARK PORTUGAL

Position: Pitcher
Team: Houston Astros
Born: October 30, 1962
  Los Angeles, CA
Height: 6' **Weight:** 190 lbs.
Bats: Right **Throws:** Right
Acquired: Traded from Twins
  for Todd McClure, 12/88

Despite spending half of 1992 on the disabled list with a sore shoulder, Mark Portugal remained one of Houston's most effective pitchers. In 10 of his first 15 starts, Portugal lasted six innings or better while holding adversaries to three runs or less. During the '92 season, Portugal posted a 6-3 record with a 2.66 ERA, though Houston provided their veteran righthander with fewer than 3.5 runs per game. In his 18 appearances for the Astros in '92, he threw in over 100 innings, striking out 62 batters. Portugal's first season with the Astros was '89, but his greatest success came in '90, thanks to an 11-10 record in 32 starts, tying him for the Houston team lead. In '91, Portugal was 10-12 with a 4.49 ERA.

Portugal may reach a dozen wins per year, but he'll never be a star pitching ace for Houston. His 1993 commons aren't positive buys. Our pick for his best 1993 card is Upper Deck. We have chosen this card because it has a distinctive look.

	W	L	ERA	G	CG	IP	H	ER	BB	SO
92 NL	6	3	2.66	18	1	101.1	76	30	41	62
Life	45	45	4.01	174	8	813.0	771	362	309	542

KIRBY PUCKETT

Position: Outfield
Team: Minnesota Twins
Born: March 14, 1961
  Chicago, IL
Height: 5'8" **Weight:** 213 lbs.
Bats: Right **Throws:** Right
Acquired: First-round pick,
  1/82 free-agent draft

Kirby Puckett, a 5'8" mass of muscle, powered his way through another phenomenal season. A seven-time All-Star, Puckett is a solid force for the Minnesota Twins. He put up great numbers again in '92, including a .329 batting average, 38 doubles, and 110 RBI. He had 210 hits in over 160 games for the '92 season. Puckett has made a career of being a line drive hitter, not a longball champion. His hits make things happen, however. That's what makes him so valuable to the Twins and so feared by everyone else. In fact, Puckett has hit for both power and average over the last seven seasons. His fielding is another facet of his game that continues to amaze. In '92, his all-around spectacular play earned him a .993 fielding percentage and his fifth Gold Glove.

Get wild and spend a few quarters on Kirby's '93s. An unnoticed but tempting early Puckett is in the '87 Donruss Diamond King at 50 cents. Our pick for his best 1993 card is Topps. We have chosen this card due to its unique photographic approach.

	BA	G	AB	R	H	2B	3B	HR	RBI	SB
92 AL	.329	160	639	104	210	38	4	19	110	17
Life	.321	1382	5645	820	1812	304	51	142	785	117

Series two cards from some companies were available at press time. If space allows, both cards are shown; if not, the most up-to-date cards are pictured.

TIM PUGH

Position: Pitcher
Team: Cincinnati Reds
Born: January 26, 1967
   Lake Tahoe, CA
Height: 6'6" **Weight:** 225 lbs.
Bats: Right **Throws:** Right
Acquired: Sixth-round pick,
   6/89 free-agent draft

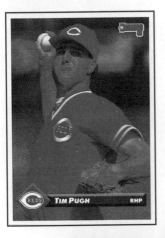 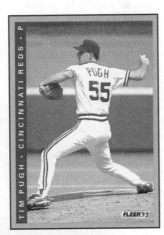

In a one-month trial, Tim Pugh emerged as a darkhorse starter for the 1993 Reds. He earned his late-season promotion in '92 on the strength of a 12-9 record and 3.55 ERA at Triple-A Nashville. His 4-2 record in the bigs is remarkable, considering that Cincinnati provided him with an average of less than three runs per game. In five of his seven starts, the righthander went at least six innings while holding the opposition to three runs or less. He posted a 2.58 ERA in his 45 ⅓ big league innings. Pugh's first success as a starter came in the Class-A South Atlantic League in '91, when he led the league with eight complete games and a 15-6 record. Before the start of his professional career, Pugh sported a 33-6 record at Oklahoma State University.

Pugh could surprise card investors in 1993. If he enjoys a solid spring training, snap up his cards at a dime or less apiece. Our pick for his best 1993 card is Upper Deck. We have chosen this card because it will increase in value.

	W	L	ERA	G	CG	IP	H	ER	BB	SO
92 AAA	12	9	3.55	27	3	169.2	165	67	65	117
92 NL	4	2	2.58	7	0	45.1	47	13	13	18

PAUL QUANTRILL

Position: Pitcher
Team: Boston Red Sox
Born: November 3, 1968
   London, Ontario, Canada
Height: 6'1" **Weight:** 175 lbs.
Bats: Left **Throws:** Right
Acquired: Sixth-round pick,
   6/89 free-agent draft

Paul Quantrill began his major league career on a high note in 1992. After coming off a good showing at spring training (1-0 with a 3.00 ERA in six games), he showed he was itching for a shot at the big leagues. Quantrill received his opportunity on July 20 against Kansas City and made the most of it. In 2 ⅔ innings, he yielded no runs on two hits while striking out three, earning the win over the Royals. For the '92 season, he posted a 2-3 record with a 2.19 ERA. He also earned one save and three holds while working in 27 games for a total of 49 ⅓ innings. He finished his first Boston season with one of the team's top ERAs.

Because Quantrill's '93 relief role remains undefined, it's tough to speculate on what will be his officially designated rookie cards. Avoid the 10- to 15-cent items now, regrouping only if Quantrill becomes a starter. Our pick for his best 1993 card is Fleer. We have chosen this card due to the outstanding photographic composition.

	W	L	ERA	G	CG	IP	H	ER	BB	SO
92 AAA	6	8	4.46	19	4	119	143	59	20	56
92 AL	2	3	2.19	27	0	49.1	55	12	15	24

Series two cards from some companies were available at press time. If space allows, both cards are shown; if not, the most up-to-date cards are pictured.

239

SCOTT RADINSKY

Position: Pitcher
Team: Chicago White Sox
Born: March 3, 1968
Glendale, CA
Height: 6'3" **Weight:** 190 lbs.
Bats: Left **Throws:** Left
Acquired: Third-round pick,
6/86 free-agent draft

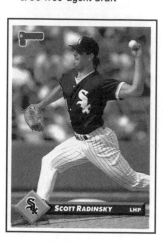

TIM RAINES

Position: Outfield
Team: Chicago White Sox
Born: September 16, 1959
Sanford, FL
Height: 5'8" **Weight:** 165 lbs.
Bats: Both **Throws:** Right
Acquired: Traded from Expos
with Jeff Carter and Mario
Brito for Barry Jones and
Ivan Calderon, 12/90

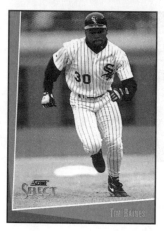

White Sox reliever Scott Radinsky got credit for clinching the AL Western Division pennant in 1992—unfortunately, not for the Sox. As he struck out Chili Davis to end the game on September 28, Chicago's win over Minnesota mathematically eliminated the Twins from the pennant race against Oakland. During the rest of '92, Radinsky's efforts were just as exciting. When stopper Bobby Thigpen faltered, Radinsky supported the team with career bests in ERA (2.73), saves (15), and appearances (27). The lefty pitcher tamed lefthanded hitters (.182 average in '92). In '91, Radinsky worked 67 games, going 5-5 with eight saves and a 2.02 ERA. His '90 rookie season consisted of five saves, a 6-1 record, and a 4.82 ERA.

Radinsky's 1992 season was ground-breaking for him, but ranks as mildly above-average in the eyes of fans and collectors. His 1993 commons don't look promising. Our pick for his best 1993 card is Donruss. We have chosen this card for its technical merits.

Tim Raines kept running with the 1992 White Sox. He stole more than 40 bases (45) for the 11th time in 12 seasons. (His "off" year was 33 steals with the '88 Expos.) Raines seems to like the new Comiskey Park. His '92 home batting average of .319 was almost 50 points higher than his batting average on the road (.271). Overall, he pumped up his average in '92 over 25 points higher than his '91 mark. The seven-time All-Star has played two years in the AL, but hasn't been able to fully recapture the production he had with Montreal. Raines batted a career-high .334 in '86, winning the NL batting championship. The Expos chose Raines in the fifth round of the '77 draft, following his Florida high school baseball and football career.

Only if you believe Raines has an outside shot at the Hall of Fame should you gamble a nickel apiece on his '93s. An '82 Donruss card of Raines is still available at $1.25. Our pick for his best 1993 card is Fleer. We have chosen this card because of its great combination of photography and design.

	W	L	ERA	G	SV	IP	H	ER	BB	SO
92 AL	3	7	2.73	68	15	59.1	54	18	34	48
Life	14	13	3.05	197	27	183.0	154	62	93	143

	BA	G	AB	R	H	2B	3B	HR	RBI	SB
92 AL	.294	144	551	102	162	22	9	7	54	45
Life	.297	1704	6465	1138	1923	315	96	108	656	730

FERNANDO RAMSEY

Position: Outfield
Team: Chicago Cubs
Born: December 20, 1965
Rainbow, Panama
Height: 6'1" **Weight:** 175 lbs.
Bats: Right **Throws:** Right
Acquired: 33rd-round pick,
6/87 free-agent draft

WILLIE RANDOLPH

Position: Second base
Team: New York Mets
Born: July 6, 1954
Holly Hill, SC
Height: 5'11" **Weight:** 171 lbs.
Bats: Right **Throws:** Right
Acquired: Signed as a free
agent, 12/91

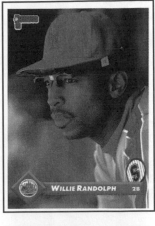

Fernando Ramsey was just another face in the Cubs' outfield parade of 1992. He started six games in center field, displaying fine speed and errorless defense. Yet, his offensive weaknesses were obvious: an .063 average against lefthanders and an .071 mark at Wrigley Field. His overall average in '92 for the Cubs was a meager .120. While he didn't have a single home run with Triple-A Iowa in '92, his 35 stolen bases led the team. The 26-year-old was promoted to Chicago when rosters were enlarged in September. In '90, his 43 swipes led Class-A Carolina League baserunners. His .276 average at Double-A Charlotte in '91 marked a personal best. Ramsey, an Olympic track competitor for Panama in '84, signed with the Cubs out of New Mexico State University.

With the arrival of outfielders Willie Wilson and Candy Maldonado, Ramsey's potential may fade faster than flyhawking flop Jerome Walton. No need to buy these common-priced cards. Our pick for his best 1993 card is Upper Deck. We have chosen this card due to the outstanding photographic composition.

Willie Randolph didn't contend for a batting title with the 1992 Mets largely because he spent much of the season on the disabled list. In '92, he was sharing second base duties with Bill Pecota before going on the DL in August with a fractured wrist. He had been hit by a pitch from Pittsburgh's Bob Walk. This turn of events was especially tough to take since he had such a great '91. That year, Randolph finished third in the AL with a career-high .327 average. The veteran second baseman's return to New York in '92 reminded fans that he was a Yankees cornerstone from 1976-89. One of his most productive seasons (.305, seven homers, 67 RBI) came with the '87 Yanks. Selected to six All-Star teams, Randolph has been active in the majors since premiering with the '75 Pirates.

Randolph may make his last ride in the majors in 1993. He may not have any clout in Cooperstown, giving his '93 commons no hopes for short-term profits. Our pick for his best 1993 card is Topps. We have chosen this card due to the outstanding photographic composition.

	BA	G	AB	R	H	2B	3B	HR	RBI	SB
92 AAA	.269	133	480	62	129	9	5	1	38	39
92 NL	.120	18	25	0	3	0	0	0	2	0

	BA	G	AB	R	H	2B	3B	HR	RBI	SB
92 NL	.252	90	286	29	72	11	1	2	15	1
Life	.276	2202	8018	1239	2210	316	65	54	687	271

JEFF REARDON

Position: Pitcher
Team: Cincinnati Reds
Born: October 1, 1955
Pittsfield, MA
Height: 6′ **Weight:** 200 lbs.
Bats: Right **Throws:** Right
Acquired: Signed as a free
agent, 1/93

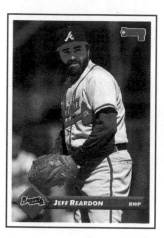

JEFF REBOULET

Position: Infield
Team: Minnesota Twins
Born: April 30, 1964
Dayton, OH
Height: 6′ **Weight:** 167 lbs.
Bats: Right **Throws:** Right
Acquired: 10th-round pick,
6/88 free-agent draft

Like Gregg Olson, Jeff Reardon relies on a curve as his primary pitch. Reardon did more than record his 11th consecutive 20-save season in 1992. He notched his 342nd career save, erasing the record of Hall of Famer Rollie Fingers, with Boston on June 15. For '92, he added 27 notches to his save belt. The only man with 40-save seasons in both leagues, Reardon was named Reliever of the Decade for the '80s in the Rolaids Relief Man Award rankings. Reardon, whose 40 saves in '91 were a Red Sox record, pitched so well that Boston won 45 of the 51 games he finished. Reardon was traded to Atlanta last August and signed with the Reds for '93.

No short-term payoffs, but Reardon's '93s could boom when he hits Cooperstown. Buy at a nickel each. At $10, his 1981 Topps may be overpriced. The card won't gain any value until the reliever makes C-town. Our pick for his best 1993 card is Score. We have chosen this card for the interesting facts included on the reverse.

Jeff Reboulet played six full years in the minors and was still not on the Twins' 40-man roster. Early in 1992, however, he finally made it to the big leagues when the Twins sustained some injuries in their infield. Reboulet is a versatile player who appeared at second, short, and third as well as serving as a DH. He hit just .208 in his first 48 big league at-bats, but he made the hits count, driving in nine runs. He can hit at home or against lefties fairly well, but will never dazzle you either with average or power. His career high in stolen bases (18) was set with Orlando in '88. Reboulet turned pro with Class-A Visalia in '86 and quickly made it to Double-A. He simmered there for a while, bouncing back and forth between Double- and Triple-A for five years before getting the call. His experience could keep him around for a few years.

Spotty hitting curses Reboulet's 1993 cards, even at a dime each. Our pick for his best 1993 card is Donruss. We have chosen this card for its technical merits.

	W	L	ERA	G	SV	IP	H	ER	BB	SO
92	5	2	3.41	60	30	58	67	22	9	39
Life	68	71	3.05	811	357	1061.0	917	360	345	838

	BA	G	AB	R	H	2B	3B	HR	RBI	SB
92AAA	.286	48	161	21	46	11	1	2	21	3
92AL	.190	73	137	15	26	7	1	1	16	3

Series two cards from some companies were available at press time. If space allows, both cards are shown; if not, the most up-to-date cards are pictured.

JODY REED

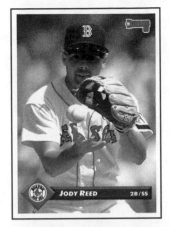

Position: Second base
Team: Los Angeles Dodgers
Born: July 26, 1962 Tampa, FL
Height: 5'9" **Weight:** 165 lbs.
Bats: Right **Throws:** Right
Acquired: Traded from Rockies
for Rudy Seanez, 11/92

STEVE REED

Position: Pitcher
Team: Colorado Rockies
Born: March 11, 1966
Los Angeles, CA
Height: 6'2" **Weight:** 200 lbs.
Bats: Right **Throws:** Right
Acquired: Third-round pick,
11/92 expansion draft

Jody Reed's 1992 struggles were reflective of Boston's overall decline. He entered the season with a career .288 average. However, for all his efforts in '92, he only accrued a .247 batting average with 27 doubles, three homers, and 40 RBI. His previous career-low mark had been a .283 batting average with the '91 Red Sox. Boston discovered the infielder out of Florida State University. Reed began with the BoSox in '88, hitting .300 with eight RBI in nine games. He finished third in AL Rookie of the Year balloting in '88, hitting .293. In '90, he moved to second base, after growing up at shortstop in the Boston organization. Now he'll join the Dodgers for '93.

Reed isn't one of the youngest or most memorable second basemen currently in baseball. Avoid his 1993 commons, especially if he falls into an infield platoon. Our pick for his best 1993 card is Topps. We have chosen this card because of its great combination of photography and design.

Steve Reed set a minor league record by gathering 43 saves in 1992. Drafted by the Rockies, he has the inside line to become the closer in 1993, an assignment that would have eluded him for several years if he had stayed with the Giants. In '92, Reed began at Double-A Shreveport, where he picked up 23 saves in his first 24 chances. Promoted to Triple-A, he was effective there as well. Reed was a *Baseball Weekly* Player of the Week in early August. He is a submariner with below-average velocity, but his ball sinks, and his unusual delivery gives him an advantage. He throws strikes and is a big believer in a good mental approach, which helps in the tight spots a closer must face. Reed was the '88 Rolaids Relief Pitcher of the Year in the rookie Pioneer League and an '89 Class-A Midwest League All-Star.

Whether Reed's velocity is enough to allow him to succeed in the bigs is uncertain. Use extreme caution when investing here. Our pick for his best 1993 card is Donruss. We have chosen this card because the design lends itself to the best use of the elements.

	BA	G	AB	R	H	2B	3B	HR	RBI	SB
92 AL	.247	143	550	64	136	27	1	3	40	7
Life	.280	715	2658	361	743	180	7	17	227	23

	W	L	ERA	G	SV	IP	H	ER	BB	SO
92 AAA	0	1	3.48	29	20	31.0	27	12	10	30
92 NL	1	0	2.30	18	0	15.2	13	4	3	11

KEVIN REIMER

Position: Outfield
Team: Milwaukee Brewers
Born: June 28, 1964
  Macon, GA
Height: 6'2" **Weight:** 230 lbs.
Bats: Left **Throws:** Right
Acquired: Traded from Rockies
  for Dante Bichette, 11/92

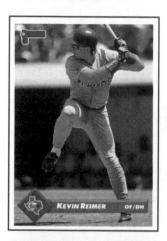

Kevin Reimer's 1992 marks dipped briefly, although he continued to supply power from the left side. While he managed a .267 batting average with 16 home runs and 58 RBI for the '92 season, the flipside of his game was in more serious trouble. He led AL left fielders in errors (11), causing speculation on how long it will be before he is made a designated hitter. He'll join the Brewers' staff in '93. In '91, Reimer spent his first full season with Texas. His marks included 20 home runs, 69 RBI, and a .269 average. Reimer began his pro career in '85 and reached Texas for the conclusion of the '88 season. He divided his time between Triple-A Oklahoma City and Arlington in '89 and '90.

Reimer could hit anywhere from 15 to 25 homers yearly. His horrid fielding, modest speed, and excessive strikeouts pose risks to his 1993 common-priced cards. Our pick for his best 1993 card is Topps. We have chosen this card for its artistic presentation.

	BA	G	AB	R	H	2B	3B	HR	RBI	SB
92 AL	.267	148	494	56	132	32	2	16	58	2
Life	.262	363	1018	109	267	63	3	39	144	2

HAROLD REYNOLDS

Position: Second base
Team: Baltimore Orioles
Born: November 26, 1960
  Eugene, OR
Height: 5'11" **Weight:** 165 lbs.
Bats: Both **Throws:** Right
Acquired: Signed as a free
  agent, 12/92

Harold Reynolds had the painful task of watching his second base job fade away with the 1992 Mariners. As Seattle tumbled into last place for the '92 season, the team handed the keystone job to rookie Bret Boone. Reynolds was being shown the door out of the Kingdome early. He rolled with the punches, though, and signed on with the Orioles for '93. In his '92 campaign, he had a .247 batting average, 23 doubles, three homers, and 33 RBI. The Oregon native contributed a career-high 57 RBI in '91. A Mariners fixture since '86, his average grew to a personal-best .300 in '89. Two All-Star appearances and three Gold Gloves highlight Reynolds' past accomplishments. Reynolds, a first-round pick by Seattle in '80, made his debut with the M's in '83.

As always, new cards of Reynolds sell at three to five cents each. Unknown outside the Northwest, his issues will have the disadvantage of his relocation to a new team. Don't invest. Our pick for his best 1993 card is Score. We have chosen this card for the interesting facts included on the reverse.

	BA	G	AB	R	H	2B	3B	HR	RBI	SB
92 AL	.247	140	458	55	113	23	3	3	33	15
Life	.260	1155	4090	543	1063	200	48	17	295	228

ARTHUR RHODES

Position: Pitcher
Team: Baltimore Orioles
Born: October 24, 1969
  Waco, TX
Height: 6'2" **Weight:** 204 lbs.
Bats: Left **Throws:** Left
Acquired: Second-round pick,
  6/88 free-agent draft

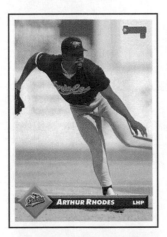 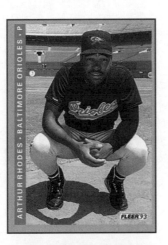

 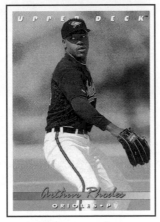

Arthur Rhodes is a top prospect who has been brought along very slowly. In '92, however, he started 15 games for the Baltimore Orioles, finishing with winning marks. His 7-5 record and 3.63 ERA were highlighted by two complete games. He struck out 77 batters, walking only 38. One year earlier, he was named Double-A Eastern League Pitcher of the Year after going 7-4 with a 2.70 ERA. Three of his wins in that '91 season were 1-0 games. That season culminated with a call-up to Baltimore, where he was the youngest player on the roster. Rhodes has more strikeouts than innings over a career that began in '88. In '89, Rhodes was leading his short-season Class-A league with 45 strikeouts when he was promoted to the Class-A Carolina League. Rhodes got another promotion in '90, pacing the Carolina League in strikeouts-to-walks ratio.

Rhodes could make 1993 memorable. Grab his cards at a dime each. Our pick for his best 1993 card is Upper Deck. We have chosen this card because of its great combination of photography and design.

	W	L	ERA	G	CG	IP	H	ER	BB	SO
92 AL	7	5	3.63	15	2	94.1	87	38	38	77
Life	7	8	4.83	23	2	130.1	134	70	61	100

DAVE RIGHETTI

Position: Pitcher
Team: San Francisco Giants
Born: November 28, 1958
  San Jose, CA
Height: 6'4" **Weight:** 210 lbs.
Bats: Left **Throws:** Left
Acquired: Signed as a free
  agent, 12/90

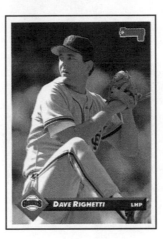 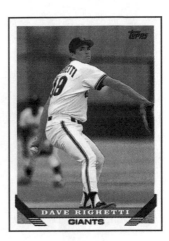

Dave Righetti had made 522 straight relief outings before the Giants gave him a start last June. Returning to the rotation did not help him, however. After an 0-2 record and 8.68 ERA in four starts, Righetti returned to the bullpen, where he had 248 saves before the '92 season. The author of an '83 no-hitter has obviously seen better days. He yielded almost a hit an inning in '92, averaged more than four walks per nine innings, and fanned fewer than six batters per game. Opponents compiled a .269 batting average, a .344 on-base percentage, and a .374 slugging percentage against him in '92. Righetti has fallen far from his 46-save form of '86.

Even though he still throws a sinker, slider, curveball, and changeup, Righetti has lost velocity on his once-feared fastball. His '93s are not a wise buy. Our pick for his best 1993 card is Topps. We have chosen this card because the design lends itself to the best use of the elements.

	W	L	ERA	G	SV	IP	H	ER	BB	SO
92 NL	2	7	5.06	54	3	78.1	79	44	36	47
Life	78	75	3.25	637	251	1286.2	1142	464	537	1038

Series two cards from some companies were available at press time. If space allows, both cards are shown; if not, the most up-to-date cards are pictured.

JOSE RIJO

Position: Pitcher
Team: Cincinnati Reds
Born: May 13, 1965
 San Cristobal,
 Dominican Republic
Height: 6'2" **Weight:** 210 lbs.
Bats: Right **Throws:** Right
Acquired: Traded from
 Athletics with Tim Birtsas for
 Dave Parker, 12/87

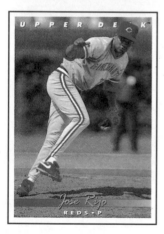

BILLY RIPKEN

Position: Second base
Team: Baltimore Orioles
Born: December 16, 1964
 Havre de Grace, MD
Height: 6'1" **Weight:** 186 lbs.
Bats: Right **Throws:** Right
Acquired: 11th-round pick,
 6/82 free-agent draft

Jose Rijo was Cincinnati's pitching ace for the second season in a row in 1992. He matched his 15-win campaign from '91, while keeping his ERA below three (2.56) for a fifth consecutive season. One of Rijo's most notable wins came in San Francisco on September 27, 1992, when he pitched what most (inaccurately) thought would be the Giants' last home game before a rumored move to Florida. Rijo's first year with Cincinnati came in '88, when he began the year as a reliever. Converted to a starter, he finished with a 13-8 record. He topped off his '90 season as the World Series MVP. When Rijo joined the NL, he escaped four years of frustration with the Yankees and Athletics. His AL totals wound up at 19-30 with a 4.75 ERA.

Rijo's nickel-priced cards will make price gains only if he becomes a league leader, wins 20, helps the Reds into postseason play, or all of the above. Our pick for his best 1993 card is Fleer. We have chosen this card for its technical merits.

Billy Ripken contributed one of his most substantial offensive seasons ever for the Orioles in 1992. The little brother of Cal Ripken Jr. posted a career-high home run total (four), still modest by most standards. Previously, the second baseman's best was three home runs in '91. At least that year his batting average was a hefty .291. Ripken's primary contributions, such as his sacrifice bunts and fine fielding, don't show up in box scores. After being selected in the 11th round of the '82 draft, Ripken labored for six minor league seasons to reach Baltimore in mid-1987. In his 58-game audition he batted .308. Since then, he's been unpredictable at the plate.

The Orioles could boot Ripken in 1993. With his shaky status in baseball, he's a card risk at any price. Don't invest in Billy's common-priced cards. Our pick for his best 1993 card is Upper Deck. We have chosen this card due to its unique photographic approach.

	W	L	ERA	G	CG	IP	H	ER	BB	SO
92 NL	15	10	2.56	33	2	211.0	185	60	44	171
Life	83	68	3.26	256	18	1287.1	1131	466	498	1096

	BA	G	AB	R	H	2B	3B	HR	RBI	SB
92 AL	.230	111	330	35	76	15	0	4	36	2
Life	.244	667	2087	217	510	92	5	13	168	20

Series two cards from some companies were available at press time. If space allows, both cards are shown; if not, the most up-to-date cards are pictured.

CAL
RIPKEN JR.

Position: Shortstop
Team: Baltimore Orioles
Born: August 24, 1960
  Havre de Grace, MD
Height: 6'4" **Weight:** 220 lbs.
Bats: Right **Throws:** Right
Acquired: Second-round pick,
  6/78 free-agent draft

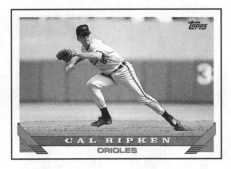

BEN
RIVERA

Position: Pitcher
Team: Philadelphia Phillies
Born: July 11, 1969
  San Pedro de Macoris,
  Dominican Republic
Height: 6'6" **Weight:** 210 lbs.
Bats: Right **Throws:** Right
Acquired: Traded from Braves
  for Donnie Elliott, 5/92

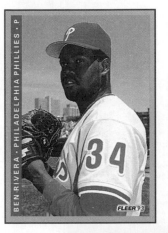

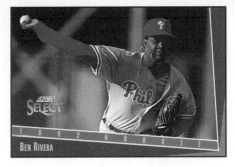

Cal Ripken suffered a slump in '92. Even though it was one of his least productive seasons for the Orioles, he managed to earn a spot in the All-Star Game for the ninth consecutive season. He also kept his playing streak alive. It began on May 30, 1982—the day after Floyd Rayford started in his place at third base in the second game of a doubleheader against Toronto. Since then, Cal Ripken Jr. has not missed a game. Heading into the '92 campaign, he had played in 1,573 consecutive games—557 short of Lou Gehrig's record. Such a workload hardly handicaps Ripken's game. In '91, he won his first Gold Glove and second MVP Award. He led the majors with 85 extra-base hits and 368 total bases, breaking Brooks Robinson's club record. He also hit personal peaks with a .323 average, 34 homers, and 114 RBI.

Is he the next Lou Gehrig? Find out at 15 cents per card. Early Ripkens are out of sight financially. Our pick for his best 1993 card is Topps. We have chosen this card due to the outstanding photographic composition.

Ben Rivera, once considered a valuable prospect in the Atlanta organization, was gone in a trade just seven weeks after making his debut for the Braves. Rivera, going to the Phillies, was immediately put to work in the bullpen. The righty, who can start and relieve, was able to provide some innings and seemed to improve as the season progressed. He made the most of this opportunity, fanning five Mets in a row on August 14. Overall for his '92 campaign, Rivera posted a 7-4 record with a 3.07 ERA. He was a little wild in his first taste of the bigs, but exposure should help that. Rivera was signed as a free agent by the Braves in '85 and went 1-5 with a 3.26 ERA at rookie-level ball. He was in the rotation most of the next four years, including '91 at Double-A Greenville, where he went 11-8. The fact that he can start and relieve makes his future role an intriguing mystery.

Although Rivera's slated to be a starter, only spend a dime on his '93s. Our pick for his best 1993 card is Fleer. We have chosen this card because of its overall appeal and pleasing looks.

	BA	G	AB	R	H	2B	3B	HR	RBI	SB
92 AL	.251	162	637	73	160	29	1	14	72	4
Life	.277	1800	6942	1043	1922	369	34	273	1014	32

	W	L	ERA	G	CG	IP	H	ER	BB	SO
91 AAA	11	8	3.86	26	3	158.2	155	63	75	116
92 NL	7	4	3.07	28	4	117.1	99	40	45	77

LUIS RIVERA

Position: Shortstop
Team: Boston Red Sox
Born: January 3, 1964
  Cidra, Puerto Rico
Height: 5'9" **Weight:** 175 lbs.
Bats: Right **Throws:** Right
Acquired: Traded from Expos
  with John Dopson for Spike
  Owen and Dan Gakeler,
  12/88

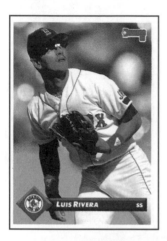

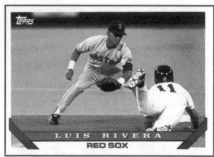

BIP ROBERTS

Position: Outfield
Team: Cincinnati Reds
Born: October 27, 1963
  Berkeley, CA
Height: 5'7" **Weight:** 165 lbs.
Bats: Both **Throws:** Right
Acquired: Traded from Padres
  with Craig Pueschner for
  Randy Myers, 12/91

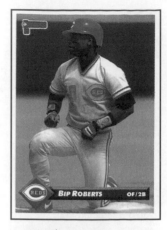

Basically, Luis Rivera filled up space in Boston's 1992 infield. The veteran provided only adequate defense at shortstop to offset one of his poorest seasons ever at the plate. He hit in the .170s against lefthanders or when facing anyone in Fenway Park. Overall in '92, he had a .215 batting average with 29 RBI and no homers. By contrast, Rivera batted .258 with eight home runs and 40 RBI in '91, all career highs. After setting those personal bests in '91, he underwent knee and shoulder surgery following the season. Rivera has been active with the Red Sox since mid-1989. Rivera played seven years in the Expos organization. With Montreal, his best effort of four round-trippers and 30 ribbies came in '88.

With rookie sensation John Valentin waiting in the wings, Rivera can't take his job for granted in 1993. Rivera's average performances don't propel his card values. Don't toy with his 1993 commons. Our pick for his best 1993 card is Topps. We have chosen this card because the design lends itself to the best use of the elements.

Bip Roberts divided his 1992 season between four different positions for the Reds. Playing at second, third, and in left and center field, Roberts was still able to maintain a .991 fielding percentage, committing one single error. He didn't fare too poorly at the plate, either, finishing '92 with a .323 average, four homers, and 45 RBI. He added 44 stolen bases just for good measure. His batting average and swipes were both ties for third best in the league in '92. Roberts rekindled his '90 excellence, when he batted .309 with nine home runs, 44 RBI, and 46 stolen bases for the Padres. The '92 All-Star went 2-for-2 with two RBI and a run scored in the midseason classic.

Roberts may be too valuable as a defensive fill-in to be limited to one position. He'll struggle for recognition if he keeps bouncing around the lineup. Furthermore, his '93 commons will struggle with him. Our pick for his best 1993 card is Score. We have chosen this card for the interesting facts included on the reverse.

	BA	G	AB	R	H	2B	3B	HR	RBI	SB
92 AL	.215	102	288	17	62	11	1	0	29	4
Life	.233	638	1940	209	452	100	9	24	187	18

	BA	G	AB	R	H	2B	3B	HR	RBI	SB
92 NL	.323	147	532	92	172	34	6	4	45	44
Life	.299	636	2091	378	626	103	22	20	158	151

Series two cards from some companies were available at press time. If space allows, both cards are shown; if not, the most up-to-date cards are pictured.

HENRY RODRIGUEZ

Position: Outfield
Team: Los Angeles Dodgers
Born: November 8, 1967
   Santo Domingo,
   Dominican Republic
Height: 6'1" **Weight:** 180 lbs.
Bats: Left **Throws:** Left
Acquired: Signed as a free
   agent, 7/85

IVAN RODRIGUEZ

Position: Catcher
Team: Texas Rangers
Born: November 30, 1971
   Vega Baja, Puerto Rico
Height: 5'9" **Weight:** 205 lbs.
Bats: Right **Throws:** Right
Acquired: Signed as a free
   agent, 7/88

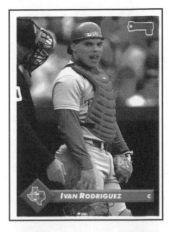

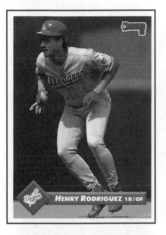

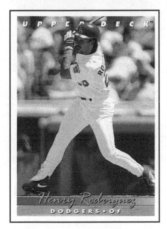

Henry Rodriguez was one of the few players to benefit from the 1992 Dodgers collapse. He was promoted to LA for the first time in his six-year career in pro ball, following injuries to starters Eric Davis and Darryl Strawberry. Rodriguez seemed to prefer lefties in '92, hitting .400 against southpaws. However, he was facing righties most of the time, foes he couldn't manage .200 against. Rodriguez played first base at Triple-A Albuquerque in 1992, batting .304 with 14 homers and 72 RBI. His Triple-A totals from '91 included 10 homers and 67 RBI. Rodriguez was touted as a future big league slugger after his 28 home runs and 109 RBI in '90 led all Double-A sluggers.

   With the Dodgers expected to make major changes in 1993, Rodriguez could see considerable playing time. His 1993 cards will average a dime each, an unstable price until Rodriguez lasts a whole season in the bigs. Our pick for his best 1993 card is Topps. We have chosen this card because of its great combination of photography and design.

Even after Carlton Fisk retires, the AL will still have a Pudge. With more than nicknames in common with Fisk, Ivan Rodriguez proved himself an able sophomore, earning an All-Star Game appearance and a Gold Glove. Despite a stress fracture in his back, Rodriguez remained a defensive standout. The rifle-armed righty ranked among baseball's best receivers throughout the year, maintaining a 51.8 caught-stealing percentage in '92. He also hit eight homers and knocked in 37 runs for the Rangers. When Rodriguez debuted with the Rangers in '91, he was only 19 years old. He was signed out of high school at age 16. Upon catching Nolan Ryan, Rodriguez formed the first battery of a teenager and over-40 mate in 30 years.

   These cards are keepers, baseball fans. Invest in his 1993s at a dime apiece, and you'll be set for some surprising payoffs. A reasonable buy is Pudge's '91 Donruss Rookie at $1.25. Our pick for his best 1993 card is Fleer. We have chosen this card because it has a distinctive look.

	BA	G	AB	R	H	2B	3B	HR	RBI	SB
92 AAA	.304	94	365	59	111	21	5	14	72	1
92 NL	.219	53	146	11	32	7	0	3	14	0

	BA	G	AB	R	H	2B	3B	HR	RBI	SB
92 AL	.260	123	420	39	109	16	1	8	37	0
Life	.261	211	700	63	183	32	1	11	64	0

RICH RODRIGUEZ

Position: Pitcher
Team: San Diego Padres
Born: March 1, 1963
  Downey, CA
Height: 6′ **Weight:** 200 lbs.
Bats: Right **Throws:** Left
Acquired: Traded from Mets for
  Brad Pounders, 12/88

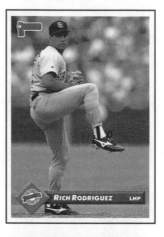

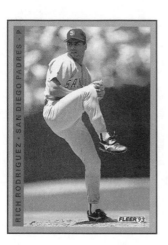

Pitcher Rich Rodriguez was a vital part of the 1992 Padres relief unit. Aside from closer Randy Myers, Rodriguez was the only lefthander in the San Diego bullpen. His ERA (2.37) shaved nearly a point off his '91 mark, and he registered a second consecutive season of 50-plus appearances (61). He was originally a sixth-round pick of the Mets in '84. However, he had never advanced beyond Double-A after five years in the Mets farm system. After the '88 season, Rodriguez was swapped to the Padres and, in '91, spent his first full season at the major league level. Before deciding to play ball at the University of Tennessee, Rodriguez had considered accepting a 17th-round draft pick from Kansas City in 1981.

Rodriguez will endure a fruitless search for stardom in his current bullpen role. If no one notices his middle relief work, how will his 1993 cards ever be worth more than a nickel apiece? Our pick for his best 1993 card is Donruss. We have chosen this card due to the outstanding photographic composition.

	W	L	ERA	G	SV	IP	H	ER	BB	SO
92 NL	6	3	2.37	61	0	91.0	77	24	29	64
Life	10	5	2.80	157	1	218.2	195	68	89	126

KENNY ROGERS

Position: Pitcher
Team: Texas Rangers
Born: November 10, 1964
  Savannah, GA
Height: 6′1″ **Weight:** 205 lbs.
Bats: Left **Throws:** Left
Acquired: 39th-round pick,
  6/82 free-agent draft

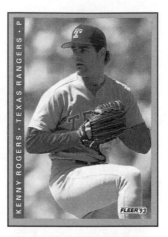

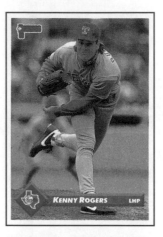

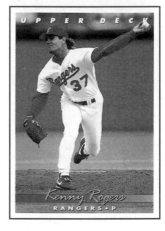

As a full-time reliever once again, Kenny Rogers polished up his stats with the 1992 Rangers. The lefthander broke his career-best mark of 73 appearances, set during his '89 rookie season, with 81 appearances in '92. In '91, Rogers won 10 games for the second season in a row. He began that season in the starting rotation, which caused his ERA to swell to 5.42 by season's end. By June, the team abandoned the experiment. Back in the bullpen in '92, his other marks include a 3-6 record with a 3.09 ERA, six saves, and 16 holds. In the 78 ⅔ innings of work that Rogers logged in with the Rangers in '92, he struck out 70 and walked 26 of the 337 batters he faced. Rogers helped set up saves for departed closer Jeff Russell. When Russell was injured in '90, Rogers took over the stopper's job, earning a personal-best 15 saves.

Even if he pitches in half the Rangers games yearly, Rogers will get little credit for working in middle relief. Our pick for his best 1993 card is Fleer. We have chosen this card for the superior presentation of information on its back.

	W	L	ERA	G	SV	IP	H	ER	BB	SO
92 AL	3	6	3.09	81	6	78.2	80	27	26	70
Life	26	26	3.78	286	28	359.2	354	151	171	280

MEL ROJAS

Position: Pitcher
Team: Montreal Expos
Born: December 10, 1966
Haina, Dominican Republic
Height: 5'11" **Weight:** 185 lbs.
Bats: Right **Throws:** Right
Acquired: Signed as a free
agent, 11/85

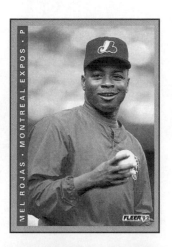

Mel Rojas was the Expos' unstoppable hurler in 1992. The right-handed reliever spun an ERA under 2.00 (1.43), tops among all NL firemen. His 10 saves ranked second on the Expo staff to John Wetteland (37). Rojas worked in over 100 innings in '92, posting a 7-1 record for the season. Of the 399 batters he faced, he struck out 70 and walked 34. In '91, Rojas was 3-3 with six saves and a 3.75 ERA in 37 games with Montreal. His first promotion to the Expos came in '90. While Rojas has worked exclusively as a reliever in his three major league seasons, the righthander concentrated on starting duties as a minor leaguer. His uncle, Jesus Alou (a Montreal scout), helped sign Rojas as an undrafted free agent in 1985.

Rojas will be playing second fiddle in the Expos bullpen to Wetteland again in 1993. He needs more wins, strikeouts, or saves before his commons will inch upward in price guides. Our pick for his best 1993 card is Fleer. We have chosen this card due to the outstanding photographic composition.

	W	L	ERA	G	SV	IP	H	ER	BB	SO
92 NL	7	1	1.43	68	10	100.2	71	16	34	70
Life	13	5	2.48	128	17	188.2	147	52	71	133

JEFF RUSSELL

Position: Pitcher
Team: Oakland Athletics
Born: September 2, 1961
Cincinnati, OH
Height: 6'3" **Weight:** 205 lbs.
Bats: Right **Throws:** Right
Acquired: Traded from Rangers
with Bobby Witt and Ruben
Sierra for Jose Canseco,
8/92

Jeff Russell's team-leading 28 saves with the 1992 Rangers turned out to be a small part of the stopper's season. He became a famed third of the deal which sent Jose Canseco to Texas. At the time, Russell had a 1.91 ERA with 43 strikeouts in 51 games. During the last week of the season, Russell had elbow problems, clouding both his future and his ability to display his talent. For the '92 season, he was able to post a 4-3 record with a 1.63 ERA and 30 saves. Russell's double-digit save count for the '92 season was good for a sixth-place tie in the National League. It also marked the second season in a row that he saved 30. In '89, he adopted the closer role with Texas, responding with a league-leading 38 saves.

Don't be fooled by the free-agent attention Russell drew before the 1993 season. Unless he can be a contributing member of a contending team, his common-priced cards will stay cold. Our pick for his best 1993 card is Score. We have chosen this card for the interesting facts included on the reverse.

	W	L	ERA	G	SV	IP	H	ER	BB	SO
92 AL	4	3	1.63	59	30	66.1	55	12	25	48
Life	50	60	3.79	404	113	923.2	889	389	354	576

NOLAN RYAN

Position: Pitcher
Team: Texas Rangers
Born: January 31, 1947
　Refugio, TX
Height: 6'2" **Weight:** 212 lbs.
Bats: Right **Throws:** Right
Acquired: Signed as a free
　agent, 12/88

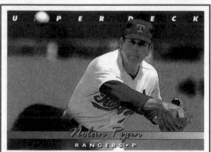

Nolan Ryan suffered through his first losing season since 1987. His '92 problems included a strained calf muscle, a sore hip, and recurring back spasms. Beginning on April 7, Ryan was a DL regular. Not since his 8-16 record with the '87 Astros had the super-human pitcher looked so mortal. The seven-time All-Star seemed ready to retire in what was his 25th major league season, especially when he was winless going into late June. Yet, in his fourth decade of big league action, Ryan continued to amaze by striking out an average of one batter per inning pitched in '92. Out of the 675 batters he faced in '92, he walked only 69.

　Speculation has it that 1993 could be Ryan's final go-round. Those last-ever player cards will be swell investments at 15 cents or less. The payoffs will come when Ryan is swept into Cooperstown. Are there any affordable Ryan's left? Maybe the '82 Donruss King at $3.50 qualifies. Our pick for his best 1993 card is Upper Deck. We have chosen this card due to the outstanding photographic composition.

	W	L	ERA	G	CG	IP	H	ER	BB	SO
92 AL	5	9	3.72	27	2	157.1	138	65	69	157
Life	319	287	3.17	794	222	5319.2	3869	1875	2755	5668

BRET SABERHAGEN

Position: Pitcher
Team: New York Mets
Born: April 11, 1964
　Chicago Heights, IL
Height: 6'1" **Weight:** 185 lbs.
Bats: Right **Throws:** Right
Acquired: Traded from Royals
　with Bill Pecota for Kevin
　McReynolds, Gregg
　Jefferies, and Keith Miller,
　12/91

The odd/even jinx is getting ridiculous. Bret Saberhagen always enjoys big seasons in odd-numbered years but endures endless ailments and suffers through hard times in even-numbered years. It happened again in 1992, his first season with the Mets. He got off to a rocky start, finally found his groove, and then moved from the rotation to the sidelines with an inflamed index finger. For his efforts in '92, he wound up with a 3-5 record and a 3.50 ERA. Saberhagen had won two Cy Young Awards and thrown a no-hitter during his career with the Royals. He was also named MVP of the '85 World Series. He was not only the youngest World Series MVP but the youngest pitcher to win an AL Cy Young Award as well. Despite his injuries, his future still seems to be ahead of him.

　Check his health before spending 10 to 15 cents on his '93s. Considering his injuries and inconsistencies, Saberhagen's '80 cards are overvalued at $4 and up. Our pick for his best 1993 card is Upper Deck. We have chosen this card since its design makes it a standout.

	W	L	ERA	G	CG	IP	H	ER	BB	SO
92 NL	3	5	3.50	17	1	97.2	84	38	27	81
Life	113	83	3.23	269	65	1758.0	1635	631	358	1174

CHRIS SABO

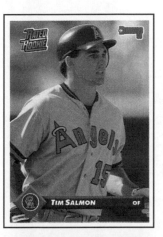

Position: Third base
Team: Cincinnati Reds
Born: January 19, 1962
Detroit, MI
Height: 6′ **Weight:** 185 lbs.
Bats: Right **Throws:** Right
Acquired: Second-round pick,
6/83 free-agent draft

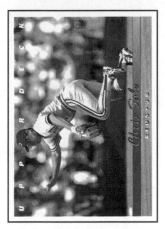

The first half of the 1992 season was nothing short of a struggle for Chris Sabo. He couldn't produce his usual power and speed because of the lingering effects of a jammed right ankle that had sent him to the DL in April. Though unable to push off his back foot while batting, Sabo convinced Cincinnati manager Lou Piniella that his presence in the lineup could help a team that had been hit hard by injuries. By June 25, Cincinnati was clinging to a one-game lead over Atlanta in the divisional title chase. Sabo contributed with his bat, too, hitting 12 homers and knocking in 43 runs in '92. When healthy, he's even better. In '91, his best season, he finished with career peaks in batting (.301), home runs (26), hits (175), and RBI (88). The three-time All-Star was NL Rookie of the Year in 1988.

Sabo is an okay card buy at a dime apiece. See Spuds in the '88 Topps Traded for $1.25. Our pick for his best 1993 card is Score. We have chosen this card because it has a distinctive look.

TIM SALMON

Position: Outfield
Team: California Angels
Born: August 24, 1968
Long Beach, CA
Height: 6′3″ **Weight:** 200 lbs.
Bats: Right **Throws:** Right
Acquired: Third-round pick,
6/89 free-agent draft

After burning up the minor leagues, outfield phenom Tim Salmon received a late-season audition with the 1992 Angels. By late August, Salmon was scorching his Triple-A league with 29 homers, 105 RBI, and a .347 average. If his average had been four points higher, Salmon would have won the PCL Triple Crown. He earned the league's MVP Award and was also named Minor League Player of the Year by *Baseball America* and *The Sporting News*. Although he didn't achieve the same success in the bigs during his '92 peek, it shouldn't take long before the desired results appear. At Double-A Midland in '91, Salmon swatted 23 homers and 94 RBI. Before deciding to play college ball, Salmon was offered an 18th-round draft selection by the Braves in '86.

Expect to see Salmon's 1993 cards at 15 cents each. Take a chance on a few. California has been praying for a young slugger for years and will immortalize anyone who comes close. Our pick for his best 1993 card is Fleer. We have chosen this card due to the outstanding photographic composition.

	BA	G	AB	R	H	2B	3B	HR	RBI	SB
92 NL	.244	96	344	42	84	19	3	12	43	4
Life	.273	616	2335	342	637	153	11	80	275	108

	BA	G	AB	R	H	2B	3B	HR	RBI	SB
92 AAA	.347	118	409	101	142	38	4	29	105	9
92 AL	.177	23	79	8	14	1	0	2	6	1

BILL SAMPEN

Position: Pitcher
Team: Kansas City Royals
Born: January 18, 1963
  Lincoln, IL
Height: 6'2" **Weight:** 195 lbs.
Bats: Right **Throws:** Right
Acquired: Traded from Expos
  with Chris Haney for Archie
  Corbin and Sean Berry, 8/92

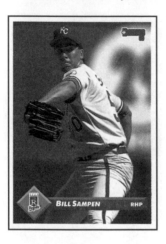

Bill Sampen brought his middle-relief act to the American League in late August 1992, after becoming excess cargo for Montreal's pennant-contending pitching staff. He had been demoted to Triple-A in mid-August, after making 44 appearances and one start with the '92 Expos. In the bigs during '92, he posted an 0-2 record with a 3.66 ERA, no saves, and one hold. Sampen led a charmed life in Montreal in '90 and '91. His '90 rookie season amounted to a 12-7 record with a 2.99 ERA, including a year-opening 6-0 streak. In '91, he returned to the Triple-A American Association for seven minor league starts, but wound up with a 9-5 effort. Sampen was brought up in the Pirates organization. He had been chosen in the 12th round of the '85 draft. In December '89, he was drafted by the Expos off Pittsburgh's Double-A roster.

Sampen isn't going to become a household name in the Kansas City bullpen. Forget investing in his 1993 commons. Our pick for his best 1993 card is Donruss. We have chosen this card because of its great combination of photography and design.

	W	L	ERA	G	SV	IP	H	ER	BB	SO
92	1	6	3.25	52	0	83	83	30	32	37
Life	22	18	3.42	154	2	265.2	273	101	111	158

REY SANCHEZ

Position: Infield
Team: Chicago Cubs
Born: October 5, 1967
  Rio Piedras, Puerto Rico
Height: 5'9" **Weight:** 165 lbs.
Bats: Right **Throws:** Right
Acquired: Traded from Rangers
  for Bryan House, 1/90

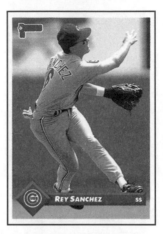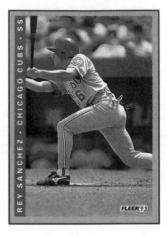

The Cubs were lucky they had Sanchez when regular shortstop Shawon Dunston went out of commission in 1992. Sanchez was bursting for a chance after a '91 campaign in which he played in the Triple-A All-Star Game and made the American Association's postseason squad. Not even a bout with chicken pox in '92 got him down. With the Cubs in '92, he had a .251 average, 14 doubles, and 19 RBI. He still has some holes in his defensive game, but he's down from a career-high 35 errors in '88. Sanchez was drafted in the 13th round of the June '86 draft by Texas. He made the Class-A All-Star team in '88. Jumping two rungs to Triple-A in '89, he hit just .224. The Rangers dealt Sanchez to the Cubs in January '90, but he missed the entire season due to an elbow operation. Sanchez, capable of hitting .250 or better, can also play second.

Life as a Shawon Dunston backup looks limited for Sanchez. Steer clear of his '93 issues. Our pick for his best 1993 card is Topps. We have chosen this card for its technical merits.

	BA	G	AB	R	H	2B	3B	HR	RBI	SB
92 NL	.251	74	255	24	64	14	3	1	19	2
Life	.252	87	278	25	70	14	3	1	21	2

RYNE SANDBERG

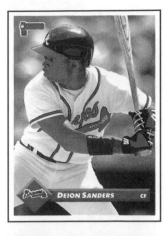

Position: Second base
Team: Chicago Cubs
Born: September 18, 1959
   Spokane, WA
Height: 6'2" **Weight:** 180 lbs.
Bats: Right **Throws:** Right
Acquired: Traded from Phillies
   with Larry Bowa for Ivan
   DeJesus, 1/82

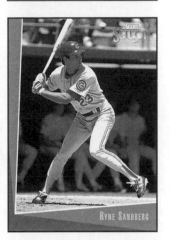

If Ernie Banks was Mr. Cub of the '50s, Ryne Sandberg is Mr. Cub of the '90s. Like Banks, Sandberg is a power-hitting infielder. Sandberg's prowess was acknowledged in '84 with the NL MVP award when the Cubs took the division crown. Sandberg produced even better numbers in '90, when he had 40 homers, 100 RBI, and 344 total bases to go with a .306 batting average. When he again hit the 100-RBI mark in '91, he became the first second baseman since Bobby Doerr in 1949-50 to reach that plateau in successive seasons. Sandberg appeared in nine All-Star Games in a row and is a nine-time Gold Glove winner. Between June 21, 1989, and May 17, 1990, Sandberg played in a record 123 consecutive games without an error, handling 584 total chances. He is also a threat on the basepaths, swiping 314 lifetime.

Ryno is a swell card buy at 15 cents apiece. Sandberg's Diamond King leads off the '85 Donruss set. Consider it at $4. Our pick for his best 1993 card is Upper Deck. We have chosen this card because it has a distinctive look.

	BA	G	AB	R	H	2B	3B	HR	RBI	SB
92 NL	.304	158	612	100	186	32	8	26	87	17
Life	.289	1705	6705	1076	1939	320	67	231	836	314

DEION SANDERS

Position: Outfield
Team: Atlanta Braves
Born: August 9, 1967
   Ft. Myers, FL
Height: 6'1" **Weight:** 195 lbs.
Bats: Left **Throws:** Left
Acquired: Signed as a free
   agent, 1/91

Dividing time between big league baseball and pro football may have slowed the progress of Deion Sanders, but he proved in 1992 that he is to be taken seriously. Rising to the challenge when the Braves needed a replacement for veteran center fielder Otis Nixon (who opened the season on the suspended list for substance abuse), Sanders won the job with a spectacular spring training. Atlanta manager Bobby Cox had to be convinced that Sanders would connect often enough to bat leadoff. Sanders let his bat do the talking. Though he had to share center field with the reinstated Nixon, Sanders had a .304 average, 26 stolen bases, eight homers, and a best-in-baseball 14 triples for his '92 efforts.

Neon Deion has to be healthy and playing regularly for his '93s to be worth more than a dime each. His '91 Upper Deck may be as low as a quarter, a "prime time" price for investing. Our pick for his best 1993 card is Fleer. We have chosen this card for its technical merits.

	BA	G	AB	R	H	2B	3B	HR	RBI	SB
92 NL	.304	97	303	54	92	6	14	8	28	26
Life	.245	222	593	101	145	11	18	17	57	46

REGGIE SANDERS

Position: Outfield
Team: Cincinnati Reds
Born: December 1, 1967
　Florence, SC
Height: 6'1"　**Weight:** 180 lbs.
Bats: Right　**Throws:** Right
Acquired: Seventh-round pick,
　6/87 free-agent draft

Reggie Sanders established himself in the majors in 1992, playing in the outfield and bringing speed and punch to Cincinnati's lineup. He did go on the DL with a sore hamstring, continuing a series of injuries that have marred his career. He put together a .270 average with 12 homers and 36 RBI for the 116 games he appeared in for the Reds in the '92 season. He also swiped 16 bases in 23 attempts during '92. Sanders began his career as a shortstop but became an outfielder in '90, winning the MVP award in his Class-A league. Managers voted him the league's top prospect and best defensive outfielder. He once stole as many as 40 bases in a minor league season and had a career high of 17 homers. Throughout his career, he has been bothered by a variety of health problems. If he manages to stay healthy and can find the handle against right-handed pitchers, he'll discover stardom soon.

　Sanders has untapped power. Tap into his 1993s at a dime each. Our pick for his best 1993 card is Upper Deck. We have chosen this card due to the outstanding photographic composition.

	BA	G	AB	R	H	2B	3B	HR	RBI	SB
92 NL	.270	116	385	62	104	26	6	12	36	16
Life	.264	125	425	68	112	26	6	13	39	17

SCOTT SANDERSON

Position: Pitcher
Team: New York Yankees
Born: July 22, 1956
　Dearborn, MI
Height: 6'5"　**Weight:** 192 lbs.
Bats: Right　**Throws:** Right
Acquired: Purchased from
　Athletics, 1/91

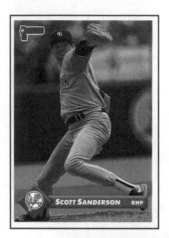

Despite a bulging ERA (4.93), Scott Sanderson won in double digits for the sixth time in his rocky career. He rivaled Melido Perez for many team leads in his second year with the Yankees. Overall, Sanderson posted a 12-11 record over the course of 33 appearances. However, he was a pale imitation of his '91 success, which included a 16-10 record. One of Sanderson's best seasons came with the '90 Athletics, when he went 17-11 in 34 starts. The right-hander's pro career began in '77 as Montreal's third-round draft pick. His first game as an Expo came in '78. In '80, Sanderson registered a 16-11 effort. He pitched with the Cubs from 1984 through '89. In '88, he missed all but 11 games of the season, due to a career-threatening back injury.

　Sanderson could keep winning a dozen or so games for the next year or three. He showed strong signs of aging, though, and could hit the skids quickly. Don't believe in his common-priced cards. Our pick for his best 1993 card is Donruss. We have chosen this card for its technical merits.

	W	L	ERA	G	CG	IP	H	ER	BB	SO
92 AL	12	11	4.93	33	2	193.1	220	106	64	104
Life	143	121	3.72	410	38	2228.1	2192	922	571	1443

Series two cards from some companies were available at press time. If space allows, both cards are shown; if not, the most up-to-date cards are pictured.

BENITO SANTIAGO

Position: Catcher
Team: Florida Marlins
Born: March 9, 1965
    Ponce, Puerto Rico
Height: 6'1" **Weight:** 185 lbs.
Bats: Right **Throws:** Right
Acquired: Signed as a free
    agent, 12/92

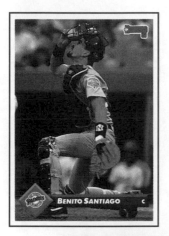 

Benito Santiago was not a happy camper in 1992. Contract problems, upcoming free agency, and health woes limited his effectiveness. He went on the DL May 31, 1992, with a broken little finger on his throwing hand. Santiago, the top All-Star vote-getter among catchers, healed and attended the midseason classic for the fourth time. He complained that he wanted to be traded, yet was stuck in San Diego throughout the year. The frustration was natural, considering that he was coming off a season of 17 homers and 87 RBI in '91. His '92 stats reflected his continued unhappiness. Hopefully, the '87 Rookie of the Year will find bliss with the Florida Marlins in '93.

A change of teams could motivate Santiago back into award-winning performances again. Don't bet more than a nickel each on his 1993 cards that it happens, however. A harmless investment is Santiago in the '87 Topps Traded edition for 35 cents. Our pick for his best 1993 card is Topps. We have chosen this card for its technical merits.

	BA	G	AB	R	H	2B	3B	HR	RBI	SB
92 NL	.251	106	386	37	97	21	0	10	42	2
Life	.264	789	2872	312	758	124	15	85	375	62

STEVE SAX

Position: Second base
Team: Chicago White Sox
Born: January 29, 1960
    Sacramento, CA
Height: 6' **Weight:** 188 lbs.
Bats: Right **Throws:** Right
Acquired: Traded from Yankees
    for Melido Perez, Bob
    Wickman, and Domingo
    Jean, 1/92

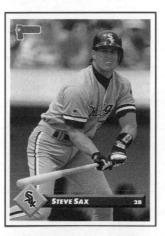 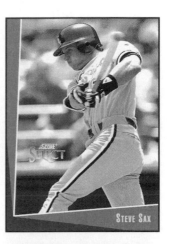

The 1992 season, Steve Sax's first with the White Sox, brought more shocks than surprises. Chicago surrendered three players to land the veteran who was coming off a season highlighted by 10 homers, 56 RBI, 31 stolen bases, and a .304 average. Instead of backing up those numbers with another solid performance, Sax fell onto hard times. For the first time in his major league career, his average fell below .240. The best Sax could do in '92 was a .236 average with four homers and 47 RBI. His fielding slipped, too, as he committed 20 errors, more than any other AL second sacker. Once a defensive joke among second basemen, Sax developed into one of baseball's top fielders with the Yanks. Before '92, the '82 NL Rookie of the Year averaged nearly 40 steals per year.

Following his flop in 1992, Sax needs another 1991 season in 1993 to jumpstart his nickel-priced cards. Investors should wait and see. Our pick for his best 1993 card is Donruss. We have chosen this card because the design lends itself to the best use of the elements.

	BA	G	AB	R	H	2B	3B	HR	RBI	SB
92 AL	.236	143	567	74	134	26	4	4	47	30
Life	.282	1705	6797	891	1915	273	46	53	541	437

BOB SCANLAN

Position: Pitcher
Team: Chicago Cubs
Born: August 9, 1966
 Los Angeles, CA
Height: 6'7" **Weight:** 215 lbs.
Bats: Right **Throws:** Right
Acquired: Traded from Phillies
 with Chuck McElroy for
 Mitch Williams, 4/91

 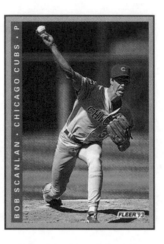

Bob Scanlan blossomed in his new bullpen role with the 1992 Cubs, quickly becoming the team's leader in saves. Despite a two-day suspension for a brawl with Philadelphia's Dave Hollins, the righthanded reliever kept the Cubs out of some trouble. His 3-6 record in '92 doesn't tell the whole story. He also earned a 2.89 ERA with 14 saves and seven holds in his 69 appearances. Scanlan almost didn't seem ready for the post in spring training as he went 1-2 with two saves and a 7.11 ERA in 11 appearances. In his previous eight pro seasons, Scanlan's season high in saves was one, achieved during his '91 rookie season with Chicago. Since being chosen in the '84 draft by Philadelphia, Scanlan had been used exclusively as a starter.

Scanlan needs to be in the 30-save range to be respected as one of the game's top relievers. Until he does that, his 1993 cards won't be worth more than a nickel apiece. Our pick for his best 1993 card is Fleer. We have chosen this card since its design makes it a standout.

	W	L	ERA	G	SV	IP	H	ER	BB	SO
92 NL	3	6	2.89	69	14	87.1	76	28	30	42
Life	10	14	3.45	109	15	198.1	190	76	70	86

CURT SCHILLING

Position: Pitcher
Team: Philadelphia Phillies
Born: November 14, 1966
 Anchorage, Alaska
Height: 6'4" **Weight:** 215 lbs.
Bats: Right **Throws:** Right
Acquired: Traded from Astros
 for Jason Grimsley, 4/92

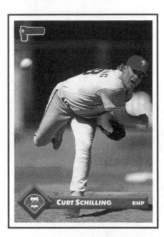 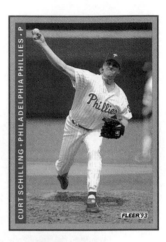

Curt Schilling joined the fourth organization of his short career in 1992, achieving a personal high in wins following the move. On April 2, the Phillies traded fellow pitcher Jason Grimsley for Schilling. Philadelphia committed robbery. While Schilling was tallying his chart-topping success, Grimsley faded into Houston's Triple-A woodwork. In '92, Schilling posted a 14-11 record with a 2.35 ERA over the course of 42 appearances, 26 of which were starts. Before the '92 season, he owned only five starts in 100 career games. His best year had been with the '91 Astros, consisting of eight saves, a 3-5 record and 3.81 ERA. After Schilling was taken in the second round of the '86 draft by the Red Sox, he worked three years as a starter. In July '88, he was swapped to Baltimore with Brady Anderson.

Schilling is a possible 20-game winner. His common-priced cards are inexpensive but promising possibilities. Our pick for his best 1993 card is Fleer. We have chosen this card because of its great combination of photography and design.

	W	L	ERA	G	CG	IP	H	ER	BB	SO
92 NL	14	11	2.35	42	10	226.1	165	59	59	147
Life	18	22	3.05	142	10	371.1	314	126	130	260

Series two cards from some companies were available at press time. If space allows, both cards are shown; if not, the most up-to-date cards are pictured.

DICK SCHOFIELD

Position: Shortstop
Team: New York Mets
Born: November 21, 1962
Springfield, IL
Height: 5'10" **Weight:** 179 lbs.
Bats: Right **Throws:** Right
Acquired: Traded from Angels
for Julio Valera, 4/92

MIKE SCHOOLER

Position: Pitcher
Team: Seattle Mariners
Born: August 10, 1962
Anaheim, CA
Height: 6'3" **Weight:** 220 lbs.
Bats: Right **Throws:** Right
Acquired: Second-round pick,
6/85 free-agent draft

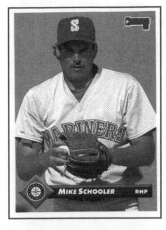

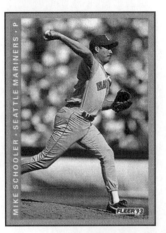

Dick Schofield's fresh start with the 1992 Mets had mixed results. While his batting average sank to .205, his lowest in 10 years, Schofield neared his '87 total of 46 RBI. He lost his starting role with the Angels in '92 spring training, due to a strong showing by Gary DiSarcina. The move was inevitable. DiSarcina batted .392 in preseason play, Schofield only .220. However, Schofield is a fine fielder with some speed. He was the lone beacon in New York's defensive fog last summer. Flashing exceptional range, reliable hands, and a good arm, he got high fielding marks. His highs came in '86, when he slammed 13 home runs and 57 RBI. Despite his limited offense, Schofield may follow his father's longevity record. Dick "Ducky" Schofield's career spanned seven teams from 1953-71.

Schofield can't survive offensively as a full-time player. Expect his common-priced cards to remain stale in 1993. Our pick for his best 1993 card is Fleer. We have chosen this card since the photograph captures the athletic ability of the player.

Mike Schooler could have been a poster boy for the hapless Mariners bullpen in 1992. Although he led the team in saves (13) for a third season, Schooler's losing record (2-7) and near-five ERA (4.70) only hinted at his problems. Schooler surrendered four grand slams during the season. Ironically, he was 3-0 with one save in '92 spring training, hurling 14 ⅔ scoreless innings with no walks. His '90 campaign ended on August 25 due to a shoulder injury. He didn't return to Seattle until July '91. Based on his performance, he should have stayed home. For three minor league seasons, the M's tried to groom the righthander as a starter. Now, Schooler is the M's all-time saves leader, thanks to 33 in '89 and 30 in '90. However, his health miseries and sheer ineffectiveness of late could change his job status soon.

Schooler will be lucky to make the 1993 Mariners, based on his 1992 woes. His common-priced cards are hopeless. Our pick for his best 1993 card is Score. We have chosen this card because of its overall appeal and pleasing looks.

	BA	G	AB	R	H	2B	3B	HR	RBI	SB
92	.206	143	423	52	87	18	2	4	36	11
Life	.229	1203	3818	452	875	122	29	52	314	109

	W	L	ERA	G	SV	IP	H	ER	BB	SO
92 AL	2	7	4.70	53	13	51.2	55	27	24	33
Life	12	29	3.30	243	98	267.1	253	98	93	232

PETE SCHOUREK

Position: Pitcher
Team: New York Mets
Born: May 10, 1969 Austin, TX
Height: 6'5" **Weight:** 195 lbs.
Bats: Left **Throws:** Left
Acquired: Second-round pick,
6/87 free-agent draft

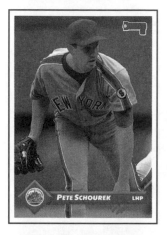 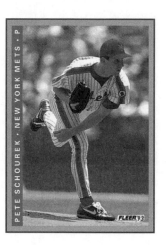

Pete Schourek didn't get much help as a 1992 Mets starter. In his first 20 starts, teammates provided him with an average of fewer than three runs per game. It's no surprise that he didn't start the '92 season in New York. He was 1-5 with a 6.52 ERA in seven spring training appearances. For the regular '92 season, he went 6-8 with a 3.64 ERA. The lefthander's career progress is notable, considering that he sat out the entire '88 campaign due to elbow surgery. Although Schourek has been a starter since his '87 beginning in the Mets organization, he was used as a reliever during his '91 rookie season in New York. That year, he made eight starts in 35 appearances, ending at 5-4 with two saves and a 4.27 ERA.

If Schourek is kept in the New York starting rotation for an entire season, he should be an easy double-digit winner. His '93s will average about a dime each. If the price dips to a nickel, invest quickly. Our pick for his best 1993 card is Topps. We have chosen this card for its technical merits.

	W	L	ERA	G	CG	IP	H	ER	BB	SO
92 NL	6	8	3.64	22	0	136.0	137	55	44	60
Life	11	12	3.89	57	1	222.1	219	96	87	127

MIKE SCIOSCIA

Position: Catcher
Team: Los Angeles Dodgers
Born: November 27, 1958
Upper Darby, PA
Height: 6'2" **Weight:** 220 lbs.
Bats: Left **Throws:** Right
Acquired: First-round pick,
6/76 free-agent draft

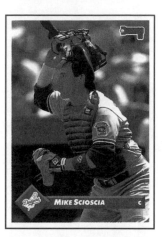 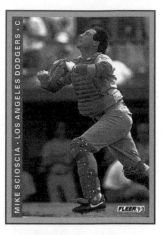

Mike Scioscia suffered through a humbling and frustrating year with the 1992 Dodgers. Knowing that his contract was up for renewal after the season, the Dodgers chose to give younger catchers Mike Piazza and Carlos Hernandez increased playing time. Scioscia, an LA regular since '81, faced being a back-up backstop for the first time in his big league existence. His stats reflect the effects. Just two seasons earlier ('90), Scioscia's offense produced career highs of 12 homers and 66 RBI. The two-time All-Star was known as one of the top-fielding receivers of the '80s, fearless at blocking the plate. Before '92, his lifetime walks (535) were nearly double his lifetime strikeouts (276). Scioscia ranks fifth in LA history in career games played.

Free-agent Scioscia wants to play full-time somewhere in 1993. Expect the veteran backstop to retire or accept platoon duty with another club. Either way, his common-priced cards lose. Our pick for his best 1993 card is Topps. We have chosen this card since the photograph captures the athletic ability of the player.

	BA	G	AB	R	H	2B	3B	HR	RBI	SB
92 NL	.221	117	348	19	77	6	3	3	24	3
Life	.259	1441	4373	398	1131	198	12	68	446	29

GARY SCOTT

Position: Infield
Team: Florida Marlins
Born: August 22, 1968
 New Rochelle, NY
Height: 6′ **Weight:** 175 lbs.
Bats: Right **Throws:** Right
Acquired: Traded from Cubs
 with Alex Arias for Greg
 Hibbard, 11/92

In 1992, Gary Scott had a couple of shots to win a major league job, but he simply hasn't been able to hit the way he did in the minors. After batting at least .280 at three minor league stops on the way to the majors, Scott failed to break the .200 mark with the Cubs—despite playing in a park that is kind to hitters. The Marlins are hoping he'll find his stride in '93 with their newly formed team. Chicago's Minor League Player of the Year in '90, Scott got an invitation to '91 spring training as a non-roster player. He batted .366 in 29 exhibition games while making all the plays at third. This performance earned him a trip north as the Opening-Day third baseman, but he hit just .165 with one homer before being sent out. Scott's problems did not end with his Triple-A demotion. At Iowa, he was batting .208 before a pitch hit his left hand, fracturing it and ending his season.

 It may be time to give up on Scott and his nickel-priced '93s. Our pick for his best 1993 card is Donruss. We have chosen this card because the design lends itself to the best use of the elements.

	BA	G	AB	R	H	2B	3B	HR	RBI	SB
92 NL	.156	36	96	8	15	2	0	2	11	0
Life	.160	67	175	16	28	5	0	3	16	0

TIM SCOTT

Position: Pitcher
Team: San Diego Padres
Born: November 16, 1966
 Hanford, CA
Height: 6′2″ **Weight:** 185 lbs.
Bats: Right **Throws:** Right
Acquired: Signed as a free
 agent, 11/90

Tim Scott's San Diego stock rose as 1992 progressed. He began the year as a non-roster invitee to spring training, but wound up in the Triple-A Pacific Coast League for a second consecutive year. A quick call-up allowed Scott to finish 16 games and earn four holds for the '92 Padres, working exclusively in relief. He saw only an inning's worth of action with San Diego in '91, constituting his major league debut. Worst of all, he earned a 9.00 ERA. Signed out of high school as a second-round draft selection by the Dodgers in '84, Scott bounced around their minor league system for seven seasons without a bow in the bigs. Following arm surgery in '87, his career came to a standstill.

 Scott's thankless bullpen role and his seesaw '92 efforts both cast doubts on his future card values. While he should last a full season with the 1993 Padres, he won't set the relief world ablaze. Our pick for his best 1993 card is Topps. We have chosen this card because the design lends itself to the best use of the elements.

	W	L	ERA	G	SV	IP	H	ER	BB	SO
92 NL	4	1	5.26	34	0	37.2	39	22	21	30
Life	4	1	5.35	36	0	38.2	41	23	21	31

SCOTT SCUDDER

Position: Pitcher
Team: Cleveland Indians
Born: February 14, 1968
  Paris, TX
Height: 6'2" **Weight:** 185 lbs.
Bats: Right **Throws:** Right
Acquired: Traded from Reds
  with Joe Turek and Jack
  Armstrong for Greg Swindell,
  11/91

A losing record and five-plus ERA were only two of Scott Scudder's problems with the 1992 Indians. A sore shoulder could have been the reason he didn't win a game after midseason. It was not the first time shoulder woes had caused him problems. The same type of problem kept him out of action for six weeks in '91, when he earned a 6-9 record with a 4.35 ERA with Cincinnati. On the plus side, '92 was the first season Scudder did not make a trip to the minors. He finished the '92 season with a 6-10 record and a 5.28 ERA. The Reds chose Scudder as a first-round draftee in '86. Before the draft, he was 19-0 for his Texas state-champion high school team. The righthander debuted in the NL in '89, giving the Reds a 4-9 effort. He returned for another partial season in '90, accumulating a 5-5 record over 21 games.

Scudder is young but won't be given forever to succeed with the Tribe. His commons are low-priced investment gambles. Think before you buy. Our pick for his best 1993 card is Topps. We have chosen this card for its technical merits.

	W	L	ERA	G	CG	IP	H	ER	BB	SO
92 AL	6	10	5.28	23	0	109.0	134	64	55	66
Life	21	33	4.76	94	0	382.1	390	202	202	225

DAVID SEGUI

Position: Outfield/first base
Team: Baltimore Orioles
Born: July 19, 1966
  Kansas City, KS
Height: 6'1" **Weight:** 200 lbs.
Bats: Both **Throws:** Left
Acquired: 18th-round pick,
  6/87 free-agent draft

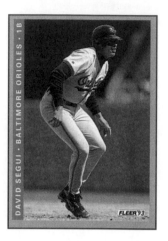

David Segui played in more than 100 games with the 1992 Orioles, but had few key hits to show for it. Segui was a defensive standout both at first base and in the outfield, but was a liability at the plate. Part of his offensive struggle was a .205 average against lefties and a .213 at home. Overall in '92, the switchhitter batted .233 with one homer and 17 RBI in 189 at-bats. By contrast, he hit .278 with the '91 O's. The first baseman/outfielder has never been a traditional power hitter. Segui started his pro career in '88. By '90, he was in Baltimore. His 40-game debut produced two home runs, 15 RBI, and a .244 average. His father, Diego Segui, pitched in the majors from 1962-77. The younger Segui is in baseball's twilight zone, too polished for the minors but unable to conquer big league hurlers.

Segui hasn't made a significant enough contribution in his pro career to validate the purchase of his cards. His 1993 cards are wasted nickels. Our pick for his best 1993 card is Fleer. We have chosen this card due to the outstanding photographic composition.

	BA	G	AB	R	H	2B	3B	HR	RBI	SB
92 AL	.233	115	189	21	44	9	0	1	17	1
Life	.254	241	524	50	133	23	0	5	54	2

Series two cards from some companies were available at press time. If space allows, both cards are shown; if not, the most up-to-date cards are pictured.

KEVIN SEITZER

Position: Third base
Team: Milwaukee Brewers
Born: March 26, 1962
  Springfield, IL
Height: 5'11" **Weight:** 190 lbs.
Bats: Right **Throws:** Right
Acquired: Signed as a free
  agent, 3/92

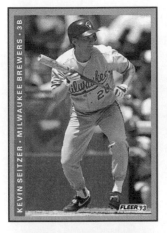

Kevin Seitzer's career came back from the brink in 1992, thanks to the faith of the Brewers. Seitzer attended spring training with the Royals, but received his unconditional release on March 26. On March 31, Milwaukee signed Seitzer to replace traded third sacker Gary Sheffield. He found his run-producing stroke and stayed healthy for the entire '92 season. He had a .270 average, 71 RBI, and 13 stolen bases. This marked his hottest RBI season since his '87 rookie campaign, when he drove in 83 runs. When he came in second that year in Rookie of the Year balloting, his totals included a .323 average, 15 home runs, and 207 hits in 161 games. Yet, Seitzer's year of overachievement made all his subsequent seasons look like failures.

A one-year comeback can't hide the prolonged downfall Seitzer faced in Kansas City. If Seitzer resumes his Royals-like offensive coma in 1993, his common-priced cards will sink quickly. Our pick for his best 1993 card is Score. We have chosen this card due to its unique photographic approach.

	BA	G	AB	R	H	2B	3B	HR	RBI	SB
92 AL	.270	148	540	74	146	35	1	5	71	13
Life	.290	889	3289	482	955	163	25	38	336	63

FRANK SEMINARA

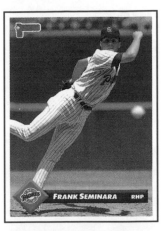

Position: Pitcher
Team: San Diego Padres
Born: May 16, 1967
  Brooklyn, NY
Height: 6'2" **Weight:** 205 lbs.
Bats: Right **Throws:** Right
Acquired: Drafted from
  Yankees, 12/90

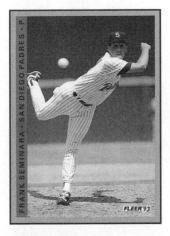

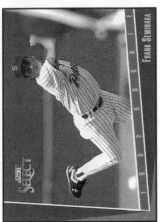

Frank Seminara has come a long way—from being an unprotected player in the major league draft to a big league starter—in less than two years. San Diego grabbed him from the Yankees at the 1990 winter meetings even though he had just been named Pitcher of the Year in the Class-A Carolina League. Seminara continued his development by going 15-10 with a 3.38 ERA at Wichita and making the All-Star team in his first look at Double-A ball. San Diego brought him to the majors in '92, and he fit right into the rotation, going 6 ⅔ shutout innings in his debut against the Cubs. For the '92 season, he went 9-4 with a 3.68 ERA. Seminara is a bulldog who likes to get the decision in games he starts. Four of his first six big league starts were quality starts. He is only the second Columbia player to play in the bigs since Lou Gehrig, the other being Gene Larkin.

San Diego likes Seminara's arm. You should like his 1993 cards for 15 cents each. Our pick for his best 1993 card is Fleer. We have chosen this card for its artistic presentation.

	W	L	ERA	G	CG	IP	H	ER	BB	SO
92 NL	9	4	3.68	19	0	100.1	98	41	46	61
Life	9	4	3.68	19	0	100.1	98	41	46	61

Series two cards from some companies were available at press time. If space allows, both cards are shown; if not, the most up-to-date cards are pictured.

263

SCOTT SERVAIS

Position: Catcher
Team: Houston Astros
Born: June 4, 1967
LaCrosse, WI
Height: 6'2" **Weight:** 195 lbs.
Bats: Right **Throws:** Right
Acquired: Third-round pick,
6/88

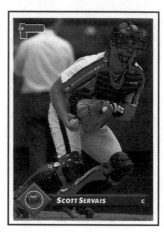 

MIKE SHARPERSON

Position: Second base
Team: Los Angeles Dodgers
Born: October 4, 1961
Orangeburg, SC
Height: 6'3" **Weight:** 190 lbs.
Bats: Right **Throws:** Right
Acquired: Traded from Blue
Jays for Juan Guzman, 9/87

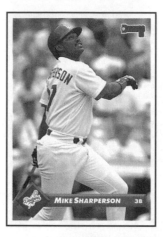 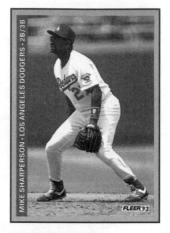

Scott Servais has played baseball around the world, including for Team USA in 1987, the U.S. Olympic team in '88, and winter ball in Venezuela from '91-'92. The place he wants to play most of all is in a major league line-up. He finally got a taste of the bigs in '92. Servais divided the workload with Ed Taubensee and Scooter Tucker. No one in the trio of backstops, however, could make the spot their own by wielding a big enough bat. In '92, Servais didn't hit righties well (.217), but showed some pop against lefties (.248). Since he has neither longball power nor base-stealing speed, a lot of his future depends on his glove. He made only two errors in his 524 innings of work for the Astros in '92. Servais was originally drafted by the Mets in the second round in '85. He got to the majors on July 12, 1991.

Servais ranks third behind Taubensee and Tucker in Houston's catching crew. His '93s are worth a shot at a nickel each. Our pick for his best 1993 card is Donruss. We have chosen this card because of its great combination of photography and design.

Mike Sharperson's best-ever season with the 1992 Dodgers ended quietly. He was named to his first All-Star team, due to a first-half effort of two home runs, 27 RBI, and a .328 average. Surprisingly, he batted only .235 in '92 spring training. In late '92, Eric Young and Lenny Harris took over at second base, while Dave Hansen and Dave Anderson monopolized third. As a result, Sharperson resumed his past duties as defensive substitute and pinch-hitter. Previously, Sharperson's most noteworthy season was in '90, when he batted .297 with three home runs, 36 RBI, and 15 stolen bases. Before Sharperson started his pro career with Toronto in '81, he turned down draft bids by the Pirates, Expos, and Tigers. He debuted with the Blue Jays in '87.

Sharperson's cards won't pull much weight at a nickel apiece. Without full-time responsibilities, he can't give collectors reason to buy his cards. Our pick for his best 1993 card is Donruss. We have chosen this card for its technical merits.

	BA	G	AB	R	H	2B	3B	HR	RBI	SB
92 NL	.239	77	205	12	49	9	0	0	15	0
Life	.227	93	242	12	55	12	0	0	21	0

	BA	G	AB	R	H	2B	3B	HR	RBI	SB
92 NL	.300	128	317	48	95	21	0	3	36	2
Life	.283	477	1106	135	313	56	5	8	111	20

Series two cards from some companies were available at press time. If space allows, both cards are shown; if not, the most up-to-date cards are pictured.

GARY SHEFFIELD

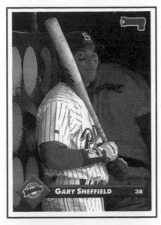

Position: Third base
Team: San Diego Padres
Born: November 18, 1968
   Tampa, FL
Height: 5'11" **Weight:** 190 lbs.
Bats: Right **Throws:** Right
Acquired: Traded from Brewers
   with Geoff Kellogg for Ricky
   Bones, Jose Valentin, and
   Matt Mieske, 3/92

Before the 1992 arrival of Gary Sheffield, San Diego's third-base situation had become a standing joke. The team had tried 73 players at the position in its 24-year history. When Sheffield started on Opening Day, he became the seventh different first-game starter in seven seasons. Fully recovered from wrist and shoulder injuries that ruined his '91 season, Sheffield responded warmly to the San Diego climate. He was just what the doctor ordered for the Padres. Because San Diego is also the home turf of Tony Fernandez, Sheffield had no objection to playing third base. His bat boomed from the start, and he claimed the NL batting crown for '92 with a .330 batting average. His other '92 stats included 33 home runs, 34 doubles, 100 RBI, and five stolen bases.

Feel lucky if you can find Sheffield's '93s at 15 cents each. The 1989 Topps Rookie of Sheffield is still within reach at 75 cents. Our pick for his best 1993 card is Upper Deck. We have chosen this card due to its unique photographic approach.

	BA	G	AB	R	H	2B	3B	HR	RBI	SB
92 NL	.330	146	557	87	184	34	3	33	100	5
Life	.283	440	1667	225	471	95	6	54	233	48

KEITH SHEPHERD

Position: Pitcher
Team: Colorado Rockies
Born: January 21, 1968
   Wabash, IN
Height: 6'2" **Weight:** 205 lbs.
Bats: Right **Throws:** Right
Acquired: Second-round pick,
   11/92 expansion draft

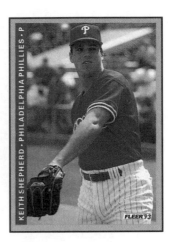

Pitcher Keith Shepherd's seven-year professional career took some strange turns in 1992. His career began as an 11th-round draft pick in '86. After five years in the Pittsburgh farm system, he signed a free-agent pact with the White Sox in '91. One season later, he was swapped to Philadelphia for shortstop Dale Sveum. The Phils had spotted his Double-A achievements of seven saves, a 3-3 mark, and 2.14 ERA in 40 appearances. Summoned to plug the leaky Phillies bullpen, the righthander answered with a 1-1 record, two saves, four holds and a 3.27 ERA in 12 relief outings. Due to his final-month heroics, Shepherd was Colorado's 12th pick in the second round of the expansion draft, the 50th selection overall.

Don't place a lot of hope on this seven-year rookie or his common-priced cards in 1993. His rocky past does just about anything but guarantee a Rockies future. Our pick for his best 1993 card is Donruss. We have chosen this card due to the outstanding photographic composition.

	W	L	ERA	G	SV	IP	H	ER	BB	SO
92 AAA	3	3	2.14	40	7	71.1	50	17	20	64
92 NL	1	1	3.27	12	2	22	19	8	6	10

RUBEN SIERRA

Position: Outfield
Team: Oakland Athletics
Born: October 6, 1965
    Rio Pedras, Puerto Rico
Height: 6'1" **Weight:** 175 lbs.
Bats: Both **Throws:** Right
Acquired: Traded from Rangers
    with Bobby Witt and Jeff
    Russell for Jose Canseco,
    8/92

 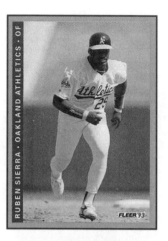

For the past six seasons, Ruben Sierra has been the most powerful switch-hitter in the AL. In '92, he batted .278 with 17 homers and 87 RBI. Sierra showed his best stuff against lefties and on the road, hitting above .300 in both situations during '92. Although these numbers were very good, he could hardly match his stats from '91. That year he ranked third in the league in doubles, total bases, and RBI, while tying for third in hits. He played in his second All-Star Game, enjoyed his third 100-RBI campaign, and became the career Texas leader in RBI, extra-base hits, and total bases. He also showed marked improvement defensively in right field. At the end of '91, he was voted Rangers' Player of the Year for the fourth time. Part of the trade that sent Canseco to Texas, Sierra should continue to shine in Oakland.

Rope in a few '93s of Sierra at a dime apiece. Quick! See if any '87 Topps cards of him are available for $2. Our pick for his best 1993 card is Fleer. We have chosen this card due to the outstanding photographic composition.

DON SLAUGHT

Position: Catcher
Team: Pittsburgh Pirates
Born: September 11, 1958
    Long Beach, CA
Height: 6'1" **Weight:** 190 lbs.
Bats: Right **Throws:** Right
Acquired: Traded by Yankees
    for Willie Smith and Jeff
    Robinson, 12/89

Don Slaught partnered with Mike LaValliere for the third year in a row to form Pittsburgh's catching platoon. Slaught's 1992 marks outdistanced his backstop companion, especially his .345 batting average. He hit an amazing .395 against righthanders. With the Bucs, Slaught has been remarkably consistent at bat. In '90, he hit .300 with four homers and 29 RBI. His '91 totals offered one homer, 29 RBI, and a .295 average. Slaught's career dates back to '80, when he was a seventh-round draft selection of the Royals. By '82, he was active in Kansas City. Slaught was involved in a six-player transaction with Texas in '85. His '86 totals for the Rangers brought career highs of 13 homers and 46 RBI.

Slaught's career looks golden as a part-time player. Yet, he hasn't excelled in full-time play, a fact which dooms his '93 common-priced cards. Our pick for his best 1993 card is Score. We have chosen this card for the interesting facts included on the reverse.

	BA	G	AB	R	H	2B	3B	HR	RBI	SB
92 AL	.278	151	601	83	167	34	7	17	87	14
Life	.280	1060	4144	588	1160	230	44	156	673	88

	BA	G	AB	R	H	2B	3B	HR	RBI	SB
92 NL	.345	87	255	26	88	17	3	4	37	2
Life	.280	1004	3071	320	859	193	26	59	351	16

Series two cards from some companies were available at press time. If space allows, both cards are shown; if not, the most up-to-date cards are pictured.

JOHN SMILEY

Position: Pitcher
Team: Cincinnati Reds
Born: March 17, 1965
  Phoenixville, PA
Height: 6'4" **Weight:** 200 lbs.
Bats: Left **Throws:** Left
Acquired: Signed as a free
  agent, 11/92

John Smiley didn't repeat his 20-win season with the Twins in 1992, but maybe it's just as well. After he turned in a career-best effort of 20-8 with the '91 Pirates, Pittsburgh rewarded the hurler with a trade to another league. Actually, the Bucs' real concern was the flow of dollars out of their pocket and into Smiley's. The relocation put Smiley in a strange fix. Minnesota grabbed him to replace staff ace Jack Morris. After he went 16-9 with a 3.21 ERA in '92 for the Twins, he was again on the bargaining table. He made another division change and will be with the Reds for '93. Drafted in '83 by Pittsburgh, Smiley was molded as a reliever. Following a 12-game tryout in '86, his first full season came in '87, featuring a 5-5 record with four saves.

In the fashion of a Dave Stewart, Smiley could become a perpetual 20-game winner for the Reds. His 1993 cards could be buried treasures at a nickel or less. Our pick for his best 1993 card is Score. We have chosen this card due to its unique photographic approach.

	W	L	ERA	G	CG	IP	H	ER	BB	SO
92 AL	16	9	3.21	34	5	241.0	205	86	65	163
Life	76	51	3.49	230	22	1095.0	992	425	294	697

DAN SMITH

Position: Pitcher
Team: Texas Rangers
Born: August 20, 1969
  St. Paul, MN
Height: 6'5" **Weight:** 190 lbs.
Bats: Left **Throws:** Left
Acquired: First-round pick,
  6/90 free-agent draft

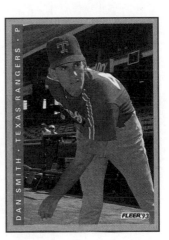

Dan Smith assembled the best showing of his three-year pro career in 1992, coming back beautifully from a disastrous '91. In '92, he was named the Double-A Texas League Pitcher of the Year and captured the ERA title. Smith ranked among the win, ERA, and strikeout leaders in the Rangers' minor league system and also compiled a five-game winning streak. He appeared in the Double-A All-Star Game and pitched two-thirds of an inning without allowing a hit or a walk. Double-A opponents compiled a .212 batting average against him last year. Smith might have collected an extra victory or two, but he had a bout with shoulder tendinitis. His size gives him presence on the mound, and he backs it up with an ability to throw the ball over the plate with something on it.

Smith, who seems ready for another crack at Triple-A and possibly the bigs in '93, may very well take off. Put a few of his '93s away for safekeeping. Our pick for his best 1993 card is Fleer. We have chosen this card due to the outstanding photographic composition.

	W	L	ERA	G	CG	IP	H	ER	BB	SO
92 AA	11	7	2.52	24	4	146.1	110	41	34	122
92 AL	0	3	5.02	4	0	14.1	18	8	8	5

DWIGHT SMITH

Position: Outfield
Team: Chicago Cubs
Born: November 8, 1963
  Tallahassee, FL
Height: 5'11" **Weight:** 175 lbs.
Bats: Left **Throws:** Right
Acquired: Third-round pick,
  6/84 free-agent draft

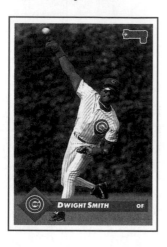

LEE SMITH

Position: Pitcher
Team: St. Louis Cardinals
Born: December 4, 1957
  Jamestown, LA
Height: 6'6" **Weight:** 250 lbs.
Bats: Right **Throws:** Right
Acquired: Traded from Red Sox
  for Tom Brunansky, 5/90

Dwight Smith spent another uneventful year riding the Cubs bench in 1992. Employed by Chicago as a reserve outfielder, defensive substitute, and pinch-hitter, Smith's '92 totals were better than expected from many part-timers. He lifted his average from its '91 mark of .228 to .276 in '92, which helped offset his three home runs and 24 RBI. His last real opportunity as a semi-starter came in '90, when he batted .262 with six homers and 27 RBI in 117 games. Smith hasn't recaptured the magic of his '89 rookie season, when he earned nine homers, 52 RBI, and a .324 average for 109 games. That was the season he finished second in Rookie of the Year balloting to teammate Jerome Walton. Smith has played in the Cubs organization since '84.

Since the Cubs lost Andre Dawson to free-agency, Smith will have a remote chance of increased playing time. His '93 season—and his common-priced cards—still face uncertain futures. Our pick for his best 1993 card is Donruss. We have chosen this card for its technical merits.

Lee Smith did it again for the St. Louis Cardinals in 1992. Smith followed up one record-setting season with another. In '91, he saved 47 games, an NL record, and finished second to Atlanta's Tom Glavine in Cy Young Award voting. He proved that, knee problems or not, he is a valuable asset to the Redbirds. The record performance placed Smith third on the career saves list and placed him within striking distance of the career mark of 341 held by Hall of Famer Rollie Fingers. Would Smith run out of smoke before accomplishing this feat? No. In '92, he posted another 43 saves, for a lifetime total of 355. Smith, still a workhorse for the Cards, made 70 appearances in '92. He struck out 60 batters over 75 innings.

Big Lee is an underrated steal at a dime per card in '93. An '82 Fleer Rookie may still remain as low as $6. Don't delay. Our pick for his best 1993 card is Fleer. We have chosen this card due to the outstanding photographic composition.

	BA	G	AB	R	H	2B	3B	HR	RBI	SB
92 NL	.276	109	217	28	60	10	3	3	24	9
Life	.280	425	1017	130	285	51	11	21	124	31

	W	L	ERA	G	SV	IP	H	ER	BB	SO
92 NL	4	9	3.12	70	43	75.0	62	26	26	60
Life	65	74	2.86	787	355	1066.2	919	339	402	1050

Series two cards from some companies were available at press time. If space allows, both cards are shown; if not, the most up-to-date cards are pictured.

LONNIE SMITH

Position: Outfield
Team: Pittsburgh Pirates
Born: December 22, 1955
 Chicago, IL
Height: 5'9" **Weight:** 170 lbs.
Bats: Right **Throws:** Right
Acquired: Signed as a free
 agent, 1/93

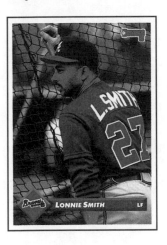

In 1992, Lonnie Smith appeared in fewer than 100 games for the first time since he joined the Braves in '88. His stats dipped to a .247 average with six homers and 33 RBI. Smith was coming off a '91 campaign of seven home runs, 44 RBI, and a .275 average. In the '91 World Series, he hit three homers, becoming the first National Leaguer ever to connect in three consecutive series games. Smith has seen action with a number of teams over the years, with one interesting slant. In addition to the Braves, he has seen Series action with the '80 Phillies, '82 Cardinals, and '85 Royals, making him the first-ever four-team competitor in post-season play. His personal bests, reached with the Braves in '89, included 21 homers and 79 RBI. That season he won the Comeback Player of the Year Award. He joins Pittsburgh for '93.

Smith is destined to a few remaining years of part-time duty. His common-priced cards will have no lasting value. Our pick for his best 1993 card is Donruss. We have chosen this card for its technical merits.

	BA	G	AB	R	H	2B	3B	HR	RBI	SB
92 NL	.247	84	158	23	39	8	2	6	33	4
Life	.289	1475	4888	853	1414	264	54	90	504	360

OZZIE SMITH

Position: Shortstop
Team: St. Louis Cardinals
Born: December 26, 1954
 Mobile, AL
Height: 5'10" **Weight:** 160 lbs.
Bats: Both **Throws:** Right
Acquired: Traded from Padres
 for Garry Templeton, 2/82

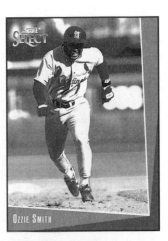

Although he no longer possesses the blinding speed that allowed him to steal 57 bases in one season, you still can't blink when Ozzie Smith is on base. Smith continues to contribute generously to the Cardinal tradition of showing speed on the basepaths. His '92 stats included an impressive .295 batting average with 20 doubles. He hit best on the road in '92, producing a .335 average away from Busch Stadium. He also provides the Redbirds with solid glove work while swallowing up anything that comes his way at short. A 10 time All-Star and winner of 12 Gold Gloves, Smith is still an acrobatic infielder who compensates for the lost step with his knowledge of how to play the hitters. Once regarded as a weak hitter, he improved steadily after coming to the Cardinals from San Diego in 1982. He hit a career-best .303 in 1987.

A St. Louis saint, Ozzie's '93s are perfect buys at 15 cents each. The first-ever Donruss card, 1981 (#1), features Smith. Our pick for his best 1993 card is Upper Deck. We have chosen this card since the photograph captures the athletic ability of the player.

	BA	G	AB	R	H	2B	3B	HR	RBI	SB
92 NL	.295	132	518	73	153	20	2	0	31	43
Life	.261	2208	8087	1079	2108	347	57	22	681	542

PETE SMITH

Position: Pitcher
Team: Atlanta Braves
Born: February 27, 1966
Abington, MA
Height: 6'2" **Weight:** 200 lbs.
Bats: Right **Throws:** Right
Acquired: Traded from Phillies
with Ozzie Virgil for Milt
Thompson and Steve
Bedrosian, 12/85

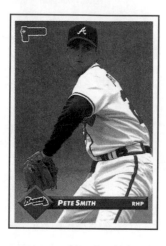

ZANE SMITH

Position: Pitcher
Team: Pittsburgh Pirates
Born: December 28, 1960
Madison, WI
Height: 6'2" **Weight:** 200 lbs.
Bats: Left **Throws:** Left
Acquired: Traded from Expos
for Scott Ruskin, Moises
Alou, and Willie Greene, 8/90

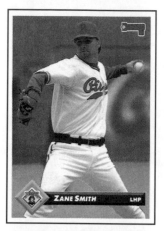 

For the first time in six major league seasons, Pete Smith seems to have a future with the Braves. His 1992 efforts in Triple-A Richmond—15 starts with a 7-4 record and a 2.14 ERA—finally paid off on July 29. That's when Atlanta summoned the righthander back to the bigs, hoping he'd simply replace ailing starter Mike Bielecki. Instead, Smith became a fixture in the Braves rotation, winning seven in a row. In seven of his first 10 starts, Smith pitched into or past the sixth inning while allowing three runs or less. His efforts for the Braves in '92 earned him a 7-0 record and a 2.05 ERA. He worked 79 innings, struck out 43 batters, and walked 28. A first-round draft pick of the Phillies in '84, Smith was traded to the Braves organization after two seasons. Going into '92, Smith's lifetime marks with Atlanta were 19-40 with a 4.37 ERA.

Don't buy his nickel-priced cards if he leaves Atlanta. Our pick for his best 1993 card is Donruss. We have chosen this card for the superior presentation of information on its back.

Zane Smith's shoulder stopped him from being a major force in Pittsburgh's 1992 title defense. He was a respectable 8-7 with a 2.96 ERA at the All-Star break, but shoulder tendinitis took him out of a July 11 game early. By July 25, he was trapped on the disabled list. Activated on August 8, he headed for the DL again August 15. Smith had finished the best year of his career (16-10, 3.20 ERA) with the '91 Bucs. He survived some horrifying seasons with Atlanta, as well as a high-water mark 15-10 season in '87. In '86, he was tagged with an 8-16 mark. Before Smith was traded to the Expos in mid-1989, the lefthander endured a 1-12 record. His '89 stay in Montreal marked the only time in Smith's major league career that he worked in relief.

Smith needs a 20-win season before collectors would consider his nickel-priced cards investments. Try one of the younger arms on the Pittsburgh staff instead. Our pick for his best 1993 card is Fleer. We have chosen this card due to the outstanding photographic composition.

	W	L	ERA	G	CG	IP	H	ER	BB	SO
92 NL	7	0	2.05	12	2	79.0	63	18	28	43
Life	26	40	4.05	105	11	573.0	554	258	233	378

	W	L	ERA	G	CG	IP	H	ER	BB	SO
92 NL	8	8	3.06	23	4	141.0	138	48	19	56
Life	75	86	3.53	281	31	1485.1	1473	583	483	828

Series two cards from some companies were available at press time. If space allows, both cards are shown; if not, the most up-to-date cards are pictured.

JOHN SMOLTZ

Position: Pitcher
Team: Atlanta Braves
Born: May 15, 1967 Detroit, MI
Height: 6'3" **Weight:** 185 lbs.
Bats: Right **Throws:** Right
Acquired: Traded from Tigers
for Doyle Alexander, 8/87

When John Smoltz threw a two-hit shutout at San Francisco on June 24, 1992, he increased his record to 8-5, dropped his ERA to 3.18, and got his fifth complete game and second shutout of the young season. Only first and ninth-inning singles by Will Clark separated Smoltz from his first no-hitter. The Smoltz victory gave the Braves three consecutive shutouts for the second time in '92. It also silenced skeptics who wondered when the magic of sports psychologist Jack Llewellyn would wear off. The sage counsel of Llewellyn had enabled Smoltz to overcome a 2-11 first half in '91 to forge a 12-2 finish. He pitched his only shutout of that season in Game 7 of the NL Championship Series against Pittsburgh. He set an Atlanta club record with a 15-strikeout game against Montreal in 1992.

Welcome 1993 cards of Smoltz at 15 cents apiece. Mull over a '88 Fleer Update of Smoltz at $3. Our pick for his best 1993 card is Topps. We have chosen this card for its technical merits.

J.T. SNOW

Position: First base
Team: California Angels
Born: February 26, 1968
Long Beach, CA
Height: 6'2" **Weight:** 202 lbs.
Bats: Both **Throws:** Left
Acquired: Traded from Yankees
with Jerry Nielsen and Russ
Springer for Jim Abbott,
12/92

If he thought there was pressure in trying to move up to New York to try and beat out Don Mattingly, wait till Snow sees what is waiting for him in Anaheim. Snow was the key player traded for Jim Abbott, who is a national hero as well as Angels' owner Gene Autry's favorite player. That's pressure. Snow is coming off the year of his life and had better be ready for the majors. Snow was the Triple-A International League's Rookie of the Year and won its MVP Award in '92. He reached career highs in batting average, homers, and RBI. His .313 average claimed the batting title. Making the '92 All-Star team for his Triple-A league marked the third year he has won that honor. His ability to switch-hit would add flexibility to the Angels lineup, and the fact that he keeps improving and adjusting makes you wonder exactly how good he'll get!

Pick up a few of his '93s, and wait for him to break it wide open in California. Our pick for his best 1993 card is Upper Deck. We have chosen this card because it will increase in value.

	W	L	ERA	G	CG	IP	H	ER	BB	SO
92 NL	15	12	2.85	35	9	246.2	206	78	80	215
Life	57	54	3.50	146	25	979.2	852	381	352	738

	BA	G	AB	R	H	2B	3B	HR	RBI	SB
92 AAA	.313	135	492	81	154	26	4	15	78	3
92 AL	.143	7	14	1	2	1	0	0	2	0

Series two cards from some companies were available at press time. If space allows, both cards are shown; if not, the most up-to-date cards are pictured.

271

CORY SNYDER

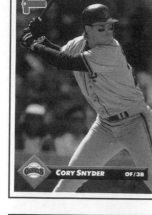

Position: Infield/outfield
Team: Los Angeles Dodgers
Born: November 11, 1962
Inglewood, CA
Height: 6'3" **Weight:** 185 lbs.
Bats: Right **Throws:** Right
Acquired: Signed as a free
agent, 12/92

Cory Snyder came to the Giants' 1992 spring training camp hoping to hook on as a utility player. By mid-June, however, his booming bat had made him the club's every-day cleanup hitter. Snyder collected his 18th RBI in 20 games on June 12, stretched his hitting streak to 10 games, and had his average at .309. He homered twice off Jose Rijo four days later. He finished the '92 campaign with a .269 average, 14 homers, and 57 RBI. He finished the '92 calendar year by signing with the Dodgers for '93. In previous years, Snyder had been a high-power, low-average performer whose play was plagued by frequent strikeouts. He had 33 homers in '87 and topped 20 in two other seasons but drew his release from the White Sox in '91 after his average fell to .175. In addition to his batting revival, Snyder gave the Giants the added bonus of his throwing arm—one of baseball's best.

Is Snyder a one-year wonder? His '93s are skeptical buys. Our pick for his best 1993 card is Upper Deck. We have chosen this card because it has a distinctive look.

	BA	G	AB	R	H	2B	3B	HR	RBI	SB
92 NL	.269	124	390	48	105	22	2	14	57	4
Life	.244	852	2987	360	729	139	12	132	414	23

LUIS SOJO

Position: Second base
Team: Toronto Blue Jays
Born: January 3, 1966
Barquisimeto, Venezuela
Height: 5'11" **Weight:** 174 lbs.
Bats: Right **Throws:** Right
Acquired: Traded from Angels
for Kelly Gruber and cash,
12/92

Luis Sojo's second year with the Angels took some strange detours in 1992. Bobby Rose beat him out of the starting second baseman's job, and Sojo began the year at Triple-A Edmonton. He was recalled May 22, when Rose was injured in the team's bus accident. Sojo barely hit .200 against lefthanders, but he was the team's starting second sacker at year's end. Sojo had only been with California since the '91 season, but reached the end of the line with the Angels late in '92. His first year with the Halos offered three homers, 20 RBI, and a .258 average. For '93, he'll join the Toronto Blue Jays. He's familiar with the Jays' organization. They had signed Sojo as an undrafted free agent in '86. His only work in Toronto at that time came as a utility infielder in '90.

Sojo's offensive inconsistencies will give the Angels and card investors fits in 1993. Don't invest in his commons. Our pick for his best 1993 card is Upper Deck. We have chosen this card since the photograph captures the athletic ability of the player.

	BA	G	AB	R	H	2B	3B	HR	RBI	SB
92 AL	.272	106	368	37	100	12	3	7	43	7
Life	.261	252	812	89	212	29	4	11	72	12

Series two cards from some companies were available at press time. If space allows, both cards are shown; if not, the most up-to-date cards are pictured.

PAUL SORRENTO

Position: First base
Team: Cleveland Indians
Born: November 17, 1965
Somerville, MA
Height: 6'2" **Weight:** 223 lbs.
Bats: Left **Throws:** Right
Acquired: Traded from Twins
for Curt Leskanic and Oscar
Munoz, 3/92

Paul Sorrento escaped the shadow of Kent Hrbek when he was traded from the Twins and won the starting first base job with the 1992 Indians. Sorrento responded to his first big league starting job with a year of double-digit homers (18). Even though he wasn't an Oriole, Sorrento earned the honor of hitting the first home run in Baltimore's new ballpark. His sole downfall in '92 was a year-long struggle against lefthanded pitching. At season's end, he had managed only a .159 average against southpaws. Overall, he had a .269 average with 60 RBI. After attending Florida State University, Sorrento began his career as California's fourth-round draft pick in '86. He was swapped to the Twins in the deal for Bert Blyleven for the '89 season and graduated to Minnesota by year's end.

You'll find Sorrento's '93 cards for a nickel or less. His encouraging power could make those values double if the Indians contend. Our pick for his best 1993 card is Donruss. We have chosen this card for its technical merits.

	BA	G	AB	R	H	2B	3B	HR	RBI	SB
92 AL	.269	140	458	52	123	24	1	18	60	0
Life	.255	221	647	71	165	30	2	27	87	1

SAMMY SOSA

Position: Outfield
Team: Chicago Cubs
Born: November 10, 1968
San Pedro de Macoris,
Dominican Republic
Height: 6' **Weight:** 175 lbs.
Bats: Right **Throws:** Right
Acquired: Traded from White
Sox with Ken Patterson for
George Bell, 3/92

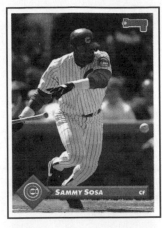

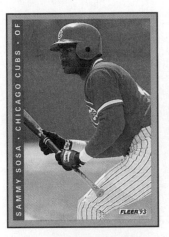

Early in 1992, the Cubs sent George Bell across town to obtain Ken Patterson and Sammy Sosa. Sosa needed only 67 games with the crosstown Cubs to nearly match his '91 White Sox totals. In '91, the streaky outfielder fell to .200 with nine home runs and 26 RBI, he was shipped back to Triple-A for a month. In '92, a fractured ankle wiped out the rest of Sosa's '92 NL debut. The Cubs hoped Sosa would regain his '90 magic, when he gave the White Sox 15 homers, 70 RBI, and 32 stolen bases, though this was tempered by a .233 average and 150 strikeouts. He began his '89 rookie season with Texas, but was swapped to the ChiSox in July.

Sosa needs a first healthy season before anyone can get excited about his nickel-priced cards. Monitor his 1993 progress before investing. You can pick up virtually any of Sosa's '90 Rookies at under a quarter. Our pick for his best 1993 card is Fleer. We have chosen this card because of its great combination of photography and design.

	BA	G	AB	R	H	2B	3B	HR	RBI	SB
92 NL	.260	67	262	41	68	7	2	8	25	15
Life	.234	394	1293	179	303	51	13	37	141	67

BILL SPIERS

Position: Infield
Team: Milwaukee Brewers
Born: June 5, 1966
Orangeburg, SC
Height: 6'2" **Weight:** 190 lbs.
Bats: Left **Throws:** Right
Acquired: First-round pick,
6/87 free-agent draft

Even on the disabled list, Bill Spiers made a valuable contribution to the 1992 Brewers. He was touted as the team's starting shortstop, but was sidelined due to off-season back surgery. As a result, rookie sensation Pat Listach inherited the position, sparking the team to surprise pennant contention. Spiers managed only 12 games for the Brew Crew in '92. His injury-filled year was a bleak turnaround from '91, when he batted .283, adding eight homers and 54 RBI. Spiers' first year as starting shortstop was in '90, when he hit .242 with two homers and 36 RBI. As an '89 Brewers rookie, Spiers socked four homers, 33 RBI, and a .255 average as a utility infielder. Expect Spiers to move to second base in '93.

Middle infielders with power are a rare breed, but Spiers needs a full, healthy season at a new position to prove his worth. Postpone buying his commons. Our pick for his best 1993 card is Upper Deck. We have chosen this card due to the outstanding photographic composition.

	BA	G	AB	R	H	2B	3B	HR	RBI	SB
92 AL	.313	12	16	2	5	2	0	0	2	1
Life	.262	371	1138	161	298	39	12	14	125	36

ED SPRAGUE

Position: Infield/catcher
Team: Toronto Blue Jays
Born: July 25, 1967
Castro Valley, CA
Height: 6'2" **Weight:** 215 lbs.
Bats: Right **Throws:** Right
Acquired: First-round pick,
6/88 free-agent draft

Ed Sprague remained one of Toronto's promising prospects again in 1992, but couldn't get noticed while surrounded by such a talented lineup. He banged out 16 homers, 50 RBI, and a .276 average at Triple-A Syracuse in '92, but had few opportunities to spell starting catcher Pat Borders. For his time served with the Jays in '92, he earned a .234 average with one homer and seven RBI in a 22 game span. Although Sprague was a first-round draft pick in '88, he spent the year as a member of the U.S. Olympic baseball team. He began his three-year minor league journey in '89, and got a '91 debut in Toronto, where he hit .275 with four homers. As late as '90, Sprague was a third baseman in the minors.

Sprague isn't starting for the 1993 Blue Jays. Even worse, catching prospects Carlos Delgado and Randy Knorr will threaten Sprague's big league survival. Common-priced Sprague cards aren't promising. Our pick for his best 1993 card is Donruss. We have chosen this card due to the outstanding photographic composition.

	BA	G	AB	R	H	2B	3B	HR	RBI	SB
92 AL	.234	22	47	6	11	2	0	1	7	0
Life	.266	83	207	23	55	9	0	5	27	0

Series two cards from some companies were available at press time. If space allows, both cards are shown; if not, the most up-to-date cards are pictured.

RUSS SPRINGER

Position: Pitcher
Team: New York Yankees
Born: November 7, 1968
   Alexandria, LA
Height: 6'4" **Weight:** 195 lbs.
Bats: Right **Throws:** Right
Acquired: Seventh-round pick,
   6/89

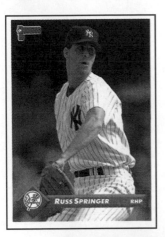

Russ Springer has come along quickly despite a shoulder injury that at one point made him wonder if he should forget his baseball career. Springer has left that doubt behind and could be ready to compete for a job in the Yankee rotation in '93. He pitched both in Class-A and Double-A ball in '91 and even made a brief appearance in the majors early in '92. He made his big league debut on April 17 against the Indians, allowing three runs in four innings. Springer is a starting pitcher, but he relieved in his first stint with the Yankees. In his '92 efforts with the Yankees, he worked 16 innings and notched two holds. For most of the season, Springer pitched for Triple-A Columbus, where he had some success but did not dominate to the extent he did in the lower classifications. Given time to gain more experience, this should change.

Springer's pitching potential is uncertain. His '93s are risks at a dime apiece. Our pick for his best 1993 card is Score. We have chosen this card for the interesting facts included on the reverse.

	W	L	ERA	G	SV	IP	H	ER	BB	SO
92 AL	0	0	6.19	14	0	16	18	11	10	12
Life	0	0	6.19	14	0	16	18	11	10	12

MATT STAIRS

Position: Outfield
Team: Montreal Expos
Born: February 27, 1969
   Fredericton, New Brunswick
Height: 5'9" **Weight:** 175 lbs.
Bats: Left **Throws:** Right
Acquired: Signed as a free
   agent, 6/89

Matt Stairs, like teammate Larry Walker, represents a chance for a Canadian-based franchise to have a native son in a starring role. Stairs certainly offers some promise for such a niche, having risen quickly through the farm system to a major league debut on May 29, 1992. In his 30 at-bats for the Expos in '92, he knocked in five runs and walked seven times. His ascent was not without distinction. He played for Double-A Harrisburg in '91 and was named MVP in the league. That year he batted .333 with 30 doubles, 13 homers, and 23 steals in making the postseason All-Star team at second base. He hit for the cycle on August 23, dropping a bunt to clinch the feat. Stairs was the Expos' minor league player of the month for June and August. He didn't hit much in his first tour in the majors, but produced in Triple-A.

Stairs fell down in his 1992 trial in Montreal. His 1993 cards are 15-cent chances. Our pick for his best 1993 card is Donruss. We have chosen this card since its design makes it a standout.

	BA	G	AB	R	H	2B	3B	HR	RBI	SB
92 NL	.167	13	30	2	5	2	0	0	5	0
Life	.167	13	30	2	5	2	0	0	5	0

ANDY STANKIEWICZ

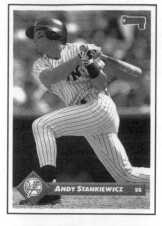

Position: Infield
Team: New York Yankees
Born: August 10, 1964
Inglewood, CA
Height: 5'9" **Weight:** 165 lbs.
Bats: Right **Throws:** Right
Acquired: 12th-round pick,
6/86 free-agent draft

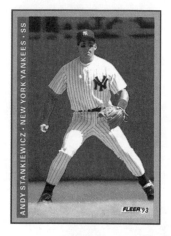

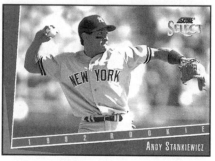

MIKE STANLEY

Position: Catcher/infield
Team: New York Yankees
Born: June 25, 1963
Fort Lauderdale, FL
Height: 6'1" **Weight:** 185 lbs.
Bats: Right **Throws:** Right
Acquired: Signed as a free
agent, 11/92

Andy Stankiewicz's career is a story about the virtue of never quitting. In 1991, he turned 27 and still had not appeared in a big league game. But his enthusiasm and skill made him an important part of New York's '92 season. He became New York's regular shortstop, but he can play third and second, too. Stankiewicz has come to be known as Stanky the Yankee, quite a compliment considering all the players who have found New York to involve too much pressure. Stankiewicz seems to be having too much fun to feel pressure. Stanky gave the Yankees the leadoff man they had needed. In his '92 campaign, he earned a .268 batting average, two homers, and 38 RBI. He feasts on lefthanded pitching and hits well on the road. His power tends to be of the extra-base variety. Showing occasional speed, he swiped nine bases in '92.

The scrappy, fun-loving New York infielder has a following. Follow his 1993 cards at a dime. Our pick for his best 1993 card is Topps. We have chosen this card for its technical merits.

Mike Stanley had one of his best offensive seasons with the 1992 Yankees. He began as a non-roster invitee to spring training, making the team with the aid of a .310 preseason average. During the regular season in '92, he posted a .249 average with eight homers and 27 RBI. After playing out his option with the '91 Rangers, Stanley didn't get an offer from a single major league team. He signed a Triple-A contract in January '92. Previously, his best offensive feats in the majors came in '87. Recalled from Triple-A that year for 46 games, he smacked 13 homers. Stanley saw action in 78 games with the Rangers, hitting .273 with six homers and 37 RBI. He was the team's starting catcher at the beginning of the '88 campaign.

Stanley will maintain his utility role with the Yankees in '93. Continuing his part-time status makes Stanley's common-priced cards unappealing. Our pick for his best 1993 card is Topps. We have chosen this card for its artistic presentation.

	BA	G	AB	R	H	2B	3B	HR	RBI	SB
92 AL	.268	116	400	52	107	22	2	2	25	9
Life	.268	116	400	52	107	22	2	2	25	9

	BA	G	AB	R	H	2B	3B	HR	RBI	SB
92 AL	.249	68	173	24	43	7	0	8	27	0
Life	.251	520	1160	138	291	50	4	24	147	6

MIKE STANTON

Position: Pitcher
Team: Atlanta Braves
Born: June 2, 1967
   Houston, TX
Height: 6'1" **Weight:** 190 lbs.
Bats: Left **Throws:** Left
Acquired: 13th-round pick,
   6/87 free-agent draft

Mike Stanton achieved a career high in saves (8) for the 1992 Braves. He pitched in over 60 games (65) for the second season in a row. However, his 4.10 ERA in '92 demonstrated a marked increase. Stanton ended '91 with a 5-5 mark, seven saves, and a 2.88 ERA in 74 outings. The lefthander was one of Atlanta's '91 postseason heroes. In NLCS play, he gave up only one run in three appearances against the Pirates. Pitching in the World Series, Stanton was 1-0 versus the Twins. In five appearances, he registered 7 ⅓ innings of shutout baseball, striking out seven. A low-round draft pick of Atlanta's in '87, Stanton worked two years as a starter. He premiered with the Braves in '89, collecting seven saves and a 1.50 ERA in 20 appearances.

Stanton's shifting duties on the Atlanta pitching staff will stop him from gaining widespread attention. His common-priced cards will remain in the dark, too. Our pick for his best 1993 card is Upper Deck. We have chosen this card because it has a distinctive look.

	W	L	ERA	G	SV	IP	H	ER	BB	SO
92 NL	5	4	4.10	65	8	63.2	59	29	20	44
Life	10	13	3.75	166	24	172.2	154	72	53	132

TERRY STEINBACH

Position: Catcher
Team: Oakland Athletics
Born: March 2, 1962
   New Ulm, MN
Height: 6'1" **Weight:** 195 lbs.
Bats: Right **Throws:** Right
Acquired: Ninth-round pick,
   6/83 free-agent draft

Terry Steinbach logged another banner season with the Oakland Athletics in 1992. While he didn't match the career-high 67 RBI he reached with the '91 Athletics, the Minnesota native showed the most power since he hit 16 home runs in his '87 rookie season. Steinbach's '92 stats include a .279 batting average with 12 homers and 53 RBI. Steinbach became a household word in '88, when fans voted him the starting catcher for the AL All-Stars. He was voted All-Star MVP for driving in the only runs of the 2-0 victory. Steinbach signed with the A's in the '83 draft. He jumped from Double-A ball directly to Oakland in '86, thanks to minor league totals of 24 homers, 132 RBI, and a .325 average. In his first-ever major league at-bat, he hit a home run.

Despite Steinbach's quiet consistency, his cards have never been big sellers. Quite likely, his '93 nickel-priced issues will be shunned, too. Our pick for his best 1993 card is Fleer. We have chosen this card for its artistic presentation.

	BA	G	AB	R	H	2B	3B	HR	RBI	SB
92 AL	.279	128	438	48	122	20	1	12	53	2
Life	.272	733	2484	278	675	114	9	61	330	9

Series two cards from some companies were available at press time. If space allows, both cards are shown; if not, the most up-to-date cards are pictured.

TODD STEVERSON

Position: Outfield
Team: Toronto Blue Jays
Born: November 15, 1971
  Culver City, CA
Height: 6'2" **Weight:** 194 lbs.
Bats: Right **Throws:** Right
Acquired: First-round pick,
  6/92 free-agent draft

Despite rave reviews, center field phenom Todd Steverson suffered through an uneven professional debut in 1992. A first-round selection of the '92 free-agent draft, Steverson played 65 games with St. Catherine's in the short-season Class-A league, hitting .209. His weak batting average was offset by a team-leading six home runs, with 24 RBI and 23 stolen bases. His '91 totals at Arizona State University included 10 home runs, 50 RBI, and a .289 average. Steverson ended his collegiate career in 1992 by batting .302, notching 12 homers, 37 RBI, and 17 stolen bases. *Baseball America* ranked Steverson as seventh-best in a list of the 100 finest prospects before the '92 draft. Steverson had turned down a sixth-round draft selection by the Cardinals in '89.

With speed and power as his primary assets, Steverson could reach the majors by 1995. His 1993 rookie cards are realistic investment choices at 10 to 15 cents apiece. Our pick for his best 1993 card is Score. We have chosen this card because it has a distinctive look.

	BA	G	AB	R	H	2B	3B	HR	RBI	SB
91 COL	.289	—	232	48	67	16	1	10	50	9
92 COL	.303	56	218	52	66	16	3	12	38	17

DAVE STEWART

Position: Pitcher
Team: Toronto Blue Jays
Born: February 19, 1957
  Oakland, CA
Height: 6'2" **Weight:** 200 lbs.
Bats: Right **Throws:** Right
Acquired: Signed as a free
  agent, 12/92

 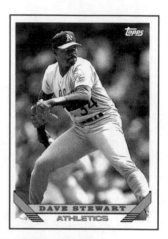

Dave Stewart improved upon some of his flaws in 1992 with the Athletics. Yet, the hurler looked like a bad imitation of the dominating winner he once was. Stewart was roughed up in '92 spring training to the tune of 1-2 with a 5.48 ERA. A sore right elbow limited his first-half efforts, influencing Stewart's '92 stats of a 12-10 record with a 3.66 ERA. The righthander's decline began in '91, when he was 11-11 with a 5.18 ERA. The slump ended a four-year reign of consecutive 20-win seasons from 1987-90. Stewart's first year with Oakland was in '86. He joined the team in late May, following his release by the Phillies, and wound up with a 9-5 mark. In '93, Stewart will join the Toronto Blue Jays. In a pro career dating back to '75, Stewart has served Los Angeles (1978-83), Texas (1983-85), Philadelphia (1985-86), and Oakland (87-92) before joining the Blue Jays.

Stew may be stewed in 1993. Don't consider his nickel-priced cards. Our pick for his best 1993 card is Topps. We have chosen this card due to the outstanding photographic composition.

	W	L	ERA	G	CG	IP	H	ER	BB	SO
92 AL	12	10	3.66	31	2	199.1	175	81	79	130
Life	146	106	3.69	459	54	2253.1	2101	925	861	1476

Series two cards from some companies were available at press time. If space allows, both cards are shown; if not, the most up-to-date cards are pictured.

DAVE
STIEB

Position: Pitcher
Team: Chicago White Sox
Born: July 22, 1957
　Santa Ana, CA
Height: 6'1" **Weight:** 195 lbs.
Bats: Right **Throws:** Right
Acquired: Signed as a free
　agent, 12/92

KURT
STILLWELL

Position: Second base
Team: San Diego Padres
Born: June 4, 1965
　Glendale, CA
Height: 5'11" **Weight:** 175 lbs.
Bats: Both **Throws:** Right
Acquired: Signed as a free
　agent, 2/92

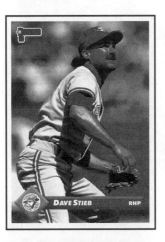 

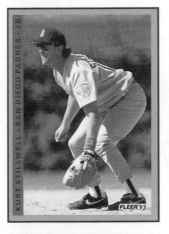 

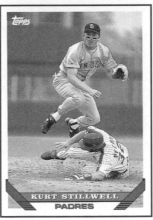 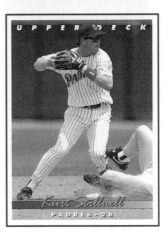

Dave Stieb was an infrequent participant in Toronto's 1992 title quest. A sore elbow kept Stieb out of action for more than half the season and hampered the rare appearances he made. At the end of '92, he went 4-6 with a 5.04 ERA. In '91, Stieb's season ended May 22. Shoulder problems shelved him for the year, requiring surgery in December. Before he became a DL regular, Stieb had reached his career peak in '90. His 10th season of double-digit wins resulted in a personal-best 18-6 record. Stieb's seventh All-Star appearance came in '90. He won the '83 midseason classic, then lost the '84 affair. In his career, he's topped 200 innings nine different times. After pitching with Toronto since '79, Stieb might be physically unfit. The Chicago White Sox, however, are counting on him in '93.

Stieb's nickel-priced cards won't be hot items in '93. His age and past injuries spook investors. Our pick for his best 1993 card is Topps. We have chosen this card for its technical merits.

Kurt Stillwell needed 1992 to adjust to the National league. In '92, he clinched a spot on San Diego's Opening-Day roster with a .268 effort in the Padres' spring training. A former Kansas City shortstop, Stillwell played a new position for the Padres in '92. While Stillwell made slow but steady adjustments, he still made 16 errors—more than any other second baseman in the NL. He hit .227 with two homers and 24 RBI. Stillwell was a starting shortstop in Kansas City from 1988-91. For four consecutive seasons, he knocked in more than 50 runs. His first AL season was highlighted with a career-best 10 homers. The Reds landed Stillwell in the first round of the '83 draft. He was Cincinnati's starting shortstop for part of '86, batting .229 in 104 games.

Although Stillwell may be better adjusted to National League pitchers in 1993, his 1993 cards shouldn't adjust from their common prices. Our pick for his best 1993 card is Donruss. We have chosen this card because the design lends itself to the best use of the elements.

	W	L	ERA	G	CG	IP	H	ER	BB	SO
92 AL	4	6	5.04	21	1	96.1	98	54	43	45
Life	174	132	3.39	420	103	2822.2	2487	1064	1003	1631

	BA	G	AB	R	H	2B	3B	HR	RBI	SB
92 NL	.227	114	379	35	86	15	3	2	24	4
Life	.250	873	2866	339	716	141	28	32	292	32

TODD STOTTLEMYRE

Position: Pitcher
Team: Toronto Blue Jays
Born: May 20, 1965
Yakima, WA
Height: 6'3" **Weight:** 195 lbs.
Bats: Left **Throws:** Right
Acquired: First-round pick,
secondary phase, 6/85 free-
agent draft

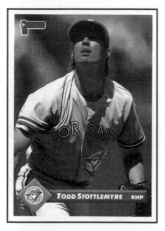

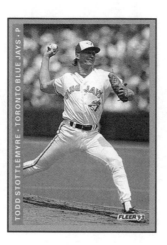

Todd Stottlemyre racked up his third season in a row of double-digit wins (12) with the Blue Jays. The righthander struggled to keep his 1992 record above .500, as a sore knee kept him shelved for nearly a month. The injury stopped the hurler from exceeding 30 starts (28) and 200 innings pitched (174) for the first time since '89. His '92 record was puzzling, considering that Toronto averaged nearly six runs per game while Stottlemyre pitched. Stottlemyre was more dominating in '91, when he carved out a career-best mark of 15-8 with a 3.78 ERA. His first full season with Toronto came in '89, ending in a 13-17 effort. Before Stottlemyre signed with the Blue Jays in '85, he turned down draft offers from the Yankees and Cardinals.

Stottlemyre may be worth a dozen wins per year. However, he's the least predictable or dependable starter on Toronto's staff. Shy away from his common-priced cards. Our pick for his best 1993 card is Fleer. We have chosen this card since its design makes it a standout.

	W	L	ERA	G	CG	IP	H	ER	BB	SO
92 AL	12	11	4.50	28	6	174.0	175	87	63	98
Life	51	51	4.32	150	11	821.2	829	394	297	459

DARRYL STRAWBERRY

Position: Outfield
Team: Los Angeles Dodgers
Born: March 12, 1962
Los Angeles, CA
Height: 6'6" **Weight:** 195 lbs.
Bats: Left **Throws:** Left
Acquired: Signed as a free
agent, 11/90

After a winter trade reunited Darryl Strawberry with pal Eric Davis in the Los Angeles Dodgers' outfield, injuries interfered with their anticipated dream season. Strawberry, idled by a herniated disc in his back, was unable to realize his preseason prediction that he would hit 45 home runs. He only played in 43 games for the Dodgers in '92, averaging a weak .237, 30 points off his '91 mark. At age 31, however, a healthy Strawberry should be able to make a formidable challenge. In three of his 10 big league seasons, most of them with the Mets, he has hit at least 37 homers three times. Heading into the '92 campaign, Strawberry had never hit less than 25 homers in a season. He has also had three 100-RBI campaigns. The LA native joined the Dodgers before the '91 season.

Investors are sour on Strawberry. Insist on paying a dime, tops, for his '93s. Feast on an '86 Topps Strawberry for $1.25. Our pick for his best 1993 card is Score. We have chosen this card because of its great combination of photography and design.

	BA	G	AB	R	H	2B	3B	HR	RBI	SB
92 NL	.237	43	156	20	37	8	0	5	25	3
Life	.262	1291	4564	768	1196	217	34	285	857	204

FRANKLIN STUBBS

Position: First base
Team: Milwaukee Brewers
Born: October 21, 1960
   Laurinburg, NC
Height: 6'2" **Weight:** 209 lbs.
Bats: Left **Throws:** Left
Acquired: Signed as a free
   agent, 12/90

 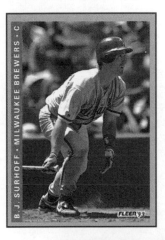

Franklin Stubbs was Milwaukee's biggest disappointment in 1992. He worked as a back-up first baseman and designated hitter, but continued to struggle offensively. His '92 numbers added up to a .229 average with nine homers and 42 RBI. The '92 season marked the second year that the Brewers have waited for Stubbs to duplicate his '90 success with Houston. He batted .213 with 11 home runs and 38 RBI for the '91 Brew Crew. For two years in a row, he's been a far cry from the 23 homers, 71 RBI, and .261 marks he achieved in his one-year stint with the Astros. However, he snagged a fat free-agent contract for his efforts. Stubbs assembled six seesaw seasons with the Dodgers dating back to '84. He was a first-round draft pick by Los Angeles in '82 and climbed to the bigs in less than three minor league seasons.

Stubbs is an overpriced liability, both as a baseball card and a player. His nickel-priced 1993s aren't serious investments. Our pick for his best 1993 card is Upper Deck. We have chosen this card due to the outstanding photographic composition.

	BA	G	AB	R	H	2B	3B	HR	RBI	SB
92 AL	.229	92	288	37	66	11	1	9	42	11
Life	.232	883	2475	310	573	98	12	102	329	74

B.J. SURHOFF

Position: Catcher
Team: Milwaukee Brewers
Born: August 4, 1964
   Bronx, NY
Height: 6'1" **Weight:** 200 lbs.
Bats: Left **Throws:** Right
Acquired: First-round pick,
   6/85 free-agent draft

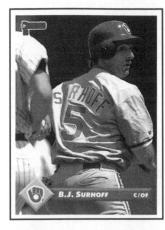

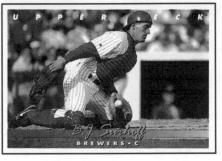

B.J. Surhoff fought off challenges from two other backstops to retain his starting job with the Brewers in 1992. Surhoff batted a mere .196 in spring training and seemed vulnerable to starting challenges by prospects Tim McIntosh and Dave Nilsson. He was mired at .234 with three homers and 37 RBI at the All-Star break. However, as Milwaukee pushed the pennant race down to the last weekend of the season, Surhoff got hot. He finished the '92 season with a .252 average, four homers, and 62 RBI. Surhoff's offense has been very predictable during his six years with the Brew Crew. His RBI totals have ranged from 55 to 68 in all but one season. Surhoff has never been the superstar some people expected after he was the first player chosen in the entire 1985 draft.

This 1984 U.S. Olympic team member offers little inspiration to card collectors. Surhoff's commons aren't smart choices. Our pick for his best 1993 card is Upper Deck. We have chosen this card because it has a distinctive look.

	BA	G	AB	R	H	2B	3B	HR	RBI	SB
92 AL	.252	139	480	63	121	19	1	4	62	14
Life	.268	797	2783	314	745	119	16	32	350	83

Series two cards from some companies were available at press time. If space allows, both cards are shown; if not, the most up-to-date cards are pictured.

RICK SUTCLIFFE

Position: Pitcher
Team: Baltimore Orioles
Born: June 21, 1956
  Independence, MO
Height: 6'7" **Weight:** 215 lbs.
Bats: Left **Throws:** Right
Acquired: Signed as a free
  agent, 12/91

RUSS SWAN

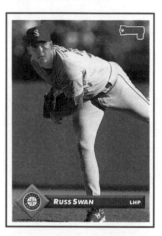

Position: Pitcher
Team: Seattle Mariners
Born: January 3, 1964
  Fremont, CA
Height: 6'4" **Weight:** 215 lbs.
Bats: Left **Throws:** Left
Acquired: Traded from Giants
  for Gary Eave, 5/90

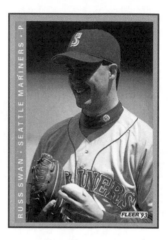

Rick Sutcliffe stabilized the 1992 Orioles rotation, keeping the team in pennant contention into the last days of the season. Along with double-digit wins (16), the hurler surpassed 30 starts (36) and 200 innings pitched (237 ⅓) for the seventh time in his career. The righthander escaped the shoulder problems that haunted him throughout '90 and '91. Sutcliffe was a first-round selection of the Dodgers back in '74. He made his debut with Los Angeles in '76. In '79, his first full year in the majors, he won the NL Rookie of the Year Award with a 17-10 effort. The Cubs won their division in '84, thanks to Sutcliffe's dazzling 16-1 Cy Young award-winning performance.

With his low winning percentage and high ERA from '92, Sutcliffe didn't overwhelm the baseball world. The aging hurler would need a Cy Young Award to enliven his '93 commons, a nearly impossible challenge. Our pick for his best 1993 card is Topps. We have chosen this card due to the outstanding photographic composition.

Russ Swan could be called the best of the worst from Seattle's dreadful 1992 pitching staff. Swan's ERA danced near five (4.74), and his walks matched his strikeouts (45 each). Yet, Swan became the dominant lefty out of the Mariners' bullpen, challenging fallen stopper Mike Schooler for the team lead in saves. Remarkably, opponents hit a meager .209 off Swan in road games. Lefthanders did worse than that. Swan honed his relief skills in '91, when he made 63 appearances for the M's. The southpaw began the '90 season with San Francisco, but was swapped to Seattle's Triple-A affiliate in May. He started for the Mariners on June 9, 1990, tossing a one-hitter against the Tigers. Swan was a fifth-round draft pick of San Francisco's in '86.

Swan may be one of the few pitching survivors in Seattle's anticipated overhaul. His 1993 common-priced cards aren't welcoming, due to his yet-unknown role with the team. Our pick for his best 1993 card is Fleer. We have chosen this card for its technical merits.

	W	L	ERA	G	CG	IP	H	ER	BB	SO
92 AL	16	15	4.47	36	5	237.1	251	118	74	109
Life	155	125	3.90	412	69	2464.0	2357	1068	975	1573

	W	L	ERA	G	SV	IP	H	ER	BB	SO
92 AL	3	10	4.74	55	9	104.1	104	55	45	45
Life	11	18	4.26	133	11	239.0	244	113	99	96

Series two cards from some companies were available at press time. If space allows, both cards are shown; if not, the most up-to-date cards are pictured.

BILL SWIFT

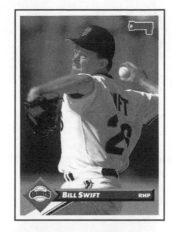

Position: Pitcher
Team: San Francisco Giants
Born: October 27, 1961
  South Portland, ME
Height: 6′ **Weight:** 180 lbs.
Bats: Right **Throws:** Right
Acquired: Traded from
  Mariners with Mike Jackson
  and Dave Burba for Kevin
  Mitchell, 12/91

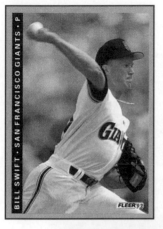

GREG SWINDELL

Position: Pitcher
Team: Houston Astros
Born: January 2, 1965
  Fort Worth, TX
Height: 6′3″ **Weight:** 225 lbs.
Bats: Right **Throws:** Left
Acquired: Signed as a free
  agent, 12/92

Before coming to the Giants in 1992, Bill Swift had been used primarily as a relief pitcher. In 1991, his best season, he had a 1-2 record, 17 saves, and 1.99 ERA for Seattle while making 71 appearances, all in relief. All but eight of his 55 outings the year before were also from the bullpen. In '92, however, San Francisco manager Roger Craig, short of quality starters, made a swift decision on his No. 1 starter. Bill Swift was on the mound on Opening Day. He went 7 ⅔ innings to beat the Dodgers 8-1, and won five more decisions in a row before missing a month with shoulder problems. The unfamiliar heavy workload—he had three complete games, including two shutouts—might have taken its toll. Back in action on June 21, Swift showed no ill effects. He hurled five scoreless innings against San Diego.

His injuries and years of pitching in relief are two demerits against his '93 issues. Our pick for his best 1993 card is Upper Deck. We have chosen this card since the photograph captures the athletic ability of the player.

	W	L	ERA	G	CG	IP	H	ER	BB	SO
92 NL	10	4	2.08	30	3	164.2	144	38	43	77
Life	40	44	3.69	283	10	923.2	971	379	296	369

Greg Swindell bounced back from a disappointing 1991 and made '92 a banner year. His numbers included a 12-8 record with a 2.70 ERA. His ERA sported a new and improved look that was much lighter than years past. He helped the Reds stay in contention, too. His efforts did not go unnoticed and the Astros picked him up for '93. In '91, his stats weren't as impressive, but that wasn't all his fault. The Indians gave him little run support and that hurt his record. Considered by many to be one of the game's most effective pitchers, Swindell's best mark came in '88 when he posted an 18-14 record. Even in college his pro potential was apparent. He earned a first-round selection by the Indians in the '86 draft. After making just three starts at Waterloo that summer, Swindell jumped directly to Cleveland.

At a nickel apiece, '93 Swindells would be a fine buy. The '87 Donruss Rookie of Swindell is a wise choice for a buck. Our pick for his best 1993 card is Score. We have chosen this card due to its unique photographic approach.

	W	L	ERA	G	CG	IP	H	ER	BB	SO
92 NL	12	8	2.70	31	5	213.2	210	64	41	138
Life	72	63	3.60	184	37	1256.2	1269	503	267	894

Series two cards from some companies were available at press time. If space allows, both cards are shown; if not, the most up-to-date cards are pictured.

JEFF TACKETT

Position: Catcher
Team: Baltimore Orioles
Born: December 1, 1965
Fresno, CA
Height: 6'2" **Weight:** 206 lbs.
Bats: Right **Throws:** Right
Acquired: Second-round pick,
6/84 free-agent draft

In June 1992, Jeff Tackett seized his chance to play when first-string catcher Chris Hoiles suffered an injury. Tackett—who before the '92 season had played only six of his 668 pro games in the majors—showed that he belonged. He threw out runners and hit for power. He even took a turn at third base. He was especially successful against lefthanded pitching, and he drove in 13 runs with his first 19 hits. Tackett spent three years at Triple-A Rochester of the International League before getting his first shot at the majors. He was named the league's best defensive catcher by *Baseball America*. Tackett led the International League two years in a row in percentage of runners he gunned down in steal attempts. He threw out 13 of the final 15 runners to try against him before his 1991 call-up to Baltimore. Tackett made his major league debut on September 11, 1991, versus the Yankees.

As a backup catcher, Tackett's cards aren't even worth the minimum. Our pick for his best 1993 card is Topps. We have chosen this card for its artistic presentation.

	BA	G	AB	R	H	2B	3B	HR	RBI	SB
92 AL	.240	66	179	21	43	8	1	5	24	0
Life	.235	72	187	22	44	8	1	5	24	0

FRANK TANANA

Position: Pitcher
Team: New York Mets
Born: July 3, 1953 Detroit, MI
Height: 6'3" **Weight:** 195 lbs.
Bats: Left **Throws:** Left
Acquired: Signed as a free
agent, 12/92

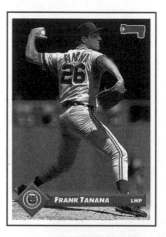

Frank Tanana will turn 40 in 1993 with a new team—the New York Mets. In 1992 with the Detroit Tigers, he celebrated with his 14th season of double-digit victories. He also passed Hall of Famer Bob Feller on the all-time list for strikeouts and innings pitched. Since joining Detroit in June 1985, Tanana has provided anywhere from nine to 15 victories per season. The Angels selected Tanana in the first round of the 1971 draft. A year after being named AL Rookie of the Year by *The Sporting News* in 1974, he won the league strikeout title with 269. Tanana climbed to a career-high 19 victories with the 1976 Halos, then presented league bests of seven shutouts and a 2.54 ERA in 1977. The wise, old lefty will begin his third decade of pro ball in 1993. Once a power pitcher, he now relies on smarts and pinpoint control.

Tanana's cards are available for a nickel or less. Longevity alone can't boost his values, so invest accordingly. Our pick for his best 1993 card is Topps. We have chosen this card because of its great combination of photography and design.

	W	L	ERA	G	CG	IP	H	ER	BB	SO
92 AL	13	11	4.39	32	3	186.2	188	91	90	91
Life	233	219	3.63	606	143	3985.2	3847	1606	1200	2657

Series two cards from some companies were available at press time. If space allows, both cards are shown; if not, the most up-to-date cards are pictured.

KEVIN TAPANI

Position: Pitcher
Team: Minnesota Twins
Born: February 18, 1964
  Des Moines, IA
Height: 6′ **Weight:** 187 lbs.
Bats: Right **Throws:** Right
Acquired: Traded from Mets
  with Jack Savage, Tim
  Drummond, David West, and
  Rick Aguilera for Frank Viola
  and Loy McBride, 7/89

 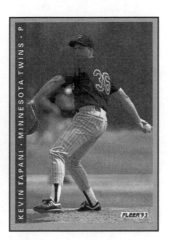

DANNY TARTABULL

Position: Outfield/designated
  hitter
Team: New York Yankees
Born: October 30, 1962
  Miami, FL
Height: 6′1″ **Weight:** 205 lbs.
Bats: Right **Throws:** Right
Acquired: Signed as a free
  agent, 1/92

Kevin Tapani proved his 1991 success with Minnesota was no fluke. He nearly duplicated his fine '91 totals in 1992, offering some comfort after the loss of 1991 star hurler Jack Morris. Tapani checked in with a 10-5 record and a 3.84 ERA at the '92 All-Star break, although he went just 6-6 from that point on. His second-half slide mirrored all of Minnesota's season-ending woes. In 1991, the Iowa native posted a 16-9 mark, along with a 2.99 ERA, in 34 starts and 244 innings pitched. In 1990, Tapani finished fifth in American League Rookie of the Year balloting thanks to a 12-8 record. Before he joined the Twins in late 1989, Tapani began the year with the Mets. He was one of the jewels that Minnesota uncovered in the Frank Viola trade. Oakland chose Tapani in the second round of the 1986 draft.

Tapani's 1993 cards are intriguing investments at a nickel or less. He seems poised for a run at a 20-win season, which excites investors. Our pick for his best 1993 card is Fleer. We have chosen this card because of its overall appeal and pleasing looks.

Even before he played a single game in 1992, Danny Tartabull was one of New York's biggest sports stories. He signed a five-year free-agency contract set to pay him more than $5 million in 1992 alone. Besides feeling the pressure of big money, Tartabull was challenged to repeat his 1991 performance of 31 homers, 100 RBI, and a personal-best .316 average with the Royals. Due to injuries, namely back spasms, Tartabull spent less than half of the '92 season in the outfield. Still, he topped 20 homers for the fifth time in his career. When Tartabull began his pro career as a Cincinnati third-round draft choice in 1980, he was considered a second baseman or shortstop. He broke in as an infielder with the 1984 Mariners. He enjoyed strong seasons with the Royals in the late 1980s, topping 100 RBI in both 1987 and 1988.

While Tartabull is not affordable to most teams, his cards are affordable to investors. You should be able to find his 1993s for a dime or less. Our pick for his best 1993 card is Fleer. We have chosen this card for the interesting facts included on the reverse.

	W	L	ERA	G	CG	IP	H	ER	BB	SO
92 AL	16	11	3.97	34	4	220.0	226	97	48	138
Life	46	30	3.62	104	9	663.1	654	267	129	397

	BA	G	AB	R	H	2B	3B	HR	RBI	SB
92 AL	.266	123	421	72	112	19	0	25	85	2
Life	.284	946	3340	507	950	193	16	177	620	35

EDDIE TAUBENSEE

Position: Catcher
Team: Houston Astros
Born: October 31, 1968
   Beeville, TX
Height: 6'4" **Weight:** 205 lbs.
Bats: Left **Throws:** Right
Acquired: Traded from Indians
   with Willie Blair for Kenny
   Lofton and Dave Rohde,
   12/91

MICKEY TETTLETON

Position: Catcher
Team: Detroit Tigers
Born: September 16, 1960
   Oklahoma City, OK
Height: 6'2" **Weight:** 212 lbs.
Bats: Both **Throws:** Right
Acquired: Traded from Orioles
   for Jeff Robinson, 1/91

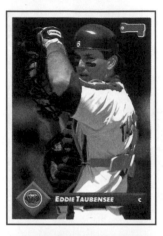
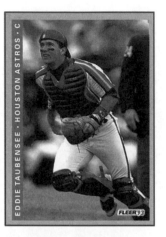
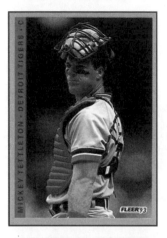

Eddie Taubensee faced an increasing amount of pressure in 1992 because of the success enjoyed by Kenny Lofton in Cleveland. Since Houston traded Lofton for Taubenssee, Astros fans naturally wanted to see a show. Taubensee, though, does not play with the same offensive flair that Lofton can, and he was hitting well south of the .200 mark when optioned to the minors in mid-June. Taubensee runs well enough to have once stolen 11 bases in a minor league campaign. He has reached double figures in homers four consecutive times in the minors. Drafted in the sixth round by Cincinnati in 1986, Taubensee was picked by Oakland in the 1990 Rule 5 draft, but he never played for the Athletics. Cleveland picked him up on waivers in April 1991, and he made his major league debut for the club on May 18. Taubensee went 23 at-bats before getting a hit in the major leagues.

Don't buy Taubensee commons unless his hitting improves substantially. Our pick for his best 1993 card is Score. We have chosen this card due to the outstanding photographic composition.

Mickey Tettleton is the best slugging catcher in the American League, if not the majors. He surpassed 30 home runs for the second year in a row with the 1992 Tigers. The veteran backstop nearly kept pace with his 1991 totals of 31 homers, 89 RBI, and a 263 average. For the third consecutive year, Tettleton surpassed 100 annual walks. Baltimore hosted Tettleton from 1988-90. His best year with the O's was an All-Star season of 26 homers and 65 RBI in 1989. After a career at Oklahoma State University, Tettleton was a fifth-round selection of Oakland's in 1981. He bounced from the minors to the majors from 1984 through 1987. Tettleton's best season with the A's, 1986, wasn't much to write home about, as he totalled 10 homers and 35 RBI. Surprisingly, Tettleton was released days before the 1988 season began.

Tettleton's 1993 nickel-priced cards could pay off if he challenges league leaders. Hunt for a 1986 Donruss Tettleton for $1.50. Our pick for his best 1993 card is Fleer. We have chosen this card since its design makes it a standout.

	BA	G	AB	R	H	2B	3B	HR	RBI	SB
92 NL	.222	104	297	23	66	15	0	5	28	2
Life	.226	130	363	28	82	17	1	5	36	2

	BA	G	AB	R	H	2B	3B	HR	RBI	SB
92 AL	.238	157	525	82	125	25	0	32	83	0
Life	.241	932	2873	416	693	121	8	137	406	18

TIM
TEUFEL

Position: Infield
Team: San Diego Padres
Born: July 7, 1958
Greenwich, CT
Height: 6′ **Weight:** 175 lbs.
Bats: Right **Throws:** Right
Acquired: Traded from Mets for
Garry Templeton, 5/91

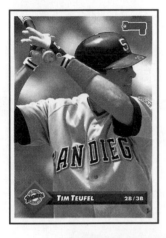

Tim Teufel's contributions to the 1992 Padres didn't always show up on the stat sheets. The veteran infielder shared second base with newcomer Kurt Stillwell and also chaired San Diego's pinch-hitting corps. Teufel couldn't duplicate the impact he made when he joined the Padres in '91, when he tallied 11 home runs and 42 RBI in only 97 games. Twice, Teufel has produced identical career highs of 14 homers and 61 RBI, with the 1987 Mets and 1984 Twins. Minnesota chose Teufel in the second round of the 1980 free-agent draft, following his collegiate performance at Clemson. He debuted with the Twins in 1983, hitting .308 in 21 games. Teufel's 1984 slugging placed him fourth in AL Rookie of the Year balloting. The Mets obtained Teufel in a five-player transaction before the 1986 season, and San Diego traded for him in 1991.

Teufel will not be a full-timer with the Padres in 1993. He won't have the necessary stats to propel values of his common-priced cards. Our pick for his best 1993 card is Donruss. We have chosen this card for its technical merits.

	BA	G	AB	R	H	2B	3B	HR	RBI	SB
92 NL	.224	101	246	23	55	10	0	6	25	2
Life	.254	977	2912	389	739	174	10	79	348	21

BOB
TEWKSBURY

Position: Pitcher
Team: St. Louis Cardinals
Born: November 30, 1960
Concord, NH
Height: 6′4″ **Weight:** 208 lbs.
Bats: Right **Throws:** Right
Acquired: Signed as a free
agent, 12/88

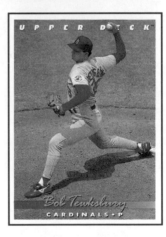

Bob Tewksbury was a two-time reject before finding a happy home with the Cardinals. Less than a year after posting a 9-5 record and 3.31 ERA as a rookie with the 1986 Yankees, he was foolishly included in a package of players sent to the Cubs for washed-up Steve Trout. Injuries interfered with his progress in both 1987 and 1988, but the Louisville Redbirds, the Triple-A affiliate of the Cardinals, allowed him another chance. Healthy again, he went 13-5 for Louisville and worked his way back to the majors. Tewksbury had 10 wins for the Cardinals in 1990 and a career-high 11 in 1991, his first full season in the majors. An artist whose work has been featured in *Sports Illustrated,* Tewksbury is also an artist on the mound. One of the top control pitchers in the majors, he kept runners off base so well in 1992 that he posted a 2.16 ERA.

Don't spend much on Tewk's cards. Despite his excellent 1992 numbers, you have to remember that he's 32 years old. Our pick for his best 1993 card is Donruss. We have chosen this card because the design lends itself to the best use of the elements.

	W	L	ERA	G	CG	IP	H	ER	BB	SO
92 NL	16	5	2.16	33	5	233.0	217	56	20	91
Life	48	39	3.22	137	14	784.1	828	281	136	305

BOBBY THIGPEN

Position: Pitcher
Team: Chicago White Sox
Born: July 17, 1963
Tallahassee, FL
Height: 6'3" **Weight:** 195 lbs.
Bats: Right **Throws:** Right
Acquired: Fourth-round pick,
6/85 free-agent draft

When talk turns to career years, fingers usually point to Bobby Thigpen's 1990 performance: 57 saves in 65 chances and league highs in games (77) and games finished (73). The hard-throwing product of Mississippi State also had a 1.83 ERA and a direct hand in 65 percent of Chicago's victories. He added another 30 saves in 1991—even though he got off to a difficult start. That performance gave the closer four consecutive 30-save campaigns. Thigpen, primarily an outfielder during his college career, broke into pro ball in 1985. For the next two years, he served as a starting pitcher in the minors. But he's been used exclusively in relief by the White Sox, who brought him to the big leagues in 1986. Before Thigpen made it a habit, the only Sox relievers who posted 30-save seasons were Ed Farmer in 1980 and Bob James in 1985. Thigpen had a tough 1992 season, falling to 22 saves.

If Thigpen regains his sterling numbers, his cards may be worth buying. Our pick for his best 1993 card is Donruss. We have chosen this card due to the outstanding photographic composition.

	W	L	ERA	G	SV	IP	H	ER	BB	SO
92 AL	1	3	4.75	55	22	55.0	58	29	33	45
Life	28	33	3.09	399	200	507.0	451	174	212	343

FRANK THOMAS

Position: First base
Team: Chicago White Sox
Born: May 27, 1968
Columbus, GA
Height: 6'5" **Weight:** 240 lbs.
Bats: Right **Throws:** Right
Acquired: First-round pick,
6/89 free-agent draft

According to Frank Thomas, patience makes perfect. In 1991, his first full season in the majors, the former Auburn football player walked more often than he struck out (138-112) while scaling the century mark in both runs scored and runs batted in. He was the only man in the majors with a .300 batting average, .400 on-base average, and .500 slugging average—even though he was hampered all season by a sore shoulder. Thomas also became the first player since Carl Yastrzemski in 1970 to record at least a .450 on-base percentage, .550 slugging percentage, 30 homers, 100 RBI, and 100 runs scored. Thomas says his ability to relax in front of big crowds helps. Although his production fell off a bit during the first half of the 1992 campaign, Thomas retained his reputation as the most dangerous hitter in the Chicago lineup.

Big Frank's 50-cent cards are worth it, as they may rise as the season progresses. Our pick for his best 1993 card is Topps. We have chosen this card because of its overall appeal and pleasing looks.

	BA	G	AB	R	H	2B	3B	HR	RBI	SB
92 AL	.323	160	573	108	185	46	2	24	115	6
Life	.322	378	1323	251	426	88	7	63	255	7

JIM THOME

Position: Infield
Team: Cleveland Indians
Born: August 27, 1970
   Peoria, IL
Height: 6'4" **Weight:** 215 lbs.
Bats: Left **Throws:** Right
Acquired: 13th-round pick,
   6/89 free-agent draft

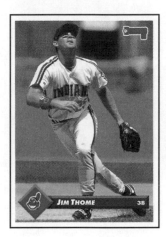 

Jim Thome became Cleveland's regular third baseman in 1992 in just his fourth year of pro ball. However, a sore right shoulder kept him from assembling the numbers expected of someone named the American League's best hitting prospect by Upper Deck and *Baseball America*. Thome was unable to get many at-bats until late June and early July, when he was inserted into the lineup batting eighth. Thome got his first look at the majors in 1991, completing a season that began in Double-A. Despite playing for three different teams and making adjustments as he moved up the ladder, Thome collected 31 doubles, seven triples, eight homers, and 82 RBI in 1991. In a *USA Today* poll, Thome placed second behind Atlanta's Mark Wohlers as Player of the Year in the minors that year. Thome played at two Class-A levels in 1990, hitting .340. He was named the top prospect in the rookie-level Appalachian League.

Try Thome's 1993 cards at a dime or less. His ratings are still high. Our pick for his best 1993 card is Donruss. We have chosen this card for its technical merits.

	BA	G	AB	R	H	2B	3B	HR	RBI	SB
92 AL	.205	40	117	8	24	3	1	2	12	2
Life	.228	67	215	15	49	7	3	3	21	3

MILT THOMPSON

Position: Outfield
Team: Philadelphia Phillies
Born: January 5, 1959
   Washington, DC
Height: 5'11" **Weight:** 200 lbs.
Bats: Left **Throws:** Right
Acquired: Signed as a free
   agent, 12/92

Milt Thompson flirted with .300 for a second season in a row with the 1992 Cardinals. He couldn't quite repeat his .307 mark from 1991, but he provided St. Louis with one of its most dependable lefthanded bats. Although he was a defensive standout at all three outfield positions, Thompson's primary role in 1992 was pinch-hitting. In 1989, his first year as a Cardinal, Thompson drove in a career-high 68 runs. Yet, he became a platoon player the next year. As a result, his batting average plunged to .218. With the 1987 Phillies, Thompson hit a career-best seven home runs. That same year, he swiped a personal high of 46 bases. Thompson was a selection of Atlanta's in the 1979 draft. He was swapped to Philadelphia in December 1985. After 1992, the Phillies picked him up again, this time as a free agent.

Thompson excels as a fourth outfielder. However, his stats will never grow as long as he's a platoon or part-time player. Bypass his 1993 commons. Our pick for his best 1993 card is Donruss. We have chosen this card for its technical merits.

	BA	G	AB	R	H	2B	3B	HR	RBI	SB
92 NL	.293	109	208	31	61	9	1	4	17	18
Life	.281	980	2982	398	838	124	35	37	258	191

ROBBY THOMPSON

Position: Second base
Team: San Francisco Giants
Born: May 10, 1962
  West Palm Beach, FL
Height: 5'11" **Weight:** 170 lbs.
Bats: Right **Throws:** Right
Acquired: First-round pick,
  secondary phase of 6/83
  free-agent draft

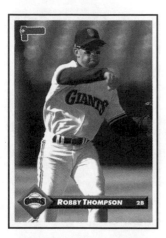

With the singular exception of Ryne Sandberg, Robby Thompson produces more power than any National League second baseman. He's hit more than a dozen home runs four years in a row and once led the league with 11 triples. He's especially productive against lefthanded pitching, batting .280 last year against southpaws. He had a .333 on-base average and a .415 slugging percentage in 1992. Definitely more than a one-dimensional player, Thompson is a solid fielder with good hands, good instincts, and the ability to turn the double play. He led NL second basemen in double plays in '91 and tied for the lead the year before. Though he's only a .260 hitter who strikes out more than he should, Thompson draws his share of walks, steals a dozen or so bases per season, and is one of baseball's best bunters. Cutting down on his penchant to strike out would be a huge improvement.

Thompson is an average card buy at under a nickel in '93. Our pick for his best 1993 card is Score. We have chosen this card because it has a distinctive look.

	BA	G	AB	R	H	2B	3B	HR	RBI	SB
92 NL	.260	128	443	54	115	25	1	14	49	5
Life	.258	983	3426	487	883	174	34	85	342	87

RYAN THOMPSON

Position: Outfield
Team: New York Mets
Born: November 4, 1967
  Chestertown, MD
Height: 6'3" **Weight:** 200 lbs.
Bats: Right **Throws:** Right
Acquired: Traded from Blue
  Jays with Jeff Kent for David
  Cone, 8/92

Escaping Toronto's talent-laden minor league system and major league outfield logjam, Ryan Thompson got a big chance in the Big Apple in 1992. Thompson's brief efforts with the Mets were notable, particularly his 15 runs scored in 30 games. In return for his efforts, New York protected him in the November expansion draft. Signed out of high school as a 13th round draft pick in '87, Thompson's first five seasons in the minors were unspectacular. However, he came of age in '92 with Syracuse, Toronto's Triple-A affiliate. The Mets snared Thompson due to his 14 homers, 45 RBI, and .289 average. As he cuts down on his strikeouts, Thompson's offensive muscle will grow.

Due to the questionable health and defense of outfielders Howard Johnson and Vince Coleman, Thompson will get lots of attention in '93. At a dime or less, cards of the gung-ho newcomer will be bright buys. Our pick for his best 1993 card is Upper Deck. We have chosen this card due to the outstanding photographic composition.

	BA	G	AB	R	H	2B	3B	HR	RBI	SB
92 AAA	.282	112	429	74	121	20	7	14	46	10
92 NL	.222	30	108	15	24	7	1	3	10	2

GARY THURMAN

Position: Outfield
Team: Kansas City Royals
Born: November 12, 1964
Indianapolis, IN
Height: 5'10" **Weight:** 175 lbs.
Bats: Right **Throws:** Right
Acquired: First-round pick,
6/83 free-agent draft

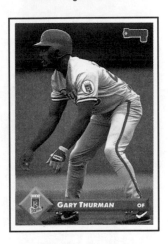

Gary Thurman played all three outfield positions and served as a part-time designated hitter for the 1992 Royals. Used most often in right field, he supplied speed and defense but no power in limited action. An overly aggressive hitter who fans four times more than he walks, Thurman succeeds when he hits down on the ball—producing grounders that skip through the artificial turf infield. He had a .281 on-base average and a .305 slugging percentage in '92. He is slightly more productive against lefthanded pitchers. He's a decent outfielder who throws well enough to man right field on occasion. In four-dozen outfield starts last year, he made only a couple of errors. Thurman is one of those players who's too good to linger in Triple-A but not quite good enough for the majors. He had three .300 years in the minors but has never come close to that figure in the majors.

His unproven ability in the big leagues casts serious doubt on his '93s. Our pick for his best 1993 card is Donruss. We have chosen this card because of its overall appeal and pleasing looks.

	BA	G	AB	R	H	2B	3B	HR	RBI	SB
92 AL	.245	88	200	25	49	6	3	0	20	9
Life	.245	325	678	96	166	23	4	2	48	53

MIKE TIMLIN

Position: Pitcher
Team: Toronto Blue Jays
Born: March 10, 1966
Midland, TX
Height: 6'4" **Weight:** 205 lbs.
Bats: Right **Throws:** Right
Acquired: Fifth-round pick,
6/87 free-agent draft

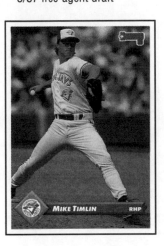 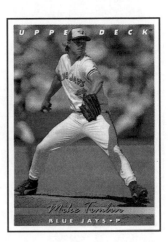

After a fine rookie year in 1991, Mike Timlin was slow to heal from off-season elbow surgery. He spent some time at Triple-A Syracuse trying to recapture his rookie form. He had a 0-1 record with an 8.74 ERA, five walks, and seven strikeouts in 11 innings and seven games at Syracuse in '92. A fastball-and-slider pitcher who averages seven strikeouts per nine innings, Timlin had control trouble last year. He also yielded more hits than innings pitched—something he did not do when healthy in '91. Opponents in '92 compiled a .271 batting average, a .351 on-base percentage, and a .307 slugging percentage against him. Although Timlin fares well when facing first batters, he often has problems with lefty hitters. At Class-A Dunedin in '90, he had a 1.43 ERA and 22 saves, and he had eight saves in Double-A.

Even at under a nickel apiece, investing in an unhealthy reliever is a big gamble. Our pick for his best 1993 card is Upper Deck. We have chosen this card for its artistic presentation.

	W	L	ERA	G	SV	IP	H	ER	BB	S
92 AL	0	2	4.12	26	1	43.2	45	20	20	35
Life	11	8	3.43	89	4	152.0	139	58	70	120

RANDY TOMLIN

Position: Pitcher
Team: Pittsburgh Pirates
Born: June 14, 1966
   Bainbridge, MD
Height: 5'10" **Weight:** 170 lbs.
Bats: Left **Throws:** Left
Acquired: 18th-round pick,
   6/88 free-agent draft

When the Pittsburgh Pirates traded 20-game winner John Smiley to the Minnesota Twins during 1992's spring training, they handed the No. 3 berth in the starting rotation to Randy Tomlin. Working behind veterans Doug Drabek and Zane Smith, Tomlin made the most of the opportunity. He went 4-0 in April, slipped a bit in May, then rebounded in June to win five decisions in a row and post a 1.40 ERA. His 5-2 win over St. Louis on June 22 made him the second National Leaguer to post 10 victories. A crafty lefthander who had only a dozen career wins before 1992, Tomlin reached Pittsburgh from the minors on August 6, 1990. In 12 starts in '90, he split eight decisions and posted a 2.55 ERA. A year later, he went 8-7 and pitched his first two big-league shutouts—back-to-back consecutive gems.

Tomlin's common-priced cards are modest investments, but nothing more. Our pick for his best 1993 card is Upper Deck. We have chosen this card since the photograph captures the athletic ability of the player.

	W	L	ERA	G	CG	IP	H	ER	BB	SO
92 NL	14	9	3.41	35	1	208.2	226	79	42	90
Life	26	20	3.10	78	7	461.1	458	159	108	236

ALAN TRAMMELL

Position: Shortstop
Team: Detroit Tigers
Born: February 21, 1958
   Garden Grove, CA
Height: 6'0" **Weight:** 175 lbs.
Bats: Right **Throws:** Right
Acquired: Second-round pick,
   6/76 free-agent draft

Alan Trammell was reunited with second baseman Lou Whitaker for a record 15th season in 1992. No double-play combination has ever been together anywhere near as long. However, the veteran shortstop was frustrated by injuries almost the whole season. Trammell was also sidelined in 1991, with a knee injury and a sprained ankle. He made his sixth All-Star appearance in 1990, hitting .304 with 14 home runs and 89 RBI. Trammell sparked the Tigers to their last division title in 1987, when he tallied 28 homers and 105 RBI for a career-best .343 average. He finished second in MVP voting to Toronto's George Bell. Trammell is one of six shortstops in history to own six seasons of .300 hitting. He is the only member of the bunch not in the Hall of Fame. Not yet anyway.

Don't miss Trammell's cards, begging for investment at a nickel apiece. They'll make steady gains once the shortstop gets Hall of Fame consideration. Also, pick out a 1981 Donruss of Trammell for $1. Our pick for his best 1993 card is Donruss. We have chosen this card due to the outstanding photographic composition.

	BA	G	AB	R	H	2B	3B	HR	RBI	SB
92 AL	.275	29	102	11	28	7	1	1	11	2
Life	.286	1965	7179	1077	2050	356	51	162	876	212

Series two cards from some companies were available at press time. If space allows, both cards are shown; if not, the most up-to-date cards are pictured.

MIKE TROMBLEY

Position: Pitcher
Team: Minnesota Twins
Born: April 14, 1967
   Springfield, MA
Height: 6'2" **Weight:** 200 lbs.
Bats: Right **Throws:** Right
Acquired: 14th-round pick,
   6/89 free-agent draft

SCOOTER TUCKER

Position: Catcher
Team: Houston Astros
Born: November 18, 1966
   Greenville, MS
Height: 6'2" **Weight:** 205 lbs.
Bats: Right **Throws:** Right
Acquired: Claimed on waivers
   from Giants, 9/91

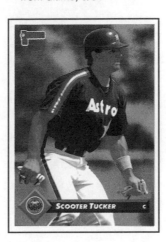

A pitcher who goes 6-22 in his college career would normally figure to look elsewhere for a profession. But Mike Trombley didn't, and he became a major leaguer on August 19, 1992. He promptly hurled one scoreless inning against the Indians. In Triple-A in '92, Trombley led his league with 138 strikeouts, finishing sixth in ERA. Trombley never suffered his collegiate problems in the minors. He has been at least a .500 pitcher at every stop, and he's shown control and a knack for quality starts. His résumé at Double-A Orlando in '91 included a seven inning no-hitter at Knoxville and a four-hit shutout in a Southern League playoff game against Greenville. He tied for the organization lead in wins and was second in strikeouts and ERA that year.

Look for him to challenge for the No. 5 starter's spot in Minnesota in 1993. Spend a few nickels here. Our pick for his best 1993 card is Upper Deck. We have chosen this card because it will increase in value.

Scooter Tucker had a tough time at the plate in 1992, batting .120 in 50 at-bats. Tucker is a good defensive player with a good arm, but he must work on his offense in order to find more than a utility role in the majors. Tucker, who got to the big leagues on June 14, 1992, might be a contributor as the righty half of a platoon. However, he has never been a big power man, and the Astrodome should do little to help him. Tucker was drafted by the Giants in the fifth round in 1988. In 1989, he led Clinton of the Midwest League with 105 hits and 20 doubles. Promoted to San Jose in 1990, Tucker earned a berth on the California League All-Star team. He threw out a league-high 59 runners trying to steal that year, and he drove in a career-high 71 runs. In 1991, Tucker led the Texas League with 71 assists and a .995 fielding percentage, committing four errors and hitting .284.

As a poor-hitting back-up catcher, Tucker's cards aren't worth it. Our pick for his best 1993 card is Donruss. We have chosen this card for its artistic presentation.

	W	L	ERA	G	CG	IP	H	ER	BB	SO
92 AAA	10	8	3.65	25	2	165.1	149	67	58	138
92 AL	3	2	3.30	10	0	46.1	43	17	17	38

	BA	G	AB	R	H	2B	3B	HR	RBI	SB
92 NL	.120	20	50	5	6	1	0	0	3	1
Life	.120	20	50	5	6	1	0	0	3	1

JOHN VALENTIN

Position: Shortstop
Team: Boston Red Sox
Born: February 18, 1967
  Minneola, NY
Height: 6′ **Weight:** 170 lbs.
Bats: Right **Throws:** Right
Acquired: Fifth-round pick,
  6/88 free-agent draft

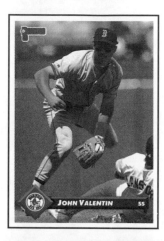 

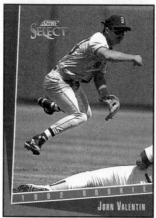 

John Valentin made the race for Boston's starting shortstop job a three-man contest in 1992. In contrast to past Red Sox occupants at shortstop—light-hitting Luis Rivera or frequently injured Tim Naehring—Valentin showed his offensive poise and defensive potential in only his fourth full professional season. Valentin nearly matched Rivera's offense in 100 fewer at-bats. Ironically, Valentin's .276 batting average was a career high, exceeding the .264 mark he posted with Pawtucket in Triple-A ball in '91. Aside from the .212 mark he endured against big league lefties, Valentin made his case for full-time employment with the '93 Red Sox.

Valentin, the college teammate of Mo Vaughn and Kevin Morton, should find playing time with the BoSox easier with the departure of second baseman Jody Reed. At a nickel each, Valentin's '93 cards look promising. Our pick for his best 1993 card is Score. We have chosen this card because it has a distinctive look.

	BA	G	AB	R	H	2B	3B	HR	RBI	SB
92 AAA	.260	97	331	47	86	18	1	9	29	1
92 AL	.276	58	185	21	51	13	0	5	25	1

JULIO VALERA

Position: Pitcher
Team: California Angels
Born: October 13, 1968
  San Sebastian, Puerto Rico
Height: 6′2″ **Weight:** 215 lbs.
Bats: Right **Throws:** Right
Acquired: Traded from Mets for
  Dick Schofield, 4/92

In 1992, Julio Valera came to California for shortstop Dick Schofield and thus earned a starting job that he wasn't going to get with the New York Mets. However, he did experience some problems with run support from the Angels. With the Halos, Valera won just four of his first 12 decisions, even though his ERA over that span was 3.76, batters hit just .233 against him, and he walked only three per nine innings. Before the trade, Valera made two trips to the majors with the Mets. He came up briefly in 1990 and pitched in three games, including a controversial start against Pittsburgh in a pennant race. He lost 7-1. Valera appeared in two games in 1991. Only once in his first six years of pro ball did Valera ever allow more hits than innings. He has, for the most part, been able to throw strikes.

Valera is young and has promise, meaning you may want to invest in his low-priced cards. Don't expect short-term profits, however. Our pick for his best 1993 card is Upper Deck. We have chosen this card for its artistic presentation.

	W	L	ERA	G	CG	IP	H	ER	BB	SO
92 AL	8	11	3.73	30	4	188.0	188	78	64	113
Life	9	12	3.90	35	4	203.0	209	88	75	120

Series two cards from some companies were available at press time. If space allows, both cards are shown; if not, the most up-to-date cards are pictured.

DAVE VALLE

Position: Catcher
Team: Seattle Mariners
Born: October 30, 1960
  Bayside, NY
Height: 6'2" **Weight:** 200 lbs.
Bats: Right **Throws:** Right
Acquired: Second-round pick,
  6/78 free-agent draft

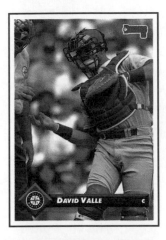

Catcher Dave Valle stayed healthier than usual last year and began to shake his horrendous 1991 slump. Still, his 1992 efforts did little to save Seattle from racking up the American League's worst record. Valle's 1992 offense was strikingly close to the marks of Rangers receiver Ivan Rodriguez. However, Rodriguez is rocketing to fame. Valle, meanwhile, has crested offensively. He was tagged by the Seattle media in 1991 as "Kill a Rally" Valle after hitting .194 in 132 games. His 1990 marks weren't much better: .214 with seven homers and 33 RBI. In 1987, Valle showed his brightest promise at bat, smacking 12 homers and driving in 53 runs with a .256 average. Although he tallied 10 homers and 50 RBI in 1988, his average slid 25 points. Valle began his professional career in 1978, but he didn't get his first dance with the M's until 1984.

Past injuries and slumps have branded Valle as an unreliable player and card investment. Save your pennies. Our pick for his best 1993 card is Fleer. We have chosen this card because of its overall appeal and pleasing looks.

	BA	G	AB	R	H	2B	3B	HR	RBI	SB
92 AL	.240	124	367	39	88	16	1	9	30	0
Life	.230	711	2079	231	479	85	10	59	255	3

JOHN VANDER WAL

Position: Outfield
Team: Montreal Expos
Born: April 29, 1966
  Grand Rapids, MI
Height: 6'2" **Weight:** 190 lbs.
Bats: Left **Throws:** Left
Acquired: Third-round pick,
  6/87 free-agent draft

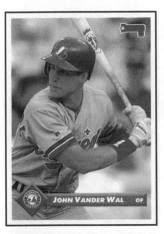
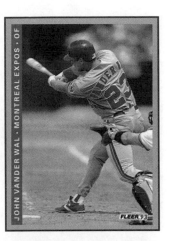

John Vander Wal was on a fast track to the majors until he suffered a broken right hand when hit by a pitch in Double-A in 1989. He reached the major leagues two seasons later, though, and has the tools to be a useful player. Vander Wal is primarily a left fielder, but he can also play right field and first base. He hits the long ball, can drive in runs, and has a little base-stealing speed. Vander Wal's best pro season came in 1991, when he played in the Triple-A All-Star Game in Louisville and was named to the post-season squad in the American Association. He hit .293 for Indianapolis, .389 when he put the ball in play. Vander Wal got promoted to the big leagues on September 6, 1991, and he hit the first pitch for a line single. He started a game two days later and tripled home a run. Vander Wal got his share of at-bats with Montreal in 1992, though he didn't hit up to his capabilities.

Vander Wal still doesn't have the numbers to instill faith in his commons. Our pick for his best 1993 card is Topps. We have chosen this card due to the outstanding photographic composition.

	BA	G	AB	R	H	2B	3B	HR	RBI	SB
92 NL	.239	105	213	21	51	8	2	4	20	3
Life	.234	126	274	25	64	12	3	5	28	3

ANDY VAN SLYKE

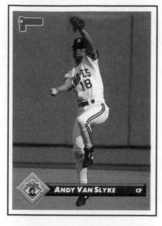

Position: Outfield
Team: Pittsburgh Pirates
Born: December 21, 1960
Utica, NY
Height: 6'2" **Weight:** 195 lbs.
Bats: Left **Throws:** Right
Acquired: Traded from
Cardinals with Mike
LaValliere and Mike Dunne
for Tony Pena, 4/87

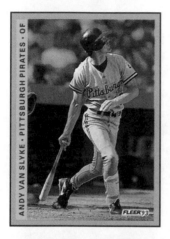

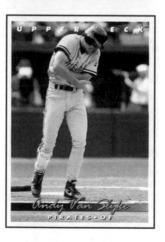

Andy Van Slyke headed into the 1992 season with four consecutive Gold Gloves and an average of 18 home runs per year. After he was diagnosed with three degenerative discs in his lower back, however, Van Slyke switched to a lighter, shorter bat and altered his swing to accommodate the sore back. The result was a higher average but less power. Never a .300 hitter in a big-league career that began in 1983, Van Slyke watched his average soar to .339 by June 20. The Pirates, playing without free agent deserter Bobby Bonilla, welcomed the "new" Van Slyke at the plate while appreciating the continued excellence of the "old" Van Slyke in the field. In 1988, his best season, he threw out nine runners at home plate en route to a fourth-place finish in MVP voting. He had 15 triples, 25 homers, 30 steals, and 100 RBI that year.

Outside of Pittsburgh, Van Slyke's cards are tough sells at a nickel apiece. A 1985 Donruss card of Van Slyke is a choice $1.50. Our pick for his best 1993 card is Score. We have chosen this card for the interesting facts included on the reverse.

	BA	G	AB	R	H	2B	3B	HR	RBI	SB
92 NL	.324	154	614	103	199	45	12	14	89	12
Life	.276	1390	4737	720	1308	251	82	144	688	220

GARY VARSHO

Position: First base/outfield
Team: Pittsburgh Pirates
Born: June 20, 1961
Marshfield, WI
Height: 5'11" **Weight:** 190 lbs.
Bats: Left **Throws:** Right
Acquired: Traded from Cubs
for Steve Carter, 3/91

Gary Varsho was one of several players who filled in for free-agent defector Bobby Bonilla as Pittsburgh's right fielder in 1992. He made better contact in '91 than he did in '92 and his averages reflect the decline. He had a .266 on-base average and a .370 slugging percentage in '92. A lefty hitter with some sting in his swing, Varsho also plays all outfield positions, fills in at first base, and makes a capable pinch-hitter against righthanded pitchers. He has some speed and steals on occasion. The speed translates to good range in the outfield, where he also has a strong arm but sometimes misjudges fly balls. An aggressive hitter who rarely walks, Varsho needs to cut his strikeout rate to retain his big league job. Varsho broke into the pros in '82 and made the majors six years later. Signed as a second baseman, he moved to the outfield because of his poor defense.

Time is running out for Varsho. Pass on his '93s. Our pick for his best 1993 card is Topps. We have chosen this card because of its overall appeal and pleasing looks.

	BA	G	AB	R	H	2B	3B	HR	RBI	SB
92 NL	.222	103	162	22	36	6	3	4	22	5
Life	.242	355	557	71	135	28	7	8	57	24

Series two cards from some companies were available at press time. If space allows, both cards are shown; if not, the most up-to-date cards are pictured.

GREG VAUGHN

Position: Outfield
Team: Milwaukee Brewers
Born: July 3, 1965
Sacramento, CA
Height: 6′ **Weight:** 193 lbs.
Bats: Right **Throws:** Right
Acquired: Selected in
secondary phase of 6/86
free-agent draft

MO VAUGHN

Position: First base
Team: Boston Red Sox
Born: December 15, 1967
Norwalk, CT
Height: 6′1″ **Weight:** 230 lbs.
Bats: Left **Throws:** Right
Acquired: First-round pick,
6/89 free-agent draft

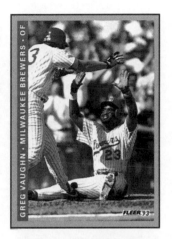
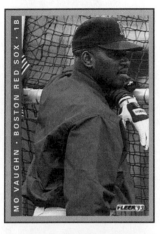
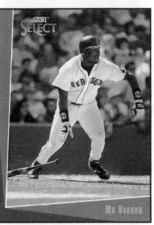

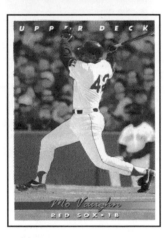

Just like clockwork, Greg Vaughn topped 20 homers for the Brewers again in 1992. However, his slugging had some drawbacks. He batted just .223, struggled against righthanded pitching, and continued to strike out more than he should. He whiffed 123 times, two fewer than his 1991 total. In 1991, Vaughn tallied 27 home runs and 98 runs batted in for the Brew Crew. His 1990 rookie-season totals were limited to 17 homers and 61 RBI. Vaughn declined to sign through four previous drafts prior to his 1986 selection by Milwaukee. He had turned down previous draft offers from the Cardinals, Brewers, Pirates, and Angels. He's hit 103 home runs and driven in 356 runs since his call-up.

Vaughn's homer and strikeout binges aren't encouraging. Unless he pumps up his average, he won't be taken seriously. Neither will his nickel-priced cards. Our pick for his best 1993 card is Fleer. We have chosen this card because it has a distinctive look.

Mo Vaughn didn't live up to his star billing with the 1992 Red Sox. Vaughn couldn't manage to hit his weight against lefthanders, or any hurlers away from Fenway Park. He wound up platooning at first base with prospect Scott Cooper, and he finished the season with a .234 batting average. Vaughn saw a clear path to starting at first base when Carlos Quintana was injured in a pre-season auto wreck. Yet, Vaughn suffered a Triple-A demotion before the All-Star break. Vaughn marked his third consecutive year serving time at Pawtucket. In 1990, he batted .295 there, busting 22 homers and driving in 72 runs. Vaughn's debut with Boston came in 1991, when he clocked in at .260 with four homers and 32 RBI in 74 games.

Vaughn's chances may lessen in 1993, due to Quintana's return and Boston's urge for a renovation. Don't risk more than a nickel each on Vaughn cards. Our pick for his best 1993 card is Fleer. We have chosen this card due to the outstanding photographic composition.

	BA	G	AB	R	H	2B	3B	HR	RBI	SB
92 AL	.228	141	501	77	114	18	2	23	78	15
Life	.234	444	1538	227	360	71	9	72	260	28

	BA	G	AB	R	H	2B	3B	HR	RBI	SB
92 AL	.234	113	335	42	83	16	2	13	57	3
Life	.244	187	574	63	140	28	2	17	89	5

RANDY VELARDE

Position: Infield
Team: New York Yankees
Born: November 24, 1962
  Midland, TX
Height: 6′ **Weight:** 190 lbs.
Bats: Right **Throws:** Right
Acquired: Traded from White
  Sox with Pete Filson for Mike
  Soper and Scott Nielsen,
  1/87

ROBIN VENTURA

Position: Third base
Team: Chicago White Sox
Born: July 14, 1967
  Santa Maria, CA
Height: 6′1″ **Weight:** 192 lbs.
Bats: Left **Throws:** Right
Acquired: First-round pick,
  6/88 free-agent draft

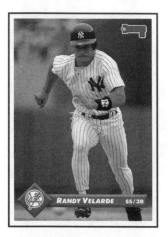

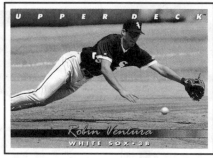

Randy Velarde rewrote all his personal highs with the 1992 Yankees, representing the team at shortstop and five other positions. Never before in the majors had Velarde played in more than 100 games in one year, as he was used previously as a pinch-hitter and defensive substitute. However, Velarde started more than 60 games in 1992. He ripped lefthanded pitching at a .300-plus clip. By contrast, he hit a mild .245 with one homer and 15 RBI in 1991. Velarde got his initial chance with the White Sox organization, which selected him in the 19th round of the 1985 draft. The Texas native spent two seasons in the White Sox chain before being traded to the Yankees.

Velarde is a fine utility man, but plan on Andy Stankiewicz or Dave Silvestri starting at shortstop in 1993. That's not enough to merit investment in Velarde's common-priced cards. Our pick for his best 1993 card is Upper Deck. We have chosen this card since the photograph captures the athletic ability of the player.

The White Sox stopped worrying about Robin Ventura's power production in 1991. After hitting five home runs as a 1990 rookie, the former No. 1 draft pick had 23 homers and 100 runs batted in in '91. That season, Ventura vaulted into the public eye with an explosive July that included a .357 average, 12 homers (including two game-enders), and 33 RBI. Three times during the month he hit two home runs in a game. After leading major league third basemen with 440 total chances and 135 putouts, Ventura won his first Gold Glove. Ventura came back in 1992 and hit an admirable .282 with 16 homers and 93 RBI. The former Oklahoma State star, who once had a 58-game hitting streak in college, is a former College Player of the Year and Olympic performer. He was named College Player of the Decade for the 1980s by *Baseball America*.

Pay up to a dime apiece for his 1993 selections. A 1989 Bowman of Ventura exists for $1.25, while his 1989 Fleer Update nears $3. Our pick for his best 1993 card is Upper Deck. We have chosen this card because it has a distinctive look.

	BA	G	AB	R	H	2B	3B	HR	RBI	SB
92 AL	.272	121	412	57	112	24	1	7	46	7
Life	.248	385	1062	128	263	51	6	20	104	11

	BA	G	AB	R	H	2B	3B	HR	RBI	SB
92 AL	.282	157	592	85	167	38	1	16	93	2
Life	.271	480	1736	230	470	83	3	44	254	5

Series two cards from some companies were available at press time. If space allows, both cards are shown; if not, the most up-to-date cards are pictured.

FRANK VIOLA

Position: Pitcher
Team: Boston Red Sox
Born: April 19, 1960
East Meadow, NY
Height: 6'4" **Weight:** 210 lbs.
Bats: Left **Throws:** Left
Acquired: Signed as a free
agent, 12/91

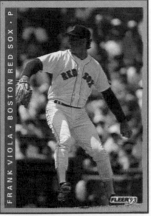
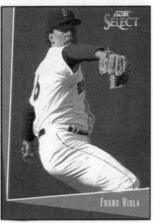
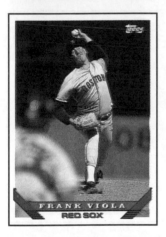

JOSE VIZCAINO

Position: Infield
Team: Chicago Cubs
Born: March 26, 1968
Palenque, Dominican
Republic
Height: 6'1" **Weight:** 150 lbs.
Bats: Both **Throws:** Right
Acquired: Traded from Dodgers
for Greg Smith, 12/90

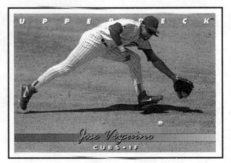

In his first year with the Boston Red Sox, Frank Viola proved that his second-half slump of 1991 was simply temporary. A former Cy Young Award winner who has had 20-win seasons in both leagues, Viola pitched his way out of New York by losing 10 of his last 11 decisions with the Mets. Nevertheless, Viola was a big fish in the free-agent pond after the 1991 season, and he signed a mega-deal with the Red Sox in December. With the Sox last year, he was a steady 13-12 with a respectable 3.44 ERA—not bad for a lefthanded pitcher in Fenway Park. Viola won MVP honors in the 1987 World Series, as well as the AL's Cy Young Award a year later. He was traded to the Mets in 1989, however, because the Twins felt he had lost some velocity off his fastball. Viola proved them wrong in 1990 with a 20-12 record and 2.67 ERA.

Don't spend more than a nickel on cards of Viola, who's no longer a star pitcher. Our pick for his best 1993 card is Topps. We have chosen this card since the photograph captures the athletic ability of the player.

In his first full major league season last year, Vizcaino served the Cubs as a three-position infielder. He mostly shared shortstop with Rey Sanchez after incumbent Shawon Dunston went down with a bad back. Vizcaino also saw lots of action at third, and he even served as Ryne Sandberg's chief understudy at second. Vizcaino didn't add much punch to the offense. His homer August 1, 1992, was his first in 446 career at-bats. Nor did Vizcaino take advantage of his natural speed. He made decent contact but poked few extra-base hits and struggled against southpaws. He had a .260 on-base average and a .298 slugging percentage in '92. A good defensive player, Vizcaino has good range and a capable arm. He was voted the best second baseman in the Triple-A Pacific Coast League in 1990.

If he boosts his on-base average by waiting for walks and starts stealing some bases, Vizcaino will improve his value. Our pick for his best 1993 card is Upper Deck. We have chosen this card since the photograph captures the athletic ability of the player.

	W	L	ERA	G	CG	IP	H	ER	BB	SO
92 AL	13	12	3.44	35	6	238.0	214	91	89	121
Life	163	137	3.70	377	72	2577	2550	1059	751	1722

	BA	G	AB	R	H	2B	3B	HR	RBI	SB
92 NL	.225	86	285	25	64	10	4	1	17	3
Life	.240	223	491	37	118	16	5	1	29	6

OMAR VIZQUEL

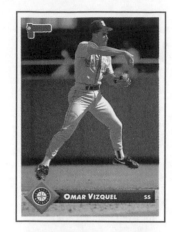

Position: Shortstop
Team: Seattle Mariners
Born: April 24, 1967
Caracas, Venezuela
Height: 5'9" **Weight:** 165 lbs.
Bats: Both **Throws:** Right
Acquired: Signed as a free
agent, 4/84

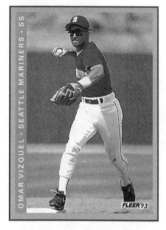

Shortstop Omar Vizquel discarded his "great hands, no stick" reputation with the 1992 Mariners. His .294 average signified a 64-point increase from his 1991 efforts. At the '92 All-Star break, he was batting an unprecedented .318. For the year, he hit above .300 against righthanded pitchers. His only drawback was power, as he hit zero home runs. Dubbed "Little O" in Seattle, Vizquel is a natural righthanded hitter. He adopted switch-hitting beginning in 1989. Vizquel never panned out in his 1989 rookie season with the M's, hitting .220 with one homer and 20 RBI in 143 games. No one has ever doubted Vizquel's fielding ability in four seasons with Seattle. While defense kept him employed for his initial career, Vizquel's new-found offense could keep him in Seattle for another decade.

If Vizquel were playing for a contender, or in a well-covered town like New York or Chicago, his cards could be contenders. But he's a Mariner, and his commons are borderline choices. Our pick for his best 1993 card is Fleer. We have chosen this card for its artistic presentation.

	BA	G	AB	R	H	2B	3B	HR	RBI	SB
92 AL	.294	136	483	49	142	20	4	0	21	15
Life	.250	502	1551	155	388	46	13	4	100	27

TIM WAKEFIELD

Position: Pitcher
Team: Pittsburgh Pirates
Born: August 2, 1966
Melbourne, FL
Height: 6'3" **Weight:** 205 lbs.
Bats: Right **Throws:** Right
Acquired: Eighth-round pick,
6/88 free-agent draft

A converted first baseman became the National League's most exciting pitcher in 1992. Tim Wakefield began the year at Triple-A Buffalo, where he was 10-3 with a 3.06 ERA, 71 strikeouts, and 51 walks in 135 innings. He debuted with the Pirates on July 31, striking out 10 in a complete-game victory against St. Louis. He joined Dodger Tom Candiotti and White Sox veteran Charlie Hough as only the third knuckleballer in the majors. Ironically, all three men wear number 49 on their jerseys. Hough provided early tutoring for Wakefield when he switched to pitching in '89. After winning three decisions in a row, Wakefield inspired The Knuckleheads, a Pittsburgh fan club present at home games.

Wakefield's 1993 cards could be 15 cents apiece. That's a fine price for investing. With his trick pitch and effortless motion, Wakefield could be in the majors well into the next century. Just look at Hough's tenure. Our pick for his best 1993 card is Donruss. We have chosen this card since its design makes it a standout.

	W	L	ERA	G	CG	IP	H	ER	BB	SO
92 NL	8	1	2.15	13	4	92.0	76	22	35	51
Life	8	1	2.15	13	4	92.0	76	22	35	51

Series two cards from some companies were available at press time. If space allows, both cards are shown; if not, the most up-to-date cards are pictured.

BOB WALK

Position: Pitcher
Team: Pittsburgh Pirates
Born: November 26, 1956
Van Nuys, CA
Height: 6'3" **Weight:** 217 lbs.
Bats: Right **Throws:** Right
Acquired: Signed as a free
agent, 4/84

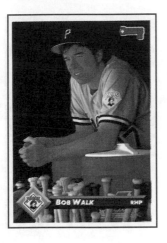

LARRY WALKER

Position: Outfield
Team: Montreal Expos
Born: December 1, 1966
Maple Ridge,
British Columbia
Height: 6'3" **Weight:** 215 lbs.
Bats: Left **Throws:** Right
Acquired: Signed as a free
agent, 11/84

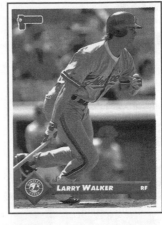

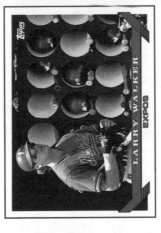

Bob "Whirlybird" Walk was Pittsburgh's secret weapon in 1992. He reached double figures in wins (10) for the fifth time in his career, continuing his domination over righthanded hitters. He also lightened his ERA to its lowest since his '88 campaign. While some players serve as utility infielders, Walk has been the Pirates' utility pitcher, working as an emergency starter, stopper, or middle reliever. Actually, the hurler has lived through two careers. A third-round Philly draft pick in '76, Walk made his big league debut in '80. Swapped to Atlanta, then dropped after three disappointing seasons, he signed a Triple-A contract with the Bucs in '84. Walk took two minor league seasons to stage a comeback. In '89, he won a career-high 13 games with Pittsburgh.

Walk is versatile, yet nearly invisible in the eyes of card collectors. Don't worry about his 1993 common-priced issues. Our pick for his best 1993 card is Upper Deck. We have chosen this card because of its great combination of photography and design.

Larry Walker picked up his 1992 season where he left off in '91. Although Walker took the long road to gaining the right field job for the Montreal Expos, now that he's there, he's decided to keep it. His efforts in '92 brought in some big returns in the form of a .301 batting average, 23 home runs, 93 RBI, and 18 stolen bases. The victim of platooning and hamstring problems in '91, Larry Walker rocketed back to regular status that season with a .338 second-half showing that included 21 doubles, a triple, 10 homers, 34 runs scored, and 41 RBI in 72 games. His second-half average in '91 was the league's best. Walker is the fifth Canadian to play for the Expos. Many baseball insiders considered the strong-armed Walker the National League's best defensive right fielder in '92.

Spend a few nickels on Walker cards. He looks hopeful. Walker's rookie card hides in the '90 Donruss set for less than 50 cents. Our pick for his best 1993 card is Topps. We have chosen this card due to its unique photographic approach.

	W	L	ERA	G	CG	IP	H	ER	BB	SO
92 NL	10	6	3.20	36	1	135.0	132	48	43	60
Life	92	67	3.82	318	13	479.0	1457	628	536	768

	BA	G	AB	R	H	2B	3B	HR	RBI	SB
92	.301	143	528	85	159	31	4	23	93	18
Life	.276	433	1481	207	409	79	9	58	212	54

TIM
WALLACH

Position: Third base
Team: Los Angeles Dodgers
Born: September 14, 1957
Huntington Beach, CA
Height: 6'3" **Weight:** 202 lbs.
Bats: Right **Throws:** Right
Acquired: Traded from Expos
for Tim Barker, 12/92

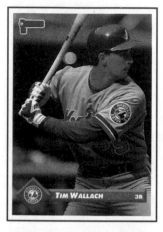

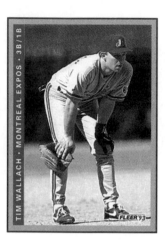

A power outage and a strange position marred Tim Wallach's 1992 progress with the Expos. Initially, he tried switching to first base, in hopes of replacing traded Andres Galarraga. New Expos manager Felipe Alou restored Wallach's hot-corner job. However, that didn't eliminate Wallach's inability to hit .200 in road games or against any righthanded pitchers. He faced similar offensive woes in '91. That season his average sank from its '90 level of .296 to .225. The five-time All-Star will try to find his groove in LA in '93. In '90, Wallach crunched 21 homers and 98 RBI. His career bests are 28 homers ('82) and 123 RBI ('87). Wallach premiered in the big league on September 1, 1980, working as a left fielder. He soared to the majors after two stellar seasons in the minor leagues.

Expect no movement on Wallach's 1993 common-priced cards, especially following his two-year offensive slide. Our pick for his best 1993 card is Fleer. We have chosen this card due to the outstanding photographic composition.

	BA	G	AB	R	H	2B	3B	HR	RBI	SB
92 NL	.223	150	537	53	120	29	1	9	59	2
Life	.259	1767	6529	737	1694	360	31	204	905	50

DAN
WALTERS

Position: Catcher
Team: San Diego Padres
Born: August 15, 1966
Brunswick, ME
Height: 6'4" **Weight:** 225 lbs.
Bats: Right **Throws:** Right
Acquired: Traded from Astros
for Ed Vosberg, 12/88

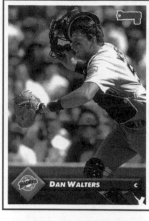

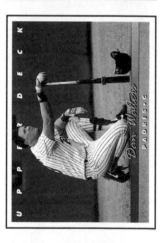

Dan Walters turned out to be one of those surprises that every team needs to have a better-than-expected year. He got a shot when Benito Santiago was injured and hit in the .280 range while making just one error in his first 29 games. He did have some trouble throwing out runners and he won't overwhelm you with power, but he was just the thing in the absence of an established star. Walters spent six years in the pros without even a taste of the majors, but a solid 1992 spring training made the Padres think of him as a late bloomer and insurance against Santiago's free agency. Walters was drafted by the Astros but was traded to San Diego for pitcher Ed Vosberg. In his first year in the Padre chain, Walters raised his average to .273. The next season, he hit a career-best 10 homers spanning Double-A and Triple-A. He spent all of 1991 in Triple-A, hitting a career-best .317.

The catcher's commons will probably never be worth an investment. Our pick for his best 1993 card is Fleer. We have chosen this card since its design makes it a standout.

	BA	G	AB	R	H	2B	3B	HR	RBI	SB
92 NL	.251	57	179	14	45	11	1	4	22	1
Life	.251	57	179	14	45	11	1	4	22	1

Series two cards from some companies were available at press time. If space allows, both cards are shown; if not, the most up-to-date cards are pictured.

DUANE WARD

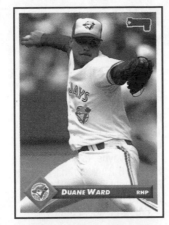

Position: Pitcher
Team: Toronto Blue Jays
Born: May 28, 1964
 Parkview, NM
Height: 6'4" **Weight:** 215 lbs.
Bats: Right **Throws:** Right
Acquired: Traded from Braves
 for Doyle Alexander, 6/86

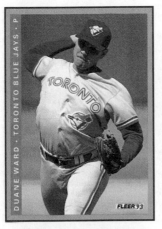

Duane Ward spent another year as a co-closer for Toronto in 1992, and he was a key figure in the team's run to the World Series championship. While his primary duty remained doing set-up work for stopper Tom Henke, Ward surpassed 10 saves for a fifth consecutive season. His 1992 excellence can be traced to his 103 strikeouts in 101 innings, along with a 1.95 ERA (lowered from 2.77 in 1991). Ward's career began as a first-round draft choice of Atlanta's in 1982. The New Mexico native posted two 11-win seasons as a Braves minor-league starter. However, he bombed with an 0-1 record and 7.31 ERA in 10 appearances with Atlanta in 1986 and was traded to Toronto that summer. Ward moved to the bullpen in 1987, a shift that uplifted and lengthened his career.

Ward deserves to be a stopper with the Blue Jays or some willing team. But until he gets that opportunity, no one will consider his 1993 commons. Our pick for his best 1993 card is Donruss. We have chosen this card because the design lends itself to the best use of the elements.

	W	L	ERA	G	SV	IP	H	ER	BB	SO
92 AL	7	4	1.95	79	12	101.1	76	22	39	103
Life	30	33	3.31	387	76	592.1	491	218	256	579

LENNY WEBSTER

Position: Catcher
Team: Minnesota Twins
Born: February 10, 1965
 New Orleans, LA
Height: 5'9" **Weight:** 192 lbs.
Bats: Right **Throws:** Right
Acquired: 21st-round pick,
 6/85 free-agent draft

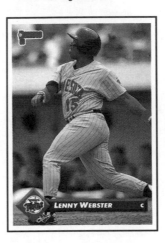

Lenny Webster had an unenviable job with the 1992 Twins: backing up iron-man catcher Brian Harper. Harper's good health and offensive success gave Webster few opportunities. Nonetheless, Webster gave Minnesota a second strong-hitting catcher, a step above departed receiver Junior Ortiz. Webster batted over .320 against lefthanded pitching, although he belted only one home run overall. Last year, Twins fans got their first substantial look at Webster, who played only 18 games in the bigs in 1991. His first two stints with Minnesota, in 1989 and '90, came before Webster had served time at Triple-A. The Twins pursued Webster twice. Initially, Minnesota selected the catcher as a 16th-round pick in the 1982 draft. Instead, he chose to attend Grambling State. Three years later, he accepted the Twins' lower-round offer.

Harper seems cemented as Minnesota's starting backstop. Webster's nickel cards won't move until he gets more playing time. Our pick for his best 1993 card is Donruss. We have chosen this card due to the outstanding photographic composition.

	BA	G	AB	R	H	2B	3B	HR	RBI	SB
92 AL	.280	53	118	10	33	10	1	1	13	0
Life	.287	87	178	21	51	14	1	4	22	0

Series two cards from some companies were available at press time. If space allows, both cards are shown; if not, the most up-to-date cards are pictured.

MITCH
WEBSTER

Position: Outfield
Team: Los Angeles Dodgers
Born: May 16, 1959
  Larned, KS
Height: 6'1" **Weight:** 185 lbs.
Bats: Both **Throws:** Left
Acquired: Traded from Pirates
  for Jose Gonzales, 7/91

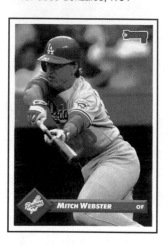

Outfielder Mitch Webster had typical part-time stats with the 1992 Dodgers. Webster's infrequent appearances limited his offensive numbers. Still, he beat the totals he posted with three different teams in 1991. Webster began the '91 season with Cleveland, but he was traded to Pittsburgh after 13 games. Active for 36 games with the Pirates, he was swapped to the Dodgers on July 3. Webster's last year as a starter came with the 1990 Indians, where he batted .252 with 12 homers and 55 RBI. Webster was a Montreal starter from 1985 through mid-1988, until he was traded to the Cubs for Dave Martinez. With the Expos, Webster earned 15 home runs and 63 RBI in 1987. Webster began his career in the Dodgers organization in 1977, but he was drafted by Toronto from the Double-A level in 1979.

Pinch-hitters and defensive replacements like Webster aren't noticed by card collectors. Don't tinker with Webster's commons. Our pick for his best 1993 card is Donruss. We have chosen this card because of its great combination of photography and design.

	BA	G	AB	R	H	2B	3B	HR	RBI	SB
92 NL	.267	135	262	33	70	12	5	6	35	11
Life	.266	1041	3107	456	825	139	52	63	313	155

ERIC
WEDGE

Position: Catcher
Team: Boston Red Sox
Born: January 27, 1968
  Fort Wayne, IN
Height: 6'3" **Weight:** 215 lbs.
Bats: Right **Throws:** Right
Acquired: Third-round pick,
  6/89 free-agent draft

Eric Wedge seems to be back on track after a couple of injuries in 1991 slowed his progress to a regular big-league job. He had moved nicely up the ladder to Pawtucket, just a rung from the majors, when a strained muscle in his right (throwing) arm bothered him. Wedge went down to New Britain, where days later he underwent surgery to remove loose cartilage from his right knee. It's a tribute to his determination that he not only got back to Pawtucket but even made it to the majors for a late-season look. He singled off Milwaukee's Chris George for his first big-league hit. Wedge attended Wichita State from 1986-89, and he led the school to the '89 College World Series title. He was one of nine finalists for the 1989 Golden Spikes Award. He can hit for a moderate average and occasional power. He will also take a walk. Don't expect stolen bases, though.

Wedge has a future as Boston's catcher. Put away a few of his 1993s at 15 cents apiece. Our pick for his best 1993 card is Donruss. We have chosen this card for its technical merits.

	BA	G	AB	R	H	2B	3B	HR	RBI	SB
92 AL	.250	27	68	11	17	2	0	5	11	0
Life	.261	28	69	11	18	2	0	5	11	0

BILL WEGMAN

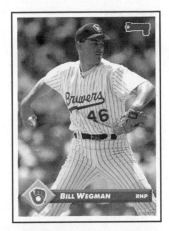

Position: Pitcher
Team: Milwaukee Brewers
Born: December 19, 1962
Cincinnati, OH
Height: 6'5" **Weight:** 220 lbs.
Bats: Right **Throws:** Right
Acquired: Fifth-round pick,
6/81 free-agent draft

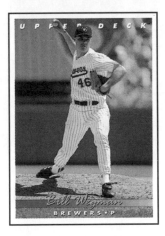

Pitcher Bill Wegman nearly got left behind in Milwaukee's season-ending pennant dash. He owned a record of 8-7 with a 3.28 ERA at the 1992 All-Star break, but he barely kept pace with his team's hot streak. His 13-14 effort didn't compare to his career-best numbers of 1991: 15-7 with seven complete games and a 2.84 ERA for the Brew Crew. The Cincinnati native premiered with Milwaukee in 1985, then became a regular in 1986. Even with his 1991 excellence, Wegman's career mark has struggled to reach .500. In 1990, Wegman's season was ruined by elbow soreness and eventual surgery. Drafted out of high school in 1981, Wegman needed five seasons to gain a starting spot with the Brewers. He enjoyed a spectacular season with Stockton in 1983, going 16-5 with a 1.30 ERA in 24 games.

Wegman's modest past and his lack of recognition in Milwaukee keep his card values down. His 1993 commons won't be booming. Our pick for his best 1993 card is Topps. We have chosen this card because of its overall appeal and pleasing looks.

	W	L	ERA	G	CG	IP	H	ER	BB	SO
92 AL	13	14	3.20	35	7	261.2	251	93	55	127
Life	64	65	4.02	186	28	1175.2	1203	525	271	537

WALT WEISS

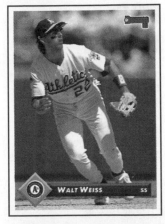

Position: Shortstop
Team: Florida Marlins
Born: November 28, 1963
Tuxedo, NY
Height: 6' **Weight:** 175 lbs.
Bats: Both **Throws:** Right
Acquired: Traded from
Athletics for Eric Helfand and
a player to be named, 11/92

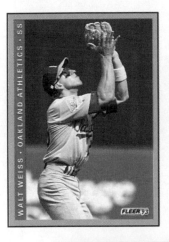

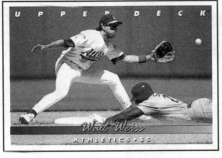

Walt Weiss gets new life with the Florida Marlins after gloom and despair followed him again in 1992. The hard-luck Oakland shortstop began the year with a rib injury. While he was recovering from yet another disability, new shortstop Mike Bordick was briefly leading the league in hitting. Weiss was recalled from the DL on June 3. Surprisingly, he wound up appearing in more games than he had during his 1991 campaign, which was also haunted by injuries. That year, he injured an ankle running out a ground ball and his season was ruined by surgery. Taken out during a double-play in the 1990 ALCS versus Boston, Weiss needed more surgery. The other knee had faced surgery in 1989, also from a double-play collision. In 1988, Weiss won the AL Rookie of the Year Award.

Even if Weiss regains his full health, his stats will never be the same. Weiss's cards are not sound investments, even at a nickel or less. Our pick for his best 1993 card is Upper Deck. We have chosen this card since the photograph captures the athletic ability of the player.

	BA	G	AB	R	H	2B	3B	HR	RBI	SB
92 AL	.212	103	316	36	67	5	2	0	21	6
Life	.246	528	1608	178	395	60	7	8	130	32

Series two cards from some companies were available at press time. If space allows, both cards are shown; if not, the most up-to-date cards are pictured.

BOB WELCH

Position: Pitcher
Team: Oakland Athletics
Born: November 3, 1956
Detroit, MI
Height: 6'3" **Weight:** 198 lbs.
Bats: Right **Throws:** Right
Acquired: Traded from Dodgers
with Matt Young and Jack
Savage for Jesse Orosco,
Alfredo Griffin, and Jay
Howell, 12/87

JOHN WETTELAND

Position: Pitcher
Team: Montreal Expos
Born: August 21, 1966
San Mateo, CA
Height: 6'2" **Weight:** 195 lbs.
Bats: Right **Throws:** Right
Acquired: Traded from Reds
with Bill Risley for Dave
Martinez, Scott Ruskin, and
Willie Greene, 12/91

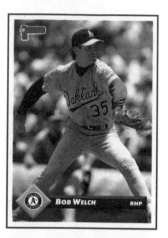

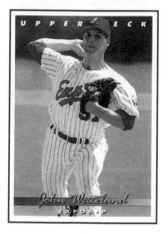

Bob Welch was one of Oakland's strongest pitchers of 1992—when he was healthy. The righthanded workhorse started the season with three problems: a sore knee, a strained back, and a possible rotator cuff injury. By the All-Star break, Welch was 7-4 with a 2.70 ERA in 11 starts. Seeing Welch on the sidelines was a rare sight. From 1986 through 1991, he exceeded 200 innings yearly. Prior to the injuries, Welch hoped to avenge his 1991 slump, which amounted to a 12-13 record and 4.58 ERA. Then again, any effort after his Cy Young Award-winning season of 27-6 in 1990 would have looked pale. Welch's first victory of 1993 will be a meaningful one: the 200th in a career dating back to the 1978 Dodgers. The two-time All-Star made 1992 his 11th career outing of 10 wins or more, as he won 11 games in just 20 starts.

After two straight years of slumps and injuries, Welch can't be hopeful for 1993. Expect his common-priced cards to go downhill. Our pick for his best 1993 card is Fleer. We have chosen this card because of its great combination of photography and design.

John Wetteland's own persistence carried him to the role of stopper with the 1992 Expos. Trapped on the Dodgers' Triple-A affiliate for a third straight year in 1991, Wetteland requested a change. He asked to work as a stopper. He was perfect in 20 save opportunities for Albuquerque in '91, then joined Los Angeles for the last month of the season. In 1992, the righthander was the pride of the Expos bullpen. Not since Jeff Reardon spun a team record 41 saves in 1985 had any Expos reliever sparkled so. Wetteland saved 37 games last year. His pitching repertoire is simple, consisting of a fastball, curve, and changeup. With those three pitches, he racked up more than one strikeout per inning. Don't expect to see this converted starter back in the rotation.

Wetteland could be in store for a fabulous flop, much like record-setting stopper Bobby Thigpen experienced in 1992. Think carefully about nickel-priced Wetteland cards. Our pick for his best 1993 card is Upper Deck. We have chosen this card because of its overall appeal and pleasing looks.

	W	L	ERA	G	CG	IP	H	ER	BB	SO
92 AL	11	7	3.27	20	0	123.2	114	45	43	47
Life	199	129	3.27	451	61	2856.2	2607	1039	935	1862

	W	L	ERA	G	SV	IP	H	ER	BB	SO
92 NL	4	4	2.92	67	37	83.1	64	27	36	99
Life	12	16	3.52	126	38	238.0	194	93	90	240

Series two cards from some companies were available at press time. If space allows, both cards are shown; if not, the most up-to-date cards are pictured.

LOU
WHITAKER

Position: Second base
Team: Detroit Tigers
Born: May 12, 1957
  Brooklyn, NY
Height: 5'11" **Weight:** 180 lbs.
Bats: Left **Throws:** Right
Acquired: Fifth-round pick,
  6/75 free-agent draft

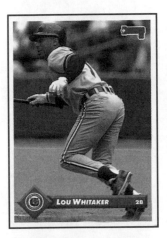

DEVON
WHITE

Position: Outfield
Team: Toronto Blue Jays
Born: December 29, 1962
  Kingston, Jamaica
Height: 6'2" **Weight:** 180 lbs.
Bats: Both **Throws:** Right
Acquired: Traded from Angels
  with Willie Fraser and
  Marcus Moore for Junior
  Felix, Luis Sojo, and Ken
  Rivers, 12/90

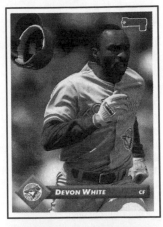

Tigers second baseman Lou Whitaker padded his distinguished résumé with another strong offensive showing in 1992. He just missed the fifth 20-plus season of homers in his career, but he did manage to become only the seventh Tiger in history with 2,000 lifetime hits. His 1992 averages at home and against lefthanded pitchers rose into the mid-.300s. Whitaker's success began in 1978, when he was AL Rookie of the Year. His career highs include a .320 average (1983), 28 home runs (1989) and 85 RBI (1989). Four All-Star team berths and three Gold Glove Awards highlight his accomplishments. When the Tigers chose Whitaker in the fifth round of the 1975 draft, he was tabbed initially for third base. He has never strayed from second base in the majors.

  Although his nickel-priced 1993 cards won't grow in value quickly, they'll blossom if Sweet Lou gets his Hall of Fame plaque. A 1981 Fleer of Whitaker is a good investment at 50 cents. Our pick for his best 1993 card is Upper Deck. We have chosen this card since the photograph captures the athletic ability of the player.

Devon White had the year of his life in 1992. Although his regular season stats were good, his postseason activities were spectacular. White made sensational plays in the field and came through at the plate for the Blue Jays during the ALCS and World Series games. His most memorable moment was a play he initiated during the World Series that should have been a triple play. Despite a blown officiating call, it was the high point of the Series and perhaps the highlight of White's career. The '92 season came on the heels of some other pretty exciting personal achievements for him. In '91, White played his first season in Toronto and set career highs, including a .282 average, 110 runs scored, 181 hits, and 55 walks. He won a Gold Glove after leading all AL outfielders with a .998 fielding percentage.

  His performance in '92 cannot make up for underachievement in years past. Pass on White's nickel-priced '93s. Our pick for his best 1993 card is Score. We have chosen this card for the interesting facts included on the reverse.

	BA	G	AB	R	H	2B	3B	HR	RBI	SB
92 AL	.278	130	453	77	126	26	0	19	71	6
Life	.274	2095	7616	1211	2088	353	62	209	930	134

	BA	G	AB	R	H	2B	3B	HR	RBI	SB
92 AL	.248	153	641	98	159	26	7	17	60	37
Life	.254	921	3514	545	891	157	41	93	361	193

Series two cards from some companies were available at press time. If space allows, both cards are shown; if not, the most up-to-date cards are pictured.

WALLY WHITEHURST

Position: Pitcher
Team: San Diego Padres
Born: April 11, 1964
  Shreveport, LA
Height: 6'3" **Weight:** 195 lbs.
Bats: Right **Throws:** Right
Acquired: Traded from Mets
  with D.J. Dozier for Tony
  Fernandez, 10/92

Wally Whitehurst endured a second consecutive year of losing records with the Mets in 1992. The "swing man" bounced between the bullpen and the starting rotation but had another hard-luck statistical year. For the '92 campaign, Whitehurst posted a 3-9 record with a 3.62 ERA, four holds, and no saves. The Padres are hoping to change his luck in '93, as they traded for him and D.J. Dozier after the '92 season. Whitehurst's first full season with the Mets, 1991, ended at 7-12 with a 4.19 ERA. The righthander's best campaign came with New York in '89. Working exclusively in relief, Whitehurst went 1-0 with a 3.29 ERA in 38 outings. The bulk of his five-year stay in the minors, however, was devoted to relief. Originally, Whitehurst was picked by Oakland in the '85 draft.

His quiet contributions aren't going to stimulate common-priced card values. Our pick for his best 1993 card is Topps. We have chosen this card for its technical merits.

MARK WHITEN

Position: Outfield
Team: Cleveland Indians
Born: November 25, 1966
  Pensacola, FL
Height: 6'3" **Weight:** 215 lbs.
Bats: Both **Throws:** Right
Acquired: Traded from Blue
  Jays with Glenallen Hill and
  Denis Boucher for Tom
  Candiotti, 6/91

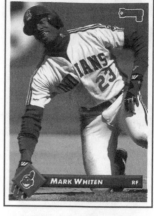

Mark Whiten's first full season with Cleveland produced both highs and lows in 1992. His offense was close to the combined nine homers and 45 RBI produced between the Blue Jays and Indians in '91. Yet, Whiten's average dipped to .254 and his strikeouts grew to 102. While he didn't match the speed of outfield teammate Kenny Lofton, Whiten regained his stolen-base skills in '92, swiping 16. He stole just four bases in '91, partially due to an ankle injury. For two years in a row, Whiten has rivaled for the AL lead in outfield assists, tossing out more than a dozen baserunners yearly. The Florida native toiled for five minor league seasons before debuting with Toronto in '90, batting .273 in his first season.

Whiten will play a huge role in any comeback made by Cleveland in 1993. His combination of power and speed is ideal for stardom. Gamble a few nickels on his cards. Our pick for his best 1993 card is Donruss. We have chosen this card due to the outstanding photographic composition.

	W	L	ERA	G	SV	IP	H	ER	BB	SO
92 NL	3	9	3.62	44	0	97.0	99	39	33	70
Life	11	22	3.83	127	3	310.0	321	132	72	212

	BA	G	AB	R	H	2B	3B	HR	RBI	SB
92 AL	.254	148	508	73	129	19	4	9	43	16
Life	.251	297	1003	131	252	38	12	20	95	22

KEVIN WICKANDER

Position: Pitcher
Team: Cleveland Indians
Born: January 4, 1965
Ft. Dodge, IA
Height: 6'2" **Weight:** 202 lbs.
Bats: Left **Throws:** Left
Acquired: Second-round pick,
6/86 free-agent draft

Kevin Wickander supported the left side of the Indians bullpen in 1992. After showing control problems in spring training, he started '92 in Triple-A. He worked his way back and appeared in 44 games for the Tribe in '92, posting a 2-0 record with a 3.07 ERA, one save, and seven holds. The Iowa native must have the trip between Triple-A Colorado Springs and Cleveland memorized. He shuttled between those two stops for several years. In '91, the lefty seemed set to spend the season in Cleveland. However, he slipped and fractured his elbow, ending that season on May 30. Wickander worked two years as a starter before converting to relief as a Double-A hurler in '88. The results were immediate, as he earned 16 saves and a win in Double-A ball.

Wickander won't get the attention in the Tribe bullpen that Steve Olin pulls. There is no need to invest in these common-priced cards. Our pick for his best 1993 card is Topps. We have chosen this card due to the outstanding photographic composition.

	W	L	ERA	G	SV	IP	H	ER	BB	SO
92 AL	2	0	3.07	44	1	41.0	39	14	28	38
Life	2	1	3.21	56	1	56.0	59	20	34	48

BOB WICKMAN

Position: Pitcher
Team: New York Yankees
Born: June 8, 1971
Los Angeles, CA
Height: 6'1" **Weight:** 207 lbs.
Bats: Both **Throws:** Left
Acquired: Traded from White
Sox with Melido Perez and
Domingo Jean for Steve Sax,
1/92

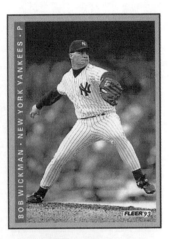
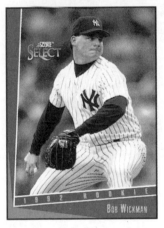

Bob Wickman is a key figure in what could prove to be one of the better trades the Yankees have made recently. Wickman reeled off an impressive winning streak in the Triple-A International League. He held International League hitters to a .227 batting average in '92. Called to the majors late in the season and joining Sam Militello as a farmhand who brought promise for the future, Wickman won three of his first four starts with the Yankees. One of his victories completed a three-game sweep of Baltimore, hurting the Orioles' chances to win the division. All this happened despite a farm accident that cost Wickman the tip of his right index finger when he was two years old. He was originally selected by the White Sox in the second round of the June '90 draft.

Expect Wickman to have a good shot at winning a job in New York in '93. Pick up a few of his '93s for a rainy day. Our pick for his best 1993 card is Fleer. We have chosen this card because of its overall appeal and pleasing looks.

	W	L	ERA	G	CG	IP	H	ER	BB	SO
92 AAA	12	5	2.92	23	2	157	131	51	55	108
92 AL	6	1	4.11	8	0	50.1	51	23	20	21

RICK WILKINS

Position: Catcher
Team: Chicago Cubs
Born: July 4, 1967
  Jacksonville, FL
Height: 6'2" **Weight:** 210 lbs.
Bats: Left **Throws:** Right
Acquired: 23rd-round pick,
  6/86 free-agent draft

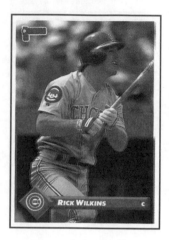

BERNIE WILLIAMS

Position: Outfield
Team: New York Yankees
Born: September 13, 1968
  San Juan, Puerto Rico
Height: 6'2" **Weight:** 196 lbs.
Bats: Both **Throws:** Right
Acquired: Signed as a free
  agent, 9/85

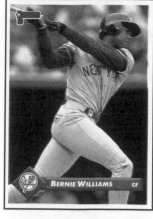

Rick Wilkins stood out among the flood of catchers appearing for the Cubs in 1992. The lefthanded-hitting Wilkins platooned with Joe Girardi, who missed most of '91 with a back injury. While both catchers were offensively similar, Wilkins showed more power. He improved from his '90 rookie totals of six homers and a .222 average in 86 games, lifting his batting average by nearly 50 points. However, Wilkins was detoured for part of '92 to Triple-A Iowa, where he batted .277 with five home runs and 28 RBI. Chicago considered him for sophomore duty in the majors when he hit .298 in '92 spring training. The Cubs discovered Wilkins out of a Florida community college, giving him little thought in the '86 free-agent draft. He flashed his long-ball promise in Double-A in '90, hitting 17 homers and 71 RBI.

Wilkins will have the starting job with the Cubs in '93. His cards, however, will remain commons. Our pick for his best 1993 card is Donruss. We have chosen this card for its technical merits.

Although his performance was seen for less than half the 1992 campaign, Bernie Williams made his case as a starting New York outfielder. The Yankees placed him on the Opening-Day roster following a preseason audition of .275. He started the year as the team's fourth outfielder. Williams played in 62 games for the Yankees in '92, earning a .280 average with five homers and 26 RBI before making yet another trip back to Triple-A Columbus. At Columbus, the switch-hitter contributed .306 with eight homers, 50 RBI, and 20 stolen bases. His achievements with the '92 Yanks provided a contrast to his '90 debut total of three homers, 34 RBI, and a .238 average. Unlike past slugging dinosaurs who've roamed Yankee Stadium pastures, Williams is a fleet baserunner and gifted defensive outfielder.

Pencil in Williams as a 1993 Yankees starter. You'll have a hopeful investment at a nickel per card. Our pick for his best 1993 card is Fleer. We have chosen this card due to the outstanding photographic composition.

	BA	G	AB	R	H	2B	3B	HR	RBI	SB
92 NL	.270	83	244	20	66	9	1	8	22	0
Life	.248	169	447	41	111	18	1	14	44	3

	BA	G	AB	R	H	2B	3B	HR	RBI	SB
92 AL	.280	62	261	39	73	14	2	5	26	7
Life	.256	147	581	82	149	33	6	8	60	17

Series two cards from some companies were available at press time. If space allows, both cards are shown; if not, the most up-to-date cards are pictured.

BRIAN WILLIAMS

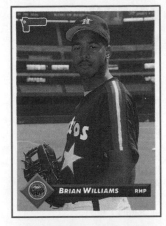

Position: Pitcher
Team: Houston Astros
Born: February 15, 1969
  Lancaster, SC
Height: 6'2" **Weight:** 195 lbs.
Bats: Right **Throws:** Right
Acquired: First-round pick,
  6/90 free-agent draft

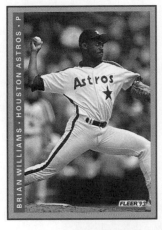

GERALD WILLIAMS

Position: Outfield
Team: New York Yankees
Born: August 10, 1966
  New Orleans, LA
Height: 6'2" **Weight:** 190 lbs.
Bats: Right **Throws:** Right
Acquired: 14th-round pick,
  6/87 free-agent draft

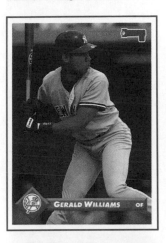

Brian Williams established himself in the majors almost as quickly as he reached the big leagues. Williams, in only his third year of pro ball, got the call in June 1992, quickly posting two wins. On June 16, he shut down the tough San Diego lineup for six innings in an 11-0 victory. Six days later, he went seven innings in a 5-2 win over the Reds. It shouldn't have surprised anyone what Williams did in '91. He made four stops, going from Class-A up the ladder to the majors. Williams was originally selected by the Pirates as a shortstop in the third round in '87 and was the highest drafted player not to sign that year. In '90, the Astros had a pick for the Giants' signing of free agent Kevin Bass, and they used it to tab Williams. He has never shown exceptional control as a pro and must work on it to stay in the majors.

Williams has moderate chances at success in Houston. His '93 cards have fewer chances, even at a nickel apiece. Our pick for his best 1993 card is Upper Deck. We have chosen this card due to its unique photographic approach.

Gerald Williams broke free of his Triple-A confinement in 1992 to become one of the New York Yankees best hopes for the future. Williams tried to make his sixth minor league season his last in '92, collecting 12 home runs, 71 RBI, 30 stolen bases, and a .277 batting average. Upon his New York debut, he provided three homers and six RBI in just 15 at-bats with the Yanks. Known as "Ice" for his unflappable ability and demeanor, Williams was the odds-on favorite for right fielder when the '92 season ended. Active in pro ball since '87, Williams is a product of Grambling State University. His speed and power potential make him a can't-miss choice for the '90s.

Williams should be a Yankees regular, due to the departure of Jesse Barfield and Mel Hall. For a nickel apiece, collectors shouldn't go wrong with 1993 cards of Williams. Our pick for his best 1993 card is Score. We have chosen this card for the superior presentation of information on its back.

	W	L	ERA	G	CG	IP	H	ER	BB	SO
92 NL	7	6	3.92	16	0	96.1	92	42	42	54
Life	7	7	3.90	18	0	108.1	103	47	46	58

	BA	G	AB	R	H	2B	3B	HR	RBI	SB
92 AL	.296	15	27	7	8	2	0	3	6	2
Life	.296	15	27	7	8	2	0	3	6	2

MATT WILLIAMS

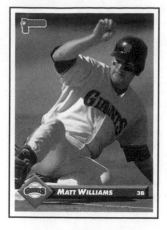

Position: Third base
Team: San Francisco Giants
Born: November 28, 1965
Bishop, CA
Height: 6'2" **Weight:** 205 lbs.
Bats: Right **Throws:** Right
Acquired: First-round pick,
6/86 free-agent draft

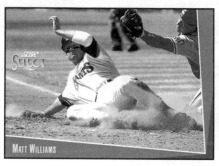

Matt Williams suffered a downturn in his performance in 1992. Williams' power stats, his real strength, were lower than in '91. Although 20 homers and 66 RBI are nothing to sneeze at, it was definitely not his best season. Overall in '92, Williams had a .227 batting average. A big part of his problem was his penchant to strike out. He had too much success in that category, as his 109 whiffs in '92 topped all other third basemen in the league. He came off a great year, too. Playing third in '91, Williams won his first Rawlings Gold Glove and reached a personal peak with 34 home runs—giving him 67 in two seasons. The native Californian had reached his RBI high a year earlier, when he led the National League with 122.

Let Williams recover from an off year before investing. Many dealers still sell Williams for a nickel apiece. If you expect a comeback, you'll expect dividends from Williams' '88 Score Rookie for 75 cents. Our pick for his best 1993 card is Donruss. We have chosen this card because it has a distinctive look.

	BA	G	AB	R	H	2B	3B	HR	RBI	SB
92 NL	.227	146	529	58	120	13	5	20	66	7
Life	.241	682	2428	293	586	97	16	121	376	24

MITCH WILLIAMS

Position: Pitcher
Team: Philadelphia Phillies
Born: November 17, 1964
Santa Ana, CA
Height: 6'4" **Weight:** 205 lbs.
Bats: Left **Throws:** Left
Acquired: Traded from Cubs
for Chuck McElroy and Bob
Scanlan, 4/91

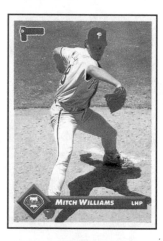

Mitch Williams drives managers crazy: he has a penchant for pitching himself into trouble, then working his way out of the self-created jam. Such heroics wreak havoc with the nervous stomachs of the men who make the decisions. Yet it is difficult to argue with the success the Wild Thing often achieves. He is a rubber-armed reliever who has worked at least 80 games in a season twice. In '92, Williams worked in 66 games for the Phillies, saving 29 and marking the sixth time in seven seasons that he has made at least 60 appearances. He also saw his ERA balloon to almost a point and a half more than his '91 career best. That season, his first with the Phils, he posted 30 saves, accented with personal bests in ERA (2.34) and wins (12). Williams was with the Chicago Cubs before joining the Phils. Since '88, he has saved at least 16 games a season.

With his ERA inflating and his save total not, wait on his '93s. Our pick for his best 1993 card is Score. We have chosen this card due to its unique photographic approach.

	W	L	ERA	G	SV	IP	H	ER	BB	SO
92 NL	5	8	3.78	66	29	81.0	69	34	64	74
Life	40	44	3.41	502	143	592.0	436	224	448	560

DAN
WILSON

Position: Catcher
Team: Cincinnati Reds
Born: March 25, 1969
   Arlington Heights, IL
Height: 6'3" **Weight:** 190 lbs.
Bats: Right **Throws:** Right
Acquired: First-round pick,
   6/90 free-agent draft

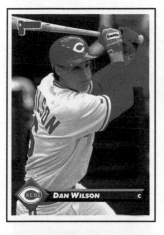

Dan Wilson reached the big leagues in just his third pro season, and the speed with which he arrived leaves him plenty of time to excel with the Reds. He made his major league debut on September 7, 1992, but spent most of his time get getting the feel of the majors. He broke into the pros with Class-A Charleston in '90 and made just one error in 32 games. He opened the following season in Class-A, threw out 44 percent of runners trying to steal, and was named the league's top defensive receiver. He was promoted to Double-A ball in June. Wilson was drafted by the Mets in '87, but chose to attend the University of Minnesota. As a Golden Gopher, he was named first team All-American by *Baseball America* in '90.

While he doesn't seem likely to wrest the starting job from Joe Oliver any time soon, Wilson does give Cincinnati depth at this important position and looms as the catcher of the future. If you believe, pick up a couple of Wilson's '93s for a dime. Our pick for his best 1993 card is Upper Deck. We have chosen this card because it will increase in value.

	BA	G	AB	R	H	2B	3B	HR	RBI	SB
92 AAA	.251	–	366	27	92	16	1	4	34	1
92 NL	.360	12	25	2	9	1	0	0	3	0

NIGEL
WILSON

Position: Outfield
Team: Florida Marlins
Born: January 12, 1970
   Oshawa, Ontario
Height: 6'1" **Weight:** 185 lbs.
Bats: Left **Throws:** Left
Acquired: First-round pick,
   11/92 expansion draft

While Toronto's Double-A Southern League affiliate in Knoxville suffered through a difficult season in 1992, Nigel Wilson was a highlight film in himself. He blossomed into a true slugger and finished third in the league with 26 homers. Wilson had twice reached double figures in his pro career, and earned a spot on the Class-A Florida State League's postseason All-Star team in '91. He hadn't, however, put things together quite the way he did in his first look at Double-A ball. He had a .325 on-base average and a .516 slugging percentage in '92. Wilson has reached double figures in stolen bases for three years in a row. He was named to the Southern League's postseason All-Star Team as a DH. If he improves his fielding, he could be Florida's Opening Day left fielder.

His '93s seem a little pricey. He could, however, be a real stand-out on the fledgling Marlins. Our pick for his best 1993 card is Upper Deck. We have chosen this card because it will increase in value.

	BA	G	AB	R	H	2B	3B	HR	RBI	SB
91 A	.301	119	455	64	137	18	13	12	55	27
92 AA	.274	137	521	85	143	34	7	26	69	13

STEVE WILSON

Position: Pitcher
Team: Los Angeles Dodgers
Born: December 13, 1964
  Victoria, British Columbia,
  Canada
Height: 6'4" **Weight:** 195 lbs.
Bats: Left **Throws:** Left
Acquired: Traded from Cubs
  for Jeff Hartsock, 9/91

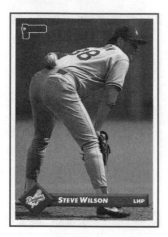

What a difference a year makes. When the Dodgers were scrapping for a divisional title in 1991, Steve Wilson pitched like Superman after his September arrival. With the Dodgers doomed to the cellar in '92, Wilson's work bore the stamp of Clark Kent. Used mostly against lefthanded hitters, Wilson wobbled from the start. He yielded more hits than innings and had trouble finding the plate. He also gave up six homers, too many in his 67 innings. His two saving graces were success against first batters and an average of seven-and-one-half strikeouts per nine innings. In '92, opponents compiled a .282 batting average, a .351 on-base percentage, and a .424 slugging percentage against him. Wilson is a good bunter, baserunner, and fielder who has trouble keeping baserunners close. His top priority is finding his control.

Spending your pennies on an on-again/off-again reliever is not a wise move. Hold off on Wilson's '93s. Our pick for his best 1993 card is Topps. We have chosen this card due to the outstanding photographic composition.

	W	L	ERA	G	SV	IP	H	ER	BB	SO
92 NL	2	5	4.18	60	0	66.2	74	31	29	54
Life	12	18	4.39	180	5	319.2	318	156	116	229

TREVOR WILSON

Position: Pitcher
Team: San Francisco Giants
Born: June 7, 1966
  Torrance, CA
Height: 6' **Weight:** 175 lbs.
Bats: Left **Throws:** Left
Acquired: Eighth-round pick,
  6/85 free-agent draft

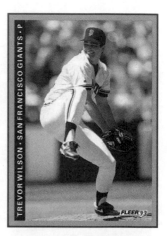

Trevor Wilson could have sued his teammates for nonsupport in 1992. He was given fewer than three runs per nine innings all year, so it is not surprising that he led the Giants in losses. Wilson had hoped to maintain the momentum of his strong '91 finish but ran into trouble before Opening Day. During surgery to remove a benign cyst from his ribs, surgeons sliced portions of two healthy ribs. Wilson later encountered elbow problems that knocked him out of action in September. In between, he had more than five strikeouts per nine innings. He threw too many home run balls and did not enjoy his usual success against lefties. Opponents compiled a .265 batting average, a .342 on-base percentage, and a .416 slugging percentage on him in '92. He does help himself as a hitter, bunter, and fielder.

Wilson should be on track for a major comeback in '93. If he controls the gopher ball, he'll dominate. His cards are a toss-up at under a nickel. Our pick for his best 1993 card is Fleer. We have chosen this card because of its overall appeal and pleasing looks.

	W	L	ERA	G	CG	IP	H	ER	BB	SO
92 NL	8	14	4.21	26	1	154.0	152	72	64	88
Life	31	37	3.92	115	6	527.2	465	230	222	330

WILLIE WILSON

Position: Outfield
Team: Chicago Cubs
Born: July 9, 1955
   Montgomery, AL
Height: 6'3" **Weight:** 200 lbs.
Bats: Both **Throws:** Right
Acquired: Signed as free agent,
   12/92

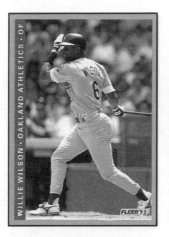

Willie Wilson was a reborn starter for Oakland in 1992, following a season-long injury to center fielder Dave Henderson. Wilson was in vintage form in his second Oakland season. On the bases, he stole 28 in 36 attempts, moving into baseball's all-time top 10 for steals. Wilson's five triples increased his career total to 142, maintaining his ranking as first among active players. Used sparingly by the A's in '91, Wilson hit a mere .238. His stay with the A's ended after the '92 season as he signed a free-agent deal that will take him to Chicago. With Kansas City before he went to Oakland, he earned five AL leads in triples, an '82 batting title (.332), and two All-Star game appearances.

Wilson isn't a sure thing for the Hall of Fame, especially due to his 1984 suspension for drug involvement. His card values won't climb on the basis of his 1993 stats, which should discourage investors who consider Wilson's commons. Our pick for his best 1993 card is Score. We have chosen this card for the superior presentation of information on its back.

	BA	G	AB	R	H	2B	3B	HR	RBI	SB
92 AL	.270	132	396	38	107	15	5	0	37	28
Life	.286	2032	7489	1136	2145	270	142	40	574	660

DAVE WINFIELD

Position: Outfield
Team: Minnesota Twins
Born: October 3, 1951
   St. Paul, MN
Height: 6'6" **Weight:** 220 lbs.
Bats: Right **Throws:** Right
Acquired: Signed as a free
   agent, 12/92

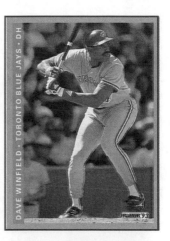

Dave Winfield proved in 1992 that life begins at 40. Signed to serve as Toronto's DH after drawing a surprise release from the Angels, Winfield had a .304 average, 11 homers, and 37 RBI after his first 68 games with the Jays. His presence in the lineup as the club's cleanup man helped Joe Carter, the No. 3 hitter, get a steady diet of pitches to hit. Pitchers quickly found it unwise to walk Carter with Winfield waiting in the wings. The Angels had mistakenly believed age was catching up with the slugger, who had only 10 homers and 29 RBI during the second half of the '91 campaign. Winfield has produced eight 100-RBI campaigns, five Gold Gloves, and a Comeback Player of the Year Award (after back surgery cost him the entire '89 season). The double-digit All-Star selection is one of a handful of big leaguers who never played in the minors.

Winfield is Cooperstown bound. Buy his '93s at a dime or less. His '82 Donruss Diamond King is affordable at 75 cents. Our pick for his best 1993 card is Score. We have chosen this card because of its overall appeal and pleasing looks.

	BA	G	AB	R	H	2B	3B	HR	RBI	SB
92 AL	.290	156	583	92	169	33	3	26	108	2
Life	.285	2707	10047	1551	2866	493	83	432	1710	218

BOBBY WITT

Position: Pitcher
Team: Oakland Athletics
Born: May 11, 1964
  Canton, MA
Height: 6'2" **Weight:** 205 lbs.
Bats: Right **Throws:** Right
Acquired: Traded from Rangers
  with Jeff Russell and Ruben
  Sierra for Jose Canseco,
  8/92

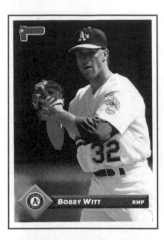

Bobby Witt escaped seven years of Texas turmoil to join Oakland's 1992 pennant chase. Witt lugged a record of 9-13 and a 4.46 ERA to the Athletics as one third of the deal that sent Jose Canseco to the Rangers. By the end of the '92 season, his record stood at 10-14 with a 4.29 ERA. Witt's wild ways began in '86, when he was 11-9 in his Texas rookie season. For the first of his three seasons with the Rangers, he led the league in walks. Witt was the third player in the nation chosen during the first round of the '85 draft. Before playing with the '84 U.S. Olympic baseball team, Witt refused Cincinnati in the '82 draft. Unlike his many talented teammates, Witt's contract runs through '93. In hopes to get his option picked up, Witt should be at his best.

Witt never leveled off in Texas and never won more than 17 games. However, the consistency shown with Oakland hints that Witt's ready to win 20. Buy his cards at a nickel apiece. Our pick for his best 1993 card is Fleer. We have chosen this card due to the outstanding photographic composition.

	W	L	ERA	G	CG	IP	H	ER	BB	SO
92 AL	10	14	4.29	31	0	193.0	183	92	114	125
Life	69	73	4.57	191	27	1173.0	1024	596	796	1076

MARK WOHLERS

Position: Pitcher
Team: Atlanta Braves
Born: January 23, 1970
  Holyoke, MA
Height: 6'4" **Weight:** 207 lbs.
Bats: Right **Throws:** Right
Acquired: 10th-round pick,
  6/88 free-agent draft

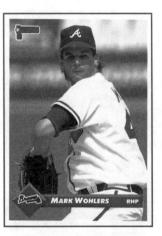
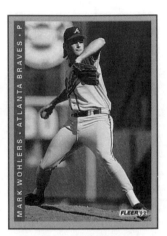

Relief pitchers are supposed to deliver in emergencies, and that's what Mark Wohlers tried to do early in 1992 when the Braves were having trouble in their bullpen. Wohlers was recalled from Triple-A Richmond and immediately was given a chance to be the closer. In his first seven games, he collected three saves and one hold with no blown saves. He also gave up enough runs to put his ERA over 5.00. Like most pitchers, Wohlers will not dominate the way he did in the minors. In '91, for instance, he posted 11 saves in 23 games for Richmond, posting a 1.03 ERA. He got a late-season call to Atlanta, where he was 3-1 with two saves in 17 games. He also got into three World Series contests. A starter for the first two years of his pro career, Wohlers was converted to a closer early in the 1990 season.

Wohlers has unlimited potential as a reliever. His '93s have unlimited futures at a dime each. Our pick for his best 1993 card is Score. We have chosen this card for its technical merits.

	W	L	ERA	G	SV	IP	H	ER	BB	SO
92 NL	1	2	2.55	32	4	35.1	28	10	14	17
Life	4	3	2.78	49	6	55.0	45	17	27	30

KERRY WOODSON

Position: Pitcher
Team: Seattle Mariners
Born: May 18, 1969
Jacksonville, FL
Height: 6′2″ **Weight:** 190 lbs.
Bats: Right **Throws:** Right
Acquired: 29th-round pick,
6/88 free-agent draft

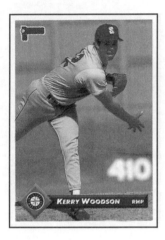 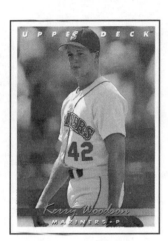

Pitcher Walter Browne "Kerry" Woodson IV endured mixed reviews following his rookie campaign. The righthander's 1992 efforts were marred by control problems. Both with Triple-A Calgary and with the Mariners in Seattle, he walked more than he struck out. In '90, the Florida native led the Class-A California League by beaning 12 batters. Yet, he wasn't homered upon once during his Mariners debut, and surrendered less than one hit per inning. Furthermore, his 3.29 ERA was a pleasant relief from the team's bloated 4.55 mark (second worst in the league). Used mainly as a starter before his '92 promotion, Woodson could see service as a "swing man" with the 1993 Mariners.

Woodson carries twice the burden of most other young pitchers. Not only is he stuck in middle relief, he's on a last-place team. At that rate, his '93 commons will never be worthwhile. Our pick for his best 1993 card is Upper Deck. We have chosen this card because of its great combination of photography and design.

	W	L	ERA	G	SV	IP	H	ER	BB	SO
92 AL	0	1	3.29	8	0	13.2	12	5	11	6
Life	0	1	3.29	8	0	13.2	12	5	11	6

TODD WORRELL

Position: Pitcher
Team: Los Angeles Dodgers
Born: September 28, 1959
Arcadia, CA
Height: 6′5″ **Weight:** 222 lbs.
Bats: Right **Throws:** Right
Acquired: Signed as a free-
agent, 12/92

 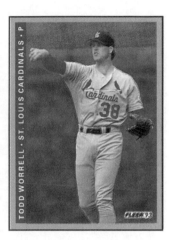

Todd Worrell was healthy but not always happy with the 1992 Cardinals. During his two-year recuperation from elbow and shoulder problems, St. Louis acquired stopper Lee Smith. When Worrell made his '92 return, he found another reliever was walking a mile in his shoes. So, Worrell decided to take a hike to LA were he hopes the turf will be greener. In '92, Worrell adapted well to the role of set-up man, gaining 25 holds. Still, he saw action in few save situations. In '86, his first full season with the Redbirds, Worrell led the NL with a career-high 36 saves. Two subsequent seasons of 30-plus saves were followed by a 20-save campaign in '89. He worked three seasons in the Cards' farm system before switching from a starting role to relief.

Although moving off the Cardinal roster will give Worrell more work, even a 40-save season isn't going to transform his nickel-priced cards. Our pick for his best 1993 card is Topps. We have chosen this card due to the outstanding photographic composition.

	W	L	ERA	G	SV	IP	H	ER	BB	SO
92 NL	5	3	2.11	67	3	64.0	45	15	25	64
Life	33	33	2.56	348	129	425.2	345	121	167	365

ANTHONY YOUNG

Position: Pitcher
Team: New York Mets
Born: January 19, 1966
  Houston, TX
Height: 6'2" **Weight:** 200 lbs.
Bats: Right **Throws:** Right
Acquired: 39th-round pick,
  6/87 free-agent draft

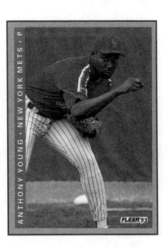

Anthony Young won a spring training competition for a berth in the New York Mets' starting rotation in '92. While not in the class of some of the more prominent members of that staff, Young seems to have a good future. He is at his best when he is throwing hard stuff down, making hitters produce ground balls, as he did in an early-season start in St. Louis. However, Young didn't always do that, which accounts for the frequency of extra base hits he yielded. His marks for the '92 campaign include a 2-14 record with a 4.17 ERA and 15 saves over the course of 52 game appearances. Young was stingy with walks (31), but perhaps some of his pitches were too fat. He could also use a tool to make him more effective against lefties, as southpaws hit him at a .324 clip in '92. Young was at his best when on the road or when facing righthanded batters.

Young's monster losing streak should put a permanent curse on his '93 cards. Our pick for his best 1993 card is Score. We have chosen this card for the superior presentation of information on its back.

	W	L	ERA	G	SV	IP	H	ER	BB	SO
92 NL	2	14	4.17	52	15	121.0	134	56	31	64
Life	4	19	3.86	62	15	170.1	182	73	43	84

ERIC YOUNG

Position: Second base
Team: Colorado Rockies
Born: May 18, 1967
  New Brunswick, NJ
Height: 5'9" **Weight:** 180 lbs.
Bats: Right **Throws:** Right
Acquired: First-round pick,
  11/92 expansion draft

As the 1992 season progressed, Eric Young's good fortunes grew. After Los Angeles released incumbent second baseman Juan Samuel, Young started 35 games. Both expansion teams knew they'd welcome the young speedster if the Dodgers would dare leave the young prospect unprotected. Before his acquisition by Colorado, Young was a 43rd-round selection by Los Angeles in the '89 free-agent draft. The Rutgers University product (a star wide receiver) captured three minor league stolen base crowns in his first three seasons, including two consecutive campaigns of 70 or more swipes annually. An outfielder in college, Young could benefit the Rockies in two different positions.

Even a mediocre player will stand out with this '93 fledgling team in search of talent. Young's untapped speed could make him a future All-Star and a sleeper investment for optimistic collectors. Gamble a few dimes on his cards. Our pick for his best 1993 card is Score. We have chosen this card for its technical merits.

	BA	G	AB	R	H	2B	3B	HR	RBI	SB
92 NL	.258	49	132	9	34	1	0	1	11	6
Life	.258	49	132	9	34	1	0	1	11	6

Series two cards from some companies were available at press time. If space allows, both cards are shown; if not, the most up-to-date cards are pictured.

ROBIN YOUNT

Position: Outfield
Team: Milwaukee Brewers
Born: September 16, 1955
　　Danville, IL
Height: 6′ **Weight:** 180 lbs.
Bats: Right **Throws:** Right
Acquired: First-round pick,
　　6/73 free-agent draft

 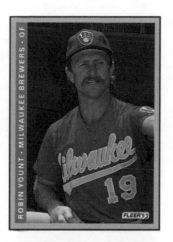

Robin Yount, a two-time American League MVP, notched a major career milestone in '92 with his 3,000th career hit. He also managed a .264 batting average, 40 doubles, and 77 RBI. Yount has spent his entire 19-year career with Milwaukee. In '82, his best year, he led the Brewers to their only pennant with a .331 average, 29 homers, 114 runs batted in, and major-league highs in hits (210), doubles (46), and total bases (367). He won the MVP award again in '89, when he had a career-best 19-game hitting streak. A solid clutch hitter, Yount is also a solid defensive center fielder. Because he won one MVP as a shortstop and one as an outfielder, Yount is one of three players to win the award while playing two different positions.

　Rockin' Robin's cards will be at least 15 cents each due to his record. Don't expect any price climbs until he reaches the Hall of Fame. Try a first-ever Fleer or Donruss Yount from '81 at $3 apiece. Our pick for his best 1993 card is Fleer. We have chosen this card due to the outstanding photographic composition.

	BA	G	AB	R	H	2B	3B	HR	RBI	SB
92 AL	.264	150	557	71	147	40	3	8	77	15
Life	.287	2729	10554	1570	3025	558	123	243	1355	262

TODD ZEILE

Position: Third base
Team: St. Louis Cardinals
Born: September 9, 1965
　　Van Nuys, CA
Height: 6′1″ **Weight:** 190 lbs.
Bats: Right **Throws:** Right
Acquired: Third-round pick,
　　6/86 free-agent draft

 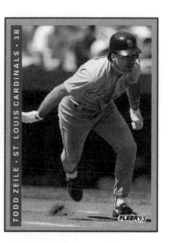

Third baseman Todd Zeile got a surprising wake-up call on August 10, 1992. The leader in four offensive categories for the '91 Cardinals was demoted to the minors. At the time, he was hitting .251 with five homers and 36 RBI. However, he had gone a month without an extra-base hit for St. Louis. After five homers, 13 RBI, and a .311 average back in Triple-A, Zeile returned to the Cards on the first of September. In '91, Zeile collected career-high marks of 81 RBI and a .280 average. During his '90 big league debut, Zeile blasted 15 homers. The converted catcher had played in four minor league campaigns before being sent down in '92.

　Zeile may not head back to the minors in '93, but his demotion proves he doesn't have guaranteed employment in St. Louis. Because Zeile may never hit .300 or 20 homers per year, his nickel-priced cards seem hazardous. Our pick for his best 1993 card is Score. We have chosen this card due to the outstanding photographic composition.

	BA	G	AB	R	H	2B	3B	HR	RBI	SB
92 NL	.257	126	439	51	113	18	4	7	48	7
Life	.261	453	1581	196	413	82	11	34	194	26

EDDIE
ZOSKY

Position: Shortstop
Team: Toronto Blue Jays
Born: February 10, 1968
   Whittier, CA
Height: 6′ **Weight:** 175 lbs.
Bats: Right **Throws:** Right
Acquired: First-round pick,
   6/89 free-agent draft

BOB
ZUPCIC

Position: Outfield
Team: Boston Red Sox
Born: August 18, 1966
   Pittsburgh, PA
Height: 6′4″ **Weight:** 225 lbs.
Bats: Right **Throws:** Right
Acquired: Second-round pick,
   6/87 free-agent draft

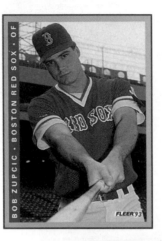

Shortstop Eddie Zosky found fewer chances awaiting him in Toronto in 1992. Although he was promoted when rosters were expanded in September, Zosky was called up mainly due to incumbent shortstop Manuel Lee's sore knee. For his '92 efforts, Zosky achieved a .286 batting average in eight games. His major league debut in '91 was an unmemorable .148 showing in 18 games. However, he was tops among Triple-A International League shortstops in four fielding categories. Following a collegiate career at Fresno State, Zosky was the 19th overall pick in the first round of the '89 draft. Originally, the Mets tempted him with a fifth-round selection in '86. Since the acquisition of Roberto Alomar in '91, Zosky's chances to crack Toronto's infield lineup seem hopeless.

After struggling offensively during his '92 Triple-A season, Zosky's stock has plummeted. His '93 cards are poison, even at a nickel each. Our pick for his best 1993 card is Donruss. We have chosen this card because of its overall appeal and pleasing looks.

Bob Zupcic could eventually become one of those players who feed off the wall at Fenway Park. He reached double figures in homers twice in the minors, including the 18 he hit in the Triple-A International League in '91. With his size and ability to hit lefthanded pitching, he could be a useful bat for a club that has traditionally used power at home. Fortunately, that power began to surface in the majors in '92 in the form of two grand slams. His .276 batting average for his '92 season was accented by three homers and 43 RBI. As a testament to his liking for lefthanded pitching, he attained a .293 average against them. He also does better at the plate when on the road (.286) than when at home (.265). Zupcic is a good defender and played all three outfield positions, as well as serving as an occasional designated hitter.

Zupcic was a pleasant surprise in '92. His cards won't be as pleasant at up to a quarter each, yet they deserve investigating. Our pick for his best 1993 card is Fleer. We have chosen this card due to the outstanding photographic composition.

	BA	G	AB	R	H	2B	3B	HR	RBI	SB
92 AL	.286	8	7	1	2	0	1	0	1	0
Life	.176	26	34	3	6	1	2	0	3	0

	BA	G	AB	R	H	2B	3B	HR	RBI	SB
92 AL	.276	124	392	46	108	19	1	3	43	2
Life	.269	142	417	49	112	19	1	4	46	2